Venkat Iyer
4 / 95
New Haven, CT

Visual Basic Multimedia Adventure Set

D1621699

Scott Jarol

Edited by Jeff Duntemann

 CORIOLIS GROUP BOOKS

Publisher	*Keith Weiskamp*
Editor	*Jeff Duntemann*
Assistant Editor	*Jenni Aloi*
Proofreader	*Diane Green Cook*
Interior Design	*Bradley Grannis*
Layout Production	*Bradley Grannis and Barbara Nicholson*
Publicist	*Shannon Bounds*
Production Coordinator	*Lisa Eads*

Trademarks: Microsoft is a trademark and Windows is a registered trademark of Microsoft Corporation. All other brand names and product names included in this book are trademarks, registered trademarks, or trade names of their respective holders.

Distributed to the book trade by IDG Books Worldwide, Inc.

Copyright © 1994 by The Coriolis Group, Inc.

All rights reserved.

Reproduction or translation of any part of this work beyond that permitted by section 107 or 108 of the 1976 United States Copyright Act without the written permission of the copyright owner is unlawful. Requests for permission or further information should be addressed to The Coriolis Group, 7721 E. Gray Rd., Suite 204, Scottsdale, Arizona 85260.

Library of Congress Cataloging-in-Publication Data

Jarol, Scott, 1960-
    Visual Basic multimedia adventure set / Scott Jarol : edited by Jeff Duntemann
       p. cm.
    Includes Index
    ISBN 1-883577-01-2 : $39.95
    1. Multimedia systems. 2. Microsoft Visual BASIC. I. Duntemann, Jeff. II. Title.
QA76.575.J37 1994
006.6--dc20   94-22435
                                                     CIP

Printed in the United States of America

10 9 8 7 6 5 4 3 2

Acknowledgments

So many people have contributed to this project that it's hard to remember everyone, but a few names stand out. I offer my deepest gratitude to Keith Weiskamp and Jeff Duntemann who made this project possible and who shepherded it through from earliest conception to completion. I also wish to thank Darrin Chandler, not only for his invaluable technical insights, but for his encouragement and support. My other technical alter-ego was Dan Haygood, programmer extraordinaire.

Several artists have contributed to this book, including Susan Haygood, who drew the moth (or if you prefer, butterfly) sprites for the animation programs; Kane Clevenger of Tier 3 Productions, who drew the dictionary pages for the FLIPBOOK program; and James Cowlin, whose gorgeous landscape photographs appear in several program examples, including the Grand Canyon demonstration program.

I also wish to thank Nels Johnson of The San Francisco Canyon Company, who contributed his knowledge and insight into the profoundly technical world of digital video; MIDI programming wizard Arthur Edstrom of Artic Software, Inc., who contributed the great program (VB MIDI Piano) described in Chapter 14, and who helped me solve several MIDI mysteries; James Tyminski, who contributed the VB Messenger custom control that made MIDI input possible; Angel Diaz of Microsoft Corporation for creating the WaveMix DLL and for his generous support of this "unsupported" product; and Rick Segal, the Multimedia Evangelist of Microsoft Corporation, for contributing the entire Video for Windows system.

Another very important contributor was Shannon Bounds of The Coriolis Group. Shannon called hundreds of companies and spent numerous hours putting together the contest and acquiring the software and goodies included in this book.

Many thanks to The Coriolis Group Books production team, including eagle-eyed copy editor Jenni Aloi, designer and layout artist Brad Grannis, Lenity Mauhar, Rob Mauhar, Diane Cook, and Barbara Nicholson. I'd also like to thank Karen Watterson and Phil Kunz.

We are all indebted to the many companies that contributed prizes to the Multimedia Contest and clip art for the companion CD-ROM. These include Adobe Systems; AJS Publishing, Inc.; Andover Advanced Technologies; Cambium Development Corp.; Crisp Technology Inc.; Data Techniques, Inc.; First Byte; Interactive Publishing Corporation; Media-Pedia Video Clips, Inc.; Media Architects; Microsoft Corporation; Rainbow Imaging; Software Interphase; and Ulead Systems, Inc.

Finally, this project has consumed nearly two years of my family's lives, and I thank them for their patience with Daddy's zombie-like behavior (muttering to myself, wandering the halls late at night). I promise, no more books—for now.

Dedication

This book is dedicated to my wife Claudia, and my children Kristen and Ryan.

About the Author

Scott Jarol is a noted author and contributing editor for *PC TECHNIQUES* Magazine who has spent the last 16 years as a consultant and programmer. A multimedia producer with his Phoenix-based company, Media Terra Inc., Scott specializes in natural history, science, and adventure travel titles. He has a wife, Claudia, and two children, Kristen and Ryan.

Contents

Chapter 10   Expanding the Hypermedia Interface   275

Chapter 11   The Magic of Animation   323

Introduction

Don't even think about developing a multimedia project until you've taken a good look at Visual Basic, Microsoft's visual programming system for Windows. Windows programming can be a bear with conventional programming languages, so most multimedia developers turn tail and opt for more generic, but less flexible *authoring systems.*

Authoring systems are the multimedia equivalent of page layout software. They make it easy to assemble photographs, illustrations, music, sound bites, animation, and video clips into lively onscreen presentations. Many offer a variety of built-in special effects and interactive controls that make it possible to produce engaging presentations with just a few mouse clicks. But most lock you into their own ways of doing things. They're not *extensible*, which means that the only effects and controls you get are the ones built into the product.

Visual Basic (VB), on the other hand, is a completely extensible development system. Almost any feature not supported directly by VB itself is available in the form of either a Windows *dynamic link library* (DLL), or a *custom control.* And with the new Windows *object linking and embedding* (OLE) system, entire programs—even other multimedia authoring systems—can become custom controls, embedded in and controlled by our own VB programs.

With VB you get the power and flexibility of a true programming language, along with the simplicity and rapid development time of an authoring system. In this book, I'm going to show you how far VB can take you. We'll use just a few custom controls and one amazing DLL, but VB is so powerful in its own right that we won't even have time to discuss the hundreds of other add-on products available right now that you can use to energize your multimedia productions.

Who Is This Book For?

If you want to learn how to get the most out of VB, then this book is for you. Although we'll be focusing "like a laser beam" on multimedia programming, the programming principles will apply to any kind of VB project. We'll be calling dozens of functions from the Windows *Application Programming Interface* (API), along with some functions not found in the core Windows libraries. We'll also hit a variety of other VB topics, including database programming, code organization, custom controls, and subclassing—a technique for adding new capabilities to an existing control.

If you're new to Windows or to VB or to both, don't worry. You won't need any prior knowledge of the Windows Multimedia System. I will, however, assume that you have at least a basic working knowledge of Windows and VB—just enough to set up VB forms and controls. Several existing books, not to mention the fine manuals packaged with the program, introduce and thoroughly explain the concepts of programming in VB. I won't rehash them. I will, however, discuss why I've chosen VB as a multimedia development system, and review concepts that pertain directly to the projects in this book. The best way to learn *how* to use something is to use it. In this book we'll work our way up from basic principles to working systems, so even with minimal knowledge of VB you'll pick up quite a bit along the way.

Programmers who work in the Holy Trinity Languages—C, C++, and Pascal—will also benefit. The concepts that we study in this book will apply to *all* multimedia programming projects in Windows. In fact, many programmers use Visual Basic as a prototyping tool for projects they intend to implement in other languages, and almost all PC programmers, regardless of their language preferences, understand code written in Basic. With Visual Basic we can concentrate on concepts peculiar to multimedia without getting lost in all the Windows overhead.

What We Will Do

Unlike most Basic language programming compendia, which offer tips, tricks, and techniques on a variety of unrelated projects, this book will focus on one unifying concept. The programs we'll create in the course of the text will all add functionality to either the presentation engine or to the authoring tools. Every bit of this book will introduce or clarify multimedia concepts, and each programming project will build upon the last.

In most of the projects, we'll be calling functions from the Windows API. Many VB programmers never crack open the API, which is a shame because they don't know what they're missing. The API is a programmer's treasure trove. Many of the capabilities that seem to be missing from VB were omitted intentionally because they are so easily accessible from the API. Most of the 1,000 or so Windows API functions belong to families. For example, the *graphic device interface* (GDI) includes dozens of drawing and typesetting functions. We won't be able to use all the functions in every group, but we'll cover enough of them to kindle your understanding of those we miss.

The API functions reside in a set of DLLs. Functions in DLLs can be called at runtime from any language that supports dynamic linking, which today include languages as diverse as C++, Word Basic, WordPerfect Macros, and VB. The Windows operating system itself is a set of DLLs. So is the multimedia system. And third-party software developers are publishing new DLLs all the time, offering everything from advanced statistical functions to spelling checkers to 3D graphics engines. VB provides an easy interface to most functions located in DLLs, which you'll discover in Chapter 1.

What You Will Need

To complete most of the projects in this book, all you need is Visual Basic Professional Edition and a multimedia-capable PC, which consists primarily of a Windows system and a sound card. To produce commercial multimedia titles, however, you'll need to invest in all kinds of stuff—a scanner, one or more image editing and drawing programs, an animation program, a WAVE audio editing program, and a video digitizer and a video source, such as a VCR or camcorder or both.

If you do decide to delve more deeply into multimedia development, or even just use some of the many commercial titles, you'll need an *MPC-compatible* computer, which includes the following hardware and software:

- A 386SX or better processor
- At least 2 Mb of memory (4 Mb or more is ideal)
- A VGA display system, preferably super VGA (SVGA)
- An MPC-compatible sound board, which must support PCM playback for WAVE files, MIDI playback through a synthesizer, and an internal audio mixer
- A CD-ROM drive with a minimum average seek time of 1 second (remarkably slow) and a sustained transfer rate of 150 kilobytes per second (you'll want a drive with an average seek time no greater than 500 milliseconds; several manufacturers now offer seek times under 350 milliseconds)
- Windows 3.1 or later

If your system isn't already equipped as an MPC, I recommend that you buy one of the many upgrade kits available through almost all PC vendors now. That's what I did, and I believe it saved me from a configuration nightmare. These kits usually include a sound board, a CD-ROM drive, software drivers, and a bundle of multimedia titles. It's the quickest way to get going and sample the state-of-the-art multimedia technology.

> **Caution:** *Look for the MPC™ logo—not all multimedia upgrade kits comply with the specification, and those that don't may not run the disks you want.*

As a general rule we'll avoid extensions to VB. We'll write all the projects in VB and use Windows API functions. In a couple of cases we'll use some functions from DLLs written in other languages. And in one case, we'll use a shareware custom control (included on the companion CD-ROM) to add capabilities otherwise unavailable to VB programmers. I wish all the code could be written in VB, but when you're dealing with real-time events, sometimes you have to program "to the metal."

Take the Test Drive

Before we get started, let's take a look at a mini-multimedia title driven entirely with code from upcoming chapters. To get the full effect, you'll need the Video for Windows (VfW) version 1.1a runtime library and the MCIWNDX.VBX custom control installed on your computer. If you haven't installed the VfW runtime on your system, you'll find everything you need on the companion CD-ROM, along with complete instructions in Chapter 16.

Also on the companion CD-ROM, you'll find a directory called \GRANDCAN, which contains a program called HYPRMED3.EXE, and three subdirectories called \GRANDCAN\IMAGES, \GRANDCAN\SOUND, and \GRANDCAN\VIDEO. To run the program, open the Windows Program Manager and use the Browse button to locate and select HYPRMED3.EXE. You will soon see a window containing a brief multimedia presentation about the Grand Canyon, as shown in Figure I.1.

Some of the highlighted words in the text window will open other text topics. Many will trigger multimedia events. Similarly, the images in the top window contain hidden *hotspots* that run video clips, play sounds, jump to text topics, or display other images when you select them. Try clicking the hypertext *hotlinks* and image hotspots. See if you can locate the video clips of two of the Grand Canyon's spectacular waterfalls.

> **Note:** *If video playback is jerky, try copying the entire \GRANDCAN directory, along with its subdirectories to your hard drive. Some CD-ROM drives may not transfer video data quickly enough for smooth playback. Most hard drives, however, will provide more than adequate throughput.*

This program is written entirely in Visual Basic, with a little help from the Windows API and the VfW Development Kit (included on the companion CD-ROM). In the coming chapters you'll learn how to do all the things you see here, along with many other fun and exciting multimedia projects.

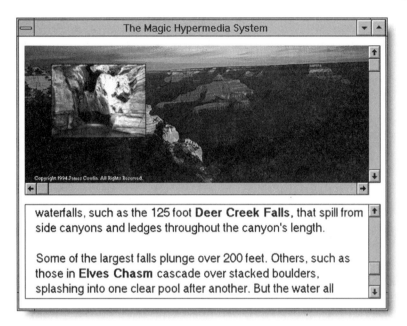

Figure I.1   *The Grand Canyon mini-title.*

Our Adventure Itinerary

The most logical way to organize this book would be in sections—sound, images, video, and so on. But that would be too dull. Instead, I've mixed up the material a little, working through all the topics, and gradually adding features to the multimedia engine along the way.

In Chapter 1, we'll begin with a couple of simple experiments to demonstrate just some of the multimedia capabilities built into Windows and VB. We'll also review a few VB programming concepts.

In Chapter 2 we'll break ground for the Magic Multimedia Engine by building the first version of the hypertext system.

Chapters 3 and 4 will take us into the Windows Multimedia API. First, we'll add some multimedia capabilities to the hypertext system. Then, we'll explore the various high-level and low-level functions of the MMSYSTEM.DLL by playing WAVE files—six different ways.

In Chapters 5 and 6 we'll seek out the Windows Palette Manager and learn to display and manipulate bitmaps entirely with API functions. Then, in Chapter 7 we'll use that knowledge to create awesome visual effects.

In Chapters 8 and 9 we'll return to hyperlinking. But instead of text, we'll learn how to place hotspots on images. We'll begin with simple rectangles,

but by the time we finish, we'll have a powerful hotspot editor that will let us draw and test a hotspot over any irregularly shaped object.

Chapter 10 brings us back to our hypertext system. For the first time, our hypertext and image hotspot systems will come together to form the Magic Hypermedia Engine. We'll also expand both subsystems by adding scrolling capabilities.

In Chapters 11 and 12 we'll explore the world of graphic animation. The emphasis here is on sprites, the interactive form of animation that powers most video games and other graphic simulations.

In Chapter 13 we return to Waveaudio. We'll use the knowledge of the low-level functions we studied in Chapter 4 to manipulate WAVE data at the byte-level. Then, we'll explore the remarkable WaveMix DLL, an experimental library distributed by Microsoft that lets us do real-time mixing of up to eight WAVE files for simultaneous playback—in stereo! I'll also show you an easy way to record WAVE files from your VB programs.

In Chapter 14 we'll tackle the Musical Instrument Digital Interface, known as MIDI (pronounced "mid'-y"), a real-time networking system originally designed to control synthesizers. MIDI's main domain is music, but the power of MIDI has barely been tapped by multimedia developers. You may be surprised to learn just what your sound card can do.

One of the major components of the Windows Multimedia System is the Media Control Interface (MCI). By the time we get to Chapter 15, we'll have used a few simple MCI commands to play multimedia files, including .WAV audio, .MID music, and .AVI video. In this chapter we'll look at some of the MCI's other capabilities by building two very different audio CD players.

Our last adventure takes us into the dazzling world of digital video. Microsoft has generously provided us with the complete VfW runtime libraries, production utilities, and Development Kit. We'll use the custom controls in the VfW DK to develop our own video capture utility (which requires a video capture card) and to perform controlled video playback (no special hardware required at all). Finally, we'll come full circle, adding video playback controls to the Magic Hypermedia Engine, which we'll use to produce the Grand Canyon mini-multimedia presentation.

Let's hit the trail!

Ready for the adventure of a lifetime? Then join in as we explore how Visual Basic can help you to create interactive multimedia projects.

The Visual Basic Multimedia Connection

A h, multimedia! Sit back, throw your feet up on your desk, fire up your computer, and get lost in a world of adventure and fun. A world where you can explore historical events and fascinating places by watching videos and participating in interactive stories. Or journey into the Grand Canyon and raft down the awesome rapids of the Colorado river. That's multimedia as it should be. But when you try to create apps like this, you'll discover multimedia development is practically a black art and you'll need all the help you can get.

Gone are the days when a program only required a few algorithms, a database, and some interface code to come to life. As multimedia takes PCs into the twenty-first century, traditional programming languages and development tools alone simply won't cut it anymore. With sound, music, video, 3D animation, scrolling images, and hypertext to support, you'll need a visual development environment that provides the right multimedia connections.

And that's where Visual Basic (VB) comes in. Instead of drowning in minute technical details in a complex language like C++ or using a dedicated multi-

media authoring system that locks you into its own way of doing things (and there are certainly many of them competing for the spotlight), you can have the best of both worlds by using VB and letting your creativity soar.

Go Interactive

The multimedia we'll be exploring in this book isn't the boring "slide show" stuff that first emerged when the multimedia world arrived at the PC's doorstep. The demand for multimedia products has been high and so has the temptation for just throwing "browse ware" software together on a CD-ROM. Our interest is in creating adventurous interactive multimedia that brings new worlds to the user.

Imagine being able to watch any part of a basketball game from any player's position. You could put yourself in Charles Barkley's shoes as he goes for a jump shot or you could follow around the official as he breaks up a fight. If you want to replay a shot, you could click your mouse and step back in time for a moment. That's interactive. You get to be part of the experience rather than just a spectator watching from a distance.

Creating quality interactive multimedia takes a lot of knowledge and the right tools. You must know how to present your information and how to manipulate it in real time. Of course, you won't become an instant content expert from reading this book, but you will learn how to create the tools to process your multimedia images, sound files, music, animation, video, and hypertext. We'll start by exploring some of the tools that Windows provides for manipulating these components, and then we'll create our own. You'll be amazed by the multimedia power and flexibility that VB brings to the table.

Exploring the Windows Multimedia System

The Windows Multimedia System, which is built into Windows, provides a set of services that you can use in your programs to manipulate sound, graphics, and video. Windows 3.1 (or Windows 3.0 with Multimedia Extensions) also includes some multimedia utilities that give you instant access to these capabilities. The Sound Recorder, for instance, will let you add digitized sounds, such as oral annotations, to Word documents, Excel spreadsheets, or other apps that support Windows Object Linking and Embedding (OLE). The Media Player utility will play back *WAVE* files, *MIDI* sequencer files, or *AVI* video files (that's video as in television video, not PC display video) right from your hard disk or CD-ROM drive. Media Player can also play standard audio CDs on your CD-ROM drive, and if you load the right drivers, it can operate video laser disks, video tape decks, and other external devices equipped with serial or *SCSI* interfaces.

An add-on product, called the Microsoft Sound System, provides various sound services to business users, including a speech synthesizer that will read numbers to you from your spreadsheet so you can check them against your accounting ledger without looking back and forth.

No Programming Necessary

Not everyone aspires to multimedia fame. Some of us just want to use sound and pictures to make a point or to assist with day to day tasks, or just to play music. Fortunately, you can use Windows Multimedia features without ever touching a programming language or an authoring system. Let's explore a simple example.

Start up any Windows app that supports Object Linking and Embedding, such as Microsoft Word or Excel. Create or load any file. Then, locate the option that enables you to insert a Windows object into a document. In Word, choose Insert, Object. Word will display the dialog box shown in Figure 1.1.

Choose Sound from the Object Type list box to open the Sound Recorder utility. Plug a microphone into your sound card, press the record button (the little microphone button) on the Sound Recorder, and say something. Try to be as profound as Alexander Graham Bell

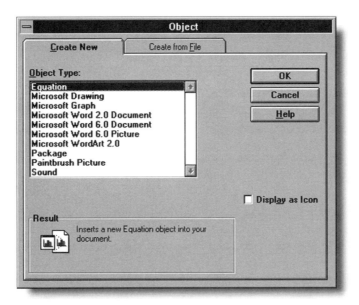

Figure 1.1 *The Microsoft Word Insert Object dialog box allows you to insert Windows objects into a document.*

when he tested his first telephone ("Watson, come here I need you!"). But keep it brief; digital audio recordings gobble disk space!

When you're done, close the Recorder. Word will display a microphone icon in your document as shown in Figure 1.2.

You may insert text as you please before or after this *embedded object*. To replay your recording, just double-click on the microphone icon. If you transmit your document by E-mail to other people who use Word for Windows, they too will see the Recorder icon and can replay your message.

By the way, you can embed existing recordings just as easily as new ones by selecting Media Clip from the Object Type list box. When the Media Player appears, choose Device, Sound from the menu. Then, open and play any WAVE file. When you're done, close Media Player. In this case, Word will display the Media Player icon rather than the Sound Recorder's microphone. Double-click on the icon to replay the sound.

If you want a little more flexibility but are truly wary of programming, you can use an authoring system to build presentations. You can get to all the same *kinds* of services (sound, graphics, animation, and video) without programming as you can with programming; you just won't have as much flexibility in how you present them.

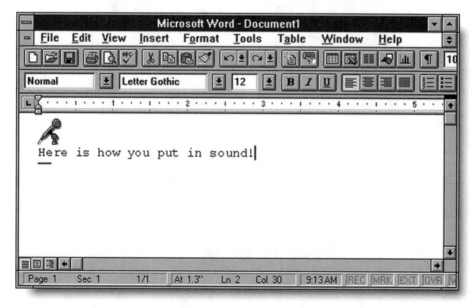

Figure 1.2   *Microsoft Word document with an embedded Recorder object.*

These handy utilities perform some amazing operations behind the scenes. And Microsoft has given us most of the functions we need to build our own programs to manipulate the devices and data that comprise the Multimedia System. They're contained in a Windows *Dynamic Link Library* (*DLL*) called MMSYSTEM.DLL. Just like any other Windows *Application Programming Interface* (*API*) functions, we can call these functions from our own apps.

Windows Programming—A Black Art?

Windows programming resembles no other type of programming that most of us have ever encountered. The Windows graphical user interface (GUI) is designed to make programs look similiar. Obviously, you can only go so far in this direction, or all programs would look exactly the same. But many apps, especially productivity programs like word processors and spreadsheets, share dozens of common operations. For example, all word processors offer cursor movement, printing, rulers, cut and paste operations, and a variety of other features. And all programs need navigation tools so you can get from one option or data field to another.

Windows provides functions that perform many of these common operations. In fact, the Windows Application Programming Interface (API) offers over 1,000 functions. Some do spectacular things, like playing back a video file with a single call; others perform small, specialized operations like reporting the position of the cursor. To program a Windows app, all you have to do is stack up a series of calls to the appropriate Windows functions.

Right!

A Windows app carries on an intimate relationship with the operating system. Like young lovers, they exchange messages at a frantic rate. Almost any time something happens in Windows, whether it's in your app or another one running at the same time, Windows sends your app a message, offering it an opportunity to respond. Often the response triggers a flurry of exchanges. You may already be familiar with the infamous *WinProc*, the often gargantuan procedure familiar to C/C++ Windows programmers, that consists primarily of a lengthy case statement piled high with procedures that respond to messages. This is where the work of a Windows app happens.

To write a Windows app—at least one that works reliably—you have to anticipate all the messages your app might receive and need to act upon.

Unless you write your application in VB.

Visual Basic As a Windows Development System

Prepare yourself for a suspicious claim:

You can accomplish a lot more in a lot less time with VB than you can with one of the traditional languages like C, C++, or Pascal. (Unless, of course, you want to explore the lower-level dungeons of Windows.)

Languages like C/C++ are necessary for writing tight, fast code for projects like device drivers or communication programs. These languages have more direct access to the lower-level capabilities of the hardware and operating system. But most of us want to write applications and utilities that solve higher-level day-to-day problems like amortizing loans or storing information about clients and patients. To create the low-level services of the Windows Multimedia System, you would need a language like C or Pascal. To reach in and grab hold of those services and bring them to life, VB provides the ticket.

Visual Basic Takes Care of Windows Housekeeping Chores for You

Huge sections of the Windows API perform routine functions like opening and closing windows, managing memory, formatting text, and displaying scroll bars. Since most Windows apps use these features, they tend to call the same functions and respond to the same messages. With VB, the details for many of the basic Windows housekeeping chores like these are taken care of for you. VB calls hundreds of API functions and responds to all the appropriate messages behind the scenes. You only need to fill in the blanks.

It's Event Driven

To program in Windows, you have to think in Windows, and Windows is a world of events. Almost anything an app does in Windows is a response to an event. Windows notifies your program of each event by sending it a message.

VB is designed around this event-driven model. If you click on a command button in a typical Windows program, some program code would need to be called to perform an operation. VB provides you with built-in event handlers for standard events, such as mouse clicks, so that you can easily create truly event-driven programs. VB even goes one step further and incorporates the event-driven nature of Windows into the VB development environment. For example, you can click on a command button to open a window and display your code as you are designing your programs.

Interactive Development Puts the User First

VB offers the most interactive way to develop interactive programs. The ease with which you can add controls helps you to design and modify your programs so that they work and feel just right for your users.

When you create a program with a traditional language, the initial focus is on the task you want to automate. Once you think you know how to solve the tough problems, you begin to grind out the code. Along the way, you build the user interface: menus, windows, interactive controls, data entry fields, and so on.

But with VB, you begin with the most important component— the user.

Visual Programming Power

Visual design is a handy feature for creating many types of Windows apps. For interactive multimedia, it's essential. Interactive multimedia is a new medium—a visual medium. The success of a project depends on how the user can interact with it. A movie director would never hand over a script to his crew and wait in his office for the final film footage. Much of what ends up on the screen is discovered on the set. When you design your multimedia title, you need feedback every step of the way. Are the buttons too big? Too small? Too many? Does the picture get lost among the controls? Can you read the text without covering the images?

With VB, you can fine tune your apps as you work. And, if you still need low-level horsepower, you'll have your map to guide you as you machete your trail through the API jungle.

Easy-to-Use Support of the API

Although some of the Windows API functions deliver their goods to us through the VB back door, many do not. Some of them must be called directly, which, thankfully, is easy. (Actually, it isn't so much that the API functions are difficult to understand individually. The tricky part is finding the right combinations to successfully complete the task at hand.) To prove just how easy, let's try one.

Playing Multimedia with a Few Lines of Code

Our first VB multimedia project shows you how to use the **mciExecute()** multimedia API call to play a WAVE file.

Start up VB and create a new form called MCIPlay. Place one control on it: a Command Button named ExecuteMCICommand. Set the **Caption** Property of this button to "Execute MCI Command."

> Next, click on the ExecuteMCICommand button. VB should display the framework for the **Click** event shown in Figure 1.3. We're going to call upon the services of the simplest function in the multimedia API—**mciExecute()**. This function executes MCI commands.

The function **mciExecute()** takes a single argument, a string, which contains a plain English command as shown in Listing 1.1. In this simple example, all we want to do is play a WAVE file. The MCI "play" command will automatically open and close the WAVE device for us.

Listing 1.1　ExecuteMCICommand_Click() Event Procedure

```
Sub ExecuteMCICommand_Click ()
    Dummy% = mciExecute("play c:\windows\tada.wav")
    End Sub
```

Make sure you add the folloing declaration:

```
Declare Function mciExecute Lib "MMSystem" (ByVal CommandString As String) As Integer
```

mciExecute() is a true *function*, not a *procedure*, or subprocedure as procedures are called in VB; it returns an integer value that indicates success or failure. Since we don't plan to act upon that result, we're just catching the result in a dummy integer variable.

If Windows is installed on a drive other than C:, make the appropriate change to the command string argument. Then, run the program and click on

Figure 1.3　*The VB Code window with the ExecuteMCICommand_Click() event procedure displayed.*

the Command Button. You can insert the name of any WAVE file into this command. Try it out and give it a listen!

Actually, you can insert the name of any MCI supported data file into the play command. Windows 3.1 comes with a sample MIDI sequencer file called CANYON.MID. Replace the WAVE filename with the name of this MIDI file and run the program again.

```
Dummy% = mciExecute("play c:\windows\canyon.mid")
```

Unlike the brief WAVE files, CANYON.MID will play for a couple of minutes.

I would be misleading you if I told you that all the Windows multimedia API calls were this easy to use. Many functions take several arguments. Often you have to follow arcane rules to pass arguments from VB to Windows functions. Some functions work only in combination with other functions. And other functions don't work from VB at all. In Chapter 3, we'll begin to look more closely at the Windows API in general and at the multimedia functions in particular. By the time we've finished with our presentation system, you'll know how to use many of the key functions that will take our programs into the multimedia age.

The Essential VB Ingredients

Before we begin programming in earnest, let's rummage around in the VB closet and figure out what we can use. We'll start by sorting the components we'll be needing into their proper compartments.

A VB program usually consists of a least one *form* on which we find one or more objects, in the form of *controls*. Controls have *properties*, which define their appearance and general behavior, and *event procedures,* which determine what will happen when the control is activated by one or several operator actions, or *events*.

Forms Present

Forms are actually objects themselves, and like control objects, they offer some event procedures. For most purposes, we generally think of a form as a frame within which to place controls. In general, we'll abide by that convention, although we'll also see that plain unpopulated forms can perform some useful functions in screen presentation, as well.

Objects Behave

Most of the real action takes place within controls. Much of the activity on the screen requires the services of more than one control. A Command Button, for example, might load a bitmap image into a Picture Box. Each type of control offers its own selection of event procedures. Some overlap; but many do not.

Properties Define

Properties determine states, such as background color or the name by which we'll reference the control elsewhere within our program.

Events Happen

Events usually trigger everything that happens in VB programs. In fact, if you write a program that loops away on its own, without regard to events—which you *can* do—you'll effectively disable Windows, and may be forced to reboot the computer. An infinite loop in a Windows program will hang your system just as well as an infinite loop in a DOS program. But thanks to multitasking, there's just more to crash.

The concept of multimedia events extends beyond Windows programming, as you'll see when we discuss the Musical Instrument Digital Interface, or MIDI, in Chapter 14.

Functions, Procedures, and Methods Work

Functions and *procedures* contain program statements that manipulate data. When we want something done, we call a procedure; when we want something back, we call a function. Event procedures are special procedures that Windows and VB call when something happens in Windows that might affect a particular form or control. VB also includes dozens of other functions that perform common operations like trimming strings of their leading or trailing spaces, or calculating the cosine of an angle.

Forms and controls offer a special type of procedure that performs work under program control rather than in response to user events. These procedures are defined as integral components of their host objects. In objected-oriented programming, such procedures are called *methods*. VB, by the way, though object-oriented in its design, doesn't permit us to define our own objects and methods, at least not from within the language itself. It is therefore, object-oriented, but not *in*ternally extensible. How's that for colliding jargon?

The difference between a method and any other procedure that is built into the language is that a method belongs to its host object and usually modifies a property of that object, whereas a general purpose procedure accepts and modifies conventional data elements, such as variables, constants and arrays—most of the time. You can write procedures that modify an object's properties. The difference between these two components will just continue to get fuzzier, and I promised a brief review, so we'll move on.

Modules Organize

The way we scatter code around in a VB program, you have to wonder whether we're still entitled to call it "structured." The VB programming system—and it is a system, not just a language—dictates not only syntax, but architecture. In fact, the apparently chaotic organization of a VB program reflects a purer form of the structured ideal than the linear listings required by traditional programming languages. Like protein molecules, procedures perform distinct operations. They offer a single entry point and a single exit. The order in which we create them matters only to the extent that one procedure cannot call another unless the one being called already exists.

Yet, within any given program, procedures do tend to cluster. So-called low-level procedures perform minute repetitive tasks and tend to call built-in language or operating system features. Higher-level procedures call on low-level procedures, so much so that the low-level procedures sometimes obscure the identity of the host language. Several procedures may perform related tasks, like disk and file management.

As we write event procedures for our VB programs, we find that we want to write procedures we can call upon over and over again without duplicating their code. We may even want to bag some of these tools and tote them from one program to another. So we place them in *modules*.

You can add general procedures and functions to a form, but if you create a separate module to store those items, they can be called by procedures in other forms, as well. And if you add that module file to another project, that same code can be called from modules or forms in both projects. Throughout this book we'll bundle code into modules that you can incorporate into your own projects.

Code Style Clarifies

The most overlooked component of any language is overlooked because it isn't a component, but a philosophy. *Code style* illuminates a program's rails and switches. A digital computer runs a program in a particular order. That order is determined by a set of critical statements that divert the processor into loops and branches. You can weave as many loops and branches into your program as you wish, and as long as you obey the language's rules of syntax, the interpreter or compiler doesn't care how your code looks to you. But *you* should care because if *you* can't follow it, it probably doesn't work the way you think.

The most obvious element of code style is *indentation*. This apparently trivial technique has fanned some hot debates. Everyone has personal views on indentation, and since none of the mainstream languages impose indentation style, we all stick to our own guidelines. This discussion won't shed any light on multimedia, so I'll just say that I try to indent my code to clarify its structure. I never write code without indentation, not even tiny programs, but I am not a purist and my style may not satisfy your needs. I recommend two things: (1) develop or adopt a style, and (2) *apply it consistently.* Inconsistent indentation can hang you as surely as no indentation, maybe worse—we don't expect any help from unformatted code, but randomly formatted code plays pranks on us.

The second key element of code style is *scoping.* The VB manuals explain scoping pretty well, as do some of the many introductory texts on the language. I won't waste your time by repeating the same technical discussion. Think of scoping as containment, like a nest of Chinese boxes. When you're done with a program, nothing should show outside those boxes, except what you need to run that program. And at each layer within, the same rule pertains: nothing more or less than you need should appear outside that level of scope. Each time you declare a variable, consider where you'll use it, then put it in the smallest box you can. By eliminating global variables, passing information around as arguments instead, you'll write more re-usable code. Remember, structured programming is the artful hiding of details. This rule too, I will try to follow as closely as possible.

Intrinsic Multimedia Features

You'll find yourself using a large assortment of VB's features to write any serious application. Thus, any VB feature could be considered useful for multimedia projects. But some of VB's features turn out to be particularly useful. Let's take a closer look.

Forms, Image Boxes, and Picture Boxes, for example, are essential multimedia tools, both in obvious and—as we'll learn in Chapter 2—in surprising ways. These three *objects* share several useful capabilities, like the **Picture** property and **Graphics** methods.

Forms are the platforms on which we'll stage our productions. To make effective presentations, we need to think carefully about forms, about how many to display, how to size them, and how to move them.

Graphics *methods* provide essential graphic capabilities to our programs at runtime, whereas Graphics *controls* take the form of lines, boxes, and circles with which we can decorate our forms at design-time.

VB also lets us add pictures to our applications either at design-time or at runtime. We can move them, resize them, and remove them. With a simple technique based on control arrays, we can even animate them. We'll use Picture Boxes, Images, Text Boxes, and forms themselves extensively in our applications. And we'll end up using most of their properties and methods. By layering these elements and manipulating their properties at runtime, we can really get the show moving. Let's try a simple example.

Moving Pictures

This project shows you how to use a few VB programming tricks to move a picture around in a window.

First, we need a form. We won't need to reference the **Name** property, so you can name the form anything you wish. On the form, place a Frame control and stretch it to proportions similar to those shown in Figure 1.4. The Frame control is represented in the toolbox by a rectangle with the letters "XYZ" in the top border.

Next, click on the Picture Box control icon in the toolbox. The Picture Box is represented by a picture of a desert vista. Place the Picture Box inside the Frame control. We need to align the upper-left corners of the Picture Box and Frame controls so that the Frame disappears, but before we do that, let's assign an image to the Picture Box so we can keep track of it.

The accompanying CD-ROM contains a subdirectory called \VBMAGIC\IMAGES. In it you will find a file called YAKIDAWN.BMP. We want to assign this file to the **Picture** property of the Picture Box.

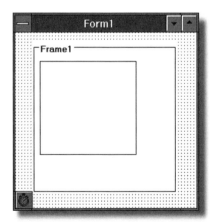

Figure 1.4 *The moving picture form with a Frame control.*

Now you can slide the Picture Box up into position. This requires a little practice; you may tend to accidentally switch contexts and find yourself dragging the Frame instead of the Picture Box, but it can be done. The easiest way to neaten the edges is to set the **Top** and **Left** properties of the Picture Box to 0 in the VB Properties Window. **Top** and **Left** determine the position of the Picture Box relative to its container, in this case, the Frame.

We need to change one other property of the Picture Box, **AutoSize**. Set this property to True.

> *NOTE:* *You can switch a* boolean *property (a property with either of two values: True or False) by double-clicking anywhere on its line in the Properties list.*

The **AutoSize** property causes the Picture Box to match its size to the height and width of the currently active Picture—the image assigned to the **Picture** property. The picture is much larger than what we can see on the screen. To see the entire picture as shown in Figure 1.5, open the file in Windows' Paintbrush application.

The Frame masks the Picture Box so we can only see the portion of the picture that is visible through the Frame.

Place a Timer control anywhere on the form. The Timer will disappear at runtime so it doesn't matter where it goes. If you put more than one Timer on a form, you may want to locate them on or near the other controls to which they're most closely related. Timers service only one event, the **Timer** event, and have only seven properties.

The only Timer properties that affect us are **Enabled**, which must be True, and **Interval**. The **Interval**, measured in milliseconds, determines how often the **Timer** event occurs. Actually, the Timer control can't tick any more often than the system timer, which ticks 18 times per second, so the shortest mean-

Copyright 1994 James Cowlin. All Rights Reserved.

Figure 1.5   *This figure shows the entire YAKIDAWN.BMP file.*

ingful interval is one eighteenth of a second, or about 56 milliseconds. We are going to use the Timer to animate our image, and we want the smoothest motion we can coax from it, so set the **Interval** to 56.

We're going to use the **Timer** event to slide the Picture Box from right to left behind the Frame, creating the illusion that we're panning the landscape. Listing 1.2 shows the code needed for the **Timer1_Timer()** event procedure.

Listing 1.2 Timer1_Timer() Event Procedure

```
Sub Timer1_Timer ()
    Picture1.Left = Picture1.Left - 15
    End Sub
```

The **Left** property indicates the position of the Picture Box control relative to the left edge of its container. We measure this value in *twips*, VB's default *Scale Mode*. Twips provide a device-independent scale for measuring screen objects. One twip equals 1/1440th of a logical inch, or 1/567th of a logical centimeter. The benefit of using the twips scale measurement is that the size of an object remains reasonably constant, regardless of screen resolution (not always the case with pixels). As we subtract twips from Picture1.Left, increasing its negative magnitude, the whole Picture control slides further and further left of the left edge of the Frame. The negative value indicates how many twips the control's left edge rests from position zero, the Frame's left edge. Run the program to see what happens.

Don't forget to stop the program after the image disappears. To prevent the Picture Box from sliding right on past us, let's add a terminating condition. The new version of our event procedure is shown in Listing 1.3.

Listing 1.3 The New Timer1_Timer() Event Procedure

```
Sub Timer1_Timer ()
    Picture1.Left = Picture1.Left - 15
    If Picture1.Left = -(Picture1.Width - Frame1.Width) Then
        Timer1.Enabled = False
        End If
    End Sub
```

With the **Width** property, we can stop the motion of the image either by diverting around the subtraction statement, or, as we've done here, by disabling the Timer. By disabling the Timer, we free some system resources. We want the motion to cease when the right edges of the image and the Frame meet. The difference between the Picture Box width and the Frame width tells us how much of the image will be hanging out to the left of the Frame when that happens. Picture1.Left will contain a negative value, so we negate the difference of the object widths before comparing the two values.

That's animation with five lines of code—seven if you're particular—no function calls, and one bitmap. If that isn't intrinsic multimedia, I don't know what is.

We'll look at some more animation techniques in Chapters 11 and 12.

The Professional Edition MCI Control

The Professional Edition of VB comes with a custom control called the *MCI control*. You can operate all kinds of devices with this control, including the system's sound card, Microsoft's AVI (Audio-Video Interleave) files, CD-Audio, and external VCRs and video disk players. But you don't *need* the MCI control to operate many of these devices. In fact, the MCI control can be cumbersome when all you want to do is play back a WAVE file or a MIDI sequence. Yet, as an interface to external devices, the MCI control can come in handy.

Missing Links

As good as VB is at displaying screens with text, still images, and controls, and at responding to user activity, it provides no intrinsic support for the most exciting multimedia elements: sound, animation, and video. If you plan to use Windows' multimedia features, unless you own the Professional Edition, you have no choice but to venture outside the secure confines of VB. And even if you do own the Professional Edition, you'll find it easier to accomplish some things without the MCI control.

In many cases, VB will serve us well as an application framework, tending to the menial tasks of Windows management. For much of what we'll do, we'll rely on VB's numerous features, especially when it comes to the user interface. With its assortment of Scroll Bars, List Boxes, Image controls, and various buttons, we can assemble some attractive, functional forms.

Where VB leaves off, we'll look to the Windows API. Sometimes we'll have to sneak past VB, intentionally avoiding its zealous attempts to protect us from the fearsome machinery below.

We'll start our multimedia presentation kit in Chapter 2 by building a hypertext system, which we'll create entirely with plain vanilla VB.

Learn about the world of
hypermedia and how to
create a useful hypertext
system with Visual Basic.

Chapter 2

Exploring Hypermedia

f you've been watching the computer industry explode over the past few years, you've probably witnessed the growth of CD-ROM. From 3-D games to dinosaur adventures to interactive encyclopedias, CD-ROM has ushered in a new age of desktop computing. And it's no wonder. A CD-ROM holding thousands of images and millions of words can bring the magical world of multimedia to your PC. But to really make use of all the interesting data forms that can be stored on a CD-ROM, you'll need a way to organize and process your crowd-generating images, intriguing sounds, dazzling video, and important text.

And that's where *hypermedia* comes in. Hypermedia isn't a new miracle cure, though. It's simply a way of organizing information—text, graphics, pictures, video, and so on—so that you can create powerful, interactive interfaces. If you've used multimedia products, you're already aware of the benefits of hypermedia. For example, when you click on the name of a street in an electronically displayed street atlas and a document window pops up to give you directions, you're experiencing the power of hypermedia at work.

Because hypermedia is the foundation of interactive multimedia, this is the best place to start. I'll introduce you to some of the hypermedia key concepts, such as hyperlinks and hypertext. Then, I'll show you how to write the VB code to support hypertext. And because hypermedia systems tend to resemble each other in many ways, you'll be able to create a hypermedia system that you can adapt to a variety of multimedia projects.

The Explosion of Hypermedia

Until recently, hypermedia-based systems were regarded as lab experiments. Apple Computer brought hypermedia into the mainstream when they released the innovative HyperCard for the Mac. Since that time, a number of unique applications have emerged that incorporate hypermedia capabilities. Even the help systems of most major software products now use hypermedia techniques.

In a hypermedia presentation, you can navigate by jumping from topic to topic, or topic to media element—picture, sound, video, and so on. You can also locate information by clicking on keywords and icons in specially-prepared documents. Such a document could consist of text or graphics, or a combination of both. For example, you could click on a particular spot in a world map and voila!—you'd have an article about the history of Portugal on your screen. Then, as you're getting your history lesson, you could click on the word "currency" and guess what?—up comes an article about Portuguese currency, along with pictures of various bank notes and coins.

Some visionaries like Ted Nelson claim that some day soon all information—magazine articles, books, newspapers, scientific papers, stock quotes, network news stories, movies, music, everything—will be available as hypermedia. This information could be available online and accessible by satellite from your personal pocket computer. Of course, someone will need to convert all of this stuff into an electronic form. The best materials will undergo information renewal, transformed into entirely new works at the hands of skilled multimedia producers.

Organized Chaos—The Magic of Hyperlinking

Hypermedia systems are designed so that you can explore information in a variety of formats by activating *hyperlinks*. A hyperlink operates like an underground tunnel to connect points of data together. These pieces of data may appear in an application as "highlighted" text, a picture with a "hot" spot, a graphic embellishment, or an icon. (Since the field of hypermedia is so new, many creative techniques for representing hyperlinks are just starting to emerge.)

In more traditional- or document-based systems, the term *hypertext* is used to refer to text-based information that is connected with hyperlinks. Some hypertext documents mix two or more kinds of markers, each one performing a different function. As an example, Figure 2.1 shows how VB uses hyperlinks with its hypertext-based help system.

Hyperlinking can serve many purposes. Sometimes you may just want to look up a term and then return to what you were doing. Other times you may

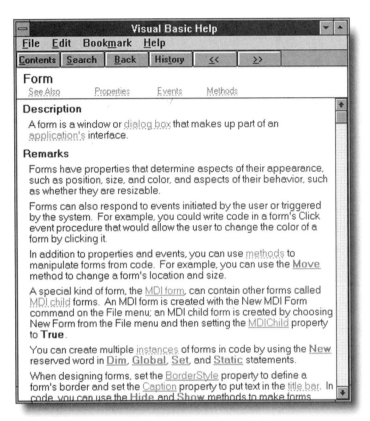

Figure 2.1 *A typical hypertext screen from the VB help system.*

discover a subtopic that you want to explore more thoroughly, so you jump to another topic, forgetting your previous work completely. And occasionally, you may want to refresh your knowledge on a subject, or acquire some background information, then return to your point of departure.

The manner in which hyperlinks are placed in a multimedia application can really determine how useful the application will be. If too few links are used, the user might feel too constrained. (After all, a multimedia application is suppose to be more fun and interesting than flipping pages in a book.) If too many links are used, on the other hand, the user might feel like he or she is trapped in a maze. Figure 2.2 shows how an organized hypermedia system stacks up against a disorganized one.

The network of linked pathways provides the first and most-used layer of interactivity. And this is where the relationship between content and interface begins. In the publishing world, authors and editors have to choose and stick to a single structure for each publication they create. Sometimes the structure

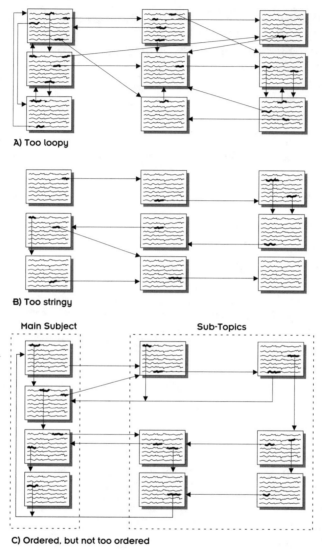

Figure 2.2 *An organized hypertext system versus a disorganized one.*

falls out of the material. But sometimes the most obvious structure ends up being the least effective—and the most boring!

Fortunately, most topics become fascinating—almost magical—when they are examined from a variety of angles. On paper, one word follows another, paragraph after paragraph, chapter after chapter. With hyperlinks, on the other hand, you can connect thoughts and ideas in much more creative ways, and that is the main benefit of the hyperlinking approach.

Before I started this book, I created a working outline. I used Microsoft Word's Outline View feature so I could move freely through my material, expanding and collapsing headings, jumping from section to section, adding and removing topics as new ideas emerged. As you can guess, the finished outline—a portion of which is shown in Figure 2.3—defined a book organized by subject categories—a section for images, one for sound, another for text, and so on.

When the outline was finished, I realized that the book really needed a different, more creative approach. So I reorganized the material into chapters that began with basic concepts, then built upon those concepts, intertwining ideas, techniques, and fun projects to complete the multimedia adventure set.

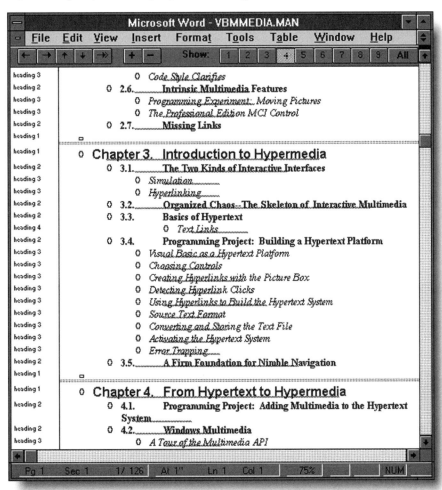

Figure 2.3 *Part of an early outline for this book as it appears in Microsoft Word.*

I actually needed to maintain two outlines, one that organized the book by subject, and another that split subjects into smaller chunks spread across multiple chapters. At one point, I even began to contemplate creating a third structure that would be organized by technical issues so I could sort through the programming projects more easily! If I had created this book as a hypermedia document, I could have offered the different views of the outline as interfaces.

Many of the hyperlinks you incorporate into your productions will be utilitarian—digressions on subtopics or simple glossary lookups. But hyperlinking is also an editorial lantern that enables you to illuminate the secret passages through your ideas and concepts.

Getting to Hypertext

So far, I've been singing the praises of hypermedia and, in particular, hyperlinks. Throughout the rest of this chapter, I'll focus on techniques for creating a hypertext system with VB. In the next chapter, we'll expand the code presented here and create more powerful hypermedia support tools. We'll also take a look at the Windows multimedia API.

Creating Text Links

To set up a hypertext system, you'll need to link up text-based information using *source* and *target* nodes. A *source node* is simply a word or phrase in your text that you want to link up to some other information. When a user selects the source node by clicking the mouse or pressing a key on the keyboard, the target node gets triggered. In a hypertext-only system, you only need to display new text when a source node is selected. In a more sophisticated hypermedia system, you could display a graphic image, run a video clip, or even play a sound.

The actual form of a hypertext link will depend on the format of the source documents you adapt or create for your hypertext system. A hyperlink may advance the user to the beginning of a topic or to a particular line within a lengthy passage. (For documents composed of many brief topics, short enough to fit entirely on the screen, either type of link would produce the same result.) In lengthy documents that remain essentially linear, you could link from word to word or from phrase to phrase. In a presentation that incorporates two or more separate but whole documents, a hyperlink might take the user directly to the top of a document, or to any point within another document. Figure 2.4 shows some examples of hyperlinks in a hypertext system.

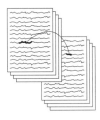

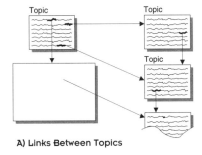

A) Links Between Topics

B) Links between two points in a lengthy, contiguous documents.

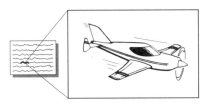

C) Play a multimedia sound, animation, or video and return.

Figure 2.4 *Types of hyperlinks used in a hypertext system.*

Creating a Hypertext System

Now that we've explored the basics of hyperlinking and hypertext, let's build our own hypertext system. We'll start by creating a simple hypertext project that uses VB's event-driven interface. Then, we'll build on this project to add additional features, such as pop-up message windows, support for hypertext source files, and a hypertext compiler. In Chapter 3, we'll use Windows API calls to attach multimedia events to our hypertext screens, linking them directly to the "hot" words embedded in the text.

Visual Basic as a Hypertext Platform

VB practically jumps up and screams to become a multimedia development platform. With its powerful controls (and more coming every day), direct support for bitmapped graphics, and remarkable event-driven interface, VB gives you more flexibility than you'll find with other multimedia development environments. VB also provides a relatively straightforward interface to the Windows API, as you'll see in the next chapter.

Unfortunately, VB doesn't provide a control for hypertext linking. So, we must roll our own. We'll need to display text that contains highlighted "hotlinks," which when selected with a mouse click, cause the system to display the text page (known as a topic or subject) that elaborates on or defines the high-lighted word.

Searching for the Right Control

Of all the controls included with VB, there are three possible options for our hypertext system:

- Text Box
- Combination of Labels and Command Buttons
- Picture Box

Let's examine each of these approaches with a critical eye.

Text Box　This control is designed to display and edit text. It even supports the standard Windows mouse techniques for selecting text and performing clipboard operations. Unfortunately, it doesn't provide many mouse events for external programmed responses because it offers its own internal mouse-dependent editing functions. The second problem is that the Text Box control doesn't support internal variable formatting. Thus, text is always displayed with the same attribute, so we can't highlight hotlinks. It looks like we'll have to scrap the Text Box control for now.

Labels and Command Buttons　We could also use a combination of labels and command buttons to implement our hypertext system (see Figure 2.5). All *plain* text (text that isn't hotlinked) could appear on the form as Labels. To display a hotlink, we could place a Command Button between Labels and set the button's caption to the word or phrase to which we wanted to link. Then, all we'd need to do is respond to the Mouse Click event for the command buttons.

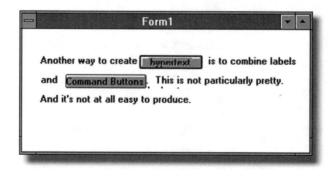

Figure 2.5　*A patchwork of Label and Command Button controls.*

Displaying text this way would require some fancy footwork. If our hypertext system had multiple screens, we would need to place controls at runtime and neatly align them into well formatted text. Although this approach might work, we'd find ourselves buried in the mechanics of formatting text. Let's forget it; this is too much work!

Picture Box   We have one option left—the Picture Box. This control provides several features to facilitate text formatting. Within a single Picture Box, we can mix *typefaces*, *type size*, *character attributes*, and even *color*. Now we're talking. We can easily highlight the hotlinks by boldfacing, underlining, or using color contrast.

But there is a catch; words displayed in the Picture Box are stored as bitmapped images—no longer words, but just pictures of words. While the Text Box can hand us its contents whole or as bits and pieces of strings, the Picture Box can't tell us anything about its contents except the coordinates of the *insertion point*, and the locations of mouse events.

Fortunately, we don't really need to know the actual word on which the user has clicked. To achieve a "hyper jump," only three things are needed:

1. *When* the user clicks on a hotlink
2. *Which* link the user clicks on
3. The *destination subject*

The Picture Box's **MouseDown** event can tell us when and where a click has occurred, and we can keep a table that correlates screen coordinates (actually Picture Box coordinates) with destination subjects. Figure 2.6 shows an example of how the Picture Box control can be used to implement our hypertext system.

Creating Hyperlinks with the Picture Box

For our first hyperlink programming project, we'll use VB's Picture Box control and set up a simple form so that we can create our basic hypertext system. Here are the steps to follow:

1. Create a form called HYPRTXT1.FRM using the instructions provided in the next section, *Creating the Form*.
2. Create a code module called GLOBCONS.BAS that will hold the VB constant declarations.

> 3. Add the code for HYPRTXT1.FRM. This form requires the function **GetWordFrom()** (Listing 2.1) and the procedure **LoadSubject()** (Listing 2.2).
>
> 4. Add the support code to handle the **OpenButton_Click** event (Listing 2.3) and the code for the **NewLine()** procedure (Listing 2.4).
>
> *This project is stored in the subdirectory \VBMAGIC in the files HYPRTXT1.MAK, HYPRTXT1.FRM, and GLOBCONS.BAS.*

Running the Simple Pre-Hypertext Program

If you run the program and click the Open Hyperbase Command Button, you should see a text string in the Picture Box with the tagged words highlighted in boldface, as shown in Figure 2.7.

Although this program displays the hotlink word in boldface, it doesn't yet respond to mouse clicks. We'll add this feature later on.

Creating the Form

Our new form actually requires two controls: a Picture Box that occupies most of the form area and a Command Button. On the Picture Box, set the **Picture** property to (none), and set **AutoRedraw** to True. On the Command

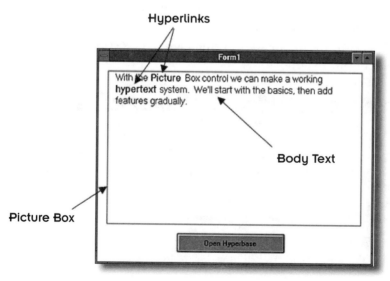

Figure 2.6 *Hypertext in a Picture Box.*

Figure 2.7 *The text with a highlighted hotlink.*

Button, set the **Caption** property to "Open Hyperbase." We'll use the default control name of Picture1, but we'll change Command1's **Name** property to "**OpenButton**." Check out Figure 2.8 to see how the form should be set up. In the form itself, we'll retain the default **Name** property of Form1 (you can use the file HYPRTXT1.FRM on the companion CD-ROM).

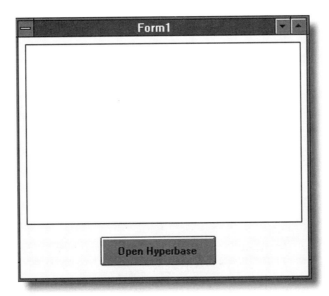

Figure 2.8 *Setting up the form HYPRTXT1.FRM.*

Getting the Text Ready

Before we can display hypertext with highlighted hotlinks, we need to define a format for our *source text*. The Microsoft help system uses several conventions that rely on *rich text format* (or *RTF*, a general-purpose file format for formatted text) to define various types of links and display formats. But you don't need all the features of the Windows help system to create usable hypertext. We want something simple.

We'll use a string constant with our first project to test the interface, then we'll switch to an *ASCII text file* for the last project presented in this chapter. To mark a hotlink, we'll precede the link word with a double pound sign (##). Then, when it's time to display the text, we just watch for this marker. When we find a word that begins with "##", we'll stripoff the tag and display the word in boldface type. Here's an example of a sentence with a hotlink:

This sentence uses the word ##hotlink as the link.

> **Note:** *The hypertext test string used with this project will be placed in* the **OpenButton_Click()** *event procedure. (For more information, see the section,* Adding the Support Code.*)*

Creating the Global Constants Code Module

Next, we'll need to create a *code module* for our project. From the VB menu bar, select File, New Module. VB will display the new module's declarations section. Next, select File, Load Text to display the Load Text dialog box. Locate the file CONSTANT.TXT, which is distributed with VB and is usually located in the VB main directory. Highlight the filename and select the Merge button to import the text file into the new module's *declarations section*. Finally, from the VB menu select File, Save File As to display the Save File As dialog box, and save the module with the filename GLOBCONS.BAS. We'll be using this code module in projects throughout this book. You can also look up the constants we use in each program (in CONSTANT.TXT) and declare them yourself either in a separate module or in the declarations section of the form.

For our first project, we're only using one constant: **BLACK**. It has a value of **&H0&**. Since our project has only one form, you could declare **BLACK** as a constant in the declarations section of the form rather than in a separate module. However, you cannot use the **Global** statement when you declare variables or constants at the form level.

Adding the Code to the Form Module

To perform the text processing tasks, we'll need the function **GetWordFrom()**. This function is designed to process one word at a time. It takes a string argument and returns the first word from the string and strips the word off the front of the string. **GetWordFrom()** won't be an event function, so we'll declare it as a general function at the form level.

Listing 2.1   GetWordFrom() Function from HYPRTXT1.FRM

```
Function GetWordFrom (AnyString As String) As String
   If InStr(AnyString, " ") = 0 Then
      GetWordFrom = AnyString
      AnyString = ""
   Else
      GetWordFrom = Left$(AnyString, InStr(AnyString, " "))
      AnyString = Mid$(AnyString, InStr(AnyString, " ") + 1)
   End If
```

Here a word is defined as any set of characters delimited by spaces or by the ends of the string. The word returned by **GetWordFrom()** includes the terminating space character, except when it's the last word in the string.

Next, we need to iterate through the source text, printing the formatted text as we go. The general procedure **LoadSubject()** performs this operation. We could just insert this code in the **OpenButton_Click()** event procedure, but to make the code re-usable for other projects, we'll create a general procedure, again at the form level.

Listing 2.2   LoadSubject() General Procedure from HYPRTXT1.FRM

```
Sub LoadSubject (StringToPrint As String)
   Dim NextWord As String
   Dim CreatingALink As Integer

   ' Set base text attributes.
   Picture1.ForeColor = BLACK
   Picture1.FontBold = False
   Picture1.FontSize = 12
   ' Indent a little from the left border.
   Picture1.CurrentX = 200
   ' Get the first word in the string.
   NextWord = GetWordFrom(StringToPrint)
   Do While NextWord <> ""
      If Left$(NextWord, 2) = "##" Then
         CreatingALink = True
         NextWord = Mid$(NextWord, 3)
      Else
         CreatingALink = False
      End If
      ' Check for word wrap.
      If ((Picture1.CurrentX + Picture1.TextWidth(NextWord$)) >
          Picture1.ScaleWidth) Then
         ' Call an external procedure to advance the line.
         NewLine
```

```
        Picture1.CurrentX = 200
    End If
If CreatingALink Then
    Picture1.FontBold = True
    Picture1.Print NextWord;
    Picture1.FontBold = False
Else
    Picture1.Print NextWord;
    End If
NextWord = GetWordFrom(StringToPrint)
Loop
End Sub
```

The first section of this procedure, following the declarations and text prop-erties, pulls each word from the front of the source string and checks to see if it has the double-pound sign prefix. If it does, meaning that it's a hotlink word, the procedure sets a flag and removes the pound signs:

```
' Get the first word in the string.
NextWord = GetWordFrom(StringToPrint)
Do While NextWord <> ""
    If Left$(NextWord, 2) = "##" Then
        CreatingALink = True
        NextWord = Mid$(NextWord, 3)
    Else
        CreatingALink = False
    End If
```

The next section checks the width of the word to determine whether it will fit on the current line. To do this, it must first call the **TextWidth** method, which takes a string and returns the width of the string in the current *scale mode* (the current unit of measure—twips, pixels, centimeters, etc.) as it would appear if printed to the client area of the window. Then, it adds the calculated width to the **CurrentX** property and compares the total to the **ScaleWidth** property. **ScaleWidth** contains the current width of the client area of the window, again in the current scale mode:

```
' Check for word wrap.
If ((Picture1.CurrentX + Picture1.TextWidth(NextWord$)) > Picture1.ScaleWidth) Then
    ' Call an external procedure to advance the line.
    NewLine
    Picture1.CurrentX = 200
End If
```

If the word will not fit on the current line, we call **NewLine** (see Listing 2.4 in the next section) and reset the **CurrentX** property to the indented position of 200 *twips* from the left edge. Twips represent VB's default scale mode. One twip equals 1/1440th of a "logical inch," which means that 200 twips equal approximately 0.14 inches. Twips come in handy when you want to determine the precise sizes of graphic objects output to the printer (screen inches depend, of course, on the size of your monitor and the resolution of the display system). Unfortunately, twips do not exist in the Windows realm outside VB, so in later projects, when we begin passing measurements to the Windows API, we'll have to switch to the pixel-based scale mode.

Finally, the last section of the **While** loop prints the word with the appropriate text attributes—bold if its a hotlink, plain otherwise. Then, the loop grabs the next word and starts over:

```
If CreatingALink Then
    Picture1.FontBold = True
    Picture1.Print NextWord;
    Picture1.FontBold = False
  Else
    Picture1.Print NextWord;
  End If
NextWord = GetWordFrom(StringToPrint)
Loop
```

Adding the Support Code

Now that we have the key procedure **LoadSubject()** in place, we can fill in the supporting code to process the **OpenButton_Click()** event procedure. This event calls **LoadSubject()** with a test string, as the code in Listing 2.3 shows.

Listing 2.3   OpenButton_Click() Event Procedure from HYPRTXT1.FRM

```
Sub OpenButton_Click ()
    Const TestString$ = "This is the first step toward ##hypertext."
    LoadSubject TestString$
    End Sub
```

Finally, Listing 2.4 shows the simple **NewLine** procedure.

Listing 2.4   NewLine Procedure from HYPRTXT1.FRM

```
Sub NewLine
    Picture1.Print
    End Sub
```

This procedure looks silly now but it will grow as we add to this project.

Detecting Hyperlink Clicks

Let's expand our first hypertext project and add a detection feature for processing hyperlinks. Now, when the user selects a hotlink, a message box will pop up. Here are the steps to follow:

1. Create a form with filename HYPRTXT2.FRM.
2. Create the array data structure called **HyperLinkElement** to process hyperlinks. This array is defined in the new code module HYPRTXT2.BAS (Listing 2.5).
3. Create the code module for the HYPRTXT2.FRM form. This form requires the function **GetWordFrom()** from the previous project (Listing 2.1) and a modified version of the procedure **LoadSubject()** (Listing 2.6).
4. Add new declarations to HYPRTXT2.FRM (Listing 2.7).
5. Update the support code including the **NewLine** procedure (Listing 2.8) and the **MouseDown()** event procedure (Listing 2.9).

This project is stored in the subdirectory \VBMAGIC in the files HYPRTXT2.MAK, HYPRTXT2.FRM, HYPRTXT2.BAS, and GLOBCONS.BAS.

Using the Program

With this project we've added a simple user interface to our hypertext system. To test it out, select Run, Start from the VB menu bar (or press F5, or click on the Run button on the Toolbar). Click on the boldface hotlink word in the program to display the message box.

Building the Form

For this project, we'll need a form module identical to the one in the previous project. If you wish, you can remove the default form from the new project and use the File, Add File option on the VB menu bar to add the form HYPRTXT1.FRM. Then, select File, Save File As from the menu and save the form with the filename HYPRTXT2.FRM. Again, you may retain the form's **Name** property of Form1.

Building the Data Structure

Highlighted hotlinks won't do us any good until we can detect and interpret mouse clicks on them. To keep track of the hotlinks, we must record their screen locations. Then, when the user clicks the mouse button, we can check the mouse coordinates against our list of hotlinks to determine whether a link has been selected, and if so, return the name of the destination subject.

To code this feature, we must define a data structure that describes the *hot zone* and the link target. Since words occupy rectangular regions, we can keep track of their locations by recording the positions of their four sides, as shown in Figure 2.9.

Since each screen may contain one or several hotlinks, we'll use an array called **HyperLinkElement** to keep track of all the links on a given screen (see Listing 2.5). An element of this array consists of a record, or in VB, a **Type** containing five fields: **Left**, **Top**, **Right**, **Bottom**, and **DestinationSubject**.

Listing 2.5 Declarations Section from HYPRTXT2.BAS

```
Type HyperLinkElement
    Left As Integer
    Top As Integer
    Right As Integer
    Bottom As Integer
    DestinationSubject As String * 128
    End Type
```

Structures defined with the **Type** statement must be declared in the declarations section of a code module, not in the form module. To create the new code module, select File, New Module from the VB menu bar. The next time you save the project, VB will ask you to name the module. Call it HYPRTXT2.BAS.

Figure 2.9 *Words occupy rectangular regions.*

To use the array, we must declare an array of **HyperLinkElement** in the declarations section of Form1 (stored in the file HYPRTXT2.FRM):

```
Dim HyperLinkArray(100) As HyperLinkElement
```

Notice here that I've assigned an arbitrary size to this array. The array needs only enough elements to hold the largest number of hotlinks that would ever appear on a single subject screen (if your topics contain 100 elements per screen, you need to re-think your structure, seriously).

Creating the New Code

We'll modify the **LoadSubject()** procedure in HYPRTXT2.FRM (Form1) so it will build the **HyperLinkElement** array as it parses the source text string (see Listing 2.6). We already know when we've stumbled across a hotlink, so all we have to do is store its coordinates.

We can determine our current position in the Picture Box at any time by checking the **CurrentX** and **CurrentY** properties. Each time we start a new line, we'll assign the value of **CurrentY** to a temporary variable called **CurrentTop**. This variable will preserve the new Y value that defines the **Top** boundary of any word in the current line. When we place a hotlink on the screen, we can set its **Left** boundary by recording **CurrentX** before printing, and its **Right** boundary by recording **CurrentX** after printing. When we advance to the next line, we'll grab the new **CurrentTop** and record it in any hotlinks we've found on the previous line as their **Bottom** boundaries.

Listing 2.6   LoadSubject() Procedure from HYPRTXT2.FRM

```
Sub LoadSubject (StringToPrint As String)
    Dim NextWord As String
    Dim CreatingALink As Integer

    ' Clear the Picture Box display.
    Picture1.Cls
    ' Initialize array indices.
    LinkArrayPos = 0
    ArrayPlaceHolder = 1
    ' Set base text attributes.
    Picture1.ForeColor = BLACK
    Picture1.FontSize = 12
    Picture1.FontBold = False
    ' Indent a little from the left border.
    Picture1.CurrentX = 200
    ' Save the current Y position before printing anything.
    CurrentTop = Picture1.CurrentY
```

```
' Get the first word from the string.
NextWord = GetWordFrom(StringToPrint)
Do While NextWord <> ""
    If Left$(NextWord, 2) = "##" Then
        CreatingALink = True
        NextWord = Mid$(NextWord, 3)
      Else
        CreatingALink = False
      End If
    ' Check for word wrap.
    If ((Picture1.CurrentX + Picture1.TextWidth(NextWord)) >
         Picture1.ScaleWidth) Then
        NewLine
        Picture1.CurrentX = 200
        End If
    If CreatingALink Then
        LinkArrayPos = LinkArrayPos + 1
        HyperLinkArray(LinkArrayPos).Left = Picture1.CurrentX
        HyperLinkArray(LinkArrayPos).Top = CurrentTop
        Picture1.FontBold = True
        Picture1.Print NextWord;
        Picture1.FontBold = False
        HyperLinkArray(LinkArrayPos).Right = Picture1.CurrentX
        HyperLinkArray(LinkArrayPos).DestinationSubject = NextWord
      Else
        Picture1.Print NextWord;
      End If
    NextWord = GetWordFrom(StringToPrint)
    Loop
HyperLinkArraySize = LinkArrayPos
' Finish out last line in case links are present.
NewLine
End Sub
```

The major change in this procedure from the previous version is the addition of the assignment statements that are used to record the graphical boundaries of the link word:

```
If CreatingALink Then
    LinkArrayPos = LinkArrayPos + 1
    HyperLinkArray(LinkArrayPos).Left = Picture1.CurrentX
    HyperLinkArray(LinkArrayPos).Top = CurrentTop
    Picture1.FontBold = True
    Picture1.Print NextWord;
    Picture1.FontBold = False
    HyperLinkArray(LinkArrayPos).Right = Picture1.CurrentX
    HyperLinkArray(LinkArrayPos).DestinationSubject = NextWord
  Else
    Picture1.Print NextWord;
  End If
```

Adding New Declarations

As I mentioned earlier, we need to add a declaration for the support array. We'll also need to add a few other declarations to support our new linking features. Listing 2.7 shows the four new declarations you should add to Form1.

Listing 2.7   Declarations Section from HYPRTXT2.FRM

```
Option Explicit

Dim HyperLinkArray(100) As HyperLinkElement
Dim HyperLinkArraySize As Integer
Dim CurrentTop As Single
Dim LinkArrayPos As Integer
Dim ArrayPlaceHolder As Integer
```

Adding the Support Code

We're just about ready to wrap up our second project. The only tasks remaining are to update the **NewLine** procedure and the **MouseDown()** event.

NewLine needs to perform some additional housekeeping. Each time we advance to the next line, we want **NewLine** to fill in the **Bottom** boundaries for all the links on the previous line. Listing 2.8 shows the new code.

Listing 2.8   NewLine Procedure from HYPRTXT2.FRM

```
Sub NewLine
    ' Start a new line.
    Picture1.Print
    CurrentTop = Picture1.CurrentY
    ' Fill in the Bottom values for any links on
    ' the previous line.
    While ArrayPlaceHolder <= LinkArrayPos
        HyperLinkArray(ArrayPlaceHolder).Bottom = CurrentTop
        ArrayPlaceHolder = ArrayPlaceHolder + 1
        Wend
End Sub
```

Now, when **LoadSubject()** parses the source text string, it will create an array of hotlinks. With this structure in place we can test our user interface.

We'll test the hotlinks by popping up a message box each time the user clicks on a hotlink, as shown in Figure 2.10. This will tell us whether our hypertext control actually works. You might expect this code to appear in the Picture Box's **Click** event, but the **Click** event does not receive position coordinates. Instead, we'll add our code to the **Picture1_MouseDown()** event procedure (Listing 2.9), which provides us with the mouse position as the single-precision, floating-point values **X** and **Y**.

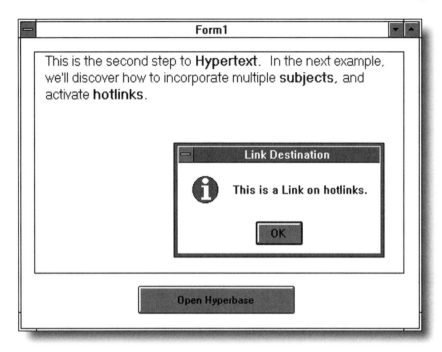

Figure 2.10 *A message box triggered by a hotlink.*

Listing 2.9 Picture1_MouseDown() Event Procedure from HYPRTXT2.FRM

```
Sub Picture1_MouseDown (Button As Integer, Shift As Integer, X As Single,
                        Y As Single)
    Dim FileType As String
    Dim Index as Integer

    For Index = 1 To HyperLinkArraySize
        If (X > HyperLinkArray(Index).Left) And
           (X < HyperLinkArray(Index).Right) And
           (Y < HyperLinkArray(Index).Bottom) And
           (Y > HyperLinkArray(Index).Top) Then
            MsgBox "This is a Link on " +
               RTrim$(HyperLinkArray(Index).DestinationSubject),
               64, "Link Destination"
        End If
    Next Index
End Sub
```

Note: *The comparisons may look confusing because the Y axis is upside down. The upper-left corner of the Picture Box is position X=0, Y=0, so the* **Bottom** *boundary has a greater value than the* **Top** *boundary, as shown in Figure 2.11.*

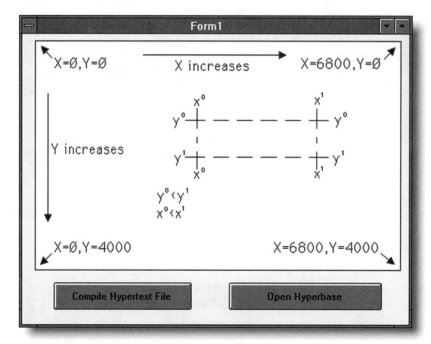

Figure 2.11   *Coordinate system within the Picture Box.*

Extending the Hypertext System

We added a useful pop-up message feature to test hypertext links in the previous project. But pop-up messages hardly constitute real hypertext. What we need is a system that can actually change the contents of the screen when hotlinks are selected. In addition, we'll want to be able to store and process longer text that has multiple hypertext links.

To create such a system, we'll need to store hypertext data in a source file and then use a hypertext compiler to process the data and put it in a format that our system can use.

Extending the Hypertext System with Text Files

Let's extend our hypertext system one more time by adding more useful hotlink processing features and a hypertext storage system. Here are the steps to follow:

1. Create a form using the filename HYPRTXT3.FRM. Once again, this form will start out with the same controls and properties as the form in the previous project.

2. Define a source text format for the hypertext data (Listing 2.10) and create a text compiler to process the source file into data records (Listing 2.11).

3. Add a Command Button and support code to the form for invoking the text compiler (Listings 2.12) and opening the hypertext files (Listing 2.13).

4. Add the required declarations to HYPRTXT3.FRM (Listing 2.14).

5. Add the code to the form module HYPRTXT3.FRM. This form requires modified versions of the **GetWordFrom()** function from the first project in this chapter (Listing 2.1) and the **LoadSubject()** procedure (Listing 2.15). Also, add the **ReadInText()** function (Listing 2.16) and the **ParseLink()** procedure (Listing 2.17).

6. Update the **Picture1_MouseDown()** event procedure (Listing 2.18) and the **OpenButton_Click()** event procedure(Listing 2.19).

7. Add the code for a **Form_Load()** event procedure (Listing 2.20) to initialize the **FilesAreOpen** variable.

This project is stored in the subdirectory \VBMAGIC in the files HYPRTXT3.MAK, HYPRTXT3.FRM, HYPRTXT3.BAS, and GLOBCONS.BAS.

Defining the New Source Text Format

First, we need to define authoring conventions to create our hypertext in a text editor. Then we'll "compile" the hypertext into a form that lends itself to random access.

To perform hyperlinks, our program has to know the *destination subject.* So each subject in the hypertext file needs a name we can link to, and each hotlink embedded in the text must indicate the destination subject, or target, to which it is linked. That's how subjects bind (or "relate") to links.

We'll tag *subject headings* with three pound signs (###) and place them on their own lines. The text of each subject will follow on any number of lines, and will end with either the next subject heading or the end of the file.

To record destination subjects in the hotlinks, we need to add more information to the embedded link element. To separate the hotlink word from the destination subject, the vertical bar character is used as the delimiter. We'll need to allow embedded spaces in subject headings, so we can't depend on a space to terminate the hotlink element. Instead, we'll use a tilde (~). As a bonus, this structure allows the hotlinks themselves to include multiple words. Here's a specification for the format we'll be using:

```
##multimedia|Types of Multimedia~
```

Listing 2.10 shows a text source file with three subjects. This is the text that we'll be using to test out our new hypertext system.

Listing 2.10 Hypertext Source File from HYPRTXT3.TXT

```
###Hypertext
Hypertext systems enable readers to jump from topic to topic by selecting key
    words or phrases embedded in the text.  These special words are sometimes known
    as ##"hotlinks"|Text Links~.
###Text Links
In this ##Hypertext|Hypertext~ system, the author creates hotlinks by tagging
    the word or phrase with a double pound sign, and providing the name of the
    ##Destination Subject|Destination Subjects~.
###Destination Subjects
When the user clicks on a ##hotlink|Text Links~, the system locates the appropriate
    topic in the ##hypertext|Hypertext~ file and displays it on the screen.
```

Type in this example—or your own—with any text editor (such as the Windows Notepad), and save it as the file HYPRTXT3.TXT. Also, if you break a line in mid-sentence, add an extra space on the end to separate the words when the program later concatenates the lines into paragraph strings.

Storing the Text File

Before we can use our text, we must get it into a manageable form. We could use a simple approach and create a flat file with one record for each subject. The record could consist of two fields: subject name and subject text. But then we would have to search the entire file to locate a particular subject. We would also have to define a maximum size for each text block and allocate that much space for every subject, which could waste a lot of space. The approach I've taken splits the text into two files:

- A text record file that stores blocked strings in linked lists
- A subject file that acts as an index to the blocked text file

To implement this approach, we'll need to define two records in VB:

```
Type HyperTextRecords
    TextBlock As String * 128
    NextBlock As Long
    End Type

Type SubjectIndexRecords
    Subject As String * 128
    TextFilePos As Long
    End Type
```

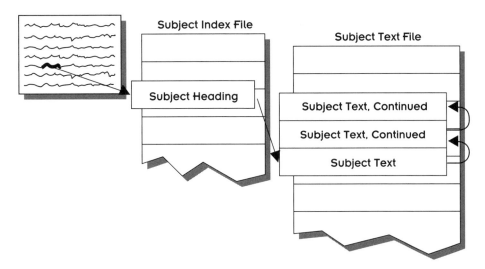

Figure 2.12 *The relationship between HyperTextRecords and SubjectIndexRecords.*

Figure 2.12 shows how these two structures relate to each other. These two **Type** definitions need to be placed at the bottom of your global module, in this case, HYPRTXT3.BAS, which should now contain the **Type** declarations for three structures: **HyperLinkElement**, **HyperTextRecords**, and **SubjectIndexRecords**.

Converting the Text File

To get our source text file into the required format, we'll need to write a simple text file compiler, called **CompileText()**. This procedure, shown in Listing 2.11, converts the source text file into a matched pair of files. The files will have the same root name as the source file. Their extensions will be .IDX for the subject index file, and .HTF for the hypertext file (subject text file).

Listing 2.11 CompileText() Procedure from HYPRTXT3.FRM

```
Sub CompileText (FileName As String)
    Dim LineOfText As String
    Dim RootFileName As String
    Dim ParagraphText As String
    Dim LinkRecordLen As Integer
    Dim IndexRecordLen As Integer
    Dim TextFileNum As Integer
    Dim PreviousTextPos As Long

    ParagraphText = ""

    LinkRecordLen = Len(HyperTextRecord)
    IndexRecordLen = Len(SubjectIndexRecord)
```

```
TextFileNum = 1
LinkFileNum = 2
IndexFileNum = 3


' Extract the root filename from the source text file.
If InStr(FileName, ".") > 0 Then
    RootFileName = Left$(FileName, InStr(FileName, ".") - 1)
  Else
    RootFileName = FileName
  End If
Open FileName For Input As #TextFileNum
If FilesAreOpen Then
    Close LinkFileNum
    Close IndexFileNum
    End If
' Eliminate pre-existing .HTF and .IDX files.
' They need to be opened first in case they don't exist
' so they will be created, otherwise we'll get an
' error when we try to Kill them.
Open RootFileName + ".HTF" For Random As #LinkFileNum Len = LinkRecordLen
Open RootFileName + ".IDX" For Random As #IndexFileNum Len = IndexRecordLen
Close #LinkFileNum
Close #IndexFileNum
Kill RootFileName + ".HTF"
Kill RootFileName + ".IDX"
Open RootFileName + ".HTF" For Random As #LinkFileNum Len = LinkRecordLen
Open RootFileName + ".IDX" For Random As #IndexFileNum Len = IndexRecordLen
FilesAreOpen = True


IndexPos = 0
LinkPos = 0
SubjectIndexRecord.Subject = ""
SubjectIndexRecord.TextFilePos = 0
' Read and process the source text file line
' by line until we reach the end.
Do While Not EOF(TextFileNum)
    Line Input #TextFileNum, LineOfText
    If (Left$(LineOfText, 3) <> "###") Then
        ' Append this line of the source text
        ' to the current Subject text buffer.
        If Len(LineOfText) = 0 Then
            ParagraphText = ParagraphText + " " + Chr$(13) + Chr$(10) + " "
          Else
            ParagraphText = ParagraphText + LineOfText
          End If
      End If
    If (Left$(LineOfText, 3) = "###") Or (EOF(TextFileNum)) Then
        ' We've reached the end of a subject, so
        ' store its accumulated text and prepare to
        ' start the next one.
        PreviousTextPos = 0
        If Len(ParagraphText) > 0 Then
            HyperTextRecord.TextBlock = ""
            HyperTextRecord.NextBlock = 0
```

```
            Do While (Len(ParagraphText) > 0)
                If Len(ParagraphText) > 128 Then
                    If Mid$(ParagraphText, 128, 1) = " " Then
                        HyperTextRecord.TextBlock = Left$(ParagraphText,
                            127) + Chr$(1)
                    Else
                        HyperTextRecord.TextBlock = Left$(ParagraphText, 128)
                    End If
                    ParagraphText = Mid$(ParagraphText, 129)
                Else
                    HyperTextRecord.TextBlock = ParagraphText
                    ParagraphText = ""
                End If
                LinkPos = LinkPos + 1
                HyperTextRecord.NextBlock = PreviousTextPos
                Put #LinkFileNum, LinkPos, HyperTextRecord
                PreviousTextPos = LinkPos
                Loop
            End If
        ' Set the file pointer in the subject record and
        ' save the record in the .IDX file.
        SubjectIndexRecord.TextFilePos = PreviousTextPos
        If Len(RTrim$(SubjectIndexRecord.Subject)) > 0 Then
            IndexPos = IndexPos + 1
            Put #IndexFileNum, IndexPos, SubjectIndexRecord
            End If
        ' Create a new subject
        If Left$(LineOfText, 3) = "###" Then
            SubjectIndexRecord.Subject = Mid$(LineOfText, 4)
            SubjectIndexRecord.TextFilePos = 0
        Else
            SubjectIndexRecord.Subject = ""
            SubjectIndexRecord.TextFilePos = 0
        End If
        End If
    Loop
    ' If the source text ends with an orphan
    ' subject header (it has no Subject text),
    ' save it anyway.
    If Len(RTrim$(SubjectIndexRecord.Subject)) > 0 Then
        IndexPos = IndexPos + 1
        Put #IndexFileNum, IndexPos, SubjectIndexRecord
        End If

    Close LinkFileNum
    Close IndexFileNum
    FilesAreOpen = False
    Close TextFileNum
End Sub
```

This is the most complex procedure in our system. **CompileText()** treats all text as simple strings; it doesn't actually interpret any of the hotlinks. It differentiates only between subject text and subject names.

To get a better understanding of how the procedure works, check out the following pseudo-code:

```
Open the files.
Repeat:
    Read a line from the text file;
    If the line does not begin with ###, then
        add it to the subject text buffer string;
    If the line does begin with ###, or we've reached the end of the file, then
        store the subject:
            If we have gathered text for the previous subject then
                record the subject text by breaking up the text buffer
                string into a reverse-linked list of fixed-length
                strings in the .HTF file;
            Insert the position of the last text record into the subject index record;
            Record the subject index record in the .IDX file;
            If the latest line we've read begins with ###, then
                start a new subject;
    until we reach the end of text file.
If the last line of the file contained a subject name, then
    store it in the subject index file, even though it has no subject text.
Close the files.
```

The hotlinks don't matter in this text conversion process. We only need to collect the text from the source file, build it into a long string, then chop it up into uniform blocks that we can store as records in the .HTF file. Each record in the .HTF file points to the previous segment in its subject text group. The first record in each subject list contains a null pointer (record number zero). Each subject index record in the .IDX file points to the last record in the .HTF file that belongs to that subject. As Figure 2.13 shows, this backward daisy-chain is called a *reverse-linked list*. You could forward-link the subject text records, but you would have to juggle more file pointers as you assemble the list.

Let's take a closer look at the most important sections of **CompileText()**:

```
Do While Not EOF(TextFileNum)
    Line Input #TextFileNum, LineOfText
    If (Left$(LineOfText, 3) <> "###") Then
        ' Append this line of the source text
        ' to the current subject text buffer.
        If Len(LineOfText) = 0 Then
            ParagraphText = ParagraphText + " " + Chr$(13) + Chr$(10) + " "
        Else
            ParagraphText = ParagraphText + LineOfText
        End If
    End If
    -
    -
```

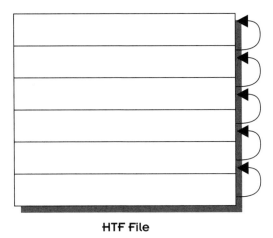

HTF File

Figure 2.13 *A reverse-linked list.*

```
    -
Loop
```

The beginning of the main loop reads a line from the source text file, and checks that line to determine if it begins with the triple-pound sign prefix, indicating a subject heading. If the line does not begin with "###", we add its contents to the current text buffer, **ParagraphText**.

When VB reads a line from a source (.TXT) text file, it doesn't include the carriage return/line feed pair that terminate the line. A blank line becomes a null string. If we just add the null string to the **ParagraphText** string—meaning that we add nothing at all—we lose the blank line altogether. By inserting the space-bracketed CR LF sequence, we create a "word" that **GetWordFrom()** can detect. We could actually substitute some other non-printing character, or we could use just the CR or LF alone, but a CR LF sequence is ideal for marking the location of an intentional (or "hard") CR LF.

The next section in the **While** loop checks the newly read line of text to determine if it's a subject heading. But this time the loop also checks for an end-of-file condition. Either condition indicates that it has come to the end of a subject block, and that it's time to re-package the text for storage in the linked text file:

```
Do While Not EOF(TextFileNum)
    -
    -
    -
```

```
If (Left$(LineOfText, 3) = "###") Or (EOF(TextFileNum)) Then
    ' We've reached the end of a subject, so
    ' store its accumulated text and prepare to
    ' start the next one.
    PreviousTextPos = 0
    -

    -

    -
```

The innermost block of code bales the text, linking it as it goes.

```
If Len(ParagraphText) > 0 Then
    HyperTextRecord.TextBlock = ""
    HyperTextRecord.NextBlock = 0
    Do While (Len(ParagraphText) > 0)
        If Len(ParagraphText) > 128 Then
            If Mid$(ParagraphText, 128, 1) = " " Then
                HyperTextRecord.TextBlock = Left$(ParagraphText, 127) + Chr$(1)
              Else
                HyperTextRecord.TextBlock = Left$(ParagraphText, 128)
              End If
            ParagraphText = Mid$(ParagraphText, 129)
          Else
            HyperTextRecord.TextBlock = ParagraphText
            ParagraphText = ""
          End If
        LinkPos = LinkPos + 1
        HyperTextRecord.NextBlock = PreviousTextPos
        Put #LinkFileNum, LinkPos, HyperTextRecord
        PreviousTextPos = LinkPos
        Loop
    End If
```

One subsection of this code deserves some special attention:

```
If Mid$(ParagraphText, 128, 1) = " " Then
    HyperTextRecord.TextBlock = Left$(ParagraphText, 127) + Chr$(1)
      Else
        HyperTextRecord.TextBlock = Left$(ParagraphText, 128)
      End If
```

VB fills fixed-length strings with spaces. When we reassemble the text for display, we'll use the **RTrim$()** function to eliminate the padding. But the last character in a full block may actually contain an intentional space. So to preserve that space, we substitute a non-printing character (I've arbitrarily chosen ASCII value 1) to mark its place. Later, when we load this text, we'll swap the space back in.

Remember, as you type your source text, you must include all the interword spaces; which means that before you type a carriage return in mid-sentence, you'll want to add a space to the end of the current line.

Before we bid farewell to the main loop, we fill in the **FilePos** field in the subject index record, which links it to the text records. And finally, if necessary (meaning we haven't yet reached the end of the file), we create the next subject index record.

```
      SubjectIndexRecord.FilePos = PreviousTextPos
      If Len(RTrim$(SubjectIndexRecord.Subject)) > 0 Then
          IndexPos = IndexPos + 1
          Put #IndexFileNum, IndexPos, SubjectIndexRecord
          End If
      ' Create a new subject
      If Left$(LineOfText, 3) = "###" Then
          SubjectIndexRecord.Subject = Mid$(LineOfText, 4)
          SubjectIndexRecord.FilePos = 0
        Else
          SubjectIndexRecord.Subject = ""
          SubjectIndexRecord.FilePos = 0
        End If
    End If
Loop
```

After we've read and digested the entire source text file, we handle any stray subject heading that might have been hanging on the end of the file without any subject text:

```
    If Len(RTrim$(SubjectIndexRecord.Subject)) > 0 Then
        IndexPos = IndexPos + 1
        Put #IndexFileNum, IndexPos, SubjectIndexRecord
        End If

    Close LinkFileNum
    Close IndexFileNum
    FilesAreOpen = False
    Close TextFileNum
End Sub
```

Using the Compiler

To invoke **CompileText()**, we'll need to add a Command Button control to Form1. As Figure 2.14 shows, the Command Button on our form has the caption "Compile Hypertext." You must also set its **Name** property to "CompileButton."

Next, in the **CompileButton_Click()** procedure, include a call for **CompileText()**, passing the name of your text file as its parameter:

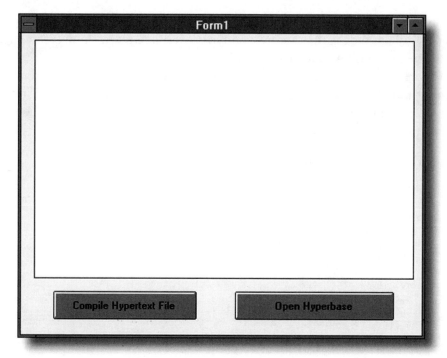

Figure 2.14   *The expanded hypertext form with the required Command Button.*

Listing 2.12   CompileButton_Click() General Procedure from HYPRTXT3.FRM

```
Sub CompileButton_Click ()
    CompileText App.Path & "\HyprTxt3.Txt"
    End Sub
```

Before we can use the compiled hypertext, we need to open it. This is accomplished in the **OpenHyperbase()** procedure, shown in Listing 2.13.

Listing 2.13   OpenHyperbase() General Procedure from HYPRTEXT3.FRM

```
Sub OpenHyperbase (FileName As String)
    Dim RootFileName As String
    Dim LinkRecordLen As Integer
    Dim IndexRecordLen As Integer

    LinkFileNum = 2
    IndexFileNum = 3
    NumberOfSubjects = 0
    LinkRecordLen = Len(HyperTextRecord)
    IndexRecordLen = Len(SubjectIndexRecord)
    If InStr(FileName, ".") > 0 Then
        RootFileName = Left$(FileName, InStr(FileName, ".") - 1)
      Else
```

```
            RootFileName = FileName
        End If
    If FilesAreOpen Then
        Close LinkFileNum
        Close IndexFileNum
        FilesAreOpen = False
        End If
    Open RootFileName + ".HTF" For Random As #LinkFileNum Len = LinkRecordLen
    Open RootFileName + ".IDX" For Random As #IndexFileNum Len = IndexRecordLen
    FilesAreOpen = True
    IndexPos = 0
    Do Until EOF(IndexFileNum)
        IndexPos = IndexPos + 1
        Get #IndexFileNum, IndexPos, SubjectIndexArray(IndexPos)
        Loop
    NumberOfSubjects = IndexPos - 1
    End Sub
```

This procedure opens the .IDX and .HTF files. It then reads the entire .IDX
file into an array. The obvious benefit of this approach is speed. By having all
of the index entries in memory, you can get away with linear searches. For
very large hyperbases, this may not be practical. Instead, you may wish to
search the .IDX file directly. File searches use less memory, but performance
lags slightly (unless you resort to hashing or indexing, of course).

We now have a control system and a data structure. After we add the necessary
declarations to our form, we'll modify **LoadSubject()** to read text from the files.

Adding the Required Declarations

Before continuing, we need to add the declarations shown in Listing 2.14 to
Form1 (filename HYPRTXT3.FRM) so that all of our new hypertext processing
features will be supported.

Listing 2.14   Declarations Section from HYPRTXT3.FRM

```
Option Explicit

Dim HyperLinkArray(100) As HyperLinkElement
Dim SubjectIndexArray(100) As SubjectIndexRecords
Dim HyperLinkArraySize As Integer
Dim HyperTextRecord As HyperTextRecords
Dim SubjectIndexRecord As SubjectIndexRecords
Dim NumberOfSubjects As Integer
Dim IndexPos As Long
Dim LinkPos As Long

Dim CurrentTop As Single
Dim LinkArrayPos As Integer
Dim ArrayPlaceHolder As Integer
Dim SubjectHeading As String
```

```
Dim LinkFileNum As Integer
Dim IndexFileNum As Integer
Dim FilesAreOpen As Integer
```

Wrapping Up the Complete Hypertext System

To wrap up the new hypertext system, we'll need to create new versions of the **LoadSubject()** procedure and the **Getword From()** function we used in the first two hypertext projects. We'll also need to create a new support function, **ReadInText()**, and a new procedure, **ParseLink()**. Then, we'll modify the **Picture1_MouseDown()** and **OpenButton_Click()** event procedures.

The final version of **LoadSubject()** (Listing 2.15) performs a few miscellaneous formatting duties, such as displaying the subject heading in a different color and larger type. It uses the new function, **ReadInText()**, to locate a subject in a .IDX file and retrieve the corresponding text from the .HTF file. **LoadSubject()** also calls the new general procedure **ParseLink()**, which parses the link element into its two components: a hotlink word (or phrase) and a destination subject (or "target").

Listing 2.15   LoadSubject() General Procedure from HYPRTXT3.FRM

```
Sub LoadSubject (Subject As String)
    Dim StringToPrint As String
    Dim CreatingALink As Integer
    Dim NextWord As String
    Dim TempWord As String

    StringToPrint = ReadInText(Subject)

    Picture1.Cls
    LinkArrayPos = 0
    ArrayPlaceHolder = 1

    ' Display subject name as heading.
    Picture1.FontBold = False
    Picture1.ForeColor = BLUE
    Picture1.FontSize = 16
    Picture1.CurrentX = 200
    Picture1.Print RTrim$(Subject)
    Picture1.Print

    ' Set base text attributes.
    Picture1.ForeColor = BLACK
    Picture1.FontSize = 12
    Picture1.CurrentX = 200

    CurrentTop = Picture1.CurrentY
    NextWord = GetWordFrom(StringToPrint)
```

```
    Do While NextWord <> ""
        If Left$(NextWord, 2) = "##" Then
            ParseLink NextWord, TempWord, Subject
            TempWord = TempWord + Left$(StringToPrint, 1)
            StringToPrint = Mid$(StringToPrint, 2)
            CreatingALink = True
        Else
            TempWord = NextWord
            CreatingALink = False
        End If
        ' Insert a blank line between paragraphs.
        If Left$(TempWord, 1) = Chr$(13) Then
            NewLine
            NewLine
            Picture1.CurrentX = 200
            TempWord = ""
            End If
        If ((Picture1.CurrentX + Picture1.TextWidth(TempWord)) >
            Picture1.ScaleWidth) Then
            NewLine
            Picture1.CurrentX = 200
            End If
        If CreatingALink Then
            LinkArrayPos = LinkArrayPos + 1
            HyperLinkArray(LinkArrayPos).Left = Picture1.CurrentX
            HyperLinkArray(LinkArrayPos).Top = CurrentTop
            Picture1.FontBold = True
            Picture1.Print TempWord;
            Picture1.FontBold = False
            HyperLinkArray(LinkArrayPos).Right = Picture1.CurrentX
            HyperLinkArray(LinkArrayPos).DestinationSubject = Subject
        Else
            Picture1.Print TempWord;
        End If
        NextWord = GetWordFrom(StringToPrint)
    Loop
    HyperLinkArraySize = LinkArrayPos
    NewLine
End Sub
```

The previous version of the function **GetWordFrom()** (as shown in Listing 2.1) searched for spaces to determine word boundaries. But a hotlink may consist of more than a single word. When **GetWordFrom()** locates a link string in the text, we'll want it to grab the whole thing, from the ## tag to the ~ terminator, so we can later parse it into its two components: a link word or phrase, and a target subject string. We'll modify **GetWordFrom()** so it treats link strings as a special case, as shown in Listing 2.16.

Listing 2.16　GetWordFrom() General Function from HYPRTXT3.FRM.

```
Function GetWordFrom (AnyString As String) As String
   If Left$(AnyString, 1) = "#" Then
      GetWordFrom = Left$(AnyString, InStr(AnyString, "~"))
      AnyString = Mid$(AnyString, InStr(AnyString, "~"") + 1)
   ElseIf InStr(AnyString, " ") = 0 Then
      GetWordFrom = AnyString
      AnyString = ""
   Else
      GetWordFrom = Left$(AnyString, InStr(AnyString, " "))
      AnyString = Mid$(AnyString, InStr(AnyString, " ") + 1)
   End If
End Function
```

Instead of passing **LoadSubject()** the actual paragraph text, we want to pass it the subject name. And that's where **ReadInText()** comes in (see Listing 2.17). Recall that this function reads the .IDX file to locate the subject, and then it reads the .HTF file to retrieve the related text. As it reads the text records belonging to a particular subject from the .HTF file, it will concatenate them into a single string, which it will then return to **LoadSubject()**.

Listing 2.17　ReadInText() General Function from HYPRTXT3.FRM

```
Function ReadInText (SubjectName As String) As String

   Dim ParagraphText As String
   Dim TempString As String

   ParagraphText = ""
   IndexPos = 1
   ' Search for subject.
   Do Until (RTrim$(SubjectIndexArray(IndexPos).Subject) = SubjectName)
            Or (IndexPos > NumberOfSubjects)
      IndexPos = IndexPos + 1
      Loop
   ' If subject is found, read in text.
   If IndexPos <= NumberOfSubjects Then
      LinkPos = SubjectIndexArray(IndexPos).TextFilePos
      Do Until (LinkPos = 0) Or (EOF(LinkFileNum))
         Get #LinkFileNum, LinkPos, HyperTextRecord
         TempString = RTrim$(HyperTextRecord.TextBlock)
         ' Replace the substituted spaces.
         If Right$(TempString, 1) = Chr$(1) Then
             TempString = Left$(TempString, Len(TempString) - 1) + " "
           End If
         ParagraphText = TempString + ParagraphText
         LinkPos = HyperTextRecord.NextBlock
         Loop
```

```
    End If
ReadInText = ParagraphText
End Function
```

Next, we need to add the new procedure **ParseLink()**, as shown in Listing 2.18.

Listing 2.18   ParseLink() General Procedure from HYPRTXT3.FRM

```
Sub ParseLink (RawLink As String, LinkWord As String, Subject As String)
    Dim DelimiterPos As Integer
    Dim TildePos As Integer
    ' Strip off the pound signs.
    While Left$(RawLink, 1) = "#"
        RawLink = Mid$(RawLink, 2)
        Wend
    ' Find the link phrase.
    DelimiterPos = InStr(RawLink, "|")
    LinkWord = Left$(RawLink, DelimiterPos - 1)
    RawLink = Mid$(RawLink, DelimiterPos + 1)
    ' Find the destination subject.
    TildePos = InStr(RawLink, "~")
    Subject = Left$(RawLink, TildePos - 1)
    End Sub
```

ParseLink() takes a hotlink string segment that starts with ## and ends with ~, and breaks it into its two constituent components: the hotlink word or phrase that needs to appear in the text, and the name of the subject to which it is linked. Parsing can be complex, but in this case there's nothing to it. We use VB's **InStr()** function to locate the delimiter characters—the pound sign (#), vertical bar (|), and tilde (~), then use VB's **Left$()** and **Mid$()** functions to strip the delimiters and pull out the strings.

Picture1_MouseDown() now needs to respond differently to a click on a hotlink. Instead of displaying a pop-up message, we want it to load and display the appropriate subject, as the code shown in Listing 2.19 indicates.

Listing 2.19   The Picture1_MouseDown() Event Procedure from HYPRTXT3.FRM

```
Sub Picture1_MouseDown (Button As Integer, Shift As Integer, X As Single, Y As
Single)
    Dim AnyString As String
    Dim Index As Integer

    For Index = 1 To HyperLinkArraySize
        If (X > HyperLinkArray(Index).Left) And
           (X < HyperLinkArray(Index).Right) And
           (Y < HyperLinkArray(Index).Bottom) And
           (Y > HyperLinkArray(Index).Top) Then
                AnyString = RTrim$(HyperLinkArray(Index).DestinationSubject)
                LoadSubject AnyString
```

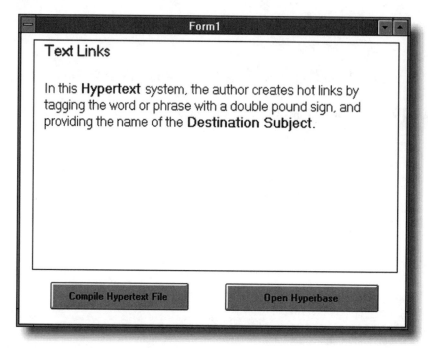

Figure 2.15   *The working hypertext system.*

```
        End If
      Next Index
   End Sub
```

Next, we change **OpenButton_Click()** (see Listing 2.20) to call **OpenHyperbase()** and load the first subject in the index:

Listing 2.20   OpenButton_Click() Event Procedure from HYPRTXT3.FRM

```
Sub OpenButton_Click ()
   OpenHyperbase App.Path & "\HyprTxt3.XXX"
   LoadSubject RTrim$(SubjectIndexArray(1).Subject)
   End Sub
```

The filename extension is irrelevant to **OpenHyperbase()** because it's going to strip off the extension and open the files HYPRTXT3.IDX and HYPRTXT3.HTF.

Before we can run the program, we need to initialize **FilesAreOpen**. We do that in the **Form_Load()** event procedure, shown in Listing 2.21.

Listing 2.21   Form_Load() Event Procedure from HYPRTXT3.FRM

```
Sub Form_Load ()
   FilesAreOpen = False
   End Sub
```

Running the Complete Hypertext Program

We're finally ready to take our new program for a test drive. To do this, click on the **CompileButton** button to compile the text file HYPRTXT3.TXT, then click on the **OpenButton** button to open the compiled hypertext file. The first subject from the source text file should appear on the screen as shown in Figure 2.15. If you have provided sufficient hotlinks, you can move freely among the subject screens. If you haven't, you might find yourself trapped in a dead end, in which case your only choice is to terminate execution using any of the three handy controls designed for this purpose: the form's own Control menu, VB's End option on the Run menu, or the End button on the Toolbar.

Adding Error Trapping Support

If we were to add error trapping to our previous project, we'd have a much larger and more complex program on our hands. In order to avoid obscuring the subject at hand, throughout this book I will neglect most error trapping. Don't follow this bad example in your own projects.

The runtime errors that you'd need to consider fall into three categories:

- I/O errors that occur as a result of missing files, invalid drive specifications, or malfunctioning hardware
- Errors in the source text that trip up the parser and prevent it from compiling the source text into the hypertext files
- Poorly designed hyperlinks that lead the user into inescapable circular traps

VB provides some valuable features for runtime error trapping. The *VB Programmer's Guide* provides detailed examples of error trapping functions for some of the file I/O operations. You should study these functions and incorporate similar error traps into your programs. The goal of runtime error trapping is to prevent the user from ever encountering an error that terminates the execution of the program. If you plan to distribute your multimedia projects, whether as a commercial release, or as a corporate information system, or for any other purpose in which other people will need to use it without your personal guidance, then you must scrutinize your programs, and plug every chink with some sort of fail-safe mechanism.

As for errors in the source text, you'll get no help from VB. In my code, I've assumed that all hyperlinks will be properly terminated and delimited, and that once compiled, the hyperlinked text will provide open passage. Neither of these assumptions is prudent. See if you can devise methods for validating your source text, and for reporting compilation errors. Once your multimedia projects grow beyond a handful of topics, you'll find that time invested in error trapping is time well spent.

A Firm Foundation for Nimble Navigation

We've now constructed the most essential mechanisms for a hypertext—or a hypermedia—platform. We discovered that the Picture Box control offered us the most flexibility with the fewest obstacles for creating our hypertext system. We then developed data structures and algorithms that we used to place hyperlinks on the screen, to detect clicks on those links, and to store, retrieve, and display the text to which those links point.

Hypertext is only one of several navigational tools we can provide to the readers of our electronic documents. I'll present some of the others in later chapters. But first, let's add some multimedia features and get to the heart of the Windows Multimedia API.

Chapter

3

Ride the wave into multimedia apps by learning how to use the Windows Multimedia System.

Getting Started with the Windows Multimedia System

Thanks to Windows and Visual Basic, the step from hypertext to full hypermedia is shorter than you might suspect. The Windows Multimedia API offers several interfaces to help you get there. In Chapter 1, you learned about ways to call the simple **mciExecute()** function to plug in multimedia features. Now, I'm going to explain the Windows multimedia system in much more detail.

This system provides both low-level and high-level sets of functions. The low-level set, which includes numerous functions for WAVE, MIDI (musical instrument digital interface), and movie player operations, is the largest of the two. The high-level set, which consists primarily of six functions, provides an easy-to-use, high-level interface. As you might guess, the low-level functions call device drivers and require more programming. The high-level functions, on the other hand, hide the details as they pass messages to the *Media Control Interface* (*MCI*), which interprets the messages and calls the low-level functions to access the appropriate device drivers.

57

To perform important low-level tasks, such as writing utilities for mixing and editing WAVE files or synchronizing sounds with other multimedia activities, such as animation, we'll need the flexibility and precision timing of the low-level interface. For now, we only want to play existing multimedia files, so the high-level interface will work just fine.

Let's continue where we left off in Chapter 2 and expand on our hypertext system. After we explore the high-level multimedia interface, we'll add a multimedia connection to our hypertext system. Then, we'll work our way through the levels of the multimedia interface by exploring a couple of ways to play WAVE files. In Chapter 4, we'll move down a few levels and show you how to get closer to the MCI and work with low-level audio functions.

A Look at the High-Level MCI

Although the high-level MCI imposes a few limitations, it's still packed with useful features. It exists mainly to isolate us from the actual device drivers by providing a common interface for all multimedia devices. Using this interface, many of the same instructions will work whether we want to play CD audio, WAVE files, MIDI sequences, or video discs.

The MCI comes in two flavors: the Command-Message Interface and the Command-String Interface. The difference between these two interfaces is simple. When you call the Command-Message function **mciSendCommand()**, you pass it a numeric constant and a data structure filled with constants, strings, or pointers to other structures that indicate what operation you want the MCI to perform. When you call the Command-String function **mciSendString()**, you pass it a text string. The two functions execute the same commands—they just expect the commands in different formats.

In their *Multimedia Programmer's Workbook*, Microsoft states that the Command-Message Interface is "more versatile if your application controls an MCI device directly." They also say that the Command-String Interface is slower (after all, it's really just a translator that converts string commands into data structures for the Command-Message interface). Both statements may well be true, but the Command-String Interface offers a couple of advantages. First, you don't need a long list of constant declarations to establish names for all the command messages. Second—and this Microsoft does mention—the Command-String Interface can execute scripts provided by the end user without intermediate interpretation (you can pass operator text directly to the **mciSendString()** function, that is, if the operator knows the MCI command syntax).

Adding Multimedia to the Hypertext System

Our goal now is to extend the hypertext system we constructed in the previous chapter by adding sound. We can easily do this by using **mciExecute()**—the function that strips the Command-String Interface down to its bare bones. This function accepts a plain english text string as a single parameter. Unlike other MCI command functions, **mciExecute()** doesn't return an error code. Instead, when we call **mciExecute()**, the MCI performs its own error trapping and displays message boxes whenever an error occurs. Because these errors are non-fatal, your programs can go about their business, even when one or more multimedia devices aren't working. Although this function won't support a complex application that requires a dialog between the user and various multimedia devices, it does offer the easiest way to play back WAVE (digitized sound), MIDI (synthesized music and sound effects), MMM (movie/animation), AVI (audio/video interleave), and other standard multimedia files.

Plugging into the High-Level MCI

This project allows you to play a multimedia file when a hyperlink is selected. To incorporate the MCI interface, follow these steps:

1. Create a new form called HYPRTXT4.FRM. Begin with the form created in the last project in Chapter 2, HYPRTXT3.FRM, or make a copy of that file and add it to the new project.

2. Add a declaration for **mciExecute()** to the project's global code module, HYPRTXT4.BAS (Listing 3.1).

3. Modify the **Picture1_MouseDown()** event procedure used in the last hypertext project in Chapter 2 (Listing 3.2).

4. Create a new hypertext file to test out the multimedia interface (Listing 3.3).

 You'll find this project in the subdirectory \VBMAGIC, in the files HYPRTXT4.MAK, HYPRTXT4.FRM, HYPRTXT4.BAS, GLOBCONS.BAS, and HYPRTXT4.TXT.

Setting Up the Multimedia Interface

Once the new form has been created, we need to add the API function declaration shown in Listing 3.1 to the global code module.

Listing 3.1 Revised Declarations Section of HYPRTXT4.BAS

```
Declare Function mciExecute Lib "MMSystem" (ByVal CommandString As String) As Integer
```

Next, we need to modify the **Picture1_MouseDown()** event procedure. (Recall that this is the event procedure we used in Chapter 2 to test our hyperlinks.) In **Picture1_MouseDown()**, we'll perform a little extra parsing on the destination subject. We can play any multimedia file by passing the command string **"Play <filename.ext>"** to **mciExecute()**. So, we need to identify which destination subjects are truly subjects, and which are filenames. For this situation, a little cheating is in order. We'll assume that whenever the fourth character from the end of the destination subject is a period, the destination subject will be a filename with a three character extension. If we find such a string, we'll feed it to **mciExecute()** as the object of a **"Play"** command sentence. Listing 3.2 provides the new version of **Picture1_MouseDown()**.

Listing 3.2 Picture1_MouseDown() Event Procedure from HYPRTXT4.FRM

```
Sub Picture1_MouseDown (Button As Integer, Shift As Integer,
                        X As Single, Y As Single)
    Dim AnyString As String
    Dim FileType As String
    Text1.Text = ""
    For Index% = 1 To HyperLinkArraySize
        If (X > HyperLinkArray(Index%).UpperX) And
           (X < HyperLinkArray(Index%).LowerX) And
           (Y < HyperLinkArray(Index%).LowerY) And
           (Y > HyperLinkArray(Index%).UpperY) Then
           AnyString =
               RTrim$(HyperLinkArray(Index%).DestinationSubject)
           If Left$(Right$(AnyString, 4), 1) = "." Then
               Text1.Text = "Playing: " + AnyString
               Dummy% = mciExecute("Play " + AnyString)
           Else
               LoadSubject AnyString
           End If
        End If
    Next Index%
End Sub
```

The function **mciExecute()** returns a boolean value to indicate if it succeds or fails. I'm ignoring it by assigning it to **Dummy%**. I also sneaked in a Text control to display the name of the file being played.

That's it. You can add a hotlink to the hypertext source file that specifies a multimedia filename, including the path if necessary, and try it out. Listing 3.3 provides a sample hypertext file.

Listing 3.3   HYPRTXT4.TXT Sample Source Text File

```
###Hypertext
Hypertext systems enable readers to jump from topic to topic by selecting
key words or phrases embedded in the text.  These special words are sometimes
known as ##"hotlinks"|Text Links~.
###Text Links
In this sytem, the author creates hotlinks by tagging the word or phrase with
a double pound sign, and providing the name of the ##Destination
Subject|Destination Subjects~.
###Destination Subjects
When the user clicks on a ##hotlink|Text Links~, the system locates the
appropriate topic in the ##hypertext|Hypertext~ file and displays it on the
screen.

Hotlinks may also trigger ##multimedia|Multimedia~ events.
###Multimedia
Multimedia systems combine elements such as text, ##sound|c:\windows\chord.wav~
and ##hypertext|Hypertext~ to create an engaging and informative presentation.

To prepare a multimedia presentation, we design forms on which to display
graphics and text.  Icons are used to invoke other media, such as sound bites
and ##MIDI|c:\windows\canyon.mid~ music.
```

Of course, you can add other multimedia features. For example, you might want to display a bitmap or activate a CD player. For true hypermedia, you may even want to create hotspot regions on bitmapped images. We'll do all of these things in later chapters using a combination of VB and a few Windows API functions. But first, let's look at the Windows Multimedia System in more detail.

Exploring the Windows Multimedia System

The Windows multimedia system functions are located in two dynamic link libraries, or DLLs. In fact, all Windows operating system functions reside in DLLs. The plain old Windows operating system, *sans* multimedia, comes in three libraries: Kernel, GDI (graphic device interface), and User. These files carry .EXE extensions rather than .DLL, but nevertheless, they contain all of the 800 or so functions that define Windows services.

Almost all of the graphics functions reside in the GDI. When you create a multimedia project, you will inevitably call numerous GDI functions, which include functions for drawing shapes, writing text, defining and changing colors, and many other graphics operations. Because the three main Windows libraries are more fundamental to Windows programming than to the multimedia system, we'll skip them for now and return to them in later chapters.

A Tour of the Multimedia API

The multimedia system provides an interface to several services:

- WAVE audio playback and recording
- Synthesizer audio and MIDI
- Animation playback
- Video playback
- Joystick services
- High-resolution timing
- Operation of external media devices

Except for the lower-level animation functions, which you'll find in MMP.DLL, the functions that control these services reside in MMSYSTEM.DLL. These functions can be further divided into two classes: the low-level and high-level multimedia interfaces. The function **mciExecute()**, which we used earlier to add multimedia playback capabilities to our hypertext system, belongs to the high-level interface. In fact, you might say that **mciExecute()** represents the *highest* level of the high-level interface because it parses MCI commands and performs its own error trapping.

Let's descend into the multimedia interface one level at a time. We'll do this by calling upon several of the functions that we can use to play WAVE files.

Using High-Level Multimedia Functions: MessageBeep() and sndPlaySound()

As I mentioned earlier, the high-level interface includes the MCI—a kind of universal control language for media devices—and two sound functions: **MessageBeep()** and **sndPlaySound()**. You could say that **MessageBeep()** and **sndPlaySound()** sit atop the summit of the multimedia interface. Why? Because they perform a single high-level function—playing WAVE files. In addition, you don't need to know anything about the underlying data structures—such as the Wave audio data itself—to use them.

Of theses two functions, **MessageBeep()** is the most specialized. It takes a single parameter, a flag that indicates a system alert level. If you've explored VB's **MsgBox** statement (or function), you may know that among the many *message types* it will accept are four special types that indicate system alerts: **MB_ICONSTOP**, **MB_ICONQUESTION**, **MB_ICONEXCLAMATION**, and **MB_ICONINFORMATION**. These four message box flags cause the message box to display icons: a stop sign, a question mark, an exclamation point, and the letter "i", respectively. These four VB message flags correspond to four Windows flags: **MB_ICONHAND**, **MB_ICONQUESTION**, **MB_ICON-**

EXCLAMATION, and **MB_ICONASTERISK**. Their names may differ, but their values match.

Now if you look in the **[sounds]** section of your WIN.INI file, you'll find a list that looks something like this:

```
[sounds]
SystemAsterisk=chord.wav,Asterisk
SystemHand=chord.wav,Critical Stop
SystemDefault=ding.wav,Default Beep
SystemExclamation=chord.wav,Exclamation
startprogram=CHIMES.WAV,Program Launch
SystemQuestion=chord.wav,Question
SystemExit=C:\WINDOWS\GLASS.WAV,Windows Exit
SystemStart=tada.wav,Windows Start
```

These entries assign sounds, in the form of WAVE files, to system events. Notice that four of the events in this list correspond to the four Windows message flags. By calling **MessageBeep()** with one of these four flags, you will cause Windows to look up the appropriate sound in WIN.INI and play it.

Actually, **MessageBeep()** is not a function at all; it's a procedure because it doesn't return anything—no error code, no handles, no success flag—nothing. If you hand it a flag value it doesn't recognize, it simply plays the **SystemDefault** sound.

You can also use **sndPlaySound()** to play message beeps. This function is actually more useful than **MessageBeep()** because it can play other WAVE files in your system and not just the sounds that you've assigned to system events in WIN.INI. The **sndPlaySound()** function takes two arguments and returns an integer value that represents a boolean result.

Integer versus Boolean Values

From now on, I'll refer to "integer values that represent boolean results" as boolean values. Technically, VB does not support a boolean data type. Instead, it uses integer values to represent the two boolean conditions: True or False. An integer value of 0, which in binary is represented by 16 bits all set to 0, indicates a boolean value of False. Any other integer value (that is, any binary value that is not purely 0), represents a boolean value of True. VB uses the value -1 to represent True because, in base 2, the integer value -1 is represented by 16 bits all set to 1, which is kind of like saying "this is absolutely True." Windows API functions, on the other hand, return +1 to represent a logical value of True. Since any integer value other than 0 means True to VB, either value will work.

Playing WAVE Files with MessageBeep()

Let's begin a new project that demonstrates **MessageBeep()**. We'll call it **MCIPlay**. As we descend into the multimedia interface, we're going to add to this project, building in new functions that demonstrate the various ways to play WAVE and other types of multimedia files.

To test out **MessageBeep()**, follow these steps:

1. Create a new form called MCIPLAY1.FRM.
2. Add the required declarations to MCIPLAY1.FRM (Listing 3.4).
3. Create a code module called MCIPLAY1.BAS, and add the required declarations (Listing 3.5).
4. Add a Command Button to MCIPLAY1.FRM to play a WAVE file.
5. Add code for the **MessageBeepButton_Click()** event procedure (Listing 3.6).

This project is located in the subdirectory \VBMAGIC, in the files MCIPLAY1.MAK, MCIPLAY1.FRM, and MCIPLAY1.BAS. These files will also be used for the second project in this chapter.

Creating the MCIPlay Project: Version 1

To start, add the declaration shown in Listing 3.4 to the declarations section of MCIPLAY1.FRM. (Remember, this is a new form that you should create.)

Listing 3.4   From the Declarations Section of MCIPLAY1.FRM

```
Declare Sub MessageBeep Lib "User" (ByVal wAlert As Integer)
```

As this declaration indicates, **MessageBeep()** actually resides in the "User" DLL.

To call **MessageBeep()**, you'll need at least one of the four values assigned to the six constants shown in Listing 3.5.

Listing 3.5   From the Declarations Section of MCIPLAY1.BAS

```
Global Const MB_ICONHAND = &H10
Global Const MB_ICONSTOP = MB_ICONHAND
Global Const MB_ICONQUESTION = &H20
Global Const MB_ICONEXCLAMATION = &H30
Global Const MB_ICONASTERISK = &H40
Global Const MB_ICONINFORMATION = MB_ICONASTERISK
```

These constants could be declared at the form level, without the **Global** keyword of course, but since we're going to need a *code module* eventually, we might as well start one now. Notice that we've named the code module **MCIPLAY1.BAS**.

Next, we'll add a Command Button to the form and set its caption to "Message Beep," as shown in Figure 3.1. It also wouldn't hurt to change its **Name** property to something more descriptive than Command1. I recommend "MessageBeepButton."

Finally, we'll need to add one statement in the **MessageBeepButton_Click()** event procedure as shown in Listing 3.6.

Listing 3.6   MessageBeepButton_Click Event Procedure from MCIPLAY1.FRM

```
Sub MessageBeepButton_Click ()
    MessageBeep MB_ICONEXCLAMATION
    End Sub
```

> **Note:** *If you wish, you can use the Sound applet in the Windows Control Panel to change the system sounds.*

MessageBeep() allows us to abandon old-fashioned beeps in favor of digitized sounds for system signals. Because of its limited capabilities, you wouldn't want to use it as a multimedia presentation function. However, when you build your multimedia apps, you could use message beeps for system signals, just as you would with other types of applications. The **[sounds]** section of the WIN.INI file is supposed to ensure that all Windows apps produce the same message beeps, whether those are the default sounds, or sounds installed by the user.

Figure 3.1 *The MCIPLAY form with its first Command Button.*

Playing WAVE Files with sndPlaySound()

This second sound project allows you to play any WAVE file using the **sndPlaySound()** function. Here are the steps to follow:

1. Add a new declaration to MCIPLAY1.FRM (Listing 3.7).
2. Add the required declarations to the MCIPLAY1.BAS code module (Listing 3.8).
4. Add the necessary controls to MCIPLAY1.FRM.
5. Update the **PlaySoundButton_Click()** event (Listing 3.9).

Running the New MCIPlay Project

To test **sndPlaySound()**, run the program MCIPlay and type the name of a WAVE file, including its path, into the Command String Text Box that appears at the top of the form. Then, click on the Command Button labeled "sndPlaySound." Figure 3.2 shows an example of the program as it is running.

You can also enter the name of a system sound, such as "SystemAsterisk" or "SystemExit." **sndPlaySound()** first searches the **[sounds]** section of WIN.INI for a matching string. If it doesn't find one, it looks in the disk directory. If it still doesn't find a match, it plays the "SystemDefault" sound. You might expect an empty string to produce either an error or the "SystemDefault" sound. Don't count on it. When you call the function with an empty (or null) string, it simply plays nothing.

The only way I have found to produce a return value of **False** is to disable the device driver for my sound card. **sndPlaySound()** is remarkably robust, which makes it handy for simple sound playback applications.

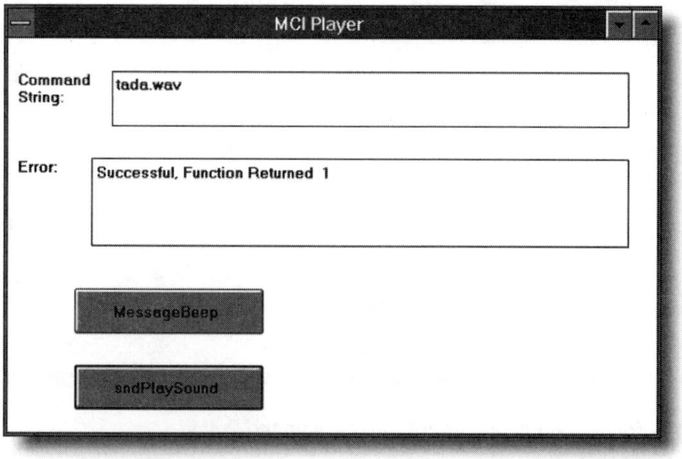

Figure 3.2 *Testing **sndPlaySound()**.*

By the way, all of the high-level MCI functions will play system sounds. We won't bother to explore that option further, but it's there if you need it.

Expanding the MCIPlay Project: Version 1

Instead of creating a whole new project, we'll add to MCIPLAY1.FRM from the previous project. This time, add the declaration shown in Listing 3.7 to the declarations section of MCIPLAY1.FRM.

Listing 3.7   From the Declarations Section of MCIPLAY1.FRM

```
Declare Function sndPlaySound Lib "MMSystem" (ByVal lpSound As String,
  ByVal flag As Integer) As Integer
```

For the first parameter, **lpSound**, we pass a *long pointer to a string* that contains either a filename or the name of a system sound. For the second parameter, **flag**, we pass an integer value that comprises one or more *Flags*.

Many of the Windows API functions take **flag** parameters. These paramaters are also an integeral component of *windows messages*. In decimal terms, the value of each flag is a factor of two. The first flag has a decimal value of 1 (2 raised to the power of 0), the second flag has a decimal value of 2, the third has a value of 4, and so on. So each flag value represents one bit in the two byte integer. An integer flag block can therefore hold up to 16 flags simultaneously (sometimes **flag** parameters are represented by 4 bytes, or in VB, *long integers*, which can hold 32 flags). To set multiple flags, we can just add their values together, or better yet, combine them with a logical **Or** operation.

The six flags that **sndPlaySound()** supports need to be added to the declarations section of MCIPLAY1.BAS (Listing 3.8).

Listing 3.8   From the Declarations Section of MCIPLAY1.BAS

```
Global Const SND_SYNC = &H0        ' decimal 0, play synchronously (the default)
Global Const SND_ASYNC = &H1       ' decimal 1, play asynchronously
Global Const SND_NODEFAULT = &H2   ' decimal 2, don't use default sound
Global Const SND_MEMORY = &H4      ' decimal 4, lpSound points to a memory file
Global Const SND_LOOP = &H8        ' decimal 8, loop the sound
Global Const SND_NOSTOP = &H10     ' decimal 16, don't stop any currently
                                               playing sound
```

For now, we'll only use the first two **SND** flags. **SND_SYNC** causes the system to play a WAVE file *synchronously*. This means that a program will stand at attention until **sndPlaySound()** has finished playing the sound. Since **SND_SYNC** has a 0 value, it actually represents the absence of a flag. It also represents the default behavior of the function. **SND_ASYNC** causes **sndPlaySound()** to return control to a program immediately after starting playback, even as the WAVE file continues to play *asynchronously* in the background. If **sndPlaySound()** succeeds, it returns **True**; otherwise, it returns **False**.

To demonstrate this function, we'll add three more controls to MCIPlay: a Command Button named **PlaySoundButton**, and two Text Boxes named **CommandStringText** and **ErrorText**, which are shown in Figure 3.3. Let's also label the Text Boxes and clear their initial **Text** properties.

In the **PlaySoundButton_Click()** event procedure, we'll accept a **SoundName** as user input through the **CommandStringText** Text Box. We'll then interpret the result of the play operation and display a message in **ErrorText** to indicate success or failure. The new version of this event is shown in Listing 3.9.

Listing 3.9 PlaySoundButton_Click() Event Procedure from MCIPLAY1.FRM

```
Sub PlaySoundButton_Click ()
    Dim Successful As Integer
    Dim SoundName As String

    SoundName = CommandStringText.Text
    Successful = sndPlaySound(SoundName, SND_ASYNC)
    If Successful Then
        ErrorText.Text = "Successful, Function Returned " + Str$(Successful)
    Else
        ErrorText.Text = "Unsuccessful, Function Returned " + Str$(Successful)
    End If
End Sub
```

In the next chapter, we'll add four more buttons to this program to demonstrate some of the other ways to play sound.

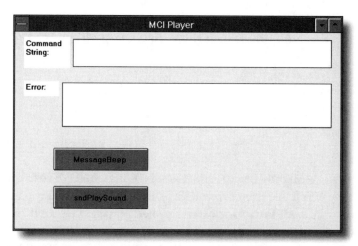

Figure 3.3 *MCIPlay with additional controls to demonstrate **sndPlaySound()**.*

**Learn how to use the
Windows Multimedia System.**

Inside the Windows Multimedia System

T he Windows Media Control Interface, or MCI, provides a common interface to a variety of multimedia devices, including *Audio Video Interleave* (AVI) playback, animation players, VCRs, video disk players, CD players, and the Waveaudio and synthesizer systems on our sound cards. In this chapter, we'll continue where we left off in the previous chapter, and I'll show you how to play WAVE files using MCI funtions. Then, we'll move down a level to show you how to use low-level audio functions.

Using the MCI

With the MCI functions we can send commands to any of these devices to start, stop, pause, or position them, like pushing the buttons on the front panel of your home VCR or CD player. The particular commands available for each device depend on the capabilities of the device itself. For example, we can order the Waveaudio device to record, but a CD player can only play. To send MCI commands to multimedia devices, we pass them as arguments to any of three MCI command functions. Along with the command functions, the MCI includes two support functions.

All MCI function names begin with the prefix *mci* and are arranged in three short groups:

- The Command-Message Interface
  mciSendCommand()
  mciGetDeviceID()
- The Command-String Interface
  mciSendString()
  mciExecute()
- Both Command-String and Command-Message Interfaces
  mciGetErrorString()
  mciSetYieldProc()

The last function, **mciSetYieldProc()**, enables the MCI to carry on a dialog with your application when you issue an MCI command with a **WAIT** flag. The **WAIT** flag instructs MCI not to return control back to your program until it completes the operation you've requested. For example, you may instruct the MCI to play a MIDI music sequencer file, which could take several minutes. Without the **WAIT** flag, the MCI will immediately return control to your program and play the MIDI file in the background. With the **WAIT** flag, the MCI will freeze your program until the entire sequence has played. Both methods have their uses. **mciSetYieldProc()** enables a program to track the progress of a command executed with the **WAIT** flag. However, VB does not support this kind of interaction with the API, so we can't use this function (unless we want to write a custom control in a holy-trinity language like C). That's fine; we don't need it.

The two high-level command interfaces, Command-Message and Command-String, both perform the same functions. They send commands to the multimedia system, instructing it to play WAVE files or MIDI files, to position the CD audio player on track 7, or any of several operations similar to those you would perform with the remote control on your home entertainment system. Recall that the difference between these two interfaces is mainly the difference between words and numbers. You've already seen one of the easiest ways to play a Waveaudio file—**mciExecute()**. For the sake of completeness, I've added a demonstration function for **mciExecute()**. I won't bother to make this a separate project, but you can easily test it out with the Command Button I've added to the MCIPLAY2.FRM, as shown in Figure 4.1, and the code shown in Listing 4.1.

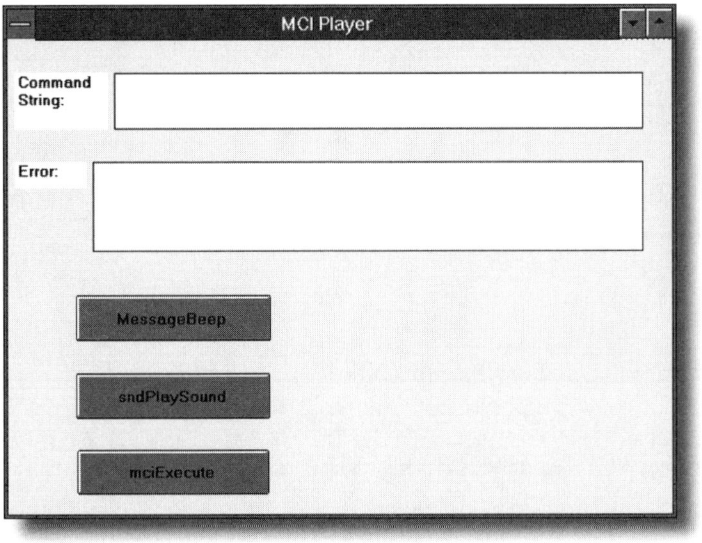

Figure 4.1   *MCIPlay with an mciExecute() Command Button.*

Listing 4.1   ExecuteButton_Click Event Procedure from MCIPLAY2.FRM

```
Sub ExecuteButton_Click ()
    Dim Successful As Integer
    Dim CommandString As String

    CommandString = CommandStringText.Text
    Successful = mciExecute(CommandString)
    If Successful Then
        ErrorText.Text = "Successful " + Str$(Successful)
      Else
        ErrorText.Text = "Unsuccessful " + Str$(Successful)
      End If
    End Sub
```

Making WAVES with mciSendString() and mciSendCommand()

Let's scoot down the ladder another rung and explore **mciSendString()** and **mciSendCommand()**. These functions are both useful for playing WAVE files. **mciSendString()** is the simplest so we'll start with this function first.

Its formal declaration (known in Windows SDK circles as its *prototype*), looks like this:

```
DWORD FAR PASCAL mciSendString(lpstrCommand, lpstrRtnString, wRtnLength, hCallback)
```

And here it is translated into VB as:

```
Declare Function mciSendString Lib "MMSystem" (ByVal lpstrCommand As String,
 lpstrRtnString As Any, ByVal wRtnLength As Integer, ByVal hCallback As Integer) As
Long
```

We can also play a WAVE file with the other MCI function, **mciSendCommand()**. Here's its standard prototype:

```
DWORD mciSendCommand(wDeviceID, wMessage, dwParam1, dwParam2)
```

Once again, we translate this into VB as:

```
Declare Function mciSendCommand Lib "MMSystem" (ByVal wDeviceID As Integer,
 ByVal wMessage As Integer, ByVal dwParam1 As Long, dwParam2 As Long) As Long
```

We can refine this definition one step further by naming the third and fourth parameters more descriptively than the ones used in the Multimedia Development Kit (MDK) documentation:

```
Declare Function mciSendCommand Lib "MMSystem" (ByVal wDeviceID As Integer, ByVal
 wMessage As Integer, ByVal dwFlags As Long, dwCommandParameters As Long) As Long
```

Here, an MCI message requires a group of parameters, which we deliver by wrapping them in a *user-defined* **Type** and passing that structure by reference. That's how the folks at Microsoft managed to consolidate all the myriad MCI operations into a single interface function. Otherwise, you would need a separate function for each operation, each with its own parameter list. Instead of all those functions with separate parameter lists, we call a single function and tell it where to find its parameters.

Playing WAVE Files with mciSendString()

In this second version of the MCIPlay project, we'll add Command Buttons that call both **mciSendString()** and **mciSendCommand()**. To play a WAVE file with the MCI command strings requires these steps:

1. Add a declaration for **mciSendString()** to MCIPLAY2.FRM (Listing 4.2).
2. Add a new Command Button and a new Text Box to MCIPLAY2.FRM.
3. Add code for the **SendStringButton_Click()** event procedure (Listing 4.3).

This project is found in the subdirectory \VBMAGIC, in the files MCIPLAY2.MAK, MCIPLAY2.FRM, and MCIPLAY2.BAS.

Creating the MCIPLAY Project: Version 2

In the sample project MCIPLAY2.MAK, we begin where we left off in MCIPLAY1.MAK in Chapter 3. If you are creating this project yourself, you may wish to copy the files from the previous project before you begin. Add the declaration shown in Listing 4.2 to the declarations section of MCIPLAY2.FRM.

Listing 4.2   From the Declarations Section of MCIPLAY2.FRM

```
Declare Function mciSendString Lib "MMSystem" (ByVal lpstrCommand As String,  →
lpstrRtnString As Any, ByVal wRtnLength As Integer, ByVal hCallback As Integer) As Long
```

Next, drop in another Command Button, set its **Name** property to **SendStringButton**, and set its **Caption** property to "mciSendString." Finally, add a Text Box, and set its **Name** property to **ReturnStringText**. You may also wish to add a label beside the new Text Box. The new version is shown in Figure 4.2.

You could play sounds by simply inserting the following trial version of the **SendStringButton_Click()** event:

Figure 4.2   *MCIPlay with four Command Buttons.*

```
Sub SendStringButton_Click ()
    Dim Dummy As Long
    Dummy = mciSendString("play c:\windows\tada.wav", ByVal 0&, 0, 0)
    End Sub
```

This minimalistic procedure illustrates how little you need to exercise the Command-String interface, but it also ignores some useful and, frankly, essential features. Unlike **mciExecute()**, **mciSendString()** doesn't benefit from the built-in error trapping dialogs. When a command fails, the user will receive no feedback unless you collect the error code returned by the function and act upon it.

In addition to error codes, the Command-String interface can also return information about an MCI device, which it does by setting **lpstrRtnString**. This opens all kinds of new capabilities not available with **mciExecute()**. To add error checking support, we'll use the version of **SendStringButton_Click()** shown in Listing 4.3.

Listing 4.3 SendStringButton_Click() Event Procedure from MCIPLAY2.FRM

```
Sub SendStringButton_Click ()
    Dim mciError As Long
    Dim ReturnString As String * 512
    Dim Dummy As Integer
    Dim mciErrorString As String * 256
    Dim CommandString As String

    ErrorText.Text = ""
    CommandString = CommandStringText.Text
    mciError = mciSendString(CommandString, ByVal ReturnString,
            Len(ReturnString) - 1, 0)
    Dummy = mciGetErrorString(mciError, mciErrorString, 255)
    ErrorText.Text = mciErrorString
    ReturnStringText.Text = ReturnString
    End Sub
```

Notice that neither the **"Play"** command, nor the target filename appear in this procedure. To play a WAVE file, type the entire command into the Text Box labeled "Command String," then press the mciSendString button as shown in Figure 4.3.

A Closer Look at mciSendString() and mciGetError String()

A closer inspection of Listing 4.2 shows that **mciSendString()** takes four parameters. This first paramater is a string that tells the MCI what to do. The second parameter supplies the memory address of a buffer through which the MCI can return a message. The third parameter specifies the length of the return buffer. (The MCI uses this information to determine the length of the

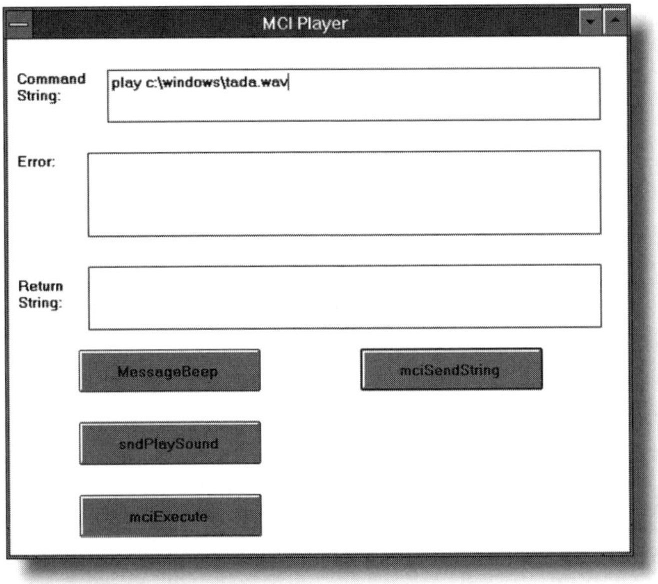

Figure 4.3   *MCIPlay loaded and cocked with a Command String.*

message that it can return.) Finally, the fourth parameter is used to set up a *callback* function. (I'll explain this a little later.)

If you look at the names of the first and second parameters, **lpstrCommand** and **lpstrRtnString**, you'll notice that their prefixes identify them as long pointers (lp) to strings (str). When we pass strings from VB to API functions, we normally declare them with the **ByVal** keyword. For most data types, **ByVal** indicates that the contents of the variable, rather than its memory address, is being passed. But, in combination with a string variable, **ByVal** performs a special function.

Normally, when we pass parameters by value, they remain unchanged. The target procedure receives a copy of the variable rather than the variable itself. Thus, if the procedure changes the variable, those changes affect only its local copy, not the original value. Once the program returns from that called function, the modified value vanishes. A variable passed by reference, VB's default behavior, enjoys no such protection. If the target function changes its value, then the value has changed outside that function as well. But when we use the **ByVal** keyword to pass strings, its meaning changes. We cannot pass VB strings to API functions by value. The **ByVal** keyword instead causes VB to convert the string to a C-style (or *zero-terminated*) string. If the API function changes the string, then when we return from the function, we will find the new value in our string variable, just as we would with a variable of any other data type passed by reference. Upon returning from the called function, VB converts the zero-terminated string back into a VB string. To pass a string to a DLL other than one written specifically for VB, we must pass the string with **ByVal**. Why then have I declared the second parameter, **lpstrRtnString**, without the **ByVal** keyword?

Many MCI commands produce return strings, containing such information as track lengths, numbers of tracks, and device mode. The **"Play"** command, however, does not produce a return string. So, rather than provide a useless buffer, we instead want to tell the API function that no buffer exists. We can do this by sending it a zero, or *NULL* value in place of a memory address. But we can't pass a **NULL** value if we declare the parameter as a string. VB would report a data type mismatch. If we sent a null string, as indicated by an empty pair of quotation marks (""), VB would just pass along the address of an empty string. But we want to pass a **NULL** *address*, indicating the complete absence of a string. To gain a little flexibility, we declare this parameter **As Any**. We may then pass either a string or a numeric value to **mciSendString()**. When we call **mciSendString()**, we must always precede the value of **lpstrRtnString** with **ByVal** to force VB to pass it either as a zero-terminated string, or as a long integer zero. That's why for the second parameter **ByVal** appears in the call to **mciSendString()** rather than in its declaration. You must still always use **ByVal** when you call **mciSendString()**, whether you pass it a **NULL** address or a string buffer. The VB documentation does not explain why you cannot just declare:

```
ByVal <string variable> As Any
```

but since Microsoft knows more about the internal workings of VB than I do, I'm inclined to follow their instructions!

When we do need **lpstrRtnString**, we pass a fixed-length string, or a variable-length string that's been pre-filled with spaces, and specify its length because the Windows API cannot extend variable-length strings. When **mciSendString()** fills in a return string, it starts with the first byte pointed to by the string reference, then continues filling as many subsequent bytes as it needs to hold the entire string. If we were to supply a variable-length string that was too short to hold the return string, **mciSendString()** would write into memory not allocated to that string, quite possibly overwriting some other crucial data. By declaring and passing a fixed-length string, we reserve a large enough block of memory, a *buffer*, to hold any value returned by the API function.

In Chapter 16, you'll see how we can use the **lpstrRtnString** parameter to retrieve status and position information from MCI devices.

We're now ready to get back to the last parameter of **mciSendString()**. It performs a function, known as a *callback*, which is not available to us from within VB. Many API functions perform callbacks. A callback is a means by which an API function can notify a program that it has completed an operation. Callbacks work in one of two ways: they either call an independent function written by the programmer to service the callback, or, like **mciSendString()**, they send a message to a window, which must then contain code to service the callback. In the latter case, the callback works just like any other Windows event, except that instead of responding to an action performed by the user—like a mouse click or a resize event—the program responds to an action requested by an API function. Unfortunately, VB provides no intrinsic support for programmer-defined events. The only way we could respond to the **MM_MCINOTIFY** message generated by **mciSendString()** would be to write a custom control in a holy-trinity language. (When we write our own controls, we also get to define which events to support.) For now, we'll just tell **mciSendString()** not to send a notification message by passing a zero value as the callback handle. It won't send the **MM_MCINOTIFY** message anyway, unless we change the command string to:

```
"play c:\windows\tada.wav notify"
```

Along with **mciSendString()**, I've also slipped in another new function, **mciGetErrorString()**. Take a look at its declaration:

```
Declare Function mciGetErrorString Lib "MMSystem" (ByVal dwError As Long,
    ByVal lpstrBuffer As String, ByVal wLength As Integer) As Integer
```

In the first parameter, I pass the error code returned by **mciSendString()** (or by **mciSendCommand()**, as you'll soon see). The second and third parameters once again define a buffer for a return string and its length, respectively. The return value of **mciGetErrorString()** is—believe it or not—an error code. After all, we could feed it an invalid error code to begin with, which would be an error (error trapping can become very convoluted).

Playing WAVE Files with mciSendCommand()

This next addition to the MCI project requires these simple steps:

1. Add the declarations shown in Listing 4.4 to MCIPLAY2.FRM.
2. Add code for the **SendCommandButton_Click()** event procedure to MCIPLAY2.FRM (Listing 4.5).

> 3. Add the global constants (Listing 4.6).

> *This project, which is a continuation of the previous project, can be found in the directory \VBMAGIC, in the files MCIPLAY2.MAK, MCIPLAY2.FRM, and MCIPLAY2.BAS.*

Expanding the MCIPlay Project: Version 2

To play a WAVE file using **mciSendCommand()**, we need two primary and one secondary data structures, as presented in Listing 4.4.

Listing 4.4   Data Structures Needed to Play a WAVE File with the MCI Command-Message Interface, Declared in MCIPLAY2.BAS

```
Type MCI_WAVE_OPEN_PARMS
    dwCallback As Long
    wDeviceID As Integer
    wReserved0 As Integer
    lpstrDeviceType As Long
    lpstrElementName As Long
    lpstrAlias As Long
    dwBufferSeconds As Long
    End Type

Type MCI_PLAY_PARMS
    dwCallback As Long
    dwFrom As Long
    dwTo As Long
    End Type

Type PseudoString
    AnyString As String * 255
    End Type
```

The **"Play"** message in the Command-Message Interface does not perform implied open and close operations. So, to play a WAVE file, we will need to issue three command messages: open, play, and close. Two of these, open and play, take parameter blocks.

MCI_WAVE_OPEN_PARMS is just a slightly extended version of the more generic structure **MCI_OPEN_PARMS**, which lacks the field **dwBufferSeconds**. If you do not wish to specify a buffer length, you can use **MCI_OPEN_PARMS**. **MCI_PLAY_PARMS** holds the parameters for the play command, although we won't use any of them in this example.

The third data structure, **PseudoString**, will help us overcome another quirky limitation in VB's ability to pass data structures to API functions.

MCI_WAVE_OPEN_PARMS (or **MCI_OPEN_PARMS**) contains three **lpstr** fields, that is, three long pointers (memory addresses) to strings. VB uses its own convention for managing strings. When we place a variable-length string field in a data structure defined with **Type**, VB actually inserts a VB *string descriptor*. On the other hand, if we declare a fixed-length string in a data structure, VB inserts neither a standard pointer nor a string descriptor. It places the whole string in the data structure, byte for byte. Don't get too upset about all these apparent quirks; VB performs myriad housekeeping chores behind the scenes and all these confusing oddities are simply the price we pay for automated memory management. Unfortunately, to noodle around in the Windows API, we have to occasionally outwit our guardians, and that's just what we're going to do. **PseudoString** cloaks a fixed-length string in a **Type** wrapper so we can ask the Windows API to generate a memory address that points to a fixed-length string. We can then assign that address to any of the three long pointer fields in the **OPEN** structure.

The next step involves adding the **SendCommandButton_Click()** event procedure code in Listing 4.5.

Listing 4.5   The SendCommandButton_Click() Event Procedure from MCIPLAY2.FRM

```
Sub SendCommandButton_Click ()
    Dim Dummy As Long
    Dim mciError As Long
    Dim DeviceType As PseudoString
    Dim ElementName As PseudoString
    Dim mciOpenParms As MCI_WAVE_OPEN_PARMS
    Dim mciPlayParms As MCI_PLAY_PARMS
    Dim mciFlags As Long
    Dim wDeviceID As Integer
    Dim mciErrorString As String * 256

    ErrorText.Text = ""
    mciOpenParms.dwCallback = 0&
    mciOpenParms.wDeviceID = 0
    mciOpenParms.wReserved0 = 0
    DeviceType.AnyString = "waveaudio" + Chr$(0)
    ElementName.AnyString = "c:\windows\tada.wav" + Chr$(0)
    mciOpenParms.lpstrDeviceType = lstrcpy(DeviceType, DeviceType)
    mciOpenParms.lpstrElementName = lstrcpy(ElementName, ElementName)
    mciOpenParms.lpstrAlias = 0&
    mciOpenParms.dwBufferSeconds = 0&
    mciFlags = MCI_OPEN_TYPE Or MCI_OPEN_ELEMENT

    mciError = mciSendCommand(0, MCI_OPEN, mciFlags, mciOpenParms)
    If Not mciError Then
```

```
        wDeviceID = mciOpenParms.wDeviceID
        mciError = mciSendCommand(wDeviceID, MCI_PLAY, MCI_WAIT, mciPlayParms)
        If Not mciError Then
            mciError = mciSendCommand(wDeviceID, MCI_CLOSE, 0, ByVal 0&)
        End If
    End If
  Dummy = mciGetErrorString(mciError, mciErrorString, 255)
  ErrorText.Text = mciErrorString

    End Sub
```

This procedure, actually a complete program except for declarations, uses several constants. Remember when I said that the difference between the Command-String Interface and the Command-Message Interface was largely the difference between words and numbers? This is what I meant. You'll find definitions of them all in the Microsoft *Multimedia Programmer's Reference*, but not their values. For their numeric values, you'll have to look in the file WINMMSYS.TXT that comes with VB (normally copied by VB Setup to the subdirectory \VB\WINAPI). For this example, we need the six standard constants shown in Listing 4.6.

Listing 4.6   The Global MCI Constants Needed to Play a WAVE File

```
Global Const MCI_OPEN = &H803          ' Command Message
Global Const MCI_PLAY = &H806          ' Command Message
Global Const MCI_CLOSE = &H804         ' Command Message
Global Const MCI_OPEN_TYPE& = &H2000&  ' Command Flag
Global Const MCI_OPEN_ELEMENT& = &H200& ' Command Flag
Global Const MCI_WAIT& = &H2&          ' Command Flag
```

The first several lines of this procedure set the parameter values required by the **Open** command message. The first three are easy.

```
mciOpenParms.dwCallback = 0&
mciOpenParms.wDeviceID = 0
mciOpenParms.wReserved0 = 0
```

VB doesn't support callbacks so we set the first field to 0. We don't know the **DeviceID** yet; the MCI will assign one and return its value in the **wDeviceID** field when we execute the **Open** command. The third field contains a 0. According to the Microsoft documentation this field is reserved, and that's that.

The next four statements twice perform the machinations that enable us to capture and pass on pointers to strings.

```
DeviceType.AnyString = "waveaudio" + Chr$(0)
ElementName.AnyString = "c:\windows\tada.wav" + Chr$(0)
```

```
mciOpenParms.lpstrDeviceType = lstrcpy(DeviceType, DeviceType)
mciOpenParms.lpstrElementName = lstrcpy(ElementName, ElementName)
```

To get the addresses of the strings, we're using the API function **lstrcpy()** in an unusual way. But first we want to make sure each string ends with a **NULL**, or in VB terms, **Chr$(0)**. A string in C (the mother language of Windows) is just a series of bytes. C programs pass around strings indirectly by passing around their memory addresses. When a C routine receives a string, it knows where the string begins, but not where it ends. The convention in C is that a string ends with a byte value of 0, known as a **NULL**. Therefore, a procedure can read a string character by character until it finds a **NULL**. The **lstrcpy()** function is a low-level API function that copies a C string and returns the memory address of the new copy. Before we can call **lstrcpy()** we need to *NULL terminate* our strings so the function knows just how much to copy; otherwise it will just run on and on through memory until it either crashes or stumbles into a **NULL** byte.

By copying **DeviceType** and **ElementName** to themselves, we change nothing, but we capture addresses that we can stuff into the **OPEN** parameter structure. This is like passing the strings by reference, only we have to do it indirectly. Unlike regular string parameters, VB won't translate its own strings into pointers to zero-terminated strings when we pass the strings as elements of structures. We need to get the address first, then pass the address, a long integer, by value.

We don't want to assign an alias to the device, and we don't need to specify a buffer length so we set both of these parameters to 0.

```
mciOpenParms.lpstrAlias = 0&
mciOpenParms.dwBufferSeconds = 0&
```

Next, we need to set the flags that tell the Command-Message Interface how to interpret the information we've passed in the **mciOpenParms** structure.

```
mciFlags = MCI_OPEN_TYPE Or MCI_OPEN_ELEMENT
```

Boolean operations like *Or* can look misleading. Unlike a boolean decision, like we find in **If** statements and **While** loops, the **Or** operator in this assignment statement performs a *bitwise* operation that actually combines the two flags. Let's look first at a trivial case.

Bits can carry one of two values, 0 or 1. Let's say we have two bits, A and B. If both A and B start out with 0 values, then the expression "A Or B" returns 0. If either A or B, or both A and B are set to 1, then the expression "A Or B" returns 1. Now let's expand that one step to two whole bytes full of bits.

```
A = 00000001
B = 00000010
```

When we **Or** A and B, VB performs the **Or** operation on each bit, comparing the first bit (or more correctly, the lowest-order bit, counting from right to left) of A with the first bit of B, then the second bit of A with the second bit of B, and so on. The result of "A Or B" in this case will produce a byte with two bits set to 1:

```
A Or B = 00000011
```

The **flag** parameter is a four-byte value. Each bit in the four bytes represents one flag for a total of 32 possible flags. Several flags are defined in Table 4.1.

By the way, these flags notify the MCI that we're supplying both the device type and the name of the file, or *element*, that we want it to play. We could actually omit the device type. The MCI can determine the device type by looking up the file extension in the **[mci extensions]** section of the WIN.INI file.

Once we've set all our flags, pointers to strings, and other parameters, we can send the messages:

```
mciError = mciSendCommand(0, MCI_OPEN, mciFlags, mciOpenParms)
If Not mciError Then
    wDeviceID = mciOpenParms.wDeviceID
    mciError = mciSendCommand(wDeviceID, MCI_PLAY, MCI_WAIT, mciPlayParms)
    If Not mciError Then
        mciError = mciSendCommand(wDeviceID, MCI_CLOSE, 0, ByVal 0&)
    End If
  End If
Dummy = mciGetErrorString(mciError, mciErrorString, 255)
ErrorText.Text = mciErrorString
```

The **MCI_WAIT** flag that accompanies the **MCI_PLAY** message instructs the MCI not to return control to our program until the play operation is complete. Without this flag we can go on about our business while the WAVE file plays in

Table 4.1 *Some of the flags defined for the MCI command.*

Flag	Hexadecimal	Binary Value
MCI_OPEN_TYPE&	&H2000&	00000000 00000000 00100000 00000000
MCI_OPEN_ELEMENT&	&H200&	00000000 00000000 00000010 00000000
MCI_OPEN_TYPE& Or MCI_OPEN_ELEMENT&	&H2200&	00000000 00000000 00100010 00000000

the background. However, when we send the **MCI_CLOSE** message, the MCI aborts the play operation. To play the WAVE file *asynchronously* we would need to find some other way to close the device upon completion. For HTL programmers this is easy; they can write a callback function and pass the **NOTIFY** flag. For VB programmers, it can be a nuisance, so for now we won't bother.

In one way, we've taken a step backward here by hard-coding the commands to play a WAVE file. Unfortunately, because of the data structures it requires for its parameters, the Command-Message Interface doesn't easily adapt to a little excerciser function like the one we created for the Command-String Interface.

For most multimedia applications that we're likely to write with VB, the Command-Message Interface dwells in purgatory between the simple, friendly Command-String Interface and the complex but truly powerful low level functions that speak directly to the multimedia device drivers. Now you know how to use it. Relax. We won't need **mciSendCommand()** for any of the other projects or exercises in *this* book.

Using the Low-Level Audio Functions

Clearly, the MCI functions that we've investigated do a lot of work behind the scenes. Waveaudio data resides in files, which contain not only the *digital sample* values, but also descriptive information that identifies the particular format of that audio data. To replay a WAVE file, the multimedia system has to open the file, read and interpret its header information, load the audio data into memory, open the Waveaudio device, play the sound, and close both the device and the file. Whew! That's a lot of work!

To accomplish all this, the MCI functions call upon the services of several low-level functions. To perform low-level replay of WAVE files we need to call about a dozen functions. These fall into two groups: functions that read *Resource Interchange File Format (RIFF)* files, and functions that manage Waveaudio playback.

Before you can even open the Waveaudio device, you have to know some things about the data you intend to send it. WAVE data comes in several formats, various combinations of sampling rate, multiple channels (mono or stereo), and different resolutions (number of bits per sample). We'll talk about WAVE formats in greater detail in Chapter 13. For now, all you need to know is that this information appears in a format block—known in RIFF terminology as a *chunk*—near the beginning of each WAVE file.

The Mysteries of RIFF Files

As Figure 4.4 indicates, RIFF files are hierarchical structures—chunks contain chunks which again may contain chunks.

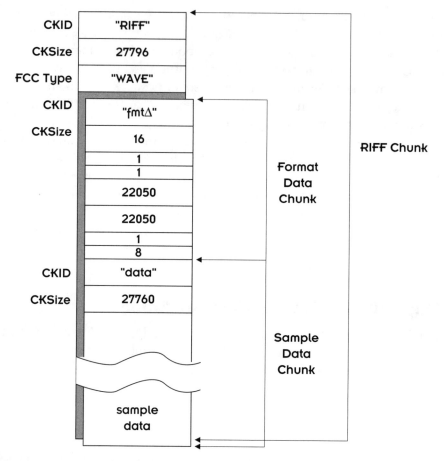

Figure 4.4 *The RIFF file structure.*

The highest level chunk is the RIFF chunk itself. Chunks carry labels, known officially as *chunk IDs*. If you peek at a WAVE file with a file viewer, you'll see that the first four bytes literally contain the characters *R,I,F,* and *F.*

To read and write RIFF files, you use a standard data structure called **MMCKINFO**, for "multimedia chunk information." In VB the structure looks like this:

```
' RIFF chunk information data structure
Type MMCKINFO
    CkId As FOURCC
    CkSize As Long
    fccType As FOURCC
    dwDataOffset As Long
    dwFlags As Long
    End Type
```

The first and third fields actually contain simple four-character, fixed-length strings:

```
Type FOURCC
    Chars As String * 4
    End Type
```

This **FOURCC** substructure is just a convention created for C programmers who don't have such straight-forward string operations.

To keep you from getting as confused as I did, let me state now that **MMCKINFO** *does not define a data file record!* We use **MMCKINFO** only to exchange information with the *multimedia file I/O functions.* Although chunks do adhere to a couple of well-defined structures, they vary in size, which means we can't just read them into, or write them from simple, fixed-length record buffers.

All chunks start with at least two common fields: the chunk ID and the chunk size, which, coincidentally, correspond to the first two fields of **MMCKINFO**. When we use the low-level multimedia function **mmioDescend()** to read a chunk, we will pass it the address of a structure of type **MMCKINFO**, which it will then fill in with the appropriate values. This is an important distinction. When we read records from a file with VB, we often use the **Get** statement. **Get** takes three arguments: the file number, a record number, and the variable name into which we want the data copied. To read a record that contains multiple fields, we can define a record with the **Type** statement, declare a variable of that type, then **Get** a record of the same structure from the disk file. If **MMCKINFO** were a file record type—which it is not—we could do something like this:

```
Dim TheChunk As MMCKINFO          ' Don't even think about doing this!
Get #WaveFile, 1, TheChunk
```

Don't do it! It won't work.

A RIFF file doesn't contain a series of records of uniform structure. Chunks vary in size. The only efficient way to read a RIFF file is to walk through it in the prescribed manner, using the **mmio** (multimedia I/O) functions.

To navigate a RIFF file you use the functions **mmioDescend()** and **mmioAscend()**. These functions are used to position the file pointer in a chunk. Depending on what type of chunk you want to find, you set either the chunk ID (**ckID**) or the form type (**fccType**), set a search flag, then call **mmioDescend()**. This function will locate the next chunk in the file with the **ckID** or **fccType** you have specified. If you want the next chunk in line, you can descend without specifying the **ckID** or the **fccType**, and the descent function will fill in those fields with the four-character codes it finds in the next chunk.

The Structure of a WAVE File

To better understand how WAVE files are accessed, let's look at a sample file. Table 4.2 shows a breakdown of the WAVE file TADA.WAV.

At minimum, a WAVE file comprises three chunks. The RIFF chunk is the largest container. The whole WAVE file is actually a RIFF chunk. The **ckSize,** which appears immediately after the "RIFF" **ckID**, contains a value equal to the file size minus eight bytes—the eight bytes required to store the RIFF chunk's own **ckID** and **ckSize**. The second and third chunks, known as *subchunks*, are contained within the RIFF chunk. The first of these, the "fmt " chunk, contains the information necessary to fill in a **PCMWAVEFORMAT** structure. The second subchunk, the "data" chunk—by far the largest portion of the file—immediately follows the "fmt" subchunk, and contains all the

Table 4.2 *The structure of a sample WAVE file.*

Position		Size in Bytes	Contents	Comments
Hex	Dec			
0000	0	4	"RIFF"	Each byte contains one character, ckId
0004	4	4	27796	Equals the file size minus eight bytes, ckSize
0008	8	4	"WAVE"	fccType
000C	12	4	"fmt "	Next ckID; notice the blank, must be four characters
0010	16	4	16	The WAVE format chunk is 16 bytes, ckSize
0014	20	2	1	1 indicates a PCM Wave format, wFormatTag
0016	22	2	1	Number of channels, nChannels
0018	24	4	22050	Sampling rate, nSamplesPerSec
001C	28	4	22050	nAvgBytesPerSec
0020	32	2	1	Effectively bytes per sample, nBlockAlign
0022	34	2	8	wBitsPerSample
0024	36	4	"data"	Next ckID; this chunk contains the wave data itself
0028	40	4	27760	Next ckID; size of wave data
002C	44	Depends on Data		The digitized audio data

digital waveform data. The end of the "data" subchunk corresponds to the end of the RIFF chunk. The **ckSize** of the RIFF chunk equals the total number of bytes occupied by the "fmt" and "data" subchunks.

To make matters worse, RIFF files may contain another type of chunk called a *LIST* chunk. LIST chunks hold additional information, such as copyright notices and other user-defined data that describes the contents of the main "data" chunk or chunks. At this point, it won't help us any to discuss LIST chunks; the WAVE files that come with Windows 3.1 don't contain any. I only mention them because their presence—or at least their potential presence—will highlight the value of the multimedia file I/O functions, which Microsoft custom-designed for RIFF data files. You'll see what I mean shortly.

A Peek at the Multimedia I/O Functions

You *could* read RIFF files with conventional file I/O functions by calculating offsets and reading blocks of the appropriate sizes. But the multimedia file I/O functions provide intrinsic support for the RIFF format. The best way to understand these functions is to use them.

All of the multimedia file I/O functions begin with the prefix *mmio*. Here is the complete set:

```
mmioOpen()
mmioClose()
mmioSeek()
mmioRead()
mmioWrite()
mmioDescend()
mmioAscend()
mmioCreateChunk()
mmioFOURCC()
mmioStringToFOURCC()
mmioAdvance()
mmioGetInfo()
mmioSetInfo()
mmioInstallIOProc()
mmioSendMessage()
```

Of these fifteen functions, we'll need just five to read and play a WAVE file: **mmioOpen()**, **mmioClose()**, **mmioRead()**, **mmioDescend()**, and **mmioAscend()**.

All of these functions can return errors, so to use them properly we have to check the result of each function call to make sure that the operation is performed correctly. Since we need to make several calls to read the WAVE file, this error-checking procedure can become a little lengthy. To minimize con-

fusion and make the code more manageable, we could create two separate VB routines, one to open and read a WAVE file, and one to play it. And that's what we'll do in the next project.

Playing WAVE Files Using Low-Level Functions

This project shows you how to read and play WAVE files using the low-level mutlimedia I/O functions. Just as MCIPLAY2.MAK began where MCIPLAY1.MAK left off, this new project, MCIPLAY3.MAK, will begin with the files from MCIPLAY2.MAK. By the time we're done, the final project will have six Command Buttons, each offering a different way to play WAVE files. Here are the steps:

1. Create the code module WAVEPLAY.BAS and add the necessary declarations.
2. Create the function named **OpenWaveFile()** (Listing 4.7) for opening and processing a WAVE file.
3. Create the function named **WaveOut()** (Listing 4.8) for playing the WAVE file.
4. Add a new Command Button to MCIPLAY3.FRM and use its Click event procedure to open and play the WAVE file.

 This version of the MCIPlay project is located in the directory \VBMAGIC, in the files MCIPLAY3.MAK, MCIPLAY3.FRM, MCIPLAY3.BAS, and WAVEPLAY.BAS.

Reading and Processing a WAVE File

To read and play a WAVE file, we'll create a separate code module named WAVEPLAY.BAS with two procedures, one named **OpenWaveFile()** to open and read the file, and one named **WaveOut()** to play it. We'll call them both from a Command Button Click event. Let's begin with **OpenWaveFile()**.

The first thing we want to do is open the file, so let's declare the low-level multimedia function, **mmioOpen()**.

```
Declare Function mmioOpen Lib "MMSystem" (ByVal szFilename As String,
lpMMIOINFO As Any, ByVal dwOpenFlags As Long) As Integer
```

The first parameter, **szFilename**, specifies the filename. We have enough experience passing strings to the API, so this is easy. Just remember to use **ByVal** in the declaration.

For the second parameter, **lpMMIOINFO**, we could pass a pointer to a **MMIOINFO** data structure, but we don't need this structure. We'll declare this parameter as type **Any** so we can pass it a **NULL** (literal value 0&) pointer.

mmioOpen() performs several operations, all selectable by passing flags with the third parameter, **dwOpenFlags**. For this example, we'll need only one flag, **MMIO_READ**.

Add the declaration for **mmioOpen()** to the declarations section of WAVEPLAY.BAS. Then, select New Procedure from the View menu, and declare a new function called **OpenWaveFile()**. Once you have the function framework on the screen, add a single parameter for passing the filename of the WAVE file we intend to open and play. Also, declare the *return type* of the function **As Integer**:

```
Function OpenWaveFile (FileNameAndPath As String) As Integer
    End Function
```

Now we can plug in the **mmioOpen()** function, along with the declaration for the file handle, **hMMIO**.

```
Function OpenWaveFile (FileNameAndPath As String) As Integer
    Dim hMMIO As Integer

    hMMIO = mmioOpen(FileNameAndPath, ByVal 0&, MMIO_READ)
```

After we've opened the file, we have to locate the *parent chunk*, that is, the RIFF chunk. RIFF files can't contain more than a single RIFF chunk in the current version of the multimedia I/O system. Thus, this process may seem non-sensical, but future releases probably will support *compound* files (RIFF files that could, for example, contain more than one WAVE sound). Besides, the search operation automatically positions the file pointer at the beginning of the data section of the chunk (in this case, the 13th byte in the file), so it isn't a completely wasted effort.

To search for chunks, we'll call upon **mmioDescend()**, which we also declare in WAVEPLAY.BAS:

```
Declare Function mmioDescend Lib "MMSystem" (ByVal hMMIO As Integer, lpCk As
Any, lpCkParent As Any, ByVal wFlags As Integer) As Integer
```

To search for a particular type of RIFF chunk—in this case, a RIFF chunk that contains WAVE data—we have to specify the *form type*. The form type identifies the type of data stored in the RIFF chunk. The form type is the third field at the head of a RIFF chunk. It's also the third field in **MMCKINFO**. We'll declare a variable of type **MMCKINFO** called **MMCkInfoParent**. To search for a RIFF chunk with a form type of WAVE, we set the **fccType** field in this record to "WAVE" and call **mmioDescend()**.

```
Function OpenWaveFile (FileNameAndPath As String) As Integer
    Dim MMCkInfoParent As MMCKINFO
    Dim hMMIO As Integer
    Dim ErrorCode As Integer

    hMMIO = mmioOpen(FileNameAndPath, ByVal 0&, MMIO_READ)
    If hMMIO <> 0 Then
        ' Find WAVE Parent Chunk
        MMCKInfoParent.fccType.Chars = "WAVE"
        ErrorCode = mmioDescend(hMMIO, MMCKInfoParent, ByVal 0&, MMIO_FINDRIFF)
```

Descending is kind of like reading. The difference is that **mmioDescend()** reads only the fields that describe the chunk. That is, it reads the rind and not the fruit—the data inside the chunk. All chunks begin with two data fields, the chunk ID (**ckID**) and the chunk size (**ckSize**). Instead of defining two different structures for chunks, Microsoft muddies the definition of a chunk with a kludge: a chunk may also contain a third data field, the form type or list type (**fccType**), which is contained in the first four bytes of the data section of the chunk. Only RIFF and LIST chunks include this "extra" field (form type for RIFF chunks, and list type for LIST chunks, both known as **fccType**).

When you descend into a chunk, **mmioDescend()** fills in the field **dwDataOffset** in the **MMCKINFO** record, which in this case is **MMCkInfoParent**. If you're decending into a RIFF or LIST chunk, **mmioDescend()** will also automatically fill in the **ckID** with either "RIFF" or "LIST."

In the call to **mmioDescend()**, we set the form type to "WAVE" and pass the flag **MMIO_FINDRIFF**. With astonishing speed, **mmioDescend()** will search the file for its one and only one RIFF chunk, the one that starts right at the beginning of the file. Truly amazing. When it has finished, we will have a complete description of the RIFF chunk contained in a record called **MMCkInfoParent**.

The RIFF chunk with the form type "WAVE" is the mother of all chunks, at least of all other chunks in a WAVE file. To search for any other type of chunk, we need to specify the **ckID** and pass (by reference) a record of type **MMCHKINFO** for the parent chunk as the third parameter:

```
Function OpenWaveFile (FileNameAndPath As String) As Integer
    Dim MMCKInfoParent As MMCKINFO
    Dim MMCkInfoChild As MMCKINFO
    Dim hMMIO As Integer
    Dim ErrorCode As Integer
```

```
hMMIO = mmioOpen(FileNameAndPath, ByVal O&, MMIO_READ)
If hMMIO <> 0 Then
    ' Find WAVE Parent Chunk
    MMCKInfoParent.fccType.Chars = "WAVE"
    ErrorCode = mmioDescend(hMMIO, MMCKInfoParent, ByVal O&, MMIO_FINDRIFF)
    If ErrorCode = 0 Then
        ' Find fmt Chunk
        MMCkInfoChild.CkId.Chars = "fmt "
        ErrorCode = mmioDescend(hMMIO, MMCkInfoChild, MMCKInfoParent, MMIO_FINDCHUNK)
```

Notice that **MMCkInfoChild.CkID.Chars** is blank-padded to four characters. In this statement, **mmioDescend()** searches the parent RIFF chunk for a
format chunk. Once again, this takes little effort because the format chunk
begins right after the form type field, at the 13th byte in the file. You can't
assume, however, that this will always be the case. Someday you may encounter a WAVE file that includes LIST chunks, which appear ahead of the
format chunk. If you were to read the file in a conventional fashion, either
with standard file I/O, or with the function **mmioRead()**, you would have to
identify and skip the LIST chunks. But when we call **mmioDescend()** with
the flag **MMIO_FINDCHUNK**, and a **CkId** of "fmt," it will automatically hop
directly to the format chunk.

Now we get to read some data:

```
Function OpenWaveFile (FileNameAndPath As String) As Integer
    Dim MMCKInfoParent As MMCKINFO
    Dim MMCkInfoChild As MMCKINFO
    Dim hMMIO As Integer
    Dim ErrorCode As Integer
    Dim BytesRead As Long

    hMMIO = mmioOpen(FileNameAndPath, ByVal O&, MMIO_READ)
    If hMMIO <> 0 Then
        ' Find WAVE Parent Chunk
        MMCKInfoParent.fccType.Chars = "WAVE"
        ErrorCode = mmioDescend(hMMIO, MMCKInfoParent, ByVal O&, MMIO_FINDRIFF)
        If ErrorCode = 0 Then
            ' Find fmt Chunk
            MMCkInfoChild.CkId.Chars = "fmt "
            ErrorCode = mmioDescend(hMMIO, MMCkInfoChild, MMCKInfoParent, MMIO_FINDCHUNK)
            If ErrorCode = 0 Then
                ' Read PCM Wave Format Record
                BytesRead = mmioRead(hMMIO, PCMWaveFmtRecord, MMCkInfoChild.CkSize)
```

mmioRead() does what you would expect. It reads from the file specified
by **hMMIO** the number of bytes specified by the third parameter, and places
the data in memory beginning at the address specified by the second parameter. Since we're passing a record of type **PCMWAVEFORMAT** by reference in

the second parameter, when we return from **mmioRead()** we should find that it has filled in the wave format record.

Declaring the Wave Format Record

We declare the wave format record in the general declarations section of WAVEPLAY.BAS:

```
Type WAVEFORMAT
      wFormatTag As Integer
      nChannels As Integer
      nSamplesPerSec As Long
      nAvgBytesPerSec As Long
      nBlockAlign As Integer
      End Type

Type PCMWAVEFORMAT
      wf As WAVEFORMAT
      wBitsPerSample As Integer
      End Type
 -
 -
 -
Dim PCMWaveFmtRecord As PCMWAVEFORMAT
```

We'll also need to declare **mmioRead()**:

```
Declare Function mmioRead Lib "MMSystem" (ByVal hMMIO As Integer, pCh As Any,
      ByVal cCh As Long) As Long
```

After we read the format chunk, we can check to see whether the WAVE file at hand contains data that's compatible with our digital waveform output device. If not, we can skip the rest of the procedure. To do this, we'll use a special case of **waveOutOpen()**. Ordinarily, this function is used to open the Waveaudio output device. In fact, we will use it for just that purpose in our function **WaveOut()**. But we can also call it with a flag named **WAVE_FORMAT_QUERY**, which will compare the contents of the wave format record with the device capabilities as defined in the Waveaudio device driver. If the file is compatible with the device, **waveOutOpen()** returns zero. We'll look at **waveOutOpen()** in more detail when we write the function **WaveOut()**:

```
Function OpenWaveFile (FileNameAndPath As String) As Integer
      Dim MMCKInfoParent As MMCKINFO
      Dim MMCkInfoChild As MMCKINFO
      Dim hMMIO As Integer
      Dim ErrorCode As Integer
      Dim BytesRead As Long
```

```
hMMIO = mmioOpen(FileNameAndPath, ByVal 0&, MMIO_READ)
If hMMIO <> 0 Then
    ' Find WAVE Parent Chunk
    MMCKInfoParent.fccType.Chars = "WAVE"
    ErrorCode = mmioDescend(hMMIO, MMCKInfoParent, ByVal 0&, MMIO_FINDRIFF)
    If ErrorCode = 0 Then
        ' Find fmt Chunk
        MMCkInfoChild.CkId.Chars = "fmt "
        ErrorCode = mmioDescend(hMMIO, MMCkInfoChild, MMCKInfoParent,
                MMIO_FINDCHUNK)
        If ErrorCode = 0 Then
            ' Read PCM Wave Format Record
            BytesRead = mmioRead(hMMIO, PCMWaveFmtRecord, MMCkInfoChild.CkSize)
            If BytesRead > 0 Then
                ErrorCode = waveOutOpen(hWaveOut, WAVE_MAPPER,
                        PCMWaveFmtRecord, 0&, 0&, WAVE_FORMAT_QUERY)
```

Somewhere after the format chunk we should find the data chunk. To find the data without making any assumptions about its location, we'll again want to use **mmioDescend()** to search the RIFF chunk for it. But before we can do that, we first have to *ascend* out of the format chunk:

```
Function OpenWaveFile (FileNameAndPath As String) As Integer
    Dim MMCKInfoParent As MMCKINFO
    Dim MMCkInfoChild As MMCKINFO
    Dim hMMIO As Integer
    Dim ErrorCode As Integer
    Dim BytesRead As Long

    hMMIO = mmioOpen(FileNameAndPath, ByVal 0&, MMIO_READ)
    If hMMIO <> 0 Then
        ' Find WAVE Parent Chunk
        MMCKInfoParent.fccType.Chars = "WAVE"
        ErrorCode = mmioDescend(hMMIO, MMCKInfoParent, ByVal 0&, MMIO_FINDRIFF)
        If ErrorCode = 0 Then
            ' Find fmt Chunk
            MMCkInfoChild.CkId.Chars = "fmt "
            ErrorCode = mmioDescend(hMMIO, MMCkInfoChild, MMCKInfoParent,
                    MMIO_FINDCHUNK)
            If ErrorCode = 0 Then
                ' Read PCM Wave Format Record
                BytesRead = mmioRead(hMMIO, PCMWaveFmtRecord,
                        MMCkInfoChild.CkSize)
                If BytesRead > 0 Then
                    ErrorCode = waveOutOpen(hWaveOut, WAVE_MAPPER,
                            PCMWaveFmtRecord, 0&, 0&, WAVE_FORMAT_QUERY)
                    If ErrorCode = 0 Then
                        ' Ascend back one level in the RIFF file.
                        ErrorCode = mmioAscend(hMMIO, MMCkInfoChild, 0)
```

The first parameter of **mmioAscend()** once again identifies the file, and the second parameter identifies the chunk from which to ascend. The third parameter may someday accept flags, but none have been defined yet by Microsoft, so we'll always set it to 0. Declare **mmioAscend()** like this:

```
Declare Function mmioAscend Lib "MMSystem" (ByVal hMMIO As Integer,
    lpCk As Any, ByVal wFlags As Integer) As Integer
```

At the end of our ascent, the file pointer will stand at the threshold of the next chunk, which coincidentally is the next chunk into which we'll descend.

```
Function OpenWaveFile (FileNameAndPath As String) As Integer
    Dim MMCKInfoParent As MMCKINFO
    Dim MMCkInfoChild As MMCKINFO
    Dim hMMIO As Integer
    Dim ErrorCode As Integer
    Dim BytesRead As Long

    hMMIO = mmioOpen(FileNameAndPath, ByVal 0&, MMIO_READ)
    If hMMIO <> 0 Then
        ' Find WAVE Parent Chunk
        MMCKInfoParent.fccType.Chars = "WAVE"
        ErrorCode = mmioDescend(hMMIO, MMCKInfoParent, ByVal 0&, MMIO_FINDRIFF)
        If ErrorCode = 0 Then
            ' Find fmt Chunk
            MMCkInfoChild.CkId.Chars = "fmt "
            ErrorCode = mmioDescend(hMMIO, MMCkInfoChild, MMCKInfoParent,
                    MMIO_FINDCHUNK)
            If ErrorCode = 0 Then
                ' Read PCM Wave Format Record
                BytesRead = mmioRead(hMMIO, PCMWaveFmtRecord, MMCkInfoChild.CkSize)
                If BytesRead > 0 Then
                    ErrorCode = waveOutOpen(hWaveOut, WAVE_MAPPER,
                            PCMWaveFmtRecord, 0&, 0&, WAVE_FORMAT_QUERY)
                    If ErrorCode = 0 Then
                        ' Ascend back one level in the RIFF file.
                        ErrorCode = mmioAscend(hMMIO, MMCkInfoChild, 0)
                        If ErrorCode = 0 Then
                            ' Read data chunk.
                            MMCkInfoChild.CkId.Chars = "data"
                            ErrorCode = mmioDescend(hMMIO, MMCkInfoChild,
                                    MMCKInfoParent, MMIO_FINDCHUNK)
```

Throughout this odyssey, our parent chunk has remained, steadfastly, the RIFF chunk. To locate the data chunk, we set the **CkID** in **MMCkInfoChild** to "data" and call **mmioDescend()** again with the flag **MMIO_FINDCHUNK**. If we strike paydirt, it's time to dig out the prize—waveform audio data.

To read in the waveform data we need to supply a buffer. In VB we have limited resources when it comes to manipulating *binary large objects* (BLOBs). WAVE files tend to be large—very large. The format of the lowest fidelity WAVE format requires 11,025 bytes per second of audio. The WAVE files that contain the Windows 3.1 message beep sounds were recorded at the next highest sampling rate of 22.05 KHz (kilohertz—*Hertz* meaning cycles per second), which means that they occupy 22,050 bytes for each second of playback time. Even the modest TADA.WAV is 27,804 bytes long (the version dated 3-10-92), and nearly all of that represents the waveform data itself.

But the largest object we can handle in VB is a string of 64 kilobytes. And to make matters worse, large strings don't easily submit to byte-by-byte manipulation. Not surprisingly, Windows will once again rescue us from this VB shortcoming, but not until Chapter 7. For now, we'll resort to an even more crippled approach; we'll use an array of 32000 bytes, where we define bytes as single-character, fixed-length strings:

```
Type byte
    Char As String * 1
    End Type

Dim WaveBuffer(1 To 32000) As byte
```

Make sure that you add these declarations to the **declarations** section of WAVEPLAY.BAS.

If we descend successfully into the data chunk we'll initialize the **WaveBuffer** by setting all its elements to **Chr$(0)**. We're going to use **lstrcpy()** again to capture the memory address of **WaveBuffer**, so we have to ensure that somewhere within the 32000 bytes, **lstrcpy()** will find a null byte, that is, a byte with a binary value of zero, which is equivalent to **Chr$(0)**:

```
        -
        -
        -
' Read data chunk.
MMCkInfoChild.CkId.Chars = "data"
ErrorCode = mmioDescend(hMMIO, MMCkInfoChild,
            MMCKInfoParent, MMIO_FINDCHUNK)
If ErrorCode = 0 Then
    For Index = 1 To 32000
        WaveBuffer(Index).Char = Chr$(0)
        Next Index
    BytesRead = mmioRead(hMMIO, WaveBuffer(1),
            MMCKInfoChild.CkSize)
    If BytesRead > 0 Then
```

```
' Get a pointer to the Wave data and fill in
  Wave Header.
WaveHeader.lpData = lstrcpy(WaveBuffer(1),
                          WaveBuffer(1))
WaveHeader.dwBufferLength = BytesRead
WaveHeader.dwFlags = 0&
WaveHeader.dwLoops = 0&
OpenWaveFile = True
Else
MsgBox "Couldn't read wave data.",
        MB_ICONSTOP, "RIFF File Error"
End If
```

Next, we call **mmioRead()**, passing the first element of the array **WaveBuffer** as the target buffer in the second parameter, and **MMCkInfoChild.ckSize** as the number of bytes to read in the third parameter.

Finally, if **mmioRead()** returns successfully, we have all the information we need to construct a **WAVEHDR** record. Wave headers are the structures that describe individual WAVE buffers. For a variety of reasons, we might wish to play Wave audio data by passing it to the driver in segments. We treat each segment as a separate buffer with its own header. The format record, a structure of type **PCMWAVEFORMAT**, describes the format of a single Wave audio recording. Each segment of that recording will have its own header, a structure of type **WAVEHDR**. One reason to segment a WAVE file into multiple buffers might be to overcome limitations on the size and number of elements of VB's strings and arrays. That's not the reason we'll do it, but it's undeniably a valid reason. For now (I'm sorry to keep simplifying like this, but we're still on the grand tour so let's not bog ourselves down in too many details) we'll use a single buffer limited to 32000 bytes:

```
Type WAVEHDR
    lpData As Long
    dwBufferLength As Long
    dwBytesRecorded As Long
    dwUser As Long
    dwFlags As Long
    dwLoops As Long
    lpNext As Long
    reserved As Long
    End Type

Dim WaveHeader As WAVEHDR
```

We'll need **WaveHeader** in both **WaveOut()** and **OpenWaveFile()**, so declare it in the **declarations** section of WAVEPLAY.BAS.

While the format record describes the sampling rate, number of channels, and bit resolution of a wave audio file, the main purpose of a wave header is to hold the length and location of the wave audio data. In **WaveOut()** we'll use the format record to open the device, and we'll use the header to play the data.

When we're done reading the file and preparing the header, we can close the file. Listing 4.7 provides the complete **OpenWaveFile()** function with all its error messages.

Listing 4.7 OpenWaveFile() from WAVEPLAY.BAS

```
Function OpenWaveFile (FileNameAndPath As String) As Integer
    Dim MMCKInfoParent As MMCKINFO
    Dim MMCkInfoChild As MMCKINFO
    Dim hMMIO As Integer
    Dim ErrorCode As Integer
    Dim BytesRead As Long
    Dim Index As Integer

    hMMIO = mmioOpen(FileNameAndPath, ByVal 0&, MMIO_READ)
    If hMMIO <> 0 Then
      ' Find WAVE Parent Chunk
      MMCKInfoParent.fccType.Chars = "WAVE"
      ErrorCode = mmioDescend(hMMIO, MMCKInfoParent, ByVal 0&, MMIO_FINDRIFF)
      If ErrorCode = 0 Then
        ' Find fmt Chunk
        MMCkInfoChild.CkId.Chars = "fmt "
        ErrorCode = mmioDescend(hMMIO, MMCkInfoChild, MMCKInfoParent, MMIO_FINDCHUNK)
        If ErrorCode = 0 Then
        ' Read PCM Wave Format Record
        BytesRead = mmioRead(hMMIO, PCMWaveFmtRecord, MMCkInfoChild.CkSize)
        If BytesRead > 0 Then
          ErrorCode = waveOutOpen(hWaveOut, WAVE_MAPPER, PCMWaveFmtRecord, 0&,
                  0&, WAVE_FORMAT_QUERY)
         If ErrorCode = 0 Then
           ' Ascend back one level in the RIFF file.
           ErrorCode = mmioAscend(hMMIO, MMCkInfoChild, 0)
           If ErrorCode = 0 Then
             ' Read data chunk.
             MMCkInfoChild.CkId.Chars = "data"
             ErrorCode = mmioDescend(hMMIO, MMCkInfoChild, MMCKInfoParent,
                     MMIO_FINDCHUNK)
            If ErrorCode = 0 Then
              For Index = 1 To 32000
                WaveBuffer(Index).Char = Chr$(0)
                Next Index
              BytesRead = mmioRead(hMMIO, WaveBuffer(1), MMCkInfoChild.CkSize)
              If BytesRead > 0 Then
                ' Get a pointer to the wave data and fill in wave header.
                WaveHeader.lpData = lstrcpy(WaveBuffer(1), WaveBuffer(1))
                WaveHeader.dwBufferLength = BytesRead
```

```
                    WaveHeader.dwFlags = 0&
                    WaveHeader.dwLoops = 0&
                    OpenWaveFile = True
                  Else
                    MsgBox "Couldn't read wave data.", MB_ICONSTOP, "RIFF File Error"
                  End If
                Else
                    MsgBox "Couldn't find data chunk.", MB_ICONSTOP, "RIFF File Error"
                End If
              Else
                MsgBox "Couldn't ascend from fmt chunk.", MB_ICONSTOP, "RIFF
                          File Error"
              End If
            Else
              MsgBox "Format not supported by Wave device.", MB_ICONSTOP, "Wave
                          Data Error"
            End If
          Else
            MsgBox "Couldn't read wave format record.", MB_ICONSTOP, "RIFF File Error"
          End If
        Else
          MsgBox "Couldn't find fmt chunk.", MB_ICONSTOP, "RIFF File Error"
        End If
      Else
        MsgBox "Couldn't find WAVE parent chunk.", MB_ICONSTOP, "RIFF File Error"
      End If
      ' Close WAVE file.
      ErrorCode = mmioClose(hMMIO, 0)
  Else
    MsgBox "Couldn't open file.", MB_ICONSTOP, "RIFF File Error"
  End If

End Function
```

Last, but not least, make sure you add the following declaration for **mmioClose()** to WAVEPLAY.BAS:

```
Declare Function mmioClose Lib "MMSystem" (ByVal hMMIO As Integer,
  ByVal wFlags As Integer) As Integer
```

We don't have to ascend back out to the RIFF chunk before we close the file. Even if we did, we would still be in the same position—at the end of the file. Some day multimedia file I/O may support compound files—RIFF files that contain multiple RIFF chunks. When that happens, we may wish to ascend out of one RIFF chunk before descending into, or searching for, the next one.

Playing the WAVE File

Once we've extracted the data from the RIFF file and created the three essential data structures (the format record, the wave audio data, and the wave data header), we can use the **Waveaudio** device to play the sound. Five steps are required to play the wave audio from the structures stored in memory:

1. Open the Waveaudio device.
2. Prepare the wave header.
3. Write the data to the device.
4. Unprepare the wave header.
5. Close the device.

As you might assume from the discussion so far, we cannot just call the five functions that perform these steps in rapid-fire succession. Like **OpenWaveFile()**, our next function, **WaveOut()**, will include conditions for verification and failure. Listing 4.8 shows the complete code for **WaveOut()**.

Listing 4.8   WaveOut() from WAVEPLAY.BAS

```
Function WaveOut () As Integer
    Dim hWaveOut As Integer
    Dim ReturnCode As Integer

    ' Open the wave device.
    ReturnCode = waveOutOpen(hWaveOut, WAVE_MAPPER, PCMWaveFmtRecord, 0&, 0&, 0&)
    If ReturnCode = 0 Then
        ' Prepare the wave output header.
        ReturnCode = waveOutPrepareHeader(hWaveOut, WaveHeader, Len(WaveHeader))
        If ReturnCode = 0 Then
            ' Write the wave data to the output device.
            ReturnCode = waveOutWrite(hWaveOut, WaveHeader, Len(WaveHeader))
            ' Wait until finished playing.
            If ReturnCode = 0 Then
                Do Until (WaveHeader.dwFlags And WHDR_DONE)
                    DoEvents
                    Loop
            End If
            WaveOut = True
            ' Unprepare the wave output header.
            ReturnCode = waveOutUnprepareHeader(hWaveOut, WaveHeader, _
                        Len(WaveHeader))
            If ReturnCode <> 0 Then
                MsgBox "Unable to Unprepare Wave Header", MB_ICONSTOP, "Wave Error"
            End If
            WaveHeader.dwFlags = 0
            ' Close the wave device.
            ReturnCode = waveOutClose(hWaveOut)
            If ReturnCode <> 0 Then
                MsgBox "Unable to Close Wave Device", MB_ICONSTOP, "Wave Error"
            End If
        Else
            ' Couldn't prepare the header, so close the device.
```

```
        MsgBox "Unable to Prepare Wave Header", 0, "Wave Error"
        ReturnCode = waveOutClose(hWaveOut)
        If ReturnCode <> 0 Then
            MsgBox "Unable to Close Wave Device", MB_ICONSTOP, "Wave Error"
        End If
    End If
Else
    ' Couldn't open the device so do nothing.
    MsgBox "Unable to Open Wave Device", MB_ICONSTOP, "Wave Error"
End If

End Function
```

We begin by opening the device. Although we called **waveOutOpen()** from our function **OpenWaveFile()**, we didn't actually open the wave device. We called the function with a special flag called **WAVE_FORMAT_QUERY**, which, instead of opening the device, just verified that the format of the wave file we read was compatible with the Waveaudio device. This time we'll call **waveOutOpen()** with no flags at all, which really will open the device.

waveOutOpen() expects six parameters. The first parameter is the address of an empty device handle, which the function will fill-in if it successfully opens a Waveaudio device. This handle is used to perform all subsequent operations with the device. For the second parameter, we specifiy which Waveaudio device to open. A Windows system may contain several Waveaudio devices (the MPC specification requires only one). They will be numbered sequentially, beginning with device 0, if your system contains more than one compatible device. If you want the multimedia system to select the first available driver, you can specify the constant **WAVE_MAPPER**, which has an integer value of -1.

For the third parameter, we pass the address of the wave format structure. The fourth and fifth parameters specify a callback function and information to be used by the callback function. Holy-trinity programmers could use the callback function to carry on a dialog with the wave playback function. Unfortunately, unless we write a custom control, we VB programmers will have to use a more primitive technique to monitor playback. We'll pass **NULL**s in these arguments.

For the last parameter of **waveOutOpen(),** we could pass a flag, as we did in our function **OpenWaveFile()**. However, the only other flags available specify the callback method, and since we won't be using callbacks, we can pass a **NULL** set of flags.

The activities of **waveOutPrepareHeader()** and **waveOutUnprepare-Header()** remain mysterious to me. I can tell you that you must prepare the header before you send wave audio data to the device driver, and that you must unprepare the header before you release the memory occupied by the header and wave audio data. But I have to confess, I can't find any explanation—not even a poor one—of what this preparation actually does. I would guess that whatever these functions do, they have been separated from the function **waveOutWrite()** to facilitate performance. Digital audio output devours processor cycles. When you consider that the Windows multimedia system can play 16 bit stereo wave data at 44.1 KHz, you realize that the output functions can't be bothered with any tasks other than those that must occur in real time. Because they are external to the output function, **waveOutPrepareHeader()** and **waveOutUnprepareHeader()** enable **waveOutWrite()** to offload some overhead. With these functions we can prepare the buffers and headers in advance and feed them to the output function in quick succession. As the device driver finishes with each buffer, it can spit it out and leave the cleanup for us to perform later. Of course, when we call the prepare and unprepare functions we're still using the processor, but not during the critical handoff between buffer segments.

After we prepare **WaveHeader**, we send it to the Waveaudio device with **waveOutWrite()**. This function takes three arguments: the handle we received when we opened the device, the memory location of the wave header, and the size of the wave header. Notice that the built-in VB function **Len()** will return the size of a data structure just as easily as it will return the length of a string. We could have supplied the size as a constant value, but it's generally better practice to avoid hard-coded references to structures that may change in the future, especially when functions like **Len()** exist.

After we write out the audio data, we need to unprepare the header and close the device. But we can't do that until the device completes playback, so we loop until **waveOutWrite()** sets the flag **WHDR_DONE** in **WaveHeader**. This is the poor man's alternative to a callback function. If we *could* supply a callback, either in the form of a function or a window handle, we could then instruct **waveOutWrite()** to notify us when it's done. Instead, we just watch for the signal. Notice that this "wait" loop repeatedly executes **DoEvents**. The **DoEvents** function enables Windows to service other events while we're waiting. If we exclude that procedure call from the loop, Windows will hang (also known as "non-preemptive multihanging").

When we spot the **WHDR_DONE** flag, we unprepare the header. Then, as always, we must close the Waveaudio device before we terminate our program or we'll be unable to re-open the device until we restart Windows.

Adding Low-Level Playback to MCIPlay

Now we can add the low-level playback functions to our test program, MCIPLAY3.MAK. We're going to re-visit the functions **OpenWaveFile()** and

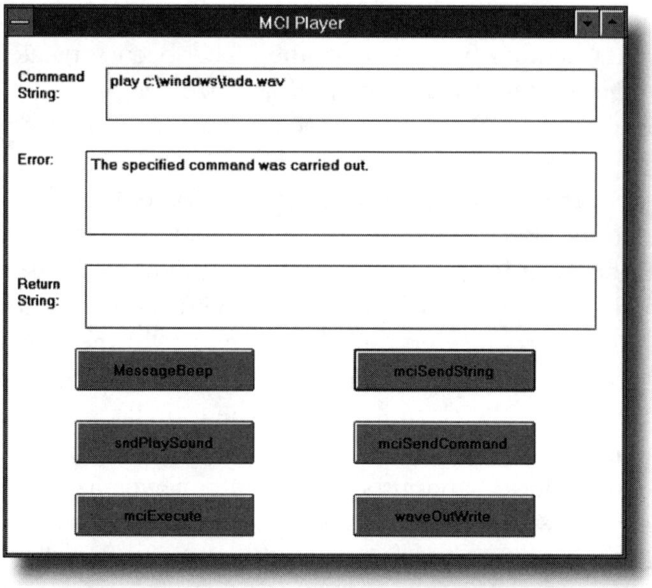

Figure 4.5   *MCIPLAY3.FRM as it appears with all six play buttons.*

WaveOut() in Chapter 13, which is why we placed them in a new code module
called WAVEPLAY.BAS. Add a new button to MCIPLAY3.FRM, and set its **Name**
property to WaveOutButton, and its **Caption** property to "waveOutWrite," as
shown in Figure 4.5. Then, insert the code that appears in Listing 4.9.

Listing 4.9   WaveOutButton_Click Event Procedure from MCIPLAY3.FRM

```
Sub WaveOutButton_Click ()
    Dim Dummy As Integer
    Dim WaveFileOpened As Integer

    If OpenWaveFile("C:\Windows\Tada.WAV") Then
        Dummy = WaveOut()
    End If

    End Sub
```

Don't forget to add the declarations to WAVEPLAY.BAS as they appear in
Listing 4.10.

Listing 4.10   From the Declarations Section of WAVEPLAY.BAS

```
Option Explicit

Type WAVEOUTCAPS
    wMid As Integer
```

```
    wPis As Integer
    vDriverVersion As Integer
    szPName As String * 32
    dwFormats As Long
    wChannels As Integer
    dwSupport, As Long
    End Type

Type WAVEFORMAT
    wFormatTag As Integer
    nChannels As Integer
    nSamplesPerSec As Long
    nAvgBytesPerSec As Long
    nBlockAlign As Integer
    End Type

Type PCMWAVEFORMAT
    wf As WAVEFORMAT
    wBitsPerSample As Integer
    End Type

Type WAVEHDR
    lpData As Long
    dwBufferLength As Long
    dwBytesRecorded As Long
    dwUser As Long
    dwFlags As Long
    dwLoops As Long
    lpNext As Long
    reserved As Long
    End Type

Type FOURCC
    Chars As String * 4
    End Type

Type MMIOINFO
    dwFlags As Long
    fccIOProc As FOURCC
    lpIOProc As Long
    wErrorRet As Integer
    wReserved As Integer
    ' Fields maintained by MMIO functions during buffered IO
    cchBuffer As Long
    pchBuffer As Long
    pchNext As Long
    pchEndRead As Long
    pchEndWrite As Long
    lBufOffset As Long
    ' Fields maintained by I/O procedure
    lDiskOffset As Long
    adwInfo As String * 12
    ' Other fields maintained by MMIO
```

```
    dwReserved1 As Long
    dwReserved2 As Long
    hMMIO As Integer
    End Type


' RIFF chunk information data structure
Type MMCKINFO
    CkId As FOURCC
    CkSize As Long
    fccType As FOURCC
    dwDataOffset As Long
    dwFlags As Long
    End Type


Declare Function waveOutGetDevCaps Lib "MMSystem" (ByVal wDeviceID As Integer,
    lpCaps As WAVEOUTCAPS, ByVal wSize As Integer) As Integer
Declare Function waveOutOpen Lib "MMSystem" (lphWaveOut As Integer, ByVal
    wDeviceID As Integer, lpFormat As Any, ByVal dwCallBack As Long, ByVal
    dwCallBack As Long, ByVal dwFlags As Long) As Integer
Declare Function waveOutClose Lib "MMSystem" (ByVal hWaveOut As Integer) As Integer
Declare Function waveOutPrepareHeader Lib "MMSystem" (ByVal hWaveOut As
    Integer, lpWaveOutHdr As Any, ByVal wSize As Integer) As Integer
Declare Function waveOutUnprepareHeader Lib "MMSystem" (ByVal hWaveOut As
    Integer, lpWaveOutHdr As Any, ByVal wSize As Integer) As Integer
Declare Function waveOutWrite Lib "MMSystem" (ByVal hWaveOut As Integer,
    lpWaveOutHdr As Any, ByVal wSize As Integer) As Integer
Declare Function mmioOpen Lib "MMSystem" (ByVal szFilename As String,
    lpMMIOINFO As Any, ByVal dwOpenFlags As Long) As Integer
Declare Function mmioClose Lib "MMSystem" (ByVal hMMIO As Integer,
    ByVal wFlags As Integer) As Integer
Declare Function mmioDescend Lib "MMSystem" (ByVal hMMIO As Integer, lpCk As
    Any, lpCkParent As Any, ByVal wFlags As Integer) As Integer
Declare Function mmioAscend Lib "MMSystem" (ByVal hMMIO As Integer,
    lpCk As Any, ByVal wFlags As Integer) As Integer
Declare Function mmioRead Lib "MMSystem" (ByVal hMMIO As Integer, pCh As Any,
    ByVal cCh As Long) As Long
Declare Function lstrcpy Lib "Kernel" (lpString1 As Any, lpString2 As Any) As Long


Global Const WAVE_MAPPER = -1        ' Device ID for Wave Mapper
Global Const MMIO_READ = &H0&
Global Const MMIO_WRITE = &H1&
Global Const MMIO_READWRITE = &H2&

Global Const MMIO_FINDCHUNK = &H10   ' mmioDescend: find a chunk by ID
Global Const MMIO_FINDRIFF = &H20    ' mmioDescend: find a LIST chunk

Global Const WHDR_DONE = &H1         ' done bit

' flags for dwFlags parameter in waveOutOpen() and waveInOpen()
Global Const WAVE_FORMAT_QUERY = &H1

Type byte
    Char As String * 1
    End Type
```

```
Dim hWaveOut As Integer
Dim PCMWaveFmtRecord As PCMWAVEFORMAT
Dim WaveBuffer(1 To 32000) As byte
Dim WaveHeader As WAVEHDR
```

You may play other WAVE files besides TADA.WAV, but remember that as it stands, this code will support only files of 32,000 bytes or less.

This may seem like too much trouble just to play WAVE files, especially when there are at least five other much simpler methods. It is. But in the most intimate form of interactivity, we will often want to manipulate not only the playback process, but the form and content of the data itself. Waveaudio data consists of lengthy streams of binary amplitude values. Those values, when used to drive an analog amplifier and speaker, translate back into sound. Once we have our hands on the binary data itself, we can chop it, filter it, loop it, splice it, mix it, and otherwise modify it—perhaps in real time—to suit our own purposes, and more importantly, to reflect the actions of our users.

The View from the Cellar

I've taken such a direct route down into the multimedia API that I've neglected to pause at each level and survey the territory. The MCI, for example, offers a whole bunch of commands that enable you to manipulate multimedia files as if they were physical media, like audio cassettes or video tapes. You can change your position, ask for the number of tracks, select tracks, set the volume, alter the playback speed, record, pause, and resume. Each device supports a few standard commands, along with a selection of commands unique to its medium.

And although I've focused on wave audio playback, the multimedia system supports several kinds of media, including MIDI for synthesizer control, the audio/video interleave format (AVI), graphic animation through the multimedia movie player (MMM), and also external devices such as video tape recorders, video disk players, CD audio players, and digital audio tape (DAT) decks.

At the low level, the Windows multimedia system includes functions to perform all kinds of operations, including buffered file I/O and MIDI sequencing and mapping. In fact, we haven't yet really reached the bottom level; we're standing on the catwalk in the deepest sub-basement, still a few feet above the floor. To perform such time-critical operations as wave audio or MIDI output, the device control functions depend on even lower-level functions, in particular, the multimedia timer, which offers much higher resolution timing than the standard Windows timer. The multimedia system even provides a standard interface for joystick input.

What we have discovered is that the Windows multimedia system offers a variety of approaches to multimedia operation, and that each technique offers unique advantages and disadvantages. For any given multimedia project, or for that matter, for any element of any project, you may choose the approach that provides the most appropriate mixture of accessibility, performance, and control over the data, from simple asynchronous message beeps to byte-by-byte manipulation of digitized sound.

In upcoming chapters, I'll apply many of these techniques, not only to wave audio, but to the other multimedia services as well. So stay tuned.

Unlock the mysteries of colors
and palettes and you'll be on
your way to creating cool
visual effects.

Fun with Imaging— Pixels and Palettes

T he world of graphics and imaging is a big black hole. The further you go
into it, the more you realize there's so much more to discover. But it's worth
the journey to see your program come alive with dazzling screen effects.

In this chapter, we'll explore how Visual Basic and Windows work together
to display images. Along the way, you'll learn about bitmaps, color display
systems, and color palettes. In the next chapter, we'll cover palette animation
and raster operations (ROPs), and a host of other low-level graphics topics.
Windows and Visual Basic provide the tools you need to step out of the
projection booth and onto the big screen. By mastering the basic imaging
techniques, you'll be able to stitch together visual information in ways that are
as captivating and expressive as movies. So, let's get to work!

The Windows Connection— The Graphics Device Interface

Every screen in Windows is a graphic image. (Even a DOS window simulates a character-based screen, drawn with a special font.) The ingenious authors of Windows, faced with a monumental graphics programming task, built a library of functions for drawing colorful borders, buttons, icons, and fonts. Fortunately, they made all those functions available to us by means of the Windows API.

VB handles many of the basic graphics tasks for us by drawing our forms and controls. VB also provides a variety of tools for drawing in Picture Boxes, Image Controls, and directly on form client areas. VB even displays *bitmapped images* on these image-ready surfaces. But when images need to be manipulated for special effects such as animation, VB tosses us back into the API.

Most Windows graphics functions reside in a Windows DLL, known as the *Graphics Device Interface* (GDI). We've already used some of them indirectly. When you create and run just about any VB program, many GDI functions are typically used behind the scenes. This frees you from needing to know about *pixels, palettes,* or *raster operations*. But to write programs that manipulate graphic images, you'll need to know about those things and how to use GDI functions directly. The easiest way to understand the GDI functions is to first understand the data structures they manipulate—in particular, bitmaps and color palettes.

Understanding Bitmaps

The PC's video system displays a matrix of pixels—little dots of light arranged into a neat grid. In a *character-based* environment, the video system contains a "hard-coded" set of shapes that represent the standard character set, along with various drawing characters (lines, corners, solid blocks, and so on) and a few symbols (smiling faces, diamonds, spades, and so on). A character is displayed by sending the system an ASCII or ANSI character code. In a *graphic* display system like Windows, the computer and its software define the shapes that appear on the screen. These shapes are represented as bitmapped images. The main benefit with this approach is that pictures and text can be displayed in a variety of sizes, fonts, and styles. Take a look at Figure 5.1 for a better idea of how this works.

What exactly are bitmapped images? They are a collection of data elements that determine which color to display at each screen position. In a *mono-*

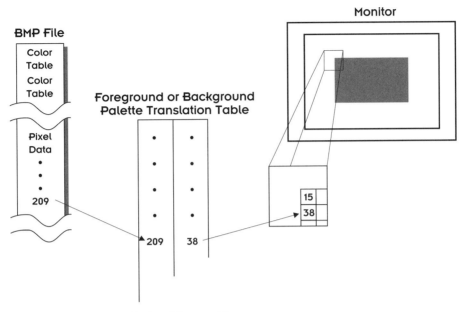

Figure 5.1 *How Windows displays bitmapped images.*

chrome (black-and-white) graphic image, each bit represents one screen pixel, zero for black (the absence of color), and one for white (the presence of color). As you'll see soon, bitmaps can describe multi-colored images. The number of bits per pixel determines the number of different colors that can appear in a single bitmap. Besides the single-bit-per-pixel monochrome version, there are three others. Four bits per pixel produces 16 colors, eight bits will support 256 colors, and 24 bits can describe 16,777,216 colors. The bits that make up a bitmap are arranged sequentially in the bitmap structure. Keep in mind, however, that the rows are stored in reverse order. That is, the first row in the pixel data section of the bitmap file is actually the bottom row of the image, as illustrated in Figure 5.2.

I'll present the actual structure of a bitmap file in Chapter 5. Then, in Chapter 6, I'll show you how to work with them in much more detail. For now, remember that each pixel represents the absence or presence of color. And that's where our exploration of the GDI begins—with color and color palettes.

Color and the PC Display System

You can ignore how color works and let Windows and VB do their own thing if you don't need to create interesting visual effects. But what good is a multimedia application if it's not visually interesting? To create the animation and

DIB Data in Memory

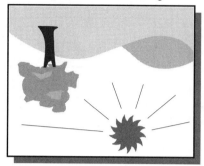

Display Image

Figure 5.2 *How bitmaps are organized.*

other imaging effects that help users enjoy what they're learning, you'll need to understand how Windows and your computer manage color.

The capabilities of your display system determine what Windows can do with color images. The systems supported today come in three classes: VGA, super VGA (SVGA), and true color. (The MPC standard specifies VGA as the minimum display capability so I'll ignore the older CGA and EGA systems.) The standard VGA system can display 16 colors simultaneously with a resolution of 640x480. As you'll see, the waters start to get a little muddy when we look at SVGA and true color systems.

SVGA systems can theoretically display a dazzling array of 16,777,216 colors. However, only 256 colors out of that vast selection can appear on the screen simultaneously. Some so-called SVGA systems display only 64 simultaneous colors, though these are usually found in color notebook computers. SVGA resolutions start at 640x480 and go up from there. Some SVGA systems even reach resolutions exceeding 1200x1000 pixels.

Systems that display the full 16 million color range are often called *true color* displays. What does "true color" mean? It is derived from the idea that if a color display shows an extensive range of colors, the images will look natural or "true." True color displays use 24 bits to determine the color of each pixel. The 24 bits are divided into three 8-bit color components that indicate the intensity of the red, green, and blue color components. For this reason, 24-bit colors are referred to as *RGB* colors. Each primary color may vary in intensity according to an integer scale of 0 through 255. When all three RGB components are set to 0, the pixel appears black; when all are set to 255, the pixel is white. The total number of RGB combinations equals 256 cubed, or 16,777,216 colors.

> **Note:** *Many true color display adapters actually use an 18-bit color model internally. Thus, many shades that have unique 24-bit identities will look identical once they reach the screen.*

Since older technology like photographs and analog television can display a virtually infinite variety of colors, it may seem presumptuous to call this digital version "true color." But right now, this is the state-of-the-art in desktop computer color technology. In fact, most hardware capable of digitizing color images provides a maximum color resolution of 24 bits, which means that a true color display displays the maximum color resolution found in current image data.

Unfortunately, SVGA systems can't display all of their colors at once because of their memory limitations. These systems display at least 307,200 pixels (640x480) and to produce full 24-bit color requires three bytes for each pixel, a total of 921,600 bytes. Until recently, having this much dedicated display memory was considered an extravagance. Many SVGA cards come configured with only 512 kilobytes of memory, enough to support 8 bits per pixel at resolutions of 800x600. Some of the latest display interfaces support resolutions up to 1280x1024, which at 24 bits of color resolution would require almost 4 Mb of display RAM! As memory prices continue to fall, more systems will include 24-bit color displays. But right now, most of the PCs being sold as Windows systems come equipped with 8-bit color displays. So this is the standard we should accommodate in our programs.

The Magic of Color Palettes

The pictures you'll display in your presentations will likely come in a multitude of different colors. Think about it; a photograph of the emerald rolling Irish hills requires a much different set of colors than a picture of Mars. If you wanted to display both images at once, you'd have a real problem on your hands. You would never have enough shades to render both images with any fidelity even with 256 colors to divide between them. Fortunately, if only one picture is displayed at a time, you can ask Windows to swap colors so that each image can activate its own selection of 256 colors—its own *color palette*.

A pixel's color on an 8-bit color display is determined by looking up its 8-bit pixel value in a color table, or *palette* as shown in Figure 5.3. A palette contains a set of 24-bit RGB color values. The maximum number of color entries in a palette is 256, numbered from 0 through 255. A palette need not contain all 256 entries. Each pixel entry in the display memory contains a value from 0 through 255. This pixel value indicates which palette entry to use to color the pixel. To change the color of a pixel, you have two options:

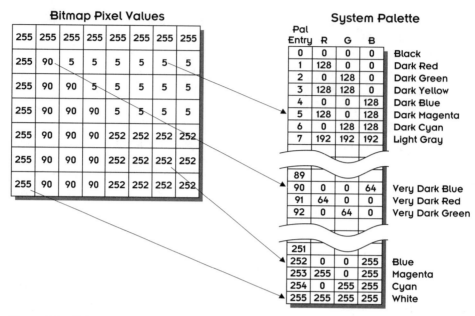

Figure 5.3   *Using a color palette to locate a pixel's color.*

You can either change the index value of the pixel to another palette entry or you can change the RGB value of the palette entry itself, which will change the color of all pixels on the screen that reference that palette entry.

Palettized color certainly imposes limitations—the 256 color limitation applies to the entire screen, not just to each window or application—but it also offers two important advantages. First, it makes your uncompressed image files two-thirds smaller than true color images. Second, you can use the built-in Windows palette manipulation functions to perform two popular (and economical) forms of animation: *palette animation* and *color cycling* (more on these techniques later).

Inside the Palette Manager

As I mentioned previously, each image you display can carry its own color palette. In addition, each active window can manipulate the current palette for its own purposes. But remember, the 256 color limitation applies to the entire screen, not just to each window or application. With such limited seating, someone has to play the role of the bouncer. And that's where the Windows *Palette Manager* comes in.

Windows uses the Palette Manager to determine which window has control of the palette at any given time. The active window, the one in the foreground, always has priority. If that window doesn't use the palette, the priority goes to the next window in the *z-order* (the order in which windows are stacked on the desktop). Once the window with the highest priority "realizes" its palette as the *foreground palette*, the other windows are signalled in order by the Palette Manager to "realize" their palettes as *background palettes*.

But what does it mean to *realize* a palette? Each image you display could have its own color palette (several palettes can be kept in memory simultaneously). A palette stored in memory is called a *logical palette*. The palette in your display system that determines which colors actually appear on the screen is called the *hardware*, or *system palette*. There is only one hardware palette and the Palette Manager maintains a copy of it. When an application wants to activate its own colors, it must select its logical palette into a *device context* and *realize* it, which means that it must ask the Palette Manager to load its logical palette into the system (hardware) palette. This process of realizing a palettte is shown in Figure 5.4.

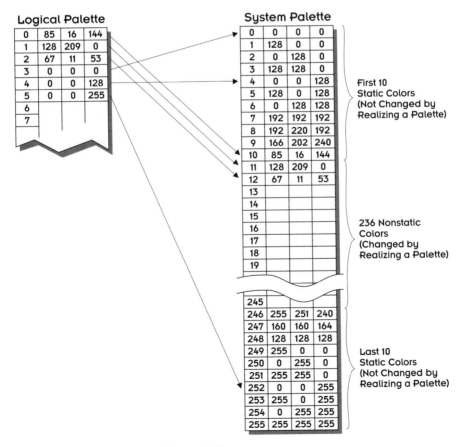

Figure 5.4 *The process of realizing a palette.*

Because palettes vary in size, the Palette Manager doesn't blindly copy a fixed-sized block of 256 color elements from the logical palette to the hardware palette. The Palette Manager loads only as many colors as it finds in each logical palette. The system palette can accommodate multiple logical palettes, as long as the total number of colors does not exceed 256. Furthermore, Windows reserves 20 of the palette entries for its *static colors*—the colors it uses to draw buttons, borders, text, icons, and so on. So we're left with only 236 changeable color slots. But this doesn't mean a palette should include only the 236 colors it needs to support its bitmap. It's wise to convert the palette of any 8-bit image into a Windows *identity palette*, which is a palette that includes the 20 reserved colors, especially if you plan to draw with the palette. Otherwise, you won't be able to use the reserved colors. If you wish, you *can* tamper with the system static colors to extend the range of definable colors all the way up to 256; the GDI provides special functions just for that purpose. But that would violate the Windows prime directive of not interfering with other active applications since it could dramatically alter their appearance.

The colors in a logical palette often do not occupy the same positions in the system palette that they do in the logical palette. So the Palette Manager must build a cross-reference table, called a *palette mapping*, as it loads a logical palette into the system palette. This table is used by GDI drawing functions to translate pixel values from logical palette indexes into system palette indexes. As I explained earlier, a pixel's color is determined by looking up its value in a color table. In the case of a *device independent bitmap* or DIB, which is the most common form of 256 color bitmap file, the bytes that make up the bitmap pixel data contain values that reference the entries in the color table contained within the file. As the GDI transfers the image from the file to the screen, that is, from a device *independent* bitmap into a device *dependent* bitmap or DDB, it uses the palette mapping to change the pixel values so they reference the correct colors in the system palette. The palette mapping that's created for a logical palette is called the *foreground mapping*.

If the active window does not hog all the palette entries, the remaining slots will be filled with colors from the inactive windows until either all the slots are occupied or no other windows ask to realize their own palettes. If the foreground window requires all 236 free color slots, all the inactive windows must conform to the active foreground palette. The Palette Manager can also perform this service automatically by mapping colors in the inactive windows to the closest matching colors in the currently realized palette, which occasionally produces amusing (or ugly) results. This is called a *background mapping*. Each time the focus changes from one palette-based application to another, the entire realization process starts over.

The difference between device independent and device dependent bitmaps is worth repeating: the pixels in a DIB contain the indexes of the colors in the logical palette that accompanies the bitmap, usually a color table stored in the DIB file; the pixels in a DDB contain the indexes of the colors in the system palette. Figure 5.5 illustrates the difference between the two structures. A DIB does not exist in a device context. It must be translated into a DDB either before it's selected into a device context or as it is painted into the device context. The foreground and background palette mappings are the tables used to translate DIBs into DDBs.

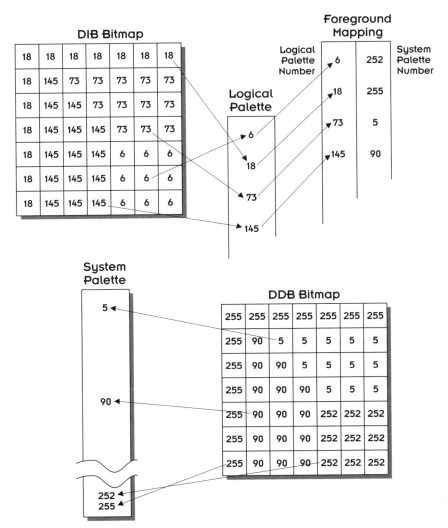

Figure 5.5 *Comparing a DIB with a DDB.*

Exploring Colors with Visual Basic

VB does a great job of hiding the details of color palette operations. If you just want to display bitmaps in Picture Boxes, you can let VB and the Windows Palette Manager handle the palette. When VB loads a bitmap that contains its own palette, it loads and realizes that palette automatically. If you load another bitmap, the palette changes again, all behind the scenes. VB can't perform miracles, however, so you'll need to keep in mind the limitations imposed by palettes and the Palette Manager as you prepare your image data. Do not, for example, expect VB to simultaneously and accurately display two or more images with dissimilar palettes.

To program image processing applications, or to perform animation or special effects, you can go over VB's head and talk directly to the Palette Manager. In this section, I'll show you how to work with colors by using both VB and Windows API functions.

Selecting Colors the Easy Way

Before we recklessly abandon VB's built-in color capabilities, let's see how far they can take us. VB provides a function named **RGB()** for creating or selecting background, text, and foreground colors. **RGB()** is like a chameleon because its behavior changes under different circumstances. For example, **RGB()** displays colors as dithered colors by default; however, other palettes can be loaded to access more "pure" colors.

Using the RGB() Function

This project shows you how to use **RGB()** to display different colors. Here are the steps to follow:

1. Create a new form named TestRGB and place a Picture Box and Scroll Bars on the form, as shown in Figure 5.6.
2. Insert code for the **ColorBar_Change()** event procedure and the Picture Box's **Paint** event.

This project is located in the directory \VBMAGIC, in the files TESTRGB.MAK and TESTRGB.FRM.

Creating the RGB() Program

To start, create the form named TestRGB and place a Picture Box somewhere on the form. Set the Picture Box's **AutoRedraw** property to False. For now, you can ignore the other properties of the Picture Box. Next, place three, side-by-side Scroll Bar controls on the form (see Figure 5.6). You may choose either variety, horizontal or vertical. We'll organize the scroll bars into a control array. To do this, simply name them all identically to **ColorBar**. After you name the second one, VB will ask you to verify that you really want a control array.

You also need to set two properties on all three Scroll Bars: Set the **Max** property to 255, and set the **LargeChange** property to a value of about 5 or 10.

Double-click on any of the three bars to display the framework for the **ColorBar_Change()** event procedure. Then, insert the following statement:

```
Picture1.Refresh
```

Because we declared a control array, all three Scroll Bars share the same event procedures. If you hadn't created a control array, you could have placed this same statement in each of the three separate Scroll Bar **Change** events.

Double-click on the Picture Box, choose the **Paint** event from the Procedure list box, and insert this line:

```
Picture1.BackColor = RGB(ColorBar(0).Value, ColorBar(1).Value, ColorBar(2).Value)
```

Now run the program. As you move the thumb on the Scroll Bars, the

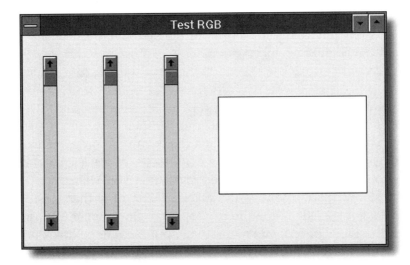

Figure 5.6 *The TestRGB form.*

Picture Box will change colors.

Remember that the VB **RGB()** function produces *dithered* colors. This means that it alternates pixels of 20 pure static colors to approximate the color value specified with the red, green, and blue color value arguments. Unless you stand at some distance from the display, dithered colors often resemble psychedelic plaids and checkerboards—not particularly exciting for high impact graphics!

Using More Colors—Loading a Palette

We can do better than dithered colors. The way to go is to use a more extensive palette of "pure colors," which are mixed at the hardware level. This can be done by loading a palette into a specific object such as a Picture Box, form, or Image Box. But none of these objects possesses a Palette property, so how do we load them?

The easiest way is to load a bitmap that contains a color table. In fact, VB comes with three special DIB files that contain a color table and a single pixel—just enough image data for them to qualify as bitmaps. If you load any of the files RAINBOW.DIB, PASTEL.DIB, or BRIGHT.DIB, either at runtime or by assigning them to the **Picture** property of a Picture Box control or a form at design time, the host object acquires access to the color palette contained in that file.

Once you load a color palette into a VB object, you need a way to select individual colors. And that is where VB's color handling begins to falter.

To see how this works, click on the Picture Box to select it and locate its **Picture** property in the Properties window. When you double-click on the **Picture** property, VB displays the Load Picture dialog box. Select the VB directory and then select one of the DIB files. I recommend using PASTEL.DIB because its colors differ substantially from the system colors, which makes them easier to recognize as you experiment.

The **Picture** property doesn't show the name of the file. Instead, it simply says "(Bitmap)." (Later, if you want to remove a bitmap from the **Picture** property, delete "(Bitmap)" from the property by selecting and deleting it from the edit control near the top of the Properties window. You do not have to delete one bitmap before you select another.) Run the program again.

As you change the Scroll Bar this time, the color of the Picture Box will jump from one palette color to another. Each time you change any of the three color values, **RGB()** locates the color palette entry that most closely matches the color specified. The three Scroll Bars can produce almost seven million combinations of red, green, and blue, but the palette holds no more than 256 colors, so as you change the RGB value, the displayed color must snap to one of those palette entries.

Using the API to Access Colors

Unless you have acutely sensitive color vision and an intuitive grasp of the relationship between numerical and actual color values, VB offers no way to select specific colors from the palette. You would think that with a table of 256 entries you could just choose colors by number. You can. But you need the Windows API.

Windows provides thirteen functions—and for C programmers, six macros—that control and retrieve information from the color palette. Among these you will find the macros used by the VB **RGB()** function to locate the closest matching color.

Whenever you reference a color from an API drawing function, you use not just the three bytes that hold the red, green, and blue color values, but also a fourth byte that contains a flag value. The lowest-order byte contains the value of the red component. The highest-order byte contains a flag that indicates whether the reference is to a dithered color, a palette matched color, or an explicit palette index. The value of the high byte determines how the three lower-order bytes will be used to select a color. When you want to specify the color of a pen or brush in one of the API functions that create those objects, you can set the high byte to one of three values listed in Table 5.1.

This double word (four bytes) value is called a COLORREF, or color reference, which means that the proper place to use it is as a parameter in API drawing functions that require a color specifier. Later we'll look at some other structures that also hold color information.

Technically, the four fields in COLORREF are byte values, but in the Windows API, COLORREF is not a record-style data structure. It is just a long integer. To construct a color reference in VB, you need to pack the three RGB values and the flag byte into a long integer value:

Table 5.1 *The possible high-order byte values in a GDI color reference.*

High-Byte Value	Result
&H00	Windows dithers the 20 reserved colors as the object is drawn. This is called an RGB color reference.
&H01	Instead of the value of the red color component, the lowest-order byte specifies the number, or index value, of a palette entry, so Windows uses the color it finds in that palette entry. The middle two bytes (bytes 1 and 2) should always contain value &H00. This is called a Palette Index reference.
&H02	Windows locates the palette entry that most closely matches the color determined by the red, green, and blue components specified in the three lower-order bytes. This is called a Palette RGB reference.

```
Dim ColorReference As Long
ColorReference = RedValue + (GreenValue  * 256) + (BlueValue * 65536) +
(FlagValue * 16777216)
```

Selecting Colors by Numbers

This project uses a handful of API functions to display a palette in a 16 x 16 unit grid, as shown in Figure 5.7. Here are the steps to follow:

1. Create a new form named PaletExp.
2. Add the declarations (Listing 5.1) and the **Form_Paint()** event procedure (Listing 5.2) to the form.

This project is located on the companion CD-ROM in the directory \VBMAGIC, in the files PALETEX1.MAK and PALETEX1.FRM.

Creating the Palette Program

This simple project requires a single, empty form—no controls. Select the form and set its **Name** property to PaletExp and load PASTEL.DIB into its **Picture** property. With the exception of a single constant and its API function declarations, our program will reside entirely in the form's **Paint()** event

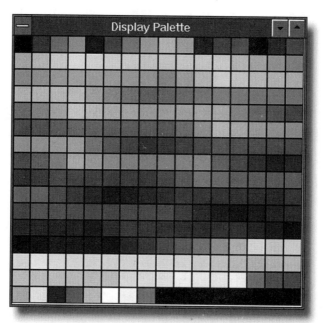

Figure 5.7 *PALETEX1 will display the form's current logical palette.*

procedure. The program won't run until we declare the API functions and specify a value for the constant **BLACK_BRUSH**. So, insert the declarations shown in Listing 5.1 to the declarations section of the form.

Listing 5.1 The Declarations Section from PALETEX1.FRM

```
Declare Function CreateSolidBrush Lib "GDI" (ByVal crColor As Long) As Integer
Declare Function SelectObject Lib "GDI" (ByVal hDC As Integer, ByVal hObject As
        Integer) As Integer
Declare Function Rectangle Lib "GDI" (ByVal hDC As Integer, ByVal X1 As Integer,
        ByVal Y1 As Integer, ByVal X2 As Integer, ByVal Y2 As Integer) As Integer
Declare Function DeleteObject Lib "GDI" (ByVal hObject As Integer) As Integer
Declare Function GetStockObject Lib "GDI" (ByVal nIndex As Integer) As Integer

Const BLACK_BRUSH = 4
```

Next, open that code window and enter the code shown in Listing 5.2.

Listing 5.2 The Form_Paint() Event Procedure from PALETEX1.FRM

```
Sub Form_Paint ()

    Dim Row As Integer
    Dim Column As Integer
    Dim BoxHeight As Integer
    Dim BoxWidth As Integer
    Dim ColorIndex As Long
    Dim hBrush As Integer
    Dim Dummy As Integer

    BoxWidth = ScaleWidth \ 16
    BoxHeight = ScaleHeight \ 16
    For ColorIndex = 0 To 255
        Row = ColorIndex \ 16 + 1
        Column = ColorIndex mod 16 + 1
        hBrush = CreateSolidBrush(&H1000000 Or ColorIndex)
        Dummy = SelectObject(hDC, hBrush)
        Dummy = Rectangle(hDC, (Column - 1) * BoxWidth, (Row - 1)
                * BoxHeight, Column * BoxWidth, Row * BoxHeight)
        Dummy = SelectObject(hDC, GetStockObject(BLACK_BRUSH))
        Dummy = DeleteObject(hBrush)
    Next ColorIndex
End Sub
```

Let's explore this procedure from the inside out. First we'll look inside the loop at the series of five function calls that draw the 256 colored rectangles.

The function **CreateSolidBrush()** performs the work of selecting colors. Its sole argument is a long integer—four bytes—which normally defines a color. But here, the logical operator **Or** sets the most significant byte to 1, which as you may recall, redefines the color reference as an index into the palette. If we omitted the logical operation leaving the high byte set to 0, the program would just display 256 shades of red, all dithered (try it). With the high byte set to 1, color number 1 means the color defined in palette entry number 1; color number 2 means the color defined in palette entry 2, and so on.

Under normal circumstances, we could use the **Line()** method to draw filled rectangles:

```
Line ((Column - 1) * BoxWidth, (Row - 1) * BoxHeight)-(Column * BoxWidth, Row *
    BoxHeight), (&H1000000 Or ColorIndex), BF
```

But the color parameter you see in this statement won't work. At runtime VB reports an illegal function call. It appears that VB intentionally prevents us from referencing the color palette by color index. In fact, we cannot insert any value into the high byte of the color reference; VB expects us to provide red, green, and blue color values, and nothing more. Since we can't use the **Line()** method, we instead call directly upon the Windows API function **Rectangle()**. (Isn't it odd that VB offers only its **Line()** method for drawing rectangles, yet Windows provides an explicit rectangle funtion?)

VB's graphic methods neatly package the steps of creating and selecting brushes, selecting colors, drawing objects and releasing brushes. But because we're circumventing VB, we have to perform these tasks ourselves.

Creating a Brush

Before we can draw rectangles in the color of our choice, we have to create a brush of that color. Windows supports two kinds of drawing objects: brushes and pens. Brushes are used for filling areas, and pens are used for writing text and for drawing lines and borders. For this program, we will use the default **BLACK_PEN** to draw the outlines of the color rectangles, and we'll create brushes to fill them with the colors from the current palette.

Here's a summary of the steps required to create and use a brush:

1. Create a solid colored brush.
2. Select the new brush into the device context.
3. Draw a rectangle.
4. Select the system default brush back into the device context.
5. Destroy the colored brush we created in step 1.

Once we create and select a brush, all of the subsequent graphic drawing functions we call within that device context will use that brush. When we wish to stop drawing or to change colors, we destroy the brush and create a new one. You cannot destroy a brush that is actively selected into the device context, so we select the system's default **BLACK_BRUSH** before we destroy the brush we've created.

Notice that in the statement that calls **CreateSolidBrush()**, you set the value of the high-order byte not by adding, but with a logical **Or** operation:

```
hBrush = CreateSolidBrush(&H1000000 Or ColorIndex)
```

It's a good idea to use logical operations when we're setting flags because it prevents us from adding them in more than once, which would produce an entirely incorrect result. Think about it. In this case we are setting the 25th bit, which appears to be equivalent to adding &H01000000 (decimal 16,777,216) to the existing flag block. If we perform a logical **Or** between values &H00000001 and &H01000000, we get &H01000001 (decimal 16,777,217). If we repeat the **Or**, this time combining our result, &H01000001 with the flag value &H01000000, we once again get &H01000001. If we perform these steps again, but add instead of **Or**ing, we start off in the right direction, because &H00000001 + &H01000000 = &H01000001 (decimal 16,777,217). But the second time we add &H01000000, we get &H02000001 (decimal 33,554,433), not the same at all.

Occasionally you may display a palette on the screen and find that it lacks some or all of the system default colors. When you request a color by its index value, you're asking for the color according to its position in the logical palette, not its position in the system palette. Windows maintains a map between the logical palette and the system palette. If the realized logical palette doesn't include the 20 system default colors, we lose access to them. This doesn't mean they go away—Windows needs those colors to properly display other objects on the desktop, including the desktop itself—we just can't get to them because we can only directly reference colors in our logical palette. If you need the system colors, add them to your logical palette. (The palette editor, PalEdit, which Microsoft includes in the Multimedia Development Kit and in Video for Windows, provides a menu option called "Make Identity Palette" which performs this function automatically.)

Now that you know how to display the logical palette, you're ready to change it, or more specifically, to set and change specific colors.

Changing Colors in the Logical Color Palette

In this project we'll use Scroll Bars again to modify colors. But this time, instead of dithering the 20 Windows reserved colors, we'll select individual colors in the logical palette and use the API's palette functions to change their actual RGB values.

1. Create a form named PaletEx2. The completed form is shown in Figure 5.8.

2. Add the **Picture1_Paint()** event procedure (Listing 5.3).

3. Add the **Picture1_MouseDown()** event procedure (Listing 5.4) to select a color for editing.

4. Add the **BigColorBox_Paint()** event procedure (Listing 5.5) to display a larger swatch of the color as it's modified.

5. Add the **ColorScrollBar_Change()** event procedure (Listing 5.6) to update the colors on the screen.

6. Define the **PALETTEENTRY** structure.

7. Add a new code module called PALETEX2.BAS and fill in its declarations section (Listing 5.7).

8. Add declarations to the form (Listing 5.8).

9. Add a **Form_Load()** event procedure to initialize the **ColorSelected** variable (Listing 5.9).

This project is located in the directory \VBMAGIC and includes the files PALETEX2.MAK, PALETEX2.FRM, and PALETEX2.BAS.

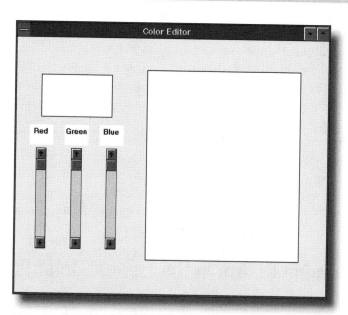

Figure 5.8   *The color editor form, PALETEX2.FRM, at design time.*

Creating the Logical Color Palette Program

For this project we need to confine the palette display to a Picture Box and re-introduce the Scroll Bar control array we used to experiment with VB's internal color control earlier in this chapter (see Figure 5.8).

We'll display the palette matrix in a Picture Box. When the user clicks in the Picture Box, we'll use the X and Y coordinates provided by the **Picture1_MouseDown()** event procedure to calculate the identity of the color cell selected. We'll then retrieve the color settings from the logical palette, highlight the selection by displaying an oversized rectangle of that color centered on the same position, and set the Scroll Bars to the present RGB values. Each time the user changes a Scroll Bar setting, we'll update the color entry in the logical palette and re-realize that palette into the system palette so the updated color will appear on the screen.

Let's begin with the **Picture1_Paint** event procedure that draws the color matrix in **Picture1**. The complete procedure is shown in Listing 5.3.

Listing 5.3   The Picture1_Paint() Event Procedure from PALETEX2.FRM

```
Sub Picture1_Paint ()
    Dim Row As Integer
    Dim Column As Integer
    Dim BoxHeight As Integer
    Dim BoxWidth As Integer
    Dim Color As Long
    Dim ColorIndex As Long
    Dim hBrush As Integer
    Dim NumPalEntries As Integer
    Dim Dummy As Integer

    hSystemPalette = GetStockObject(DEFAULT_PALETTE)
    hCurrentPalette = SelectPalette(Picture1.hDC, hSystemPalette, False)
    hSystemPalette = SelectPalette(Picture1.hDC, hCurrentPalette, False)

    BoxWidth = Picture1.ScaleWidth / 16
    BoxHeight = Picture1.ScaleHeight / 16
    For ColorIndex = 0 To 255
        Row = ColorIndex \ 16 + 1
        Column = ColorIndex Mod 16 + 1
        hBrush = CreateSolidBrush(&H1000000 Or ColorIndex)
        Dummy = SelectObject(Picture1.hDC, hBrush)
        Dummy = Rectangle(Picture1.hDC, (Column - 1) * BoxWidth, (Row - 1) *
            BoxHeight, Column * BoxWidth, Row * BoxHeight)
        Dummy = SelectObject(Picture1.hDC, GetStockObject(BLACK_BRUSH))
        Dummy = DeleteObject(hBrush)
        Next ColorIndex
    If ColorSelected >= 0 Then
        Row = ColorSelected \ 16 + 1
```

```
        Column = ColorSelected Mod 16 + 1
        hBrush = CreateSolidBrush(&H1000000 Or ColorSelected)
        Dummy = SelectObject(Picture1.hDC, hBrush)
        Dummy = Rectangle(Picture1.hDC, MaxVal((Column - 1.5) * BoxWidth, 0),
            MaxVal((Row - 1.5) * BoxHeight, 0), (Column + .5) * BoxWidth,
            (Row + .5) * BoxHeight)
        Dummy = SelectObject(Picture1.hDC, GetStockObject(BLACK_BRUSH))
        Dummy = DeleteObject(hBrush)
    End If
End Sub
```

Much of this procedure comes from **Form_Paint()**, which was used in the previous project. Since we now have several objects in hand, we will explicitly de-reference **Picture1**'s properties. We could leave them alone—since they appear in **Picture1**'s **Paint** event, they default to **Picture1**'s properties—but for the sake of clarity, I have used the verbose form.

The **Paint** event performs two additional operations. To understand the first block of code we've added to **Picture1_Paint()**, we have to look ahead a little.

To *paint* with colors from the logical palette, we need just a color reference with a high byte value of 1 and a handle to the Picture Box's device context, which VB's designers have thoughtfully provided. But to *set* colors in the logical palette, we will also need a handle to the palette itself, which we'll have to fish out ourselves. The intuitive way to accomplish this would be to call an API function that would return a handle. Too bad no such function exists. Instead we'll have to play a little shell game with the palette handles.

The API function **GetStockObject()** returns the handle to the default system palette. Actually, this useful function returns a handle to any number of system objects, depending on the constant we supply as its one and only parameter. The constant used is called **DEFAULT_PALETTE**, which is defined in theWindows 3.1 API Declaration Reference as:

```
Global Const DEFAULT_PALETTE = 15
```

You'll need to add this declaration to the declarations section of the code module.

Before we can capture the palette handle, we'll need a place to store it. For the shell game we're also going to need a place to hold a second handle.

```
Dim hCurrentPalette As Integer
Dim hSystemPalette As Integer
```

Here's the problem. We can't just ask VB for the handle to the palette referenced by **Picture1**. We can, however, select a palette into **Picture1**, or rather into **Picture1**'s device context. You select a palette by passing a handle to a device context and a handle to a palette into a function called **SelectPalette()**. It just so happens that **SelectPalette()** returns the handle of the previously selected palette, so we can con Windows into giving us the handle to the PASTEL palette by using **SelectPalette()** to switch **Picture1** over to the system palette. Then, once we have the handle to the PASTEL palette, we switch it back into the device context by calling **SelectPalette()** again.

```
hSystemPalette = GetStockObject(DEFAULT_PALETTE)
hCurrentPalette = SelectPalette(Picture1.hDC, hSystemPalette, False)
hSystemPalette = SelectPalette(Picture1.hDC, hCurrentPalette, False)
```

In the first statement, **hSystemPalette** receives the handle to the system default palette, the standard VGA colors. VB has already secretly selected PASTEL's palette into **Picture1**'s device context upon loading the file PASTEL.DIB, so in the second statement we throw in **hSystemPalette** to trick it into tossing us the handle to PASTEL's palette, which we capture into **hCurrentPalette**. Finally, we re-select PASTEL's palette back into the device context from which we snatched it, which harmlessly and uselessly reassigns to **hSystemPalette** the handle to the system default palette.

Later we'll use **SelectPalette()** again to select the same logical palette into the device context of the other Picture Box, which we'll call **BigColorBox**. **BigColorBox** will display an even larger sample of the selected color.

The second operation we'll add to **Picture1_Paint()** will display the enlarged version of the selected color rectangle. The **Picture1_MouseDown()** event procedure (coming up next) will identify the color and set a form level variable named **ColorSelected** to the color's index value. In **Picture1_Paint()**, we'll use **ColorSelected** to position and draw the expanded rectangle:

```
If ColorSelected >= 0 Then
   Row = ColorSelected \ 16 + 1
   Column = ColorSelected Mod 16 + 1
   hBrush = CreateSolidBrush(&H1000000 Or ColorSelected)
   Dummy = SelectObject(Picture1.hDC, hBrush)
   Dummy = Rectangle(Picture1.hDC, MaxVal((Column - 1.5) * BoxWidth, 0),
          MaxVal((Row - 1.5) * BoxHeight, 0), (Column + .5) * BoxWidth,
          (Row + .5) * BoxHeight)
   Dummy = SelectObject(Picture1.hDC, GetStockObject(BLACK_BRUSH))
   Dummy = DeleteObject(hBrush)
   End If
```

Now that we've finished with **Picture1_Paint()**, let's examine **Picture1_MouseDown()**. This event procedure (Listing 5.4) identifies the color index and sets the three Scroll Bar **Value** properties.

Listing 5.4 The Picture1_MouseDown() Event Procedure from PALETEX2.FRM

```
Sub Picture1_MouseDown (Button As Integer, Shift As Integer, X As Single, Y As Single)

    Dim CurrentPaletteEntry As PALETTEENTRY
    Dim Row As Integer
    Dim Column As Integer
    Dim BoxHeight As Integer
    Dim BoxWidth As Integer
    Dim Dummy As Integer

    BoxWidth = Picture1.ScaleWidth / 16
    BoxHeight = Picture1.ScaleHeight / 16
    Row = (Y \ BoxHeight)
    Column = X \ BoxWidth
    ColorSelected = Row * 16 + Column
    Dummy = GetPaletteEntries(hCurrentPalette, ColorSelected, 1, CurrentPaletteEntry)
    SelectingAColor = True
    ColorScrollBar(0).Value = 255 - Asc(CurrentPaletteEntry.peRed)
    ColorScrollBar(1).Value = 255 - Asc(CurrentPaletteEntry.peGreen)
    ColorScrollBar(2).Value = 255 - Asc(CurrentPaletteEntry.peBlue)
    SelectingAColor = False
    Picture1_Paint
    BigColorBox_Paint

    End Sub
```

Adding the PALETTEENTRY Data Structure

To retrieve the RGB values for an entry in the logical palette, we have to construct a **PALETTEENTRY**, a four-byte data structure that comprises three color bytes and a flag byte.

```
Type PALETTEENTRY
    peRed As String * 1
    peGreen As String * 1
    peBlue As String * 1
    peFlags As String * 1
    End Type
```

Technically, the four fields in this record structure are byte values, but since VB doesn't support a byte data type, we use single-character strings to hold the four byte values. You may recall that in VB you can declare a fixed-length string by tacking on an asterisk followed by the length (for example, Dim AnyString As String * 256), a kind of twisted expression of multiplication. Remember, the characters we find in each of these strings is irrelevant; the ASCII value of that character simply determines the integer value of the field. We treat bytes like very short integers, integers limited to values from 0 through 255.

Notice the similarity between a **PALETTEENTRY** and a **COLORREF**—but there's a catch. They're not the same. First of all, the flag values of a **PALETTEENTRY** are not the same as the flag values of a color reference (more on those later). Second, the bytes are in the wrong order. If we were to declare a **COLORREF** structure—which would be entirely theoretical because there isn't one—it would look like this:

```
Type COLORREF (WARNING! THIS IS NOT AN OFFICIAL DATA STRUCTURE)
    crReferenceType As String * 1
    crBlue As String * 1
    crGreen As String * 1
    crRed As String * 1
    End Type
```

Remember, a color reference is just a long integer, four bytes. The lowest-order byte contains the value of the red component. The highest-order byte contains a flag that indicates whether the reference is to a dithered color, a palette matched color, or an explicit palette index. In the **PALETTEENTRY** structure, however, the whole thing is inverted. If we were to view the four bytes of a **PALETTEENTRY** as a long integer, the lowest-order byte would contain a flag value, and the highest-order byte would contain the value of the red component.

Type declarations are always global so they must be made in the declarations section of a code module, not within a form. Once you define the new data type, you may declare a variable of the defined type anywhere, either locally or globally. The declaration of **PALETTEENTRY** will go into the file PALETEX2.BAS.

We can obtain the RGB color settings for any palette element, or for multiple elements, with the API function **GetPaletteEntries()**, as shown in Listing 5.4. The **PALETTEENTRY** structure is the component from which a logical palette is built. We use it either to set the palette entries in a logical palette, or, as in this example, to retrieve them. This procedure retrieves a single palette entry each time it is called. To get two or more contiguous entries, we would change the third argument to the appropriate number, and we would pass an array element as the fourth parameter. Of course, the array must extend far enough beyond the given element to accommodate the number of entries we request. In other words, if you ask for 50 palette entries, and you pass in an array element called PaletteEntries(100), then the array **PaletteEntries()** had better be dimensioned to at least 149 elements.

Sometimes the Best Event Is No Event

The global boolean variable, **SelectingAColor**, is used in the **MouseDown()** event procedure to eliminate unnecessary updates to the palette. Each time the user changes a Scroll Bar, we'll want to update the palette. We'll do that in the **ColorScrollBar_Change()** event procedure. But when the user first selects a color for editing, we need to set the **Value** property of all three Scroll Bars to represent the RGB values for that color. When we set the **Value** property, VB also automatically generates an unwanted Scroll Bar **Change** event. We'll use **SelectingAColor** to communicate with the **ColorScrollBar_Change()** event procedure so that it doesn't waste time updating the palette three times as we set the Scroll Bar **Values** here in **Picture1_MouseDown()**. This is one of the pitfalls of event-driven programming; sometimes we trigger events that we would rather not.

Finally, we'll call the **Paint** events for **Picture1** and **BigColorBox** so that **BigColorBox** fills itself with the correct color, and **Picture1** displays its enlarged color cell. Notice that all the actual screen updates take place in the **Paint** events. By confining graphic operations to the **Paint** events, we enable Windows to redraw our application window correctly whenever it is moved or uncovered.

In the Picture Box named **BigColorBox**, we'll place the **Paint** event shown in Listing 5.5.

Listing 5.5   The BigColorBox_Paint() Event Procedure from PALETEX2.FRM

```
Sub BigColorBox_Paint ()

    Dim hBrush As Integer
    Dim Dummy as Integer

    hSystemPalette = SelectPalette(BigColorBox.hDC, hCurrentPalette, False)
    Dummy = RealizePalette(BigColorBox.hDC)
    hBrush = CreateSolidBrush(&H1000000 Or ColorSelected)
    Dummy = SelectObject(BigColorBox.hDC, hBrush)
    Dummy = Rectangle(BigColorBox.hDC, 0, 0, BigColorBox.ScaleWidth,
        BigColorBox.ScaleHeight)
    Dummy = SelectObject(BigColorBox.hDC, GetStockObject(BLACK_BRUSH))
    Dummy = DeleteObject(hBrush)

    End Sub
```

This procedure paints the entire Picture Box with the solid color selected in the **Picture1_MouseDown** event.

Handling the Scroll Bars

Now we're ready for the scroll bars. All three scroll bars perform the same operations in their **Change** events, so we declare them as a control array, as shown in Listing 5.6.

Listing 5.6   The ColorScrollBar_Change() Event Procedure from PALETEX2.FRM

```
Sub ColorScrollBar_Change (Index As Integer)

    Dim Dummy As Integer
    Dim NewPaletteEntry As PALETTEENTRY

    If (Not SelectingAColor) And (ColorSelected > -1) Then
        NewPaletteEntry.peRed = Chr$(255 - ColorScrollBar(0).Value)
        NewPaletteEntry.peGreen = Chr$(255 - ColorScrollBar(1).Value)
        NewPaletteEntry.peBlue = Chr$(255 - ColorScrollBar(2).Value)
        NewPaletteEntry.peFlags = Chr$(0)

        hSystemPalette = GetStockObject(DEFAULT_PALETTE)
        hCurrentPalette = SelectPalette(Picture1.hDC, hSystemPalette, False)
        Dummy = SetPaletteEntries(hCurrentPalette, ColorSelected, 1, NewPaletteEntry)
        hSystemPalette = SelectPalette(Picture1.hDC, hCurrentPalette, False)
        Dummy = RealizePalette(Picture1.hDC)
    End If

End Sub
```

To invert the Scroll Bars so that the colors reach their maximum intensity when the thumb is at the top of each bar, we subtract the Scroll Bar values from 255. Since VB doesn't support a byte data type, we use single-character strings to represent the byte values. To set them, we convert the integer color values into characters before assigning them to the color bytes.

As I explained earlier, the Scroll Bars can change in response to two distinct events: when the user moves the thumb or when the user clicks the mouse in **Picture1** to select a palette color. By setting **SelectingAColor** in **Picture1**'s **MouseDown** event, we can prevent the Scroll Bar **Change** event from performing unnecessary updates to the palette. If **SelectingAColor** is **False**, then we can update the color.

The functions **SetPaletteEntries()** and **RealizePalette()** perform the real work. **SetPaletteEntries()**, like its sibling **GetPaletteEntries()**, takes four parameters. The first is a handle to the logical palette. The second and third parameters contain the number of the first palette entry we wish to change and the number of entries to change respectively. Just as we can retrieve several palette entries with a single call to **GetPaletteEntries()**, we can also set several palette entries with a single call to **SetPaletteEntries()**. The fourth parameter is a variable of type **PALETTEENTRY**, which contains the new color settings for the first palette entry we want to change. To change two or more palette entries in the same call, we would declare an array of **PALETTEENTRY** and pass the first element of the array as the fourth parameter of **SetPaletteEntries()**.

Once we've set the new color value, we have to instruct Windows to activate the new logical palette by mapping it into the system palette, which is the purpose of **RealizePalette()**. The new color will not appear on the screen until Windows realizes the logical palette. Technically, we should call the **RealizePalette()** function from within **Picture1**'s **Paint** event. At any time, our program could lose the input focus to another application that realizes a different palette. When our program regains the input focus, Windows will instruct it to repaint itself, and the first thing it must do before repainting is reactivate its own colors by realizing its logical palette. In this case, however, VB does this for us, so we don't need to worry about it.

On to the Final Details

Finally, let's take care of the details. We need to add a code module named PALETEX2.BAS and insert the code from Listing 5.7 into its declarations section.

Listing 5.7   The Declarations Section of PALETEX2.BAS

```
Type PALETTEENTRY
    peRed As String * 1
    peGreen As String * 1
    peBlue As String * 1
    peFlags As String * 1
    End Type

Global Const BLACK_BRUSH = 4
Global Const DEFAULT_PALETTE = 15
```

In the form's declaration section you'll need to declare all the API functions we've used, along with a few form level variables (Listing 5.8).

Listing 5.8   The Declarations Section of PALETEX2.FRM

```
Declare Function SelectPalette Lib "User" (ByVal hDC As Integer, ByVal hPalette
        As Integer, ByVal bForceBackground As Integer) As Integer
Declare Function RealizePalette Lib "User" (ByVal hDC As Integer) As Integer
Declare Function CreateSolidBrush Lib "GDI" (ByVal crColor As Long) As Integer
Declare Function SelectObject Lib "GDI" (ByVal hDC As Integer, ByVal hObject As
        Integer) As Integer
Declare Function Rectangle Lib "GDI" (ByVal hDC As Integer, ByVal X1 As Integer,
        ByVal Y1 As Integer, ByVal X2 As Integer, ByVal Y2 As Integer) As Integer
Declare Function DeleteObject Lib "GDI" (ByVal hObject As Integer) As Integer
Declare Function GetStockObject Lib "GDI" (ByVal nIndex As Integer) As Integer
Declare Function GetPaletteEntries Lib "GDI" (ByVal hPalette As Integer, ByVal
        wStartIndex As Integer, ByVal wNumEntries As Integer, lpPaletteEntries
        As PALETTEENTRY) As Integer
Declare Function SetPaletteEntries Lib "GDI" (ByVal hPalette As Integer, ByVal
        wStartIndex As Integer, ByVal wNumEntries As Integer, lpPaletteEntries
        As PALETTEENTRY) As Integer
```

```
Dim ColorSelected As Long
Dim hSystemPalette As Integer
Dim hCurrentPalette As Integer
Dim CurrentPaletteEntry As PALETTEENTRY
Dim NewPaletteEntry As PALETTEENTRY
Dim SelectingAColor As Integer
```

And just for good measure, we should initialize **ColorSelected** by setting it to -1 in the **Form_Load()** event procedure (Listing 5.9).

Listing 5.9 The Form_Load() Event Procedure from PALETEX2.FRM

```
Sub Form_Load ()
    ColorSelected = -1
    End Sub
```

Although our program won't permanently update a color table (for that we would have to create or update a device independent bitmap file), it does demonstrate how to manipulate a logical palette and how the logical palette interacts with the system palette. From this kernel you could construct a complete palette editor, an essential component of any image manipulation system.

If it were not for VB's inclination to repaint the Picture Box every time we change and realize the palette, we could perform some interesting real-time operations on a bitmap by altering its colors dynamically. Fortunately, Windows once again comes to the rescue with a function that will enable us to do this.

Using AnimatePalette() to Edit the Palette

This project shows you how to change colors in the system palette instantly by using the **AnimatePalette()** API function.

1. Copy the files from PALETEX2.MAK and remove the PASTEL.DIB bitmap from the **Picture** property of the Picture Box controls.
2. Add the **Form_Load()** event procedure (Listing 5.10) to create a logical palette from scratch.
3. Modify the **Picture1_Paint()** event procedure (Listing 5.11) to select in our custom palette.
4. Add calls at the end of **Picture1_MouseDown()** (Listing 5.12) to repaint the Picture Boxes.
5. Modify **ColorScrollBar_Change()** (Listing 5.13) to call **AnimatePalette()**.
6. Add the **Form_Unload()** event procedure (Listing 5.14) to dispose of the logical palette.

This project is located in the directory \VBMAGIC, in the files PALETEX3.MAK, PALETEX3.FRM, and PALETEX3.BAS.

Creating the AnimatePalette() Project

For this project, we'll modify the program from the previous project so that instead of loading a bitmap and mangling its palette, it will create a new logical palette from scratch. We'll then modify the Scroll Bar **Change** event so it calls the API function **AnimatePalette()** instead of **SetPaletteEntries()**. These changes will affect several of the event procedures.

If you wish, copy the files PALETEX2.FRM and PALETEX2.BAS to PALETEX3.FRM and PALETEX3.BAS, respectively. Then start a new project called PALETEX3.MAK and use the VB menu option File, Add File to add these new copies of the form and code modules.

Next remove the PASTEL.DIB file from the **Picture** property of **Picture1** and, if necessary, from **BigColorBox**. To remove a file from the **Picture** property, select the **Picture** property from the list box, select **(Bitmap)** in the edit box at the top of the property window, then press the Delete key.

We'll begin with the new **Form_Load()** event procedure (see Listing 5.10), where we'll build and activate our custom palette.

Building the Palette

To create a new logical palette, we have to build a Windows data structure called **LOGPALETTE**, then call **CreatePalette()** with that structure. **LOGPALETTE** includes three elements:

```
Type LOGPALETTE
    palVersion As Integer
    palNumEntries As Integer
    palPalEntry(255) As PALETTEENTRY
    End Type
```

The first field in **LOGPALETTE** contains a constant, the hexadecimal value 300 (entered as &H300) which indicates the Windows version number. The value 300 works for either Windows 3.0 or 3.1. The second field specifies the number of palette entries in the new palette. The third field in **LOGPALETTE** is not really a field at all, but an array of **PALLETTEENTRY** structures.

You must exercise extreme caution when you pass VB arrays to DLL functions. You could not, for example, pass an array of variable-length strings, because an array of VB's variable-length strings does not contain the actual string data. Instead, the array consists of a series of *descriptors* for strings stored elsewhere in memory. If you think about it, this makes complete sense. How else could you build an array of variable-length strings, especially when you consider that they can range in length from zero characters to more than 65,000? You run into the same problem when you include a variable-length string inside a structure declared with **Type**; structures that contain variable-length strings also contain only the string descriptors, not the actual string data.

Fixed-length strings, however, are another story entirely. The VB *Programmer's Guide* says that you cannot pass arrays of strings to DLL functions. It does not differentiate between fixed-length and variable-length strings in this situation. But when it comes to user-defined structures, variable-length and fixed-length strings behave differently. When a structure contains a fixed-length string, it contains the actual string data. Fortunately, the **PALETTEENTRY** structure contains nothing but four single-byte, fixed-length strings, which are packed into memory as four contiguous bytes. So the array **palPalEntry(255)** consists of 256 (0 through 255) contiguous 4-byte elements.

Listing 5.10 The Form_Load() Event Procedure from PALETEX3.FRM

```
Sub Form_Load ()
    Dim LogicalPalette As LOGPALETTE
    Dim ColorIndex As Integer
    Dim R As Integer, G As Integer, B As Integer

    LogicalPalette.PalVersion = &H300
    LogicalPalette.palNumEntries = 216
    For R = 1 To 6
        For G = 1 To 6
            For B = 1 To 6
                ColorIndex = ((R - 1) * 36) + ((G - 1) * 6) + (B - 1)
                LogicalPalette.palPalEntry(ColorIndex).peRed = Chr$(R * (255 \ 6))
                LogicalPalette.palPalEntry(ColorIndex).peGreen = Chr$(G * (255 \ 6))
                LogicalPalette.palPalEntry(ColorIndex).peBlue = Chr$(B * (255 \ 6))
                LogicalPalette.palPalEntry(ColorIndex).peFlags = Chr$(PC_RESERVED)
            Next B
        Next G
    Next R
    hCurrentPalette = CreatePalette(LogicalPalette)
    ColorSelected = -1
    End Sub
```

For simplicity's sake, the loop in the middle of the **Form_Load()** event procedure creates only 216 colors, the maximum cubed integer under 256. You may substitute any method you wish as a color generator. Remember though, that Windows reserves 20 entries in the system palette for default system colors, so unless you modify the system palette (which requires a special set of API functions, and is *not* recommended), Windows will never realize more than 236 of your colors.

CreatePalette() takes the information stored in the **LOGPALETTE** structure, makes a living logical palette out of it, and returns the palette handle. The colors in our new palette, however, will not become available for screen painting until we realize the palette, which we'll do in the **Picture1_Paint()** event procedure.

Using the Custom Palette

In **Picture1_Paint()** (Listing 5.11) we can dispense with the shell game we used before to grab the palette handle—our call to **CreatePalette()** in **Form_Load** has returned a palette handle, which we've captured in the form level variable **hCurrentPalette**.

Listing 5.11   The Picture1_Paint() Event Procedure from PALETEX3.FRM

```
Sub Picturel_Paint ()
    Dim Row As Integer
    Dim Column As Integer
    Dim BoxHeight As Integer
    Dim BoxWidth As Integer
    Dim ColorIndex As Long
    Dim hBrush As Integer
    Dim Dummy As Integer

    hSystemPalette = SelectPalette(Picturel.hDC, hCurrentPalette, False)
    Dummy = RealizePalette(Picturel.hDC)
    BoxWidth = Picturel.ScaleWidth / 16
    BoxHeight = Picturel.ScaleHeight / 16
    For ColorIndex = 0 To 255
        Row = ColorIndex \ 16 + 1
        Column = ColorIndex Mod 16 + 1
        hBrush = CreateSolidBrush(&H1000000 Or ColorIndex)
        Dummy = SelectObject(Picturel.hDC, hBrush)
        Dummy = Rectangle(Picturel.hDC, (Column - 1) * BoxWidth,
                (Row - 1) * BoxHeight, Column * BoxWidth, Row * BoxHeight)
        Dummy = SelectObject(Picturel.hDC, GetStockObject(BLACK_BRUSH))
        Dummy = DeleteObject(hBrush)
        Next ColorIndex
    If ColorSelected >= 0 Then
        Row = ColorSelected \ 16 + 1
        Column = ColorSelected Mod 16 + 1
        hBrush = CreateSolidBrush(&H1000000 Or ColorSelected)
        Dummy = SelectObject(Picturel.hDC, hBrush)
        Dummy = Rectangle(Picturel.hDC, MaxVal((Column - 1.5) * BoxWidth, 0),
                MaxVal((Row - 1.5) * BoxHeight, 0), (Column + .5) * BoxWidth,
                (Row + .5) * BoxHeight)
```

```
        Dummy = SelectObject(Picture1.hDC, GetStockObject(BLACK_BRUSH))
        Dummy = DeleteObject(hBrush)
        End If
    End Sub
```

The rest of this procedure remains unchanged from the example shown in Listing 5.3.

You'll also want to modify **Picture1_MouseDown()** (Listing 5.12) slightly by adding calls at the end to the Picture **Paint** event procedures.

Listing 5.12   The Picture1_MouseDown() Event Procedure from PALETEX3.FRM

```
Sub Picture1_MouseDown (Button As Integer, Shift As Integer, X As Single, Y As Single)

    Dim CurrentPaletteEntry As PALETTEENTRY
    Dim Row As Integer
    Dim Column As Integer
    Dim BoxHeight As Integer
    Dim BoxWidth As Integer
    Dim Dummy As Integer
    Dim Index As Integer

    BoxWidth = Picture1.ScaleWidth / 16
    BoxHeight = Picture1.ScaleHeight / 16
    Row = (Y \ BoxHeight)
    Column = X \ BoxWidth
    ColorSelected = Row * 16 + Column
    Dummy = GetPaletteEntries(hCurrentPalette, ColorSelected, 1, CurrentPaletteEntry)
    SelectingAColor = True
    ColorScrollBar(0).Value = 255 - Asc(CurrentPaletteEntry.peRed)
    ColorScrollBar(1).Value = 255 - Asc(CurrentPaletteEntry.peGreen)
    ColorScrollBar(2).Value = 255 - Asc(CurrentPaletteEntry.peBlue)
    SelectingAColor = False
    Picture1_Paint
    BigColorBox_Paint

    End Sub
```

In the previous project, where we used **SetPaletteEntries()** to change colors, each time we changed the color and realized the palette, the Windows Palette Manager issued a **WM_PALETTECHANGED** message to all the active windows, including VB. This caused **Picture1** to refresh repeatedly as we moved the color change Scroll Bars. **AnimatePalette()**, however, will not only change colors in the logical palette, but also directly in the system palette, which means we don't have to call **RealizePalette()** every time we change the selected color. Without the call to **RealizePalette()**, the Picture Boxes never receive Paint messages from the Palette Manager. So unless we call the **Paint** events explicitly after we set the Scroll Bar values, **Picture1** and

BigColorBox won't always refresh, which means that the enlarged color cell won't appear and **BigColorBox** won't display the selected color.

Plugging In the AnimatePalette() API Function

Next, let's modify the **ColorScrollBar_Change()** event procedure so it calls **AnimatePalette()** instead of **SetPaletteEntries()**.

Listing 5.13   The ColorScrollBar_Change() Event Procedure from PALETEX3.FRM

```
Sub ColorScrollBar_Change (Index As Integer)

    Dim Dummy As Integer
    Dim NewPaletteEntry As PALETTEENTRY

    NewPaletteEntry.peRed = Chr$(255 - ColorScrollBar(0).Value)
    NewPaletteEntry.peGreen = Chr$(255 - ColorScrollBar(1).Value)
    NewPaletteEntry.peBlue = Chr$(255 - ColorScrollBar(2).Value)
    NewPaletteEntry.peFlags = Chr$(PC_RESERVED)
    If Not SelectingAColor Then
        AnimatePalette hCurrentPalette, ColorSelected, 1, NewPaletteEntry
        End If

    End Sub
```

Only palette entries flagged as **PC_RESERVED** can be altered by **AnimatePalette()**. That's why we have to set the palette entry's flag byte to this value (hex 01) here and when we create the logical palette. This flag also prevents other windows from mapping their logical palettes to the reserved color entries, which confines the effects of color changes to the active window. Consequently, if you set all or most of the palette entries to **PC_RESERVED**, as I've done here, other windows will have to make do with the remaining colors. Sometimes that means that other bitmaps have no colors available to them except the 20 Windows reserved colors.

> **Note:** *Do not confuse colors defined with **PC_RESERVED** with the Windows reserved colors. The sole purpose of **PC_RESERVED** is to enable palette animation and to confine its effects to the active window. Colors marked as **PC_RESERVED** are reserved not by Windows, but by the application.*

To round out this program we need to dispose of the palette we created in the **Form_Load()** procedure. This is accomplished by using the **Form_Unload()** event procedure shown in Listing 5.14. We'll call again upon the **DeleteObject()** API function, but first we have to "unselect" our palette from the device contexts of the two Picture Boxes.

Listing 5.14   The Form_Unload() Event Procedure from PALETEX3.FRM

```
Sub Form_Unload (Cancel As Integer)
    Dim Dummy As Integer
    Dim hSystemPalette As Integer
    Dim hDummyPalette As Integer

    hSystemPalette = GetStockObject(DEFAULT_PALETTE)
    hDummyPalette = SelectPalette(Picture1.hDC, hSystemPalette, False)
    hDummyPalette = SelectPalette(BigColorBox.hDC, hSystemPalette, False)
    Dummy = DeleteObject(hCurrentPalette)

    End Sub
```

If we were to call **DeleteObject()** without first unselecting the palette from the device contexts, we would likely crash Windows. I know. I've done it—several times.

By the way, VB won't run the **Form_Unload()** event procedure unless you use the Control menu button or the Control menu Close option to end your program. If you click on the End button on the Toolbar, your program will stop running, but you may leave behind unfinished business. Each time you run this particular program, it will eat enough memory to hold the newly created palette. If you repeatedly run and end the program with the Toolbar controls, you'll gnaw away at memory by about a kilobyte at a time. If you double-click on the Control menu button to stop the program properly, **Form_Unload()** will release the memory occupied by the palette.

The projects we've completed in this chapter have used about half of the 14 API palette functions. In the next two chapters, we'll use these functions, along with many other GDI functions to perform some fancy graphical effects.

Chapter 6

Explore the worlds of color palettes and raster operations and how they help you to produce some truly amazing images.

Palette Animations and ROPs

W ould you like to be able to get down to the hardware level and create some animated visual effects? With the help of a few powerful Windows API calls and some unique pixel and raster operations, you can bring your Visual Basic apps to life.

We're now ready to embark on the second phase of our amazing journey into imaging techniques. This time, we'll go a little deeper into the graphics black hole and see what new mysteries we can uncover. Along the way we'll add to our imaging construction set.

The Magic of Color Palette Animations

With direct access to the system palette, we can perform certain kinds of animation, animations that require no actual changes to the displayed bitmap. With this technique, sometimes known as color cycling, we can simulate running water, atmospheric effects, lighting changes, and even moving objects without resorting to more resource-intensive, multi-frame animation methods.

But don't let the terminology mislead you. Remember, **AnimatePalette()** doesn't activate a process; it just sets the palette entries indicated by its second and third parameters to the new colors you specify in its fourth parameter. These changes appear immediately on the screen, without the usual intermediate step of realization, which, when called repeatedly, creates the illusion of movement. Think of **AnimatePalette()** as a way to change displayed colors in real time—a tool with which to animate, not an engine.

Marquee Lights with Palette Animation

We'll now draw a series of colored dots to represent light bulbs around the perimeter of an otherwise blank form, then use palette animation to set them in motion, like the traveling lights on a theater marquee. Here's what we'll do:

1. Create a form with filename MARQUEE.FRM with no visible controls.
2. Insert the global and form level declarations (Listings 6.1 and 6.2).
3. Add these four form event procedures: **Form_Load()**, **Form_Paint()**, **Form_Resize()**, and **Form_Unload()** (Listings 6.3 through 6.5).
4. Add the Timer control and write its **Timer()** event procedure (Listing 6.6).

 This project is located in the directory \VBMAGIC, in the files MARQUEE.MAK, MARQUEE.FRM, and MARQUEE.BAS.

Creating the Marquee Project

Start a new project and set the form's **Scale Mode** property to type 3 - Pixel. We'll borrow most of the global declarations we used in the last project of Chapter 4. Listing 6.1 shows the complete set of global variables that should be assigned to MARQUEE.BAS.

Listing 6.1 The Global Declarations from MARQUEE.BAS

```
Type PALETTEENTRY
    peRed As String * 1
    peGreen As String * 1
    peBlue As String * 1
    peFlags As String * 1
    End Type
```

```
Type LOGPALETTE
  palVersion As Integer
  palNumEntries As Integer
  palPalEntry(255) As PALETTEENTRY
    End Type

Global Const BLACK_BRUSH = 4
Global Const PC_RESERVED = &H1  ' palette index used for animation
```

You won't need the constant **DEFAULT_PALETTE** for this program, so I've removed it from the global declarations.

We can also pare down the form level declarations as shown in Listing 6.2.

Listing 6.2   The Declarations Section of MARQUEE.FRM, Based on the Declarations in PALETEX3.FRM

```
Declare Function CreatePalette Lib "GDI" (lpLogPalette As LOGPALETTE) As Integer
Declare Function SelectPalette Lib "User" (ByVal hDC As Integer, ByVal hPalette
        As Integer, ByVal bForceBackground As Integer) As Integer
Declare Function RealizePalette Lib "User" (ByVal hDC As Integer) As Integer
Declare Function CreateSolidBrush Lib "GDI" (ByVal crColor As Long) As Integer
Declare Function SelectObject Lib "GDI" (ByVal hDC As Integer, ByVal hObject As
        Integer) As Integer
Declare Function DeleteObject Lib "GDI" (ByVal hObject As Integer) As Integer
Declare Function GetStockObject Lib "GDI" (ByVal nIndex As Integer) As Integer
Declare Function Ellipse Lib "GDI" (ByVal hDC As Integer, ByVal X1 As Integer,
        ByVal Y1 As Integer, ByVal X2 As Integer, ByVal Y2 As Integer) As Integer
Declare Sub AnimatePalette Lib "GDI" (ByVal hPalette As Integer, ByVal
        wStartIndex As Integer, ByVal wNumEntries As Integer, lpPaletteColors As
        PALETTEENTRY)

Dim hSystemPalette As Integer
Dim hCurrentPalette As Integer
Dim PaletteEntries(4) As PALETTEENTRY
Dim hPaintBrush(3) As Integer
Dim LogicalPalette As LOGPALETTE
```

I've eliminated a few of the API function declarations we used in PALETEX3.BAS, and added a new one, **Ellipse()**. We also don't need all the variables we used for palette editing, and we can trim the **PaletteEntries** array down to five elements (0 through 4). I've added the array **hPaintBrush** to hold the handles of four individually colored brushes. With this approach, we don't have to create and destroy the brushes repeatedly as we draw the four separate shades of yellow, which we use to indicate varying degrees of brightness along the series of light bulbs. I've also moved the declaration of **LogicalPalette** to the form level because we'll need it in two event procedures.

Adding the Event Procedures

We'll support four form events: **Load**, **Paint**, **Unload**, and **Resize**. The **Form_Load()** event procedure will again create the palette (see Listing 6.3).

Listing 6.3   The Form_Load() Event Procedure from MARQUEE.FRM

```
Sub Form_Load ()

  Dim ColorIndex As Integer

  LogicalPalette.PalVersion = &H300
  LogicalPalette.palNumEntries = 4

  For ColorIndex = 0 To 3
    LogicalPalette.palPalEntry(ColorIndex).peRed = Chr$(127 + ColorIndex * 128 / 3)
    LogicalPalette.palPalEntry(ColorIndex).peGreen = Chr$(127 + ColorIndex * 128 / 3)
    LogicalPalette.palPalEntry(ColorIndex).peBlue = Chr$(0)
    LogicalPalette.palPalEntry(ColorIndex).peFlags = Chr$(PC_RESERVED)
    Next ColorIndex
  hCurrentPalette = CreatePalette(LogicalPalette)

  Form_Paint
End Sub
```

In this program, we declare the structure **LOGPALETTE** (in MARQUEE.BAS) with an array of only five elements:

```
Type LOGPALETTE
    palVersion As Integer
    palNumEntries As Integer
    palPalEntry(4) As PALETTEENTRY
    End Type
```

You'll also notice that in the field **LogicalPalette.palNumEntries** I've specified only four elements. For this program we only need to create four live palette entries, but we'll use the fifth entry as a temporary buffer when we begin the palette cycling. You'll see what I mean when we get to the **Timer** event. It doesn't hurt to declare a **palPalEntry** array that's larger than the size specified in **palNumEntries**; the extra entries will be ignored by **CreatePalette()**.

The other big event procedure is **Form_Paint()**, which is shown in Listing 6.4. Once we finish writing this procedure, the rest is easy.

Listing 6.4   The Form_Paint() Event Procedure from MARQUEE.FRM

```
Sub Form_Paint ()
    Dim TopPos As Integer
    Dim LeftPos As Integer
```

```
Dim BoxHeight As Integer
Dim BoxWidth As Integer
Dim ColorIndex As Long
Dim Dummy As Integer


hSystemPalette = SelectPalette(MarqueeForm.hDC, hCurrentPalette, False)
Dummy = RealizePalette(MarqueeForm.hDC)
For ColorIndex = 0 To 3
    hPaintBrush(ColorIndex) = CreateSolidBrush(&H1000000 Or ColorIndex)
    Next ColorIndex
MarqueeForm.Cls
DotWidth = MarqueeForm.ScaleWidth / 24
ColorIndex = 0
TopPos = DotWidth / 2
MarqueeForm.CurrentX = DotWidth * 1.5
Do While CurrentX < (ScaleWidth - DotWidth * 2)
    Dummy = SelectObject(MarqueeForm.hDC, hPaintBrush(ColorIndex))
    Dummy = Ellipse(MarqueeForm.hDC, CurrentX, TopPos, CurrentX + DotWidth,
            TopPos + DotWidth)
    CurrentX = CurrentX + DotWidth * 1.5
    If ColorIndex = 3 Then
        ColorIndex = 0
      Else
        ColorIndex = ColorIndex + 1
      End If
    Loop
LeftPos = MarqueeForm.ScaleWidth - DotWidth * 1.5
CurrentY = DotWidth * 1.5
Do While CurrentY < (ScaleHeight - DotWidth * 1.5)
    Dummy = SelectObject(MarqueeForm.hDC, hPaintBrush(ColorIndex))
    Dummy = Ellipse(MarqueeForm.hDC, LeftPos, CurrentY, LeftPos + DotWidth,
            CurrentY + DotWidth)
    CurrentY = CurrentY + DotWidth * 1.5
    If ColorIndex = 3 Then
        ColorIndex = 0
      Else
        ColorIndex = ColorIndex + 1
      End If
    Loop
TopPos = MarqueeForm.ScaleHeight - DotWidth * 1.5
CurrentX = MarqueeForm.ScaleWidth - DotWidth * 2.5
Do While CurrentX > DotWidth * 1.5
    Dummy = SelectObject(MarqueeForm.hDC, hPaintBrush(ColorIndex))
    Dummy = Ellipse(MarqueeForm.hDC, CurrentX, TopPos, CurrentX + DotWidth,
            TopPos + DotWidth)
    CurrentX = CurrentX - DotWidth * 1.5
    If ColorIndex = 3 Then
        ColorIndex = 0
      Else
        ColorIndex = ColorIndex + 1
      End If
    Loop
LeftPos = DotWidth / 2
CurrentY = MarqueeForm.ScaleHeight - 2 * DotWidth
```

```
Do While CurrentY > DotWidth * 1.5
    Dummy = SelectObject(MarqueeForm.hDC, hPaintBrush(ColorIndex))
    Dummy = Ellipse(MarqueeForm.hDC, LeftPos, CurrentY, LeftPos + DotWidth,
        CurrentY + DotWidth)
    CurrentY = CurrentY - DotWidth * 1.5
    If ColorIndex = 3 Then
        ColorIndex = 0
      Else
        ColorIndex = ColorIndex + 1
      End If
    Loop
Dummy = SelectObject(MarqueeForm.hDC, GetStockObject(BLACK_BRUSH))
For ColorIndex = 0 To 3
    Dummy = DeleteObject(hPaintBrush(ColorIndex))
    Next ColorIndex

End Sub
```

As you can see, this procedure is pretty complex. Let's break it down into manageable pieces. First, we do some initialization.

```
hSystemPalette = SelectPalette(MarqueeForm.hDC, hCurrentPalette, False)
Dummy = RealizePalette(MarqueeForm.hDC)
```

Remember, when you work with logical palettes you should always select and realize your palette in the **Paint** event. This effectively returns control of the system palette to your program whenever it regains the focus.

This next segment, the **For** loop, creates one GDI brush for each of the four colors we created in **Form_Load()**:

```
For ColorIndex = 0 To 3
    hPaintBrush(ColorIndex) = CreateSolidBrush(&H1000000 Or ColorIndex)
    Next ColorIndex
```

Next, we'll clear the form, set a variable to the diameter we want to use for the colored dots, and initialize a counter called **ColorIndex** to the first color, zero.

```
MarqueeForm.Cls
DotWidth = MarqueeForm.ScaleWidth / 24
ColorIndex = 0
```

The bulk of the **Paint** event consists of four loops, each of which draws a series of dots along one edge of the form's client area. Except in the details of positioning and vertical versus horizontal orientation, all these loops are similar. The first one draws the dots along the top edge of the form:

```
ColorIndex = 0
'Get a starting Y position.
TopPos = DotWidth / 2
'Get a starting X position.
MarqueeForm.CurrentX = DotWidth * 1.5
Do While CurrentX < (ScaleWidth - DotWidth * 2)
    Dummy = SelectObject(MarqueeForm.hDC, hPaintBrush(ColorIndex))
    Dummy = Ellipse(MarqueeForm.hDC, CurrentX, TopPos, CurrentX + DotWidth,
            TopPos + DotWidth)
    CurrentX = CurrentX + DotWidth * 1.5
    ColorIndex = ColorIndex + 1
    ColorIndex = ColorIndex Mod 4
    Loop
```

The **Ellipse()** API function takes a handle to the device context and two pair of coordinates, the upper-left and lower-right corners of the rectangle that bound the ellipse.

```
Declare Function Ellipse Lib "GDI" (ByVal hDC As Integer, ByVal X1 As Integer,
        ByVal Y1 As Integer, ByVal X2 As Integer, ByVal Y2 As Integer) As Integer
```

To draw a circle, make sure the two corners define a square instead of a rectangle.

I bet you're wondering why we just don't consolidate these four loops into two: one for the top and bottom rows and one for the left and right columns. Here's the reason. The separation of the loops allow us to easily keep track of which color we're on (or more precisely, which palette entry we're on) as we start to draw each row or column. Since the dot diameter depends on the width of the form and not its height, we won't know how many dots will fit in each column until we draw them. Okay, we could pre-calculate that, but then we would have to deal with still more numbers to determine the correct starting color for each of the four sides. In any case, you may wish to refine the arithmetic to produce more consistent alignment of the dots within the boundaries of the form.

When we finish painting the dots, we select the default **BLACK_BRUSH** back into the device context and destroy our four colored brushes.

```
Dummy = SelectObject(MarqueeForm.hDC, GetStockObject(BLACK_BRUSH))
For ColorIndex = 0 To 3
    Dummy = DeleteObject(hPaintBrush(ColorIndex))
    Next ColorIndex

End Sub
```

The other two form event procedures, shown in Listing 6.5, perform the required housekeeping chores.

Listing 6.5 The Form_Unload() and Form_Resize() Event Procedures from MARQUEE.FRM

```
Sub Form_Unload (Cancel As Integer)
    Dim Dummy As Integer
    Timer1.Enabled = False
    Dummy = DeleteObject(hCurrentPalette)
    End Sub

Sub Form_Resize ()
    Form_Paint
    End Sub
```

Supporting the Timer Event

Finally, we reach the climax of this story, the **Timer** event. Before you can add this event, you'll need a Timer control. You can place it anywhere on the form. I left mine in the center. The Timer comes in handy for animation, because after all, it can be made to fire—if somewhat irregularly—several times per second. Listing 6.6 shows the complete **Timer1_Timer()** event procedure.

Listing 6.6 The Timer1_Timer() Event Procedure from MARQUEE.FRM

```
Sub Timer1_Timer ()

    Dim ColorIndex As Integer

    For ColorIndex = 4 To 1 Step -1
        LogicalPalette.palPalEntry(ColorIndex) = LogicalPalette.palPalEntry(ColorIndex - 1)
        Next ColorIndex
    LogicalPalette.palPalEntry(0) = LogicalPalette.palPalEntry(4)
    AnimatePalette hCurrentPalette, 0, 4, LogicalPalette.palPalEntry(0)
    End Sub
```

The **For** loop and the following assignment statement shift the colors one position to the right in the four-element palette array, and rotate the last element (array element 3) back to the beginning (array element Ø). Array element 4 serves only as a temporary storage position.

We call **AnimatePalette()** with four arguments. The first specifies the handle of the currently realized palette. The second specifies the index of the first entry in the currently realized logical palette, in this case entry 0. The third argument indicates the number of entries we want to change (four). And for the last argument we pass a pointer (which we do by not using the **ByVal** keyword) to the first element in the palette entry array, which contains the new color values for the entries in the logical palette. Each time the Timer ticks, the colors rotate their positions in the logical palette, and

AnimatePalette() updates the system palette directly so the changes appear on the screen almost instantaneously.

That's it. Take the program out for a test drive and you'll see the marquee lights shown in Figure 6.1.

Remember to stop your program from the Control-menu button on the form rather than with the VB End button or the Run, End menu option. Otherwise, you'll leave an orphan palette in memory. I cannot stress enough how diligent we must be in releasing resources, and how carefully this must be done. At best, a failure to release resources will gradually eat away at available memory. At worst, a release performed without unselecting the object from all device contexts will cause an instant General Protection Failure.

Pixels and Raster Operations

When you get right down to it, drawing on a graphics display amounts to nothing more than setting color values for individual pixels. That is, as long as we begin with a neutral background.

But what is a "neutral" background? In our display systems, white, the most common background color, is represented by 24 bits set to 1 (or true), which means literally the maximum presence of color. The opposite of white is, of course, black, which is represented by 24 bits set to 0, the total absence of color. To display a bitmapped image we could disregard the existing colors of

Figure 6.1   *Marquee lights simulated with the AnimatePalette() API function.*

the drawing context, and replace every bit of every pixel with the bits from our new image. That's what happens when we invoke the **LoadPicture()** function to display a bitmap in a form, Picture Box, or Image control.

But sometimes, instead of replacing an existing image altogether, we need to draw on top of it, or combine images. How do you do this? It's relatively easy with the addition of *raster operations*, or *ROP*s. Raster operations determine what happens when we try to place one pixel on top of another. (Impossible? Yes and no, but more on this in a moment.) Windows provides two sets of raster operation codes in Windows, the *ROP* codes and the *ROP2* codes. But just what is a raster operation? Let's begin another project to see.

When Is a Pen a "Not Pen"?

In this simple project we'll take our first look at ROPs. Follow these steps to see how a raster operation affects a simple box drawing.:

1. Open a new VB project. Go to the **Form_MouseDown** event procedure and insert the following line:

```
Line (X, Y)-Step(1000, 1000), , B
```

This command draws a square measuring 1001 twips on a side, beginning at the present cursor location, each time you click the left mouse button.

2. In the Properties window, set the **DrawMode** to 6, which in VB is called *Invert*. Figure 6.2 shows you the effect Invert has in a drawing. It will be easier to see what's happening with thicker lines, so set the **DrawWidth** property to at least 5.

You'll find this project in the subdirectory \VBMAGIC, in the files NOTPEN.MAK and NOTPEN.FRM.

That's it. Run the program. When you click the mouse anywhere on the form's client area, VB will draw an outline of a square. You may be surprised to learn that the color of the square's borders will depend entirely on the color of the background. To prove this, stop the program and change the **BackColor** property of the form (double-click on the **BackColor** property in the Properties window to display the VB Color Palette, then click any color cell to select it). Now, when you run the program again and click the mouse, the squares will be

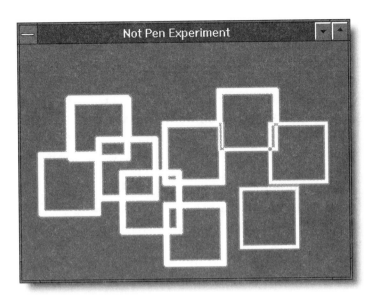

Figure 6.2   *Use the Invert drawing mode to draw boxes.*

drawn in a different color. Ordinarily you would expect the **ForeColor** property to determine the current drawing color, but when the **DrawMode** is set to Invert, the foreground color is irrelevant. Try it. Change the **ForeColor** property and run the program again. You'll get the same result. The color of the square will always depend exclusively on the background color.

As I mentioned previously, there are two sets of raster operation codes in Windows, the *ROP* codes and the *ROP2* codes. The raster operations available in the **DrawMode** property of a form or Picture Box control are the simpler *binary raster operation*, or ROP2 codes, so-called because they define the effects of combining only two pixels, a pen pixel and a destination pixel. As you can see in the **DrawMode** property, there are 16 ROP2 codes. (Later we'll talk about the ternary raster operators or ROP codes, which combine as many as three pixels.)

Mixing Pixels

As I pointed out earlier, it is these raster operations that determine what happens when we try to place one pixel on top of another. This is, of course, impossible. Our display systems can display only one pixel at a time in each pixel position. But by combining the values of pixels in various ways, we can produce electronic effects that imitate physical effects such as color blending and transparency. And as an added bonus, we can do things that would be impossible with that goop we call paint.

Let's dissect the ROP2 code we used in the previous project. A raster operation is a boolean operation performed on two or more pixel values. That's all. Take the simplest case, a black pen on a white background. In the Windows default palette, black is stored in palette location 0, or binary 00000000, and white is stored in position 255, or binary 11111111. In the language of the Windows API, the raster operation that VB calls **Invert** is actually called **R2_NOT**. The logical **Not** operator performs the simplest of all boolean operations—it flips the bits, so zeros become ones and ones become zeros. In fact, in the strictest sense, the **Invert** drawing mode doesn't perform a *binary* raster operation at all because it doesn't combine the values of two pixels. It just flips the bits of the pixel that's already displayed in the device context. If the background is white, then drawing with the **Not** pen changes pixels to black; drawing over the pixels that have changed to black will change them back to white.

This works for other colors, too. If you set the background to the color stored in logical palette position 5, for example, the **Not** pen will change the color to the one stored in position 250.

```
Not      0000 0101      5
=        1111 1010      250
```

In all, Windows offers 16 binary raster operations. For the complete list, see Table 6.1.

> **Note:** *I don't know who created the term binary raster operation, but as terminology goes, this one is a real dog. Technically, all raster operations are binary, because they perform bitwise logical operations on pixel values. But in API terms, a binary raster operation is a ROP performed on two pixels. So, although all raster operations are performed on binary values, some raster operations are* binary *binary raster operations. Just remember that the binary raster operations are the 16 ROP2 codes.*

ROPs and the Split System Palette

In a true color display system, raster operations are performed on the whole RGB values of the pixels. This approach makes the results predictable. If you invert red, which is RGB value &H0000FF, you get cyan, RGB value &HFFFF00. If you invert blue (&HFF0000), you get yellow (&H00FFFF). But on a palette-based display, the ROPs operate on the pixels' palette references, not on their actual RGB values.

The division of the Windows system colors into two groups of ten, positioned at opposite ends of the palette, is meant to provide some semblance of

Table 6.1 *The 16 Binary Raster Operations*

Windows Name	Visual Basic Name	Boolean Operation
R2_BLACK	1 - Blackness	&H00
R2_NOTMERGEPEN	2 - Not Merge Pen	Not (Pen Or Destination)
R2_MASKNOTPEN	3 - Mask Not Pen	(Not Pen) And Destination
R2_NOTCOPYPEN	4 - Not Copy Pen	Not Pen
R2_MASKPENNOT	5 - Mask Not Pen	Pen And (Not Destination)
R2_NOT	6 - Invert	Not Destination
R2_XORPEN	7 - Xor Pen	Pen XOr Destination
R2_NOTMASKPEN	8 - Not Mask Pen	Not (Pen And Destination)
R2_MASKPEN	9 - Mask Pen	Pen And Destination
R2_NOTXORPEN	10- Not Xor Pen	Not (Pen XOr Destination)
R2_NOP	11 - Nop	Destination {Do nothing}
R2_MERGENOTPEN	12- Merge Not Pen	(Not Pen) Or Destination
R2_COPYPEN	13 - Copy Pen	Pen
R2_MERGEPENNOT	14 - Merge Pen Not	Pen Or (Not Destination)
R2_MERGEPEN	15 - Merge Pen	Pen Or Destination
R2_WHITE	16 - Whiteness	&HFF

meaningful behavior when colors are inverted. White inverts to black, dark blue inverts to bright yellow, light blue inverts to dark yellow, and so on. When raster operations apply to system palette references 10 through 245, however, the results can become meaningless. If, for example, palette entries 15 and 240 (which are binary complements) contained similar colors, the inversion could become so subtle that it may not even be visible. On a display system that works internally on an 18-bit model, the two colors may even look identical.

Unfortunately, we have to learn to live with this problem. It isn't practical to re-organize the palettes of most 256 color images to pair up the complementary colors. For one thing, the logical palettes of most photographic images tend to contain many similar colors in subtle shades. Some images may contain no complementary colors at all. For most purposes, it hardly matters that inverted colors don't produce their complements. The Inverted pen and its close cousin, the XOr pen, are used primarily to draw contrasting lines across background bitmaps. In most cases, lines and filled shapes drawn with these pens will contrast enough with the background to stand out.

We've only scratched the surface of the binary raster operations, and they only hint at the power of the *blt* (pronounced "blit") raster operations. In later chapters we'll use some of the ROP2 codes. But right now, let's move on to the even more powerful ROP codes, and the API functions that bring them to life.

Processing Bitmaps—Using BitBlt Functions

Although VB does support the Windows drawing modes, and provides reasonably flexible methods and controls for drawing bitmaps, it lacks an interface to one of Windows most powerful graphical features, the ***BitBlt*** functions (pronounced "bit blit"). In a nutshell, **BitBlt()** and its cousins **PatBlt()**, **StretchBlt()**, **SetDIBitsToDevice(),** and **StretchDIBits()**, copy bitmaps or pieces of bitmaps from one device context to another.

The blt functions not only copy images from place to place, some of them can combine as many as three bitmaps, using any of 256 distinct raster operations. The grandaddy of all blt functions is **BitBlt()**:

```
Declare Function BitBlt Lib "GDI" (ByVal hDC As Integer, ByVal X As Integer, ByVal Y As
    Integer, ByVal nWidth As Integer, ByVal nHeight As Integer, ByVal hSrcDC As Integer,
    ByVal XSrc As Integer, ByVal YSrc As Integer, ByVal dwROP As Long) As Integer
```

With nine arguments, the declaration for this function can look pretty intimidating. But it's not at all difficult to use. Let's review the parameters in order.

hDC	This is the handle to the *destination* device context. For example, if you were using **BitBlt()** to copy an image from Picture1 to Picture2, you would pass Picture2.hDC as the first argument.
X	A two-byte integer representing the X coordinate, usually in pixels, of the upper-left corner of the destination rectangle. This need not be zero; you may blt the source image to any location within the destination device context.
Y	A two-byte integer representing the Y coordinate of the upper-left corner of the destination rectangle.
nWidth	A two-byte integer representing the width of the destination rectangle. These measurements are given in *logical units*. For most of our purposes that means pixels, but Windows does support other measurement systems, most notably inches and millimeters. Watch out, though; Windows API functions do not support VB twips!
nHeight	A two-byte integer representing the height of the destination rectangle.

hSrcDC   The handle to the *source* device context. In our example, from the description of the first argument, you would pass Picture1.hDC as this parameter.

XSrc   An integer representing the X coordinate of the upper-left corner of the source rectangle. Keep in mind that the *origin* (coordinates 0,0) is in the upper-left corner of any client area. X values increase from left to right; Y values increase from top to bottom (you can change this, but we'll stick to the default).

YSrc   An integer representing the Y coordinate of the upper-left corner of the source rectangle.

dwROP   A long integer representing one of the 256 raster operation codes. For a simple copy, this would be set to **SRCCOPY**, which is a Windows constant with a value of &HCC0020.

BitBlting—The Quick and Easy Recipe

The easiest way to understand **BitBlt()** is to see it in action. Let's do a simple experiment in which we'll copy part of an image in one Picture Box to a second Picture Box on the same form. Follow these steps to try out the **BitBlt()** function:

1. Start a new VB program with a single form, and place two Picture Box controls on the form side by side.

2. Set the **ScaleMode** properties of both Picture Boxes to type 3 - Pixel. Set the **Picture** property of Picture1 to any bitmap you have handy. Then add a Command Button, setting its **Name** property to CopyButton and its caption to Copy Picture.

3. Fill in the **CopyButton_Click()** event procedure and the declarations section of the form as they appear in Listings 6.7 and 6.8.

 This project is located in the subdirectory \VBMAGIC, in the files BITBLTEX.MAK and BITBLTEX.FRM.

Listing 6.7   The CopyButton_Click() Event Procedure from BITBLTEX.FRM

```
Sub CopyButton_Click ()
  Dim Dummy As Integer
  Dummy = BitBlt(Picture2.hDC, 0, 0, Picture2.ScaleWidth, Picture2.ScaleHeight,
       Picture1.hDC, 0, 0, SRCCOPY)
End Sub
```

Listing 6.8 The Declarations Section from BITBLTEX.FRM

```
Option Explicit

Declare Function BitBlt Lib "GDI" (ByVal hDC As Integer, ByVal X As Integer,
        ByVal Y As Integer, ByVal nWidth As Integer, ByVal nHeight As Integer,
        ByVal hSrcDC As Integer, ByVal XSrc As Integer, ByVal YSrc As Integer,
        ByVal dwROP As Long) As Integer

Const SRCCOPY = &HCC0020
```

I've oversimplified this experiment for the sake of clarity. For one thing, I've assumed that Picture2 will be no larger than Picture1. **BitBlt()** doesn't automatically *clip* to the dimensions of the source device context when the source is smaller than the destination, which means it would copy portions of the screen outside the Picture Box to fill the client area of Picture2. I also have failed to grab the palette from Picture1 and select it into Picture2. The colors display properly, however, because the image has already been mapped in Picture1 to the system palette by VB. **BitBlt()** makes no attempt to re-map the pixel values; it just copies them as they are to the new device context. As long as the appropriate logical palette remains selected and realized into the system palette, both the original image and the copy will display correctly.

I'll show you how to use the blt functions to do a bunch of exciting things in later chapters. But before you can do much more than blast pieces of pictures from window to window, you have to understand the effects of raster operations. In the our next project we're going to combine ROPs and **BitBlt()** to demonstrate what happens when you run bitmaps through the boolean wringer.

The Standard Windows Raster Operations

In this project, we'll try out the 15 standard raster operations. Because they're so useful, the creators of Windows have given these ROP codes their own names, in the form of Windows constants. Here's what we'll do:

1. Build the TestROPS form stored in the file ROPEXP1.FRM.
2. Add the **Form_Load()** event procedure to the form (Listing 6.9).
3. Add the **ResultPic_Paint()** event procedure (Listing 6.10) and the **ROPList_Click()** event procedure (Listing 6.11) to the form.
4. Add the necessary declarations to the form (Listing 6.12).

This project is located in the subdirectoy \VBMAGIC, in the files ROPEXP1.MAK and ROPEXP1.FRM.

Creating the Form

For this program, we'll need a single form, with three small Picture Box controls and a List Box. Set the **Name** property of the form to TestROPS. The first Picture Box, which we'll call SourcePic, will contain a bitmap in the form of a monochrome icon called WHITEDOT.ICO. The second Picture Box, called DestPic, will contain another monochrome icon called CORNERS.ICO. We're using black-and-white images here because their trivial mappings to palette entries &H00 and &HFF make it much easier to discern the effects of raster operations; remember, black represents a binary value of all zeros, white represents all ones. Any logical operation we perform on black and white pixels will produce black or white pixels as a result—no funny colors to worry about here.

You might try to size the Picture Box controls so they just fit the icon images, which are always 32 x 32 pixels. Set the **ScaleMode** to 3 - Pixel for all three Picture Boxes, which allows you to specify the **ScaleWidth** and **ScaleHeight** properties in pixels. By specifying this **ScaleMode** for the form, you will also be able specify the external control dimensions, determined by the **Height** and **Width** properties, in pixels. Otherwise, you must use VB's own peculiar scale mode, *twips* (1/1440 of an inch—based on average screen size). You may have to play with the dimensions to get them neatly framed, but don't worry too much about it because the program will work even if the Picture Boxes are oddly sized. Name the third Picture Box ResultPic, leave its **Picture** property unassigned, and set its **AutoRedraw** property to False.

Loading the List Box with the ROP Codes

In the List Box we'll build a list of the fifteen ROP codes that have been blessed with names. With 256 possible raster operations, many look pretty esoteric. Some have probably never been used. But fifteen of them turn up often enough that they earned their place among the named Windows constants. These widely used ROPs are listed in Table 6.2, along with the logical operations they perform. The code that loads the List Box resides in the **Form_Load()** event procedure as shown in Listing 6.9.

Table 6.2 *The 15 Named Ternary ROP Codes*

Name	Logical Operation	Value
SRCCOPY	Source	&HCC0020&
SRCPAINT	Source Or Destination	&HEE0086&
SRCAND	Source And Destination	&H8800C6&
SRCINVERT	Source XOr Destination	&H660046&
SRCERASE	Source And (Not Destination)	&H440328&
NOTSRCCOPY	Not Source	&H330008&
NOTSRCERASE	Not (Source Or Destination)	&H1100A6&
MERGECOPY	Source And Pattern	&HC000CA&
MERGEPAINT	(Not Source) Or Destination	&HBB0226&
PATCOPY	Pattern	&HF00021&
PATPAINT	((Not Source) Or Pattern) Or Destination	&HFB0A09&
PATINVERT	Pattern XOr Destination	&H5A0049&
DSTINVERT	Not Destination	&H550009&
BLACKNESS	0	&H000042&
WHITENESS	1	&HFF0062&

Listing 6.9   The Form_Load() Event Procedure from ROPEXP1.FRM

```
Sub Form_Load ()
    ROPSList.AddItem "SRCCOPY = &HCC0020"
    ROPSList.AddItem "SRCPAINT = &HEE0086"
    ROPSList.AddItem "SRCAND = &H8800C6"
    ROPSList.AddItem "SRCINVERT = &H660046"
    ROPSList.AddItem "SRCERASE = &H440328"
    ROPSList.AddItem "NOTSRCCOPY = &H330008"
    ROPSList.AddItem "NOTSRCERASE = &H1100A6"
    ROPSList.AddItem "MERGECOPY = &HC000CA"
    ROPSList.AddItem "MERGEPAINT = &HBB0226"
    ROPSList.AddItem "PATCOPY = &HF00021"
    ROPSList.AddItem "PATPAINT = &HFB0A09"
    ROPSList.AddItem "PATINVERT = &H5A0049"
    ROPSList.AddItem "DSTINVERT = &H550009"
    ROPSList.AddItem "BLACKNESS = &H000042&"
    ROPSList.AddItem "WHITENESS = &HFF0062"
    End Sub
```

The Paint Event

The **ResultPic_Paint()** event procedure (Listing 6.10) will do the work of "blting" the two images to ResultPic, with the ROP code chosen from the List

Box. Things are a little turned around here. We refer to the two bitmaps as the source and destination images. The purpose of the ROP is to control what happens when we lay the source bitmap over the destination. If you look at the **Paint** event, you'll see that although it looks like we're picking up both images and combining them into **ResultPic**, we're really copying the bitmap contained in **DestPic** to **ResultPic** before each ROP-based transfer. We do use a ROP code to do this, **SRCCOPY**, but as its name implies, **SRCCOPY** performs no transformation on the image. It just copies an image from one device context to another, overwriting any image that may have been there before. We then use the selected ROP code with **BitBlt()** to blt the **SourcePic** into the copy of the destination bitmap that sits in **ResultPic**.

Listing 6.10 The ResultPic_Paint() Event Procedure from ROPEXP1.FRM

```
Sub ResultPic_Paint ()
    Dim ROPType As Long
    Dim Param As String
    Dim Dummy As Integer

    DestPic.Cls
    Param = ROPSList.Text
    ROPType = Val(Mid$(Param, InStr(Param, "=") + 1))

    Dummy = BitBlt(ResultPic.hDC, 0, 0, 31, 31, DestPic.hDC, 0, 0, SRCCOPY)
    Dummy = BitBlt(ResultPic.hDC, 0, 0, 31, 31, SourcePic.hDC, 0, 0, ROPType)

    End Sub
```

The second **BitBlt()** in the **Paint** event performs the raster operation selected from the List Box by combining the image in SourcePic with the image in ResultPic.

Finishing the Program

The **ROPSList_Click()** event procedure will do nothing but call **ResultPic_Paint()**.

Listing 6.11 The ROPSList_Click() Event Procedure from ROPEXP1.FRM

```
Sub ROPSList_Click ()
    ResultPic_Paint
    End Sub
```

Before you can run this program, you'll need to declare the **BitBlt()** function and **SRCCOPY** (Listing 6.12).

Listing 6.12   The Declarations Section of ROPEXP1.FRM

```
Option Explicit

Declare Function BitBlt Lib "GDI" (ByVal hDC As Integer, ByVal X As Integer,
        ByVal Y As Integer, ByVal nWidth As Integer, ByVal nHeight As Integer,
        ByVal hSrcDC As Integer, ByVal XSrc As Integer, ByVal YSrc As Integer,
        ByVal dwROP As Long) As Integer

Const SRCCOPY = &HCC0020
```

The SRCINVERT ROP Code—Up Close and Personal

The **SRCINVERT** ROP code demonstrates a logical operation that finds its way into all kinds of situations. When you run ROPEXP1 and select **SRCINVERT** from the List Box, you'll notice that the resulting image more closely resembles a combination of the source and destination images than that produced by any of the other ROPs. The image retains the entire dot shape, as well as the opposed corners. **SRCINVERT** performs an exclusive-or operation, annotated as **XOr**, between the source and destination image pixel values. An XOr sets to 1 only those bits that are set in either the destination or source pixel, but not those that are set in both. The color inversion of half of the dot in the lower-right corner is caused by this property of the **XOr** operator. This area in both the source and destination images is colored white, all bits set to 1 (only because logical palette entry 255 happens to reference RGB color &HFFFFFF, which also represents all bits set). When **XOr** finds a bit set to 1 in both pixels, it changes the result to 0, resulting in a negative image wherever the dot overlaps the white areas of the other image.

The other interesting property of **SRCINVERT** is that it can reverse itself. If you could reapply the source image to the resulting image, again with the **XOr** operation, the dot would disappear (try modifying the program to test this). The semi-circle in the upper-left corner in both the source image and the resulting image is white. When you apply **XOr** to two white pixels, you get black, which would remove the semi-circle from that corner. The semi-circle in the lower-right corner is white in the source image and black in the resulting image. **XOr** would change those pixels to white, removing the black semi-circle from the lower corner. Poof—no more dot! See Table 6.3 to get a better understanding of this unique occurrence. You might find it difficult to imagine this effect in multi-colored images, but it works just the same. Just think of the pixels as binary numbers. Bits is bits. And for any given destination bit, two **XOr** operations with the same source bit cancel out. In fact, the same operation works on full 24-bit color bitmaps.

Table 6.3 *Repeating an XOr Operation Results in the Same Value as the Original Destination Bit*

Source Bit	Destination Bit	Result A	Source Bit	Result B
0	XOr 0	= 0	XOr 0	= 0
1	XOr 0	= 1	XOr 1	= 0
0	XOr 1	= 1	XOr 0	= 1
1	XOr 1	= 0	XOr 1	= 1

The **XOr** operation turns up in many other useful ROP codes, and we'll be using it in the next chapter to do some cool things to pictures.

Some of the ROP codes we've tested with the program ROPEXP1.MAK appear to produce identical results. **MERGECOPY**, **PATPAINT**, **PATCOPY**, and **PATINVERT** all appear to do nothing to the destination image. There's a perfectly good explanation for this. They don't. The ternary ROP codes (as opposed to the binary ROP2 codes) combine the pixels of not just two, but three bitmaps. In Chapter 7, you'll not only meet this mysterious stranger, but in the process you'll learn how to build a bitmap from the inside out. Then you'll learn how to combine all this knowledge of pixels, palettes, and raster operations to perform knockout visual effects.

Chapter 7

Learn how to take our basic techniques of raster operations one step further to create cool visual effects, just like in the movies.

Advanced Imaging—Special Visual Effects

In the previous two chapters, we explored how Windows displays pictures. You learned how the Palette Manager works in 8-bit color mode, and how to modify and transfer images, or portions of images with some simple blts and raster operations. Now it's time to pull this information together and expand on it so you can perform some visual trickery like dissolving one picture into another.

Introducing the Dissolve

Filmmakers have been using dissolves for decades in their movies to produce the dazzling visual effect of fading from one image into another. To produce this effect on movie film, all you have to do is expose each frame of the film to both pictures (the original and the end result), gradually decreasing the intensity of one and increasing the intensity of the other, frame by frame until the original image has vanished.

Creating a dissolve with your computer, however, is another story. You could simulate the photographic process on a true color display by shifting the value of each pixel from its color in the first image to its color in the second image. Unfortunately, this process would take a long time for bitmaps of any significant size even on a lightning fast PC. Of course, you could perform the dissolve steps, capture them, then play the whole thing back as an animation. That would be fine if you knew the order of all the transitions you wanted in your presentation, but it could prohibit spontaneous dissolves, especially if you have a large number of images.

Another approach is to replace one image with the other, pixel by pixel. But this process *looks* digital. Also, when you try to use this technique on an 8-bit display, you once again bump into the palette problem. If each image is composed from a palette of 256 colors, then the combined images that appear during the dissolve could require as many as 512 colors, which the display system can't provide. It's easy to dissolve from one image to another if the images share a common palette, or if each of the images uses only a few colors so that their combined palettes don't require more than 256 palette entries. But the most general purpose solution to this problem needs to allow for the worst case.

There is a compromise. By combining the pixel-by-pixel replacement technique with a color translation, you can generate a pretty attractive dissolve. Raster operations will work on either a true color or palettized display, but for 8-bit images, the color translation becomes practical only with the assistance of the Palette Manager.

Let's begin by digging deeper into raster operations and bitmaps.

ROPs Revisited

At the end of Chapter 6, I pointed out that some of the raster operations we tested in the ROPEXP1 project produced identical results because some of the 15 named ROP codes manipulate three bitmaps instead of just two.

The third bitmap, the one conspicuously absent from our last project, is the *Pattern Brush*. Brushes are special square bitmaps, eight pixels on a side, that fill an area with a repeating pattern. You most often see them used with GDI functions that draw shapes. But you can also use them with **BitBlt()** to add repeating patterns to entire bitmaps, or to combinations of bitmaps.

In ROPEXP2, our next project, we'll add the brush bitmap to **BitBlt()**. To do that, we have to create the brush, which we can do either by drawing it or by generating it from within our program. Because brushes are such itty-bitty bitmaps, I think this is a good time to show you how a bitmap is built from the ground up. Although it will take us off on a side route, building bitmaps is a skill you need to master before we get to the dissolve project later in this chapter.

Building a Bitmap

This project shows you how to create a brush and use it in the **BitBlt()** function. Here are the steps to follow:

1. Create a new form with filename ROPEXP2.FRM.
2. Add the function **CreateTheBrush()** (Listing 7.1) to the form.
3. Add the event procedures, **BrushPic_Paint()**, **ResultPic_Paint()**, and **Form_Load()** (Listings 7.2 through 7.4).
4. Place the ROP names and their hex codes in a text file named ROPSLIST.TXT.
5. Create a code module named ROPEXP2.BAS and add the required declarations (Listing 7.5).

 You'll find this project in the subdirectory \VBMAGIC, in the files ROPEXP2.MAK, ROPEXP2.FRM, ROPEXP2.BAS, and ROPSLIST.TXT.

Inside the Bitmap Data Structures

The entire bitmap creation process for this project resides in the **CreateTheBrush()** function. The **Type** declarations for the structures used by this function are located in ROPEXP2.BAS. Let's start by looking at the device-independent bitmap (DIB) data structures needed and then we'll write the **CreateTheBrush()** function.

The DIB data structure consists of either four or five major elements, depending on whether the structure is in memory or on a disk file. In this project, we'll be using the four-headed variety (we'll get to the fifth element later). The first of these components, the **BITMAPINFOHEADER** indicates, among other things, the dimensions of the bitmap, the total number of bytes in the image, and the number of color bits per pixel:

```
Type BITMAPINFOHEADER '40 bytes
    biSize As Long
    biWidth As Long
    biHeight As Long
    biPlanes As Integer
    biBitCount As Integer
    biCompression As Long
    biSizeImage As Long
    biXPelsPerMeter As Long
    biYPelsPerMeter As Long
```

```
biClrUsed As Long
biClrImportant As Long
End Type
```

The second DIB element is the color table, which consists of a series of four-byte structures of type **RGBQUAD**, similar, but not identical to **PALETTEENTRY** and the long integer color reference. This is the third type of four-byte color structure, and once again, its fields have been shuffled:

```
Type RGBQUAD
    rgbBlue        As String * 1
    rgbGreen       As String * 1
    rgbRed         As String * 1
    rgbReserved    As String * 1
    End Type
```

The **BITMAPINFOHEADER** and its related **RGBQUAD**s are gathered together under one roof in the third type of DIB element, a structure called **BITMAPINFO**:

```
Type BITMAPINFO
    bmiHeader As BITMAPINFOHEADER
    bmiColors(1) As RGBQUAD
    End Type
```

The number of elements in the array **bmiColors()** depends on the number of colors specified in the field **biClrUsed** in the **BITMAPINFOHEADER**. If you set **biClrUsed** to 0, then the **bmiColors()** must contain the exact number of colors defined by **biBitCount**. In other words, if **biBitCount** equals 8, then **bmiColors()** must include 256 elements, which requires an upper bound of 255. For a bit count of 4, dimension the array to 15, for a total of 16 elements. You may enter a number other than zero in **biClrUsed** to specify a number of colors fewer than the maximum allowed by the bit count. In a true color bitmap, **biBitCount** equals 24, **biClrUsed** equals 0, and **BITMAPINFO** includes no **RGBQUAD**s.

The first field in our **BITMAPINFOHEADER**, which is named **biSize**, must equal 40, the number of bytes in the structure itself. In the second and third fields, **biWidth** and **biHeight**, specify the bitmap dimensions in pixels. A brush is always 8 by 8, so we enter 8 for both dimensions.

The field **biPlanes** reflects a method of organizing pixel data normally not used in Windows bitmaps. Instead of lining up the three-byte RGB values of a 24-bit image sequentially, you could create three separate 8-bit bitmaps— one for the red, green, and blue color components—each with one byte per pixel. This would be a three plane bitmap. Since Windows bitmaps are not organized in planes, we always set **biPlanes** to 1.

biCompression may be set to one of three values. The constant names for those values are **BI_RGB**, **BI_RLE4**, and **BI_RLE8**, whose values are &H0, &H2, and &H1, respectively. **BI_RGB** indicates that the bitmap is not compressed. The other two values indicate which of the two *run length encoding* (RLE) methods have been used to compress the bitmap. The advantage of RLE bitmaps is that they occupy less memory and disk space. Their disadvantage is that they have to be decompressed as they are displayed so they slow things down, sometimes considerably. I won't discuss RLE bitmaps any further in this book, but you should note that compressed bitmaps do exist.

By pretending that RLE bitmaps don't exist, we also get to skip the field **biSizeImage**. For non-compressed bitmaps, the GDI can figure out the number of bytes in the pixel buffer from the dimensions and the color depth. But when you specify a compression method of **BI_RLE4** or **BI_RLE8**, the GDI wants to know the number of bytes in the compressed image data.

biXPelsPerMeter and **biYPelsPerMeter** can be used to specify the resolution of the bitmap on the absolute scale of pixels per meter. You may never encounter a bitmap in which these fields contain any value other than zero, meaning that they are ignored.

The last field in **BITMAPINFOHEADER**, **biClrImportant**, is also rarely used. It specifies how many of the colors in the color table you need to reasonably display the image. Almost all bitmap files assume that all colors are critical, so this field is set to 0. The display of 256 color images is at the whim of the Palette Manager anyway!

The fourth DIB element is the series of bytes that contain the pixel data itself, not a structure declared with the **Type** command, but a contiguous data buffer large enough to hold the entire bitmap. For the little bitmap in this project, we use a fixed-length string as the pixel buffer. You might expect the entire monchrome brush bitmap to fit into 8 bytes (8 pixels by 8 pixels, 1 bit per pixel). But the number of bytes in each row of bitmap pixels must be evenly divisible by 4, meaning that each row uses a minimum of four bytes. (No such restriction exists on the *number* of rows.) So we have to build our brush in a 32 byte buffer, in which each row will contain one byte of pixel data and three bytes of padding.

Adding CreateTheBrush()

We're now ready to add the main bitmap function, which is shown in Listing 7.1.

Listing 7.1 The CreateTheBrush() Function from ROPEXP2.FRM

```
Function CreateTheBrush () As Integer
    Dim hCompBitmap As Integer
    Dim BrushBitmapInfo As BITMAPINFO
    Dim Counter As Integer
    Dim PixelData As String * 32
    Dim Dummy As Integer
    Dim Row As Integer
    Dim Column As Integer

    ' Fill in BITMAPINFOHEADER
    BrushBitmapInfo.bmiHeader.biSize = 40
    BrushBitmapInfo.bmiHeader.biWidth = 8
    BrushBitmapInfo.bmiHeader.biHeight = 8
    BrushBitmapInfo.bmiHeader.biPlanes = 1
    BrushBitmapInfo.bmiHeader.biBitCount = 1
    BrushBitmapInfo.bmiHeader.biCompression = BI_RGB
    BrushBitmapInfo.bmiHeader.biSizeImage = 0
    BrushBitmapInfo.bmiHeader.biXPelsPerMeter = 0
    BrushBitmapInfo.bmiHeader.biYPelsPerMeter = 0
    BrushBitmapInfo.bmiHeader.biClrUsed = 0
    BrushBitmapInfo.bmiHeader.biClrImportant = 0

    ' Set the color table values for the brush to
    ' black and white.
    BrushBitmapInfo.bmiColors(0).rgbBlue = Chr$(0)
    BrushBitmapInfo.bmiColors(0).rgbGreen = Chr$(0)
    BrushBitmapInfo.bmiColors(0).rgbRed = Chr$(0)
    BrushBitmapInfo.bmiColors(0).rgbReserved = Chr$(0)
    BrushBitmapInfo.bmiColors(1).rgbBlue = Chr$(255)
    BrushBitmapInfo.bmiColors(1).rgbGreen = Chr$(255)
    BrushBitmapInfo.bmiColors(1).rgbRed = Chr$(255)
    BrushBitmapInfo.bmiColors(1).rgbReserved = Chr$(0)

    ' Initialize brush bitmap pixel data to all white.
    For Counter = 0 To 7
        Mid$(PixelData, Counter * 4 + 1, 1) = Chr$(&HFF)
        Next Counter
    ' Create a checkerboard monochrome bitmap, i.e. 50% gray dither.
    For Counter = 0 To 63
        Row = Counter \ 8
        Column = Counter Mod 8
        If (Row Mod 2 = 0) Xor (Column Mod 2 = 0) Then
            Mid$(PixelData, Row * 4 + 1, 1) = Chr$(Asc(Mid$(PixelData, Row * 4 +
                                        1, 1)) And (Not (2 ^ Column)))
        End If
    Next Counter

    hCompBitmap = CreateDIBitmap(BrushPic.hDC, BrushBitmapInfo.bmiHeader,
                CBM_INIT, PixelData, BrushBitmapInfo, DIB_RGB_COLORS)
    CreateTheBrush = CreatePatternBrush(hCompBitmap)
    Dummy = DeleteObject(hCompBitmap)
End Function
```

Let's take this function apart. The first part fills in the data needed for the **BITMAPINFOHEADER** structure. Then, we move on to the color table. Notice here that we need two entries in our color table, one for black and one for white. We use single-byte, fixed-length strings in **RGBQUAD** to hold the color values (just as we did when we used the structure **PALETTEENTRY** in the previous chapter). For black, set all the color fields to 0, and for white, set them all to their maximum value of 255. Since these are string fields, we have to convert the values with the **Chr$()** function as we assign them.

Next, we initalize the bitmap so all its pixel bits reference the white color table entry:

```
For Counter = 0 To 7
    Mid$(PixelData, Counter * 4 + 1, 1) = Chr$(&HFF)
Next Counter
```

You could easily set all the byte values to &HFF, including the pad bytes. I just want to make it clear that *only* the first byte of each four affects the outcome. Did you notice anything unusual about the **Mid$()** function? Instead of counting characters in strings beginning with 0, we begin with 1. That's why the expression in the position parameter in **Mid$()** adds 1 to **Counter * 4**.

After we've initialized the brush, we can set every other pixel bit to reference the black color table entry. And that's exactly what happens in the second **For** loop:

```
For Counter = 0 To 63
    Row = Counter \ 8
    Column = Counter Mod 8
    If (Row Mod 2 = 0) Xor (Column Mod 2 = 0) Then
        Mid$(PixelData, Row * 4 + 1, 1) =   Chr$(Asc(Mid$(PixelData, Row * 4
                                            + 1, 1)) And (Not (2 ^ Column)))

    End If
Next Counter
```

Bitwise Boolean Trickery

We have to use a little bitwise boolean trickery to change individual bits from a value of 1, which represents white, to a value of 0, which represents black. We use the VB functions **Mid$()** and **Asc()** to pull out an individual byte. Then, to set one bit in that byte, we create a pattern of bits, called a *bit mask*, in which the bit we want to change equals 0, and all the other bits equal 1. To get the pattern, we first create a complementary value in which the bit we want to change equals 1 and all other bits equal 0. The decimal equivalent of a binary number with one bit set always equals a power of 2. So we set one

Chapter 7

bit by raising 2 to the power of the column number (0 through 7). We then **Not** that result to get the complement, which leaves us with a binary mask in which one bit equals 0 and the other seven bits equal 1. When we **And** that mask with the existing byte, all the bits remain unchanged except the single bit we have selected, which will switch from a 1 to a 0. This technique is illustrated in Figure 7.1.

A checkerboard bitmap in which pixels alternate between black and white will produced a 50% gray dither.

Working with Brushes

It takes two steps to convert our DIB into a GDI brush. First, we have to convert it into a device-dependent bitmap (DDB). Believe it or not, that's the job of the API function **CreateDIBitmap()**. Despite its name, this function does not create a DIB; instead it converts a DIB into a DDB. You see, before you can display a device *independent* bitmap, you must convert it into a device *dependent* bitmap. The conversion process transforms a bitmap from its native color mode into the color mode supported by the active display system. When your display system is set to 256 color mode, each pixel represents one byte in video memory. Our monochrome brush bitmap contains one bit per pixel. **CreateDIBitmap()** converts each bit of the monochrome DIB into one byte in the corresponding DDB by first looking up the color reference in the DIB's color table. Next, the function compares that color to the colors in the logical palette currently selected into the device context specified in the first argument. Since we have not explicitly selected a palette into the device context of **BrushPic**, Windows will use the **DEFAULT_PALETTE**, which contains the 20 reserved colors, including black and white. The first and last entries in the system palette contain black and white respectively, so each byte of the DDB will reference either palette entry &H00 or palette entry &HFF. The monochrome DIB becomes a 256 color

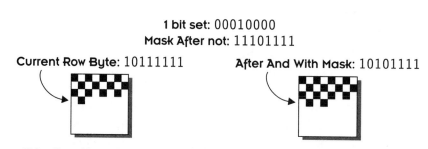

1 bit set: 00010000
Mask After not: 11101111

Current Row Byte: 10111111   **After And With Mask:** 10101111

Figure 7.1   *Use a bit mask to change monochrome pixel values.*

DDB that uses only two of the 256 available colors. The GDI stores this DDB in memory and returns a handle to it through **CreateDIBitmap()**.

CreateDIBitmap() takes six arguments:

```
Declare Function CreateDIBitmap Lib "GDI" (ByVal hDC As Integer, lpInfoHeader As
    BITMAPINFOHEADER, ByVal dwUsage As Long, ByVal lpInitBits As String,
    lpInitInfo As BITMAPINFO, ByVal wUsage As Integer) As Integer
```

The first argument specifies the device context. The function will convert the DIB to a DDB based on the capabilities of this device context. In other words, if the device context belongs to an 8-bit color display buffer, **CreateDIBitmap()** will return a handle to an 8-bit bitmap.

A long pointer to a **BITMAPINFOHEADER** is passed as the second argument. As we've done many times in previous experiments, we pass a pointer to a structure by declaring this argument *without* the **ByVal** keyword.

The third argument determines whether **CreateDIBitmap()** creates an initialized bitmap. If you pass the function a value of 0 in this argument, it will create a raw bitmap. You may then use other GDI functions to draw on that bitmap. The pixels of the uninitialized bitmap will contain whatever values happen to lie in memory. If you choose to create a new bitmap this way, be sure to initialize it with one of the drawing functions. Also, to create an uninitialized bitmap, pass the next three arguments to the function as NULL (zero). To create a bitmap based on the values in the **BITMAPINFOHEADER** and the pixel data, however, set this third argument to the constant **CBM_INIT**, which has a long integer value of &H4&.

For the fourth argument we pass the 32-byte, fixed-length string that we're using as a pixel buffer. By declaring this argument **ByVal**, we instruct VB to convert it to a null-terminated string. Since this is a fixed-length string, VB will make sure Windows allocates enough space for all 32 bytes, plus the null terminator.

The fifth argument takes a pointer to the **BITMAPINFO** structure, which contains not only a second copy of the **BITMAPINFOHEADER**, but more importantly, the color table.

Finally, for the last argument, we specify whether the color table values inside the **BITMAPINFO** structure passed in parameter five contain references to the currently realized palette, or to explicit RGB colors. In this case, we'll ask for RGB colors. We'll use the other method in a later project.

To make a brush from the bitmap, we call another API function, **CreatePatternBrush()**, which takes as its sole argument a handle to a bitmap, and returns a handle to a brush. A pattern brush is just a special class of bitmap, one that GDI painting functions can repeat like a rubber stamp to fill an area. In ROPEXP2, the drawing areas measure 32 pixels on a side, so **BitBlt()** will automatically repeat the 8 x 8 brush pattern 16 times as it draws the **ResultPic**.

Other Ways to Build a Brush

In Windows programming you often find more than one trail through the API wilderness. As an alternative to **CreateDIBitmap()**, take a look at **CreateBitmap()** and **CreateBitmapIndirect()**. With **CreateBitmap()** you can create a monchrome bitmap using nothing more than the pixel data itself—no **BITMAPINFOHEADER**, no color table, just bits. Watch out for the structure of the pixel data however, because this function does not expect the bitmap lines to end on 32 bit boundaries, so an 8 x 8 monochrome bitmap would fit neatly into 8 bytes. To create a color bitmap with this function, you must know which colors are located where in the system palette, because the function does not convert a DIB into a DDB. The pixel data must already represent a DDB when you hand it over. The other function, **CreateBitmapIndirect()**, also expects DDB pixel data, which is indirectly referenced (hence its name) by its single argument, a pointer to a structure called **BITMAP**.

For the most direct method of creating a pattern brush, use the function **CreateDIBPatternBrush(),** which consolidates the two functions **CreateDIBitmap()** and **CreatePatternBrush()** into one. To use this function, you'll need to construct a *packed DIB*, which consists of a complete DIB stored contiguously in memory, which includes the **BITMAPINFO** structure followed immediately by the pixel data. The word *packed* simply means that the elements are contiguous, not that they are compressed in any way. Later in this chapter we'll be studying some handy memory management functions that you could use to pack the DIB.

For more information on these functions and structures, see the Windows SDK or any good API reference.

Brushes 'n' Bits

It doesn't pay to go any further until we know that the pattern brush we've created has come out as we intended. We'll fill a Picture Box control with the brush pattern, which will give us a chance to use another blt function called **PatBlt()**. This function is called from the **BrushPic_Paint()** event procedure as shown in Listing 7.2.

Listing 7.2 The BrushPic_Paint() Event Procedure from ROPEXP2.FRM

```
Sub BrushPic_Paint ()
    Dim hBrush As Integer
    Dim hOldBrush As Integer
    Dim Dummy As Integer

    hBrush = CreateTheBrush()
    hOldBrush = SelectObject(BrushPic.hDC, hBrush)
```

```
Dummy = PatBlt(BrushPic.hDC, 0, 0, BrushPic.ScaleWidth,
        BrushPic.ScaleHeight, PATCOPY)
' You could also use BitBlt() to paint the
' pattern into the BrushPic DC:
' Dummy = BitBlt(BrushPic.hDC, 0, 0, BrushPic.ScaleWidth,
          BrushPic.ScaleHeight. 0. 0. 0. PATCOPY)
Dummy = SelectObject(BrushPic.hDC, hOldBrush)
Dummy = DeleteObject(hBrush)
End Sub
```

Notice that **PatBlt()** takes only six arguments:

```
Declare Function PatBlt Lib "GDI" (ByVal hDestDC As Integer, ByVal X As Integer,
  ByVal Y As Integer, ByVal nWidth As Integer, ByVal nHeight As Integer, ByVal
  dwROP As Long) As Integer
```

Just like **BitBlt()**, the first argument takes the destination device context. The second and third arguments determine the starting position of the pattern fill operation, while the fourth and fifth arguments specify the width and height of the area to be painted with the brush. The last argument takes a ROP code. The ROP code determines how **PatBlt()** will combine the pattern with

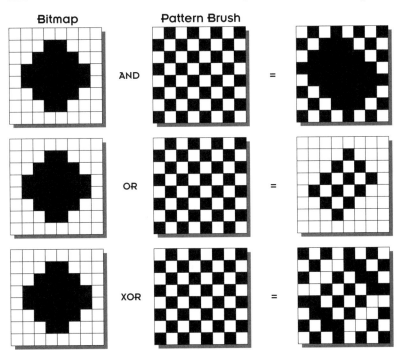

Figure 7.2 *How pattern brushes combine with monochrome or colored bitmaps in boolean raster operations.*

the exisiting bitmap as shown in Figure 7.2. You could pass any of the 256 ternary ROP codes to **PatBlt()**, but only those that include the brush or the destination will do anything (**BLACKNESS** or **WHITENESS** will also work, in their usual ways).

> **NOTE:** *For a complete list of the ternary ROP codes, see the Microsoft Windows 3.1 Programmers's Reference: Vol. 3, Messages, Structures, and Macros.*

To use the brush, we first select it into the device context of **BrushPic**. The function **SelectObject()** returns the handle of the previously selected object of the same type, which we save in **hOldBrush**. In this case, that happens to be the handle to the default **BLACK_BRUSH**. We then call **PatBlt()** with the **PATCOPY** ROP code, which replaces the current contents of the device context with the repeating brush pattern. Finally, we restore the old brush and delete our pattern brush.

We have to perform a similar set of steps in **ResultPic_Paint()** (see Listing 7.3), except that we use **BitBlt()** instead of **PatBlt()**, and we send everything to the device context of ResultPic.

Listing 7.3   The ResultPic_Paint() Event Procedure from ROPEXP2.FRM

```
Sub ResultPic_Paint ()
    Dim hBrush As Integer
    Dim hOldBrush As Integer
    Dim ROPType As Long
    Dim Param As String
    Dim Dummy As Integer


    DestPic.Cls
    Param = ROPSList.Text
    ROPType = Val(Mid$(Param, InStr(Param, " &") + 1, 11))

    hBrush = CreateTheBrush()
    hOldBrush = SelectObject(ResultPic.hDC, hBrush)
    Dummy = BitBlt(ResultPic.hDC, 0, 0, 31, 31, DestPic.hDC, 0, 0, SRCCOPY)
    Dummy = BitBlt(ResultPic.hDC, 0, 0, 31, 31, SourcePic.hDC, 0, 0, ROPType)

    'Dummy = BitBlt(ResultPic.hDC, 0, 0, ResultPic.ScaleWidth,
            ResultPic.ScaleHeight, 0, 0, 0, PATCOPY)
    Dummy = SelectObject(ResultPic.hDC, hOldBrush)
    Dummy = DeleteObject(hBrush)

    End Sub
```

I've made another change in ROPEXP2. In the ROP project presented in Chapter 6, I hard-coded the initialization of the **ROPSList** List Box. But this

time I moved the ROP names and their hex codes into a text file named
ROPSLIST.TXT. Some day when you have nothing better to do, you may add
the 241 remaining ROP codes to that file. The **Form_Load()** event procedure
shown in Listing 7.4 picks up whatever it finds there.

Listing 7.4   The Form_Load() Event Procedure from ROPEXP2.FRM

```
Sub Form_Load ()
    Dim TempString As String
    Const ROPSListFile = 1
    Open App.Path + "\ROPSList.Txt" For Input As ROPSListFile
    Do While Not EOF(ROPSListFile)
        Input #ROPSListFile, TempString
        If InStr(TempString, "&") > 0 Then
            ROPSList.AddItem TempString
          End If
        Loop
    Close #ROPSListFile
    End Sub
```

Adding the Data Structures

To wrap up the project, we need to create the code module and add the
declarations in Listing 7.5. I had to create a separate code module to accommodate the **Type** declarations, so for clarity, I moved the external function
declarations and constants there as well.

Listing 7.5   The Declarations Section from ROPEXP2.BAS

```
Option Explicit

Type BITMAPINFOHEADER '40 bytes
    biSize As Long
    biWidth As Long
    biHeight As Long
    biPlanes As Integer
    biBitCount As Integer
    biCompression As Long
    biSizeImage As Long
    biXPelsPerMeter As Long
    biYPelsPerMeter As Long
    biClrUsed As Long
    biClrImportant As Long
    End Type

Type RGBQUAD
    rgbBlue        As String * 1
    rgbGreen       As String * 1
    rgbRed         As String * 1
    rgbReserved    As String * 1
    End Type
```

```
Type BITMAPINFO
    bmiHeader As BITMAPINFOHEADER
    bmiColors(1) As RGBQUAD
    End Type

Declare Function CreateDIBitmap Lib "GDI" (ByVal hDC As Integer, lpInfoHeader As
    BITMAPINFOHEADER, ByVal dwUsage As Long, ByVal lpInitBits As String,
    lpInitInfo As BITMAPINFO, ByVal wUsage As Integer) As Integer
Declare Function CreatePatternBrush Lib "GDI" (ByVal hBitmap As Integer) As Integer
Declare Function DeleteObject Lib "GDI" (ByVal hObject As Integer) As Integer
Declare Function SelectObject Lib "GDI" (ByVal hDC As Integer, ByVal hObject As
    Integer) As Integer
Declare Function BitBlt Lib "GDI" (ByVal hDestDC As Integer, ByVal X As Integer,
    ByVal Y As Integer, ByVal nWidth As Integer, ByVal nHeight As Integer, ByVal
    hSrcDC As Integer, ByVal XSrc As Integer, ByVal YSrc As Integer, ByVal dwROP
    As Long) As Integer
Declare Function PatBlt Lib "GDI" (ByVal hDestDC As Integer, ByVal X As Integer,
    ByVal Y As Integer, ByVal nWidth As Integer, ByVal nHeight As Integer, ByVal
    dwROP As Long) As Integer

'  Pre-defined raster operation constants

Global Const SRCCOPY = &HCC0020
Global Const SRCPAINT = &HEE0086
Global Const SRCAND = &H8800C6
Global Const SRCINVERT = &H660046
Global Const SRCERASE = &H440328
Global Const NOTSRCCOPY = &H330008
Global Const NOTSRCERASE = &H1100A6
Global Const MERGECOPY = &HC000CA
Global Const MERGEPAINT = &HBB0226
Global Const PATCOPY = &HF00021
Global Const PATPAINT = &HFB0A09
Global Const PATINVERT = &H5A0049
Global Const DSTINVERT = &H550009
Global Const BLACKNESS = &H42&
Global Const WHITENESS = &HFF0062

Global Const BI_RGB = 0&
Global Const CBM_INIT = &H4&
Global Const DIB_RGB_COLORS = 0
'Global Const DIB_PAL_COLORS = 1
```

Now you can try out the ROPs that use pattern brushes. As an exercise, work out the results you would expect from **PATPAINT**. The funny-looking code that appears beside each ROP hex code in the list box represents the boolean raster operation in *reverse polish notation* (RPN). I've included these for reference only; you can't pass them to any API function, but most reference guides to the Windows API present ROPs in this form. The RPN expression for **PATPAINT** is DPSnoo (*not* pronounced "Dee Pee Snoo"). For the VB translation of this expression, see Table 6.2.

Combining Bitmaps

We now have many tools under our belts for working with palettes, blts, and raster operations. We're well on our way to the image dissolve effect. Next, let's figure out which ROP code will enable us to combine two images.

Imagine that you're holding two photographs in your hands, one on top of the other. You can't see the bottom photo because photographic prints are opaque. You can simulate the digital dissolve process by poking hundreds of tiny holes in the top image, evenly spaced across the entire picture. Through the holes you could then see little bits of the bottom photo. You could go over the entire image again with your needle, this time adding more holes between the first set. As the holes increase in number, first by hundreds then by thousands, the bottom image becomes clearer and clearer. After several rounds of hole poking, the top picture disintegrates, leaving the bottom image unobscured.

To speed things up a little, you could make a little hole puncher by sticking several pins through a piece of cork or rubber. Then you could punch dozens of holes with each pop. And that's exactly what we're going to do with a pattern brush.

The brush we created in the ROPEXP2 project consists of alternating white and black pixels—a checkerboard pattern. If we think of that pattern not as a checkerboard, however, but as a fine mesh, we can easily imagine that we could see a bitmap through the holes represented by the black pixels. As we step through the dissolve, we'll create brushes with ever increasing numbers of black pixels.

Now all we need to do is deduce which ROP code will combine the brush and the two images to generate the proper effect.

Hunting through Raster Operations

Windows raster operations have an undeserved reputation as a black art. Choosing a raster operation is one of the hardest things to do in Windows graphics programming. But like any programming problem, all you need to do is break the process into manageable steps. To mix the pixels of two images, we need to do two things:

1. Use the pattern brush to make black holes in the destination bitmap.
2. Fill the holes with the corresponding pixels from the source bitmap.

For the first step, only one logical operator is needed. If you **And** a pixel with a binary value of 00000000—representing the black palette entry—with any other pixel value, you can get only one result, 00000000. 10101010 **And** 00000000 equals 00000000, 11110000 **And** 00000000 equals 00000000, and so on. In boolean logic, only 1 **And** 1 equals 1. But what happens to the pixels in the destination when we **And** them with the white pixels in the pattern brush? Nothing. Because once again, only the pixel bits that equal 1 in the destination will yield 1 when we **And** them with pattern pixel bits that equal 1. 10101010 **And** 11111111 equals 10101010; 11110000 **And** 11111111 equals 11110000. Pixels that are black in the pattern brush become black in the destination bitmap, while pixels that are white in the pattern brush remain unchanged in the destination bitmap. So step one looks like this:

(Pattern **And** Destination)

Next we have to combine the source bitmap with the result of step 1 so that only the pixels that lie under the black holes show through. This step is trickier. Any of the three logical operators will blend the bits of the colored pixels from both images. So we have to perform another masking operation to eliminate from the source image the pixels we don't want. Step 2 splits into two steps. First we change all the unwanted pixels to black, then we press the two pictures together.

To mask all but the pixels we want added to the awaiting destination bitmap, we invert the mask with a **Not** operator. In boolean logic, **Not** changes all 1s to 0s and all 0s to 1s. Then in the third step, we use the **And** operator again, this time between the inverted pattern and the source image:

((**Not** Pattern) **And** Source)

Whoops. Still one step to go. Now there will be four. In this last step, we want to combine the results of steps 1 through 3. We know that **And** won't work because each pair of pixels includes one colored pixel from either of the images, facing one black pixel from the opposite image. Thus, an **And** would blacken the whole picture. But an **Or** will retain the bits from each colored pixel exactly as they appear in their native bitmaps. In fact, since one member of each pixel pair is black, an **Xor** would work just as well. The complete raster operation expression looks like this:

(Pattern **And** Destination) **Or** ((**Not** Pattern) **And** Source)

In reverse polish notation it looks like this:

PDaSPnao

Don't bother looking in the table of the 15 named ROP codes for that one. You won't find it. With a little boolean algebra, we could derive an equivalent expression, one that does appear in the table. But there's an easier way. The Windows API defines a set of pre-defined binary constants, one representing each of the three types of bitmaps, which we can grind through our equation to directly calculate the hexadecimal identification number of the correct ROP code.

Let's work through the steps:

1. Combine the pattern brush and the destination to make black holes in the destination.

   The pattern brush and the destination bitmap are represented by the binary constants 11110000 and 10101010, respectively. 11110000 **And** 10101010 equals 10100000.

2. Invert the pattern brush.

   Not 11110000 equals 00001111.

3. Combine the result of step 2 with the source bitmap, which is represented by the binary constant 11001100.

   00001111 **And** 11001100 equals 00001100.

4. **Or** the results of steps 1 and 3.

   10100000 **Or** 00001100 equals 10101100.

The ROP code we want is 10101100, which is hexadecimal value &HAC. ROP codes are actually long integers. The highest-order byte always equals &H00. The second highest-order byte represents the ROP identification number. The two lower-order bytes contain codes that help the ROP engine construct the correct sequence of machine instructions to perform the raster operation. ROPs are like tiny programs, or macros. For the sake of speed, the GDI assembles a temporary program in memory, enabling the blt function to perform the raster operation without calling subfunctions. The lower-order bytes don't help us identify the ROP code, but we must include them when we reference the ROP code in a blt operation.

If we look up raster operation &HAC in the ROP table, we find that its logical expression looks a little different from ours:

SPDSxax

But regardless of appearance, the two expressions are logically equivalent, which we could prove by again grinding the bitmap binary constants. Go right ahead.

> **NOTE:** *The expression given in the ROP table may seem less intuitive than the one we derived step-by-step, but you can still make sense of it if you remember that an **Xor** operation is reversible (just do it over again). In the expression SPDSxax, you see two **Xor** operations. The first*

*combines the source and destination bitmaps. The second un-combines all the pixels left untouched by the pattern brush. The middle step combines the effects of the **Not** and both **And** operations in our version of the expression. Instead of performing one **And**, then inverting the pattern to perform the second **And**, you can perform the **And** on the combined bitmaps. When you perform the final **Xor**, the blackened pixels are filled with the pixels from the source bitmap, while simultaneously the source pixels are reversed out of the unblackened destination pixels.*

According to the standard table of Windows ternary ROP codes, the complete hex value of the &HAC ROP code is &H00AC0744. To test this raster operation, add it to ROPSLIST.TXT and run ROPEXP2, as shown in Figure 7.3.

That takes care of the ROP code. Now we can start the dissolve project.

Creating the Basic Digital Dissolve

In the program BITBLTEX, which we created in Chapter 6, we used **BitBlt()** and the simple **SRCCOPY** raster operation to copy an image from one Picture

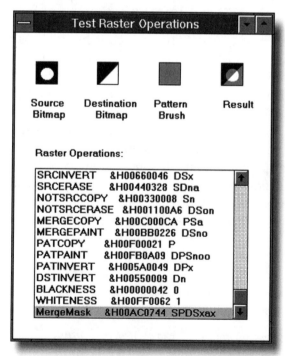

Figure 7.3 *You can use the program ROPEXP2 to test a raster operation.*

Box to another. Let's make that program more interesting by creating a series of black and white pattern brushes, tossing in our newly discovered ROP code, and dissolve the image from one Picture Box to the other.

The First Dissolve

This project shows you how to dissolve two bitmap images.

1. Create the new form DSLVEXP.FRM.
2. Add the **CreateDissolveBrush()** function (Listing 7.6) and the **CreatePixelSetSequence()** procedure (Listing 7.7) to the form.
3. Add the supporting event procedures, **Picture2_Paint()**, **DissolveButton_Click()**, **Timer1_Timer()**, **Picture2_Click()**, and **Form_Load()** (Listings 7.8 through Listings 7.12).
4. Add the necessary declarations to DSLVEXP.FRM (Listing 7.13) and DSLVEXP.BAS (Listing 7.14).

This project is located in the directory \VBMAGIC in the files DSLVEXP.MAK, DSLVEXP.FRM, DSLVEXP.FRX, DSLVEXP.BAS, and PIXELLST.TXT.

Setting Up the Dissolve

In the ROPEXP2 project presented earlier, we created a function named **CreateTheBrush()**, which built a DIB from the ground up, then converted it to a DDB, from which it made a pattern brush. For this new project, we need to modify that function to produce one of a series of pattern brushes. Each successive version of the brush will contain a greater percentage of black pixels than its predecessor. We'll call the new function **CreateDissolveBrush()**, and we'll tell it which version of the brush we want by passing it an integer argument by the name of **DissolveStep** (see Listing 7.6).

Listing 7.6 The CreateDissolveBrush() Function from DSLVEXP.FRM

```
Function CreateDissolveBrush (DissolveStep As Integer) As Integer
    Dim hCompBitmap As Integer
    Dim BrushBitmapInfo As BITMAPINFO
    Dim Counter As Integer
    Dim PixelData As String * 32
    Dim Dummy As Integer
    Dim Row As Integer
    Dim Column As Integer
```

```
BrushBitmapInfo.bmiHeader.biSize = 40
BrushBitmapInfo.bmiHeader.biWidth = 8
BrushBitmapInfo.bmiHeader.biHeight = 8
BrushBitmapInfo.bmiHeader.biPlanes = 1
BrushBitmapInfo.bmiHeader.biBitCount = 1
BrushBitmapInfo.bmiHeader.biCompression = 0
BrushBitmapInfo.bmiHeader.biSizeImage = 0
BrushBitmapInfo.bmiHeader.biXPelsPerMeter = 0
BrushBitmapInfo.bmiHeader.biYPelsPerMeter = 0
BrushBitmapInfo.bmiHeader.biClrUsed = 0
BrushBitmapInfo.bmiHeader.biClrImportant = 0

' Set the color table values for
' the brush to black and white.
BrushBitmapInfo.bmiColors(0).rgbBlue = Chr$(0)
BrushBitmapInfo.bmiColors(0).rgbGreen = Chr$(0)
BrushBitmapInfo.bmiColors(0).rgbRed = Chr$(0)
BrushBitmapInfo.bmiColors(0).rgbReserved = Chr$(0)
BrushBitmapInfo.bmiColors(1).rgbBlue = Chr$(255)
BrushBitmapInfo.bmiColors(1).rgbGreen = Chr$(255)
BrushBitmapInfo.bmiColors(1).rgbRed = Chr$(255)
BrushBitmapInfo.bmiColors(1).rgbReserved = Chr$(0)

' Initialize brush bitmap pixel data to all white.
For Counter = 0 To 7
    Mid$(PixelData, Counter * 4 + 1, 1) = Chr$(&HFF)
    Next Counter

' Set the bits representing the black pixels to 0.
For Counter = 1 To DissolveStep * (64 / NumberOfSteps)
    Row = (PixelSetSequence(Counter) - 1) \ 8
    Column = (PixelSetSequence(Counter) - 1) Mod 8
    Mid$(PixelData, Row * 4 + 1, 1) = Chr$(Asc(Mid$(PixelData, Row * 4 + 1,
                                1)) And (Not (2 ^ Column)))
    Next Counter

' Convert the DIB into a DDB and create the pattern brush.
hCompBitmap = CreateDIBitmap(Disolve1.hDC, BrushBitmapInfo.bmiHeader,
            CBM_INIT, PixelData, BrushBitmapInfo, DIB_RGB_COLORS)
CreateDissolveBrush = CreatePatternBrush(hCompBitmap)
Dummy = DeleteObject%(hCompBitmap)
End Function
```

The code that distinguishes **CreateDissolveBrush()** from **CreateThe-Brush()** is the **For** loop that sets the black pixels:

```
For Counter = 1 To DissolveStep * (64 / NumberOfSteps)
    Row = (PixelSetSequence(Counter) - 1) \ 8
    Column = (PixelSetSequence(Counter) - 1) Mod 8
    Mid$(PixelData, Row * 4 + 1, 1) = Chr$(Asc(Mid$(PixelData, Row * 4 + 1,
                                1)) And (Not (2 ^ Column)))
    Next Counter
```

Instead of simply flipping every other bit, this code uses a series of pixel numbers, stored in an array called **PixelSetSequence()**, to identify the pixels that should be changed to black for any given step in the dissolve. I tried several approaches to generate this sequence algorithmically, and failed. Every series I created caused the resulting brush to produce visible patterns in the combined bitmaps. Some made nice plaids, others drew stripes. But I wanted brushes that would produce gray-scale dithers, so that when the blt repeated the brush you would see one uniform pattern of points instead of wallpaper patterns. So I gave up and hand dithered it. The results of my intensive research efforts (I drew them with pencil on graph paper) are contained in a text file called PIXELLST.TXT, and the procedure that reads the contents of that file into the array **PixelSetSequence()** is called **CreatePixelSetSequence()** (Listing 7.7).

Listing 7.7   The CreatePixelSetSequence() Procedure from DSLVEXP.FRM.

```
Sub CreatePixelSetSequence ()
    Dim Counter As Integer
    Dim PixelNumberString As String * 5
    Const PixelListFile = 1

    Open "PixelLst.TXT" For Input As #PixelListFile
    For Counter = 1 To 64
        Input #PixelListFile, PixelNumberString
        PixelSetSequence(Counter) = Val(PixelNumberString)
        Next Counter

    End Sub
```

I've numbered the pixels from 1 to 64. I'll leave it to you to find the magic pattern and do away with this kluge.

The constant **NumberOfSteps** determines the number of pixels that are set to black at each step. I have set it to 8, so each successive brush adds 8 black pixels. If you set **NumberOfSteps** to 16, each brush will add 4 black pixels. The value of **NumberOfSteps** must divide evenly into 64. I believe my hand-picked pixel list works best for a value of 8 or 16.

> NOTE: *Let me remind you that DIB data begins with the last row, so row 0 in the* ***CreateDissolveBrush()*** *is actually row 7 on the screen. The whole pattern is upside down.*

Adding the Event Procedures

It's now time to add the five event procedures that we'll need. Once again, the brush meets blt and ROP in the event procedure **Picture2_Paint()** (Listing 7.8).

Listing 7.8 The Picture2_Paint() Event Procedure from DSLVEXP.FRM

```
Sub Picture2_Paint ()
    Dim hRgn As Integer
    Dim Dummy As Integer
    Dim hOldBrush As Integer

    hBrush = CreateDissolveBrush(DissolveStep)
    hOldBrush = SelectObject(Picture2.hDC, hBrush)
    Dummy = BitBlt(Picture2.hDC, 0, 0, Picture2.ScaleWidth,
            Picture2.ScaleHeight, Picture1.hDC, 0, 0, &HAC0744)
    Dummy = SelectObject(Picture2.hDC, hOldBrush)
    Dummy = DeleteObject%(hBrush)

    End Sub
```

With the form level variable **DissolveStep**, we create the appropriate brush. We then select it into the device context of Picture2, and **BitBlt()** the image over from Picture1, using ROP code &HAC0744. Finally, we replace the default **BLACK_BRUSH**, and delete the brush we created. The brushes live only briefly.

The rest of this program is easy. We'll need a trigger to get things going, and some way to fire off and keep track of the dissolve steps. For these tasks, we'll add a Command Button named DissolveButton and a Timer control. The **DissolveButton_Click()** event procedure starts the timer as Listing 7.9 indicates.

Listing 7.9 The DissolveButton_Click() Event Procedure from DSLVEXP.FRM

```
Sub DissolveButton_Click ()
    DissolveButton.Enabled = False
    Timer1.Enabled = True
    End Sub
```

The **Timer1_Timer()** event procedure advances the **DissolveStep** timer, as shown in Listing 7.10.

Listing 7.10 The Timer1_Timer() Event Procedure from DSLVEXP.FRM

```
Sub Timer1_Timer ()

    If DissolveStep < NumberOfSteps Then
        DissolveStep = DissolveStep + 1
        Picture2_Paint
     Else
        Timer1.Enabled = False
     End If
    End Sub
```

I've also added similar code to **Picture2_Click()** (Listing 7.11) so you can single-step through the dissolve. Just click on the Picture2 Command Button instead of the DissolveButton Command Button.

Listing 7.11   The Picture2_Click() Event Procedure from DSLVEXP.FRM

```
Sub Picture2_Click ()

    If DissolveStep < NumberOfSteps Then
        DissolveStep = DissolveStep + 1
        Picture2_Paint
    End If
End Sub
```

To complete the set of event procedures, add **Form_Load()** from Listing 7.12.

Listing 7.12   The Form_Load() Event Procedure from DSLVEXP.FRM

```
Sub Form_Load ()
    CreatePixelSetSequence
    DissolveStep = 0
    End Sub
```

Adding the Declarations

The dissolve project requires two sets of declarations. One set is placed in the DSLVEXP.FRM form (Listing 7.13) and the other set should be placed in the declarations section of DSLVEXP.BAS (Listing 7.14).

Listing 7.13   The Declarations Section from DSLVEXP.FRM

```
Option Explicit

Dim hBrush As Integer
Dim PixelSetSequence(64) As Integer
Dim DissolveStep As Integer
Const NumberOfSteps = 8
```

Listing 7.14   The Declarations Section from DSLVEXP.BAS

```
Option Explicit

Type BITMAPINFOHEADER
    biSize As Long
    biWidth As Long
    biHeight As Long
    biPlanes As Integer
```

```
        biBitCount As Integer
        biCompression As Long
        biSizeImage As Long
        biXPelsPerMeter As Long
        biYPelsPerMeter As Long
        biClrUsed As Long
        biClrImportant As Long
        End Type

    Type RGBQUAD
        rgbBlue As String * 1
        rgbGreen As String * 1
        rgbRed As String * 1
        rgbReserved As String * 1
        End Type

    Type BITMAPINFO
        bmiHeader As BITMAPINFOHEADER
        bmiColors(1) As RGBQUAD
        End Type


Declare Function CreateDIBitmap Lib "GDI" (ByVal hDC As Integer, lpInfoHeader As
    BITMAPINFOHEADER, ByVal dwUsage As Long, ByVal lpInitBits As String,
    lpInitInfo As BITMAPINFO, ByVal wUsage As Integer) As Integer
Declare Function CreatePatternBrush Lib "GDI" (ByVal hBitmap As Integer) As Integer
Declare Function DeleteObject Lib "GDI" (ByVal hObject As Integer) As Integer
Declare Function SelectObject Lib "GDI" (ByVal hDC As Integer, ByVal hObject As
    Integer) As Integer
Declare Function BitBlt Lib "GDI" (ByVal hDestDC As Integer, ByVal X As Integer,
    ByVal Y As Integer, ByVal nWidth As Integer, ByVal nHeight As Integer, ByVal
    hSrcDC As Integer, ByVal XSrc As Integer, ByVal YSrc As Integer, ByVal dwROP
    As Long) As Integer


Global Const SRCCOPY = &HCC0020
Global Const SRCPAINT = &HEE0086
Global Const SRCAND = &H8800C6
Global Const SRCINVERT = &H660046
Global Const SRCERASE = &H440328
Global Const NOTSRCCOPY = &H330008
Global Const NOTSRCERASE = &H1100A6
Global Const MERGECOPY = &HC000CA
Global Const MERGEPAINT = &HBB0226
Global Const PATCOPY = &HF00021
Global Const PATPAINT = &HFB0A09
Global Const PATINVERT = &H5A0049
Global Const DSTINVERT = &H550009
Global Const BLACKNESS = &H42&
Global Const WHITENESS = &HFF0062
Global Const BLACKONWHITE = 1
Global Const WHITEONBLACK = 2
Global Const COLORONCOLOR = 3
Global Const BI_RGB = 0&
Global Const BI_RLE8 = 1&
```

```
Global Const BI_RLE4 = 2&
Global Const TRANSPARENT = 1
Global Const OPAQUE = 2

Global Const CBM_INIT = &H4&

Global Const DIB_RGB_COLORS = 0
Global Const DIB_PAL_COLORS = 1
```

To run this program, you'll need a couple of images. For Picture1, select any 8-bit color bitmap. We haven't dealt with the color palette yet at all, so for Picture2 start with a bitmap that uses only the Windows reserved colors—try a Windows wallpaper bitmap, such as WINLOGO.BMP. Once you've installed the pictures, run the program.

Ghost of a Window

We started with a simple **BitBlt()** test program. It wasn't especially useful but it did show you how to use the blt functions. Then, we added the ability to dissolve from one Picture Box to another. Still not particularly useful—why would you want to dissolve to an image that already appears in the Picture Box next door? You wouldn't. But there is a way to make the source Picture Box invisible, and it doesn't require any changes to the program code.

DSLVEXP.FRM has two Picture Box controls, Picture1 and Picture2. Just change the **Visible** property of Picture1 to False, and change its **AutoRedraw** property to True, then run the program again. Picture1 will disappear from the form, but when you click the Do Dissolve Command Button, the image assigned to the

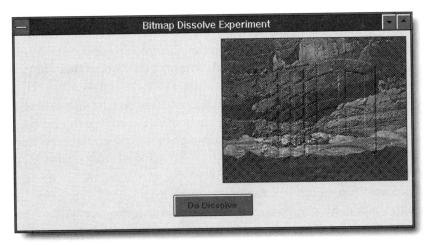

Figure 7.4   *DSLVEXP.FRM with an invisible Picture1.*

Picture property of Picture1 will still materialize in Picture2. Figure 7.4 shows this new approach. It looks as if we've pulled a rabbit out of our hat.

By activating its **AutoRedraw** property and making it invisible, we turned a simple Picture Box control into a special kind of GDI phantom, known as a *memory device context.* Just like a screen device context, we can draw on a memory device context, and we can transfer pixel data to or from its bitmap with blt functions. We just can't see it. We'll take a closer look at memory device contexts in the next project.

Dueling Palettes Revisited

The dissolve project we just created looked pretty good. Unfortunately, it's easy to break. To see what I mean, set the **Picture** property of Picture2 to any 256 color image, then run the program again. If both Picture controls are visible, you'll see that the colors of only one or the other are active in the system palette, so one image will look as if it's been re-touched by Andy Warhol. The dissolve doesn't improve the situation. Although the final image contains only the pixels of the source, their colors all come from the logical palette that VB selected into the device context of Picture2 when it loaded the original bitmap. The pixels in both images belong to DDBs. By definition, all bitmaps become device dependent by the time they reach the display. The pixel values in those bitmaps reference system palette entries and not logical palette entries. So the color of any given pixel will depend on the color that occupies the entry in the system palette referenced by the pixel value, even if that color happens to belong to another bitmap.

As I explained in the previous chapter, a palette-aware window should respond to certain messages sent by the Palette Manager by attempting to temporarily remap its logical palette to the current system palette. VB Picture controls do not always do this. Instead, whenever a Picture Box control loses the focus to another window that uses the palette, its colors may go haywire.

Copying the bitmap to a new device context won't fix the problem. The **BitBlt()** function simply copies pixel values from the source device context to the destination device context, which means that if they reference nonsensical colors to begin with, they will point to the same nonsensical colors when they arrive in their new locations. To solve this problem, we have to grab the DIBs before VB gets hold of them and turns them into DDBs. We can then remap the pixels by comparing the color tables in the two DIBs. That may sound like a time-consuming job, but the API includes a blt function that can convert the images to DDBs, combine their pixels with raster operations, and map their colors to a common palette all at the same time. In the next project, I'll show you how to suck a DIB right out of its file and blast it on to the screen with the hardest-working blt function of all. By the time we finish, we'll be doing complete 256-color digital dissolves.

Dissolve-in-a-Box

1. Create the form DSLVEXP.FRM and add its code (Listing 7.15).
2. Add the code for the DIB2.BAS code module (Listing 7.16 and 7.17).
3. Add the code for the PALETTE.BAS code module (Listing 7.18).
4. Add the code for the DISSOLVE.BAS code module (Listings 7.19 through 7.23).
5. Add the declarations section for GLBLMEM.BAS (Listing 7.24).

Creating the Amazing Dissolve

To demonstrate the code modules that perform the dissolve, we'll create a simple form with three controls, a Picture Box, a Command Button, and a Timer. When the form first loads, it will dissolve the Picture Box from its pure background color to the first image. When you click on the Command Button, the first image will dissolve to a second image, as shown in Figure 7.5.

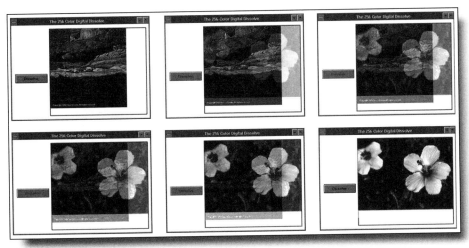

Figure 7.5 *A dissolve in progress in the form DISSOLVE.FRM from the program DISSOLVE.MAK.*

If you take a look at Listing 7.15 you'll see that DISSOLVE.FRM contains little code; it simply calls functions and subprocedures in the other code modules.

Listing 7.15 The DISSOLVE.FRM Program Code

```
VERSION 2.00
Begin Form DslvF1
    AutoRedraw        =    -1   'True
    Caption           =    "The 256 Color Digital Dissolve"
    ClientHeight      =    6780
    ClientLeft        =    312
    ClientTop         =    1800
    ClientWidth       =    11268
    Height            =    7200
    Left              =    264
    LinkTopic         =    "Form1"
    ScaleHeight       =    6780
    ScaleWidth        =    11268
    Top               =    1428
    Width             =    11364
    Begin Timer DissolveTimer
        Enabled       =    0     'False
        Interval      =    56
        Left          =    1140
        Top           =    3900
    End
    Begin CommandButton DissolveButton
        Caption       =    "Dissolve"
        Enabled       =    0     'False
        Height        =    435
        Left          =    660
        TabIndex      =    1
        Top           =    2460
        Width         =    1635
    End
    Begin PictureBox Picture1
        Height        =    6375
        Left          =    3300
        ScaleHeight   =    529
        ScaleMode     =    3    'Pixel
        ScaleWidth    =    629
        TabIndex      =    0
        Top           =    180
        Width         =    7575
    End
End
Option Explicit

Sub DissolveButton_Click ()
    'DissolveToImage Left$(App.Path, 2) & "\vbmagic\images\housrock.bmp",
    DissolveTimer, DissolveButton
```

```
   'DissolveToImage Left$(App.Path, 2) & "\vbmagic\images\kaibab.bmp",
    DissolveTimer, DissolveButton
   'DissolveToImage Left$(App.Path, 2) & "\vbmagic\images\sad1fall.bmp",
    DissolveTimer, DissolveButton
   DissolveToImage Left$(App.Path, 2) & "\vbmagic\images\hibiscus.bmp",
    DissolveTimer, DissolveButton
   End Sub

Sub DissolveTimer_Timer ()
   DoDissolveStep Picture1, DissolveTimer, DissolveButton
   End Sub

Sub Form_Load ()
   InitializeDissolve
   DissolveToImage Left$(App.Path, 2) & "\vbmagic\images\housrock.bmp",
    DissolveTimer, DissolveButton
   End Sub

Sub Form_QueryUnload (Cancel As Integer)
   DissolveUnload Picture1
   End Sub

Sub Picture1_Click ()
   DoDissolveStep Picture1, DissolveTimer, DissolveButton
   End Sub

Sub Picture1_Paint ()
   DissolvePaint Picture1
   End Sub
```

The code that does the real work resides in four modules: DISSOLVE.BAS, PALETTE.BAS, DIB2.BAS, and GLBLMEM.BAS. The majority of the code is found in the ten functions assigned to DISSOLVE.BAS. You should already be familiar with two of the functions in DISSOLVE.BAS—**CreatePixelSetSequence()** and **CreateDissolveBrush()**—since we used them in the previous project. The code modules—DSLVEXP.FRM, DIB2.BAS, and PALETTE.BAS—contain only a few functions and some declarations. GLBLMEM.BAS just contains the declarations for eight API functions and two constants. Let's put this project together by writing each of the four code modules.

Reading Bitmaps—DIB2.BAS

We now need to add a set of functions for reading and manipulating bitmaps and their palettes. To resolve the palette debacle we're going to relieve VB of its artistic responsibilities by extracting images ourselves from their disk files, loading them into memory, then blting them to their device contexts. The procedure that reads DIB files is called **ReadBitmapFile()**, and you'll find it in DIB2.BAS (Listing 7.16).

Listing 7.16　The ReadBitmapFile() Procedure from DIB2.BAS

```
Sub ReadBitmapFile (ByVal FileName As String, bmFileHeader As BITMAPFILEHEADER,
    bmInfo As BITMAPINFO, hPixelData As Integer)

    Const BitmapFile% = 1
    Const BufferSize% = 1024
    Dim wPixelDataSelector As Integer
    Dim PixelBytesToRead As Long
    Dim PixelBuffer As String * 1024
    Dim BytesStored As Long
    Dim MemOffset As Long

    Open FileName For Binary As BitmapFile%
    ' Read the header structures.
    Get BitmapFile%, 1, bmFileHeader
    Get BitmapFile%, Len(bmFileHeader) + 1, bmInfo
    PixelBytesToRead = bmInfo.bmiHeader.biSizeImage
    MemOffset = 0
    ' Allocate memory on Windows' global heap.
    hPixelData = GlobalAlloc(GMEM_MOVEABLE Or GMEM_ZEROINIT, PixelBytesToRead)
    wPixelDataSelector = GlobalHandleToSel(hPixelData)
    Do While PixelBytesToRead > 0
        Get BitmapFile%, , PixelBuffer
        BytesStored = MemoryWrite(wPixelDataSelector, MemOffset, ByVal
                        PixelBuffer, MinLong(BufferSize%, PixelBytesToRead))
        MemOffset = MemOffset + BufferSize%
        PixelBytesToRead = PixelBytesToRead - BufferSize%
        Loop
    Close
End Sub
```

Only three commands are needed to open the file and read the header information:

```
Open FileName For Binary As BitmapFile%
' Read the header structures.
Get BitmapFile%, 1, bmFileHeader
Get BitmapFile%, Len(bmFileHeader) + 1, bmInfo
```

The bulk of the code in this procedure deals with the pixel data. The field **biSizeImage** in the **BITMAPINFOHEADER** structure tells us how many bytes to read. That's where we begin to run into one of VB's limitations. Bitmaps tend to be large. The bitmap we built to create the dissolve brush was only 32 bytes, so we used a string as a buffer. But pictures often run into the hundreds of thousands of bytes. VB strings can't hold more than about 65,000 bytes. We need to find a bigger bucket.

We could try to use an array. VB arrays can exceed 65,000 bytes, as long as they don't include more than 65,536 elements. For example, you could declare an array of long integers with a dimension of 65,536 (actually dimensioned with a range of -32,768 to 32,767) elements, for a total of 262,144 bytes. But then you have to mess with offsets and subrecords. C and Pascal programmers don't have to fool around with this kind of nonsense because they can place large objects on the *heap*. The heap is the global memory that Windows makes available to programs for temporary data storage. When you create a string in VB, for example, it goes on the heap. VB does all the work of requesting the appropriate amount of space from Windows and keeping track of its location so you can just use assignment statements to store and retrieve your data. Once again, however, VB assumes its role as the mother of all programmers and denies us direct access to the heap. You can declare all the variables you want; VB will cast them out into memory and reel them back in for you, but you can't go wading off into the lake yourself.

But we VB programmers also need a way to manipulate large binary objects, and fortunately Windows gives us the means to do so. To reserve and release memory, you call the API functions **GlobalAlloc()** and **GlobalFree()**:

```
Declare Function GlobalAlloc Lib "Kernel" (ByVal wFlags As Integer, ByVal
   dwBytes As Long) As Integer
Declare Function GlobalFree Lib "Kernel" (ByVal hMem As Integer) As Integer
```

The argument **wFlags** will accept any of fourteen available flags. We need only two of them, **GMEM_ZEROINIT**, which has a value of &H40, and **GMEM_MOVEABLE**, which has a value of &H2. The first flag causes Windows to initialize every byte in the allocated block to &H00. The second flag tells Windows that it can move the block of memory around if it needs to. Because Windows is a multi-tasking environment, any active program can allocate and release memory as it runs. Without proper management, the heap could eventually become like swiss cheese and none of the active programs could find a contiguous chunk large enough to hold its data. Windows would be forced to return an Out of Memory error, even if plenty of memory is still available. To keep that from happening, Windows frequently asks everyone to scoot over and fill in the empty seats. For some applications, that could become a problem, so Windows assumes it can't touch your memory block unless you flag it with **GMEM_MOVEABLE**. Most of the time you reference global memory by way of its handle, so you really shouldn't care where it happens to lay out on the heap. In our program, we'll let the Windows memory manager do its work.

The second argument, **dwBytes**, specifies the amount of memory to allocate. If Windows can find enough space to fulfill your request, it returns a handle to the memory block. If not, it returns zero, in which case you'll probably need to notify the user that the program cannot continue unless they can free some memory by closing some other applications.

GlobalFree() does just the opposite. You pass this function the handle to your memory block, and it returns zero if Windows successfully released it. If not, it throws the handle back.

With a block of global memory in hand, our next step is to store data there. In the Holy Trinity languages you have to jump through all kinds hoops to snag the memory, lock it in place, get a *huge pointer* to it, calculate *offsets* into it, and so forth. Not so from VB. Instead, Windows provides a shortcut in the form of a library called TOOLHELP.DLL (yes, HTL programmers can use this library too). Instead of the pointers familiar to HTL programmers, we can use three of the functions in the ToolHelp DLL to manipulate a block of global memory with a *selector*. This less direct method of reading and writing memory may, in some cases, sacrifice a little performance, but it also helps prevent us from making serious errors that could crash other programs, or even Windows itself. It also requires fewer steps.

To get a selector for a memory block, we pass its handle to a ToolHelp function called **GlobalHandleToSel()**:

```
Declare Function GlobalHandleToSel Lib "ToolHelp.DLL" (ByVal hMem As Integer) As
    Integer
```

A selector is like a cross between a handle and a long pointer in that it refers to the block of memory indirectly. That is, the selector is not the physical address at which the block begins. Instead, it references an entry in the *descriptor table*, a place where the operating system keeps track of memory blocks. The entries in the descriptor table hold the physical addresses of all the *segments* that belong to any given block of memory.

The mechanics of memory management in Windows can become pretty complicated. But we can sidestep them by letting the ToolHelp functions handle them for us. Once we have a selector for our memory block, we can write to and read from it with a pair of functions called **MemoryWrite()** and **MemoryRead()**, much like we do with a disk file.

```
Declare Function MemoryWrite Lib "ToolHelp.DLL" (ByVal wSel As Integer, ByVal
    dwOffSet As Long, lpvBuf As Any, ByVal dwcb As Long) As Long
Declare Function MemoryRead Lib "ToolHelp.DLL" (ByVal wSel As Integer, ByVal
    dwOffSet As Long, lpvBuf As Any, ByVal dwcb As Long) As Long
```

In the first parameter, **wSel**, we pass the selector returned by **GlobalHandleToSel()**. **dwOffSet** indicates the offset into the memory block where we want to begin reading or writing. An offset is not the same as a position. The 500th byte has an offset of 499, in other words, 499 bytes from the beginning. To read or write from the first byte, pass a **dwOffSet** of 0. In **lpvBuf** we have to pass a pointer to a buffer. **MemoryWrite()** will copy the contents of the buffer to the global memory block; **MemoryRead()** will copy data from the global memory block to the buffer. The last parameter, **dwcb**, specifies the number of bytes to read or write.

I've used a fixed-length string called **PixelBuffer** as the data buffer. When you open a file in Binary mode, the **Get** statement will read a number of bytes from the file equivalent to the length of the string passed as the buffer. When the buffer size exceeds the remaining number of bytes in the file, **Get** will copy whatever remains into the buffer. In the declarations for **MemoryWrite()** and **MemoryRead()**, you'll notice that **dwcb** is declared as **Any**. When I call **MemoryWrite()** from **ReadBitmapFile()**, I use the **ByVal** keyword to convert the contents of **PixelBuffer** into a long pointer to a null-terminated string, also known as a C string (we used the same technique in Chapter 3).

Wrapping Up DIB2.BAS

DIB2.BAS also contains a "Min" function, which will return the lesser of two long integers passed as arguments, along with the DIB-related declarations (Listing 7.17).

Listing 7.17   The Function MinLong() and the Declarations Section from DIB2.BAS

```
Option Explicit

Type BITMAPINFOHEADER
     biSize          As Long
     biWidth         As Long
     biHeight        As Long
     biPlanes        As Integer
     biBitCount      As Integer
     biCompression   As Long
     biSizeImage     As Long
     biXPelsPerMeter As Long
     biYPelsPerMeter As Long
     biClrUsed       As Long
     biClrImportant  As Long
     End Type

Type RGBQUAD
     rgbBlue         As String * 1
     rgbGreen        As String * 1
```

```
    rgbRed          As String * 1
    rgbReserved     As String * 1
    End Type


Type BITMAPINFO
    bmiHeader         As BITMAPINFOHEADER
    bmiColors(0 To 255)  As RGBQUAD
    End Type


Type INDEXBITMAPINFO
    bmiHeader As BITMAPINFOHEADER
    bmiColorIndexes(0 To 255) As Integer
    End Type


Type BITMAPFILEHEADER
    bfType          As Integer
    bfSize          As Long
    bfReserved1     As Integer
    bfReserved2     As Integer
    bfOffBits       As Long
    End Type


Global Const SRCCOPY = &HCC0020
Global Const SRCPAINT = &HEE0086
Global Const SRCAND = &H8800C6
Global Const SRCINVERT = &H660046
Global Const SRCERASE = &H440328
Global Const NOTSRCCOPY = &H330008
Global Const NOTSRCERASE = &H1100A6
Global Const MERGECOPY = &HC000CA
Global Const MERGEPAINT = &HBB0226
Global Const PATCOPY = &HF00021
Global Const PATPAINT = &HFB0A09
Global Const PATINVERT = &H5A0049
Global Const DSTINVERT = &H550009
Global Const BLACKNESS = &H42&
Global Const WHITENESS = &HFF0062
Global Const BLACKONWHITE = 1
Global Const WHITEONBLACK = 2
Global Const COLORONCOLOR = 3
Global Const BI_RGB = 0&
Global Const BI_RLE8 = 1&
Global Const BI_RLE4 = 2&
Global Const TRANSPARENT = 1
Global Const OPAQUE = 2

Global Const CBM_INIT = &H4&

Declare Function CreateCompatibleDC Lib "GDI" (ByVal hDC As Integer) As Integer
Declare Function DeleteDC Lib "GDI" (ByVal hDC As Integer) As Integer
Declare Function CreateCompatibleBitmap Lib "GDI" (ByVal hDC As Integer, ByVal
    nWidth As Integer, ByVal nHeight As Integer) As Integer
Declare Function CreateDIBitmap Lib "GDI" (ByVal hDC As Integer, lpInfoHeader As
```

```
    BITMAPINFOHEADER, ByVal dwUsage As Long, ByVal lpInitBits As String,
    lpInitInfo As BITMAPINFO, ByVal wUsage As Integer) As Integer
Declare Function CreateDIBitmapByPal Lib "GDI" Alias "CreateDIBitmap" (ByVal hDC As
    Integer, lpInfoHeader As BITMAPINFOHEADER, ByVal dwUsage As Long, ByVal
    lpInitBits As String, lpInitInfo As INDEXBITMAPINFO, ByVal wUsage As Integer) As Integer
Declare Function DeleteObject Lib "GDI" (ByVal hObject As Integer) As Integer
Declare Function SelectObject Lib "GDI" (ByVal hDC As Integer, ByVal hObject As
    Integer) As Integer
Declare Function BitBlt Lib "GDI" (ByVal hDestDC As Integer, ByVal X As Integer,
    ByVal Y As Integer, ByVal nWidth As Integer, ByVal nHeight As Integer, ByVal
    hSrcDC As Integer, ByVal XSrc As Integer, ByVal YSrc As Integer, ByVal dwROP
    As Long) As Integer
Declare Function SetDIBitsToDevice Lib "GDI" (ByVal hDC As Integer, ByVal DestX
    As Integer, ByVal DestY As Integer, ByVal nWidth As Integer, ByVal nHeight As
    Integer, ByVal SrcX As Integer, ByVal SrcY As Integer, ByVal nStartScan As
    Integer, ByVal nNumScans As Integer, ByVal lpBits As Long, lpBitsInfo As
    BITMAPINFO, ByVal wUsage As Integer) As Integer
Declare Function StretchDIBits Lib "GDI" (ByVal hDC As Integer, ByVal DestX As
    Integer, ByVal DestY As Integer, ByVal nDestWidth As Integer, ByVal
    nDestHeight As Integer, ByVal SrcX As Integer, ByVal SrcY As Integer, ByVal
    nSrcWidth As Integer, ByVal nSrcHeight As Integer, ByVal lpBits As Long,
    lpBitsInfo As BITMAPINFO, ByVal wUsage As Integer, ByVal dwROP As Long) As Integer


Function MinLong (A As Long, B As Long)
    If A < B Then
        MinLong = A
      Else
        MinLong = B
      End If
    End Function
```

Inside PALETTE.BAS

PALETTE.BAS will require one procedure—**ConstructPaletteFromColorTable()**.
Of course, we'll also need to include some declarations in this module. Listing
7.18 shows the complete code for PALETTE.BAS.

Listing 7.18   The Declarations Section and the ConstructPaletteFromColorTable() Procedure from PALETTE.BAS

```
Option Explicit

Type PALETTEENTRY
    peRed As String * 1
    peGreen As String * 1
    peBlue As String * 1
    peFlags As String * 1
    End Type

Type LOGPALETTE
    palVersion As Integer
```

```
        palNumEntries As Integer
        palPalEntry(255) As PALETTEENTRY
        End Type

Type ColorSteps
    iRed As Integer
    iGreen As Integer
    iBlue As Integer
    End Type


Global Const BLACK_BRUSH = 4
Global Const DEFAULT_PALETTE = 15
Global Const PC_RESERVED = &H1  '  palette index used for animation
Global Const CF_PALETTE = 9
Global Const DIB_RGB_COLORS = 0 '  color table in RGBTriples
Global Const DIB_PAL_COLORS = 1


Declare Function SelectPalette Lib "User" (ByVal hDC As Integer, ByVal hPalette
    As Integer, ByVal bForceBackground As Integer) As Integer
Declare Function RealizePalette Lib "User" (ByVal hDC As Integer) As Integer
Declare Function GetDC Lib "User" (ByVal hWnd As Integer) As Integer
Declare Function ReleaseDC Lib "User" (ByVal hWnd As Integer, ByVal hDC As
    Integer) As Integer
Declare Function CreateSolidBrush Lib "GDI" (ByVal crColor As Long) As Integer
Declare Function SelectObject Lib "GDI" (ByVal hDC As Integer, ByVal hObject As
    Integer) As Integer
Declare Function Rectangle Lib "GDI" (ByVal hDC As Integer, ByVal X1 As Integer,
    ByVal Y1 As Integer, ByVal X2 As Integer, ByVal Y2 As Integer) As Integer
Declare Function DeleteObject Lib "GDI" (ByVal hObject As Integer) As Integer
Declare Function GetStockObject Lib "GDI" (ByVal nIndex As Integer) As Integer
Declare Function GetPaletteEntries Lib "GDI" (ByVal hPalette As Integer, ByVal
    wStartIndex As Integer, ByVal wNumEntries As Integer, lpPaletteEntries As
    PALETTEENTRY) As Integer
Declare Function SetPaletteEntries Lib "GDI" (ByVal hPalette As Integer, ByVal
    wStartIndex As Integer, ByVal wNumEntries As Integer, lpPaletteEntries As
    PALETTEENTRY) As Integer
Declare Function CreatePalette Lib "GDI" (lpLogPalette As LOGPALETTE) As Integer
' This function isn't used in this program, but it's a member of the family:
' Declare Sub AnimatePalette Lib "GDI" (ByVal hPalette As Integer, ByVal
    wStartIndex As Integer, ByVal wNumEntries As Integer, lpPaletteColors As
    PALETTEENTRY)


Global ColorSelected As Long
Global hSystemPalette As Integer
Global hCurrentPalette As Integer
Global CurrentPaletteEntry As PALETTEENTRY
Global NewPaletteEntry As PALETTEENTRY
Global PaletteEntries(256) As PALETTEENTRY


Sub ConstructPaletteFromColorTable (ColorTable() As RGBQUAD, LogicalPalette As
    LOGPALETTE)
    Dim Counter As Integer
    Dim TempString As String
```

```
     TempString = ""
     For Counter = 0 To 255
         LogicalPalette.palPalEntry(Counter).peRed = ColorTable(Counter).rgbRed
         LogicalPalette.palPalEntry(Counter).peGreen = ColorTable(Counter).rgbGreen
         LogicalPalette.palPalEntry(Counter).peBlue = ColorTable(Counter).rgbBlue
         If (Counter > 9) And (Counter < 246) Then
             LogicalPalette.palPalEntry(Counter).peFlags = Chr$(PC_RESERVED)
         Else
             LogicalPalette.palPalEntry(Counter).peFlags = Chr$(0)
         End If
     Next Counter
     LogicalPalette.palVersion = &H300
     LogicalPalette.palNumEntries = 256
     End Sub
```

By declaring the first parameter of this function with a pair of empty paren-
theses, we enable VB to pass it an entire array, which, in this case, is the color
table from our freshly read DIB.

ConstructPaletteFromColorTable() translates color table entries into logical palette entries. The logical palette is also an array, but it belongs to the
Type-declared structure **LOGPALETTE**, so instead of passing in the array, we
just pass the entire structure by reference. That way we can also set **palVersion**
and **palNumEntries**, rounding out a complete logical palette.

We'll be calling **ConstructPaletteFromColorTable()** from the general
procedure **DissolveToImage()**, which we'll cover in the next section.

Inside DISSOLVE.BAS

We're now ready for the workhorse module. Here we have a lot of ground to
cover, so let's break the module into its different functions. We'll start by
making a subtle, but essential change to the function **CreateDissolveBrush()**,
as shown in Listing 7.19

Listing 7.19   The function CreateDissolveBrush() from DISSOLVE.BAS.

```
Function CreateDissolveBrush (DissolveStep As Integer, ByVal hDC As Integer) As
    Integer
    Dim hCompBitmap As Integer
    Dim BrushBitmapInfo As INDEXBITMAPINFO
    Dim Counter As Integer
    Dim PixelData As String * 32
    Dim Dummy As Integer
    Dim Row As Integer
    Dim Column As Integer

    BrushBitmapInfo.bmiHeader.biSize = 40
    BrushBitmapInfo.bmiHeader.biWidth = 8
```

```
BrushBitmapInfo.bmiHeader.biHeight = 8
BrushBitmapInfo.bmiHeader.biPlanes = 1
BrushBitmapInfo.bmiHeader.biBitCount = 1
BrushBitmapInfo.bmiHeader.biCompression = 0
BrushBitmapInfo.bmiHeader.biSizeImage = 0
BrushBitmapInfo.bmiHeader.biXPelsPerMeter = 0
BrushBitmapInfo.bmiHeader.biYPelsPerMeter = 0
BrushBitmapInfo.bmiHeader.biClrUsed = 0
BrushBitmapInfo.bmiHeader.biClrImportant = 0

BrushBitmapInfo.bmiColorIndexes(0) = 0
BrushBitmapInfo.bmiColorIndexes(1) = 255

For Counter = 0 To 7
    Mid$(PixelData, Counter * 4 + 1, 1) = Chr$(&HFF)
    Next Counter
For Counter = 1 To DissolveStep * (64 / NumberOfSteps)
    Row = (PixelSetSequence(Counter) - 1) \ 8
    Column = (PixelSetSequence(Counter) - 1) Mod 8
    Mid$(PixelData, Row * 4 + 1, 1) = Chr$(Asc(Mid$(PixelData, Row * 4 + 1,
        1)) And ((Not (2 ^ (7 - Column))) - &HFF00))
    Next Counter

hCompBitmap = CreateDIBitmapByPal(hDC, BrushBitmapInfo.bmiHeader, CBM_INIT,
            PixelData, BrushBitmapInfo, DIB_PAL_COLORS)
CreateDissolveBrush = CreatePatternBrush(hCompBitmap)
Dummy = DeleteObject%(hCompBitmap)
End Function
```

As we discussed in the previous project, we normally create a bitmap by preparing a structure of type **BITMAPINFO**, which contains a **BITMAPINFOHEADER** followed by a color table in the form of an array of **RGBQUADs**. When the GDI converts this bitmap to a DDB, it maps the colors by matching the RGB values in the table to the RGB values in the currently realized logical palette. Here's the problem I discovered. Colors are matched in order, starting at the beginning of the palette. If the currently realized logical palette contains a pure white color entry in its non-reserved color list—the colors in entries 10 through 245—then when the color matching takes place, the white pixels in the monochrome bitmap will be set to reference that earlier entry instead of entry 255. When that happens, the ROPs will no longer be manipulating white pixels with values of 255, so the monochrome bitmap no longer functions as a mask.

Fortunately there is an alternate way to specify the color information. Instead of building a table of RGB values, we can create an array of 16-bit integers that specify color indexes into the currently realized logical palette. Oddly enough, although the Windows 3.1 Programmer's Reference clearly discusses this approach, there is no pre-defined structure, like **BITMAPINFO**, to handle a color palette index array. So I made one up:

```
Type INDEXBITMAPINFO
    bmiHeader As BITMAPINFOHEADER
    bmiColorIndexes(0 To 255) As Integer
    End Type
```

We declare the **BrushBitmapInfo** structure with this type:

```
Dim BrushBitmapInfo As INDEXBITMAPINFO
```

Then we set the color values to the palette entries for black and white:

```
BrushBitmapInfo.bmiColorIndexes(0) = 0
BrushBitmapInfo.bmiColorIndexes(1) = 255
```

And finally, we call **CreateDIBitmapByPal()**, an *alias* of the API function **CreateDIBitmap()**:

```
hCompBitmap = CreateDIBitmapByPal(hDC, BrushBitmapInfo.bmiHeader, CBM_INIT,
    PixelData, BrushBitmapInfo, DIB_PAL_COLORS)
```

Here's the declaration for the aliased form of the **CreateDIBitmap()** API function:

```
Declare Function CreateDIBitmapByPal Lib "GDI" Alias "CreateDIBitmap" (ByVal hDC As
    Integer, lpInfoHeader As BITMAPINFOHEADER, ByVal dwUsage As Long, ByVal lpInitBits
    As String, lpInitInfo As INDEXBITMAPINFO, ByVal wUsage As Integer) As Integer
```

In the **lpInitInfo** argument we pass the **INDEXBITMAPINFO** structure instead of **BITMAPINFO**, and we set the **wUsage** parameter to **DIB_PAL_COLORS** to indicate that the color table contains integer palette indices.

Next, we'll write **CreatePaletteSequenceArray()** (Listing 7.20), which will create the series of palettes we'll need to handle the dissolve.

Listing 7.20   The CreatePaletteSequenceArray() procedure from DISSOLVE.BAS

```
Sub CreatePaletteSequenceArray (CurrentPalette As LOGPALETTE, NewPalette As LOGPALETTE)
    '   This procedure will take the palette belonging to
    '   the currently displayed image, and the palette
    '   belonging to the new image, and will construct a
    '   series of six intermediate palettes.  The eight
    '   palettes will then be used to soften the transition
    '   between images.
    '
    '   The palette array is declared globally.

    Dim PalCounter As Integer
    Dim PalEntryCounter As Integer
```

```
    If CurrentPalette.palNumEntries <> 256 Then
        LSet Palettes(1) = NewPalette
      Else
        LSet Palettes(1) = CurrentPalette
      End If
    LSet Palettes(8) = NewPalette
    For PalEntryCounter = 0 To 255
        PalStepArray(PalEntryCounter).Red =
          (Asc(NewPalette.palPalEntry(PalEntryCounter).peRed) -
          Asc(Palettes(1).palPalEntry(PalEntryCounter).peRed)) \ 7
        PalStepArray(PalEntryCounter).Green =
          (Asc(NewPalette.palPalEntry(PalEntryCounter).peGreen) -
          Asc(Palettes(1).palPalEntry(PalEntryCounter).peGreen)) \ 7
        PalStepArray(PalEntryCounter).Blue =
          (Asc(NewPalette.palPalEntry(PalEntryCounter).peBlue) -
          Asc(Palettes(1).palPalEntry(PalEntryCounter).peBlue)) \ 7
      Next PalEntryCounter
    For PalCounter = 2 To 7
      For PalEntryCounter = 0 To 255
          Palettes(PalCounter).palPalEntry(PalEntryCounter).peRed =
            Chr$(MaxInt(MinInt((Asc(Palettes(PalCounter -
            1).palPalEntry(PalEntryCounter).peRed) +
            PalStepArray(PalEntryCounter).Red), 255), 0))
          Palettes(PalCounter).palPalEntry(PalEntryCounter).peGreen =
            Chr$(MaxInt(MinInt((Asc(Palettes(PalCounter -
            1).palPalEntry(PalEntryCounter).peGreen) +
            PalStepArray(PalEntryCounter).Green), 255), 0))
          Palettes(PalCounter).palPalEntry(PalEntryCounter).peBlue =
            Chr$(MaxInt(MinInt((Asc(Palettes(PalCounter -
            1).palPalEntry(PalEntryCounter).peBlue) +
            PalStepArray(PalEntryCounter).Blue), 255), 0))
          If (PalEntryCounter > 9) And (PalEntryCounter < 246) Then
              Palettes(PalCounter).palPalEntry(PalEntryCounter).peFlags =
                Chr$(PC_RESERVED)
            Else
              Palettes(PalCounter).palPalEntry(PalEntryCounter).peFlags = Chr$(0)
            End If
        Next PalEntryCounter
      Palettes(PalCounter).palVersion = &H300
      Palettes(PalCounter).palNumEntries = 256
      Next PalCounter
    End Sub
```

To understand what this procedure does, imagine that a particular palette entry, say entry 217, contains a color consisting of pure red in the palette of the current image and pure blue in the palette of the new image (this is unlikely, or at least unnecessary in the real world because the reserved colors include pure red and pure blue at palette entries 249 and 252). In seven steps, we want to gradually change the color &H00 &H00 &HFF into the color &HFF &H00 &H00. If you take the difference of the red component in the two colors, you get &HFF, or decimal 255. 255 divided by 7 equals approximately

Table 7.1   *A Seven-Step Transition from Pure Red to Pure Blue*

Palette Number	Blue Component	Green Component	Red Component
1	0	0	255
2	36	0	219
3	72	0	183
4	108	0	147
5	144	0	111
6	180	0	75
7	216	0	39
8	255	0	0

36. So with each step we need to add decimal value -36 to the red component. For the blue component, we do just the reverse. The blue component of palette entry 217 begins with a value of 0, and must end at decimal 255, so we need to add +36 at each step. The eight versions of palette entry 217 would contain the values that appear in Table 7.1.

In the final step of the dissolve, we just jump directly to the correct palette for the new image instead of adding the palette step values.

The first loop in **CreatePaletteSequenceArray()** builds an array of these step values, one for each red, green, and blue component of each palette entry for a total of 768 values. The second loop uses these values to build the six intermediate logical palettes.

Notice that I've set the flags of the 236 modifiable colors to **PC_RESERVED**. Although this program doesn't use **AnimatePalette()** to shift colors, the **PC_RESERVED** flags prevents colors from mapping too wildly (when we're done, try setting the flag both ways to compare the results).

At this point, we have a DIB waiting in the wings, a set of palettes to ease the transition from one image to the other, and a function to generate the brushes as we step through the dissolve. We'll pull everything together in a procedure called **DissolvePaint()** as shown in Listing 7.21.

Listing 7.21   The DissolvePaint() Procedure from DISSOLVE.BAS

```
Sub DissolvePaint (DissolvePicture As PictureBox)
    Dim hMemDC As Integer
    Dim hMemBitmap As Integer
    Dim hOldMemBitmap As Integer
    Dim ErrCode As Integer
    Dim lpDIBits As Long
    Dim lpOldDIBits As Long
```

```
Dim hOldPalette As Integer
Dim hDisolveBrush As Integer
Dim hOldBrush As Integer
Dim OldImage As Integer
Dim OldImageWidth As Integer
Dim OldImageHeight As Integer
Dim NewImageWidth As Integer
Dim NewImageHeight As Integer


' Builds a memory device context where the dissolve
' will be performed.
hMemDC = CreateCompatibleDC(DissolvePicture.hDC)
hMemBitmap = CreateCompatibleBitmap(DissolvePicture.hDC,
          DissolvePicture.ScaleWidth, DissolvePicture.ScaleHeight)
hOldMemBitmap = SelectObject(hMemDC, hMemBitmap)
ErrCode = Rectangle(hMemDC, 0, 0, DissolvePicture.ScaleWidth,
        DissolvePicture.ScaleHeight)


' Switch the context index.
OldImage = (NewImage + 1) Mod 2
' Assign image dimension info to shorthand reference variables.
OldImageWidth = bmInfo(OldImage).bmiHeader.biWidth
OldImageHeight = bmInfo(OldImage).bmiHeader.biHeight
NewImageWidth = bmInfo(NewImage).bmiHeader.biWidth
NewImageHeight = bmInfo(NewImage).bmiHeader.biHeight


' Select the palette activated by DoDissolveStep() into
' the memory and display device contexts.
ErrCode = SelectPalette(hMemDC, hPalette, False)
hOldPalette = SelectPalette(DissolvePicture.hDC, hPalette, False)
ErrCode = RealizePalette(DissolvePicture.hDC)
' Throw away the palette belonging to the previous step or image,
' unless this is the first image (you can't delete the default palette).
If (hOldPalette <> GetStockObject(DEFAULT_PALETTE)
And (hOldPalette <> hPalette) Then
    ErrCode = DeleteObject(hOldPalette)
  End If
' Lock the memory blocks that contain the pixel data for the two images.
lpDIBits = GlobalLock(hPixelData(NewImage))
If hPixelData(OldImage) <> 0 Then
    lpOldDIBits = GlobalLock(hPixelData(OldImage))
  End If
If lpDIBits <> 0 Then
    ' Create the appropriate dissolve brush for the current step,
    ' and select it into the MemDC.
    hDisolveBrush = CreateDissolveBrush(DissolveStepForPainting,
                DissolvePicture.hDC)
    hOldBrush = SelectObject(hMemDC, hDisolveBrush)
    ' Paint the old image into the MemDC with an inverted brush.
    If (hPixelData(OldImage) <> 0) Then
        ErrCode = StretchDIBits(hMemDC, 0, 0, OldImageWidth, OldImageHeight,
                0, 0, OldImageWidth, OldImageHeight, lpOldDIBits,
                bmInfo(OldImage), DIB_RGB_COLORS, &HCF0224) ' Performs ROP SPno
      End If
```

```
' Paint the new image into the MemDC with the dissolve ROP.
ErrCode = StretchDIBits(hMemDC, 0, 0, NewImageWidth, NewImageHeight, 0, 0,
            NewImageWidth, NewImageHeight, lpDIBits, bmInfo(NewImage),
            DIB_RGB_COLORS, &HAC0744) ' Performs ROP SPDSxax
' Rapidly transfer the contents of the MemDC to the screen.
ErrCode = BitBlt(DissolvePicture.hDC, 0, 0, DissolvePicture.ScaleWidth,
            DissolvePicture.ScaleHeight, hMemDC, 0, 0, SRCCOPY)
' Unlock the global memory blocks.
ErrCode = GlobalUnlock(hPixelData(NewImage))
If hPixelData(OldImage) <> 0 Then
    ErrCode = GlobalUnlock(hPixelData(OldImage))
  End If
' Replace the default brush in the MemDC and
' delete the dissolve brush.
ErrCode = SelectObject(hMemDC, hOldBrush)
ErrCode = DeleteObject(hDissolveBrush)
Else
  DissolvePicture.Print "Unable to Set Bits!"
End If
' Delete the MemDC, then delete the MemBitmap.
ErrCode = SelectObject(hMemDC, hOldMemBitmap)
ErrCode = SelectPalette(hMemDC, GetStockObject(DEFAULT_PALETTE), False)
ErrCode = DeleteDC(hMemDC)
ErrCode = DeleteObject(hMemBitmap)

End Sub
```

The first part of **DissolvePaint()** creates a memory device context.

```
hMemDC = CreateCompatibleDC(DissolvePicture.hDC)
hMemBitmap = CreateCompatibleBitmap(DissolvePicture.hDC,
            DissolvePicture.ScaleWidth, DissolvePicture.ScaleHeight)
hOldMemBitmap = SelectObject(hMemDC, hMemBitmap)
ErrCode = Rectangle(hMemDC, 0, 0, DissolvePicture.ScaleWidth,
                    DissolvePicture.ScaleHeight)
```

A memory device context is like a shadow of a screen device context. You can perform all the same operations on a memory device context that you can perform on the screen, but they're invisible. The only way to see the bitmap created or changed in a memory device context is to transfer the image to a visible device context, usually the screen. I've chosen to use a memory device context as a scratch pad for the dissolve because it helps disguise some of the slower painting that occurs with complex raster operations. It still takes longer than straight **SRCCOPY** blting, but the messy mechanics remain hidden backstage. Then when we're done with each dissolve step, we can use **SRCCOPY** and **BitBlt()** to rapidly transfer the resulting image to the screen.

There is another, perhaps more important reason for using a memory device context. Windows is a multitasking environment. When one window covers another, the covered bitmap is lost. When its parent window rises back to the top of the z order, it needs some way to redraw the rectangular area, or areas, that have just been uncovered. In some cases, it's just as easy to redraw each element whenever necessary, for example, when the only things drawn in the device context are text or controls or simple graphic elements. But for complex bitmap patterns, such as photographs, you can use a memory device context as a buffer to manipulate and store the image behind the scenes. Then whenever you need to display or restore the screen image, you can just blt it from the memory device context. That's exactly what happens when you enable the **AutoRedraw** property of a Picture Box or form in VB.

To build a memory device context, you call the function **Create-CompatibleDC()**, passing it a single argument, the handle to the screen device context you want to shadow. You then use **CreateCompatibleBitmap()** to make a bitmap with the same dimensions and color resolution as the screen device context. Before you can draw on the bitmap, you have to select it into the memory device context with **SelectObject()**. The GDI doesn't automatically initialize the bitmap, so it will contain a random pattern of pixels determined by whatever happens to lie in memory. To clean things up, I've used the **Rectangle()** function to draw a filled rectangle that covers the entire bitmap. **Rectangle()** will use whatever brush it finds selected into the device context. The default brush is pure white, so **Rectangle()** will whitewash the bitmap to a nice clean drawing surface. See the declaration sections in DISSOLVE.BAS and DIB2.BAS for the declarations of these GDI functions.

The next line of code in **DissolvePaint()** identifies which image is which.

```
OldImage = (NewImage + 1) Mod 2
```

During a dissolve we have two DIBs in memory, the **OldImage** and the **NewImage**. To keep track of them, I've declared three arrays of two elements each:

```
Global bmFileHeader(1) As BITMAPFILEHEADER
Global bmInfo(1) As BITMAPINFO
Global hPixelData(1) As Integer
Global NewImage As Integer
```

Each time we dissolve to a new image, we load the bitmap header information, and the handle to the pixel data into whichever of the two elements is free at the time. When the program first loads, we set **NewImage** to 0, so the first DIB goes into the first array element. When we load the second image, we change the value of **NewImage** to 1 and load the DIB data into the second array element. During the dissolve we know that the elements that do not hold the new image must hold the old image, so in **DissolvePaint()**,

OldImage equals **(NewImage + 1) Mod 2**. A little later when we get to the higher-level procedures, I'll show you how we ping-pong the images between the two sets of array elements.

The next four statements do nothing but provide a shorthand for the lengthy references to the image dimensions:

```
OldImageWidth = bmInfo(OldImage).bmiHeader.biWidth
OldImageHeight = bmInfo(OldImage).bmiHeader.biHeight
NewImageWidth = bmInfo(NewImage).bmiHeader.biWidth
NewImageHeight = bmInfo(NewImage).bmiHeader.biHeight
```

Next, we select the appropriate palette into both the memory device context and the screen device context:

```
' Select the palette activated by DoDissolveStep() into
' the memory and display DCs.
ErrCode = SelectPalette(hMemDC, hPalette, False)
hOldPalette = SelectPalette(DissolvePicture.hDC, hPalette, False)
ErrCode = RealizePalette(DissolvePicture.hDC)
' Throw away the palette belonging to the previous step or image,
' unless this is the first image (you can't delete the default palette).
If (hOldPalette <> GetStockObject(DEFAULT_PALETTE) And (hOldPalette <> hPalette)
Then
    ErrCode = DeleteObject(hOldPalette)
  End If
```

We have to realize the palette into the screen device context, **DissolvePicture.hDC**, to get the Palette Manager to load it into the system palette. Under normal circumstances, a memory device context cannot control the system palette.

The palettes we create for each step of the dissolve exist only until the next dissolve step, so after we select the next palette into the device context, we can destroy the previous palette, unless that happens to be the system default palette.

To prepare for the blting operations, we next lock the memory blocks that contain the pixel data:

```
lpDIBits = GlobalLock(hPixelData(NewImage))
If hPixelData(OldImage) <> 0 Then
    lpOldDIBits = GlobalLock(hPixelData(OldImage))
  End If
```

The function **GlobalLock()** takes a handle to a global memory block and returns a long pointer to the block. The pointer will remain valid as a literal address until we unlock the blocks. While a block is locked, Windows cannot move it. A friendly Windows program should keep as little global memory locked as possible and for as little time as possible. Otherwise the Windows memory manager cannot slide things around, which can cause unnecessary out-of-memory conditions in any of the active programs, including the one that's caused the problem by hogging memory!

The final step before we perform the dissolve is to create the pattern brush:

```
If lpDIBits <> 0 Then
    ' Create the appropriate dissolve brush for the current step,
    ' and select it into the MemDC.
    hDisolveBrush = CreateDissolveBrush(DissolveStepForPainting,
                   DissolvePicture.hDC)
    hOldBrush = SelectObject(hMemDC, hDisolveBrush)
```

We don't need the brush in the screen device context because we're going to perform all our complex raster operations in the memory device context. We'll use **SRCCOPY**, which doesn't use a pattern brush, to blt the image from the memory device context to the screen device context.

Once we've created the memory device context, selected the palette, locked the pixel data, and created the pattern brush, we can perform the blting operations that combine the DIBs into the memory device context.

```
' Paint the old image into the MemDC with an inverted brush.
If (hPixelData(OldImage) <> 0) Then
    ErrCode = StretchDIBits(hMemDC, 0, 0, OldImageWidth, OldImageHeight,
             0, 0, OldImageWidth, OldImageHeight, lpOldDIBits,
             bmInfo(OldImage), DIB_RGB_COLORS, &HCF0224) ' Performs ROP SPno
    End If
' Paint the new image into the MemDC with the dissolve ROP.
ErrCode = StretchDIBits(hMemDC, 0, 0, NewImageWidth, NewImageHeight, 0,
         0, NewImageWidth, NewImageHeight, lpDIBits, bmInfo(NewImage),
         DIB_RGB_COLORS, &HAC0744) ' Performs ROP SPDSxax
' Rapidly transfer the contents of the MemDC to the screen.
ErrCode = BitBlt(DissolvePicture.hDC, 0, 0, DissolvePicture.ScaleWidth,
         DissolvePicture.ScaleHeight, hMemDC, 0, 0, SRCCOPY)
```

This section of code performs three separate blt operations. In the first two, we use a new function, **StretchDIBits()**, to combine the two images with the pattern brush. **StretchDIBits()** looks a lot like **StretchBlt()**, and it performs a similar function. However, unlike **StretchBlt()**, which copies a DDB from one device context into another, **StretchDIBits()** copies a DIB from memory directly into a device context, converting it into a DDB as it goes. Compare the declarations for these two blt functions:

```
Declare Function StretchBlt Lib "GDI" (ByVal hDestDC As Integer, ByVal DestX As
    Integer, ByVal DestY As Integer, ByVal nDestWidth As Integer, ByVal
    nDestHeight As Integer, ByVal hSrcDC As Integer, ByVal SrcX As Integer, ByVal
    SrcY As Integer, ByVal nSrcWidth As Integer, ByVal nSrcHeight As Integer,
    ByVal dwRop As Long) As Integer

Declare Function StretchDIBits Lib "GDI" (ByVal hDC As Integer, ByVal DestX As
    Integer, ByVal DestY As Integer, ByVal nDestWidth As Integer, ByVal nDestHeight
    As Integer, ByVal SrcX As Integer, ByVal SrcY As Integer, ByVal nSrcWidth As
    Integer, ByVal nSrcHeight As Integer, ByVal lpBits As Long, lpBitsInfo As
    BITMAPINFO, ByVal wUsage As Integer, ByVal dwROP As Long) As Integer
```

In the declaration of **StretchBlt()** you find two parameters that specify device contexts, one for the destination, the first argument, and one for the source, the sixth argument. In the **StretchDIBits()** you find a place for only the destination device context. In place of the source device context, this function requires a pointer to the pixel data, a pointer to the **BITMAPINFO** structure that describes that pixel data, and an argument called **wUsage**, which specifies whether the color table data in **BITMAPINFO** contains palette indexes or RGB colors (just like the **dwUsage** argument in the **CreateDIBitmap()** function, which we used to make the pattern brush).

We have to use **StretchDIBits()** instead of **BitBlt()** or **StretchBlt()** because we want to map the colors of both images to the palette currently selected into the memory device context. Remember, **BitBlt()** copies literal pixel values from one location to another. It makes no attempt to match colors from one device context to the other. But because **StretchDIBits()** starts out with the DIB data, it has to map each color in its color table to the system palette as it converts the image to a DDB. That's how we get the two images to share the six intermediate palettes. The first call to **StretchDIBits()** re-translates the existing image to the intermediate palette. The second call to **StretchDIBits()** then translates the pixel values of the new image as it combines its pixels with those of the pattern brush and the existing image. When the dissolve ends, we have two versions of the new image, the DDB that appears on the screen, and the DIB that we hold in memory for the next dissolve.

I've added another raster operation in the first call to **StretchDIBits()**. This is just a refinement. The real work is done by the ROP code we derived earlier in this chapter. But this additional raster operation solves one slight problem. When dissolving from a larger image to a smaller image, you must get rid of the portions of the old image that lie outside the dimensions of the new image. Let me briefly explain how I arrived at this ROP code.

To make the periphery of the larger image fade away as the new image dissolves in, I realized that I could invert the pattern brushes and use them to gradually change the pixels in the image to pure white, the background color.

After I inverted each brush, I used an **Or** operation between the inverted brush and the image, which made an image full of white holes. To calculate the correct ROP code, I performed these two steps on the binary constants that represent a brush and a source image. Then I looked up the code in the ROP table.

For the final blt operation, I use **BitBlt()**, the quickest blt function, to **SRCCOPY** the image to the screen. The rest is cleanup:

```
                ' Unlock the global memory blocks.
                ErrCode = GlobalUnlock(hPixelData(NewImage))
                If hPixelData(OldImage) <> 0 Then
                    ErrCode = GlobalUnlock(hPixelData(OldImage))
                End If
                ' Replace the default brush in the MemDC and
                ' delete the dissolve brush.
                ErrCode = SelectObject(hMemDC, hOldBrush)
                ErrCode = DeleteObject(hDisolveBrush)
            Else
                DissolvePicture.Print "Unable to Set Bits!"
            End If
        ' Delete the MemDC, then delete the MemBitmap.
        ErrCode = SelectObject(hMemDC, hOldMemBitmap)
        ErrCode = SelectPalette(hMemDC, DEFAULT_PALETTE, False)
        ErrCode = DeleteDC(hMemDC)
        ErrCode = DeleteObject(hMemBitmap)

    End Sub
```

When we're done with each **Paint** event, we unlock the global memory blocks, restore the default brush to the memory device context, delete the dissolve brush, and delete the memory device context and its bitmap.

Now that we have the underlying elements of the dissolve in place, we need a mechanism to trigger a dissolve and tick off the steps. Listing 7.22 shows the procedures that fulfill those roles.

Listing 7.22   The DissolveToImage() and DoDissolveStep() Procedures from DISSOLVE.BAS

```
Sub DissolveToImage (FileName As String, DissolveTimer As Timer, DissolveTrigger
As Control)
    Dim NewPalette As LOGPALETTE

    DissolveTrigger.Enabled = False
    NewImage = (NewImage + 1) Mod 2
    DissolveStep = 1
    If hPixelData(NewImage) <> 0 Then
        hPixelData(NewImage) = GlobalFree(hPixelData(NewImage))
    End If
    If hPixelData(NewImage) = 0 Then
```

```
        ReadBitmapFile FileName, bmFileHeader(NewImage), bmInfo(NewImage),
          hPixelData(NewImage)
        ' Build a logical palette from the DIB color table.
        ConstructPaletteFromColorTable bmInfo(NewImage).bmiColors(), NewPalette
        ' Call sub function to interpolate an array of
        ' logical palettes between the logical palettes
        ' of the two images.
        CreatePaletteSequenceArray palettes(8), NewPalette
        DissolveTimer.Enabled = True
    Else
        MsgBox "Unable To Free Memory from Previous Image", 16, "Memory
        DeAllocation Error"
    End If
End Sub

Sub DoDissolveStep (DissolvePicture As PictureBox, DissolveTimer As Timer,
  DissolveTrigger As Control)

    hPalette = CreatePalette(Palettes(DissolveStep))
    DissolveStepForPainting = DissolveStep
    InvalidateRect DissolvePicture.hWnd, ByVal 0, False
    'DissolvePicture.Refresh
    If DissolveStep >= 8 Then
        DissolveTimer.Enabled = False
        DissolveTrigger.Enabled = True
    Else
        DissolveStep = DissolveStep + 1
    End If

End Sub
```

DissolveToImage() disables the control that initiated the dissolve, passed in as the third parameter. It then switches the value of **NewImage** to the free index into the DIB information arrays (either 1 or 0), and sets the **DissolveStep** to 1.

After it has read the DIB into its memory structures by calling **ReadBitmapFile()**, **DissolveToImage()** then calls **ConstructPaletteFromColorTable()**, followed by **CreatePaletteSequenceArray()**, which takes the two logical palettes belonging to the current image on the screen and the newly read image in memory, and interpolates six intermediate palettes.

Finally, after it has read the bitmap and set up the palettes, **DissolveToImage()** enables the Timer control specified in the second parameter.

The next procedure, **DoDissolveStep()** performs one step of the dissolve by building a logical palette and invalidating the client area of the Picture Box control, which triggers a **Paint** event. It then increments **DissolveStep**. When the dissolve is complete, it disables the Timer control passed in as the second parameter, and enables the control that triggers a new dissolve, passed in as the third parameter.

You'll notice that these procedures won't do anything until they're called by an event procedure somewhere. Instead of embedding this code directly in the event procedures, I've placed it in a code module. Things get turned a little inside out. Instead of code embedded in event procedures, we end up with procedures that expect to receive controls as arguments. In this sample program **DoDissolveStep()** is called by a **Timer** event. Any timer will do because the procedure never explicity references a Timer by its own name. Instead, it expects the event procedure that controls the dissolve to pass the Timer control as a parameter. Since the dissolve will likely be controlled by a Timer control, the event procedure will be the **Timer** event, which means that with each tick, the Timer control will pass itself to **DoDissolveStep()**, along with the control that initiated the dissolve and the Picture Box control on which the image will appear. Similarly, the Picture Box control will pass itself to **DissolvePaint()** whenever it executes its **Paint** event. By placing this code in a separate module, we make it a general purpose library that we can add to any program that needs to perform dissolves.

In the sample program, I call **DissolveToImage()** first from the **Form_Load** event, and then from a Command Button **Click** event. I could just as easily have used a List Box, or the hypertext system we built in Chapters 2 and 3.

Wrapping Up DISSOLVE.BAS

DISSOLVE.BAS also contains a few support functions and some declarations. You'll find them in Listing 7.23.

Listing 7.23　The Declarations and Remaining Functions from DISSOLVE.BAS

```
Option Explicit

Declare Function CreatePatternBrush Lib "GDI" (ByVal hBitmap As Integer) As Integer
Declare Function Rectangle Lib "GDI" (ByVal hDC As Integer, ByVal LeftX As
   Integer, ByVal TopY As Integer, ByVal RightX As Integer, ByVal BottomY As
   Integer) As Integer
Declare Sub InvalidateRect Lib "User" (ByVal hWnd As Integer, ByVal lpRect As
   Long, ByVal bErase As Integer)

Const NumberOfSteps = 8
Dim PixelSetSequence(64) As Integer
Dim DissolveStep As Integer
Dim DissolveStepForPainting As Integer

Dim bmFileHeader(1) As BITMAPFILEHEADER
Dim bmInfo(1) As BITMAPINFO
Dim hPixelData(1) As Integer
Dim NewImage As Integer
```

```
Dim hPalette As Integer
Global Palettes(1 To 8) As LOGPALETTE

Type PALSTEP
    Red As Integer
    Green As Integer
    Blue As Integer
    End Type


Dim PalStepArray(255) As PALSTEP

Sub DissolveUnload (DissolvePicture As PictureBox)
    Dim ResultCode As Integer
    If hPixelData(NewImage) <> 0 Then
        ResultCode = GlobalFree(hPixelData(NewImage))
      End If
    If hPixelData((NewImage + 1) Mod 2) <> 0 Then
        ResultCode = GlobalFree(hPixelData((NewImage + 1) Mod 2))
      End If
    ResultCode = SelectPalette(DissolvePicture.hDC, DEFAULT_PALETTE, False)
    If hPalette <> 0 Then
        ResultCode = DeleteObject(hPalette)
      End If

    End Sub


Sub InitializeDissolve ()

    NewImage = 0
    hPixelData(NewImage) = 0
    hPixelData((NewImage + 1) Mod 2) = 0
    hPalette = 0
    CreatePixelSetSequence

    End Sub

Function MaxInt (A As Integer, B As Integer)
    If A > B Then
        MaxInt = A
      Else
        MaxInt = B
      End If
      End Function

Function MinInt (A As Integer, B As Integer) As Integer
    If A < B Then
        MinInt = A
      Else
        MinInt = B
      End If
    End Function
```

The primary purpose of **DissolveUnload()** is to release the global memory blocks that we used to hold the bitmap pixel data, and to reselect the default system palette into Picture1 before destroying the latest logical palette.

Finally, Here's GLBLMEM.BAS

To wrap up our project, we just need to add the declarations to GLBLMEM.BAS, as shown in Listing 7.24. Nothing tricky here!

Listing 7.24   The Declarations Section from GLBLMEM.BAS

```
Option Explicit

Declare Function GlobalAlloc Lib "Kernel" (ByVal wFlags As Integer, ByVal dwBytes
    As Long) As Integer
Declare Function GlobalHandleToSel Lib "ToolHelp.DLL" (ByVal hMem As Integer) As
    Integer
Declare Function MemoryWrite Lib "ToolHelp.DLL" (ByVal wSel As Integer, ByVal
    dwOffSet As Long, lpvBuf As Any, ByVal dwcb As Long) As Long
Declare Function MemoryRead Lib "ToolHelp.DLL" (ByVal wSel As Integer, ByVal
    dwOffSet As Long, lpvBuf As Any, ByVal dwcb As Long) As Long
Declare Function GlobalFree Lib "Kernel" (ByVal hMem As Integer) As Integer
Declare Function AnsiNext Lib "User" (ByVal lpString As String) As Long
Declare Function GlobalLock Lib "Kernel" (ByVal hMem As Integer) As Long
Declare Function GlobalUnlock Lib "Kernel" (ByVal hMem As Integer) As Integer


Global Const GMEM_MOVEABLE = &H2
Global Const GMEM_ZEROINIT = &H40
```

Using the Dissolve Program

Our program works best with DIBs that use a Windows *identity palette*. An identity palette is a logical palette that includes the 20 reserved colors in their proper locations, 10 at the beginning and 10 at the end. Identity palettes help to prevent all kinds of odd mapping effects. Since a logical palette can really claim only 236 of the system palette entries, an image with 256 colors will have 20 of its colors mapped to other colors in the palette. Sometimes the Palette Manager does less than an ideal job of performing that palette reduction. Your images will look much better if you pre-process them with a utility, such as Microsoft's BitEdit/PalEdit combination, which comes with Video for Windows and with the Multimedia Development Kit. Some shareware image editing tools also offer this function.

Expanding the Dissolve

The dissolve construction set leaves plenty of room for optimization. I have intentionally sacrificed performance for clarity. But that shouldn't stop you from poking around in the GDI and experimenting with alternative approaches. Here are just a few suggestions:

- Use **AnimatePalette()** instead of creating and realizing new palettes for each step.
- Maintain the memory device context throughout the dissolve.
- Build all the pattern brushes before you begin the dissolve.

Now that you understand bitmaps inside out and backwards, from pixels to palettes to raster operations, you're ready to create your own special effects. Knock someone's socks off.

Jazz up your multimedia apps
by adding basic hotspots to
your images.

The World
of Hyperimaging

Y ou've probably heard this phrase a million times:
"Multimedia is a visual medium."

If something in a picture grabs your attention, you should be able to click
on it and find out what it is or does. In this chapter we'll look at a few ways
to create hotspots on pictures that can activate any of the multimedia features
we've been presenting. We'll explore a few hypermedia projects to see how
Windows operates as a hypermedia system. I'll show you some basic techniques you can use to define rectangular hotspots by creating a useful hotspot
editor. With this editor, you'll be able to define hotspots and save them in a
format so that they can be used in other multimedia apps. In Chapter 9 we'll
create a more powerful hotspot editor for defining irregular-shaped regions.
Then, in Chapter 10 we'll build a powerful hypermedia engine that handles
hotspots of any shape or size. You'll be able to use this engine for your own
multimedia projects.

We have a lot of ground to cover, so let's get started.

Windows Is Hypermedia!

Everytime you click on a button, drag a scroll bar, or select a list box item in a
Windows app, you're engaging in one kind of hypermedia or another. When you

click your mouse pointer on a button, Windows detects that the click has occurred within a particular region of the display. It then performs the appropriate actions, which usually include re-drawing the button to create the illusion that it has been depressed and released. Some controls even open entire dialog boxes. If you click in the right place on one picture, Windows may display another picture with its own hotspot regions in the form of controls.

Using Controls as Pictures

You probably won't want to use controls for every type of visual hyperlinking but they provide a good starting point. Besides, it's a good idea to step back every once in a while and try to imagine new uses for old tools. Figure 8.1 shows a simple experiment where I have built a bar chart from a control array of six Command Buttons.

You might expect Command Buttons to be short and fat rather than tall and thin. You might also expect them to keep their shapes when you click on them. But in this program, I have turned buttons into bars that shrink and grow.

Rather than stretch them randomly, I set up a simple relationship between them. Any bar (button), when clicked on, will change its size in proportion to the difference in size between itself and its neighbor to the left. The procedure that performs this operation, **BarButton_Click()**, is shown in Listing 8.1.

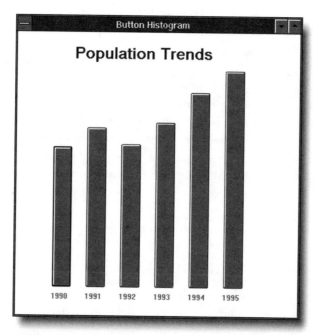

Figure 8.1　*HISTOBTN.FRM creates this bar chart at runtime.*

Listing 8.1   The BarButton_Click() Procedure

```
Sub BarButton_Click (Index As Integer)
    If Index > 0 Then
        BarButton(Index).Top = BarButton(Index).Top - .05 *
          (BarButton(Index).Height - BarButton(Index - 1).Height)
        BarButton(Index).Height = BarButton(Index).Height + .05 *
          (BarButton(Index).Height - BarButton(Index - 1).Height)
    Else
        BarButton(Index).Top = BarButton(Index).Top - .05 *
                   BarButton(Index).Height
        BarButton(Index).Height = BarButton(Index).Height * 1.05
    End If
End Sub
```

This code actually exaggerates the curve formed by the tops of the bars in a somewhat less than predictable fashion. You could also use the **Click** event to pop up a Message Box that explains the reasons for the rise or fall in population for that particular year.

To jazz up this demonstration, you could easily substitute Labels or some other control for the Command Buttons. But Command Buttons have their own qualities. They expect to be touched. You don't need a label that says "Press the Bars for Further Information."

Using Controls as Hotspot Buttons

Now let's move on to the core of this chapter—how to add hotspots to images. By images, I mean bitmap graphics. You could scan photographs or drawings to create your images. You could also paint them with a drawing program such as Fractal Painter. You could even use VB to draw them directly into your Picture Box controls. It doesn't matter how you create your images, because pixels are pixels, and as we discovered in Chapter 2, a hotspot is nothing more than a region on the screen. Once you define that region, you can use the **MouseDown()** event procedure to fire off any multimedia event you wish.

As you disovered in the bar chart program, Command Buttons don't make the greatest hotspots. For one thing, they're opaque; you don't want to cover up your attractive images with boring Command Buttons. Fortunately, VB provides us with two other controls that can hide invisibly on top of pictures, and yet remain active. These are the Label and Image controls. Let's see what they can do for us.

Creating Hotspots with Label and Image Controls

This project uses Labels and Image controls to set up hotspots on an image. To create the project, all you'll need to do is make a new form, add a picture, and include the controls.

There is a simple example of this hotspot technique in the directory \VBMAGIC, in the files HOTSPOT1.MAK, HOTSPOT1.FRM, and HOTSPOT1.FRX.

Start a new VB project, select the **Picture** property of the form, and add a bitmap. Anything will do. Next, place a Label control on the picture. It will appear as blank rectangle. Size the Label so it covers some object in the image as closely as possible. Remove the caption from the Label by double-clicking on the **Caption** property in the Properties window and pressing the Delete key. Finally, change the **BackStyle** property to 0 - Transparent. The only sign of the Label will be its frame handles. Once you click elsewhere on the form, all visible traces of it will vanish from the image. But when you click on the area it covers, it reappears. When you double-click on the area, VB will display its **Click** event procedure. All you need to do is add the code to kick off the appropriate multimedia event.

You can do the same thing with an Image control. And, as a bonus, the Image control will work with its default property settings. The other advantage of the Image control over a Label is that it will display a border during development time so you won't lose track of it.

To use the control-based method of hyperimaging for a large number of images, you would need a way to create and place controls over the images at runtime. You could keep track of their locations and sizes in a simple database, either using VB's ordinary file I/O, or with its Data Access features. You could then use a control array to generate as many controls as you need to cover all the hotspots of any particular image. When you finished displaying an image, you could delete all but the one Label or Image control that must remain as a placeholder for the control array.

Since you have to keep track of the locations and dimensions of the hotspots anyway, it would be nice if you could just create them directly on the client area of the form or Picture Box, without scattering controls all over the place. I'm sure you won't be surprised when I tell you that the Windows API once again comes to our aid with a pair of almost unbelievably simple functions that do just what we need. Follow me to the next project in our multimedia adventure.

Using Rectangular Window Regions

The GDI includes a family of functions that create and manipulate *regions*. A region is simply a bounded area of the screen. Just like the other GDI objects we explored in Chapters 4 and 5, regions have handles. One function, named **CreateRectRgn()**, contructs a Windows region from two pair of coordinates that specify the upper-left corner and lower-right corner of a rectangle, and return a handle that we can store in an integer variable:

```
Declare Function CreateRectRgn Lib "GDI" (ByVal X1 As Integer, ByVal Y1 As
    Integer, ByVal X2 As Integer, ByVal Y2 As Integer) As Integer
```

Thanks to another GDI function named **PtInRegion()**, regions make handy mouse traps.

```
Declare Function PtInRegion Lib "GDI" (ByVal hRgn As Integer, ByVal X As
    Integer, ByVal Y As Integer) As Integer
```

In Chapter 2, we kept track of hotlink words or phrases in hypertext topic windows by recording their rectangular boundaries. Then, in the **MouseDown()** event procedure, we compared the mouse position coordinates to the rectangular boundaries to determine whether a mouse click occurred within any of those rectangles. With these two new API functions, we can do the same thing with fewer steps.

To intercept mouse clicks in a particular section of the screen, we can mark that area with a region, then pass the handle to that region and the coordinates of the **MouseDown()** event procedure to **PtInRegion()**, which will return either **True** or **False**.

Before calling the **CreateRectRgn()** and **PtInRegion()** functions, we need some way to determine the positions and dimensions of the rectangular regions we want to use as hotspots. Here's our solution. We can write a VB hotspot editor that lets us draw rectangles over bitmaps, test them, and save them in a file so we can use them later in our hypermedia system. The editor will be a great addition to our multimedia construction set.

Creating a Visual Basic Hotspot Editor

This is one of the bigger projects we've created so far—so hold on to your hat. A number of steps are required but the editor is actually easy to put together.

1. Create the main form HOTSPOT2.FRM and add the **Form_Load()** and **Form_Unload()** event procedures (Listing 8.1).

2. Add the global variables for the project to the module HOTSPOT2.BAS (Listing 8.2).

3. Add the form's **Mouse** events for drawing hotspot regions (Listings 8.3 through 8.5).

4. Add the **TestOption_Click()** event procedure (Listing 8.6) to test out hotspots and the **DefineOption_Click()** event procedure (Listing 8.7) to define hotspots.

5. Add the **DeleteRegion()** procedure (Listing 8.8) to HOTSPOT2.BAS to delete hotspot regions.

6. To support a menu system, add the **LoadOption_Click()** event procedure to HOTSPOT2.FRM (Listing 8.9) and the **InitRecordBuffer()** procedure to HOTSPOT2.BAS (Listing 8.10).

7. To save hotspot records, add the **SaveOption_Click()** event procedure to HOTSPOT2.FRM (Listing 8.11) and the **SaveHotspotRecord()** procedure to HOTSPOT2.BAS (Listing 8.12).

8. Almost there! Create the form HTSPT2F2.FRM and add the necessary support event procedures (Listings 8.13 and 8.16).

9. Add the **EditOption_Click()** event procedure (Listing 8.17), the **NewOption_Click()** event procedure (Listing 8.18), and the **DeleteOption_Click()** event procedure (Listing 8.19).

This project is located in the directory \VBMAGIC in the files HOTSPOT2.MAK, HOTSPOT2.FRM, HOTSPOT2.BAS, HTSPT2F2.FRM, and GLOBCONS.BAS. You will also need the Common Dialog custom control, located in the file CMDIALOG.VBX. VB Setup normally installs this file in your \WINDOWS\SYSTEM directory.

How the Hotspot Editor Works

Before you explore this project, take a few minutes to run the editor just to see how it works. Figure 8.2 shows the editor with a bitmap image loaded. The editor allows you to load in a bitmap image, draw your hotspots with the mouse, and then save them.

To display an image, choose File, Load Picture, then use the Open file dialog box to locate and select a bitmap image. When the picture appears on the form, you may use the mouse to draw and test hotspot regions.

Figure 8.2   *The rectangular hotspot editor.*

Each time you press the mouse button, the editor will begin drawing a new rectangle. You won't see the new figure until you stretch it into one or two dimensions by moving the mouse. When you release the mouse button, the rectangle will remain locked at its last position and size until you start the process over by pressing the mouse button again.

After you draw a rectangle, choose Mode, Test. When you click inside the rectangle, you should hear TADA.WAV. When you click outside the rectangle, you should hear DING.WAV.

Designing the Hotspot Editor

Our editor requires two forms: HOTSPOT2.FRM and HTSPTF2.FRM. The first form contains the **Mouse** event procedures for drawing hotspot regions and the menu system for the project. We'll create the HTSPTF2.FRM form to retrieve and edit hotspots that we have already saved in a file. We'll be taking a closer look at this form later. For now, let's create the main form.

Create a new form and set its **Name** property to HotSpot2F1. Next, set the **DrawMode** property to 6 - Invert, and save it in a file named HOTSPOT2.FRM. We'll need a pair of event procedures for loading and unloading the form. These procedures are shown in Listing 8.1.

Listing 8.1   The Form_Load() and Form_Unload() Event Procedures from HOTSPOT2.FRM

```
Sub Form_Load ()
    NewOption.Enabled = False
```

```
    EditOption.Enabled = False
    SaveOption.Enabled = False
    DeleteOption.Enabled = False
    CurrentHotspotRecordNumber = 0
    DrawingRectangle = False
    Open App.Path + "\ImagLink.Dat" For Random As ImageLinkFile Len = Len(HotSpotRecord)
    InitRecordBuffer
    End Sub

Sub Form_Unload (Cancel As Integer)
    DeleteRegion hRectRgn
    End Sub
```

Form_Load() is needed to initialize the variables we'll be using. It also contains the code for opening a data file so that the editor can store the newly created hotspot regions. We'll look at this procedure in a little more detail when we discuss how hotspot regions are saved. The **Form_Unload()** procedure is responsible for removing any stray regions that have been left lying around in memory.

Speaking of variables, where should we declare them? In HOTSPOT2.FRM? No. Remember that our project requires two forms and both of them will need to access the variables and the four API functions that are used. We'll need to put declarations in HOTSPOT2.BAS. Listing 8.2 shows the complete set.

Listing 8.2　The Declarations Section of HOTSPOT2.BAS

```
Option Explicit

Type HotSpotRecords
    Image As String * 128
    Target As String * 128
    TopX As Integer
    TopY As Integer
    BottomX As Integer
    BottomY As Integer
    End Type

Global Const ImageLinkFile = 1
Global HotSpotRecord As HotSpotRecords
Global hRectRgn As Integer
Global CurrentImageFilename As String
Global CurrentHotspotRecordNumber As Long
Global AnchorX As Integer
Global AnchorY As Integer
Global EndX As Integer
Global EndY As Integer

Declare Function CreateRectRgn Lib "GDI" (ByVal X1 As Integer, ByVal Y1 As
    Integer, ByVal X2 As Integer, ByVal Y2 As Integer) As Integer
```

```
Declare Function PtInRegion Lib "GDI" (ByVal hRgn As Integer, ByVal X As
    Integer, ByVal Y As Integer) As Integer
Declare Function DeleteObject Lib "GDI" (ByVal hObject As Integer) As Integer
Declare Function mciExecute Lib "MMSystem" (ByVal CommandString As String) As
    Integer
```

We start out with the declaration of the data structure **HotSpotRecords**. This structure is used to store and retrieve file records containing hotspot information. Next, you'll find the declarations of the nine global variables needed. Finally, HOTSPOT2.BAS declares the API functions we'll be using to draw and define hotspot regions. Let's take a closer look.

Setting the Bait—Outlining Hot Regions

We need to create the three event procedures to support the mouse. So let's get to it. Double-click on the main form and open the **MouseDown()** event procedure. Listing 8.3 provides the code required for **Form_MouseDown()**.

Listing 8.3   TheForm_MouseDown() Event Procedure of HOTSPOT2.FRM

```
Sub Form_MouseDown (Button As Integer, Shift As Integer, x As Single, y As
    Single)
    Dim Dummy As Integer

    If DefineOption.Checked Then
        Line (AnchorX, AnchorY)-(EndX, EndY), , B
        AnchorX = x
        AnchorY = y
        EndX = x
        EndY = y
        DrawingRectangle = True
    Else
        ' Test whether click is in region.
        If PtInRegion(hRectRgn, x, y) Then
            Dummy = mciExecute("play c:\windows\tada.wav")
        Else
            Dummy = mciExecute("play c:\windows\ding.wav")
        End If
    End If
End Sub
```

This procedure initiates the drawing process. We need a flag to tell the other mouse event procedures that we're in the middle of drawing a rectangle, so we set **DrawingRectangle** to **True**. Next, we call the **Line()** method to erase any rectangle we may have drawn previously. The first time we press the mouse button, both vertices lie at the origin (upper-left corner) of the client area so nothing will happen. We then initialize both vertices to the current position of the mouse, as returned by the **x** and **y** arguments of the **Form_MouseDown()** procedure.

Next, we need to add the **Form_MouseMove()** event procedure (Listing 8.4).

Listing 8.4   The Form_MouseMove() Event Procedure from HOTSPOT2.FRM

```
Sub Form_MouseMove (Button As Integer, Shift As Integer, x As Single, y As Single)
    If DrawingRectangle Then
        HotSpot2F1.Line (AnchorX, AnchorY)-(EndX, EndY), , B
        EndX = x
        EndY = y
        HotSpot2F1.Line (AnchorX, AnchorY)-(EndX, EndY), , B
    End If
End Sub
```

Each time we move the mouse, we need to erase the previously drawn rectangle and draw a new one from the anchor point to the new mouse location. Because we have set the **DrawMode** to **Invert**, the first call to the **Line()** method erases the old rectangle by drawing right over it. We then grab the new end points and draw the new rectangle.

Finally, to complete the drawing operation, we turn to the **Form_MouseUp()** event procedure shown in Listing 8.5.

Listing 8.5   The Form_MouseUp() Event Procedure from HOTSPOT2.FRM

```
Sub Form_MouseUp (Button As Integer, Shift As Integer, x As Single, y As Single)
    If DrawingRectangle Then
        EndX = x
        EndY = y
        DrawingRectangle = False
    End If
End Sub
```

Nothing complicated here. We just capture the final end point and set **DrawingRectangle** to **False**. Now we need to convert the rectangle we drew into a Windows region.

Drawing or Testing?

Our editor must be set up so that we can switch between drawing mode and testing mode. I've added a menu to the form with an option called Mode. This option itself contains two suboptions labeled Define and Test. We'll use check marks to indicate which option is active. Define will turn on the drawing mode, and Test will create the rectangular Windows region. Listing 8.6 shows the **TestOption_Click()** event procedure.

Listing 8.6 The TestOption_Click() Event Procedure from HOTSPOT2.FRM.

```
Sub TestOption_Click ()
   DefineOption.Checked = False
   TestOption.Checked = True
   hRectRgn = CreateRectRgn(AnchorX, AnchorY, EndX, EndY)
   End Sub
```

The first two lines of this procedure just switch the check mark on the menu from the Define option to the Test option. The third and last line calls the API function **CreateRectRgn()** to register the rectangle with Windows as an official region.

Go back and look closely at the **Form_MouseDown()** event procedure (Listing 8.3). Notice we used the **Checked** property of the **DefineOption** menu item to split the **MouseDown()** event procedure into two clauses, one for each mode. The truth clause of the **If** statement performs this procedure's part in the drawing operation. The **Else** clause, which handles test mode, calls the API function **PtInRegion()**, passing it the handle to the rectangular region, along with the **x** and **y** coordinates of the mouse pointer. **PtInRegion()** returns **True** or **False**, so we can use another **If** statement to respond to the **MouseDown()** event procedure. I've called upon the services of our old friend **mciExecute()** to announce whether the event occurs inside or outside of the region.

For proper symmetry we'll need to support the **DefineOption_Click** event. Listing 8.7 provides the required event procedure.

Listing 8.7 The DefineOption_Click() Event Procedure from HOTSPOT2.FRM

```
Sub DefineOption_Click ()

   DefineOption.Checked = True
   TestOption.Checked = False
   DeleteRegion hRectRgn
   End Sub
```

First, we switch the check mark. Then we call **DeleteRegion()**, a new general procedure shown in Listing 8.8. We must place this procedure in the code module, HOTSPOT2.BAS, because it will be called from two different forms.

Listing 8.8 The DeleteRegion() General Procedure from HOTSPOT2.BAS

```
Sub DeleteRegion (hRgn As Integer)
   If hRgn <> 0 Then
       If DeleteObject(hRgn) Then
```

```
        hRgn = 0
    Else
      MsgBox "Unable to Delete Region", 48, "GDI Error"
    End If
  End If
End
```

This simple procedure checks whether **hRgn** has been set, presumably with a previous call to **CreateRectRgn()**. If it has, it deletes the region referenced by the handle by calling the API function **DeleteObject()**, then sets **hRgn** to zero. If it cannot delete the region, it displays a warning. A failure to delete a region will not prevent the program from continuing, but it will leave an orphan region in memory, which will remain there otherwise harmlessly, for the rest of the Windows session.

That's all it takes to create and use hotspots with Windows regions. First, you define the boundaries. Then, you create the region. And finally, you test whether a mouse click has ocurred within the region.

Adding the Menu System

Most of the work we've done on this program so far just helps us define our region boundaries. But to use these regions, you must associate them with images and save them somewhere.

(It's time to add the menu system for loading images and creating and saving hotspots. First, view the form and display the Menu Design window.) Second, add a File menu to the menu bar. Then add the options listed in Table 8.1.

Add the file CMDIALOG.VBX to the project. This custom control allows you to invoke the *Common Dialog* for opening files. This dialog box, shown in Figure 8.3, looks and operates like the file dialog boxes you find throughout the VB development environment. When you add CMDIALOG.VBX to the project, VB will add its icon to the Toolbox (a little schematic window with a dark caption bar and a few controls). Double-click on the Toolbox button (or click

---

Table 8.1   *File MENU Suboptions from HOTSPOT2.FRM*

Menu Caption	Menu Name
Load Picture	LoadOption
New Hotspot	NewOption
Edit Saved Hotspot	EditOption
Save Hotspot	SaveOption
Delete Hotspot	DeleteOption
Quit	QuitOption

Open

File **N**ame:
```
*.bmp;*.dib
```
hibiscus.bmp
housrk2.bmp
kaibab2.bmp
sadfall2.bmp
winterb.bmp

Director**i**es:
d:\vbmagic\images

📂 d:\
📂 vbmagic
📁 images

OK

Cancel

☐ **R**ead Only

List Files of **T**ype:
Pictures

Dri**v**es:
💾 d: disk_2

Figure 8.3 *We'll use the Common Dialog for opening files.*

once and drag) to place one Common Dialog control on the form. It doesn't matter where you place it because it's invisible at runtime. Change the **Name** property of the Common Dialog control to ImageFileDialog. Set the **DefaultExt** property to *.BMP;*.DIB, and the **Filter** property to Pictures|*.BMP;*.DIB.

To support our menu system, we'll need to add event procedures for each of the menu options shown in Table 8.1. The **LoadOption_Click()** event procedure has three distinct groups of statements, as shown in Listing 8.9.

Listing 8.9   The LoadOption_Click() Menu Event Procedure from HOTSPOT2.FRM

```
Sub LoadOption_Click ()

    NewOption.Enabled = True
    EditOption.Enabled = True
    SaveOption.Enabled = False
    DeleteOption.Enabled = False

    CurrentHotspotRecordNumber = 0
    DrawingRectangle = False
    InitRecordBuffer
    AnchorX = 0
    AnchorY = 0
    EndX = 0
    EndY = 0
    DeleteRegion hRectRgn

    ImageFileDialog.Action = 1
    If ImageFileDialog.Filename <> "" Then
        CurrentImageFilename = ImageFileDialog.Filename
        HotSpot2F1.Picture = LoadPicture(CurrentImageFilename)
      End If
End Sub
```

The first four lines turn on or off four of the other options in the File menu. Once an image is loaded, you can ask to create a new hotspot or edit an existing hotspot. You can't save or delete a hotspot until you create one or retrieve one from the hotspot file (which we haven't yet created).

The next eight lines initialize the hotspot editor. The variable **CurrentHotspot-RecordNumber** will eventually hold the record number of a hotspot that has already been recorded in the hotspot file. The general procedure **InitRecordBuffer()** will clear all the fields in a global structure called **HotSpotRecord**, which we'll use to store and retrieve hotspot records from the file.

The last five lines of code activate the **ImageFileDialog** in its "Open" file mode. The user may then use the drive, directory, and file list boxes to select an image file. When the program returns from the Open file dialog box, the **FileName** property of **ImageFileDialog** will contain the path and filename of the selected file. We'll need that again later, so we copy it to a variable called **CurrentImageFilename**, then pass it to the VB function **LoadPicture()** to assign the image to the **Picture** property of the form.

Before this procedure will work, we need to add the general procedure **InitRecordBuffer()**, which is shown in Listing 8.10.

Listing 8.10　The General Procedure InitRecordBuffer() from HOTSPOT2.BAS

```
Sub InitRecordBuffer ()
    HotSpotRecord.Image = ""
    HotSpotRecord.Target = ""
    HotSpotRecord.TopX = 0
    HotSpotRecord.TopY = 0
    HotSpotRecord.BottomX = 0
    HotSpotRecord.BottomY = 0
    End Sub
```

Drawing with Inverted Colors

You'll notice that the lines that form the rectangles are not solid, but look more like negative versions of the pixels they cover. The **DrawMode** we selected for the form, **6 - Invert**, flips the bits of each pixel value, either from one to zero, or zero to one. The pixel values then reference colors in the opposite side of the system palette. The result often looks like a photographic negative, but it isn't, unless each color in the palette happens to be paired with its RGB complement at the position in the palette determined by its 8-bit binary complement. Most of the Windows reserved colors try to look like complementary pairs, but even they are impostors. The only colors in the system palette that always enjoy such symmetry are black and white.

Saving Hotspots—A Simple Filing System

Now that we can draw hotspots over images, we need a way to store and edit them so we can use them in the hypermedia system. At the beginning of this project, we defined a data structure in HOTSPOT2.BAS called **HotSpotRecords** (Listing 8.2). Let's now explore how it is used to store and retrieve file records:

```
Type HotSpotRecords
    Image As String * 128
    Target As String * 128
    TopX As Integer
    TopY As Integer
    BottomX As Integer
    BottomY As Integer
    End Type
```

First, we'll need a data file. In the **Form_Load()** event procedure for the main form we'll open or create a file called IMAGLINK.DAT.

```
Sub Form_Load ()
    NewOption.Enabled = False
    EditOption.Enabled = False
    SaveOption.Enabled = False
    DeleteOption.Enabled = False
    CurrentHotspotRecordNumber = 0
    DrawingRectangle = False
    Open App.Path + "\ImagLink.Dat" For Random As ImageLinkFile Len = Len(HotSpotRecord)
    InitRecordBuffer
    End Sub
```

This procedure also disables most of the other File menu options, since they won't mean anything until we load an image file. If the files exists, the **Open** statement will open it; if it doesn't exist, **Open** will create and open it. The application property **App.Path** will force the data file into the same directory from which the program was invoked.

After you open an image file and draw a hotspot, you'll want to save its coordinates, along with the name of the image file and a hotlink target. That will be the job of the File, Save Hotspot menu option and its event procedure **SaveOption_Click()**, shown in Listing 8.11.

Listing 8.11   The SaveOption_Click() Menu Event Procedure from HOTSPOT2.FRM

```
Sub SaveOption_Click ()
    Dim TempString As String

    TempString = RTrim$(HotSpotRecord.Target)
    TempString = InputBox$("Enter a Hyperlink Target string of up to 128 characters:", _
            "Enter Target", TempString)
```

```
   If Len(TempString) > 0 Then
      HotSpotRecord.Image = CurrentImageFilename
      HotSpotRecord.Target = TempString
      HotSpotRecord.TopX = AnchorX
      HotSpotRecord.TopY = AnchorY
      HotSpotRecord.BottomX = EndX
      HotSpotRecord.BottomY = EndY
      SaveHotspotRecord HotSpotRecord, CurrentHotspotRecordNumber
      DeleteOption.Enabled = True
   End If
End Sub
```

We already know the filename and path of the image because we saved it in the string variable **CurrentImageFilename** when we loaded the picture into the form. We also know the hotspot coordinates, which we created with the drawing operation. The only thing we don't know is the target to which we want the hotspot linked, so we have to ask for it.

The VB function **InputBox$()** will display a simple dialog box with a prompt, a title, and a text box into which the user may type a response. (See Figure 8.4 to see what this function accomplishes.) The third parameter of **InputBox$()** enables us to display a default response. For a new hotspot, this default will come from a freshly initialized **HotSpotRecord**, which means it will be blank. Later, when we implement the Edit Hotspot option, the variable **TempString** will pass the existing target string to **InputBox$()**.

After we set the fields of the **HotSpotRecord**, we call the general procedure **SaveHotspotRecord()** (Listing 8.12), passing the record and a file position.

Listing 8.12 The SaveHotspotRecord() General Procedure from HOTSPOT2.BAS

```
Sub SaveHotspotRecord (HotSpotRecord As HotSpotRecords, RecordPos As Long)
   Dim Counter As Long
   Dim FileSize As Long
   Dim TempRecord As HotSpotRecords
   Dim BlankFound As Integer

   If RecordPos = 0 Then
      BlankFound = False
      FileSize = LOF(ImageLinkFile) \ Len(HotSpotRecord)
      Counter = 0
      Do Until (Counter >= FileSize) Or BlankFound
         Counter = Counter + 1
         Get ImageLinkFile, Counter, TempRecord
         BlankFound = (Len(RTrim$(TempRecord.Image)) = 0)
         Loop
      If BlankFound Then
         RecordPos = Counter
        Else
         RecordPos = FileSize + 1
```

```
      End If
   End If
Put ImageLinkFile, RecordPos, HotSpotRecord
End Sub
```

For new records, **SaveHotspotRecord()** looks for the first available record position in the file. A record that contains a blank filename in the **Image** field is considered to be free. If all the records are occupied, it appends the new record to the end of the file. If **RecordPos** contains a value other than zero, **SaveHotspotRecord()** writes the record back to the specified position.

Retrieving Hotspot Records

Our next requirement is to be able to retrieve and edit hotspots that we have already saved in the file. And that's where the HTSPT2F2.FRM, shown in Figure 8.5, comes in. Create this form and set its **Name** property to HotSpot2F2. Remember to save it in a file named HTSPT2F2.FRM.

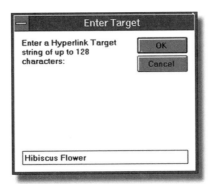

Figure 8.4   *The InputBox$() function will display a dialog box to request the target string for the hotspot.*

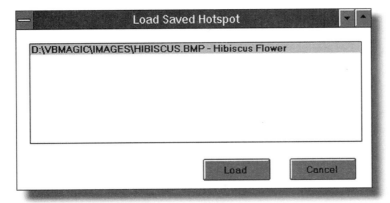

Figure 8.5   *The HTSPT2F2.FRM form will allow us to retrieve and edit existing hotspots.*

The form has three controls: a List Box named **HotSpotList** and two Command Buttons named **CancelButton** and **LoadButton**. The **Form_Load()** event procedure, shown in Listing 8.13, loads **HotSpotList** with the names of all the hotspots in the file that belong to the currently loaded image.

Listing 8.13   The Form_Load() Event Procedure from HTSPT2F2.FRM

```
Sub Form_Load ()
    Dim RecordCounter As Long
    Dim FileLength As Integer
    Dim TempHotspotRecord As HotSpotRecords

    LoadButton.Enabled = False
    HotSpotList.Clear
    FileLength = LOF(ImageLinkFile) / Len(TempHotspotRecord)
    For RecordCounter = 1 To FileLength
        Get ImageLinkFile, RecordCounter, TempHotspotRecord
        If RTrim$(TempHotspotRecord.Image) = CurrentImageFilename Then
            HotSpotList.AddItem RTrim$(TempHotspotRecord.Image) +
    " - " + RTrim$(TempHotspotRecord.Target)
            HotSpotList.ItemData(HotSpotList.NewIndex) = RecordCounter
        End If
    Next RecordCounter
End Sub
```

We use the **ItemData** property of the List Box to store the record positions of the hotspot records, so we can replace one or more of them later without searching for them.

To select a hotspot for editing and display it on HotSpot2F1, we'll accept either a double-click on the **HotSpotList** item, or a single click on the Load Command Button. The procedures that handle this work are shown in Listing 8.14.

Listing 8.14   The HotspotList_DblClick() and LoadButton_Click() Event Procedures from HTSPT2F2.FRM

```
Sub HotspotList_DblClick ()
    CurrentHotSpotRecordNumber = HotSpotList.ItemData(HotSpotList.ListIndex)
    LoadHotSpot CurrentHotSpotRecordNumber
    End Sub

Sub LoadButton_Click ()
    CurrentHotSpotRecordNumber = HotSpotList.ItemData(HotSpotList.ListIndex)
    LoadHotSpot CurrentHotSpotRecordNumber
    End Sub
```

These simple event procedures both call a general procedure, **LoadHotSpot()**, shown in Listing 8.15.

Listing 8.15 The LoadHotSpot() General Procedure from HTSPT2F2.FRM

```
Sub LoadHotSpot (RecordPos As Long)

    Get ImageLinkFile, RecordPos, HotSpotRecord
    AnchorX = HotSpotRecord.TopX
    AnchorY = HotSpotRecord.TopY
    EndX = HotSpotRecord.BottomX
    EndY = HotSpotRecord.BottomY
    HotSpot2F1.SaveOption.Enabled = True
    HotSpot2F1.DeleteOption.Enabled = True

    Unload HotSpot2F2

    End Sub
```

The other Command Button, **CancelButton**, just unloads the form. Its event procedure is provided in Listing 8.16.

Listing 8.16 The CancelButton_Click() Event Procedure from HTSPT2F2.FRM

```
Sub CancelButton_Click ()
    Unload HotSpot2F2
    End Sub
```

Defining the Other Menu Options

Back in the main form, HOTSPOT2.FRM, the File, Edit Saved Hotspot option kicks off the process of loading a hotspot record. Listing 8.17 shows the procedure needed for this task.

Listing 8.17 The EditOption_Click() Menu Event Procedure from HOTSPOT2.FRM

```
Sub EditOption_Click ()
    HotSpot2F1.Line (AnchorX, AnchorY)-(EndX, EndY), , B
    DeleteRegion hRectRgn
    HotSpot2F2.Show 1
    If TestOption.Checked Then
        hRectRgn = CreateRectRgn(AnchorX, AnchorY, EndX, EndY)
      End If
    HotSpot2F1.Refresh
    End Sub
```

EditOption_Click() first uses the **Line()** method to erase any rectangle already visible in the client area. It then deletes any lingering Windows region, and opens HotSpot2F2 as a *modal* form. One difference between a modal and a *modeless* form is that when Windows displays a modal form, no other window in the application can receive input, either from the keyboard or the mouse, until the modal form is unloaded or hidden. The other difference has a more profound impact on the code in this **Click** event. The five lines of code that follow **HotSpot2F2.Show** build the new rectangular region and redraw the screen to display the rectangle on the image. If we showed the second form *modelessly*, these last lines would excecute immediately. Then when the user selected a hotspot from the Hotspot List Box and returned to **HotSpot2F1**, the region and the rectangular coordinates might belong to two different region records. When you **Show** a modal form, execution of code in the calling procedure is suspended until the modal form is hidden or unloaded. In effect, the modal form behaves like a subprocedure (Message Boxes are modal forms). You should specify the modal option on a form whenever it makes no sense to continue program execution until the subform gathers information from the user. The global constant **MODAL**, which has a value of 1, is located in the file GLOBCONS.TXT, which we've imported into GLOBCONS.BAS.

Next, we need a way to clear an existing hotspot from the editor window and start a new one. For that, we'll write the **NewOption_Click()** event procedure as shown in Listing 8.18.

Listing 8.18   The NewOption_Click() Menu Event Procedure from HOTSPOT2.FRM

```
Sub NewOption_Click ()

    SaveOption.Enabled = False
    DeleteOption.Enabled = False
    CurrentHotspotRecordNumber = 0
    InitRecordBuffer
    Line (AnchorX, AnchorY)-(EndX, EndY), , B
    AnchorX = 0
    AnchorY = 0
    EndX = 0
    EndY = 0
    TestOption.Checked = False
    DefineOption.Checked = True
    DeleteRegion hRectRgn
    End Sub
```

Once again, we use the **Line()** method and the **Invert DrawMode** to undraw the current rectangle. We then initialize all the variables, set the Mode menu options to indicate that the program is in Define mode, and if necessary, delete the current region.

Deleting Hotspot Records

We have one more menu option to finish, Delete Hotspot. The procedure that processes this menu option is **DeleteOption_Click()**, which is shown in Listing 8.19.

Listing 8.19   The DeleteOption_Click() Menu Event Procedure from
HOTSPOT2.FRM

```
Sub DeleteOption_Click ()
    Dim Response As Integer

    If CurrentHotspotRecordNumber > 0 Then
        Response = MsgBox("Are you sure you want to delete this Hotspot?",
                MB_YESNO + MB_ICONQUESTION, "Warning!")
        If Response = IDYES Then
            SaveOption.Enabled = False
            DeleteOption.Enabled = False
            InitRecordBuffer
            SaveHotspotRecord HotSpotRecord, CurrentHotspotRecordNumber
            CurrentHotspotRecordNumber = 0
            Line (AnchorX, AnchorY)-(EndX, EndY), , B
            AnchorX = 0
            AnchorY = 0
            EndX = 0
            EndY = 0
            TestOption.Checked = False
            DefineOption.Checked = True
            DeleteRegion hRectRgn
        End If
    Else
        MsgBox "There is no region to delete.", 48, "Delete Error"
    End If
End Sub
```

This procedure performs many of the same operations as
NewOption_Click(). The only significant differences are the **MsgBox()** prompt
that offers an opportunity to cancel the deletion, and the call to
SaveHotspotRecord. The second **MsgBox()**, the one that warns when users
try to delete an undefined region, should never appear if you have properly
enabled and disabled menu options throughout the program.

What's Next?

Wow. Creating our rectangular hotspot editor was a big job. In our hyperimaging
adventures, we've uncovered some powerful Windows programming techniques to help automate the process of defining hotspot regions.

We're now ready to move on and enter the next dimension of hyperimaging.
When we arrive, you'll learn how to create a much more versatile hotspot
editor for defining irregular-shaped hotspots.

Chapter 9

It's now time to explore real-world objects, and create more functional hyperimaging projects.

Hyperimaging: The Next Dimension

magine if you could bring the feel of the Grand Canyon into your home. You could hang up a big photograph in your living room but it wouldn't be very interactive. What you really want is to feel like you're there. Almost as if you could soar over the canyon like an eagle, locate a hidden gorge, dive down into the canyon, and jump on a raft and splash down the Colorado river.

In Chapter 8, we learned to create rectangular hotspot regions. Unfortunately, the real world isn't made up of rectangles. (If it were, think how boring life would be!) To create multimedia adventures like the real-world, Grand Canyon project, you'll need a way to jig-saw pictures of the real world into irregularly-shaped hotspots. Once you accomplish this task, you'll be able to click on any part of a picture and set off a multimedia event like playing a video or zooming in for greater detail.

Mastering Irregular Hotspots

To bring the non-rectangular world of cars, planes, dinosaurs, and nature into our multimedia apps, we need to create irregular hotspots.

Let's begin by developing another hotspot editor for our multimedia construction set. For now, we'll start with the drawing and testing features. Then, in the next project we'll adapt the code we wrote in Chapter 8 for the rectangular hotspot editor into an editor for irregular-shaped regions.

Drawing Irregular-Shaped Images

This project shows you how to draw irregular-shaped images using the mouse and then test out the regions you've drawn.

1. Create the form HOTSPOT3.FRM to use as the hotspot drawing area.
2. Add the event procedures that make it possible to quickly draw complex shapes on the form's client area (Listings 9.1 through 9.4).
3. Add the **DeleteRegion()** general procedure to HOTSPOT3.BAS (Listing 9.5).
4. Fill in the **Paint** event to redraw the current polygon (Listing 9.6).
5. Add the menu support procedures (Listing 9.7 and 9.8).
6. Add the necessary declarations (Listing 9.9 and 9.10).

> *This project is located in the directory \VBMAGIC, in the files HOTSPOT3.MAK, HOTSPOT3.FRM, and HOTSPOT3.BAS.*

Running the Program—Testing the Polygon Hotspots

Run the HOTSPOT3 program and you'll see that it starts in Define mode as shown in Figure 9.1. To begin drawing a polygon, click the mouse button and release it anywhere on the client area of the form. The first line segment will then follow your cursor around until you click again to lock in the second point. Then the second line will follow the cursor. Add several sides to the figure. When you feel you've made a complex enough region, place the cursor near the first point and click again. The line that was following you will let go of the cursor and join the first vertex, sealing off the polygon. If you click again anywhere on the client area, the program will display the message box that tells you the polygon is closed. To draw a different polygon, you must first select New from the File menu.

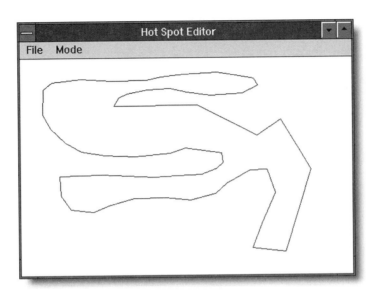

Figure 9.1 *Drawing irregularly-shaped regions with HOTSPOT3.*

To test the hotspot region, select Testing Region from the Mode menu. Then click in and around your polygon to prove that it works. To stop the program, choose Close from the Control menu of the form or select Quit from the File menu. If you stop the program from the VB menu bar, you may leave an orphaned region in memory, which will remain there throughout your Windows session.

Creating the Form

We'll begin the project with a new form. Set the Form's **Name** property to **HotSpot3F1** and save it as HOTSPOT3.FRM. Set the **AutoRedraw** and **ClipControls** properties to False, set the **ScaleMode** to 3 - Pixel, and set the **DrawMode** to 6 - Invert.

We won't need to place any controls on the form, but we do need to begin with a few menu options. Open the Menu Design window and add the menus and options shown in Table 9.1. Figure 9.2 shows the completed form.

Drawing Polygons

In this project we'll use the **MouseDown** and **MouseMove** events to draw the outlines of our polygon hotspot regions. But unlike the editor in Chapter 8, this drawing program doesn't use the **MouseUp** event to complete a figure. When we were drawing rectangles, we needed to define only two points, opposite corners. The procedure for drawing a rectangle meshed nicely with

Table 9.1　*The HOTSPOT3.FRM Menus.*

Menu Caption Property	Menu Name Property	Option Caption Property	Option Name Property
File	FileMenu	New	NewOption
		Quit	QuitOption
Mode	ModeMenu	Defining Region	DefineOption
		Testing Region	TestOption

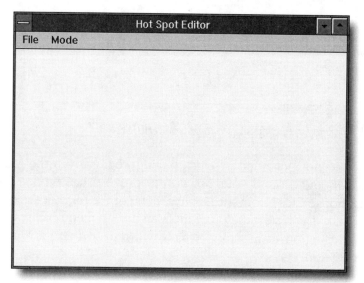

Figure 9.2　*The HotSpot3F1 form, the main form for our polygon hotspot test editor.*

the **MouseDown-MouseMove-MouseUp** sequence of events. Unfortunately, it takes more than two points to define a non-rectangular polygon. To mark each corner, or *vertex*, we need to click and release the mouse button repeatedly, which means we can't use the **MouseUp** event to wrap things up.

So when is a polygon complete? When it's closed. For each mouse click, we'll add a new vertex to the polygon and check the distance to the starting point. We'll close the loop either when the latest click comes within 10 pixels of the starting point, or when we fill up the array of vertex points, whichever comes first.

The **Form_MouseDown()** event procedure we'll need looks similar to the one in HOTSPOT2.FRM, but there's a big difference as shown in Listing 9.1.

Listing 9.1   The Form_MouseDown() Event Procedure from HOTSPOT3.FRM

```
Sub Form_MouseDown (Button As Integer, Shift As Integer, X As Single, Y As Single)

    Dim Dummy As Integer

    If DefineOption.Checked Then
        If DrawingPolygon Then
            DrawingPolygon = Not VertexFinishesPolygon(X, Y)
            PreviousX = X
            PreviousY = Y
        Else
            Dummy = mciExecute("play c:\windows\ding.wav")
            MsgBox "This polygon region is closed", 16, "Drawing Error"
        End If
    Else
        ' Test whether click is in region.
        If PtInRegion(hPolyRgn, X, Y) Then
            Dummy = mciExecute("play c:\windows\tada.wav")
        Else
            Dummy = mciExecute("play c:\windows\ding.wav")
        End If
    End If
End Sub
```

In HOTSPOT2.FRM, the **MouseDown** event erased the previously drawn rectangle by drawing over it in **Invert DrawMode**. It then set new anchor and end points. The version of **MouseDown** in this program doesn't draw or erase anything itself. It leaves that task to **MouseMove**. For each click of the mouse button, until the polygon is finished, **MouseDown** calls a general function named **VertexFinishesPolygon()**, as shown in Listing 9.2

Listing 9.2   The VertexFinishesPolygon() General Function from HOTSPOT3.FRM

```
Function VertexFinishesPolygon (X As Single, Y As Single) As Integer
    If (CurrentPointIndex > 0) And ((Sqr((X - PolygonVertices(0).X) ^ 2 + (Y -
        PolygonVertices(0).Y) ^ 2) <= 10) Or (CurrentPointIndex = 99)) Then
        HotSpot3F1.Line (PolygonVertices(CurrentPointIndex).X,
            PolygonVertices(CurrentPointIndex).Y)- (PreviousX, PreviousY)
        HotSpot3F1.Line (PolygonVertices(CurrentPointIndex).X,
                    PolygonVertices(CurrentPointIndex).Y)- (PolygonVertices(0).X,
                    PolygonVertices(0).Y)
        VertexFinishesPolygon = True
    Else
        CurrentPointIndex = CurrentPointIndex + 1
        PolygonVertices(CurrentPointIndex).X = X
        PolygonVertices(CurrentPointIndex).Y = Y
        VertexFinishesPolygon = False
    End If
End Function
```

The first thing this function does is check whether the polygon has more than one vertex and whether it's time to close it. If so, it erases the last line segment drawn by **MouseMove**, draws the line that closes the polygon, and returns **True**. Otherwise it adds the new vertex to the array and returns **False**. I've split out this function only for clarity; it's called from just one place, **Form_MouseDown**.

Listing 9.3 shows the **Form_MouseMove()** event procedure.

Listing 9.3 The Form_MouseMove() Event Procedure from HOTSPOT3.FRM

```
Sub Form_MouseMove (Button As Integer, Shift As Integer, X As Single, Y As Single)
    If DrawingPolygon And (CurrentPointIndex > -1) Then
        Line (PolygonVertices(CurrentPointIndex).X,
                PolygonVertices(CurrentPointIndex).Y)- (PreviousX, PreviousY)
        PreviousX = X
        PreviousY = Y
        Line (PolygonVertices(CurrentPointIndex).X,
                PolygonVertices(CurrentPointIndex).Y)- (PreviousX, PreviousY)
    End If
End Sub
```

Like the **Form_MouseMove()** event procedure we used in HOTSPOT2.FRM, this procedure erases and redraws the lines as you move the mouse across the client area. But instead of a rectangle, it stretches a single line from the latest vertex to the mouse pointer. Until you close the polygon by clicking within the 10-pixel radius of ground zero, or by filling up the vertex array, the line will follow you wherever you go.

With all these things to keep track of—the array of vertices and its number of points stored, the current state of completion, the lines on the screen, the region handle—you know we're going to need an initalization procedure. Listing 9.4 shows **InitPolygonEditor()**—the right guy for this job.

Listing 9.4 The InitPolygonEditor() General Procedure from HOTSPOT3.FRM

```
Sub InitPolygonEditor ()
    Dim I As Integer

    DeleteRegion hPolyRgn
    If CurrentPointIndex > 1 Then
        For I = 1 To CurrentPointIndex
            Line (PolygonVertices(I - 1).X, PolygonVertices(I - 1).Y)-
              (PolygonVertices(I).X, PolygonVertices(I).Y)
        Next I
        If Not DrawingPolygon Then
            Line (PolygonVertices(CurrentPointIndex).X,
              PolygonVertices(CurrentPointIndex).Y)- (PolygonVertices(0).X,
```

```
            PolygonVertices(0).Y)
        End If
    End If
  CurrentPointIndex = -1
  DrawingPolygon = True
  End Sub
```

This procedure cleans up any polygon, or polygon pieces, we have lying around by disposing of the region handle, drawing over the polygon in the client area with the Invert pen, and resetting **CurrentPointIndex** to **-1**. The general procedure **DeleteRegion()**, shown in Listing 9.5, comes from the previous hotspot projects, and it resides in HOTSPOT3.BAS.

Listing 9.5   The DeleteRegion() General Procedure from HOTSPOT3.BAS

```
Sub DeleteRegion (hRgn As Integer)
    If hRgn <> 0 Then
        If DeleteObject(hRgn) Then
            hRgn = 0
        Else
            MsgBox "Unable to Delete Region", 48, "GDI Error"
        End If
    End If
  End Sub
```

Redrawing Polygons

Event-driven programming really begins to test us when we write drawing programs. To get predictable results, we have to consider not only how the various mouse events need to behave, but also all the things that can happen to our client area during and after the drawing process. What happens, for example, when you bring the hotspot editor back to the foreground after switching to another application? We expect the program to return the picture to the state it was in before we covered it. And to do that, it's going to need a **Form_Paint()** event procedure. So that's what we'll do. Take a look at Listing 9.6 to see how this is done.

Listing 9.6   The Form_Paint() Event Procedure from HOTSPOT3.FRM

```
Sub Form_Paint ()
    Dim I As Integer

    If CurrentPointIndex > 1 Then
        For I = 1 To CurrentPointIndex
            Line (PolygonVertices(I - 1).X, PolygonVertices(I - 1).Y)-
              (PolygonVertices(I).X, PolygonVertices(I).Y)
        Next I
```

```
    If Not DrawingPolygon Then
        Line (PolygonVertices(CurrentPointIndex).X,
                    PolygonVertices(CurrentPointIndex).Y)-
(PolygonVertices(0).X,
                    PolygonVertices(0).Y)
        End If
    End If
End Sub
```

This procedure will redraw the outline of the polygonal hotspot whenever the client area becomes uncovered, moves, or changes size. But it won't work unless you've properly set both the **AutoRedraw** and **ClipControls** properties of the form HotSpot3F1. If you set **AutoRedraw** to True, you don't need the **Paint** event at all, and you don't need to worry about **ClipControls**. However, if you set **AutoRedraw** to **False** then you must also set **ClipControls** to **False**. When **AutoRedraw** is **False** and **ClipControls** is **True**, VB will repaint the entire client area whenever it detects the need to repaint any portion of it. The problem with indiscriminately repainting everything is that the Invert pen will erase the areas that were never covered in the first place, so the lines in the newly exposed area re-appear and all the others vanish. When you set **ClipControls** to **False**, however, VB repaints only newly exposed areas, restoring the image to its original condition.

Starting a New Polygon

We have one last drawing detail to handle before we fill in the remaining menu options and the declarations. If you decide to select the New menu option before you've closed off a polygon, you'll trail a stray line from the last point you set to the edge of the client area. To make sure the extra line gets cleaned up we have to check whether we're in drawing mode, and if so, erase the line by redrawing it. Listing 9.7 shows the menu procedure that handles this task.

Listing 9.7 The NewOption_Click() Event Procedure from HOTSPOT3.FRM

```
Sub NewOption_Click ()
    If DrawingPolygon Then
        Line (PolygonVertices(CurrentPointIndex).X,
                PolygonVertices(CurrentPointIndex).Y)-(PreviousX, PreviousY)
    End If
    InitPolygonEditor
    TestOption.Checked = False
    DefineOption.Checked = True
    End Sub
```

The **MouseMove()** event procedure won't draw any lines when **DrawingPolygon** is **False**, so we want to execute the **Line()** method in the **NewOption_Click()** event procedure only when **DrawingPolygon** is **True**.

The last three lines of the **NewOption_Click()** event procedure set things up so we can draw a new polygon. Obviously, if we've cleared the current polygon, we have to make sure the program is in Define mode, not Test mode.

Tidying Up—The Remaining Code for HOTSPOT3

The last three menu option **Click** events and the **Form_Load()** and **Form_Unload()** event procedures perform some simple housekeeping, such as switching the check mark on the Define and Test mode options, and creating and deleting the hotspot region. This code is shown in Listing 9.8.

Listing 9.8   The Remaining Event Procedures in HOTSPOT3.FRM

```
Sub DefineOption_Click ()
    TestOption.Checked = False
    DefineOption.Checked = True
    DeleteRegion hPolyRgn
    End Sub

Sub Form_Load ()
    InitPolygonEditor
    End Sub

Sub Form_Unload (Cancel As Integer)
    DeleteRegion hPolyRgn
    End Sub

Sub TestOption_Click ()
    If DrawingPolygon Then
        MsgBox "Cannot Test Incomplete Polygon", 48, "Error"
      Else
        DefineOption.Checked = False
        TestOption.Checked = True
        hPolyRgn = CreatePolygonRgn(PolygonVertices(0), CurrentPointIndex + 1, 0)
      End If
    End Sub

Sub QuitOption_Click ()
    Form_Unload (0)
    End
    End Sub
```

Finally, we need to add the declarations to HOTSPOT3.FRM (Listing 9.9) and HOTSPOT3.BAS (Listing 9.10).

Listing 9.9   The Declarations Section from HOTSPOT3.FRM

```
Option Explicit

Dim hPolyRgn As Integer
Dim PolygonVertices(99) As POINTAPI
Dim PreviousX As Integer
Dim PreviousY As Integer
Dim CurrentPointIndex As Integer
Dim DrawingPolygon As Integer
```

Listing 9.10   The Declarations Section from HOTSPOT3.BAS

```
Option Explicit

Type POINTAPI
    X As Integer
    Y As Integer
    End Type

Declare Function CreatePolygonRgn Lib "GDI" (lpPoints As POINTAPI, ByVal nCount
    As Integer, ByVal nPolyFillMode As Integer) As Integer
Declare Function PtInRegion Lib "GDI" (ByVal hRgn As Integer, ByVal X As
    Integer, ByVal Y As Integer) As Integer
Declare Function DeleteObject Lib "GDI" (ByVal hObject As Integer) As Integer
Declare Function mciExecute Lib "MMSystem" (ByVal CommandString As String) As
    Integer
```

Adding Polygon Hotspots to Images

Now we'll combine what we learned in our last two projects, HOTSPOT2.MAK (Chapter 7) and HOTSPOT3.MAK, to write a polygon editor that lets us draw irregular-shaped hotspots over bitmap images and save them in a data file. In the next chapter, we'll pull them back out and put them to work in our hypermedia system.

Although this program closely resembles HOTSPOT2, it varies considerably in the details. I'll highlight the most significant differences here, but don't make any assumptions about the housekeeping procedures. One flaky flag can break the whole thing. Study the code.

Watch for three important differences between this and the two previous projects. First, we'll add a Picture Box control, where we'll do all our drawing. Second, we'll shift around some code, primarily from the main form to the code module. Finally, we'll use the data access features of VB to store our hotspots in a Microsoft Access database. These changes will help us get ready to add hyperimaging to our hypermedia system.

The Powerful (Irregular) Hotspot Editor

This editor draws and saves irregular (polygon) hotspot regions. Here are the steps we'll follow:

1. Create two forms, HotSpot4F1, saved as the file HOTSPOT4.FRM, and HotSpot4F2, saved as the file HTSPT4F2.FRM.
2. Set up the **Mouse** events to perform the drawing operations (Listings 9.11 through 9.13).
3. Create the database file structure.
4. Save and retrieve hotspots from the database file (Listings 9.14 through 9.17).

> *This project is located in the directory \VBMAGIC, in the files HOTSPOT4.MAK, HOTSPOT4.FRM, HOTSPOT4.BAS, HTSPT4F2.FRM, DATACONS.BAS, and GLOBCONS.BAS. You'll also need the Common Dialog control, which is located in the file CMDIALOG.VBX. VB Setup normally installs this, and its other .VBX files in your \WINDOWS\SYSTEM directory.*

Running the New Hotspot Editor

When you start the HOTSPOT4 program, you'll see the form shown in Figure 9.3. The first time you run this program, it will create an Access database file

Figure 9.3 *Running HOTSPOT4.*

called IMAGES.MDB. The file should appear in the same directory as HOTSPOT4.MAK. Before you can begin drawing polygons, you must first load a picture into the Picture Box by choosing File, Load Picture. Use the resulting dialog box to select any Windows bitmap image file (*.BMP or *.DIB).

Draw a polygon outline around some portion of the image, and then choose File, Save Hotspot. The program prompts you to enter a hyperlink target string. For now, enter anything; we'll create working target strings in the next chapter. When you click on OK, the program will add a new record to the Image Table in IMAGES.MDB.

Of course, you have to properly terminate the program and dispose of any active region. Simply choose File, Quit, or choose Close from the form's Control menu. That's all there is to it.

Creating the Forms

Start with a new project and set the **Name** property of the first form to HotSpot4F1. You won't need to worry about the **DrawMode**, **ScaleMode**, **AutoRedraw**, or **ClipControls** properties of the form because we're going to do all our drawing in a Picture Box.

Open the Menu Design window and create two menus, one labeled &File and one labeled &Mode. Under the File menu, add the options listed in Table 9.2.

Under the Mode menu, add the &Defining Region and &Testing Region options. Name them **DefineOption** and **TestOption**, respectively.

We'll need two controls on this form. First, drop in a Picture Box. We'll only have one Picture Box in the whole project, so we'll just leave its **Name** property set to the default, Picture1. This is where we'll be drawing our polygon hotspots, so stretch it out to fill most of the client area of the form, as shown in Figure 9.4. Set the Picture Box's **AutoRedraw** and **ClipControls** properties to False, set its **ScaleMode** to 3 - Pixel, and set its **DrawMode** to 6 - Invert.

Table 9.2 *The File menu options from HOTSPOT2.FRM*

Menu Caption	Menu Name
&Load Picture	LoadOption
&New Hotspot	NewOption
&Edit Saved Hotspot	EditOption
&Save Hotspot	SaveOption
&Delete Hotspot	DeleteOption
&Quit	QuitOption

The second control we'll be adding will be a Common Dialog. Make sure the file CMDIALOG.VBX is listed in the Project window. If not, select File, Add File from the VB menu bar, and locate this file in the Windows System directory (usually C:\WINDOWS\SYSTEM). Once you've added the .VBX file to the project, you'll find the Common Dialog control in the VB Toolbox. The icon for the control looks like a miniature window with a few controls drawn on it. You can place the Common Dialog control anywhere on the form's client area; remember, it will become invisible at runtime.

To add the second form, select File, New Form. Set the **Name** property of the form to HotSpot4F2. Also, set its **BorderStyle** to 1 - Fixed Single and its **Caption** to "Open a Hotspot."

On this form we'll need three controls, one List Box and two Command Buttons. Set the **Name** property of the List Box to HotSpotList. Set the **Caption** properties of the two Command Buttons to "Load Hotspot" and "Cancel." Set their **Name** properties to LoadButton and CancelButton, respectively. Figure 9.5 shows what this form looks like.

Programming the Main Form

The **MouseDown()** and **MouseMove()** event procedures have changed hardly at all, except that they now belong to Picture1 rather than the form. The **Line()** methods inside **MouseMove()** include explicit de-references to Picture1 although their relationship to the control is implied. Listing 9.11 shows the complete code for **Picture1_MouseMove()**.

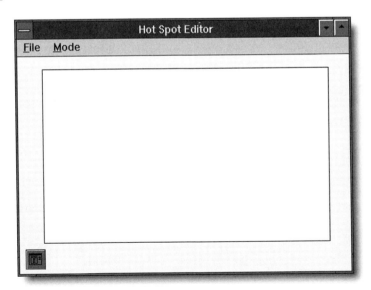

Figure 9.4   *Creating the main form for the hotspot editor.*

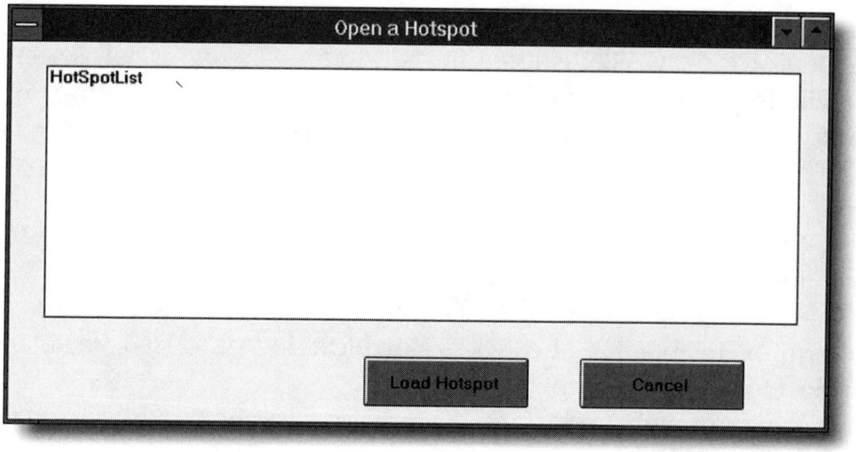

Figure 9.5 *The HotSpot4F2 form.*

Listing 9.11 The Picture1_MouseMove() Event Procedure from HOTSPOT4.FRM

```
Sub Picture1_MouseMove (Button As Integer, Shift As Integer, X As Single, Y As Single)
    If DrawingPolygon And (CurrentPointIndex > -1) Then
        Picture1.Line (PolygonVertices(CurrentPointIndex).X,
                PolygonVertices(CurrentPointIndex).Y)-(PreviousX, PreviousY)
        PreviousX = X
        PreviousY = Y
        Picture1.Line (PolygonVertices(CurrentPointIndex).X,
                PolygonVertices(CurrentPointIndex).Y)-(PreviousX, PreviousY)
    End If
End Sub
```

We have to modify the general function **VertexFinishesPolygon()** in the same way, but this time the change is necessary. Here's why. General functions defined in a form module belong to that form, and any method we use without an explicit object reference would belong to the form. To guarantee that the **Line()** methods draw on the Picture Box instead of the form, we have to change their object references to Picture1, as shown in Listing 9.12.

Listing 9.12 The VertexFinishesPolygon() General Function from HOTSPOT4.FRM

```
Function VertexFinishesPolygon (X As Single, Y As Single) As Integer
    If (CurrentPointIndex > 0) And
        ((Sqr((X - PolygonVertices(0).X) ^ 2 + (Y - PolygonVertices(0).Y) ^ 2)
                <= 10) Or (CurrentPointIndex = 99)) Then
        Picture1.Line (PolygonVertices(CurrentPointIndex).X,
                PolygonVertices(CurrentPointIndex).Y)-(PreviousX, PreviousY)
        Picture1.Line (PolygonVertices(CurrentPointIndex).X,
```

```
                    PolygonVertices(CurrentPointIndex).Y)-(PolygonVertices(0).X,
                    PolygonVertices(0).Y)
    VertexFinishesPolygon = True
    SaveOption.Enabled = True
  Else
    CurrentPointIndex = CurrentPointIndex + 1
    PolygonVertices(CurrentPointIndex).X = X
    PolygonVertices(CurrentPointIndex).Y = Y
    VertexFinishesPolygon = False
  End If
End Function
```

In HOTSPOT3.FRM we duplicated the code that draws (or erases) the polygon in **InitPolygonEditor()** and the **Form_Paint()** event procedure. In our new version, we'll place that code in a general procedure called **DrawPolygon()**, which will now reside in HOTSPOT4.BAS as shown in Listing 9.13.

Listing 9.13   The DrawPolygon() General Procedure from HOTSPOT4.BAS

```
Sub DrawPolygon (VertexArray() As POINTAPI, LastArrayIndex As Integer,
  ThePicture As PictureBox, CompletePolygon As Integer)
  Dim I As Integer

  If LastArrayIndex > 0 Then
    For I = 1 To LastArrayIndex
      ThePicture.Line (VertexArray(I - 1).X, VertexArray(I - 1).Y)-
                      (VertexArray(I).X, VertexArray(I).Y)
    Next I
  If CompletePolygon Then
      ThePicture.Line (VertexArray(LastArrayIndex).X,
                      VertexArray(LastArrayIndex).Y)-(VertexArray(0).X,
VertexArray(0).Y)
    End If
  End If
End Sub
```

This procedure reveals the reason for plugging in Picture1 instead of continuing to use the form as the drawing surface. When we later use the hotspots we've created with this program in actual multimedia presentations, we may occasionally want to draw the outlines of the hotspot regions. To produce such a general purpose version of the procedure, we'll need to pass in the display control as an argument, which means that we have to give it an *object type*. We can't use the types **Form** and **PictureBox** interchangeably, so we have to pick one or the other. Since Picture Boxes will give us the most flexibility in later programming projects (not just those in this book), that's what we'll use here.

Storing Polygon Regions

In the project HOTSPOT2.MAK, we used VB's regular file I/O to store records in a binary data file. We defined the record with the **Type** statement:

```
Type HotSpotRecords
    Image As String * 128
    Target As String * 128
    TopX As Integer
    TopY As Integer
    BottomX As Integer
    BottomY As Integer
    End Type
```

We then used the **Put** and **Get** statements to store and retrieve records from the data file.

To use the same method for polygon hotspots, we would need to modify the record structure to accommodate a complete set of vertices:

```
Type PolygonHotSpotRecords
    Image As String * 128
    Target As String * 128
    VertexArray(99) As POINTAPI
    End Type
```

The record structure looks simpler, but it's much larger. Each record of type **HotSpotRecords** occupies 264 bytes, the sum of its two string fields and four two-byte integers. A record of the hypothetical type **PolygonHotSpotRecords** would fill 656 bytes, no matter whether the polygon it represented consisted of only three or eighty-three vertices.

We could split the record into two structures, and therefore two files, one to hold the image filename and target string, and one to hold each vertex. Then we could store just as many points as we needed to define each polygon. To keep track of the vertex records, we could use a linked list structure, like the one we created to store hypertext in Chapter 2.

Even if we were to get all that working, we would still have to figure out ways sort and search the primary file, and to manage deleted records in both files. Fortunately, VB offers us an alternative to building our own database manager. With version 3.0 of VB, Microsoft introduced the *Data Access* system, which includes a whole bunch of features that enable us to create and maintain databases using the Microsoft Access database engine. With the Data Access features, we can use simple methods to add, change, or delete records. And to top it all off, records in Access databases can store special binary fields, which may vary in length from record to record.

Building the Hotspot Database

Unlike ordinary binary data files, Access data files are not built from records defined with the **Type** statement. Instead, Access records are collections of *field objects* that belong to a *table definition object*. The table definition object, in turn, belongs to the mother of all Access objects, a *database object*.

Let's take a look at the inner workings of the Access database engine. We build a useable database by first creating all the necessary objects. We then assemble them with the **Append** method. First we declare and define **Field** objects, which we **Append** to the **Fields** collection of the **TableDef** object. Next we define an **Index** object based on the fields in the **Fields** collection and **Append** it to the **Indexes** collection of the **TableDef** object. And finally, we **Append** the whole **TableDef** object to the **Database** object. A **Table** may contain many fields, and a **Database** may contain many **Tables**. And these are just some of the object types available to us in the Access database system.

We'll call our database ImageDB and store it in a file called IMAGES.MDB. ImageDB will contain only one table, which we'll call ImageTable. The table definition that corresponds to ImageTable will be called **ImageTableDef**, and will contain four field definitions: **ImageFilename**, a 128-byte *text* field; **HotSpotNum**, a long integer field; **LinkTarget**, another 128-byte text field; and **VertexArray**, a *long binary* field. We'll also create one index for the table called **PrimaryKey**, which will be ordered according to the combination of two fields, the **ImageFilename** plus the **HotSpotNum**.

The general function **OpenImageDatabase()**, which resides in HOTSPOT4.BAS as shown in Listing 9.14, will open the database for business. If the file doesn't exist, it will create it by assembling all the appropriate objects.

Listing 9.14   The OpenImageDatabase() General Function from HOTSPOT4.BAS

```
Function OpenImageDatabase () As Integer
    ' Opens the file IMAGES.MDB.  If file does
    ' not exist, this function will create it.
    Dim Fld() As New Field
    Dim Idx() As New Index
    Dim ImageTableDef As New TableDef
    Dim Counter As Integer

    If Len(Dir$(App.Path + "\Images.MDB")) > 0 Then
        Set ImageDB = OpenDatabase(App.Path + "\Images.MDB")
        Set ImageTable = ImageDB.OpenTable("ImageTable")
      Else
        ' Create the database Images.MDB
        Set ImageDB = CreateDatabase(App.Path + "\Images.MDB", DB_LANG_GENERAL)
        ' Create the ImageTable
```

```
        ImageTableDef.Name = "ImageTable"
        ' Create the Fields.
        ReDim Fld(1 To 4)
        Fld(2).Attributes = DB_AUTOINCRFIELD      ' Counter field.
        For Counter = 1 To 4  ' Set properties for fields.
            Fld(Counter).Name = Choose(Counter, "ImageFileName", "HotSpotNum",
                            "LinkTarget", "VertexArray")
            Fld(Counter).Type = Choose(Counter, DB_TEXT, DB_LONG, DB_TEXT,
                            DB_LONGBINARY)
            Fld(Counter).Size = Choose(Counter, 128, 4, 128, 400)
            ImageTableDef.Fields.Append Fld(Counter)
            Next Counter

        ' Create the Table Index.
        ReDim Idx(1)
        Idx(1).Name = "PrimaryKey"
        Idx(1).Fields = "ImageFileName;HotSpotNum"
        Idx(1).Primary = True
        Idx(1).Unique = True
        ImageTableDef.Indexes.Append Idx(1)

        ' Create the Table.
        ImageDB.TableDefs.Append ImageTableDef
        ImageDB.Close
        Set ImageDB = OpenDatabase(App.Path + "\Images.MDB")
        Set ImageTable = ImageDB.OpenTable("ImageTable")
    End If
End Function
```

Although it looks a little lengthy, this function is simple. The only decision it needs to make is whether to open an existing database file or create a new one. The VB **Dir$()** function will return a null string ("") if it can't locate the filename and path you've passed it. If we find the file, we use the **Set** statement and the **OpenDatabase()** function to open the object variable **ImageDB**. There is no permanent relationship between the object variable and the database file. We could use any legal variable name to reference the database object, as long as we declare it as a database object:

```
Dim AnyDatabase As Database
```

The declaration for **ImageDB** is **Global** and you'll find it in the declarations section of HOTSPOT4.BAS, along with the declaration for **ImageTable**. Inside this function we declare three types of local object variables:

```
Dim Fld() As New Field
Dim Idx() As New Index
Dim ImageTableDef As New TableDef
```

Here we use the reserved word **New** to indicate that these objects don't yet exist. To create a new child object, you must declare it as **New**.

To open an existing database, we use two **Set** statements:

```
If Len(Dir$(App.Path + "\Images.MDB")) > 0 Then
    Set ImageDB = OpenDatabase(App.Path + "\Images.MDB")
    Set ImageTable = ImageDB.OpenTable("ImageTable")
```

The **Path** property of the **App** object will return the path of the .MAK file for a program running in the VB development environment, or the path of the .EXE file for a compiled program. This is an arbitrary restriction I've placed in the program to make it easier for you to run the sample program. You may wish to remove it. To turn the project into a general purpose hotspot editor, you'll probably want to add a file dialog box that will let the user select a specific image database file, or choose the location for a new one.

To create a new database we begin with VB's **CreateDatabase()** function:

```
Set ImageDB = CreateDatabase(App.Path + "\Images.MDB", DB_LANG_GENERAL)
```

This statement sets **ImageDB** to the **Database** object type, referencing an empty database definition. Now all we need to do is fill it out.

We begin by assigning the **Name** "ImageTable" to the new table definition. Then we define its four fields:

```
ReDim Fld(1 To 4)
Fld(2).Attributes = DB_AUTOINCRFIELD    ' Counter field.
For Counter = 1 To 4  ' Set properties for fields.
    Fld(Counter).Name = Choose(Counter, "ImageFileName", "HotSpotNum",
        "LinkTarget", "VertexArray")
    Fld(Counter).Type = Choose(Counter, DB_TEXT, DB_LONG, DB_TEXT, DB_LONGBINARY)
    Fld(Counter).Size = Choose(Counter, 128, 4, 128, 400)
    ImageTableDef.Fields.Append Fld(Counter)
Next Counter
```

The order in which we set the field properties doesn't matter as long as we set all the properties of any given field *before* we **Append** it to the **Fields** collection of the table definition. Since we're going to set most of the properties and **Append** the fields inside the **For** loop, we need to get the one oddball property out of the way first.

The second field, **HotSpotNum** is an *autoincrement* field. That is, every time we add a new record to the table, the database engine automatically sets this field to the next available long integer value. Unlike ordinary binary files, indexed database files provide no meaningful record numbers. So to make sure that every record has a unique identity, it's often useful to add an autoincrement field to the record definition. Since this type of field increments indefinitely (or up to 2,147,483,647, the maximum long integer value), and never re-uses the values assigned to deleted records, it also enables us to build indexes that reflect the order in which the records were added to the table. We set the **Attributes** property of the second field before we begin the loop because none of the other fields has special attributes.

Inside the **For** loop, we use the VB **Choose()** function to select the values of the field properties based on the loop index, an integer variable named **Counter**. The constants **DB_AUTOINCRFIELD**, **DB_TEXT**, **DB_LONG**, **DB_TEXT**, and **DB_LONGBINARY** are defined in the code module DATACONS.BAS. After we assign the field **Name**, **Type**, and **Size** properties, we use the **Append** method to add the fields to the table definition's **Fields** collection, the Access equivalent of a record definition.

Next, we define an **Index** object for the table:

```
ReDim Idx(1)
Idx(1).Name = "PrimaryKey"
Idx(1).Fields = "ImageFileName;HotSpotNum"
Idx(1).Primary = True
Idx(1).Unique = True
ImageTableDef.Indexes.Append Idx(1)
```

By setting the **Primary** property to **True** we instruct VB to enforce a couple of rules. First, the values of the fields that make up the index, in this case the fields called **ImageFileName** and **HotSpotNum**, must never contain null values. Second, these fields, when combined, must always produce a unique value. In this case, we've guaranteed uniqueness by making **HotSpotNum** an autoincrement field. The **Unique** property is redundant when **Primary** is set to **True**. *A table can have only one primary index, and the key values in the primary index must be unique for each entry.*

Finally, we append the entire table definition to the database:

```
ImageDB.TableDefs.Append ImageTableDef
```

However, we must first close, then re-open the database before we can use it:

```
ImageDB.Close
Set ImageDB = OpenDatabase(App.Path + "\Images.MDB")
Set ImageTable = ImageDB.OpenTable("ImageTable")
```

Saving Hotspot Records

Now that we have our database, we're going to have to add records to it. Don't worry, adding records to an Access database is easy. You just call the **AddNew** method, assign your values to the fields, and call the **Update** method. To replace an existing record you use the **Edit** method instead of **AddNew**. Unlike conventional file systems, in which you explicitly read or write a whole record at once, in the VB Data Access system, you position yourself over a record, then assign values to or from individual fields. The record buffer is like a sliding porthole. When you want to edit an existing record, you ask VB to position the porthole over it using one of the various search methods. Then you tell it that you intend to change the contents of the record by calling the **Edit** method. You can copy data to one field or several, but you don't necessarily have to update them all. When you ask to add a new record with the **AddNew** method, VB positions the buffer over an empty record. Other than that, there is no difference between adding and replacing a record. In either case, you commit your changes to the file by calling the **Update** method. Listing 9.15 shows the **SaveHotspotRecord()** general procedure that handles all of this for us.

Listing 9.15 The SaveHotspotRecord() General Procedure from HOTSPOT4.BAS

```
Sub SaveHotspotRecord ()
    Dim TempTarget As String
    Dim ArrayString As String

    ArrayString = StringFromArray(PolygonVertices(), CurrentPointIndex)
    If CurrentHotspotRecordID = 0 Then
        ' Add a new record.
        TempTarget = ""
        TempTarget = InputBox$("Enter a Hyperlink Target string of up to 128
                    characters: ", "Enter Target", TempTarget)
        If Len(TempTarget) > 0 Then
            ImageTable.AddNew
            ImageTable!ImageFilename = CurrentImageFilename
            ImageTable!LinkTarget = TempTarget
            ImageTable!VertexArray = ArrayString
            ImageTable.Update
        End If
    Else
        ' Replace an existing record.
        ImageTable.Seek "=", CurrentImageFilename, CurrentHotspotRecordID
        If Not ImageTable.NoMatch Then
            TempTarget = ImageTable!LinkTarget
            TempTarget = InputBox$("enter a Hyperlink Target string of up to 128
                        characters: ", "Enter Target", TempTarget)
```

```
        If Len(TempTarget) > 0 Then
            ImageTable.Edit
            ImageTable!ImageFilename = CurrentImageFilename
            ImageTable!LinkTarget = TempTarget
            ImageTable!VertexArray = ArrayString
            ImageTable.Update
        End If
    Else
        MsgBox "Unable to Relocate Record", 48, "Database Error"
    End If
  End If
End Sub
```

Before we can perform either type of update to our hotspot records, we need to set the values of the variables **CurrentImageFilename**, **TempTarget**, and **ArrayString**. We can get the first of these out of the way easily. When we load the image into Picture1, we set **CurrentImageFilename** to the name of the bitmap file chosen from the file dialog box. That value will remain unchanged until we either select another picture to work on, or exit the program. The next easiest field to capture is **TempTarget**. We'll just display an Input Box and ask the user to enter the target string:

```
TempTarget = ""
TempTarget = InputBox$("Enter a Hyperlink Target string of up to 128 characters:
            ", "Enter Target", TempTarget)
```

To fill in the third field, **ArrayString**, we'll need to be a little trickier. You set a field of type **DB_LONGBINARY** by assigning it the value of a string. So before we can store our vertex array in the database record, we first need to convert it into a string. That's the job of the general function **StringFromArray()**, which is shown in Listing 9.16.

Listing 9.16   The StringFromArray() General Function from HOTSPOT4.BAS

```
Function StringFromArray (VertexArray() As POINTAPI, LastArrayIndex As Integer)
    As String
    Dim I As Integer
    Dim TempString As String

    TempString = ""
    For I = 0 To LastArrayIndex
        TempString = TempString + Chr$(VertexArray(I).X \ 256)
        TempString = TempString + Chr$(VertexArray(I).X Mod 256)
        TempString = TempString + Chr$(VertexArray(I).Y \ 256)
        TempString = TempString + Chr$(VertexArray(I).Y Mod 256)
    Next I
```

```
    StringFromArray = TempString
    End Function
```

We store the **X** and **Y** values by converting them into characters and appending them to the variable-length string **TempString**. A character can have any ANSI value from 0 to 255, which means that any single-byte value can be represented by a character. To break a two-byte integer into two character values, we extract the high and low bytes with the integer divide (\) and **Mod** operators. When we're done, we can return a string just long enough to hold the current vertex array.

There's one precaution you should take before you replace a record. You should make sure that the current record buffer and position match the record you retrieved for editing. To re-position yourself on the record, use the **Seek** method:

```
ImageTable.Seek "=", CurrentImageFilename, CurrentHotspotRecordID
If Not ImageTable.NoMatch Then
    ...
```

The **NoMatch** property will tell you whether you've managed to re-locate the record. In most situations you don't need to worry about this step, but in a multi-user environment, unless you provide adequate protection in the form of record locking, it's possible for another user to delete a record while you're working on it.

Retrieving Hotspot Records

To read a hotspot record from the database table, we first locate the record with the **Seek** method. If VB finds the record we've requested, we can set our variables with simple assignment statements. Once it has been located, reading a record requires no special commands or methods. This is the job of the general function **LoadHotSpot()**, shown in Listing 19.17.

Listing 9.17   TheLoadHotSpot() General Function from HOTSPOT4.BAS

```
Function LoadHotSpot (ImageFilename As String, ByVal RecordID As Long) As Integer
    Dim TempString As String

    ImageTable.Index = "PrimaryKey"
    ImageTable.Seek "=", ImageFilename, RecordID
    If Not ImageTable.NoMatch Then
        CurrentImageFilename = ImageTable!ImageFilename
        TempString = ImageTable!VertexArray
        CurrentPointIndex = ArrayFromString(PolygonVertices(), TempString)
```

```
        CurrentHotspotRecordID = ImageTable!HotSpotNum
        LoadHotSpot = True
    Else
        LoadHotSpot = False
    End If
End Function
```

The index we've defined for **ImageTable** consists of two fields, **ImageFileName** and **HotSpotNum**. To retrieve a hotspot record, we pass those two values to **LoadHotSpot()**. Inside the function we set the current **Index** to **PrimaryKey**, which is the name we gave to the one and only index of **ImageTable**. Then we use the **Seek** method to search for a match. If we find the record, we assign the field values into our program variables, convert the long binary field back from a string into an array of **POINTAPI** structures, and return **True**.

The Complete Listing of HOTSPOT4

Listings 9.18, 9.19, and 9.20 show the complete listings of HOTSPOT4.FRM, HTSPT4F2.FRM, and HOTSPOT4.BAS. The code modules GLOBCONS.BAS and DATACONS.BAS contain the text files CONSTANT.TXT and DATACONS.TXT that ship with VB. You will most likely find them in your VB directory.

Listing 9.18   HOTSPOT4.FRM

```
VERSION 2.00
Begin Form HotSpot4F1
    Caption         =   "Hot Spot Editor"
    ClientHeight    =   4056
    ClientLeft      =   1764
    ClientTop       =   2736
    ClientWidth     =   6420
    Height          =   4800
    Left            =   1716
    LinkTopic       =   "Form1"
    ScaleHeight     =   4056
    ScaleWidth      =   6420
    Top             =   2040
    Width           =   6516
    Begin CommonDialog ImageFileDialog
        Left        =     120
        Top         =    3600
    End
    Begin PictureBox Picture1
        ClipControls    =   0    'False
        DrawMode        =   6    'Invert
        Height          =   3252
```

```
          Left            =    480
          ScaleHeight     =    269
          ScaleMode       =    3   'Pixel
          ScaleWidth      =    459
          TabIndex        =    0
          Top             =    240
          Width           =    5532
       End
    Begin Menu FileMenu
       Caption          =    "&File"
       Begin Menu LoadOption
          Caption          =    "&Load Picture"
       End
       Begin Menu NewOption
          Caption          =    "&New"
       End
       Begin Menu EditOption
          Caption          =    "&Edit Saved Hotspot"
       End
       Begin Menu SaveOption
          Caption          =    "&Save Hotspot"
       End
       Begin Menu DeleteOption
          Caption          =    "&Delete Hotspot"
       End
       Begin Menu QuitOption
          Caption          =    "&Quit"
       End
    End
    Begin Menu ModeMenu
       Caption          =    "&Mode"
       Begin Menu DefineOption
          Caption          =    "&Defining Region"
          Checked          =    -1  'True
       End
       Begin Menu TestOption
          Caption          =    "&Testing Region"
       End
    End
End
Option Explicit

Dim DrawingPolygon As Integer

Sub DefineOption_Click ()
    TestOption.Checked = False
    DefineOption.Checked = True
    DeleteRegion hPolyRgn
    End Sub

Sub DeleteOption_Click ()
    Dim Response As Integer
```

```
    If CurrentHotspotRecordID > 0 Then
        Response = MsgBox("Are you sure you want to delete this Hotspot?", _
                    MB_YESNO + MB_ICONQUESTION, "Warning!")
        If Response = IDYES Then
            ImageTable.Seek "=", CurrentImageFilename, CurrentHotspotRecordID
            If Not ImageTable.NoMatch Then
                ImageTable.Delete
                SaveOption.Enabled = False
                DeleteOption.Enabled = False
                InitPolygonEditor
                DrawPolygon PolygonVertices(), CurrentPointIndex, Picture1, Not
                  DrawingPolygon
                PreviousX = 0
                PreviousY = 0
                TestOption.Checked = False
                DefineOption.Checked = True
                DeleteRegion hPolyRgn
            Else
                MsgBox "Unable to Relocate Hotspot Record.", 48, "Database Error"
            End If
        End If
    Else
        MsgBox "There is no region to delete.", 48, "Delete Error"
    End If
End Sub

Sub EditOption_Click ()
    DrawPolygon PolygonVertices(), CurrentPointIndex, Picture1, Not
  DrawingPolygon
    DeleteRegion hPolyRgn
    DrawingPolygon = False
    HotSpot4F2.Show MODAL
    If CurrentHotspotRecordID > 0 Then
        SaveOption.Enabled = True
        DeleteOption.Enabled = True
    End If
    If TestOption.Checked Then
        hPolyRgn = CreatePolygonRgn(PolygonVertices(0), CurrentPointIndex + 1, 0)
    End If
    HotSpot4F1.Refresh
End Sub

Sub Form_Load ()
    NewOption.Enabled = False
    EditOption.Enabled = False
    SaveOption.Enabled = False
    DeleteOption.Enabled = False
    CurrentHotspotRecordID = 0&
    DatabaseOpen = OpenImageDatabase()
    InitPolygonEditor
End Sub

Sub Form_Resize ()
    Picture1.Width = .9 * HotSpot4F1.ScaleWidth
```

```
    Picture1.Height = .9 * HotSpot4F1.ScaleHeight
    Picture1.Left = HotSpot4F1.ScaleWidth \ 2 - Picture1.Width \ 2
    Picture1.Top = HotSpot4F1.ScaleHeight \ 2 - Picture1.Height \ 2
    End Sub

Sub Form_Unload (Cancel As Integer)
    DeleteRegion hPolyRgn
    ImageTable.Close
    ImageDB.Close
    End Sub

Sub InitPolygonEditor ()
    DeleteRegion hPolyRgn
    DrawPolygon PolygonVertices(), CurrentPointIndex, Picture1, Not DrawingPolygon
    CurrentPointIndex = -1
    CurrentHotspotRecordID = 0&
    PreviousX = 0
    PreviousY = 0
    DrawingPolygon = True
    End Sub

Sub LoadOption_Click ()
    NewOption.Enabled = True
    EditOption.Enabled = True
    SaveOption.Enabled = False
    DeleteOption.Enabled = False
    CurrentHotspotRecordID = 0&
    InitPolygonEditor
    ImageFileDialog.Filter = "Bitmaps *.BMP|*.BMP|Device Independent Bitmaps *.DIB|*.DIB"
    ImageFileDialog.Action = 1
    If ImageFileDialog.Filename <> "" Then
        CurrentImageFilename = Mid$(ImageFileDialog.Filename,3)
        Picture1.Picture = LoadPicture(CurrentImageFilename)
      End If
    End Sub

Sub NewOption_Click ()
    SaveOption.Enabled = False
    DeleteOption.Enabled = False
    CurrentHotspotRecordID = 0&
    If DrawingPolygon And (CurrentPointIndex > -1) Then
        Picture1.Line (PolygonVertices(CurrentPointIndex).X,
                   PolygonVertices(CurrentPointIndex).Y)-(PreviousX, PreviousY)
      End If
    InitPolygonEditor
    TestOption.Checked = False
    DefineOption.Checked = True
    DeleteRegion hPolyRgn
    End Sub

Sub Picture1_MouseDown (Button As Integer, Shift As Integer, X As Single, Y As Single)

    Dim Dummy As Integer
```

```
    If DefineOption.Checked And (Len(CurrentImageFilename) > 0) Then
        If DrawingPolygon Then
            DrawingPolygon = Not VertexFinishesPolygon(X, Y)
            PreviousX = X
            PreviousY = Y
          Else
            Dummy = mciExecute("play c:\windows\ding.wav")
            MsgBox "This polygon region is closed", 16, "Drawing Error"
          End If
          Else
        ' Test whether click is in region.
          If PtInRegion(hPolyRgn, X, Y) Then
            Dummy = mciExecute("play c:\windows\tada.wav")
          Else
            Dummy = mciExecute("play c:\windows\ding.wav")
          End If
    End If

    End Sub


Sub Picture1_MouseMove (Button As Integer, Shift As Integer, X As Single, Y As Single)
    If DrawingPolygon And (CurrentPointIndex > -1) Then
        Picture1.Line (PolygonVertices(CurrentPointIndex).X,
                    PolygonVertices(CurrentPointIndex).Y)-(PreviousX, PreviousY)
        PreviousX = X
        PreviousY = Y
        Picture1.Line (PolygonVertices(CurrentPointIndex).X,
                    PolygonVertices(CurrentPointIndex).Y)-(PreviousX, PreviousY)
    End If
End Sub


Sub Picture1_Paint ()
    DrawPolygon PolygonVertices(), CurrentPointIndex, Picture1, Not DrawingPolygon
End Sub


Sub QuitOption_Click ()
    Form_Unload (0)
    End
End Sub


Sub SaveOption_Click ()
    SaveHotspotRecord
End Sub


Sub TestOption_Click ()
    If DrawingPolygon Then
        MsgBox "Cannot Test Incomplete Polygon", 48, "Error"
      Else
        DefineOption.Checked = False
        TestOption.Checked = True
        hPolyRgn = CreatePolygonRgn(PolygonVertices(0), CurrentPointIndex + 1, 0)
    End If
End Sub
```

```
Function VertexFinishesPolygon (X As Single, Y As Single) As Integer
    If (CurrentPointIndex > 0) And ((Sqr((X - PolygonVertices(0).X) ^ 2 +
                  (Y - PolygonVertices(0).Y) ^ 2) <= 10) Or (CurrentPointIndex =
99)) Then
        Picture1.Line (PolygonVertices(CurrentPointIndex).X,
          PolygonVertices(CurrentPointIndex).Y)- (PreviousX, PreviousY)
        Picture1.Line (PolygonVertices(CurrentPointIndex).X,
                  PolygonVertices(CurrentPointIndex).Y)-(PolygonVertices(0).X,
                  PolygonVertices(0).Y)
        VertexFinishesPolygon = True
        SaveOption.Enabled = True
      Else
        CurrentPointIndex = CurrentPointIndex + 1
        PolygonVertices(CurrentPointIndex).X = X
        PolygonVertices(CurrentPointIndex).Y = Y
        VertexFinishesPolygon = False
      End If
    End Function
```

Listing 9.19   HTSPT4F2.FRM

```
VERSION 2.00
Begin Form HotSpot4F2
    BorderStyle     =   1   'Fixed Single
    Caption         =   "Open a Hotspot"
    ClientHeight    =   3780
    ClientLeft      =   876
    ClientTop       =   1524
    ClientWidth     =   8460
    Height          =   4200
    Left            =   828
    LinkTopic       =   "Form1"
    ScaleHeight     =   3780
    ScaleWidth      =   8460
    Top             =   1152
    Width           =   8556
    Begin CommandButton CancelButton
        Caption     =   "Cancel"
        Height      =   492
        Left        =   5940
        TabIndex    =   2
        Top         =   3120
        Width       =   1692
    End
    Begin CommandButton LoadButton
        Caption     =   "Load Hotspot"
        Enabled     =   0   'False
        Height      =   492
        Left        =   3720
        TabIndex    =   1
        Top         =   3120
        Width       =   1692
    End
```

```
    Begin ListBox HotSpotList
        Height          =     2520
        Left            =     360
        TabIndex        =     0
        Top             =     240
        Width           =     7812
    End
End
Option Explicit

Sub CancelButton_Click ()
    Unload HotSpot4F2
    End Sub

Sub Form_Load ()
    Dim Done As Integer

    LoadButton.Enabled = False
    HotSpotList.Clear
    ImageTable.Index = "PrimaryKey"
    ImageTable.Seek ">=", CurrentImageFilename
    If (Not ImageTable.NoMatch) And (ImageTable!ImageFilename =
      CurrentImageFilename) Then
        Done = False
        Do While Not Done
            HotSpotList.AddItem ImageTable!ImageFilename + " - " +
              ImageTable!LinkTarget
            HotSpotList.ItemData(HotSpotList.NewIndex) = ImageTable!HotSpotNum
            ImageTable.MoveNext
            Done = ImageTable.EOF
            If Not Done Then
                Done = (ImageTable!ImageFilename <> CurrentImageFilename)
              End If
            Loop
      End If
    End Sub

Sub HotSpotList_Click ()
    LoadButton.Enabled = True
    End Sub

Sub HotSpotList_DblClick ()
    Dim LoadedHotspot As Integer
    LoadedHotspot = LoadHotSpot(CurrentImageFilename,
                              HotSpotList.ItemData(HotSpotList.ListIndex))
    Unload HotSpot4F2
    End Sub

Sub LoadButton_Click ()
    Dim LoadedHotspot As Integer
    LoadedHotspot = LoadHotSpot(CurrentImageFilename,
                              HotSpotList.ItemData(HotSpotList.ListIndex))
    Unload HotSpot4F2
    End Sub
```

Listing 9.20   HOTSPOT4.BAS

```
Option Explicit

Type POINTAPI
    X As Integer
    Y As Integer
    End Type

Declare Function CreatePolygonRgn Lib "GDI" (lpPoints As POINTAPI, ByVal nCount
    As Integer, ByVal nPolyFillMode As Integer) As Integer
Declare Function PtInRegion Lib "GDI" (ByVal hRgn As Integer, ByVal X As
    Integer, ByVal Y As Integer) As Integer
Declare Function DeleteObject Lib "GDI" (ByVal hObject As Integer) As Integer
Declare Function mciExecute Lib "MMSystem" (ByVal CommandString As String) As
    Integer

Global ImageDB As Database
Global ImageTable As Table
Global CurrentHotspotRecordID As Long
Global CurrentImageFilename As String
Global hPolyRgn As Integer
Global PolygonVertices(99) As POINTAPI
Global PreviousX As Integer
Global PreviousY As Integer
Global CurrentPointIndex As Integer
Global DatabaseOpen As Integer

Function ArrayFromString (TheVertexArray() As POINTAPI, ByVal TheString As
    String) As Integer
    Dim I As Integer
    Dim LastElement As Integer

    LastElement = Len(TheString) \ 4 - 1
    For I = 0 To LastElement
        TheVertexArray(I).X = Asc(Mid$(TheString, I * 4 + 1, 1)) * 256 +
                                                            Asc(Mid$(TheString,
    I * 4 + 2, 1))
        TheVertexArray(I).Y = Asc(Mid$(TheString, I * 4 + 3, 1)) * 256 +
                                                            Asc(Mid$(TheString,
    I * 4 + 4, 1))
        Next I
    ArrayFromString = LastElement
    End Function

Sub DeleteRegion (hRgn As Integer)
    If hRgn <> 0 Then
        If DeleteObject(hRgn) Then
            hRgn = 0
          Else
            MsgBox "Unable to Delete Region", 48, "GDI Error"
          End If
      End If
```

```
        End Sub

Sub DrawPolygon (VertexArray() As POINTAPI, LastArrayIndex As Integer,
    ThePicture As PictureBox, CompletePolygon As Integer)
    Dim I As Integer

    If LastArrayIndex > 0 Then
        For I = 1 To LastArrayIndex
            ThePicture.Line (VertexArray(I - 1).X, VertexArray(I - 1).Y)-
                (VertexArray(I).X, VertexArray(I).Y)
            Next I
        If CompletePolygon Then
            ThePicture.Line (VertexArray(LastArrayIndex).X,
                VertexArray(LastArrayIndex).Y)-(VertexArray(0).X, VertexArray(0).Y)
        End If
    End If
End Sub

Function LoadHotSpot (ImageFilename As String, ByVal RecordID As Long) As Integer
    Dim TempString As String

    ImageTable.Index = "PrimaryKey"
    ImageTable.Seek "=", ImageFilename, RecordID
    If Not ImageTable.NoMatch Then
        CurrentImageFilename = ImageTable!ImageFilename
        TempString = ImageTable!VertexArray
        CurrentPointIndex = ArrayFromString(PolygonVertices(), TempString)
        CurrentHotspotRecordID = ImageTable!HotSpotNum
        LoadHotSpot = True
    Else
        LoadHotSpot = False
    End If
End Function


Function OpenImageDatabase () As Integer
    '  Opens the file IMAGES.MDB.  If file does
    '  not exist, this function will create it.
    Dim Fld() As New Field
    Dim Idx() As New Index
    Dim ImageTableDef As New TableDef
    Dim Counter As Integer

    If Len(Dir$(App.Path + "\Images.MDB")) > 0 Then
        Set ImageDB = OpenDatabase(App.Path + "\Images.MDB")
        Set ImageTable = ImageDB.OpenTable("ImageTable")
    Else
        ' Create the database Images.MDB
        Set ImageDB = CreateDatabase(App.Path + "\Images.MDB", DB_LANG_GENERAL)
        ' Create the ImageTable.
        ImageTableDef.Name = "ImageTable"
        ' Create the Fields.
        ReDim Fld(1 To 4)
        Fld(2).Attributes = DB_AUTOINCRFIELD    ' Counter field.
        For Counter = 1 To 4 ' Set properties for fields.
```

```
            Fld(Counter).Name = Choose(Counter, "ImageFileName", "HotSpotNum",
                "LinkTarget", "VertexArray")
            Fld(Counter).Type = Choose(Counter, DB_TEXT, DB_LONG, DB_TEXT,
                DB_LONGBINARY)
            Fld(Counter).Size = Choose(Counter, 128, 4, 128, 400)
            ImageTableDef.Fields.Append Fld(Counter)
            Next Counter

        ' Create the Table Index.
        ReDim Idx(1)
        Idx(1).Name = "PrimaryKey"
        Idx(1).Fields = "ImageFileName;HotSpotNum"
        Idx(1).Primary = True
        Idx(1).Unique = True
        ImageTableDef.Indexes.Append Idx(1)

        ' Create the Table.
        ImageDB.TableDefs.Append ImageTableDef
        ImageDB.Close
        Set ImageDB = OpenDatabase(App.Path + "\Images.MDB")
        Set ImageTable = ImageDB.OpenTable("ImageTable")
    End If
End Function

Sub SaveHotspotRecord ()
    Dim TempTarget As String
    Dim ArrayString As String

    ArrayString = StringFromArray(PolygonVertices(), CurrentPointIndex)
    If CurrentHotspotRecordID = 0 Then
        ' Add a new record.
        TempTarget = ""
        TempTarget = InputBox$("Enter a Hyperlink Target string of up to 128
                                        characters: ", "Enter Target",
    TempTarget)
        If Len(TempTarget) > 0 Then
            ImageTable.AddNew
            ImageTable!ImageFilename = CurrentImageFilename
            ImageTable!LinkTarget = TempTarget
            ImageTable!VertexArray = ArrayString
            ImageTable.Update
        End If
    Else
        ' Replace an existing record.
        ImageTable.Seek "=", CurrentImageFilename, CurrentHotspotRecordID
        If Not ImageTable.NoMatch Then
            TempTarget = ImageTable!LinkTarget
            TempTarget = InputBox$("enter a Hyperlink Target string of up to
                                        128 characters: ", "Enter
    Target", TempTarget)
            If Len(TempTarget) > 0 Then
                ImageTable.Edit
                ImageTable!ImageFilename = CurrentImageFilename
```

```
                ImageTable!LinkTarget = TempTarget
                ImageTable!VertexArray = ArrayString
                ImageTable.Update
            End If
        Else
            MsgBox "Unable to Relocate Record", 48, "Database Error"
        End If
    End If
End Sub

Function StringFromArray (VertexArray() As POINTAPI, LastArrayIndex As Integer)
    As String
    Dim I As Integer
    Dim TempString As String

    TempString = ""
    For I = 0 To LastArrayIndex
        TempString = TempString + Chr$(VertexArray(I).X \ 256)
        TempString = TempString + Chr$(VertexArray(I).X Mod 256)
        TempString = TempString + Chr$(VertexArray(I).Y \ 256)
        TempString = TempString + Chr$(VertexArray(I).Y Mod 256)
        Next I
    StringFromArray = TempString
    End Function
```

Hotspots: The Next Generation

The programs we've written in this chapter work just well enough to get some hotspots on to our images. You'll find many other ways to expand their capabilities—you just need to look. For one thing, as I said in an earlier chapter, you should take greater pains to trap errors. You may also want to add an option that displays or tests all the hotspots for an image simultaneously, just as they'll be used in a working presentation. Or, you may want to fix up HOTSPOT4 so you can change a hotspot's vertex array without first deleting the whole record from the database. The more you look, the more you'll find.

As a matter of fact, there's one way great way to improve on polygon regions. With the API function we've used in HOTSPOT3 and HOTSPOT4, **CreatePolygonRgn()**, we have been able to make regions that consist of either one polygon, or multiple polygons joined at common vertices (just cross over some of your own lines when you draw the polygon). But what do you do when you have several separate hotspots on your image that all have the same hyperlink target? You could make separate hotspot regions for each of them. Or you could call upon the services of yet another API function, called **CreatePolyPolygonRgn()**.

```
Declare Function CreatePolyPolygonRgn Lib "GDI" (lpPoints As POINTAPI,
```

```
lpPolyCounts As Integer, ByVal nCount As Integer, ByVal nPolyFillMode As
Integer) As Integer
```

The difference between this function and **CreatePolygonRgn()** is in the second argument, **lpPolyCounts**. In this parameter, we would pass a pointer to a second array, a simple array of integer values in which each integer specifies how many points in the first array belong to each separate polygon. For example, let's say we had an array of 25 vertices, and a second array of three integers that contained the values 3, 12, and 10. This would describe a Windows region that consisted of three distinct polygons. The first three points in the vertex array would define a triangle, the next 12 points would describe a second polygon, and the last 10 would describe a third.

When we called **PtInRegion()** with the handle to the PolyPolygon region, it would return **True** if the click had occurred anywhere within any of the three polygons. Three regions act like one. Pretty neat, huh?

To implement PolyPolygon regions, you would have to modify both the drawing functions of the program and the storage system, but if you need this much flexibility, you should be able to modify HOTSPOT4 to support it.

Now that you know how to create and activate hotspots in both text and images, let's put all this knowledge to work. Our next adventure takes us into a true hypermedia realm—one of sound, music, images, and video.

Chapter 10

Adventures like this come once in a lifetime, so come with me as we combine our hypertext and hyperimaging systems into one dazzling hypermedia event!

Expanding the Hypermedia Interface

Strap on your toolbelt. It's time to pull together some of the things we've learned in the first nine chapters and build a hypermedia construction set that will let us link pictures with text, sound, music, and video.

In Chapter 1 I showed you how easily you can use VB to trigger multimedia events. Then, in Chapter 2, we used VB to build a hypertext engine that let us jump from topic to topic by clicking on hotlinked words in the text itself. In Chapter 3 we added some multimedia features to the hypertext engine so hotlinked words in the hypertext could play back video, or MIDI music, or any other event supported by the Windows Multimedia API. In Chapter 4 we delved deeper into the API, using waveform audio to try a variety of functions. In Chapters 5, 6, and 7 we covered the elements of image display and special effects. And in the previous two chapters, we built an editor that enabled us to map out hotspots on our images. We've come a long way.

Now, in this chapter we're going to draw on this knowledge to expand our hypermedia system. First, we're going to briefly re-visit hypertext and turn our hypertext system into a code module that we can call from any program. Then, we'll hook in image hotspots so we can hop back and forth between pictures and text. Later in the chapter we'll flesh out the hypermedia engine with some powerful new navigation and display features.

Repackaging the Hypertext

In Chapter 5 we wrote a program that dissolved one 8-bit color picture into another. But instead of adding the functions and procedures that performed the dissolve to the program's main form, we placed them in their own code module called DISSOLVE.BAS. Other functions went into code modules too, including DIB.BAS, PALETTE.BAS, and GLBLMEM.BAS. We put related functions together in these handy packages so that we could tote them from one project to another without extensive modifications.

In general, lower-level functions package more neatly than higher-level, program-specific functions. There are no clear guidelines to follow as you write your program. When I write a new VB program, I often place more code than I should in the form module. After all, when I want to use the **MouseDown** event, why not put the code in the event procedure that belongs to the form or control? Once I get everything working though, I try to find ways to pull my code out of the form and into its own module. Then, when I want to write another program with the same functions, I can just select File, Add File from the VB menu bar and hook the module right into my project.

Before we try to write a general-purpose multimedia engine, we need to finish the job of sorting out our code. Let's start by tidying up the hypertext system we wrote in Chapters 2 and 3. The last version of this program was called HYPRTXT4.MAK. In this section we'll create one more version called HYPRTXT5.MAK. One of the files in this project will be HYPRTXT5.BAS, a *re-useable* code module that contains all the essential hypertext functions.

The General Purpose Hypertext Engine

This project presents the new and improved hypertext engine:

1. Copy the form and code modules from HYPRTXT4.MAK.
2. Open a new VB project file called HYPRTXT5.MAK.
3. Move all the key procedures and functions from the form module to the code module.

4. Modify the code to make it re-useable for future projects.

 You'll find this project in the subdirectory \VBMAGIC in the files HYPRTXT5.MAK, HYPRTXT5.FRM, HYPRTXT5.BAS, GLOBCONS.BAS, and HYPRTXT5.TXT.

Preparing the Project

We're going to use most of the code in HYPRTXT4.FRM and HYPRTXT4.BAS with only a few changes here and there, so the best way to start this project is to make copies of those files. Follow these steps:

1. Use the Windows File Manager or the DOS Copy command to copy HYPRTXT4.FRM to HYPRTXT5.FRM.
2. Use the Windows File Manager or the DOS Copy command to copy HYPRTXT4.BAS to HYPRTXT5.BAS.
3. Choose File, New Project from the VB menu bar.
4. In the Project window, highlight FORM1.FRM, usually the first entry in the list, and choose File, Remove File from the VB menu bar.
5. If you wish, use the File, Remove File option to remove all the .VBX files from the project. We won't use any of them for this project.
6. To add the form module to the project, select File, Add File from the VB menu bar. Use the controls in the Add File dialog box to locate and select HYPRTXT5.FRM.
7. To add the first code module to the project, choose File, Add File from the VB menu bar. Then use the Add File dialog to select HYPRTXT5.BAS.
8. To add the second code module to the project, choose File, Add File and use the Add File dialog box to select GLOBCONS.BAS.
9. Choose File, Save Project As and save the project as HYPRTXT5.MAK.

You should now have a project consisting of one form module and two code modules. Don't try to run it yet!

Modifying the Form Module

When we first wrote HYPRTXT4, we added the code module only to hold the global constants and three **Type** declarations. In this project, we'll remove the global constants and move all the code from HYPRTXT5.FRM into the new version of the code module, HYPRTXT5.BAS.

HYPRTXT5.FRM currently contains fifteen variable declarations, seven general procedures, and four event procedures. Table 10.1 lists all of these declarations and procedures.

Table 10.1   *A Current Inventory of HYPRTXT5.FRM*

Declarations:

Dim HyperLinkArray(100) As HyperLinkElement

Dim SubjectIndexArray(100) As SubjectIndexRecords

Dim HyperLinkArraySize As Integer

Dim HyperTextRecord As HyperTextRecords

Dim SubjectIndexRecord As SubjectIndexRecords

Dim NumberOfSubjects As Integer

Dim IndexPos As Long

Dim LinkPos As Long

Dim CurrentTop As Single

Dim LinkArrayPos As Integer

Dim ArrayPlaceHolder As Integer

Dim SubjectHeading As String

Dim LinkFileNum As Integer

Dim IndexFileNum As Integer

Dim FilesAreOpen As Integer

General Procedures:

Sub CompileText (FileName As String)

Function GetWordFrom (AnyString As String) As String

Sub LoadSubject (Subject As String)

Sub NewLine ()

Sub OpenHyperbase (FileName As String)

Sub ParseLink (RawLink As String, LinkWord As String, Subject As String)

Function ReadInText (SubjectName As String) As String

Event Procedures:

Sub CompileButton_Click ()

Sub Form_Load ()

Sub OpenButton_Click ()

Sub Picture1_MouseDown (Button As Integer, Shift As Integer, X As Single, Y As Single)

Let's begin by moving all the declarations and general procedures to HYPRTXT5.BAS. We'll perform the following steps eight times to move all the general procedures and the declarations to the code module.

1. Select the entire function or procedure in HYPRTXT5.FRM, then select Edit, Cut from the VB menu bar.
2. Open the code window of HYPRTXT5.BAS, and display the declarations section. Place the insertion point on a new line at the end of the declarations section.
3. Select Edit, Paste from the VB menu. VB will move the procedure into its own section and add its name to the procedure list box at the top of the code window.

For reasons that won't become clear until we combine the hypertext and hyperimaging systems, we'll also modify the **Picture1_MouseDown()** event procedure. We'll rearrange and split its code into one function and one procedure—**TargetFromPointInText()** and **DoHyperTextJump()** in the code module. This new code is shown in Listings 10.1 and 10.2.

Listing 10.1   The New TargetFromPointInText() General Function from HYPRTXT5.BAS

```
Function TargetFromPointInText (X As Single, Y As Single) As String
    Dim Counter As Integer
    Dim Found As Integer
    Dim TempTargetString As String

    TempTargetString = ""
    Found = False
    Counter = 0
    Do While (Counter < HyperLinkArraySize) And (Not Found)
        Counter = Counter + 1
        If (X > HyperLinkArray(Counter).Left) And (X < HyperLinkArray(Counter).Right) And
            (Y < HyperLinkArray(Counter).Bottom) And
            (Y > HyperLinkArray(Counter).Top) Then
            TempTargetString = RTrim$(HyperLinkArray(Counter).DestinationSubject)
            Found = True
        End If
    Loop
    TargetFromPointInText = TempTargetString
End Function
```

Listing 10.2   The New DoHyperTextJump() General Procedure from HYPRTXT5.BAS

```
Sub DoHyperTextJump (TargetString As String, ThePicture As PictureBox)
    Dim Dummy As Integer

    If Left$(Right$(TargetString, 4), 1) = "." Then
        Dummy = mciExecute("Play " + TargetString)
    Else
```

```
      LoadSubject TargetString, ThePicture
   End If
End Sub
```

When we're done, we'll end up with a nearly empty version of
HYPRTXT5.FRM as shown in Listing 10.3.

Listing 10.3　The New, Lean Version of HYPRTXT5.FRM

```
VERSION 2.00
Begin Form Form1
   AutoRedraw        =    -1   'True
   Caption           =    "Form1"
   ClientHeight      =    5412
   ClientLeft        =    1248
   ClientTop         =    1632
   ClientWidth       =    6912
   Height            =    5832
   Left              =    1200
   LinkMode          =    1   'Source
   LinkTopic         =    "Form1"
   ScaleHeight       =    5412
   ScaleWidth        =    6912
   Top               =    1260
   Width             =    7008
   Begin TextBox Text1
      Height         =      312
      Left           =      2040
      TabIndex       =      3
      Top            =      4920
      Width          =      4332
   End
   Begin CommandButton OpenButton
      Caption        =      "Open Hyperbase"
      Height         =      495
      Left           =      3600
      TabIndex       =      2
      Top            =      4200
      Width          =      2895
   End
   Begin CommandButton CompileButton
      Caption        =      "Compile Hypertext File"
      Height         =      495
      Left           =      300
      TabIndex       =      1
      Top            =      4200
      Width          =      2655
   End
   Begin PictureBox Picture1
      ClipControls   =      0   'False
      Height         =      3732
      Left           =      240
      ScaleHeight    =      3708
```

```
          ScaleWidth     =    6288
          TabIndex       =    0
          Top            =    120
          Width          =    6312
       End
       Begin Label Label1
          Caption        =    "Multimedia Activity:"
          Height         =    252
          Left           =    300
          TabIndex       =    4
          Top            =    4920
          Width          =    1632
       End
    End
End
Option Explicit

Sub CompileButton_Click ()
    CompileText App.Path & "\Hyprtxt5.Txt"
    End Sub

Sub Form_Load ()
    FilesAreOpen = False
    Picture1.AutoRedraw = True
    End Sub

Sub OpenButton_Click ()
    OpenHyperbase App.Path & "\Hyprtxt5.XXX"
    Picture1.AutoRedraw = False
    DisplayFirstTopic Picture1
    End Sub

Sub Picture1_MouseDown (Button As Integer, Shift As Integer, X As Single, Y As Single)
    Dim TempTarget As String

    TempTarget = TargetFromPointInText(X, Y)
    If Len(TempTarget) > 0 Then
        Text1.Text = TempTarget
        DoHyperTextJump TempTarget, Picture1
      End If
    End Sub

Sub Picture1_Paint ()
    LoadSubject CurrentSubject, Picture1
    End Sub
```

Passing Controls As Arguments

Notice that when we call certain procedures, we pass the Picture Box as an argument. When the program was self-contained and all the code was contained within the form module, the general procedures could directly reference the Picture Box control. But to encapsulate the code in a code module, we need to pass the control in by reference. That way, when we later re-use the code, we can name the control whatever we wish without having to modify the code module. Take a look at the abbreviated version of **LoadSubject()** in Listing 10.4. In HYPRTXT4.FRM, this procedure had only one parameter, **Subject**, which specified the name of the next subject to display in **Picture1**. In the previous version all the **Print** method calls in the procedure directly referenced **Picture1** (for instance, **Picture1.Print**). In the new version of this procedure, we pass in the Picture Box as an argument, then reference it by its argument name, **ThePicture**.

Listing 10.4   A Portion of the LoadSubject() General Procedure from HYPRTXT5.BAS

```
Sub LoadSubject (ByVal Subject As String, ThePicture As PictureBox)
    ...
    ThePicture.Cls
    ...
    ' Display Subject name as heading.
    ThePicture.FontBold = False
    ThePicture.ForeColor = BLUE
    ThePicture.FontSize = 16
    ThePicture.CurrentX = 200
    ThePicture.Print RTrim$(Subject)
    ThePicture.Print
    ...
    End Sub
```

Three other procedures take the Picture Box control as an argument: the new version of **NewLine()**, and the two new procedures **DisplayFirstTopic()** and **DoHyperTextJump()**.

You may have also noticed that I added a **Paint** event to Picture1. In the **OpenButton_Click()** event procedure, I set the **AutoRedraw** property of Picture1 to False. This disables VB's own device context shadowing, which means that it will not automatically redraw the Picture Box when it is uncovered by another window. To make sure the text reappears on cue, we just call **LoadSubject()**. We keep track of the current subject in a global variable named—appropriately enough—**CurrentSubject**, which is set by **LoadSubject()**.

The Mysterious Case of the Missing Subject String

When I first added the **Paint()** event procedure to Picture1, I discovered a bug. The first time I covered then uncovered the Picture Box, the program would redraw the text correctly. But when I immediately repeated the test, the subject text would be replaced either by another subject or by the filename and path of one of the media elements. For some reason, the **Paint()** event procedure appeared to be losing track of the current subject string which I had so cleverly taken pains to store in its own global variable.

With a little help from VB's Breakpoints, I soon discovered the source of the problem. First of all, I was passing the string argument **Subject** by reference (no **ByVal** keyword), VB's default method. But in **Picture1_Paint()**, I was calling **LoadSubject()** with **CurrentSubject** as the argument. This didn't work, because **LoadSubject()** was changing the string. The next time the Picture Box received the paint message, it called **LoadSubject()** with an invalid **Subject** string. But why was I changing the string in the first place?

I goofed. I re-used the variable **Subject** for an entirely separate purpose in the procedure. When **LoadSubject()** identifies a hotlink in the text, it calls another function, **ParseLink()** to break the link into two parts, the hotlinked words or phrase and the target subject. Instead of creating a new local variable for that purpose, I passed **Subject** along to **ParseLink()** to use as the buffer for the target string. This error never showed itself before because once I called **LoadSubject()**, I no longer needed to know the contents of **Subject**. It wasn't until I added the **Paint()** event procedure to Picture1 that I discovered my mistake. In this new version of the procedure, I have declared a local string variable called **TargetString** for this purpose.

I could also have swept the problem under the carpet by adding the **ByVal** keyword to the declaration of **LoadSubject()**:

```
Sub LoadSubject (ByVal Subject As String, ThePicture As PictureBox)
```

But that would have been cheating. Multi-purposed variables can cause some of the trickiest bugs, especially when they tunnel their way into your programs through arguments passed by reference (*referential arguments*). Hunt them down and kill them.

We're now ready to present the complete code for HYPRTXT5.BAS, which is shown in Listing 10.5.

Listing 10.5   HYPRTXT5.BAS

```
Option Explicit

Declare Function mciExecute Lib "MMSystem" (ByVal CommandString As String) As Integer

Type HyperLinkElement
    Left As Integer
    Top As Integer
    Right As Integer
    Bottom As Integer
    DestinationSubject As String * 128
    End Type

Type HyperTextRecords 'To store text as linked list of lines
    TextBlock As String * 128
```

```
        NextBlock As Long
        End Type

    Type SubjectIndexRecords
        Subject As String * 128
        FilePos As Long
        End Type

    Dim CurrentTop As Single
    Dim LinkArrayPos As Integer
    Dim ArrayPlaceHolder As Integer

    Dim HyperLinkArray(100) As HyperLinkElement
    Dim SubjectIndexArray(100) As SubjectIndexRecords
    Dim HyperLinkArraySize As Integer

    Dim HyperTextRecord As HyperTextRecords
    Dim SubjectIndexRecord As SubjectIndexRecords
    Dim NumberOfSubjects As Integer

    Dim LinkFileNum As Integer
    Dim IndexFileNum As Integer

    Global FilesAreOpen As Integer
    Global CurrentSubject As String

    Sub CompileText (ByVal FileName As String)
        Dim LineOfText As String
        Dim RootFileName As String
        Dim ParagraphText As String
        Dim LinkRecordLen As Integer
        Dim IndexRecordLen As Integer
        Dim TextFileNum As Integer
        Dim PreviousTextPos As Long
        Dim IndexPos As Long
        Dim LinkPos As Long

        ParagraphText = ""

        LinkRecordLen = Len(HyperTextRecord)
        IndexRecordLen = Len(SubjectIndexRecord)
        TextFileNum = 1
        LinkFileNum = 2
        IndexFileNum = 3

        ' Extract the root filename from the source text file.
        If InStr(FileName, ".") > 0 Then
            RootFileName = Left$(FileName, InStr(FileName, ".") - 1)
          Else
            RootFileName = FileName
          End If
        Open FileName For Input As #TextFileNum
        If FilesAreOpen Then
            Close LinkFileNum
            Close IndexFileNum
```

```
      End If
' Eliminate pre-existing .HTF and .IDX files.
' They need to be opened first, so that they will be created in case they
' don't exist, otherwise we'll get an
' error when we try to Kill them.
Open RootFileName + ".HTF" For Random As #LinkFileNum Len = LinkRecordLen
Open RootFileName + ".IDX" For Random As #IndexFileNum Len = IndexRecordLen
Close #LinkFileNum
Close #IndexFileNum
Kill RootFileName + ".HTF"
Kill RootFileName + ".IDX"
Open RootFileName + ".HTF" For Random As #LinkFileNum Len = LinkRecordLen
Open RootFileName + ".IDX" For Random As #IndexFileNum Len = IndexRecordLen
FilesAreOpen = True


IndexPos = 0
LinkPos = 0
SubjectIndexRecord.Subject = ""
SubjectIndexRecord.FilePos = 0
' Read and process the source text file line-
' by-line until we reach the end.
Do While Not EOF(TextFileNum)
    Line Input #TextFileNum, LineOfText
    If (Left$(LineOfText, 3) <> "###") Then
        ' Append this line of the source text
        ' to the current Subject text buffer.
        If Len(LineOfText) = 0 Then
            ParagraphText = ParagraphText + " " + Chr$(13) + Chr$(10) + " "
        Else
            ParagraphText = ParagraphText + LineOfText
        End If
    End If
    If (Left$(LineOfText, 3) = "###") Or (EOF(TextFileNum)) Then
        ' We've reached the end of a Subject, so
        ' store its accumulated text and prepare to
        ' start the next one.
        PreviousTextPos = 0
        If Len(ParagraphText) > 0 Then
            HyperTextRecord.TextBlock = ""
            HyperTextRecord.NextBlock = 0
            Do While (Len(ParagraphText) > 0)
                If Len(ParagraphText) > 128 Then
                    If Mid$(ParagraphText, 128, 1) = " " Then
                        HyperTextRecord.TextBlock = Left$(ParagraphText,
                            127) + Chr$(1)
                    Else
                        HyperTextRecord.TextBlock = Left$(ParagraphText, 128)
                    End If
                    ParagraphText = Mid$(ParagraphText, 129)
                Else
                    HyperTextRecord.TextBlock = ParagraphText
                    ParagraphText = ""
                End If
                LinkPos = LinkPos + 1
```

```
                        HyperTextRecord.NextBlock = PreviousTextPos
                        Put #LinkFileNum, LinkPos, HyperTextRecord
                        PreviousTextPos = LinkPos
                        Loop
                End If
            ' Set the file pointer in the Subject record and
            ' save the record in the Subject Index file.
            SubjectIndexRecord.FilePos = PreviousTextPos
            If Len(RTrim$(SubjectIndexRecord.Subject)) > 0 Then
                IndexPos = IndexPos + 1
                Put #IndexFileNum, IndexPos, SubjectIndexRecord
                End If
            ' Create a new subject.
            If Left$(LineOfText, 3) = "###" Then
                SubjectIndexRecord.Subject = Mid$(LineOfText, 4)
                SubjectIndexRecord.FilePos = 0
                Else
                SubjectIndexRecord.Subject = ""
                SubjectIndexRecord.FilePos = 0
                End If
            End If
        End If
    Loop
' If the source text ends with an orphan
' Subject header (it has no Subject text),
' save it anyway.
If Len(RTrim$(SubjectIndexRecord.Subject)) > 0 Then
    IndexPos = IndexPos + 1
    Put #IndexFileNum, IndexPos, SubjectIndexRecord
    End If

Close LinkFileNum
Close IndexFileNum
FilesAreOpen = False
Close TextFileNum
End Sub

Sub DisplayFirstTopic (ThePicture As PictureBox)
    LoadSubject RTrim$(SubjectIndexArray(1).Subject), ThePicture
    End Sub

Sub DoHyperTextJump (TargetString As String, ThePicture As PictureBox)
    Dim Dummy As Integer

    If Left$(Right$(TargetString, 4), 1) = "." Then
        Dummy = mciExecute("Play " + TargetString)
      Else
        LoadSubject TargetString, ThePicture
      End If
    End Sub

Function GetWordFrom (AnyString As String) As String
    If Left$(AnyString, 1) = "#" Then
        GetWordFrom = Left$(AnyString, InStr(AnyString, "~"))
        AnyString = Mid$(AnyString, InStr(AnyString, "~") + 1)
```

```
      ElseIf InStr(AnyString, " ") = 0 Then
        GetWordFrom = AnyString
        AnyString = ""
      Else
        GetWordFrom = Left$(AnyString, InStr(AnyString, " "))
        AnyString = Mid$(AnyString, InStr(AnyString, " ") + 1)
      End If
    End Function

Sub InitializeHyperEngine ()
    CurrentSubject = RTrim$(SubjectIndexArray(1).Subject)
    End Sub

Sub LoadSubject (Subject As String, ThePicture As PictureBox)
    Dim StringToPrint As String
    Dim CreatingALink As Integer
    Dim NextWord As String
    Dim TempWord As String
    Dim TargetString As String

    CurrentSubject = Subject
    StringToPrint = ReadInText(Subject)

    ThePicture.Cls
    LinkArrayPos = 0
    ArrayPlaceHolder = 1

    ' Display the Subject name as heading.
    ThePicture.FontBold = False
    ThePicture.ForeColor = BLUE
    ThePicture.FontSize = 16
    ThePicture.CurrentX = 200
    ThePicture.Print RTrim$(Subject)
    ThePicture.Print

    ' Set the base text attributes.
    ThePicture.ForeColor = BLACK
    ThePicture.FontSize = 12
    ThePicture.CurrentX = 200

    CurrentTop = ThePicture.CurrentY
    NextWord = GetWordFrom(StringToPrint)
    Do While NextWord <> ""
        If Left$(NextWord, 2) = "##" Then
            ParseLink NextWord, TempWord, TargetString
            TempWord = TempWord + Left$(StringToPrint, 1)
            StringToPrint = Mid$(StringToPrint, 2)
            CreatingALink = True
          Else
            TempWord = NextWord
            CreatingALink = False
          End If
        ' Insert a blank line between paragraphs.
        If Left$(TempWord, 1) = Chr$(13) Then
```

```
            NewLine ThePicture
            NewLine ThePicture
            ThePicture.CurrentX = 200
            TempWord = ""
          End If
        If ((ThePicture.CurrentX + ThePicture.TextWidth(TempWord)) >
          ThePicture.ScaleWidth) Then
            NewLine ThePicture
            ThePicture.CurrentX = 200
            End If
        If CreatingALink Then
            LinkArrayPos = LinkArrayPos + 1
            HyperLinkArray(LinkArrayPos).Left = ThePicture.CurrentX
            HyperLinkArray(LinkArrayPos).Top = CurrentTop
            ThePicture.FontBold = -1
            ThePicture.Print TempWord;
            ThePicture.FontBold = 0
            HyperLinkArray(LinkArrayPos).Right = ThePicture.CurrentX
            HyperLinkArray(LinkArrayPos).DestinationSubject = TargetString
          Else
            ThePicture.Print TempWord;
          End If
        NextWord = GetWordFrom(StringToPrint)
        Loop
    HyperLinkArraySize = LinkArrayPos
    NewLine ThePicture
    End Sub

Sub NewLine (ThePicture As PictureBox)
    ThePicture.Print

    CurrentTop = ThePicture.CurrentY
    While ArrayPlaceHolder <= LinkArrayPos
        HyperLinkArray(ArrayPlaceHolder).Bottom = ThePicture.CurrentY
        ArrayPlaceHolder = ArrayPlaceHolder + 1
        Wend
    End Sub

Sub OpenHyperbase (ByVal FileName As String)
    Dim RootFileName As String
    Dim LinkRecordLen As Integer
    Dim IndexRecordLen As Integer
    Dim IndexPos As Long

    LinkFileNum = 2
    IndexFileNum = 3
    NumberOfSubjects = 0
    LinkRecordLen = Len(HyperTextRecord)
    IndexRecordLen = Len(SubjectIndexRecord)
    If InStr(FileName, ".") > 0 Then
       RootFileName = Left$(FileName, InStr(FileName, ".") - 1)
     Else
       RootFileName = FileName
     End If
```

```
If FilesAreOpen Then
    Close LinkFileNum
    Close IndexFileNum
    FilesAreOpen = False
    End If
Open RootFileName + ".HTF" For Random As #LinkFileNum Len = LinkRecordLen
Open RootFileName + ".IDX" For Random As #IndexFileNum Len = IndexRecordLen
FilesAreOpen = True
IndexPos = 0
Do Until EOF(IndexFileNum)
    IndexPos = IndexPos + 1
    Get #IndexFileNum, IndexPos, SubjectIndexArray(IndexPos)
    Loop
NumberOfSubjects = IndexPos - 1
End Sub

Sub ParseLink (RawLink As String, LinkWord As String, Subject As String)
    Dim DelimiterPos As Integer
    Dim TildePos As Integer
    While Left$(RawLink, 1) = "#"
        RawLink = Mid$(RawLink, 2)
        Wend
    DelimiterPos = InStr(RawLink, "|")
    LinkWord = Left$(RawLink, DelimiterPos - 1)
    RawLink = Mid$(RawLink, DelimiterPos + 1)
    TildePos = InStr(RawLink, "~")
    Subject = Left$(RawLink, TildePos - 1)

    End Sub

Function ReadInText (SubjectName As String) As String

    Dim ParagraphText As String
    Dim TempString As String
    Dim IndexPos As Integer
    Dim LinkPos As Long

    ParagraphText = ""
    IndexPos = 1
    ' Search for subject.
    Do Until (RTrim$(SubjectIndexArray(IndexPos).Subject) = SubjectName) Or
            (IndexPos > NumberOfSubjects)
        IndexPos = IndexPos + 1
        Loop
    ' If subject is found, read in text.
    If IndexPos <= NumberOfSubjects Then
        LinkPos = SubjectIndexArray(IndexPos).FilePos
        Do Until (LinkPos = 0) Or (EOF(LinkFileNum))
            Get #LinkFileNum, LinkPos, HyperTextRecord
            TempString = RTrim$(HyperTextRecord.TextBlock)
            ' Replace the substituted spaces.
            If Right$(TempString, 1) = Chr$(1) Then
                TempString = Left$(TempString, Len(TempString) - 1) + " "
                End If
```

```
        ParagraphText = TempString + ParagraphText
        LinkPos = HyperTextRecord.NextBlock
        Loop
    End If
    ReadInText = ParagraphText
End Function

Function TargetFromPointInText (X As Single, Y As Single) As String
    Dim Counter As Integer
    Dim Found As Integer
    Dim TempTargetString As String

    TempTargetString = ""
    Found = False
    Counter = 0
    Do While (Counter < HyperLinkArraySize) And (Not Found)
        Counter = Counter + 1
        If (X > HyperLinkArray(Counter).Left) And
           (X < HyperLinkArray(Counter).Right) And
           (Y < HyperLinkArray(Counter).Bottom) And
           (Y > HyperLinkArray(Counter).Top) Then
            TempTargetString = RTrim$(HyperLinkArray(Counter).DestinationSubject)
            Found = True
        End If
    Loop
    TargetFromPointInText = TempTargetString
End Function
```

Creating the Hypermedia Engine

At last, it's time to join words with pictures. In this project we'll build a code
module that handles image hotspots to go along with our hypertext system.
Then, we'll plug them both into a program that will let us leap from words to
pictures and back again with the click of a mouse button.

Creating the Hypermedia Engine

This project creates the complete hypermedia engine. Here are the
steps to follow:

1. Create a new form with two Picture Box controls, one for text and
   one for images.
2. Add the code module HYPRTXT5.BAS to the project.
3. Copy HOTSPOT4.BAS to HOTSPOT5.BAS and fill in the functions
   we need to use the polygon hotspots we created in Chapter 9
   (Listings 10.6 through 10.8).

4. Create a new code module called HYPRMED1.BAS with its one and only procedure **DoHypermediaJump()** (Listing 10.9), and fill in the **MouseDown()** event procedures in the two Picture Boxes so they call this new general procedure (Listings 10.10 and 10.11).

5. Complete the remaining event procedures in HYPRMED1.FRM (Listings 10.12 through 10.14).

6. Copy HYPRTXT5.TXT to HYPRMED1.TXT and modify it so we can test out our new hypermedia system (Listing 10.15).

 You'll find this program in the subdirectory \VBMAGIC in the files HYPRMED1.MAK, HYPRMED1.FRM, HYPRMED1.BAS, HOTSPOT5.BAS, HYPRTXT5.BAS, GLOBCONS.BAS, DATACONS.BAS, and HYPRMED1.TXT.

Running the Magic Hypermedia Engine

Run the program and you'll see the window shown in Figure 10.1. Notice that the subject "HyperText" is displayed just as it was in all the previous hypertext projects. But when you click on the word "Pictures" it will display the photograph in ImagesPictureBox. If you have your paths set correctly in the text file and in the **ImageTable**, clicking on the larger flower, the one in the foreground, should cause the TextPictureBox to display the subject "Hotspots."

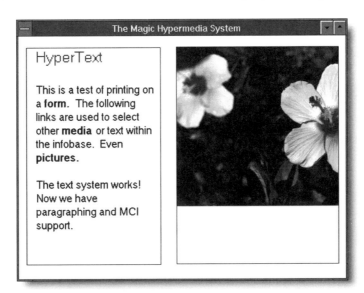

Figure 10.1 *The hypermedia engine at work.*

I've drawn the hotspot with some care, following the outline of the flower's petals, so clicking between petals won't do anything.

If the program can't find the bitmap file, it will display a message box that indicates where it's looking for it. Make the necessary corrections to the text file. Keep in mind that the **ImageTable** in IMAGES.MDB won't change by itself. You have to update the field **ImageFilename**, so it contains the correct path for the bitmap file.

Try adding your own images to the system. Use the hotspot editor we built in Chapter 9 to define the hotspots, then add hotlinks to the text file to load the pictures. Remember not to create any dead ends (if you do, you can always stop the program). If you get really ambitious, you can always increase the size of **SubjectIndexArray** (in the declarations section of HYPRTXT5.BAS) to support more hypertext subjects.

Creating the Form

Now that we've seen what the project will do, let's get going. Start a new project called HYPRMED1.MAK. This project will have one form, which we'll save as HYPRMED1.FRM. Set the form's **Name** property to HyperMedia1F1. Set the form's **ScaleMode** property to the default, 1 - Twip. You may also wish to set the caption. I've used the title *The Magic Hypermedia System.*

We'll need two Picture Box controls on the form, as shown in Figure 10.2.

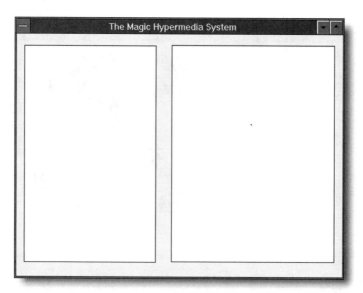

Figure 10.2 *The HyperMedia1F1 form stored in the file HYPRMED1.FRM.*

Place the first Picture Box on the form and set its **Name** property to TextPictureBox. Set the **ScaleMode** to 1 - Twip, and set both **AutoRedraw** and **ClipControls** to False. Place the second Picture Box to the right of the first, and set its **Name** property to ImagesPictureBox. Again, set **AutoRedraw** and **ClipControls** to False, but set this Picture Box's **ScaleMode** property to 3 - Pixel.

Adding the Code Modules

For this project we'll need four of the code modules we developed in previous projects. First, select File, Add File on the VB menu bar and add GLOBCONS.BAS. Use this same procedure to add DATACONS.BAS and HYPRTXT5.BAS.

You'll also need the hotspot code module, but before you add it to the project, use the Windows File Manager or the DOS Copy command to make a new copy of HOTSPOT4.BAS (called HOTSPOT5.BAS). Add the new copy to the project.

Hyperlinking Hotspots

In the project HOTSPOT4.MAK, we wrote a code module called HOTSPOT4.BAS that included the functions and procedures we needed to create and test hotspot regions on images. Now we're going to add two new procedures and one function to the new copy of that code module, HOTSPOT5.BAS, which we'll use to arm those hotspots.

In our hotspot editor we could activate and test only one hotspot at a time. But for our hypermedia system we'll need to activate all of the hotspots that belong to an image simultaneously. For that job, we'll write a procedure called **ActivateHotspots()**, which is shown in Listing 10.6.

Listing 10.6 The ActivateHotspots() General Procedure from HOTSPOT5.BAS

```
Sub ActivateHotspots (ByVal TheTarget As String)
    Dim VertexCount As Integer
    Dim TempString As String
    Dim StillOnCurrentPicture As Integer

    DeactivateHotspots
    ImageTable.Index = "PrimaryKey"
    ImageTable.Seek ">=", TheTarget, 1
    If (Not ImageTable.NoMatch) And (Not ImageTable.EOF) Then
        StillOnCurrentPicture = (UCase$(ImageTable!ImageFilename) = UCase$(TheTarget))
        Do While StillOnCurrentPicture
            ActiveHotspotCount = ActiveHotspotCount + 1
            ActiveHotspots(ActiveHotspotCount).TargetString = ImageTable!LinkTarget
            TempString = ImageTable!VertexArray
            VertexCount = ArrayFromString(PolygonVertices(), TempString)
```

```
        ActiveHotspots(ActiveHotspotCount).hPolygonRgn =
          CreatePolygonRgn(PolygonVertices(0), VertexCount + 1, 0)
        ImageTable.MoveNext
        If ImageTable.EOF Then
            StillOnCurrentPicture = False
        Else
            StillOnCurrentPicture = (UCase$(ImageTable!ImageFilename) =
              UCase$(TheTarget))
        End If
      Loop
    End If

  End Sub
```

The first thing this procedure does is call **DeactivateHotspots()**, another new procedure, which we'll cover shortly. For now, suffice to say that **DeactivateHotspots()** simply disposes of all the currently active Windows polygon regions.

To keep track of the currently active hotspots, we'll maintain an array of structures that each hold a region handle and the hotspot's target string:

```
Type ActiveHotspotEntry
    hPolygonRgn As Integer
    TargetString As String * 128
    End Type

Dim ActiveHotspots(25) As ActiveHotspotEntry
Dim ActiveHotspotCount As Integer
```

ActivateHotspots() takes a target string as its sole argument, which must always be the path and filename of a bitmap (BMP) or device-independent bitmap (DIB). The procedure then searches the **ImageTable** in the **Images** database to locate all the hotspots for the specified picture. For each entry it finds in the table, **ActivateHotspots()** performs three tasks: it unpacks the vertex array, calls the API function **CreatePolygonRgn()**, and stores the new region handle, along with the hotspot's own target—the target to which the system will jump when the user clicks on the hotspot, *not* the target passed into the procedure—in the next available entry in the **ActiveHotspots** array.

Searching Access Databases

More than half the code in the **ActivateHotspots()** procedure deals with the mechanics of the table search. In particular, you may have noticed that I used a separate variable, **StillOnCurrentPicture**, to control the **Do While** loop. At first, I tried to place the termination test expressions in the **Do While** statement itself:

```
Do While (UCase$(ImageTable!ImageFilename) = UCase$(TheTarget)) And (Not
    ImageTable.EOF)
        _
        _

        _
    ImageTable.MoveNext
    Loop
```

This looks like it should work, but it doesn't. You run into trouble when you run off the end of the file. The MoveNext method will shove the file pointer off into limbo where the EOF property returns True, but the record buffer no longer contains a valid record. At that point, instead of returning a null string, any reference to ImageTable!ImageFilename causes VB to produce a runtime error. Many computer languages help you out of this conundrum by supporting a feature called short-circuit boolean evaluation. If this feature detects one boolean test in the expression that will cause the whole expression to produce a False result, it doesn't bother to evaluate the remaining subexpressions. Sometimes short-circuit evaluation works from right to left, and sometimes from left to right. In VB it doesn't work at all. We can't perform both tests in the same expression. That's why we have used a separate variable to determine when the search has ended. After each turn around the loop we must check first for the EOF condition:

```
ImageTable.MoveNext
If ImageTable.EOF Then
    StillOnCurrentPicture = False
  Else
    StillOnCurrentPicture = (UCase$(ImageTable!ImageFilename) =
      UCase$(TheTarget))
  End If
```

If **EOF** is **True**, we set **StillOnCurrentPicture** to **False**—our own short-circuit. If **EOF** is **False**, we can then check whether the new record belongs to the current picture. If not, we set **StillOnCurrentPicture** to **False**, which terminates the loop.

Once we have a bunch of active hotspots, we'll also need some way to get rid of them. For that job we'll write the **DeactivateHotspots()** general procedure, shown in Listing 10.7.

Listing 10.7   The DeactivateHotspots() General Procedure from HOTSPOT5.BAS

```
Sub DeactivateHotspots ()
    Dim HotspotCounter As Integer

    If ActiveHotspotCount > 0 Then
        For HotspotCounter = 1 To ActiveHotspotCount
```

```
            DeleteRegion ActiveHotspots(HotspotCounter).hPolygonRgn
          Next HotspotCounter
      End If
   ActiveHotspotCount = 0
   End Sub
```

This simple procedure steps through the **ActiveHotspots** array, deleting the polygon hotspot regions, then setting the **ActiveHotspotCount** to zero.

In the HOTSPOT4.MAK project, we tested our new hotspots by passing the mouse coordinates to the API function **PtInRegion()**. We still need to do that, but now we also need to check the mouse position against all the active hotspots until we either find a match or run out of hotspots on the image. If we find that the user has clicked on one of the hotspots, we'll need to know the target string so we can perform the appropriate action. To solve this problem, we'll write a function called **TargetFromPointInImage()**, shown in Listing 10.8, that takes the mouse coordinates as arguments, and returns the target string.

Listing 10.8   The TargetFromPointInImage() General Function from HOTSPOT5.BAS

```
Function TargetFromPointInImage (X As Single, Y As Single) As String
   Dim Counter As Integer
   Dim Found As Integer
   Dim TempTargetString As String

   TempTargetString = ""
   Found = False
   Counter = 0
   Do While (Counter < ActiveHotspotCount) And (Not Found)
      Counter = Counter + 1
      If PtInRegion(ActiveHotspots(Counter).hPolygonRgn, X, Y) Then
         TempTargetString = RTrim$(ActiveHotspots(Counter).TargetString)
         Found = True
      End If
   Loop
   TargetFromPointInImage = TempTargetString
   End Function
```

This function steps through the **ActiveHotspots** array, testing the mouse coordinates against each hotspot by passing them to **PtInRegion()** with the handle for the region held in the array element. If it finds a match, it returns the corresponding **TargetString**; otherwise it returns a null string ("").

With the additions of **ActivateHotspots()**, **DeactivateHotspots()**, and **TargetFromPointInRegion()**, we've rounded out the HOTSPOT5.BAS code module. Now we can hitch together the hotspot and hypertext systems.

Hotspots Meet Hypertext

In the project HYPRTXT5.MAK, presented earlier in this chapter, we added the **DoHyperTextJump()** general procedure to HYPRTXT5.BAS. This procedure took two arguments, a target string and a Picture Box control. If the target string looked like a filename and path (it ended with a period followed by three characters), **DoHyperTextJump()** assumed that the file was a multimedia file and called **mciExecute()** to play it. If the target string didn't look like a filename, **DoHyperTextJump()** assumed that it was a subject name, and called **LoadSubject()**, passing on the target string and the Picture Box.

Now we need to introduce a third possibility—that the target string contains the path and filename of a bitmap image. And on top of that, we have to trigger the same process whether the user clicks on a hotlink word in the TextPictureBox or on a hotspot in ImagesPictureBox. To handle these two **MouseDown** events, we'll write one over-arching procedure called **DoHypermediaJump()** that can do any of three things:

- Call the multimedia API function **mciExecute()** to play a multimedia file
- Call the VB function **LoadPicture()** and call **ActivateHotspots()** in the hotspot code module
- Call **LoadSubject()** in the hypertext code module

We'll place this procedure all by itself in a new code module called HYPRMED1.BAS, which is shown in Listing 10.9.

Listing 10.9   The DoHypermediaJump() General Procedure from HYPRMED1.BAS

```
Sub DoHypermediaJump (TargetString As String, TheTextPicture As PictureBox,
   TheImagePicture As PictureBox)
    Dim Dummy As Integer
    Dim FileExt As String

    If Left$(Right$(TargetString, 4), 1) = "." Then
        If Mid$(TargetString,2,1) <> ":" Then
            TargetString = Left$(App.Path,2) & TargetString
        End If
        If Len(Dir$(TargetString)) > 0 Then
            FileExt = UCase$(Right$(TargetString, 3))
            If (FileExt = "MID") Or (FileExt = "WAV") Or (FileExt = "AVI") Then
                Dummy = mciExecute("Play " + TargetString)
            ElseIf (FileExt = "BMP") Or (FileExt = "DIB") Then
                TheImagePicture.Picture = LoadPicture(TargetString)
                ActivateHotspots UCase$(Mid$(TargetString,3))
            Else
```

```
            MsgBox "Unknown media file type: " & TargetString, 48,
               "Hyperlink Error"
          End If
      Else
         MsgBox "Unable to locate media file " & TargetString, 48, "Hyperlink Error"
      End If
  Else
     LoadSubject TargetString, TheTextPicture
  End If
End Sub
```

Although we'll leave **DoHyperTextJump()** in the hypertext code module—we may need it someday—for the remainder of the projects in this book, we'll retire that procedure. Instead, we'll use **DoHypermediaJump()**.

Just as in **DoHyperTextJump()**, when the fourth character from the end of any target string is a period, **DoHypermediaJump()** assumes that the string contains a path and filename. If so, it uses the VB **Dir$()** and **Len()** functions to determine whether the file exists; if not, it displays a VB Message Box to report the error. Otherwise, it copies the last three characters of the string into a temporary variable called **FileExt,** which it then compares to the known media file extensions to determine whether to play the file with an MCI command, or to load a bitmap into the ImagesPictureBox (which has been passed into **DoHypermediaJump()** under the argument name **TheImagePicture**). If it can't identify the file type from its extension, it displays an error message.

Two event procedures in HYPRMED1.FRM, **TextPictureBox_MouseDown()**, shown in Listing 10.10, and **ImagesPictureBox_MouseDown()**, shown in Listing 10.11, will now call **DoHypermediaJump()**.

Listing 10.10   The TextPictureBox_MouseDown() Event Procedure from HYPRMED1.FRM

```
Sub TextPictureBox_MouseDown (Button As Integer, Shift As Integer, X As Single,
   Y As Single)
   Dim TargetString As String

   TargetString = TargetFromPointInText(X, Y)
   If Len(TargetString) > 0 Then
      DoHypermediaJump TargetString, TextPictureBox, ImagesPictureBox
    End If
End Sub
```

Listing 10.11   The ImagesPictureBox_MouseDown Event Procedure from HYPRMED1.FRM

```
Sub ImagesPictureBox_MouseDown (Button As Integer, Shift As Integer, X As
   Single, Y As Single)
   Dim TargetString As String
```

```
    TargetString = TargetFromPointInImage(X, Y)
    If Len(TargetString) > 0 Then
        DoHypermediaJump TargetString, TextPictureBox, ImagesPictureBox
    End If
End Sub
```

These two event procedures are nearly identical. The only difference between them is that **TextPictureBox_MouseDown()** calls **TargetFromPointInText()** to retrieve the **TargetString**, while **ImagesPictureBox_MouseDown()** calls **TargetFromPointInImage()** to retrieve the **TargetString**.

Filling In the Remaining Event Code

Since we've eliminated the Compile Hypertext File and Open Hyperbase Command Buttons from the project, we need to handle those tasks in the **Form_Load()** event procedure, as shown in Listing 10.12.

Listing 10.12   The Form_Load() Event Procedure from HYPRMED1.FRM

```
Sub Form_Load ()
    Dim OpenedImageDatabase As Integer

    FilesAreOpen = False
    CompileText App.Path & "\HyprMed1.Txt"
    OpenHyperbase App.Path & "\HyprMed1.XXX"
    OpenedImageDatabase = OpenImageDatabase()
    DisplayFirstTopic TextPictureBox
    End Sub
```

We'll also need to handle the **Unload** event to clean up any active hotspots. For that we'll add one procedure call to the **Form_Unload()** event procedure, as shown in Listing 10.13.

Listing 10.13   The Form_Unload() Event Procedure from HYPRMED1.FRM

```
Sub Form_Unload (Cancel As Integer)
    DeactivateHotspots
    End Sub
```

Finally, we'll fill in the **TextPictureBox_Paint()** event procedure, as shown in Listing 10.14.

Listing 10.14   The TextPictureBox_Paint() Event Procedure from HYPRMED1.FRM

```
Sub TextPictureBox_Paint ()
    LoadSubject CurrentSubject, TextPictureBox
    End Sub
```

Creating the Text File

To test the multimedia engine, we'll need to make at least one change to the text file. Copy the previous version, HYPRTXT5.TXT to HYPRMED1.TXT and open it in any text editor, such as the Windows Notepad. The new text file is shown in Listing 10.15.

Listing 10.15   The HYPRMED1.TXT Text File

```
###HyperText
This is a test of printing on a ##form|Forms Design~.  The following links are
used to select other ##media|Multimedia~ or text within the infobase.  Even
##pictures|\vbmagic\images\hibiscus.bmp~.

The text system works!  Now we have paragraphing and MCI support.
###Multimedia
Multimedia systems combine elements such as text, ##sound|c:\windows\tada.wav~,
and ##Hypertext|HyperText~ to create an engaging and informative presentation.
###Forms Design
To prepare a ##Multimedia|Multimedia~ presentation, we design forms on which to
display graphics and text.  ##Hotspots|Hotspots~ trigger sound bites,
##video|\vbmagic\video\deercrk.avi~, or even ##MIDI|c:\windows\canyon.mid~ music.
###Hotspots
Hotspots are areas on a control that when clicked on, cause the system to
display another ##Hypertext|HyperText~ screen, load another picture, or activate
a ##Multimedia|Multimedia~ event.
```

In the fourth line of this file I've added the phrase "Even ##pictures|\vbmagic\images\hibiscus.bmp~." You'll find the file HIBISCUS.BMP on the companion CD-ROM in the subdirectory \VBMAGIC\IMAGES. The IMAGES.MDB database file contains a hotspot for this picture under the path and filename \VBMAGIC\IMAGES\HIBISCUS.BMP. If you want to use the pre-defined hotspot, but the file is installed on your system in a subdirectory with a different path, you can use the VB Data Manager to open IMAGES.MDB and edit the hotspot record in the **ImageTable**. You can also use HOTSPOT4.MAK to add a new entry to the database table.

As it stands, the program looks for the text file in the same directory as the file HYPRMED1.MAK (or HYPRMED1.EXE if you've compiled the program). Either make sure the text file is in the right place, or modify the **Form_Load()** event procedure to specify an alternate path.

The Art of Scrolling Hypermedia

Unless you plan to limit your presentations to extremely brief topics and small pictures, you'll probably want to add scrolling to the hypertext system. In the previous project we joined the hypertext and image hotspot systems to support hyperjumps between text and pictures. We now need to explore how we can enhance our hypermedia engine to provide scrolling features.

Hypermedia Engine with Scrolling

In this project we'll enhance the hypermedia engine by adding Scroll Bars to both the text and image Picture Boxes. Here's what we'll do:

1. Create the new project HYPRMED2.MAK.
2. Copy and update the hypermedia form by adding three Scroll Bar controls—one for text and two for images—and one Frame control.
3. Copy HYPRTXT5.BAS to HYPRTXT6.BAS and add the new file to the project.
4. Link one vertical and one horizontal Scroll Bar to the image Picture Box so we can view and click on hotspot images that are too big to fit completely within the client area of ImagesPictureBox.
5. Link one vertical Scroll Bar to the text Picture Box so we can view and click on hotspots in lengthy hypertext topics.

You'll find this program in the subdirectory \VBMAGIC in the files HYPRMED2.MAK, HYPRMED2.FRM, HYPRMED2.BAS, HOTSPOT5.BAS, HYPRTXT6.BAS, GLOBCONS.BAS, DATACONS.BAS, MINMAX.BAS, and HYPRMED2.TXT.

Running the Scrolling Hypermedia Engine

When you run the program, it will load the first hypertext subject into the Picture Box on the left, as shown in Figure 10.3. To display an image, locate a hyperlink that references a picture and click on it. If you're using the sample text file, try clicking on the word *Pictures* in either the HyperText or Value Property subjects.

Remember to use the Close option on the form's Control menu to stop the program, or you may leave behind some stray polygon regions, which will remain in memory for the remainder of your Windows session.

Creating the Form

Start a new project called HYPRMED2.MAK. Remove the new project's default form, Form1. Copy HYPRMED1.FRM to HYPRMED2.FRM, then add this file to the new project. Set the form's **Name** property to HyperMedia2F1. Leave the form's **ScaleMode** property set to the default, 1 - Twip. You may also wish to

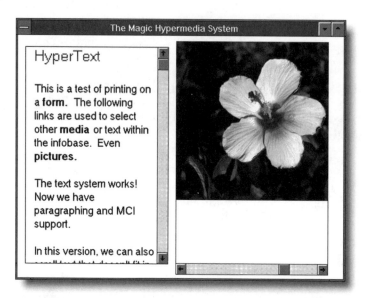

Figure 10.3　*The scrolling version of the Magic VB Hypermedia Engine in action.*

set the caption. (I've used the title *The Magic Hypermedia System.*) Select Options, Project from the VB menu bar, and set the Start Up Form to HyperMedia2F1.

We'll need a total of six controls on the form, two Picture Boxes, three Scroll Bars, and one Frame, as shown in Figure 10.4. The first Picture Box will be TextPictureBox from the previous project. Make sure its **ScaleMode** is still set

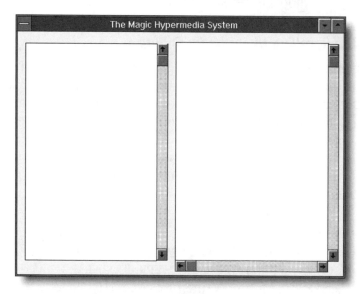

Figure 10.4　*The new hypermedia form from HYPRMED2.MAK.*

to 1 - Twip, and that both **AutoRedraw** and **ClipControls** are set to False. Place one vertical Scroll Bar on the right side of this Picture Box, and set its **Name** to TextVScroll. We'll set the other properties of TextVScroll at runtime.

From the remaining four controls we'll build a scrollable Picture Box system. In Chapter 1 I showed you a simple technique with which you could slide a large picture behind a Frame control to produce a form of animation. In this program we'll use a similar technique, but instead of driving the Picture Box with a Timer, we'll use a pair of Scroll Bars, one vertical and one horizontal. First place a Frame on the form. In the sample program on the CD-ROM, the Frame is on the right side of the form's client area. Set the Frame's **Name** property to PictureFrame. Next, move the ImagesPictureBox into the Frame by following these steps:

1. Select the Picture Box called ImagesPictureBox by clicking on it once; the sizing handles should appear around its perimeter.
2. Select Edit, Cut from the VB menu bar (or press Ctrl+X, or Shift+Delete) to transfer the Picture Box to the Clipboard.
3. Click anywhere in the Frame to select it.
4. Select Edit, Paste from the VB menu bar (or press Ctrl+V, or Shift+Insert) to drop the Picture Box into the Frame.

This Picture Box will become a *child* of the Frame. You'll see what I mean if you slide it around—the Picture Box will be clipped by the Frame, meaning that it will never appear outside the Frame's borders. Make sure the Picture Box's **Name** property is still set to ImagesPictureBox, that its **ScaleMode** is set to 3 - Pixel, and that both its **AutoRedraw** and **ClipControls** properties are set to False. For this project, you must change the **AutoSize** property to **True**. You may also wish to set its **BorderStyle** to 0 - None.

Finally, place two Scroll Bars outside and adjacent to the PictureFrame, one horizontal and one vertical. **Name** them ImageHScroll and ImageVScroll, respectively. Again, we'll set the remaining properties of the Scroll Bars at runtime.

Adding the Code Modules

For this project we'll need five of the code modules we've developed in previous projects. First, select File, Add File on the VB menu bar and add GLOBCONS.BAS. Use the same procedure to add DATACONS.BAS and HOTSPOT5.BAS. Use the Windows File Manager (or any other means) to copy HYPRTXT5.BAS to HYPRTXT6.BAS, and to copy HYPRMED1.BAS to HYPRMED2.BAS. Using the procedure described previously, add these two new files to the project HYPRMED2.MAK.

Scrolling Pictures

It doesn't take much code to move a Picture Box around inside a Frame. Take a look at Listing 10.16.

Listing 10.16 The ImageHScroll_Change() and ImageVScroll_Change() Event Procedures from HYPRMED2.FRM

```
Sub ImageHScroll_Change ()
    ImagesPictureBox.Left = -ImageHScroll.Value
    End Sub

Sub ImageVScroll_Change ()
    ImagesPictureBox.Top = -ImageVScroll.Value
    End Sub
```

When the Scroll Bars are at their zero positions—extreme left for the horizontal bar and top for the vertical bar—the ImagesPictureBox control will align itself with the upper-left corner of the Frame, exposing as much of the upper-left corner of the image as possible within the borders of the Frame (see Figure 10.5).

Figure 10.5 *This figure shows a Picture Box masked by a Frame.*

When the horizontal Scroll Bar thumb moves right to a position with a positive value, the ImagePictureBox will slide off to the left, behind the Frame, exposing the previously hidden area of the image to the right. When the vertical Scroll Bar thumb moves down to a position with a positive value, the image will slide up, exposing the lower portion.

To set the value ranges and limits of the Scroll Bars correctly for each image that is loaded into the Picture Box, we use the **Change** event of the Picture Box, as shown in Listing 10.17.

Listing 10.17 The ImagesPictureBox_Change() Event Procedure from HYPRMED2.FRM

```
Sub ImagesPictureBox_Change ()
    Dim Difference As Integer

    ImagesPictureBox.Left = 0
    ImagesPictureBox.Top = 0
    ImagesPictureBox.Visible = True
    If ImagesPictureBox.Width > PictureFrame.Width Then
        Difference = ImagesPictureBox.Width - PictureFrame.Width
        ImageHScroll.Value = 0
        ImageHScroll.LargeChange = MinInt(Difference, .33 * PictureFrame.Width)
        ImageHScroll.SmallChange = ImageHScroll.LargeChange \ 10
        ImageHScroll.Max = Difference
        ImageHScroll.Visible = True
    Else
        ImageHScroll.Visible = False
    End If
    If ImagesPictureBox.Height > PictureFrame.Height Then
        Difference = ImagesPictureBox.Height - PictureFrame.Height
        ImageVScroll.Value = 0
        ImageVScroll.LargeChange = MinInt(Difference, .33 * PictureFrame.Height)
        ImageVScroll.SmallChange = ImageVScroll.LargeChange \ 10
        ImageVScroll.Max = Difference
        ImageVScroll.Visible = True
    Else
        ImageVScroll.Visible = False
    End If
End Sub
```

For each Scroll Bar we want to determine first whether the Scroll Bar is even needed. That is, if the image is small enough in either dimension, we can dispense with the corresponding Scroll Bar. For the horizontal Scroll Bar, ImageHScroll, we compare the **Width** property of ImagesPictureBox with the **Width** of PictureFrame. Remember that we set the **AutoSize** property of ImagesPictureBox to True, so the Picture Box will automatically resize itself to the dimensions of the bitmap assigned to its **Picture** property. If

ImagesPictureBox is narrower than PictureFrame, we hide the horizontal Scroll Bar by setting its **Visible** property to False. Otherwise, we set the four properties that determine the behavior of the Scroll Bar: **Value**, **LargeChange**, **SmallChange**, and **Max**.

I've arbitrarily set the **LargeChange** property—which determines how far the thumb will move when you click in the interior of the Scroll Bar—to either the **Difference** in width between the Picture Box and Frame, or to one-third the width of the Frame, whichever is less. Also arbitrarily, I've set the value of **SmallChange**—which determines how far the thumb will move when you click either of the Scroll Bar arrows—to one-tenth the value of **LargeChange**. With these property settings, the Scroll Bar will never cause the Picture Box to over-scroll; in other words, the user cannot scroll the image past its right edge. After we set up the horizontal Scroll Bar, we repeat the process for the Vertical Scroll Bar, ImageVScroll.

The **ImagesPictureBox_Change()** event procedure uses a new general function called **MinInt()**. We'll be using a variety of minimum and maximum value functions in upcoming projects, so let's add a new code module called MINMAX.BAS, and insert the **MinInt()** function, as shown in Listing 10.18.

Listing 10.18 The MinInt() General Function from the Code Module MINMAX.BAS

```
Function MinInt (A As Integer, B As Integer) As Integer
    If A < B Then
        MinInt = A
    Else
        MinInt = B
    End If
End Function
```

We'll also want to initialize the Scroll Bars in the **Form_Load()** event procedure, as shown in Listing 10.19.

Listing 10.19 The Form_Load() Event Procedure from HYPRMED2.FRM

```
Sub Form_Load ()
    Dim OpenedImageDatabase As Integer

    FilesAreOpen = False
    CompileText App.Path & "\HyprMed2.Txt"
    OpenHyperbase App.Path & "\HyprMed2.XXX"
    OpenedImageDatabase = OpenImageDatabase()
    ImagesPictureBox.Left = 0
    ImagesPictureBox.Top = 0
    ImageHScroll.Visible = False
    ImageHScroll.Left = PictureFrame.Left
    ImageHScroll.Width = PictureFrame.Width
```

```
ImageVScroll.Visible = False
ImageVScroll.Top = PictureFrame.Top
ImageVScroll.Height = PictureFrame.Height
TextVScroll.Top = TextPictureBox.Top
TextVScroll.Height = TextPictureBox.Height
DisplayFirstTopic TextPictureBox, TextVScroll
End Sub
```

The main thing we want to accomplish in **Form_Load()** is to hide the Scroll Bars by setting their **Visible** properties to False. Sometimes it's difficult to align other controls with Frame controls at design time, so I've also taken the opportunity here to align the Scroll Bars on the form by setting their position and size properties to the corresponding properties of the Frame control.

Now, when you run the program, you'll be able to scroll your images. The **ImagesPictureBox_MouseDown()** event procedure will receive coordinates relative to the actual origin (upper-left corner) of the Picture Box, not the origin of PictureFrame. This means that all your hotspots will function normally, even when you need to scroll the image to find them.

We've managed to add Scroll Bars to the image Picture Box without modifying any of the existing code modules. All our changes have been confined to the form module. Now that's encapsulation! Unfortunately, although it will have only one Scroll Bar, the text Picture Box will not be as easy to handle.

Scrolling Hypertext

One way to scroll text would be to create a long Picture Box, and roll it up and down behind a Frame, just as we did for images. This will work, but for topics of more than a few paragraphs, it can get a little out of hand. Just the small client area of TextPictureBox occupies about 100K of memory, and in 12 point type, it can display only 70 words or so at one time. As we increase the quantity of text, we can quickly eat up large hunks of RAM. And it doesn't matter how much white space the text contains—black or white, a pixel fills a byte.

Text itself is pretty economical in terms of memory requirements, especially compared to image data. An 8-bit color picture of 320 by 240 pixels, which would occupy just one quarter of a 640 by 480 VGA display, would fill 76,800 bytes. That's enough memory to hold the text of this entire chapter!

The reason we're converting the text into a bitmap image in the first place is to display and trigger hypertext. But you can't click on a hotlink that's scrolled off the screen anyway, so why bother to keep it in bitmap format? The only portion of the text that needs to be printed to the Picture Box is the portion that's visible. The rest of it can remain in ASCII until it gets its stage call.

If we want the text to retain consistent line breaks from one end to the other, regardless of how the user skips through the "pages," we'll need to pre-format it to fit the current proportions of the TextPictureBox before we display any of it. To do this, we'll run through the text of the entire topic, chopping it into strings that, when printed, would fit within the **ScaleWidth** of the Picture Box. When we're ready to display the text, the **Value** property of the Scroll Bar will determine which line will appear at the top of the TextPictureBox. We'll then print as many successive lines as we can until we run out of either client area or text.

Preparing the Scrollable Hypertext

We've been using a single procedure called **LoadSubject()** to format and print the hypertext in the Picture Box. Now we'll strip the code out of **LoadSubject()** and peel it apart into one new function and one new procedure. The new function, called **PrepareSubject()**, will build the array of line strings and will return the number of formatted lines. The new procedure, **DisplaySubject()**, will display a section of the text beginning with the specified line.

Let's begin by renaming the existing procedure from **LoadSubject()** to **LoadShortSubject()**. Just edit its name in its declaration statement (the first line of the procedure). Don't change the calls to **LoadSubject()** elsewhere in the project because eventually we'll be writing a new **LoadSubject()** procedure.

PrepareSubject() closely resembles **LoadSubject()**. In fact, it does many of the same things. Take a look at Listing 10.20.

Listing 10.20 The PrepareSubject() General Function from HYPRTXT6.BAS

```
Function PrepareSubject (Subject As String, ThePicture As PictureBox) As Integer
        Dim StringToPrint As String
        Dim CreatingALink As Integer
        Dim NextWord As String
        Dim TempWord As String
        Dim TargetString As String
        Dim TextLineArrayPos As Integer
        Dim UnparsedLink As String
        Dim TempLine As String
        Dim AccumulatedLineLength As Integer

        For TextLineArrayPos = 0 To 500
            TextLineArray(TextLineArrayPos) = ""
            Next TextLineArrayPos
        CurrentSubject = Subject
        StringToPrint = ReadInText(Subject)

        TextLineArray(0) = RTrim$(Subject)
        TextLineArrayPos = 2
        ' Set base text attributes.
        ThePicture.ForeColor = BLACK
        ThePicture.FontSize = 12
```

```
AccumulatedLineLength = 200
TempLine = ""
NextWord = GetWordFrom(StringToPrint)
Do While NextWord <> ""
    If Left$(NextWord, 2) = "##" Then
        UnparsedLink = NextWord
        ParseLink NextWord, TempWord, TargetString
        TempWord = TempWord + Left$(StringToPrint, 1)
        UnparsedLink = UnparsedLink + Left$(StringToPrint, 1)
        StringToPrint = Mid$(StringToPrint, 2)
        CreatingALink = True
        ThePicture.FontBold = True
      Else
        TempWord = NextWord
        CreatingALink = False
        ThePicture.FontBold = False
      End If
    ' Insert a blank line between paragraphs.
    If Left$(TempWord, 1) = Chr$(13) Then
        TextLineArrayPos = TextLineArrayPos + 2
        AccumulatedLineLength = 200
        TempLine = ""
        TempWord = ""
        End If
    If ((AccumulatedLineLength + ThePicture.TextWidth(TempWord)) >
      ThePicture.ScaleWidth) Then
        TextLineArrayPos = TextLineArrayPos + 1
        TempLine = TempWord
        AccumulatedLineLength = 200 + ThePicture.TextWidth(TempWord)
      Else
        TempLine = TempLine + TempWord
        AccumulatedLineLength = AccumulatedLineLength +
                                ThePicture.TextWidth(TempWord)
      End If
    If CreatingALink Then
        TextLineArray(TextLineArrayPos) = TextLineArray(TextLineArrayPos) +
                                UnparsedLink
      Else
        TextLineArray(TextLineArrayPos) = TextLineArray(TextLineArrayPos) +
                                TempWord
      End If
    NextWord = GetWordFrom(StringToPrint)
    Loop
  TextLineArrayPos = TextLineArrayPos + 1
  PrepareSubject = TextLineArrayPos

End Function
```

We start by initializing the array to empty lines and reading in the subject text from the file:

```
For TextLineArrayPos = 0 To 500
    TextLineArray(TextLineArrayPos) = ""
```

```
    Next TextLineArrayPos
CurrentSubject = Subject
StringToPrint = ReadInText(Subject)
```

We know that the first line of the subject is its title so we place it in the first array element. We want to leave a blank line after the subject heading so we advance **TextLineArrayPos** to position 2:

```
TextLineArray(0) = RTrim$(Subject)
TextLineArrayPos = 2
```

Even though we're not printing to the Picture Box yet, we're going to use the Picture Box's **TextWidth** method to determine where to break the lines. To get meaningful results from that method, we need to set the text attributes of the Picture Box, which has been passed into the function as the argument **ThePicture**:

```
' Set base text attributes.
ThePicture.ForeColor = BLACK
ThePicture.FontSize = 12
```

We won't activate the hotlinks until we display the lines, so in each line we need to store the entire hotlink expression, including the double-pound sign tag (##), the hotlink word, the vertical bar (|), the target subject, and the tilde (~) terminator, as shown in Figure 10.6.

But to properly measure the lines, we still need to temporarily extract the hotlink word. Just as in the newly renamed procedure **LoadShortSubject()**, we step through the subject text, pulling off words with our general function **GetWordFrom()**. When we find a hotlink, we parse it and set both the **CreatingALink** variable and the **FontBold** property to True:

```
AccumulatedLineLength = 200
TempLine = ""
NextWord = GetWordFrom(StringToPrint)
Do While NextWord <> ""
    If Left$(NextWord, 2) = "##" Then
        UnparsedLink = NextWord
        ParseLink NextWord, TempWord, TargetString
        TempWord = TempWord + Left$(StringToPrint, 1)
        UnparsedLink = UnparsedLink + Left$(StringToPrint, 1)
        StringToPrint = Mid$(StringToPrint, 2)
        CreatingALink = True
        ThePicture.FontBold = True
    Else
        TempWord = NextWord
        CreatingALink = False
        ThePicture.FontBold = False
    End If
```

Array Index	String Value
0	HyperText
1	
2	This is a test of printing on
3	a ##form|Forms Design~. The following
4	links are used to select
5	other ##media|Multimedia~ or text within
6	the infobase. Even
7	##pictures|c:\vb\vbmagic\images\hibiscus.bmp~.
8	
9	The text system works!
10	Now we have
11	paragraphing and MCI
12	support.
13	
14	In this version, we can also
15	scroll text that doesn't fit in
16	the Picture Box control.
17	##Hotspots|Hotspots~ will move as the
18	text is scrolled. Each time
19	the user changes the
20	position of the thumb on
21	the scroll bar, the Paint
22	event will redraw the text
23	beginning with the line
24	specified by the ##Value|Value Property~
25	property of the Scroll Bar.
26	

Figure 10.6   *The subject HyperText from HYPRMED2.TXT as it would be stored in the TextLineArray.*

If we find a hyperlink, we save both the **TempWord** and the **UnparsedLink**. We'll use the **TempWord** to measure the formatted text against the dimensions of the Picture Box for proper wordwrap, but we'll save the **UnparsedLink** in the **TextLineArray** so we'll have it later when it's time to display and activate the hotlinks.

If we find a carriage return character (**Chr$(13)**) instead of a word, we'll insert a blank line:

```
If Left$(TempWord, 1) = Chr$(13) Then
    TextLineArrayPos = TextLineArrayPos + 2
```

```
      AccumulatedLineLength = 200
      TempLine = ""
      TempWord = ""
   End If
```

The next **If** statement measures the lines of text:

```
If ((AccumulatedLineLength + ThePicture.TextWidth(TempWord)) >
   ThePicture.ScaleWidth) Then
      TextLineArrayPos = TextLineArrayPos + 1
      TempLine = TempWord
      AccumulatedLineLength = 200 + ThePicture.TextWidth(TempWord)
   Else
      TempLine = TempLine + TempWord
      AccumulatedLineLength = AccumulatedLineLength + ThePicture.TextWidth(TempWord)
   End If
```

In **LoadShortSubject()** we used the **CurrentX** property to keep track of line length. Since we're not actually printing to the Picture Box, we accumulate the line length—which in this case is measured in Twips—in a local integer variable called **AccumulatedLineLength**. The 200 Twip offset is arbitrary; you may set the left margin at any value you wish.

Next, we add the current word to the current line in the **TextLineArray**. If the current word is a hotlink, we append the entire **UnparsedLink** to the string; otherwise we append only the **TempWord**:

```
   If CreatingALink Then
       TextLineArray(TextLineArrayPos) = TextLineArray(TextLineArrayPos) +
                                  UnparsedLink
     Else
       TextLineArray(TextLineArrayPos) = TextLineArray(TextLineArrayPos) + TempWord
     End If
   NextWord = GetWordFrom(StringToPrint)
   Loop
TextLineArrayPos = TextLineArrayPos + 1
PrepareSubject = TextLineArrayPos

End Function
```

Once it has processed the text of the entire subject, the function returns the current **TextLineArrayPos**, whose value is actually one greater than the last occupied array element.

Displaying Scrollable Hypertext

Even when most of the formatting issues are already out of the way, it's not much easier to display and activate the hypertext. We still have to re-parse the hyperlink expressions, build the array of active hyperlinks, and print the text to the Picture Box. That's why the new procedure **DisplaySubject()**, like **PrepareSubject()**, so closely resembles its parent procedure, **LoadShortSubject()**, as shown in Listing 10.21.

Listing 10.21 The New DisplaySubject() General Procedure from HYPRTXT6.BAS

```
Sub DisplaySubject (ThePicture As PictureBox, StartLine As Integer, MaxLine As
   Integer)
    Dim StringToPrint As String
    Dim CreatingALink As Integer
    Dim NextWord As String
    Dim TempWord As String
    Dim LineCounter As Integer
    Dim TargetString As String

    ThePicture.Cls
    LinkArrayPos = 0
    ArrayPlaceHolder = 1
    LineCounter = StartLine

    If StartLine = 0 Then
        ' Display Subject name as heading.
        ThePicture.FontBold = False
        ThePicture.ForeColor = BLUE
        ThePicture.FontSize = 16
        ThePicture.CurrentX = 200
        ThePicture.Print RTrim$(TextLineArray(0))
        ThePicture.Print
        LineCounter = 2
    End If
    ' Set base text attributes.
    ThePicture.ForeColor = BLACK
    ThePicture.FontSize = 12
    Do Until (ThePicture.CurrentY > ThePicture.ScaleHeight) Or (LineCounter > MaxLine)
        If TextLineArray(LineCounter) = "" Then
            NewLine ThePicture
        Else
            ThePicture.CurrentX = 200
            StringToPrint = TextLineArray(LineCounter)
            CurrentTop = ThePicture.CurrentY
            NextWord = GetWordFrom(StringToPrint)
            Do While NextWord <> ""
                If Left$(NextWord, 2) = "##" Then
                    ParseLink NextWord, TempWord, TargetString
                    TempWord = TempWord + Left$(StringToPrint, 1)
                    StringToPrint = Mid$(StringToPrint, 2)
                    CreatingALink = True
                Else
                    TempWord = NextWord
                    CreatingALink = False
                End If
                If CreatingALink Then
```

```
                LinkArrayPos = LinkArrayPos + 1
                HyperLinkArray(LinkArrayPos).Left = ThePicture.CurrentX
                HyperLinkArray(LinkArrayPos).Top = CurrentTop
                ThePicture.FontBold = True
                ThePicture.Print TempWord;
                ThePicture.FontBold = False
                HyperLinkArray(LinkArrayPos).Right = ThePicture.CurrentX
                HyperLinkArray(LinkArrayPos).DestinationSubject = TargetString
            Else
                ThePicture.Print TempWord;
            End If
          NextWord = GetWordFrom(StringToPrint)
          Loop
        NewLine ThePicture
      End If
    LineCounter = LineCounter + 1
    Loop
  HyperLinkArraySize = LinkArrayPos

  End Sub
```

The main difference between **DisplaySubject()** and **LoadShortSubject()** is that the new procedure doesn't check line lengths and insert line breaks. The only reason it parses the lines is to identify and inventory the hyperlinks for the section of text that will appear in the Picture Box. Other differences are apparent from the procedure's argument list. **DisplaySubject()** no longer takes the **Subject** as an argument. It displays whatever subject has been stored in the **TextLineArray** by **PrepareSubject()**. The new procedure also takes two new arguments: **StartLine**, which specifies the line that should appear first in the Picture Box, and **MaxLine**, which indicates the total number of lines in the subject.

Modifying the Form Code to Support Scrollable Hypertext

To activate the new version of the hypertext system we need to make several small but significant changes. Let's begin with the event procedures in HYPRMED2.FRM. First, we need to pass the Scroll Bar to **DisplayFirstSubject()** when we call the procedure from the **Form_Load()** event procedure, as shown in the last line of Listing 10.22.

Listing 10.22   The Form_Load() Event Procedure from HYPRMED2.FRM

```
Sub Form_Load ()
    Dim OpenedImageDatabase As Integer

    FilesAreOpen = False
    CompileText App.Path & "\HyprMed2.Txt"
    OpenHyperbase App.Path & "\HyprMed2.XXX"
```

```
OpenedImageDatabase = OpenImageDatabase()
ImagesPictureBox.Left = 0
ImagesPictureBox.Top = 0
ImageHScroll.Visible = False
ImageHScroll.Left = PictureFrame.Left
ImageHScroll.Width = PictureFrame.Width
ImageVScroll.Visible = False
ImageVScroll.Top = PictureFrame.Top
ImageVScroll.Height = PictureFrame.Height
TextVScroll.Top = TextPictureBox.Top
TextVScroll.Height = TextPictureBox.Height
DisplayFirstTopic TextPictureBox, TextVScroll
End Sub
```

You'll notice that I've also added two lines of code to square up the TextVScroll Scroll Bar with the TextPictureBox.

In the **TextPictureBox_MouseDown()** and **ImagesPicture-Box_MouseDown()** event procedures we'll add a new argument to the call to **DoHypermediaJump()**, as shown in Listing 10.23. Whenever the hypertext system loads a new subject, it will also need to set the properties of the Scroll Bar. When we added Scroll Bars to the ImagesPictureBox, we used the **ImagesPictureBox_Change()** event procedure and the properties of the Picture Box itself to set the Scroll Bar properties. But the **Print** method does not trigger the **Change** event, so when we pass the TextPictureBox to **DoHypermediaJump()**, we'll also need to pass TextVScroll. I'll show you what we do with it there shortly.

Listing 10.23   The TextPictureBox_MouseDown() and ImagesPictureBox_MouseDown() Event Procedures from HYPRMED2.FRM

```
Sub TextPictureBox_MouseDown (Button As Integer, Shift As Integer, X As Single,
   Y As Single)
   Dim TargetString As String

   TargetString = TargetFromPointInText(X, Y)
   If Len(TargetString) > 0 Then
       DoHypermediaJump TargetString, TextPictureBox, ImagesPictureBox, TextVScroll
     End If
   End Sub

Sub ImagesPictureBox_MouseDown (Button As Integer, Shift As Integer, X As
   Single, Y As Single)
   Dim TargetString As String

   TargetString = TargetFromPointInImage(X, Y)
   If Len(TargetString) > 0 Then
       DoHypermediaJump TargetString, TextPictureBox, ImagesPictureBox, TextVScroll
     End If
   End Sub
```

Now that we've split off the task of displaying the subject into its own procedure, we can respond properly to the **Paint** event. Listing 10.24 shows how the **TextPictureBox_Paint()** event procedure now works. This procedure is now the only place in the entire project from which we call **DisplaySubject()**.

Listing 10.24   The TextPictureBox_Paint() Event Procedure from HYPRMED2.FRM

```
Sub TextPictureBox_Paint ()
    DisplaySubject TextPictureBox, FirstTextLineNumber, LastTextLineNumber
    End Sub
```

Whenever the user moves the thumb on the Scroll Bar, the **TextVScroll_Change()** event procedure will set the new **FirstTextLineNumber** and force VB to issue a Paint message to the TextPictureBox by calling the Picture Box's **Refresh** method, as shown in Listing 10.25.

Listing 10.25   The TextVScroll_Change() Event Procedure from HYPRMED2.FRM

```
Sub TextVScroll_Change ()
    FirstTextLineNumber = TextVScroll.Value
    TextPictureBox.Refresh
    End Sub
```

Modifying LoadSubject() in the Hypertext Code Module to Support Scrolling

The new version of **LoadSubject()** will take two arguments: the Picture Box and the Scroll Bar, as shown in Listing 10.26.

Listing 10.26   The LoadSubject() General Procedure from HYPRTXT6.BAS

```
Sub LoadSubject (Subject As String, ThePicture As PictureBox, TheScrollBar As
    VScrollBar)
    LastTextLineNumber = PrepareSubject(Subject, ThePicture)
    FirstTextLineNumber = 0

    TheScrollBar.Min = 0
    TheScrollBar.SmallChange = 1
    TheScrollBar.LargeChange = MinInt((ThePicture.ScaleHeight \
        ThePicture.TextHeight("Any Text")) - 2, LastTextLineNumber - 1)
    If TheScrollBar.Value > 0 Then
        TheScrollBar.Value = 0
      Else
        ThePicture.Refresh
      End If
    TheScrollBar.Max = MaxInt((LastTextLineNumber - (ThePicture.ScaleHeight \
                    ThePicture.TextHeight("Any Text"))), 0)
    End Sub
```

After calling **PrepareSubject()**, this procedure now concerns itself primarily with the setting of the Scroll Bar properties. The expressions that set the **LargeChange** and **Max** properties limit the scroll range so that the text cannot scroll completely off the screen. The **If** statement prevents VB from double-painting the Picture Box when we load a new subject:

```
If TheScrollBar.Value > 0 Then
    TheScrollBar.Value = 0
  Else
    ThePicture.Refresh
  End If
```

When we load a new subject, we want it to begin at the first line, so we set the **Value** property of the Scroll Bar to 0. If the previous subject had been scrolled to a line other than 0, this assignment statement would trigger a Scroll Bar **Change** event, which, as we've already seen, would call the Picture Box **Refresh** method, which would trigger **TextPictureBox_Paint()**, which in turn, would call **DisplaySubject()**. If, on the other hand, the previous subject was in the home position, meaning that the Scroll Bar's **Value** property was already set to 0, then reassigning it the same value would not trigger the Scroll Bar **Change** event. To make sure we trigger **TextPictureBox_Paint()** we'll need to call the Picture Box's **Refresh** method (all-in-all a good illustration of event-driven programming, wouldn't you say?).

Before we leave the Hypertext code module again, we have two remaining details to handle. **DisplayFirstTopic()** and **DoHyperTextJump()** need to receive the Scroll Bar as an argument and pass it along to **LoadSubject()**, as shown in Listing 10.27.

Listing 10.27   The DisplayFirstTopic() and DoHyperTextJump() General Procedures from HYPRTXT6.BAS

```
Sub DisplayFirstTopic (ThePicture As PictureBox, TheScrollBar As VScrollBar)
    LoadSubject RTrim$(SubjectIndexArray(1).Subject), ThePicture, TheScrollBar
    End Sub

Sub DoHyperTextJump (TargetString As String, ThePicture As PictureBox,
   TheScrollBar As VScrollBar)
    Dim Dummy As Integer

    If Left$(Right$(TargetString, 4), 1) = "." Then
       Dummy = mciExecute("Play " + TargetString)
      Else
        LoadSubject TargetString, ThePicture, TheScrollBar
      End If
    End Sub
```

Updating the Hypermedia Code Module to Support Scrolling Hypertext

The HYPRMED2.BAS code module contains just one procedure, **DoHypermedia-Jump()**. Just as we modified **DisplayFirstTopic()** and **DoHyperTextJump()** in the hypertext code module, we need to modify this procedure to pass along the Scroll Bar control as an argument, as shown in Listing 10.28.

Listing 10.28   The DoHypermediaJump() General Procedure from HYPRMED2.BAS

```
Sub DoHypermediaJump (TargetString As String, TheTextPicture As PictureBox,
   TheImagePicture As PictureBox, TheScrollBar As VScrollBar)
    Dim Dummy As Integer
    Dim FileExt As String

    If Left$(Right$(TargetString, 4), 1) = "." Then
        If Mid$(TargetString, 2, 1) <> ":" Then
            TargetString = Left$(App.Path, 2) & TargetString
        End If
        If Len(Dir$(TargetString)) > 0 Then
            FileExt = UCase$(Right$(TargetString, 3))
            If (FileExt = "MID") Or (FileExt = "WAV") Or (FileExt = "AVI") Then
                Dummy = mciExecute("Play " + TargetString)
            ElseIf (FileExt = "BMP") Or (FileExt = "DIB") Then
                TheImagePicture.Picture = LoadPicture(TargetString)
                TheImagePicture.Left = 0
                TheImagePicture.Top = 0
                ActivateHotspots UCase$(Mid$(TargetString, 3))
            Else
                MsgBox "Unknown media file type " & TargetString, 48, "Hyperlink
                  Error"
            End If
        Else
            MsgBox "Unable to locate media file " & TargetString, 48, "Hyperlink
              Error"
        End If
    Else
        LoadSubject TargetString, TheTextPicture, TheScrollBar
    End If
End Sub
```

Modifying the Hypertext Source File

I've copied the file HYPRMED1.TXT to a file called HYPRMED2.TXT, and added some text to demonstrate the scrolling feature. The new version appears in Listing 10.29.

Listing 10.29   The HYPRMED2.TXT Text File

```
###HyperText
This is a test of printing on a ##form|Forms Design~.  The following links are
```

```
used to select other ##media|Multimedia~ or text within the infobase.  Even
##pictures|\vbmagic\images\hibiscus.bmp~.

The text system works!  Now we have paragraphing and MCI support.

In this version, we can also scroll text that doesn't fit in the Picture Box
control.  ##Hotspots|Hotspots~ will move as the text is scrolled.  Each time the
user changes the position of the thumb on the Scroll Bar, the Paint event will
redraw the text beginning with the line specified by the ##Value|Value Property~
property of the Scroll Bar.
###Multimedia
Multimedia systems combine elements such as text, ##sound|c:\windows\tada.wav~,
and ##Hypertext|HyperText~ to create an engaging and informative presentation.
###Forms Design
To prepare a ##Multimedia|Multimedia~ presentation, we design forms on which to
display graphics and text.  ##Hotspots|Hotspots~ trigger sound bites,
##video|\vbmagic\images\watrfall.avi~, or even ##MIDI|c:\windows\canyon.mid~.
###Hotspots
Hotspots are areas on a control that when clicked on, cause the system to
display another ##Hypertext|HyperText~ screen, load another picture, or activate
a ##Multimedia|Multimedia~ event.
###Value Property
This is a property of the Scroll Bar that indicates the
current position of the thumb.  In this program we use Scroll Bars to
scroll both ##Hypertext|HyperText~ and ##Pictures|\vbmagic\images\housrock.bmp~.
```

Verify the paths for all the hypermedia elements, including the pictures. If you wish, change the hyperlink expressions to load or play your own multimedia files. You may modify this file with any text editor, including the Windows Notepad. By default, the Hypermedia engine will look for the text file HYPRMED2.TXT in its default directory, the directory that holds the file HYPRMED2.MAK (or HYPRMED2.EXE if you've compiled the program). To use an alternate path or filename, make sure to modify the **Form_Load()** event procedure in HYPRMED2.FRM. You may also wish to add a menu to the form, with a proper File menu and Open dialog box so that you can choose the text file at runtime.

Don't Stop Here

There are more ways to spruce up the hypermedia engine than we could possibly cover in this book, especially if we ever want to get to sound, MIDI, and video. But by combining the techniques we've developed with some of VB's powerful features, you can add all kinds of handy features.

Hyperlinking is just one way to navigate an information base. The Windows Help system, for example, includes features for alphabetical lookups, forward and backward paging, and bookmarks. It even maintains a visitation history—a list of topics visited by the user from most recent to least recent. The navigation tools you add to the hypermedia engine should fit the material in your presentation. For multimedia encyclopedias, you may want to add all kinds of ways to sift through the information. For interactive books, you may restrict your readers more, to keep them from wandering too far. Whatever navigational tools you offer, you'll need to weigh the demands of the content against the requirements of interactivity.

Start with the basic system we've built in this chapter and add new features as you need them. Here are some suggestions for new features and enhancements:

Add a visitation history. With VB's Data Access features it's easy to keep records in order. Create a new database with a table that keeps track of user activity. Add fields to hold the subject name, the target string, and a counter to preserve the order. Index the table on the target string (or subject name) and the counter field. Use a List Box to display the user's visitation path, and use the List Box **Click** event to call **DoHypermediaJump()**.

Store the hypertext in an Access Database. Instead of storing hypertext as linked lists of records in an ordinary binary file, use a Memo field in the data access system to store entire topics in variable-length records. Index the file both by subject name and by subject number so you can scan the file either alphabetically or in logical subject order.

Use rectangular Windows regions for hypertext hotspots. Right now, the images hotspot functions and the hypertext hotspot functions use two different methods of displaying hotspots and detecting mouse clicks. As we discussed in Chapter 2, words occupy rectangular areas. It wouldn't take much effort to modify HYPRTEXT6.BAS to use rectangular Windows regions for hotlinks.

Add glossary lookups. The Windows Help system supports two kinds of hyperlinks. So far we have implemented only one, the regular hyperjump. The second type allows the user to pop up a temporary window, similar to a Message Box, which remains open only until they click somewhere else on the screen. This type of window comes in handy when you want to display a definition or a clarification without skipping to another topic entirely.

Support the multiple document interface (MDI). If you intend your presentation to be useful as a research tool, you may wish to allow the user to open multiple hypertext and image windows. The multiple document interface is the Windows system that enables applications such as WordPerfect for Windows and Microsoft Excel to open multiple documents in *child windows* contained within the confines of the main program window, or *parent window*, as shown in Figure 10.7.

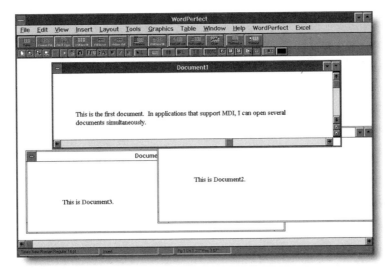

Figure 10.7 *WordPerfect for Windows with three documents open in separate child windows.*

With VB you can write your own MDI applications. Just choose File, New MDI Form from the VB menu bar to add an MDI parent form. You can add only one MDI form to a VB program, but you can define multiple child windows. To make a form into an MDI child, you set its **MDIChild** property to True. You may then open multiple *instances* of that form within the main MDI form. The VB manuals describe the entire process (see Chapter 14, "Multiple-Document Interface (MDI) Applications," in the VB Version 3.0 *Programmer's Guide*). You'll need to modify the hypertext and hotspot code modules to support multiple, simultaneous child windows. In particular, watch out for those global variables. By adding another argument to procedures like **LoadSubject()** (in HYPRTXT6.BAS), you can specify not only which Picture Box control should display the hypertext or picture, but also which instance of several child forms that Picture Box belongs to.

You can convert the multimedia engine into an MDI application, but, as you can tell, it will take some work!

Chapter 11

From flip books to moths in flight, this chapter will show you the basics of animation. Prepare yourself for some mighty exciting work.

The Magic of Animation

A nimation packs a potent punch when it's used right. Here's an amazing fact: video games generated more income than movies in the U.S. last year. What was their big attraction? Their dazzling interactive animation. If you want your multimedia apps to really grab your user's attention, don't underestimate the power of pictures in motion.

The animation used in interactive multimedia comes in two basic forms:

- Movies or video clips
- Graphical simulations

With an animation authoring tool, such as Autodesk's Animator Pro, you can create animated movies that illustrate anything from the formation of solar systems to the proper way to swing a tennis racket. To play them back, you can load them up with our old friend the Media Control Interface (MCI) and let them fly. You can also use MCI commands to pause them, to rewind them, or to skip to specific frames. Playback is a snap—the hard part is creating the animation in the first place. And since this book is not about how to create multimedia elements, but how to use them in presentations, we'll skip the complex subject of animation authoring. In fact, we'll skip this *frame-base* type of animation entirely, until Chapter 15, where we'll talk about Video for Windows.

In this chapter, we'll introduce you to some basic graphics animation techniques. These are the techniques that game developers use to create fast action adventures. We'll continue our graphics animation adventures in Chapter 12 as we show you how to create fast, smooth, flicker-free animation.

Exploring Flip Books

Although they often resemble other types of pre-recorded, frame-based animation, flip books give you a little more control at the cost of smaller size. The principle is simple. To create a paper flip book you draw each frame of the animation on a separate page. To view the result, you drag your thumb across the edges of the pages, flipping them past quickly enough that the figures in the drawings appear to move. To create a VB flip book, you place each frame of the animation in a separate Picture Box or Image control. You position the controls in a stack, then use the **Visible** property to quickly cycle through them, displaying one at a time.

The Flip Book

In this simple experiment, we'll use an array of Image controls to turn the pages of an animated book. Follow these steps:

1. Add the SPIN.VBX custom control to your new project.
2. Create the form FLIPBOOK.FRM.
3. Create a **Timer()** event procedure (Listing 11.1).
4. Add the necessary event procedures to the spin control (Listing 11.2).
5. Add the **Form_Load()** event procedure and the declarations section (Listings 11.3 and 11.4) to the form.

You'll find this project in the subdirectory \VBMAGIC in the files FLIPBOOK.MAK and FLIPBOOK.FRM. You'll also need the VB custom control SPIN.VBX, which VB usually installs in your \WINDOWS\SYSTEM subdirectory. The artwork for the project is in the file FLIPBOOK.BMP.

Running the Program

Figure 11.1 shows what the flip book looks like when you run the program. Try clicking on the spin button. The page will turn either to the left or to the

Figure 11.1   *This figure shows the flip book at runtime.*

right, depending on which side of the spin button you choose. You may also reverse the process while the page is turning by clicking the opposite button.

Creating the Form

Start a new VB project and name the form FlipBook. Place an Image control on the form, and set its **Name** property to DictionaryImage, and set the **Stretch** property to False. This will be the first frame of the animation, so set its **Visible** property to True. The next step is to set the **Picture** property. Usually you do this by selecting **Picture** in the Properties window to display the Load Picture dialog box. You then select a bitmap or metafile. But there is another way. You can also paste pictures into the control from the Clipboard.

Run Windows Paintbrush and load the file FLIPBOOK.BMP from the companion CD-ROM. This file contains a series of pictures that illustrate the turning of pages in a book, as shown in Figure 11.2.

Follow these steps to copy each frame from the Paintbrush file to an Image control:

1. Use Paintbrush's Pick tool (the top-right button that looks like scissors with a rectangle) to outline the first picture, the one in which the book's pages lay flat. You'll need to precisely align the upper-left corners of all the pictures, which means that you'll need to line up the Pick Tool's bounding box (the dashed outline) just outside the image, against the top and left edges. The bottom and right edges don't require such careful alignment. Just make sure the bounding box completely encloses the picture. The size of each frame may vary, but the upper-left corners must match.

2. Once you've selected the picture, choose Edit, Copy from the Paintbrush menu bar to copy the image to the Clipboard.

Figure 11.2   *These pictures are found in FLIPBOOK.BMP.*

3. Click on the Image control to select it (the handles should appear around its edges).

4. Choose Edit, Paste from the VB menu bar to copy the image to the Image control. The **Picture** property will now contain (Bitmap). The control should automatically resize itself to fit the picture clip. If it doesn't, make sure the **Stretch** property is set to False.

Add another image control to the form, and set its **Name** property to DictionaryImage. VB will display a message box telling you that you already have a control named DictionaryImage and will ask you if you wish to create a control array. Answer yes. Set the **Visible** property of this and all subsequent image controls to False. Then use the copy and paste operations described in the previous steps to transfer the next image to the control. Place the second Image control directly over the first. To align them perfectly, set their **Top** and **Left** properties to identical values. Setting the same property for multiple controls is easy. Simply select both controls by clicking and holding the mouse button in the form client area, then dragging the selection box around them. When you release the mouse button, the Properties windows will display a property list whose settings will affect all selected controls. After you set the **Top** and **Left** properties, de-select the controls by clicking the form anywhere outside the selection.

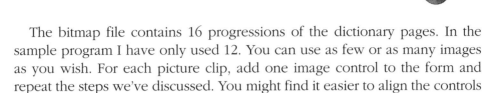

The bitmap file contains 16 progressions of the dictionary pages. In the sample program I have only used 12. You can use as few or as many images as you wish. For each picture clip, add one image control to the form and repeat the steps we've discussed. You might find it easier to align the controls after you've added them all.

We'll need two more controls to animate the dictionary, a Timer and a spin button. You can place the Timer anywhere on the form; it will disappear at runtime. Set its **Enabled** property to False, and its **Interval** to 56 (the fastest meaningful value).

Place the spin button anywhere near—but not overlapping—the stack of image controls, and set its **Orientation** property to 1 - Horizontal.

Coding the Event Procedures

To make the dictionary look as if its page is turning, we have to cycle through the image controls, displaying one at a time. We can't just run through them with a **For** loop though, because they would change too quickly. Instead, we'll use the Timer control to set a more reasonable pace. The **Interval** of 56 milliseconds should produce a rate of about 18 frames per second. In reality, it probably won't because Windows can't always handle **Timer** events that quickly. Actually, the standard Timer is not accurate enough for most time critical applications, but it works well enough for many types of animation.

With each tick, the Timer will hide the current image and display either the next or previous image in the series. Take a look at Listing 11.1 to see how this works.

Listing 11.1   The Timer1_Timer() Event Procedure from FLIPBOOK.FRM

```
Sub Timer1_Timer ()
    DictionaryImage(FrameCounter).Visible = False
    If TurnForward Then
        FrameCounter = (FrameCounter + 1) Mod 12
      Else
        FrameCounter = (FrameCounter + 11) Mod 12
      End If
    DictionaryImage(FrameCounter).Visible = True
    If FrameCounter = 0 Then
        Timer1.Enabled = False
      End If
    End Sub
```

When the form level integer variable **FrameCounter** reaches zero, the Timer disables itself. The form level variable **TurnForward** will contain ei-

ther **True** or **False**, and will be set by the **Spin1_SpinUp()** or **Spin1_SpinDown()** event procedures as shown in Listing 11.2.

Listing 11.2 The Spin1_SpinDown() and Spin1_SpinUp() Event Procedures from FLIPBOOK.FRM

```
Sub Spin1_SpinDown ()
    TurnForward = False
    Timer1.Enabled = True
    End Sub

Sub Spin1_SpinUp ()
    TurnForward = True
    Timer1.Enabled = True
    End Sub
```

When you click on the spin button, one of these two event procedures will set **TurnForward** to the appropriate direction and enable the Timer.

Finishing the Form's Code

The **Form_Load()** event procedure shown in Listing 11.3 disables the Timer, and initializes the two form level variables shown in Listing 11.4.

Listing 11.3 The Form_Load() Event Procedure from FLIPBOOK.FRM

```
Sub Form_Load ()
    Timer1.Enabled = False
    TurnForward = True
    FrameCounter = 1
    End Sub
```

Listing 11.4 The Declarations Section from FLIPBOOK.FRM

```
Option Explicit

Dim TurnForward As Integer
Dim FrameCounter As Integer
```

Adventures with Sprite Animation

The most interactive form of animation lets the user move objects around on the screen, usually to do something like shooting alien monsters or scrambling up and down ladders. In video games, you often find that you can move objects in more than one direction at various speeds, and that other objects, sometimes quite a few of them, whiz around the screen at the same time. If the authors of these games had to create completely rendered frames for every possible combination of background and moving objects, they would find themselves buried in artwork. Every flick of the joystick would need to send the blting engine off on another path, spitting out screen-sized images quickly enough to simulate motion.

Film animators solved a similar problem decades before the invention of video games—actually, decades before the invention of video. They call their solution *cel animation*, which comes from *celluloid animation*. A feature-length animated movie requires thousands of drawings. Each second of screen time requires twelve images (in most animation, each frame is photographed twice to produce the standard film speed of 24 frames per second). That's 720 frames per minute. Animated feature films tend to run about 100 minutes, for a total of 72,000 drawings. But most of the stuff in each frame doesn't move, or when it does, it just scrolls (*pans* in film language) right or left, up or down. So why redraw the background over and over again, hundreds of times for each scene? Instead, the background is drawn once. The characters are then painted on to clear acetate sheets (before the invention of plastics, they were painted on celluloid), which the camera operator lays over the background to compose each frame. This labor-saving method revolutionized animation, and later made it practical to produce television shows like *Rocky and Bullwinkle* or *The Simpsons*, because once the cels of a TV cartoon are painted, they can be re-used for other scenes and future episodes.

In computer animation, cels become *sprites*, bitmapped graphical objects that move around on the screen independently of the background—and each other. Just as cels make it practical to produce animated film, sprites make it practical to do real-time computer animation, which means that instead of just playing back pre-recorded animated clips, we can make animated graphics that respond to user activity.

Sprites Over Easy

In this brief project, we'll use the simplest method to move a bitmap around on the screen—with no API function calls.

1. Create a new form named SPRITE1.FRM.
2. Add the code shown in Listing 11.5 to the form.

 You'll find this project in the subdirectory \VBMAGIC in the files SPRITE1.MAK, SPRITE1.FRM, and SPRITE1.FRX.

Figure 11.3   *The SPRITE1.FRM form.*

Start a new project and place a Timer and an Image control on the form, as shown in Figure 11.3. Set the **Picture** property of the form by loading a bitmap (try the file HIBISC2.BMP on the companion CD-ROM). This will become the background image. If you wish, resize the form so its dimensions match the size of the background bitmap. Set the Timer **Interval** property to 56 or some similar value, and set its **Enabled** property to True. Set the **Stretch** property of the Image control to False and load an image into its **Picture** property. You'll find a set of four bitmap files in the \VBMAGIC subdirectory with the names MOTH1.DIB through MOTH4.DIB. You may load any of these images into the **Picture** property of the Image control, or you may use any other picture you wish.

You'll find all the code for this project in Listing 11.5.

Listing 11.5   SPRITE1.FRM

```
VERSION 2.00
Begin Form Form1
   Caption      =  "Sprite Animation Project 1"
   ClientHeight =  3504
   ClientLeft   =  876
   ClientTop    =  1524
   ClientWidth  =  5256
   Height       =  3924
   Left         =  828
   LinkTopic    =  "Form1"
```

```
    Picture     =  SPRITE1.FRX:0000
    ScaleHeight   =  292
    ScaleMode   =  3 'Pixel
    ScaleWidth   =  438
    Top       =  1152
     Width         =   5352
     Begin Timer Timer1
        Interval       =    50
        Left          =    684
        Top          =    2196
     End
     Begin Image Image1
        Height       =    960
        Left          =    1332
        Picture       =    SPRITE1.FRX:0000
        Top          =    1548
        Width       =    960
     End
End
Option Explicit

Dim Forward As Integer
Dim Down As Integer

Sub Timer1_Timer ()
    Dim NewLeft As Integer
    Dim NewTop As Integer

    If (((Image1.Left + Image1.Width) > Form1.ScaleWidth) And Forward) Or
       ((Image1.Left < 0) And Not Forward) Then
        Forward = Not Forward
     End If
    If Forward Then
        NewLeft = Image1.Left + 10
     Else
        NewLeft = Image1.Left - 10
     End If
    If (((Image1.Top + Image1.Height) > Form1.ScaleHeight) And Down) Or
       ((Image1.Top < 0) And Not Down) Then
        Down = Not Down
     End If
    If Down Then
        NewTop = Image1.Top + 7
     Else
        NewTop = Image1.Top - 7
     End If
    Image1.Move NewLeft, NewTop
    End Sub
```

The **Timer1_Timer()** event procedure uses the **Move** method of the Image
control to change its position with each tick. The variables just keep track of
position and direction. When you run this program, the Image control (with its

contents, of course) will bounce around the screen—not too complicated—not too exciting, either. Let's face it, there are a lot of things lacking here:

- The sprite and its host image control cut a rectangular block out of the background.
- The image moves in a slow, jerky motion.
- The sprite looks dead.

Let's explore how we can address these shortcomings.

Animating Sprites with BitBlt()

Image and Picture Box controls will work when we want to move sprites around on a plain background, and when we don't care much about smoothness of motion. But to get anywhere near the quality of game animation, we're going to need the power of the Windows GDI functions.

A faster way to perform sprite animation would be to blt our sprites to the device context holding the background image. This will introduce a new problem: How do we restore the background once we've poked a hole in it? I'll also show you how to perform a *transparent* blt, which will enable us to display the sprite without its white, rectangular background. We'll also cycle between two versions of the sprite to breathe a little life into our moth from the previous project.

Blt Animation

This project shows you how to produce faster and smoother animation by using blting techniques. Here are the steps to follow:

1. Create a form named SPRITE2.FRM.
2. Make special versions of the sprite bitmaps to help us perform the transparent bitblt.
3. Fill in the code for the **Paint** event (Listing 11.6).
4. Set up the **Timer** event (Listing 11.7).
5. Finish the declarations and initializations (Listing 11.8) and add the MINMAX.BAS code (Listing 11.9).

You'll find this project in the subdirectory \VBMAGIC in the files SPRITE2.MAK, SPRITE2.FRM, SPRITE2.FRX, and MINMAX.BAS The original bitmaps are in the files HIBISC2.BMP, MOTHSPT1.BMP, MOTHSPT4.BMP, MOTHMSK1.BMP, and MOTHMSK4.BMP in the same directory.

Running the Program

When you run this program, the moth will fly around AnimationPicture's client area, as shown in Figure 11.4. You can hide the sprites and masks if you wish by stopping the program and changing their **Visible** properties to False. We'll set them to **AutoRedraw** when we create the program so they behave as memory device contexts. We've omitted two of the four versions of the sprite bitmap, so the animation won't be too smooth, but that's the least of our problems.

You'll notice that the animation flickers badly. Each update of the sprite triggers three blts to the screen. On some systems you'll be able to detect the separate steps as the mask appears, followed by the sprite, then by the restoration of the background, especially if Windows is busy handling events triggered by other applications. I'll show you how to fix these problems a little later.

Creating the Form

In this version of the sprite project, we'll stop drawing on the form and use it simply as the container. Place six Picture Boxes on the form. Set the **ScaleMode** property of the form and all six Picture Boxes to 3 - Pixel. Set the **Name** property of the first picture box to AnimationPicture. Use the Load Picture dialog box to load the background bitmap and assign it to the **Picture** property. In the sample program, I have loaded the file HIBISC2.BMP. This will

Figure 11.4 *The SPRITE2 animation program.*

become the largest Picture Box, and will become the stage for the animation. Set its **AutoRedraw** property to False, and if you wish, set its **AutoSize** property to True (the Picture Box will automatically resize itself to the dimensions of the loaded bitmap). Figure 11.5 shows how the completed form should look.

From two of the remaining five pictures, create a control array called SpritePicture, and from two more, create the control array MaskPicture. These four smaller pictures will hold the sprite images and their *masks* (more on masks later). Set the **AutoRedraw** and **AutoSize** properties of all four of these Picture Boxes to True.

Name the last Picture Box BufferPicture, and once again, set its **AutoRedraw** property to True. Its **AutoSize** property is irrelevant. Once we've finished loading the sprite bitmaps into the SpritePicture and MaskPicture Picture Boxes, we'll want to make sure that BufferPicture is at least as large as they are. To be safe, I've drawn this control a little larger than it needs to be.

Preparing the Sprites—Transparent Bitmaps

In the previous project the Image control that contained the sprite bitmap cut a rectangular swatch out of the background. It's pretty hard to create the illusion that the sprite belongs to the background when it always appears against its own white mat. But there is a way to trim it neatly around the edges and display just the moth itself. To do that we need a couple of raster operations and two modified versions of the sprite bitmap.

Figure 11.5   *The SPRITE2.FRM form at design-time.*

In effect, we want the sprite bitmap to work like an animation cel. The moth should overlay the background, while the "blank" area that surrounds it should become transparent, allowing the background to show through. This is easier than you might think.

The first thing we need to do is decide which color in the orignal sprite bitmap will become transparent. The moth bitmaps are drawn on a white background, so let's assume that white pixels are transparent. We can't just blt the sprite to the background in a single operation because any raster operation we use will either blend the images in some way, ignore the sprite bitmap entirely, or transfer the entire rectangle. The problem is that we need the sprite's own background and foreground to each behave differently when we combine them with the background image. The background of the sprite must not appear at all, while the sprite's foreground shape must opaquely cover the background image. Clearly, we need to prepare the sprite and the background image in some way that they can be combined without disrupting each other.

Bear with me while we work backwards. Imagine that the white pixels of the sprite bitmap have been changed to black, which means they reference palette entry &H00 in an identity palette, and that an area in the shape of the moth has been colored black in the background image. If we could get this far, we could use an **Or** raster operation (**SRCPAINT**) to align and combine the images, because wherever we combined the black pixels in the sprite with the colored pixels in the background, the background pixels would determine the colors of the combined bitmaps; and wherever we combined the black pixels of the background with the colored pixels in the sprite, the sprite's pixels would determine the colors (remember, when you **Or** any value with &H00, you get the original value).

That's fine. But, if we can't blt the moth shape on to the background in the first place, how are we supposed to punch a moth-shaped hole? The answer to that question begins with yet another variation of the original sprite. Use your imagination again, and think what happens when you use an **And** raster operation (**SRCAND**) to blt a monochrome (black and white) bitmap on to a colored background. This time, the pixels in the monochrome bitmap that reference palette entry **&H00** (black in the system default palette and all identity palettes) will force the colored pixels in the background to turn black, and the pixels that reference palette entry **&HFF** (white in the system default palette and all identity palettes) will leave the background pixels set to their original colors. So if we begin with a monchrome version of the sprite in which the moth is colored completely black, and the surrounding pixels are colored white, their original color, then the **SRCAND** raster operation will paint a black silhouette of the moth on to the background. This monochrome version of the sprite bitmap is called a *mask*.

That's all there is to it. You take your original bitmap with its white background and make two new copies of it. In one you change the background from white to black; and in the other, you leave the white background as it is, but change all the other pixels—the ones that depict the sprite itself—to black.

Working forward this time, you first blt the monochrome mask on to the background with the **SRCAND** raster operation to punch the black silhouette. Then you blt the sprite, the version with the black background, to the same position with the **SRCPAINT** raster operation.

Converting Bitmaps to Sprites and Masks

To create the sprites and masks for this project, I used Adobe Photoshop. The sprite was easy—I flood-filled the white areas with black and saved them under new names. To make the masks I started again with the original bitmaps, changed their color mode to RGB (true color), and tweaked the threshold curve and contrast until I produced solid monochrome versions. I then saved these in 8-bit Windows bitmap format, again under new names. Next, I opened each mask in Microsoft's BitEdit and converted them back to the palette RAINBOW.DIB that ships with VB (usually located in the \VB program directory). This last step produced monochrome bitmaps that contained identity palettes so the images would be compatible with the other versions of the sprites and with the background, which I also converted to the RAINBOW.DIB palette.

Converting bitmaps to sprites and masks can be tedious work. We'll deal with that in the next project. For now, you'll find the results of my efforts in the files MOTHSPT1.BMP and MOTHSPT4.BMP (I skipped versions 2 and 3—too much work!). Use the Load Picture dialog box to load these into the two SpritePicture and two MaskPicture Picture Box controls. When you're done, the form should appear as in Figure 11.6.

The Paint Event

Now that we have all our bitmaps in place, let's put together the code to display the sprite. Besides the two blt operations that will transfer the mask and sprite to the background, we'll need a way to save the contents of the background at the sprite position so we can later restore it. That's why we have an extra Picture Box control called BufferPicture. Take a look at Listing 11.6.

Figure 11.6 SPRITE2.FRM with all bitmaps loaded.

Listing 11.6 The AnimationPicture_Paint() Event Procedure from SPRITE2.FRM

```
Sub AnimationPicture_Paint ()
    Dim Dummy As Integer
    Dim SrcWidth As Integer
    Dim CurrentX As Integer

    If Forward Then
        SrcWidth = SpritePicture(CurrentSpriteCel).ScaleWidth
        CurrentX = CurrentLeft
      Else
        SrcWidth = -SpritePicture(CurrentSpriteCel).ScaleWidth
        CurrentX = CurrentLeft + SpritePicture(CurrentSpriteCel).ScaleWidth - 1
      End If

    Dummy = BitBlt(AnimationPicture.hDC, OldLeft, OldTop,
            SpritePicture(CurrentSpriteCel).ScaleWidth,
            SpritePicture(CurrentSpriteCel).ScaleHeight, BufferPicture.hDC, 0,
            0, SRCCOPY)
    Dummy = BitBlt(BufferPicture.hDC, 0, 0,
            SpritePicture(CurrentSpriteCel).ScaleWidth,
            SpritePicture(CurrentSpriteCel).ScaleHeight, AnimationPicture.hDC,
            CurrentLeft, CurrentTop, SRCCOPY)
    Dummy = StretchBlt(AnimationPicture.hDC, CurrentX, CurrentTop, SrcWidth,
            SpritePicture(CurrentSpriteCel).ScaleHeight,
            MaskPicture(CurrentSpriteCel).hDC, 0, 0,
            SpritePicture(CurrentSpriteCel).ScaleWidth,
```

```
        SpritePicture(CurrentSpriteCel).ScaleHeight, SRCAND)
Dummy = StretchBlt(AnimationPicture.hDC, CurrentX, CurrentTop, SrcWidth,
        SpritePicture(CurrentSpriteCel).ScaleHeight,
        SpritePicture(CurrentSpriteCel).hDC, 0, 0,
        SpritePicture(CurrentSpriteCel).ScaleWidth,
        SpritePicture(CurrentSpriteCel).ScaleHeight, SRCPAINT)
OldLeft = CurrentLeft
OldTop = CurrentTop
' This next statement is optional.
BufferPicture.Refresh
End Sub
```

First of all, since the moth flies back and forth across the Picture Box, we'll want to display it so it always faces the direction it's flying. Rather than drawing a set of mirror image sprite and mask bitmaps, we can use the **StretchBlt()** function to draw a horizontally inverted version of the moth whenever it's moving from right to left. The **If** statement at the top of this procedure sets a working variable called **SrcWidth** to either the positive or negative value of the sprite width. When you pass a negative width to **StretchBlt()**, it draws the image backwards. When we flip the sprite, we also need to start drawing at the right edge of the imaginary square that bounds the sprite. This is because the blt function will draw the image to the left of the position we pass as the destination X, the second argument of the blt function. So unless we compensate, the sprite will flip to the left, effectively causing the moth to leap a distance equal to its total width when we switch from forward to backward motion, as shown in Figure 11.7. We'll use the variable **CurrentX** as a shorthand for the expression that determines the proper starting position for the blt. When the moth is flying toward the right, **CurrentX** will equal the left position of the imaginary bounding square; when the moth is flying toward the left, **CurrentX** will equal the position of the square's right edge.

The first **BitBlt()** restores the background by copying the contents of BufferPicture back to the position currently occupied by the sprite, effectively erasing the sprite. The second **BitBlt()** saves the portion of the background that lies under the next sprite position by copying it to BufferPicture. The two calls to **StretchBlt()** copy the mask and sprite to the background. **StretchBlt()** is slower than **BitBlt()**, but it enables us to mirror the sprite bitmaps at runtime.

After we've drawn the sprite, we copy **CurrentLeft** and **CurrentTop** to **OldLeft** and **OldTop**, respectively. The last line of the **Paint()** event procedure performs an optional call to the **Refresh** method for BufferPicture. Since the **AutoRedraw** property of BufferPicture is set to True, this Picture Box acts like a memory device context. In other words, the two **BitBlt()** operations copy the saved background rectangles to and from the VB persistent bitmap,

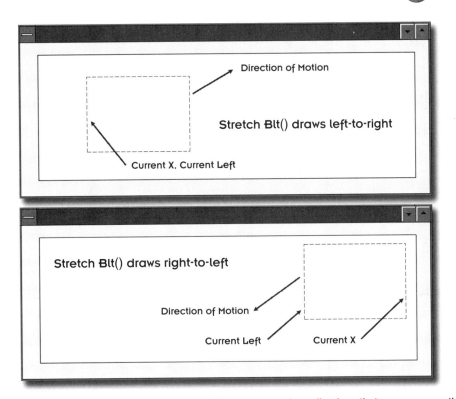

Figure 11.7   *The sprite is drawn in an imaginary square, a bounding box, that moves across the client area. When it moves from left to right, we start the StretchBlt() at the left edge, and when it moves from right to left, we start the blt at the right edge.*

which is in a memory device context. By calling the **Refresh** method, we force VB to copy the contents of the persistent bitmap to the screen device context of the control so we can see what it's doing. But we don't need to see it. It will work correctly either way.

Programming the Timer

Just as in the previous project, the job of setting the sprite position will be assigned to the Timer control, as shown in Listing 11.7.

Listing 11.7   The Timer1_Timer() Event Procedure from SPRITE2.FRM

```
Sub Timer1_Timer ()
    Dim Limit As Single

    CurrentSpriteCel = (CurrentSpriteCel + 1) Mod 2
    If (((CurrentLeft + SpritePicture(CurrentSpriteCel).ScaleWidth) >=
      AnimationPicture.ScaleWidth) And Forward) Then
```

```
        Forward = False
     ElseIf ((CurrentLeft <= 0) And Not Forward) Then
        Forward = True
     End If
  If Forward Then
       Limit = AnimationPicture.ScaleWidth -
              SpritePicture(CurrentSpriteCel).ScaleWidth
       CurrentLeft = MinSingle(CurrentLeft + 20, Limit)
     Else
       Limit = SpritePicture(CurrentSpriteCel).ScaleWidth
       CurrentLeft = MaxSingle(CurrentLeft - 20, 0)
     End If
  If (((CurrentTop + SpritePicture(CurrentSpriteCel).ScaleHeight) >=
     AnimationPicture.ScaleHeight) And Down)
     Or ((CurrentTop <= 0) And Not Down) Then
       Down = Not Down
     End If
  If Down Then
       Limit = AnimationPicture.ScaleHeight -
              SpritePicture(CurrentSpriteCel).ScaleHeight
       CurrentTop = MinSingle(CurrentTop + 7, Limit)
     Else
       CurrentTop = MaxSingle(CurrentTop - 7, 0)
     End If

  'AnimationPicture.Refresh
  AnimationPicture_Paint
  End Sub
```

It's easy to become distracted by all the activity in this procedure. None of it has anything to do with the process of displaying transparent sprites. We handled all that in the **Paint** event. The **Timer** event is responsible for four clerical tasks: (1) cycling between the two versions of the sprite, (2) changing the vertical and horizontal position of the sprite relative to the background, (3) reversing the direction of motion when the sprite bumps into one of the edges of the background, and (4) calling the **AnimationPicture_Paint()** event procedure to update the display.

I've included two lines that perform similar functions. To update the image in **AnimationPicture**, we can either call **AnimationPicture_Paint()** directly, like any other procedure, or we can invoke the **Refresh** method, which will send a Paint message to the control. When VB detects the Paint message, it will automatically re-copy some or all of the background image to the screen, then execute the **Paint()** event procedure. The advantage of the **Refresh** method is that it will properly clean up the image after it has been covered and re-exposed by another window. The disadvantage is that it tends to be slower. Depending on available system resources, these two approaches can look similar on-screen, or quite different. Try them both.

Declarations and Initializations

Before we can start up the program, we need to do some initialization. First of all, it's always wise to initialize global or form level variables like **Forward**, **Down**, **CurrentLeft**, and **CurrentTop**. Even more importantly, the BufferPicture is empty—or rather, it contains a plain white bitmap. The first time the **AnimationPicture_Paint()** event procedure runs, it will copy that white block over the upper-left corner of the background, leaving a permanent hole. To prevent that from happening, we'll initialize the background buffer by calling the **BitBlt()** function from the **Form_Activate()** event procedure. Listing 11.8 contains the declarations from SPRITE2.FRM, along with the **Form_Load()** and **Form_Activate()** event procedures.

Listing 11.8   The Declarations Section and the Form_Load() and Form_Activate() Event Procedures from SPRITE2.FRM

```
Option Explicit

Declare Function BitBlt Lib "GDI" (ByVal hDestDC As Integer, ByVal X As Integer,
    ByVal Y As Integer, ByVal nWidth As Integer, ByVal nHeight As Integer, ByVal
    hSrcDC As Integer, ByVal XSrc As Integer, ByVal YSrc As Integer, ByVal dwRop
    As Long) As Integer
Declare Function StretchBlt Lib "GDI" (ByVal hDC As Integer, ByVal X As Integer,
    ByVal Y As Integer, ByVal nWidth As Integer, ByVal nHeight As Integer, ByVal
    hSrcDC As Integer, ByVal XSrc As Integer, ByVal YSrc As Integer, ByVal nSrcWidth
    As Integer, ByVal nSrcHeight As Integer, ByVal dwRop As Long) As Integer

Const SRCCOPY = &HCC0020
Const SRCAND = &H8800C6
Const SRCPAINT = &HEE0086

Dim Forward As Integer
Dim Down As Integer
Dim CurrentLeft As Integer
Dim CurrentTop As Integer
Dim OldLeft As Integer
Dim OldTop As Integer
Dim CurrentSpriteCel As Integer

Sub Form_Load ()
    Forward = True
    Down = True
    CurrentLeft = 0
    CurrentTop = 0
    End Sub

Sub Form_Activate ()
    Dim Dummy As Integer
    Dummy = BitBlt(BufferPicture.hDC, 0, 0,
```

```
            SpritePicture(CurrentSpriteCel).ScaleWidth,
                SpritePicture(CurrentSpriteCel).ScaleHeight,
    AnimationPicture.hDC,
                CurrentLeft, CurrentTop, SRCCOPY)

    End Sub
```

Now for the MINMAX Code Module

The code module MINMAX.BAS, shown in Listing 11.9, contains some miscella-neous functions, all of which return either the lesser or greater of two values in the various numeric formats **Integer**, **Long** integer, and **Single** precision real.

Listing 11.9　MINMAX.BAS

```
Option Explicit

Function MaxInt (A As Integer, B As Integer) As Integer
    If A > B Then
        MaxInt = A
     Else
        MaxInt = B
     End If
    End Function

Function MaxLong (A As Long, B As Long) As Long
    If A > B Then
        MaxLong = A
     Else
        MaxLong = B
     End If
    End Function

Function MaxSingle (A As Single, B As Single) As Single
    If A > B Then
        MaxSingle = A
     Else
        MaxSingle = B
     End If
    End Function

Function MinInt (A As Integer, B As Integer) As Integer
    If A < B Then
        MinInt = A
     Else
        MinInt = B
     End If
    End Function

Function MinLong (A As Long, B As Long) As Long
    If A < B Then
        MinLong = A
     Else
```

```
        MinLong = B
      End If
   End Function

Function MinSingle (A As Single, B As Single) As Single
   If A < B Then
      MinSingle = A
   Else
      MinSingle = B
   End If
   End Function
```

In the next version of the sprite program we'll begin to tackle flicker. But first, let's find an easier way to convert bitmaps to sprites and masks.

Making Masks and Sprites Automatically

To keep things from getting too mixed up, let's take a break from sprite animation and concentrate on sprite creation, in other words, the conversion of bitmaps into transparent sprites and masks. Let's explore how we can convert an 8-bit bitmap with a white background into a monochrome mask (still 8-bits, but only two colors) and a sprite with a black background. We'll use the code we develop here for the sprite animation program that we're going to create in the next chapter.

The Animation Mask Maker

This project creates an animation mask for a sprite animation. Here are the steps to follow:

1. Create a form named MAKEMASK.FRM with three Picture Boxes.
2. Write the **LoadBitmapOption_Click()** event procedure (Listing 11.10).
3. Create the code module MAKEMASK.BAS, and write the general functions **ConvertImageToSprite()** and **ConvertImageToMask()** (Listings 11.11 and 11.12).
4. Fill in the remaining event procedures and declarations in MAKEMASK.FRM (Listing 11.13).

You'll find this project in the subdirectory \VBMAGIC in the files MAKEMASK.MAK, MAKEMASK.FRM, and MAKEMASK.BAS, along with DIB.BAS, PALETTE2.BAS, and GLBLMEM2.BAS (a slightly more advanced variation of GLBLMEM.BAS). You'll also need the Common

Dialog custom control, located in the file CMDIALOG.VBX, which the VB setup program should have copied to your \WINDOWS\SYSTEM subdirectory.

Running the Program

Run MAKEMASK.EXE, or load and run the project MAKEMASK.MAK. Figure 11.8 shows the program. This program has only one form. Choose File, Load Bitmap from the menu bar, and use the Load Sprite Bitmap dialog box to select an 8-bit bitmap. To produce a useable sprite, you must begin with a bitmap based on an identity palette. This will ensure that the first and last entries in the logical palette contain black and white respectively. For best performance, an animation background and its sprites should share a common palette.

The image you load will appear in the first of the three Picture Boxes. When you choose File, Make Mask from the form's menu, the program generates two alternative versions of the bitmap, a monochrome mask and a sprite with a black background, and displays them in the second and third Picture Boxes, respectively (see Figure 11.8). This program only demonstrates the conversion functions—it does not save the new images as bitmap files. In fact, that would defeat the purpose, since the idea of writing these functions is to generate the mask and sprite bitmaps at runtime. We'll put this code to work in the next version of the sprite animation program.

To close the program and release all its resources, choose File, Quit from the form's menu, or use the form's Control menu.

Creating the Form

Set the **Name** property of the form to MakeMask. Place three Picture Box controls in a row on the form, and name them BitmapPictureBox,

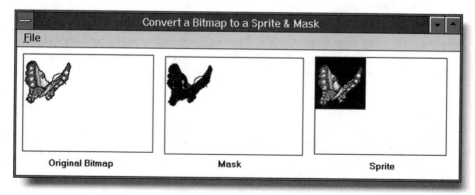

Figure 11.8 *This figure shows the animation mask program at runtime.*

MaskPictureBox, and SpritePictureBox. Set all their **AutoRedraw** and **AutoSize** properties to False, and their **ScaleMode** properties to 3 - Pixel.

Add a Common Dialog control to the form. Set its **Name** property to LoadBitmapDialog. Set the **DialogTitle** property to "Load Sprite Bitmap," and set the **Filter** property to "Pictures|*.BMP;*.DIB;*.ICO".

Next, choose Window, Menu Design from the VB menu bar to open the Menu Design window. Add a File menu to the form with three suboptions: Load Bitmap, Make Mask, and Quit. Set the **Name** property of the File menu to FileMenu. Set the **Name** properties of the three suboptions to LoadBitmapOption, MakeMaskOption, and QuitOption, respectively.

Loading the Bitmap File into Memory

In Chapters 6 and 7 we looked at the structure of device-independent bitmaps (DIBs) and how to construct them and read them from files. In this project we'll re-use that knowledge, and in fact, re-use some of the code we originally developed for the dissolve program. Once we get the pixel data out of the DIB file and into memory, we can change it as we wish. In this case, we wish to make two alternate versions, one with a normally colored sprite on a black background, and one monochrome version in which the sprite is colored completely black, while its background remains pure white.

For the code module DIB.BAS we wrote a general procedure called **ReadBitmapFile()** (Listing 7.16 in Chapter 7), which would open a bitmap file, read its header information, and transfer its pixel data to a global memory block. In this program, we'll call that procedure from the Load Bitmap menu option, as shown in Listing 11.10.

Listing 11.10   The LoadBitmapOption_Click() Event Procedure from MAKEMASK.FRM

```
Sub LoadBitmapOption_Click ()
    Dim RetValue As Integer
    Dim SpritePalette As LOGPALETTE
    Dim lpSpritePixelData As Long

    If PictureLoaded Then
        Form_QueryUnload 0, 0
        CleanUp
      End If
    LoadBitmapDialog = 1
    If Len(LoadBitmapDialog.Filename) > 0 Then
        ReadBitmapFile LoadBitmapDialog.Filename, bmBitmapFileHeader,
          bmBitmapInfo, hBitmapPixelData
        If bmBitmapInfo.bmiHeader.biBitCount <> 8 Then
```

```
        MsgBox "Please load an 8-bit image.", 16, "Load Error"
        RetValue = GlobalFree(hBitmapPixelData)
      Else
        ConstructPaletteFromColorTable bmBitmapInfo.bmiColors(), SpritePalette
        hSpritePal = CreatePalette(SpritePalette)
        RetValue = SelectPalette(BitmapPictureBox, hSpritePal, False)
        RetValue = SelectPalette(SpritePictureBox, hSpritePal, False)
        RetValue = SelectPalette(MaskPictureBox, hSpritePal, False)
        RetValue = RealizePalette(SpritePictureBox)
        PictureLoaded = True
        BitmapPictureBox.Refresh
      End If
    End If
  End Sub
```

This event procedure first checks whether a bitmap has already been loaded, and if so, calls the **Form_QueryUnload()** event procedure and the general procedure **CleanUp()** to dispose of the various global memory blocks and the palette used by the previous image.

After calling **ReadBitmapFile()** the procedure checks the **biBitCount** field in the **BITMAPINFOHEADER** to make certain that the DIB file contains an 8-bit (256 color) bitmap. If so, it creates the palette, selects it into the device contexts of all three Picture Boxes, and realizes it. It then sets the form level variable **PictureLoaded** to **True** and calls **BitmapPictureBox.Refresh** to display the bitmap.

Once we have the pixel data in a global memory block, we can get to work on it.

Converting the Pixel Data

Now we need a function that can take a handle to bitmap pixel data, duplicate it, and convert it. Actually, we'll write two functions, one called **ConvertImageToSprite()** and one called **ConvertImageToMask()**. We'll need these functions for our next sprite animation project, so we'll place them in a code module, which for now we'll call MAKEMASK.BAS (later this will become SPRITE.BAS).

Here's what we're going to do. To make the sprite, we'll first copy the pixel data. Then we'll step through it pixel by pixel (byte by byte) looking for any pixel set to &HFF (which references white in the system palette or any identity palette) and changing it to **&H00** (which references black). For the mask, we'll make a second copy of the original, and step through it changing any pixel with a value less than &HFF to &H00. Let's begin with **ConvertImageToSprite()**, which is shown in listing 11.11.

Listing 11.11 The ConvertImageToSprite() General Function from MAKEMASK.BAS.

```
Function ConvertImageToSprite (bmInfo As BITMAPINFO, hBitmapPixelData As Inte-
  ger) As Integer
```

```
Dim PixelBytesToCopy As Long
Dim hSpritePixelData As Integer
Dim lpBitmapPixelData As Long
Dim lpSpritePixelData As Long
Dim SpritePixelSelector As Integer
Dim LastLine As Integer
Dim LineCounter As Integer
Dim ColumnCounter As Integer
Dim LastColumn As Integer
Dim PaddedLineWidth As Integer
Dim BufferString As String
Dim MemOffset As Long
Dim TempChar As String * 1
Dim RetValue As Integer
Dim ColorTableIndex As Integer


' Copy the original bitmap pixels to another buffer,
' which will become the Mask pixel data.
PixelBytesToCopy = bmInfo.bmiHeader.biSizeImage
hSpritePixelData = GlobalAlloc(GMEM_MOVEABLE Or GMEM_ZEROINIT, PixelBytesToCopy)
lpBitmapPixelData = GlobalLock(hBitmapPixelData)
lpSpritePixelData = GlobalLock(hSpritePixelData)
hmemcpy lpSpritePixelData, lpBitmapPixelData, PixelBytesToCopy
lpBitmapPixelData = GlobalUnlock(hBitmapPixelData)
lpSpritePixelData = GlobalUnlock(hSpritePixelData)

SpritePixelSelector = GlobalHandleToSel(hSpritePixelData)
LastLine = bmInfo.bmiHeader.biHeight - 1
LastColumn = bmInfo.bmiHeader.biWidth
PaddedLineWidth = ((LastColumn - 1) \ 4 + 1) * 4
For LineCounter = 0 To LastLine
    BufferString = String$(PaddedLineWidth, Chr$(0))
    MemOffset = LineCounter * PaddedLineWidth
    RetValue = MemoryRead(SpritePixelSelector, MemOffset, ByVal
            BufferString, PaddedLineWidth)
    For ColumnCounter = 1 To LastColumn
        TempChar = Mid$(BufferString, ColumnCounter, 1)
        ColorTableIndex = Asc(TempChar)
        If (Asc(bmInfo.bmiColors(ColorTableIndex).rgbRed) = 255) And
           (Asc(bmInfo.bmiColors(ColorTableIndex).rgbBlue) = 255) And
           (Asc(bmInfo.bmiColors(ColorTableIndex).rgbGreen) = 255) Then
            Mid$(BufferString, ColumnCounter, 1) = Chr$(0)
        End If
      Next ColumnCounter
    RetValue = MemoryWrite(SpritePixelSelector, MemOffset, ByVal
            BufferString, PaddedLineWidth)
    Next LineCounter
ConvertImageToSprite = hSpritePixelData

End Function
```

The first block of code following the local variable declarations creates a new

global memory block, the same size as the one holding the original bitmap pixel data. We've already discussed the API functions **GlobalAlloc()**, **GlobalLock()**, and **GlobalUnlock()** before, in Chapter 7, but **hmemcpy()** is a newcomer:

```
Declare Sub hmemcpy Lib "Kernel" (ByVal lpDest As Long, ByVal lpSrc As Long,
   ByVal BytesToCopy As Long)
```

This function takes three arguments. The first, **lpDest** is a long pointer to the destination memory block. The second, **lpSrc** is a long pointer to the data we want copied. And the last argument specifies how many **BytesToCopy**.

To duplicate the pixel data, we just allocate a global memory block with the same size as the one holding the original pixel data, use **GlobalLock()** to lock both the old and new blocks, which will give us the long pointers, and feed these results to **hmemcpy()**. After we're done copying the data, we unlock the memory blocks so Windows can move them around to keep memory tidy. After the blocks are unlocked, the long pointers are no longer valid. In fact, **GlobalUnlock()** returns zero if it successfully unlocks the given memory block, so by assigning the result of **GlobalUnlock()** back to **lpBitmapPixelData** and **lpSpritePixelData** we set them back to &H00000000, which should remind us that they no longer contain memory addresses. If we were performing the proper error trapping, we would be monitoring such things. When you use this code in your own projects, you should spackle this chink.

To read and write bytes from and to the new global memory block, we'll use the **MemoryRead()** and **MemoryWrite()** functions, which we discussed in Chapter 7. These functions don't use pointers; instead they refer to a global memory block by way of a selector, which we get by calling **GlobalHandle-ToSel()**, which we also discussed in Chapter 7.

We'll read and write one scan line at a time. For that we'll need a buffer padded to the number of bytes in each line, which we'll call **BufferString**. Remember, 8-bit pixel data is padded to the nearest 4-byte boundary, so we'll need to round up to the nearest multiple of 4 to get the correct number of bytes. To read a line of pixels, we pass the **SpritePixelSelector**, the position in the memory block, known as the **MemOffset**, the pre-sized **BufferString**, and the number of bytes to read, as stored in the integer variable **PaddedLineWidth**.

Once we have the line of pixels in the string buffer, we use the VB functions **Mid$()**, **Asc()**, and **Chr$()** to examine their values and make the appropriate changes. This can get a little more complicated than you might expect. We should be able to get all the information we need from the pixel values themselves. But that won't always work. If the palette contains duplicate color entries, some white pixels, for example, might reference one palette entry, while other white pixels might reference a different palette entry. This is not uncommon in DIBs that have been converted to identity palettes. To ensure that all white pixels would convert to black in the sprite, I have looked a step beyond the pixel value by looking up the actual palette entry and checking its RGB value. If the pixel references a pure white palette entry, no matter where that entry appears in the color table, I convert it to black by forcing it to reference palette entry &H00. If you know that your device-independent bitmap files don't contain redundant color entries (unlike the moth bitmaps we're using in this chapter), you can simplify the test:

```
If Asc(TempChar) = 255 Then
 Mid$(BufferString, ColumnCounter, 1) = Chr$(0)
End If
```

After the string buffer containing the line of pixels has been scanned and modified, we use **MemoryWrite()** to drop it back into the global memory block. And when the entire bitmap has been processed, we return the handle to the new global memory block.

ConvertImageToMask() works much the same way (Listing 11.12), except in the details of pixel value conversion:

```
ColorTableIndex = Asc(TempChar)
If (Asc(bmInfo.bmiColors(ColorTableIndex).rgbRed) <> 255) Or
  (Asc(bmInfo.bmiColors(ColorTableIndex).rgbBlue) <> 255) Or
  (Asc(bmInfo.bmiColors(ColorTableIndex).rgbGreen) <> 255) Then
    Mid$(BufferString, ColumnCounter, 1) = Chr$(0)
  Else
    Mid$(BufferString, ColumnCounter, 1) = Chr$(255)
  End If
```

To help distinguish one function from the other, I've also used different names for some of the variables: **hMaskPixelData**, **lpMaskPixelData**, and **MaskPixelSelector** instead of **hSpritePixelData**, **lpSpritePixelData**, and **SpritePixelSelector**. If you're thinking that these could be merged into a single function, you are absolutely correct. Have at it.

Listing 11.12 The ConvertImageToMask() General Function from MAKEMASK.BAS

```
Function ConvertImageToMask (bmInfo As BITMAPINFO, hBitmapPixelData As Integer)
   As Integer
    Dim PixelBytesToCopy As Long
    Dim hMaskPixelData As Integer
    Dim lpBitmapPixelData As Long
    Dim lpMaskPixelData As Long
    Dim MaskPixelSelector As Integer
```

```
    Dim LastLine As Integer
    Dim LineCounter As Integer
    Dim ColumnCounter As Integer
    Dim LastColumn As Integer
    Dim PaddedLineWidth As Integer
    Dim BufferString As String
    Dim MemOffset As Long
    Dim TempChar As String * 1
    Dim RetValue As Integer
    Dim ColorTableIndex As Integer

    ' Copy the original bitmap pixels to another buffer,
    ' which will become the Mask pixel data.
    PixelBytesToCopy = bmInfo.bmiHeader.biSizeImage
    hMaskPixelData = GlobalAlloc(GMEM_MOVEABLE Or GMEM_ZEROINIT, PixelBytesToCopy)
    lpBitmapPixelData = GlobalLock(hBitmapPixelData)
    lpMaskPixelData = GlobalLock(hMaskPixelData)
    hmemcpy lpMaskPixelData, lpBitmapPixelData, PixelBytesToCopy
    lpBitmapPixelData = GlobalUnlock(hBitmapPixelData)
    lpMaskPixelData = GlobalUnlock(hMaskPixelData)

    MaskPixelSelector = GlobalHandleToSel(hMaskPixelData)
    LastLine = bmInfo.bmiHeader.biHeight - 1
    LastColumn = bmInfo.bmiHeader.biWidth
    PaddedLineWidth = ((LastColumn - 1) \ 4 + 1) * 4
    For LineCounter = 0 To LastLine
        BufferString = String$(PaddedLineWidth, Chr$(0))
        MemOffset = LineCounter * PaddedLineWidth
        RetValue = MemoryRead(MaskPixelSelector, MemOffset, ByVal BufferString,
                PaddedLineWidth)
        For ColumnCounter = 1 To LastColumn
            TempChar = Mid$(BufferString, ColumnCounter, 1)
            ColorTableIndex = Asc(TempChar)
            If (Asc(bmInfo.bmiColors(ColorTableIndex).rgbRed) <> 255) Or
              (Asc(bmInfo.bmiColors(ColorTableIndex).rgbBlue) <> 255) Or
              (Asc(bmInfo.bmiColors(ColorTableIndex).rgbGreen) <> 255) Then
                Mid$(BufferString, ColumnCounter, 1) = Chr$(0)
            Else
                Mid$(BufferString, ColumnCounter, 1) = Chr$(255)
            End If
        Next ColumnCounter
        RetValue = MemoryWrite(MaskPixelSelector, MemOffset, ByVal BufferString,
                PaddedLineWidth)
    Next LineCounter
    ConvertImageToMask = hMaskPixelData
End Function
```

Finishing the Code in the Form Module

The remaining code in MAKEMASK.FRM performs the housekeeping tasks, such
as painting the Picture Boxes and disposing of the global memory blocks and the
palette when the program is terminated. By now, you're pretty familiar with this
stuff, so we'll skip the detailed analysis. Listing 11.13 contains the complete listing

of MAKEMASK.FRM, including the event procedures we just discussed.

Listing 11.13   MAKEMASK.FRM

```
VERSION 2.00
Begin Form MakeMask
   Caption          =    "Convert a Bitmap to a Sprite & Mask"
   ClientHeight     =    2196
   ClientLeft       =    876
   ClientTop        =    1848
   ClientWidth      =    8532
   Height           =    2940
   Left             =    828
   LinkTopic        =    "Form1"
   ScaleHeight      =    183
   ScaleMode        =    3   'Pixel
   ScaleWidth       =    711
   Top              =    1152
   Width            =    8628
   Begin PictureBox BitmapPictureBox
      Height        =    1812
      Left          =    120
      ScaleHeight   =    1788
      ScaleWidth    =    2520
      TabIndex      =    2
      Top           =    120
      Width         =    2544
   End
   Begin PictureBox MaskPictureBox
      Height        =    1812
      Left          =    2880
      ScaleHeight   =    149
      ScaleMode     =    3  'Pixel
      ScaleWidth    =    220
      TabIndex      =    1
      Top           =    132
      Width         =    2664
   End
   Begin PictureBox SpritePictureBox
      Height        =    1812
      Left          =    5760
      ScaleHeight   =    149
      ScaleMode     =    3  'Pixel
      ScaleWidth    =    209
      TabIndex      =    0
      Top           =    120
      Width         =    2532
   End
   Begin CommonDialog LoadBitmapDialog
      DialogTitle   =    "Load Sprite Bitmap"
      Filter        =    "Pictures|*.BMP;*.DIB;*.ICO"
      Left          =    -12
      Top           =    1812
```

```
        End
        Begin Menu FileMenu
            Caption        =    "&File"
            Begin Menu LoadBitmapOption
                Caption        =    "&Load Bitmap"
            End
            Begin Menu MakeMaskOption
                Caption        =    "&Make Mask"
            End
            Begin Menu SaveMaskOption
                Caption        =    "&Save Mask"
                Enabled        =    0    'False
            End
            Begin Menu QuitOption
                Caption        =    "&Quit"
            End
        End
    End
End
Option Explicit

Dim bmBitmapFileHeader As BITMAPFILEHEADER
Dim bmBitmapInfo As BITMAPINFO
Dim hSpritePal As Integer
Dim PictureLoaded As Integer
Dim hBitmapPixelData As Integer
Dim hMaskPixelData As Integer
Dim hSpritePixelData As Integer

Sub BitmapPictureBox_Paint ()
    Dim RetValue As Integer
    Dim lpBitmapPixelData As Long

    If hBitmapPixelData <> 0 Then
        RetValue = SelectPalette(BitmapPictureBox.hDC, hSpritePal, False)
        RetValue = RealizePalette(BitmapPictureBox.hDC)
        lpBitmapPixelData = GlobalLock(hBitmapPixelData)
        RetValue = SetDIBitsToDevice(BitmapPictureBox.hDC, 0, 0,
                bmBitmapInfo.bmiHeader.biWidth,
                bmBitmapInfo.bmiHeader.biHeight, 0, 0, 0,
                bmBitmapInfo.bmiHeader.biHeight, lpBitmapPixelData,
                bmBitmapInfo, DIB_RGB_COLORS)
        RetValue = GlobalUnlock(hBitmapPixelData)
    End If
    End Sub

Sub CleanUp ()
    Dim RetValue As Integer

    If hSpritePal <> 0 Then
        RetValue = DeleteObject(hSpritePal)
        hSpritePal = 0
    End If
    If hBitmapPixelData <> 0 Then
        hBitmapPixelData = GlobalFree(hBitmapPixelData)
```

```
        End If
      If hMaskPixelData <> 0 Then
         hMaskPixelData = GlobalFree(hMaskPixelData)
        End If
      If hSpritePixelData <> 0 Then
         hSpritePixelData = GlobalFree(hSpritePixelData)
        End If
      PictureLoaded = False
      End Sub

  Sub Form_Load ()
      PictureLoaded = False
      End Sub

  Sub Form_QueryUnload (Cancel As Integer, UnloadMode As Integer)
      Dim RetValue As Integer

      RetValue = SelectPalette(BitmapPictureBox.hoc,
        GetStockObject(DEFAULT_PALETTE), False)
      RetValue = SelectPalette(SpritePictureBox.hoc,
        GetStockObject(DEFAULT_PALETTE), False)
      RetValue = SelectPalette(MaskPictureBox.hoc,
        GetStockObject(DEFAULT_PALETTE), False)
      End Sub

  Sub Form_Unload (Cancel As Integer)
      CleanUp
      End Sub

  Sub LoadBitmapOption_Click ()
      Dim RetValue As Integer
      Dim SpritePalette As LOGPALETTE
      Dim lpSpritePixelData As Long

      If PictureLoaded Then
         Form_QueryUnload 0, 0
         CleanUp
        End If
      LoadBitmapDialog = 1
      If Len(LoadBitmapDialog.Filename) > 0 Then
         ReadBitmapFile LoadBitmapDialog.Filename, bmBitmapFileHeader,
           bmBitmapInfo, hBitmapPixelData
         If bmBitmapInfo.bmiHeader.biBitCount <> 8 Then
            MsgBox "Please load an 8-bit image.", 16, "Load Error"
            RetValue = GlobalFree(hBitmapPixelData)
           Else
            ConstructPaletteFromColorTable bmBitmapInfo.bmiColors(), SpritePalette
            hSpritePal = CreatePalette(SpritePalette)
            RetValue = SelectPalette(BitmapPictureBox, hSpritePal, False)
            RetValue = SelectPalette(SpritePictureBox, hSpritePal, False)
            RetValue = SelectPalette(MaskPictureBox, hSpritePal, False)
            RetValue = RealizePalette(SpritePictureBox)
            PictureLoaded = True
            BitmapPictureBox.Refresh
```

```
            End If
        End If
    End Sub


Sub MakeMaskOption_Click ()
    hMaskPixelData = ConvertImageToMask(bmBitmapInfo, hBitmapPixelData)
    hSpritePixelData = ConvertImageToSprite(bmBitmapInfo, hBitmapPixelData)
    BitmapPictureBox.Refresh
    MaskPictureBox.Refresh
    SpritePictureBox.Refresh
    End Sub


Sub MaskPictureBox_Paint ()
    Dim RetValue As Integer
    Dim lpMaskPixelData As Long

    If hMaskPixelData <> 0 Then
        RetValue = SelectPalette(MaskPictureBox.hDC, hSpritePal, False)
        RetValue = RealizePalette(MaskPictureBox.hDC)
        lpMaskPixelData = GlobalLock(hMaskPixelData)
        RetValue = SetDIBitsToDevice(MaskPictureBox.hDC, 0, 0,
                bmBitmapInfo.bmiHeader.biWidth,
                bmBitmapInfo.bmiHeader.biHeight, 0, 0, 0,
                bmBitmapInfo.bmiHeader.biHeight, lpMaskPixelData,
                bmBitmapInfo, DIB_RGB_COLORS)
        lpMaskPixelData = GlobalUnlock(hMaskPixelData)
    End If
    End Sub

Sub QuitOption_Click ()
    Unload MakeMask
    End
    End Sub


Sub SpritePictureBox_Paint ()
    Dim RetValue As Integer
    Dim lpSpritePixelData As Long

    If hSpritePixelData <> 0 Then
        RetValue = SelectPalette(SpritePictureBox.hDC, hSpritePal, False)
        RetValue = RealizePalette(SpritePictureBox.hDC)
        lpSpritePixelData = GlobalLock(hSpritePixelData)
        RetValue = SetDIBitsToDevice(SpritePictureBox.hDC, 0, 0,
                bmBitmapInfo.bmiHeader.biWidth,
                bmBitmapInfo.bmiHeader.biHeight, 0, 0, 0,
                bmBitmapInfo.bmiHeader.biHeight, lpSpritePixelData,
                bmBitmapInfo, DIB_RGB_COLORS)
        lpSpritePixelData = GlobalUnlock(hSpritePixelData)
    End If
    End Sub
```

In the next chapter, we'll use the new bitmap conversion functions to load and prepare all four versions of the moth sprite, which will make for much smoother animation.

Chapter

12

Our latest adventure with animation will help you to create smooth-motion images with a mimimum of new code.

Better Animation

The animation effects we created in Chapter 11 weren't as smooth as we really want. Besides the jerky motion, the other major flaw we discovered was the flickering caused by the multiple, overlapping bitblts.

In this chapter, we are going to explore a few ways we can create faster, smoother animation. We'll develop one more animation project, but this time we'll use a few tricks to enhance the animation.

Creating Flicker Free Animation

The easiest way to solve our flicker problems would be to create a compatible bitmap and memory device context, perform all the updates there, then copy the entire bitmap to the screen device context with one **BitBlt()**. But blts take time, so what we gain in image stability, we will likely lose in speed.

Another approach would be to work on just the parts of the screen that are affected by each change in the sprite position. For this approach, all you need to do is place those portions of the screen in a separate memory device context. Take a look at Figure 12.1. Each time we move the sprite, we need to erase it from the background and redraw it in its new position. No matter which direction it's traveling—up, down, right, or left—its two positions de-

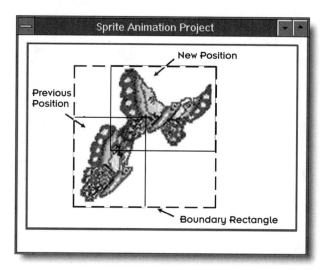

Figure 12.1 *The previous and new positions of the sprite occupy a bounding rectangle.*

fine a bounding rectangle. The only part of the background bitmap that changes is that small section. So instead of transferring the whole image with each tick of the Timer, we could work just on this smaller piece, then copy it into position on the background.

For each position change of the sprite, you must complete these six steps:

1. Copy the bounding rectangle—the one that includes the previous position and the new position—from the screen to a buffer device context.
2. Erase the sprite from this small section of the background by restoring the sprite-sized chunk we saved before we last bltted the sprite (see step 3).
3. Save the sprite-sized rectangle that we're about to cover with the new sprite (see step 2).
4. Copy the mask to the sprite's new position in the bounding rectangle.
5. Copy the sprite to its new position, over the mask.
6. Copy the whole bounding rectangle back to its original position on the background.

*In the \VBMAGIC subdirectory, you'll find a program called SPRITE3.MAK that uses this method to display and move the moth sprite. We won't cover this project in detail here, but you may want to take a look at its key procedure, the one that does all this copying, the **AnimationPicture_Paint()** event procedure, which is shown in Listing 12.1.*

Listing 12.1   The AnimationPicture_Paint() Event Procedure from SPRITE3.FRM

```
Sub AnimationPicture_Paint ()
    Dim Dummy As Integer
    Dim SpriteWidth As Integer
    Dim SpriteHeight As Integer
    Dim CurrentX As Integer
    Dim OffscreenCompositeWidth As Integer
    Dim OffscreenCompositeHeight As Integer
    Dim lpMaskPixelData As Long
    Dim lpSpritePixelData As Long

    If Forward Then
        SpriteWidth = bmBitmapInfo.bmiHeader.biWidth
        CurrentX = CurrentLeft
      Else
        SpriteWidth = -bmBitmapInfo.bmiHeader.biWidth
        CurrentX = CurrentLeft + bmBitmapInfo.bmiHeader.biWidth - 1
      End If
    SpriteHeight = bmBitmapInfo.bmiHeader.biHeight
    OffscreenCompositeWidth = Abs(SpriteWidth) + Abs(CurrentLeft - OldLeft)
    OffscreenCompositeHeight = SpriteHeight + Abs(CurrentTop - OldTop)
    ' Copy the bounding rectangle of the old and new positions to an offscreen
      composite buffer.
    Dummy = BitBlt(OffscreenCompositePicture.hDC, 0, 0, OffscreenCompositeWidth,
            OffscreenCompositeHeight, AnimationPicture.hDC, MinInt(OldLeft,
            CurrentLeft), MinInt(OldTop, CurrentTop), SRCCOPY)
    ' Restore the previously covered area by copying the hold buffer to the
      composite buffer.
    Dummy = BitBlt(OffscreenCompositePicture.hDC, MaxInt(0, OldLeft -
            CurrentLeft), MaxInt(0, OldTop - CurrentTop), Abs(SpriteWidth),
            SpriteHeight, BufferPicture.hDC, 0, 0, SRCCOPY)
    ' Copy the area that will become next position from composite buffer to the
      hold buffer.
    Dummy = BitBlt(BufferPicture.hDC, 0, 0, Abs(SpriteWidth), SpriteHeight,
            OffscreenCompositePicture.hDC, MaxInt(0, CurrentLeft - OldLeft),
            MaxInt(0, CurrentTop - OldTop), SRCCOPY)
    ' Copy the mask and the sprite to the composite buffer.
    lpMaskPixelData = GlobalLock(SpriteDIBHandles(CurrentSpriteCel, 1))
    lpSpritePixelData = GlobalLock(SpriteDIBHandles(CurrentSpriteCel, 2))
    Dummy = StretchDIBits(OffscreenCompositePicture.hDC, MaxInt(CurrentX -
            CurrentLeft, CurrentX - OldLeft), MaxInt(0, CurrentTop - OldTop),
            SpriteWidth, SpriteHeight, 0, 0, Abs(SpriteWidth), SpriteHeight,
            lpMaskPixelData, bmBitmapInfo, DIB_RGB_COLORS, SRCAND)
    Dummy = StretchDIBits(OffscreenCompositePicture.hDC, MaxInt(CurrentX -
            CurrentLeft, CurrentX - OldLeft), MaxInt(0, CurrentTop - OldTop),
            SpriteWidth, SpriteHeight, 0, 0, Abs(SpriteWidth), SpriteHeight,
            lpSpritePixelData, bmBitmapInfo, DIB_RGB_COLORS, SRCPAINT)
    ' Copy the composite buffer to the screen device context.
    Dummy = BitBlt(AnimationPicture.hDC, MinInt(OldLeft, CurrentLeft),
            MinInt(OldTop, CurrentTop), OffscreenCompositeWidth,
            OffscreenCompositeHeight, OffscreenCompositePicture.hDC, 0, 0, SRCCOPY)
    lpMaskPixelData = GlobalUnlock(SpriteDIBHandles(CurrentSpriteCel, 1))
    lpSpritePixelData = GlobalUnlock(SpriteDIBHandles(CurrentSpriteCel, 2))
```

```
OldLeft = CurrentLeft
OldTop = CurrentTop
BufferPicture.Refresh
'OffscreenCompositePicture.Refresh
End Sub
```

For all the bltting it does, this **Paint** event doesn't handle the most basic responsibility of any **Paint** event—to restore the screen after it has been uncovered by another window. To plug that hole, we could create a memory device context, perform all this work on that copy, then blt the results to the screen—which would put us right back where we started. Only now, instead of five blts, we would be up to seven. Before this gets any more out of hand, we had better simplify it.

Animation with Flicker Free Sprites

In this sprite animation project, we'll make three major revisions to the project in Chapter 11. First, we'll start a code module called SPRITE4.BAS, which you can expand on your own into a re-useable, general-purpose sprite animation module. Next, we'll use the functions **ConvertImageToMask()** and **ConvertImageToSprite()** to construct masks and sprites at runtime. And finally, we'll write a general procedure called **MoveSprite()** that will perform flicker-free sprite animation with the bare minimum of calls to **BitBlt()** and **StretchDIBits()**.

1. Start a new project and create the form.
2. Fill in the **Form_Load()** event procedure (Listing 12.2).
3. Write the **MoveSprite()** general procedure (Listing 12.3).
4. Fill in the rest of code in the form and code modules (Listings 12.4 and 12.5).

 You'll find this project in the subdirectory \VBMAGIC in the files SPRITE4.MAK, SPRITE4.FRM, SPRITE4.BAS, DIB.BAS, GLBLMEM2.BAS, MINMAX.BAS, and PALETTE2.BAS. The project also uses five bitmap files: HIBISC2.BMP and MOTH1.DIB through MOTH4.DIB.

Running the Program

Run SPRITE4.EXE, or load and run the project SPRITE4.MAK. During the **Load** event, the program will read the four moth bitmaps and convert them to six masks and six sprites. This step will take some time. When the animation finally does begin, click on either of the check boxes, labeled Reversible and Flippable, to change the orientation of the sprite, depending on which direction it's flying. From four drawings, we get sixteen variations, all thanks to **StretchDIBits()**. Figure 12.2 shows the program at runtime.

Creating the Form

To demonstrate the SPRITE4.BAS code module, we'll create a form called SpriteAnimationForm with one Picture Box control, a timer control, and two Check Box controls. Once again, set the **Name** property of the picture box to AnimationPicture. Set its **AutoRedraw** and **AutoSize** properties to False, and set its **ScaleMode** to 3 - Pixel. Do not set the form's **Picture** property—we'll load the background at runtime.

Set the **Enabled** property of Timer1 (we'll keep the default name) to False, and set its **Interval** property to 56 milliseconds. Change the **Name** property of the first check box to ReverseBox, set its caption to "Reversible," and set its **Value** property to 1 - Checked. Name the second check box FlipBox, set its caption to "Flippable," and set its **Value** property to 0 - Unchecked.

The Form_Load() Event Procedure

To understand what we're going to need in SPRITE4.BAS in the way of declarations and general procedures, let's begin with the **Form_Load()** event procedure, which is where we'll call the code that loads all the bitmaps. The code for this procedure is shown in Listing 12.2.

Figure 12.2 *SPRITE4.MAK at runtime.*

Listing 12.2 The Form_Load() Event Procedure from SPRITE4.FRM

```
Sub Form_Load ()
    Dim RetValue As Integer

    Forward = True
    Down = True
    CurrentLeft = 0
    CurrentTop = 0
    ReDim SpriteBitmapFiles(6)
    ReDim SpriteDIBHandles(6, 2)
    SpriteBitmapFiles(1) = App.Path & "\Moth1.DIB"
    SpriteBitmapFiles(2) = App.Path & "\Moth2.DIB"
    SpriteBitmapFiles(3) = App.Path & "\Moth3.DIB"
    SpriteBitmapFiles(4) = App.Path & "\Moth4.DIB"
    SpriteBitmapFiles(5) = App.Path & "\Moth3.DIB"
    SpriteBitmapFiles(6) = App.Path & "\Moth2.DIB"
    Screen.MousePointer = 11 ' Hourglass
    NumberOfSpriteCels = LoadAndPrepareSprites(6)
    hBackgroundDC = MakeBackgroundShadow(App.Path & "\Hibisc2.BMP",
                                         AnimationPicture, hSpritePal)
    Screen.MousePointer = 0
    If hBackgroundDC <> 0 Then
        OpenSprites AnimationPicture, hSpritePal
        Timer1.Enabled = True
    Else
        MsgBox "Unable to load background image.", 16, "File Error"
        Unload SpriteAnimationForm
        End
    End If
End Sub
```

In the array **SpriteBitmapFiles**, which we'll declare in SPRITE4.BAS, we specify the filenames of the sprite bitmaps. To produce a complete motion cycle, from wings closed to wings spread and back again, we need to duplicate the second and third bitmaps. Obviously, you could optimize the program so it wouldn't need to create two sets of masks and sprites for images two and three. For the sake of simplicity I've sacrificed some memory.

The function **LoadAndPrepareSprites()** (see Listing 12.4), which will become part of SPRITE4.BAS, will take as its sole argument the number of sprite bitmaps. It will call the bitmap conversion functions, and return the number of sprites it successfully created. The handles for those sprites and for their masks will be stored in the array **SpriteDIBHandles**, which, like **SpriteBitmapFiles**, is declared in SPRITE4.BAS, but re-dimensioned in this **Form_Load()** event procedure.

After we prepares the sprites, we call another general function, also located in SPRITE4.BAS, called **MakeBackgroundShadow()** (see Listing 12.4). This function will create a memory device context and bitmap compatible with the

AnimationPicture control, which we pass to it as an argument. It will then load the background bitmap from its file, transfer it to the memory device context, and create its palette. The return value of the function is the handle to the memory device context, which we assign to **hBackgroundDC**. The handle to the palette is returned by assigning it to the variable passed in the third argument, in this case, **hSpritePal**.

If **MakeBackgroundShadow()** manages to locate and load the background image, **Form_Load()** calls one more general procedure in SPRITE4.BAS, **OpenSprites()** (see Listing 12.5). This procedure creates the other memory device context used by the program, the scratch pad referenced by **hOffscreen-CompositeDC**.

And finally, with all the bitmaps in place, we kick in the Timer.

Programming the New SpriteMove() Procedure

The most significant difference between the **Timer** event in SPRITE4.FRM, which appears in the complete listing of the form (Listing 12.5), and the version in SPRITE2.FRM (Chapter 11) is the call to the new general procedure **MoveSprite()**, another addition to SPRITE4.BAS.

In previous versions of the sprite project, we handled the blting in the **AnimationPicture_Paint** event procedure. But, as always, to create a general-purpose library, we need to move that code out of the event procedure in the form module and into a general procedure in the code module. **MoveSprite()** is shown in Listing 12.3

Listing 12.3   The MoveSprite() General Procedure from SPRITE4.BAS

```
Sub MoveSprite (OldLeft As Integer, OldTop As Integer, NewLeft As Integer,
   NewTop As Integer, ByVal HorizontallyReversible As Integer, ByVal
   VerticallyReversible As Integer, bmBitmapInfo As BITMAPINFO, hSpritePixelData
   As Integer, hMaskPixelData As Integer, ResultPicture As PictureBox,
   hAnimationPalette As Integer)
  Dim Dummy As Integer
  Dim RetValue As Integer
  Dim SpriteWidth As Integer
  Dim SpriteHeight As Integer
  Dim CurrentX As Integer
  Dim CurrentY As Integer
  Dim OffscreenCompositeWidth As Integer
  Dim OffscreenCompositeHeight As Integer
  Dim lpMaskPixelData As Long
  Dim lpSpritePixelData As Long
  Dim CompositeXOffset As Integer
  Dim CompositeYOffset As Integer
```

```
If NewLeft > OldLeft Then
    SpriteWidth = bmBitmapInfo.bmiHeader.biWidth
    CurrentX = NewLeft
    OffscreenCompositeWidth = MinInt((SpriteWidth + NewLeft - OldLeft),
                                (ResultPicture.ScaleWidth - OldLeft))
  Else
    If HorizontallyReversible Then
        SpriteWidth = -bmBitmapInfo.bmiHeader.biWidth
        CurrentX = NewLeft + bmBitmapInfo.bmiHeader.biWidth - 1
      Else
        SpriteWidth = bmBitmapInfo.bmiHeader.biWidth
        CurrentX = NewLeft
      End If
    OffscreenCompositeWidth = MinInt(OldLeft + Abs(SpriteWidth),
                                (Abs(SpriteWidth) + OldLeft - NewLeft))
  End If
If HorizontallyReversible Then
    CompositeXOffset = MaxInt(CurrentX - NewLeft, CurrentX - ldLeft)
  Else
    CompositeXOffset = MaxInt(0, NewLeft - OldLeft)
  End If

If NewTop > OldTop Then
    SpriteHeight = bmBitmapInfo.bmiHeader.biHeight
    CurrentY = NewTop
    OffscreenCompositeHeight = MinInt((SpriteHeight + NewTop - OldTop),
                                (ResultPicture.ScaleHeight - OldTop))
  Else
    If VerticallyReversible Then
        SpriteHeight = -bmBitmapInfo.bmiHeader.biHeight
        CurrentY = NewTop + bmBitmapInfo.bmiHeader.biHeight - 1
      Else
        SpriteHeight = bmBitmapInfo.bmiHeader.biHeight
        CurrentY = NewTop
      End If
    OffscreenCompositeHeight = MinInt((OldTop + Abs(SpriteHeight)),
                                (Abs(SpriteHeight) + OldTop - NewTop))
  End If
If VerticallyReversible Then
    CompositeYOffset = MaxInt(CurrentY - NewTop, CurrentY - OldTop)
  Else
    CompositeYOffset = MaxInt(0, NewTop - OldTop)
  End If
Dummy = SelectPalette(hOffscreenCompositeDC, hAnimationPalette, False)
Dummy = RealizePalette(hOffscreenCompositeDC)
' Copy the bounding rectangle of the old and new positions to the offscreen
  composite buffer.
Dummy = BitBlt(hOffscreenCompositeDC, 0, 0, OffscreenCompositeWidth,
        OffscreenCompositeHeight, hBackgroundDC, MinInt(OldLeft, NewLeft),
        MinInt(OldTop, NewTop), SRCCOPY)
' Copy the mask and sprite to the composite buffer.
lpMaskPixelData = GlobalLock(hMaskPixelData)
lpSpritePixelData = GlobalLock(hSpritePixelData)
```

```
Dummy = StretchDIBits(hOffscreenCompositeDC, CompositeXOffset,
        CompositeYOffset, SpriteWidth, SpriteHeight, 0, 0, Abs(SpriteWidth),
        Abs(SpriteHeight), lpMaskPixelData, bmBitmapInfo, DIB_RGB_COLORS, SRCAND)
Dummy = StretchDIBits(hOffscreenCompositeDC, CompositeXOffset,
        CompositeYOffset, SpriteWidth, SpriteHeight, 0, 0, Abs(SpriteWidth),
        Abs(SpriteHeight), lpSpritePixelData, bmBitmapInfo, DIB_RGB_COLORS,
        SRCPAINT)
' Copy the composite buffer to the screen device context.
Dummy = BitBlt(ResultPicture.hDC, MinInt(OldLeft, NewLeft), MinInt(OldTop,
        NewTop), OffscreenCompositeWidth, OffscreenCompositeHeight,
        hOffscreenCompositeDC, 0, 0, SRCCOPY)
lpMaskPixelData = GlobalUnlock(hMaskPixelData)
lpSpritePixelData = GlobalUnlock(hSpritePixelData)

OldLeft = NewLeft
OldTop = NewTop

End Sub
```

This procedure begins by calculating the positions and dimensions for the next screen update. The arguments **HorizontallyReversible** and **VerticallyReversible** specify whether the sprite should be inverted when it is moving from right to left, or from bottom to top (I've assumed that the original bitmaps are drawn to appear correct when the sprite is moving from left to right or from top to bottom). The moth sprite looks pretty silly when you let it fly upside-down, but many other types of sprites need to be flipped vertically. Just as it will reverse a bitmap horizontally when you pass it a negative width, **StretchDIBits()** will flip a bitmap vertically when you pass it a negative value in the **nDestHeight** argument.

The blt operations in this procedure are simpler than those in the **AnimationPicture_Paint()** event procedure in SPRITE3.FRM. Instead of fiddling with so many little patches of background bitmap, this procedure uses a reserved copy of the background, stored in a memory device context referenced by the handle in **hBackgroundDC**. With each tick of the timer, **MoveSprite()** transfers a clean copy of the bounding rectangle from this pristine bitmap to **hOffscreenCompositeDC**, replacing the previous sprite at its previous position with the new sprite at its new position. This eliminates the two steps that reserve and restore the rectangular section of the bitmap covered by the sprite. The only thing we need from the previous instance of the sprite is its location, which in combination with the new position, determines the dimensions and location of the the bounding rectangle. Now we can update the sprite in only four steps:

1. Copy the bounding rectangle—the one defined by the previous position and the new position—from the uncontaminated memory device context

to a scratch pad device context (in this case, the offscreen composite device context).

2. Copy the mask to the sprite's new position in the clean bounding rectangle.

3. Copy the sprite to its new position, covering the mask.

4. Copy the whole bounding rectangle to the screen device context (in this case, AnimationPicture), simultaneously erasing the previous instance of the sprite and replacing it with the next one.

Because it shadows the entire background bitmap, this method uses more memory than the six step version, but it requires fewer blts, which *may* improve performance. I empasize "may" because Windows sometimes defies intuition. The performance of blt operations depends on several factors, including display hardware, display drivers, the availability of runtime resources, planetary alignment, fashion trends, etc. It is however, safe to assume that performance will not get any worse, and it rarely hurts to simplify code.

There is one significant performance factor you *can* control—the palette. This version of the program uses the identity palette from the background bitmap. You may recall from Chapter 5 that when the Palette Manager realizes an identity palette, it assumes a one-to-one mapping between the system palette and the logical palette, which eliminates the foreground mapping. **StretchDIBits()** must map the colors of the DIB as it copies the pixels to the device context. It does this by looking up the color referenced by each DIB pixel in the color table belonging to the DIB, then looking for the closest matching color in the currently realized logical palette. If the realized palette is not an identity palette, **StretchDIBits()** must then look up the correct pixel value in the foreground mapping table to reference the chosen color in the system palette. By realizing an identity palette you save **StretchDIBits()** a step, for which it rewards you with speedier service.

The Program Listings

We've covered most of the libraries used in this project in previous chapters. Here are the complete listings of SPRITE4.FRM and SPRITE4.BAS.

Listing 12.4 SPRITE4.FRM

```
VERSION 2.00
Begin Form SpriteAnimationForm
   Caption        =   "Sprite Animation Project 7"
   ClientHeight   =   4584
   ClientLeft     =   1308
   ClientTop      =   1968
   ClientWidth    =   5664
```

```
    Height          =    5004
    Left            =    1260
    LinkTopic       =    "Form1"
    ScaleHeight     =    382
    ScaleMode       =    3   'Pixel
    ScaleWidth      =    472
    Top             =    1596
    Width           =    5760
    Begin CheckBox FlipBox
        Caption         =    "Flippable"
        Height          =    288
        Left            =    2556
        TabIndex        =    2
        Top             =    4092
        Width           =    1428
    End
    Begin CheckBox ReverseBox
        Caption         =    "Reversible"
        Height          =    300
        Left            =    492
        TabIndex        =    1
        Top             =    4092
        Value           =    1   'Checked
        Width           =    1392
    End
    Begin Timer Timer1
        Enabled         =    0    'False
        Interval        =    56
        Left            =    216
        Top             =    3348
    End
    Begin PictureBox AnimationPicture
        Height          =    3540
        Left            =    168
        ScaleHeight     =    293
        ScaleMode       =    3   'Pixel
        ScaleWidth      =    441
        TabIndex        =    0
        Top             =    144
        Width           =    5316
    End
End
Option Explicit

Dim Forward As Integer
Dim Down As Integer
Dim CurrentLeft As Integer
Dim CurrentTop As Integer
Dim OldLeft As Integer
Dim OldTop As Integer
Dim CurrentSpriteCel As Integer
Dim hSpritePal As Integer
Dim hBackgroundDC
```

```
Sub AnimationPicture_Paint ()
    Dim RetValue As Integer

    RetValue = SelectPalette(AnimationPicture.hDC, hSpritePal, False)
    RetValue = RealizePalette(AnimationPicture.hDC)
    RetValue = BitBlt(AnimationPicture.hDC, 0, 0, AnimationPicture.ScaleWidth,
             AnimationPicture.ScaleHeight, hBackgroundDC, 0, 0, SRCCOPY)

End Sub

Sub Form_Load ()
    Dim RetValue As Integer

    Forward = True
    Down = True
    CurrentLeft = 0
    CurrentTop = 0
    ReDim SpriteBitmapFiles(6)
    ReDim SpriteDIBHandles(6, 2)
    SpriteBitmapFiles(1) = App.Path & "\Moth1.DIB"
    SpriteBitmapFiles(2) = App.Path & "\Moth2.DIB"
    SpriteBitmapFiles(3) = App.Path & "\Moth3.DIB"
    SpriteBitmapFiles(4) = App.Path & "\Moth4.DIB"
    SpriteBitmapFiles(5) = App.Path & "\Moth3.DIB"
    SpriteBitmapFiles(6) = App.Path & "\Moth2.DIB"
    Screen.MousePointer = 11 ' Hourglass
    NumberOfSpriteCels = LoadAndPrepareSprites(6)
    hBackgroundDC = MakeBackgroundShadow(App.Path & "\Hibisc2.BMP",
                   AnimationPicture, hSpritePal)
    Screen.MousePointer = 0
    If hBackgroundDC <> 0 Then
        OpenSprites AnimationPicture, hSpritePal
        Timer1.Enabled = True
    Else
        MsgBox "Unable to load background image.", 16, "File Error"
        Unload SpriteAnimationForm
        End
    End If
End Sub

Sub Form_QueryUnload (Cancel As Integer, UnloadMode As Integer)
    Timer1.Enabled = False
    CloseSprites AnimationPicture
    End Sub

Sub Form_Unload (Cancel As Integer)
    Dim RetValue As Integer
    Dim SpriteCelCounter As Integer
    Dim Counter As Integer

    For SpriteCelCounter = 1 To NumberOfSpriteCels
        For Counter = 1 To 2
            If SpriteDIBHandles(SpriteCelCounter, Counter) <> 0 Then
```

```
              SpriteDIBHandles(SpriteCelCounter, Counter) =
                GlobalFree(SpriteDIBHandles(SpriteCelCounter, Counter))
            End If
          Next Counter
        Next SpriteCelCounter

    RetValue = DeleteObject(hSpritePal)
    End Sub


Sub Timer1_Timer ()
    Dim Limit As Single
    Dim SpriteWidth As Single

    SpriteWidth = bmSpriteInfo.bmiHeader.biWidth
    CurrentSpriteCel = CurrentSpriteCel Mod NumberOfSpriteCels + 1
    If (((CurrentLeft + SpriteWidth) >= AnimationPicture.ScaleWidth) And Forward) Then
        Forward = False
      ElseIf ((CurrentLeft <= 0) And Not Forward) Then
        Forward = True
      End If
    If Forward Then
        Limit = AnimationPicture.ScaleWidth - SpriteWidth
        CurrentLeft = MinSingle(CurrentLeft + 20, Limit)
      Else
        Limit = bmSpriteInfo.bmiHeader.biWidth
        CurrentLeft = MaxSingle(CurrentLeft - 20, 0)
      End If
    If (((CurrentTop + bmSpriteInfo.bmiHeader.biHeight) >=
      AnimationPicture.ScaleHeight) And Down) Or ((CurrentTop <= 0) And Not Down) Then
        Down = Not Down
      End If
    If Down Then
        Limit = AnimationPicture.ScaleHeight - bmSpriteInfo.bmiHeader.biHeight
        CurrentTop = MinSingle(CurrentTop + 7, Limit)
      Else
        CurrentTop = MaxSingle(CurrentTop - 7, 0)
      End If
    MoveSprite OldLeft, OldTop, CurrentLeft, CurrentTop, (ReverseBox.Value = 1),
      (FlipBox.Value = 1), bmSpriteInfo, SpriteDIBHandles(CurrentSpriteCel, 2),
      SpriteDIBHandles(CurrentSpriteCel, 1), AnimationPicture, hSpritePal
    End Sub
```

Listing 12.5   SPRITE4.BAS

```
Option Explicit

Dim hOffscreenCompositeDC As Integer
Dim hOffscreenCompositeBitmap As Integer
Dim hOldOffscreenCompositeBitmap As Integer
Dim hBackgroundPixelData As Integer

Dim lpBackgroundPixelData As Long
Dim hBackgroundDC As Integer
```

```
Dim hBackgroundBitmap As Integer
Dim hOldBackgroundBitmap As Integer
Dim hBitmapPixelData As Integer

Dim bmBackgroundBitmapFileHeader As BITMAPFILEHEADER
Global bmBackgroundBitmapInfo As BITMAPINFO
Dim bmSpriteFileHeader As BITMAPFILEHEADER
Global bmSpriteInfo As BITMAPINFO

Global SpriteBitmapFiles() As String
Global SpriteDIBHandles() As Integer
Global NumberOfSpriteCels As Integer

Sub CloseSprites (ResultPicture As PictureBox)
    Dim RetValue As Integer

  RetValue = SelectPalette(ResultPicture.hDC, GetStockObject(DEFAULT_PALETTE), False)
  RetValue = SelectObject(hOffscreenCompositeDC, hOldOffscreenCompositeBitmap)
  RetValue = SelectPalette(hOffscreenCompositeDC,
    GetStockObject(DEFAULT_PALETTE), False)
  RetValue = DeleteDC(hOffscreenCompositeDC)
  RetValue = DeleteObject(hOffscreenCompositeBitmap)
  RetValue = SelectObject(hBackgroundDC, hOldBackgroundBitmap)
  RetValue = SelectPalette(hBackgroundDC, GetStockObject(DEFAULT_PALETTE), False)
  RetValue = DeleteDC(hBackgroundDC)
  RetValue = DeleteObject(hBackgroundBitmap)

    If hBitmapPixelData <> 0 Then
        hBitmapPixelData = GlobalFree(hBitmapPixelData)
    End If
    If hBackgroundPixelData <> 0 Then
        hBackgroundPixelData = GlobalFree(hBackgroundPixelData)
    End If
End Sub

Function ConvertImageToMask (bmInfo As BITMAPINFO, hBitmapPixelData As Integer)
  As Integer
    Dim PixelBytesToCopy As Long
    Dim hMaskPixelData As Integer
    Dim lpBitmapPixelData As Long
    Dim lpMaskPixelData As Long
    Dim MaskPixelSelector As Integer
    Dim LastLine As Integer
    Dim LineCounter As Integer
    Dim ColumnCounter As Integer
    Dim LastColumn As Integer
    Dim PaddedLineWidth As Integer
    Dim BufferString As String
    Dim MemOffset As Long
    Dim TempChar As String * 1
    Dim RetValue As Integer
    Dim ColorTableIndex As Integer

    ' Copy the original bitmap pixels to another buffer,
    ' which will become the Mask pixel data.
```

```
    PixelBytesToCopy = bmInfo.bmiHeader.biSizeImage
    hMaskPixelData = GlobalAlloc(GMEM_MOVEABLE Or GMEM_ZEROINIT,
                    PixelBytesToCopy)
    lpBitmapPixelData = GlobalLock(hBitmapPixelData)
    lpMaskPixelData = GlobalLock(hMaskPixelData)
    hmemcpy lpMaskPixelData, lpBitmapPixelData, PixelBytesToCopy
    lpBitmapPixelData = GlobalUnlock(hBitmapPixelData)
    lpMaskPixelData = GlobalUnlock(hMaskPixelData)


    MaskPixelSelector = GlobalHandleToSel(hMaskPixelData)
    LastLine = bmInfo.bmiHeader.biHeight - 1
    LastColumn = bmInfo.bmiHeader.biWidth
    PaddedLineWidth = ((LastColumn - 1) \ 4 + 1) * 4
    For LineCounter = 0 To LastLine
        BufferString = String$(PaddedLineWidth, Chr$(0))
        MemOffset = LineCounter * PaddedLineWidth
        RetValue = MemoryRead(MaskPixelSelector, MemOffset, ByVal BufferString,
                    PaddedLineWidth)
        For ColumnCounter = 1 To LastColumn
            TempChar = Mid$(BufferString, ColumnCounter, 1)
            ColorTableIndex = Asc(TempChar)
            If (Asc(bmInfo.bmiColors(ColorTableIndex).rgbRed) <> 255) Or
               (Asc(bmInfo.bmiColors(ColorTableIndex).rgbBlue) <> 255) Or
               (Asc(bmInfo.bmiColors(ColorTableIndex).rgbGreen) <> 255) Then
                Mid$(BufferString, ColumnCounter, 1) = Chr$(0)
              Else
                Mid$(BufferString, ColumnCounter, 1) = Chr$(255)
              End If
          Next ColumnCounter
        RetValue = MemoryWrite(MaskPixelSelector, MemOffset, ByVal BufferString,
                    PaddedLineWidth)
      Next LineCounter
    ConvertImageToMask = hMaskPixelData
    End Function

Function ConvertImageToSprite (bmInfo As BITMAPINFO, hBitmapPixelData As Integer)
  As Integer
    Dim PixelBytesToCopy As Long
    Dim hSpritePixelData As Integer
    Dim lpBitmapPixelData As Long
    Dim lpSpritePixelData As Long
    Dim SpritePixelSelector As Integer
    Dim LastLine As Integer
    Dim LineCounter As Integer
    Dim ColumnCounter As Integer
    Dim LastColumn As Integer
    Dim PaddedLineWidth As Integer
    Dim BufferString As String
    Dim MemOffset As Long
    Dim TempChar As String * 1
    Dim RetValue As Integer
    Dim ColorTableIndex As Integer
```

```
' Copy the original bitmap pixels to another buffer,
' which will become the mask pixel data.
PixelBytesToCopy = bmInfo.bmiHeader.biSizeImage
hSpritePixelData = GlobalAlloc(GMEM_MOVEABLE Or GMEM_ZEROINIT,
                   PixelBytesToCopy)
lpBitmapPixelData = GlobalLock(hBitmapPixelData)
lpSpritePixelData = GlobalLock(hSpritePixelData)
hmemcpy lpSpritePixelData, lpBitmapPixelData, PixelBytesToCopy
lpBitmapPixelData = GlobalUnlock(hBitmapPixelData)
lpSpritePixelData = GlobalUnlock(hSpritePixelData)

SpritePixelSelector = GlobalHandleToSel(hSpritePixelData)
LastLine = bmInfo.bmiHeader.biHeight - 1
LastColumn = bmInfo.bmiHeader.biWidth
PaddedLineWidth = ((LastColumn - 1) \ 4 + 1) * 4
For LineCounter = 0 To LastLine
    BufferString = String$(PaddedLineWidth, Chr$(0))
    MemOffset = LineCounter * PaddedLineWidth
    RetValue = MemoryRead(SpritePixelSelector, MemOffset, ByVal
               BufferString, PaddedLineWidth)
    For ColumnCounter = 1 To LastColumn
        TempChar = Mid$(BufferString, ColumnCounter, 1)
        ColorTableIndex = Asc(TempChar)
        If (Asc(bmInfo.bmiColors(ColorTableIndex).rgbRed) = 255) And
           (Asc(bmInfo.bmiColors(ColorTableIndex).rgbBlue) = 255) And
           (Asc(bmInfo.bmiColors(ColorTableIndex).rgbGreen) = 255) Then
             Mid$(BufferString, ColumnCounter, 1) = Chr$(0)
        End If
    Next ColumnCounter
    RetValue = MemoryWrite(SpritePixelSelector, MemOffset, ByVal
               BufferString, PaddedLineWidth)
Next LineCounter
ConvertImageToSprite = hSpritePixelData

End Function

Function LoadAndPrepareSprites (SpritesToLoad As Integer) As Integer
    Dim SpriteCounter As Integer
    Dim MsgString As String
    Dim RetValue As Integer
    Dim SpritePalette As LOGPALETTE

    SpriteCounter = 1
    Do While SpriteCounter <= SpritesToLoad
        ReadBitmapFile SpriteBitmapFiles(SpriteCounter), bmSpriteFileHeader,
          bmSpriteInfo, hBitmapPixelData
        If bmSpriteInfo.bmiHeader.biBitCount <> 8 Then
            MsgString = "File " & SpriteBitmapFiles(SpriteCounter) & " has " &
                        Str$(bmSpriteInfo.bmiHeader.biBitCount) & " bit pixels." &
                        Chr$(13) & Chr$(10)
            MsgString = MsgString & "Please load only 8-bit images."
            MsgBox MsgString, 16, "Load Error"
            LoadAndPrepareSprites = False
```

```
            SpriteDIBHandles(SpriteCounter, 1) =
                ConvertImageToMask(bmSpriteInfo, hBitmapPixelData)
            SpriteDIBHandles(SpriteCounter, 2) =
                ConvertImageToSprite(bmSpriteInfo, hBitmapPixelData)
            SpriteCounter = SpriteCounter + 1
        End If
        hBitmapPixelData = GlobalFree(hBitmapPixelData)
        Loop
    LoadAndPrepareSprites = SpriteCounter - 1

    End Function

Function MakeBackgroundShadow (Filename As String, ResultPicture As PictureBox,
    ByVal hAnimationPalette As Integer)
    Dim RetValue As Integer
    Dim SpritePalette As LOGPALETTE

    ReadBitmapFile Filename, bmBackgroundBitmapFileHeader,
                bmBackgroundBitmapInfo, hBackgroundPixelData
    If hBackgroundPixelData <> 0 Then
        hBackgroundDC = CreateCompatibleDC(ResultPicture.hDC)
        ConstructPaletteFromColorTable bmBackgroundBitmapInfo.bmiColors(),
                        SpritePalette
        hAnimationPalette = CreatePalette(SpritePalette)
        RetValue = SelectPalette(hBackgroundDC, hAnimationPalette, False)
        RetValue = SelectPalette(ResultPicture.hDC, hAnimationPalette, False)
        RetValue = RealizePalette(hBackgroundDC)
        lpBackgroundPixelData = GlobalLock(hBackgroundPixelData)
        hBackgroundBitmap = CreateDIBitmapFromGlobalMem(ResultPicture.hDC,
         bmBackgroundBitmapInfo.bmiHeader,CBM_INIT,lpBackgroundPixelData,
        bmBackgroundBitmapInfo,DIB_RGB_COLORS)
        lpBackgroundPixelData = GlobalUnlock(hBackgroundPixelData)
        hOldBackgroundBitmap = SelectObject(hBackgroundDC, hBackgroundBitmap)
        MakeBackgroundShadow = hBackgroundDC
    Else
        hBackgroundDC = 0
    End If

    End Function

Sub MoveSprite (OldLeft As Integer, OldTop As Integer, NewLeft As Integer,
    NewTop As Integer, ByVal HorizontallyReversible As Integer, ByVal
    VerticallyReversible As Integer, bmBitmapInfo As BITMAPINFO, hSpritePixelData
    As Integer, hMaskPixelData As Integer, ResultPicture As PictureBox,
    hAnimationPalette As Integer)
    Dim Dummy As Integer
    Dim RetValue As Integer
    Dim SpriteWidth As Integer
    Dim SpriteHeight As Integer
    Dim CurrentX As Integer
    Dim CurrentY As Integer
```

```
Dim OffscreenCompositeWidth As Integer
Dim OffscreenCompositeHeight As Integer
Dim lpMaskPixelData As Long
Dim lpSpritePixelData As Long
Dim CompositeXOffset As Integer
Dim CompositeYOffset As Integer

If NewLeft > OldLeft Then
    SpriteWidth = bmBitmapInfo.bmiHeader.biWidth
    CurrentX = NewLeft
    OffscreenCompositeWidth = MinInt((SpriteWidth + NewLeft - OldLeft), _
                        (ResultPicture.ScaleWidth - OldLeft))
  Else
    If HorizontallyReversible Then
        SpriteWidth = -bmBitmapInfo.bmiHeader.biWidth
        CurrentX = NewLeft + bmBitmapInfo.bmiHeader.biWidth - 1
      Else
        SpriteWidth = bmBitmapInfo.bmiHeader.biWidth
        CurrentX = NewLeft
      End If
    OffscreenCompositeWidth = MinInt(OldLeft + Abs(SpriteWidth), _
                        (Abs(SpriteWidth) + OldLeft - NewLeft))
  End If
If HorizontallyReversible Then
    CompositeXOffset = MaxInt(CurrentX - NewLeft, CurrentX - OldLeft)
  Else
    CompositeXOffset = MaxInt(0, NewLeft - OldLeft)
  End If

If NewTop > OldTop Then
    SpriteHeight = bmBitmapInfo.bmiHeader.biHeight
    CurrentY = NewTop
    OffscreenCompositeHeight = MinInt((SpriteHeight + NewTop - OldTop), _
                        (ResultPicture.ScaleHeight - OldTop))
  Else
    If VerticallyReversible Then
        SpriteHeight = -bmBitmapInfo.bmiHeader.biHeight
        CurrentY = NewTop + bmBitmapInfo.bmiHeader.biHeight - 1
      Else
        SpriteHeight = bmBitmapInfo.bmiHeader.biHeight
        CurrentY = NewTop
      End If
    OffscreenCompositeHeight = MinInt((OldTop + Abs(SpriteHeight)), _
                        (Abs(SpriteHeight) + OldTop - NewTop))
  End If
If VerticallyReversible Then
    CompositeYOffset = MaxInt(CurrentY - NewTop, CurrentY - OldTop)
  Else
    CompositeYOffset = MaxInt(0, NewTop - OldTop)
  End If
Dummy = SelectPalette(hOffscreenCompositeDC, hAnimationPalette, False)
Dummy = RealizePalette(hOffscreenCompositeDC)
' Copy the bounding rectangle of the old and new positions to the offscreen
' composite buffer.
```

```
    Dummy = BitBlt(hOffscreenCompositeDC, 0, 0, OffscreenCompositeWidth,
            OffscreenCompositeHeight, hBackgroundDC, MinInt(OldLeft, NewLeft),
            MinInt(OldTop, NewTop), SRCCOPY)
    ' Copy the mask and sprite to the composite buffer.
    lpMaskPixelData = GlobalLock(hMaskPixelData)
    lpSpritePixelData = GlobalLock(hSpritePixelData)
    Dummy = StretchDIBits(hOffscreenCompositeDC, CompositeXOffset,
            CompositeYOffset, SpriteWidth, SpriteHeight, 0, 0, Abs(SpriteWidth),
            Abs(SpriteHeight), lpMaskPixelData, bmBitmapInfo, DIB_RGB_COLORS, SRCAND)
    Dummy = StretchDIBits(hOffscreenCompositeDC, CompositeXOffset,
            CompositeYOffset, SpriteWidth, SpriteHeight, 0, 0, Abs(SpriteWidth),
            Abs(SpriteHeight), lpSpritePixelData, bmBitmapInfo, DIB_RGB_COLORS,
            SRCPAINT)
    ' Copy the composite buffer to the screen device context.
    Dummy = BitBlt(ResultPicture.hDC, MinInt(OldLeft, NewLeft), MinInt(OldTop,
            NewTop), OffscreenCompositeWidth, OffscreenCompositeHeight,
            hOffscreenCompositeDC, 0, 0, SRCCOPY)
    lpMaskPixelData = GlobalUnlock(hMaskPixelData)
    lpSpritePixelData = GlobalUnlock(hSpritePixelData)

    OldLeft = NewLeft
    OldTop = NewTop

End Sub

Sub OpenSprites (ResultPicture As PictureBox, hAnimationPalette As Integer)
    Dim RetValue As Integer

    hOffscreenCompositeDC = CreateCompatibleDC(ResultPicture.hDC)
    hOffscreenCompositeBitmap = CreateCompatibleBitmap(ResultPicture.hDC,
        ResultPicture.ScaleWidth, ResultPicture.ScaleHeight)
    RetValue = SelectPalette(hOffscreenCompositeDC, hAnimationPalette, False)
    RetValue = RealizePalette(hOffscreenCompositeDC)
    hOldOffscreenCompositeBitmap = SelectObject(hOffscreenCompositeDC,
                                   hOffscreenCompositeBitmap)

    End Sub
```

Enhancing the Sprite Animation

As always, you can improve upon the animation techniques we've used. The first, and most complex improvement would be to translate all the masks and sprites into device-dependent bitmaps at the outset. To do this you would have to create a memory device context and device compatible bitmap for each image, then transfer the DIBs to them with **StretchDIBit()**. For the moth sprite, you would want at least 16 memory device contexts: a sprite and a mask for each of the four versions, plus the mirror images of each. By pre-translating the DIBs into DDBs, you could improve the performance of the animation dramatically.

Another useful enhancement you might want to try out would be to enable the functions **ConvertImageToSprite()** and **ConvertImageToMask()** to accept the RGB value of the transparent color as an argument, instead of assuming that the transparent pixels are always pure white. That way, you could use white in your sprites as an opaque color.

Finally, for all my emphasis on interactivity, these demonstration programs don't offer much. Try using other events to control the motion of the sprites. You could, for example, limit the timer to cycling the sprite images, and use the **MouseMove** event to control the moth's position on the screen.

Now that you know how to display and move sprites, you can expand the construction set we've developed in this chapter to add all kinds of interesting motion to your VB programs.

Chapter 13

Prepare yourself to ride a most awesome WAVE as we expand our sound capabilities with some amazing effects.

Exploring Waveform Audio

I've been been telling you over and over that multimedia is a visual medium. But what about sound? You certainly don't want to underestimate its value when it comes to creating entertaining or educational multimedia applications. After all, imagine what it would be like seeing Steven Spielberg's latest action adventure movie without sound. It's the roar of the T. Rex that makes you cling to your seat.

A Potent Medium

Movie and television producers spend a small fortune on their soundtracks. Often, the sound production can cost almost as much as all of the visual work. But as you sit in the dark theater, watching pictures twenty feet high and forty feet wide you probably don't think about all the things you hear—the low tones that peak your anxiety, the reverberating footsteps, and the rhythm of the musical soundtrack.

Few people realize that most of what they hear in a movie theater, on a music CD, or on television has been carefully fabricated. In the movies, a gunshot may reverberate from cliff to canyon, but when you record the sound of a gunshot, all you usually catch on tape is a popping noise, no more impressive sounding than a kid's capgun. The sound engineers craft that recording. To give it weight, they filter out noise, stretch its duration, and mix in low frequency subharmonics. To locate it in space, whether that's the ringing confines of an underground garage or an echoing Rocky Mountain pass, they adjust the volume, balance, and Surround Sound™ effects, and run it through a digital effects processor to add reverberation.

The people who use sound to communicate know how powerful it can be, and if we're going to produce multimedia that can draw people away from their televisions, we had better learn the methods of sound production and make the necessary tools to apply them to our projects.

Checking Out the Options

Unfortunately, VB provides no intrinsic support for sound. But as you learned in Chapter 3, that won't hold us back at all. The Windows multimedia system has so many sound options, it can be hard to decide which to use. Let's sort them out.

Redbook Audio

When you pop a music CD into your Discman™ and press the Play button, you're listening to redbook audio. The specifications for the various data formats available on compact disks come in color-coded books. The cover of the standard audio specification is red, hence "redbook audio." With the MCI you can play audio CDs on your CD-ROM drive. That's how the Windows Media Player works. You don't even need a sound card to play music. Just plug the analog audio output of your CD-ROM drive into any amplifier. If both the Microsoft MSCDEX.EXE CD driver and the Windows [MCI] CD Audio drivers are loaded, you can use the Media Player—or any other Windows CD player—to operate the drive and listen to your favorite tunes. In fact, I'm doing that right now. If you have an internal CD-ROM drive and a sound card, you may have connected the drive to the card with a thin, three-wire audio cable. This cable does nothing more than act as an external audio cable. It simply connects the analog audio outputs of the drive to the line-level analog inputs of the mixer/amplifier on the sound card.

It's true that redbook audio is digital. It's also true that many sound cards can play and record digital audio at the same 16-bit, 44.1 KHz sampling rate as redbook. However, no standard drivers—and as far as I know, no commercially available CD-ROM drives or sound cards—will let you read the digital sound data on the redbook audio tracks. You may use the MCI driver to select tracks, query the drive for timing or other information, play tracks, or manipulate the disk in a variety of other ways. But the conversion of the digital audio into an analog signal is handled entirely by the digital to analog converter (DAC) inside the drive.

Does this mean we can't use redbook audio in our multimedia projects? Not by a long shot. Although the mastering process is different, redbook audio and CD-ROM data can, and often do, co-habitate on the same disk. That's how titles like Microsoft/Voyager's *Multimedia Beethoven* or 7th Level's *Tuneland with Howie Mandel* work. In Chapter 15 we'll take a closer look at the MCI string commands, and how we can use them to monitor and control audio CDs.

MIDI

The musical instrument digital interface (MIDI) actually makes no sound at all. MIDI is just a protocol that enables computers, synthesizers, keyboards, and other musical devices to communicate with each other. Almost every sound card you can buy today for your PC includes some kind of built-in synthesizer. To play music on it, though, you have to send it messages that tell it which instrument sound (known as a *patch)* to use and which note to play. You'll also need to provide information for volume control and other sound qualities. MIDI is a specification that defines both the serial interface used by instruments to communicate with each other, and the message codes that travel over those links.

MIDI is the most economical type of multimedia sound. For example, to hold a single synthesizer note for an hour would require just 6 bytes—a 3 byte message to start the note, and a 3 byte message to stop it. In contrast, one hour of the lowest-fidelity waveform data would fill 39,690,000 bytes! MIDI enables you to store lengthy musical passages in just a few kilobytes, or tens of kilobytes. Another advantage is that it allows you to change music on the fly. For example, you can transpose an entire piece to another key just by adding or subtracting a constant from all the note numbers. You can also change the playback speed of MIDI music without affecting its pitch.

The major disadvantage of MIDI is that the quality of sound it produces depends entirely on the synthesizer on which it is played, whether that is a sound card or an external synthesizer. Even two cards that use the same synthesizer chip can have different sounds programmed into it.

We'll look at MIDI in more detail in the next chapter.

Waveform Audio

Waveform audio is the workhorse of PC multimedia sound. With waveform audio you can do anything, within the practical limitations of memory, disk storage, processor speed, and the capabilities of your sound card. That doesn't mean you should skip MIDI and redbook audio altogether. It just means that waveform audio offers the most general-purpose sound system. You can record and play music, sound effects, narration—anything you could do with a tape recorder, you can do with waveform audio.

Like CD audio, waveform audio is a digital medium. Unlike CD audio, however, it supports a variety of formats, from 8-bit monophonic at a sampling rate of 11,025 samples per second (11,025 bytes per second) to 16-bit stereo at rate of 44,100 samples per second (176,400 bytes per second!). And also unlike CD audio, you can read and write it, store and retrieve it, and in short, manipulate it to your heart's content.

The waveform data format you choose—in other words, the sampling rate, number of channels (mono versus stereo), and bit resolution (8 versus 16)—should depend not only on the capabilities of the sound card on which you develop your presentations but on the capabilities of the sound card(s) on which they must eventually play.

Digital Audio Basics

Waveform audio is stored in a format known as *pulse code modulation,* or PCM, which is the ten-dollar term for the seven-and-a-half-dollar term *digital sampling.* The principle is actually pretty simple.

Sound consists of a pressure wave moving through a medium, such as air. For each wave pulse there is a traveling zone of compressed air, trailed by a zone of rarified air. To represent sound electronically, the compression is represented by a positive voltage and the rarification by a negative voltage. The voltage level determines the amplitude of the wave. A pure sine wave forms a nice rolling voltage, gradually switching from a positive value to a negative value of the same degree, and back again, as illustrated in the top portion of Figure 13.1. But most sounds aren't so pure. They include numerous sine waves, and possibly other waveforms, all added together to form a more irregular pattern, as shown in the bottom portion of Figure 13.1.

To represent an analog waveform digitally, the voltage levels of the wave are sampled at regular intervals and stored as numbers. Audible frequencies range from about 50 Hz (cycles per second) to over 20,000 Hz. So to record a meaningful digital representation you need to sample the waveform frequently.

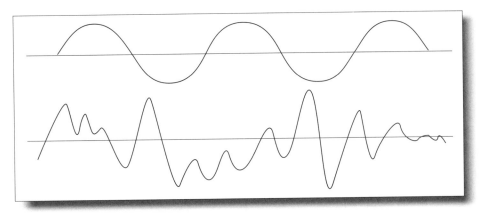

Figure 13.1 *A pure and not so pure sound waveform.*

In fact, it was proven mathematically in 1948, by Claude Shannon of Bell Laboratories, that you can accurately represent any analog signal with a digital sampling rate equal to twice the maximum frequency contained in the source. That's why CD audio is recorded at a frequency of 44.1 KHz—twice the maximum audible frequency (to humans at least).

You needn't preserve the full fidelity of the original analog signal, however. By sampling at lower rates you don't lose the sound entirely, just the higher frequencies. This can produce the "AM radio" effect—the conversion of rich, full-bodied sound into tinny cracker-box sound.

Sampling rate isn't the only factor that determines fidelity. The resolution of the sample—that is, the number of bits per sample—can also have a major impact. 8-bit samples, regardless of the sampling rate, cannot accurately represent sound. The human brain, by way of its audio sensors—ears—can distinguish very subtle differences in amplitude and frequency. With only 256 recordable levels, many of the subtler elements of a complex sound disappear. This loss is called *aliasing*. This is the audio equivalent of the stairstep aliasing that appears when you blow up bitmap images, or the color banding you often see when you convert a true color image to an 8-bit palette—especially in broad areas of graduated color, such as a clear blue sky. On the other hand, 16-bit sampling can differentiate over 65,000 signal levels, which makes it possible to represent a sound with much greater fidelity, while only doubling the storage demand.

Whatever the sampling rate and bit resolution of the digital waveform, the format of the data is simple. In 8-bit samples, each byte represents an amplitude. If the sample contains two channels of audio—in other words, stereo—the left channel is recorded in the even numbered bytes, beginning with byte zero, and the right channel is recorded in the odd numbered bytes, beginning with byte one. 8-bit values have no sign, so a value of 128 represents the *baseline* of the data. Values higher than 128 represent positive amplitudes; values lower than 128 represent negative amplitudes. Since 8 bits represent an even number of possible values, the choice of 128 as the baseline is arbitrary; 127 would work just as well. But 128 is the standard.

In 16-bit wave files, each sample occupies two bytes, which happen to represent an ordinary signed integer. Amplitudes range in value from -32,768 to 32,767. In stereo 16-bit wave files, every other pair of bytes contains the data for one channel. So bytes zero and one contain the first sample of the left channel, bytes two and three contain the first sample of the right channel, bytes four and five contain the second sample of the left channel, and so on.

The best way to understand waveform audio, and to appreciate its simplicity, is to fiddle with it. In the next project, we'll expand on the code we developed in Chapter 3 to read, play, and modify waveform data (WAVE) files with the low-level audio API functions.

Playing and Modifying Wave Data

In the last section of Chapter 4 we used the multimedia IO functions and the low-level audio functions to read and play a brief waveaudio file. In this project, we'll use the Windows global memory management functions to break the 32,000 byte barrier we encountered before. Then we'll use some simple audio processing techniques to adjust the overall loudness, or *level*, of a sample, and to add echo effects. Here are the steps to follow:

1. Create the form WAVPLAY2.FRM (Listing 13.1).
2. Copy WAVEPLAY.BAS to WAVPLAY2.BAS.
3. Change **OpenWaveFile()** and **WaveOut()** in WAVPLAY2.BAS to add support for global memory blocks (Listings 13.2 and 13.3).
4. Add **CloseWavePlay()** to WAVPLAY2.BAS (Listing 13.4).
5. Add the **DeviceCapsOption_Click()** event procedure to WAVPLAY2.FRM (Listing 13.5).
6. Add the general functions **WaveFormatStringFromConstant()** and **WaveFunctionStringFromConstant()** to WAVPLAY2.BAS (Listings 13.6 and 13.7).
7. Add the general procedure **ChangeLevel()** to WAVPLAY2.BAS (Listing 13.8).

8. Add the general function **WaveFormatConstantFromFormat()** to WAVPLAY2.BAS (Listing 13.9).

9. Add the general procedure **AddEcho()** to WAVPLAY2.BAS (Listing 13.10).

10. Add the general function **ExtendGlobalMemBlock()** to WAVPLAY2.BAS (Listing 13.11).

11. Finish the declarations for WAVPLAY2.BAS (Listing 13.12).

12. Complete the code in WAVPLAY2.FRM (Listing 13.13).

You'll find this project in the subdirectory \VBMAGIC in the files WAVPLAY2.MAK, WAVPLAY2.FRM, WAVPLAY2.BAS, GLBLMEM2.BAS, GLOBCONS.BAS, and MINMAX.BAS. It also uses the Common Dialog custom control, which is located in the file CMDIALOG.VBX. VB Setup usually installs this file in the \WINDOWS\SYSTEM subdirectory.

Running the Program

When you run the program, your screen should look similar to Figure 13.2. Choose File, Get Device Capabilities to display information about your sound card and its driver. You can use this information to decide whether any particular WAVE file will play on your card. Next, choose File, Open Wave File to display the Open Wave File dialog box. Use this dialog box to choose a WAVE file, then select Play.

You have two options when it comes to adding special effects to your audio files; choose Effects, Change Volume or Effects, Add Echo. When the mouse pointer changes back to an arrow, again select Play to hear the result of the effects option. The Change Volume option is hard-coded to reduce the amplitude of the WAVE file by 50%. The Add Echo option will repeatedly echo the sound at a period of one second, with a decay factor of 50% per iteration. As you'll soon see, you can easily change these parameters.

Creating the Form

The form for this project requires only two controls: a Picture Box and a Common Dialog. For the Picture Box, keep the default **Name** of Picture1. For the second, set the **Name** property to FileOpenDialog. In the sample program, I have also placed a Shape control behind Picture1 to give it a drop-shadow—an entirely cosmetic effect. All the features of this program will be activated from menu options. See Listing 13.1 for the property settings in WAVPLAY2.FRM.

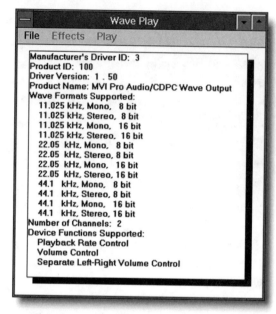

Figure 13.2 *The program WavPlay2 at runtime.*

Listing 13.1 The Property Listing of WAVPLAY2.FRM

```
VERSION 2.00
Begin Form WavePlay
    Caption          =    "Wave Play"
    ClientHeight     =    4920
    ClientLeft       =    1188
    ClientTop        =    1872
    ClientWidth      =    5040
    Height           =    5664
    Left             =    1140
    LinkTopic        =    "Form1"
    ScaleHeight      =    4920
    ScaleWidth       =    5040
    Top              =    1176
    Width            =    5136
    Begin CommonDialog FileOpenDialog
        DialogTitle  =    "Open Wave File"
        Filename     =    "*.wav"
        Filter       =    "Wave Audio|*.wav"
        Left         =    0
        Top          =    4536
    End
    Begin PictureBox Picture1
        Height       =    4455
        Left         =    240
        ScaleHeight  =    4428
        ScaleWidth   =    4428
```

```
        TabIndex       =   0
        Top            =   120
        Width          =   4455
    End
    Begin Shape Shape1
        FillStyle      =   0  'Solid
        Height         =   4452
        Left           =   360
        Top            =   240
        Width          =   4452
    End
    Begin Menu FileMenu
        Caption          =   "File"
        Begin Menu DeviceCapsOption
            Caption          =   "Get Device Capabilities"
        End
        Begin Menu OpenOption
            Caption          =   "Open Wave File"
        End
        Begin Menu QuitOption
            Caption          =   "Quit"
        End
    End
    Begin Menu EffectsMenu
        Caption          =   "Effects"
        Begin Menu VolumeOption
            Caption          =   "Change Volume"
        End
        Begin Menu EchoOption
            Caption          =   "Add Echo"
        End
    End
    Begin Menu PlayOption
        Caption          =   "Play"
    End
End
```

The Code Module

All the code that reads, plays, and processes wave files is located in the code module WAVPLAY2.BAS. To create this file, we'll begin with a copy of WAVEPLAY.BAS, which we developed for the program MCIPLAY.MAK back in Chapter 4.

You'll recall that we left that program hobbled with a 32,000 byte limit on the length of the wave data. Given the data rates for waveaudio that we covered earlier in this chapter, it's apparent that 32,000 bytes won't hold much digital audio. But we've come a long way since Chapter 4, and with a little help from the Windows memory manager, we can do away with that limit.

In the middle of the original **OpenWaveFile()** procedure, as it appeared in WAVEPLAY.BAS, we prepared an array of characters (actually single-character strings)

as a buffer, passed it to the **mmioRead()** API function, and used the **lstrcpy()** API function to capture an address that we could store in the **WaveHeader**:

```
For Index = 1 To 32000
    WaveBuffer(Index).Char = Chr$(0)
    Next Index
BytesRead = mmioRead(hMMIO, WaveBuffer(1), MMCkInfoChild.CkSize)
If BytesRead > 0 Then
    ' Get a pointer to the wave data and fill in wave header.
    WaveHeader.lpData = lstrcpy(WaveBuffer(1), WaveBuffer(1))
    WaveHeader.dwBufferLength = BytesRead
    WaveHeader.dwFlags = 0&
    WaveHeader.dwLoops = 0&
    OpenWaveFile = True
```

In the new version, we'll use the API function **GlobalAlloc()** to reserve a block of global memory large enough to hold the waveaudio sample data:

```
hWaveSampleData = GlobalAlloc(GMEM_MOVEABLE Or GMEM_ZEROINIT,
                    MMCkInfoChild.CkSize)
If hWaveSampleData <> 0 Then
    lpWaveSampleData = GlobalLock(hWaveSampleData)
    BytesRead = mmioReadToGlobal(hMMIO, lpWaveSampleData, MMCkInfoChild.CkSize)
    lpWaveSampleData = GlobalUnlock(hWaveSampleData)
    If BytesRead > 0 Then
        WaveHeader.lpData = 0
        WaveHeader.dwBufferLength = BytesRead
        WaveHeader.dwFlags = 0&
        WaveHeader.dwLoops = 0&
        OpenWaveFile = True
```

To get a long pointer to that block, we simply call **GlobalLock()**. In this version, we've also corrected another serious problem. Notice that this time we don't store the pointer to the global memory block in **WaveHeader.lpData**. We won't do that until it's time to feed the data to the waveaudio output function. We took a risk before, because we prematurely acquired a memory address for the data buffer. The array we used as a buffer was a global memory block, just like the one we're creating here. But that block was under the control of VB, and since VB had no particular reason to keep it locked, that block was free to move. If sometime between opening the file and playing it, the Windows memory manager decided to rearrange things, we could have found ourselves trying to play whatever new data happened to reside at that address. You should never obtain the address of a global memory block until you are ready to use it; and when you're finished, you should unlock the block and forget that you ever knew its location.

Other than the changes to add support for global memory blocks, including the declaration of **lpWaveSampleData**, **OpenWaveFile()** hasn't changed much, as you can see from Listing 13.2.

Listing 13.2 TheOpenWaveFile() General Procedure from WAVPLAY2.BAS

```
Function OpenWaveFile (ByVal FileNameAndPath As String) As Integer
    Dim MMCKInfoParent As MMCKINFO
    Dim MMCkInfoChild As MMCKINFO
    Dim hMMIO As Integer
    Dim ErrorCode As Integer
    Dim BytesRead As Long
    Dim Index As Integer
    Dim lpWaveSampleData As Long

    hMMIO = mmioOpen(FileNameAndPath, ByVal 0&, MMIO_READ)
    If hMMIO <> 0 Then
        ' Find WAVE parent chunk.
        MMCKInfoParent.fccType.Chars = "WAVE"
        ErrorCode = mmioDescend(hMMIO, MMCKInfoParent, ByVal 0&, MMIO_FINDRIFF)
        If ErrorCode = 0 Then
            ' Find fmt chunk.
            MMCkInfoChild.CkId.Chars = "fmt "
            ErrorCode = mmioDescend(hMMIO, MMCkInfoChild, MMCKInfoParent, _
                    MMIO_FINDCHUNK)
            If ErrorCode = 0 Then
                ' Read PCM Wave format record.
                BytesRead = mmioRead(hMMIO, PCMWaveFmtRecord, _
                        MMCkInfoChild.CkSize)
                If BytesRead > 0 Then
                    ErrorCode = waveOutOpen(hWaveOut, WAVE_MAPPER, _
                            PCMWaveFmtRecord, 0&, 0&, WAVE_FORMAT_QUERY)
                    If ErrorCode = 0 Then
                        ' Ascend back one level in the RIFF file.
                        ErrorCode = mmioAscend(hMMIO, MMCkInfoChild, 0)
                        If ErrorCode = 0 Then
                            ' Read data chunk.
                            MMCkInfoChild.CkId.Chars = "data"
                            ErrorCode = mmioDescend(hMMIO, MMCkInfoChild, _
                                    MMCKInfoParent, MMIO_FINDCHUNK)
                            If ErrorCode = 0 Then
                                hWaveSampleData = GlobalAlloc(GMEM_MOVEABLE Or _
                                            GMEM_ZEROINIT, _
                                            MMCkInfoChild.CkSize)
                                If hWaveSampleData <> 0 Then
                                    lpWaveSampleData = GlobalLock(hWaveSampleData)
                                    BytesRead = mmioReadToGlobal(hMMIO, _
                                            lpWaveSampleData, _
                                            MMCkInfoChild.CkSize)
                                    lpWaveSampleData = GlobalUnlock(hWaveSampleData)
                                    If BytesRead > 0 Then
                                        WaveHeader.lpData = 0
```

```
                                WaveHeader.dwBufferLength = BytesRead
                                WaveHeader.dwFlags = 0&
                                WaveHeader.dwLoops = 0&
                                OpenWaveFile = True
                            Else
                                MsgBox "Couldn't read wave data.",
                                    MB_ICONSTOP, "RIFF File Error"
                            End If
                        Else
                          MsgBox "Unable to Allocate Global Memory.",
                              MB_ICONSTOP, "Memory Error"
                        End If
                    Else
                      MsgBox "Couldn't find data chunk.", MB_ICONSTOP,
                          "RIFF File Error"
                    End If
                Else
                  MsgBox "Couldn't ascend from fmt chunk.",
                      MB_ICONSTOP, "RIFF File Error"
                End If
            Else
              MsgBox "Format not supported by Wave device.",
                  MB_ICONSTOP, "Wave Data Error"
            End If
        Else
          MsgBox "Couldn't read wave format record.", MB_ICONSTOP,
              "RIFF File Error"
        End If
    Else
      MsgBox "Couldn't find fmt chunk.", MB_ICONSTOP, "RIFF File Error"
    End If
  Else
    MsgBox "Couldn't find WAVE parent chunk.", MB_ICONSTOP, "RIFF File Error"
  End If
  ' Close the WAVE file.
  ErrorCode = mmioClose(hMMIO, 0)
Else
  MsgBox "Couldn't open file.", MB_ICONSTOP, "RIFF File Error"
End If

End Function
```

Like the changes to **OpenWaveFile()**, the modifications to **WaveOut()** are short and simple. In the first line of code after the declarations, we lock the global memory block and store its address in **WaveHeader.lpData**. In the last line, we unlock it. That's it. Take a look at Listing 13.3.

Listing 13.3   The WaveOut() General Function from WAVPLAY2.BAS

```
Function WaveOut () As Integer
    Dim hWaveOut As Integer
    Dim ReturnCode As Integer
```

```
WaveHeader.lpData = GlobalLock(hWaveSampleData)
' Open the wave device.
ReturnCode = waveOutOpen(hWaveOut, WAVE_MAPPER, PCMWaveFmtRecord, 0&, 0&, 0&)
If ReturnCode = 0 Then
    ' Prepare the wave output header.
    ReturnCode = waveOutPrepareHeader(hWaveOut, WaveHeader, Len(WaveHeader))
    If ReturnCode = 0 Then
        ' Write the wave data to the output device.
        ReturnCode = waveOutWrite(hWaveOut, WaveHeader, Len(WaveHeader))
        ' Wait until it's finished playing.
        If ReturnCode = 0 Then
            Do Until (WaveHeader.dwFlags And WHDR_DONE)
                DoEvents
                Loop
        End If
        WaveOut = True
        ' Unprepare the wave output header.
        ReturnCode = waveOutUnprepareHeader(hWaveOut, WaveHeader, Len(WaveHeader))
        If ReturnCode <> 0 Then
            MsgBox "Unable to Unprepare Wave Header", MB_ICONSTOP, "Wave Error"
        End If
        WaveHeader.dwFlags = 0
        ' Close the wave device.
        ReturnCode = waveOutClose(hWaveOut)
        If ReturnCode <> 0 Then
            MsgBox "Unable to Close Wave Device", MB_ICONSTOP, "Wave Error"
        End If
    Else
        ' Couldn't prepare the header, so close the device.
        MsgBox "Unable to Prepare Wave Header", 0, "Wave Error"
        ReturnCode = waveOutClose(hWaveOut)
        If ReturnCode <> 0 Then
            MsgBox "Unable to Close Wave Device", MB_ICONSTOP, "Wave Error"
        End If
    End If
Else
    ' Couldn't open the device so do nothing.
    MsgBox "Unable to Open Wave Device", MB_ICONSTOP, "Wave Error"
End If
WaveHeader.lpData = GlobalUnlock(hWaveSampleData)
End Function
```

Later, when we write the **Form_Unload()** event procedure for WAVPLAY2.FRM to terminate the program, we'll need to dispose of the global memory block. For that, we'll create another brief general procedure called **CloseWavePlay()**, shown in Listing 13.4.

Listing 13.4   The CloseWavePlay() General Procedure from WAVPLAY2.BAS

```
Sub CloseWavePlay ()
    Dim Dummy As Integer
```

```
If hWaveSampleData <> 0 Then
    Dummy = GlobalFree(hWaveSampleData)
  End If
End Sub
```

Checking the Capabilities of Your Sound Card

Although Windows supports device independence, it can't magically grant to hardware devices capabilities that they lack. The first generation of sound cards supported only 8-bit monophonic sample playback and recording at maximum sampling rates of 22.05 KHz. Hundreds of thousands of computers are still equipped with these cards, so if we plan to write commercial multimedia titles, we had better support them. The Windows multimedia API provides a function called **waveOutGetDevCaps()** with which we can query the device driver for information about the waveaudio device built into the installed sound card (other functions ask for MIDI and mixer information).

To get the device capabilities, you must first declare a structure of type **WAVEOUTCAPS**:

```
Type WAVEOUTCAPS
    wMid As Integer
    wPid As Integer
    vDriverVersion As Integer
    szPName As String * 32
    dwFormats As Long
    wChannels As Integer
    dwSupport As Long
    End Type
```

Here's a brief rundown of these fields:

- **wMid** holds the manufacturer's ID for the device driver.
- **wPid** holds the product ID (the manufacturer's ID for the sound card).
- **vDriverVersion** is an integer field that specifies the version number of the device driver. The high-order byte contains the major version number, while the low-order byte contains the minor version (or release) number.
- **szPName** contains the name of the product.
- **dwFormats** is a flag field, in which each bit represents a waveform audio format. For the list of available formats, see Table 13.1.
- **wChannels** is an integer field that contains a value of either 1 or 2, to indicate support for just monophonic output, or for both mono and stereo.
- **dwSupport**, another flag field, indicates whether the device supports any of the extended wave output capabilities, as listed in Table 13.2. If it does, you can call the three **waveOut** functions that control these fea-

Table 13.1 *The Standard Wave Format Constants*

Constant Name	Sampling Rate	Bit Resolution	Channels	Hexadecimal Value
WAVE_FORMAT_1M08	11.025 kHz	8	Mono	&H00000001
WAVE_FORMAT_1S08	11.025 kHz	8	Stereo	&H00000002
WAVE_FORMAT_1M16	11.025 kHz	16	Mono	&H00000004
WAVE_FORMAT_2M08	22.05 kHz	8	Mono	&H00000010
WAVE_FORMAT_2S08	22.05 kHz	8	Stereo	&H00000020
WAVE_FORMAT_2M16	22.05 kHz	16	Mono	&H00000040
WAVE_FORMAT_2S16	22.05 kHz	16	Stereo	&H00000080
WAVE_FORMAT_4M08	44.1 kHz	8	Mono	&H00000100
WAVE_FORMAT_4S08	44.1 kHz	8	Stereo	&H00000200
WAVE_FORMAT_4M16	44.1 kHz	16	Mono	&H00000400
WAVE_FORMAT_4S16	44.1 kHz	16	Stereo	&H00000800

Table 13.2 *The Constants That Indicate Support for Optional Wave Output Capabilities*

Constant Name	Value
WAVECAPS_PITCH	&H00000001
WAVECAPS_PLAYBACKRATE	&H00000002
WAVECAPS_VOLUME	&H00000004
WAVECAPS_LRVOLUME	&H00000008

tures: **waveOutSetPitch()**, **waveOutSetPlaybackRate()**, and **waveOutSetVolume()**, along with the three corresponding query functions: **waveOutGetPitch()**, **waveOutGetPlaybackRate()**, and **waveOutGetVolume()**.

To retrieve the device information, you pass the address of a **WAVEOUTCAPS** data structure to **waveOutGetDevCaps()**, as shown in Listing 13.5. Here's the function declaration:

```
Declare Function waveOutGetDevCaps Lib "MMSystem" (ByVal wDeviceID As Integer,
    lpCaps As WAVEOUTCAPS, ByVal wSize As Integer) As Integer
```

The first argument, **wDeviceID**, specifies the waveaudio output device to query. It's possible to install more than one waveaudio device in a single computer (if you can resolve all the IRQs, DMA channels, IO addresses, and memory buffer addresses!). Each device is given a number. The first is device number 0.

In the second argument, **lpCaps**, we must pass a pointer to the **WAVEOUTCAPS** structure, which we do by omitting the **ByVal** keyword. And in the third argument, **wSize**, we pass the size of the **WAVEOUTCAPS** record.

Listing 13.5   The DeviceCapsOption_Click() Event Procedure from WAVPLAY2.FRM

```
Sub DeviceCapsOption_Click ()
    Dim Result As Integer
    Dim CapsRecord As WAVEOUTCAPS
    Dim MajorVersion As Integer
    Dim MinorVersion As Integer
    Dim ProductName As String
    Dim Counter As Integer

    Result = waveOutGetDevCaps(0, CapsRecord, Len(CapsRecord))
    If Result = 0 Then
        Picture1.Cls
        Picture1.Print "Manufacturer's Driver ID: "; CapsRecord.wMid
        Picture1.Print "Product ID: "; CapsRecord.wPid
        MajorVersion = CapsRecord.vDriverVersion \ 256
        MinorVersion = CapsRecord.vDriverVersion Mod 256
        Picture1.Print "Driver Version: "; MajorVersion; "."; MinorVersion
        ProductName = Left$(CapsRecord.szPName, InStr(CapsRecord.szPName, Chr$(0)) - 1)
        Picture1.Print "Product Name: "; ProductName
        Picture1.Print "Wave Formats Supported:"
        For Counter = 0 To 11
            If CapsRecord.dwFormats And 2 ^ Counter Then
                Picture1.Print "    "; WaveFormatStringFromConstant(2 ^ Counter)
            End If
        Next Counter
        Picture1.Print "Number of Channels: "; Str$(CapsRecord.wChannels)
        Picture1.Print "Device Functions Supported:"
        For Counter = 0 To 4
            If CapsRecord.dwSupport And 2 ^ Counter Then
                Picture1.Print "    "; WaveFunctionStringFromConstant(2 ^ Counter)
            End If
        Next Counter
    End If
End Sub
```

This event procedure calls two support functions located in WAVPLAY2.BAS, **WaveFormatStringFromConstant()**, shown in Listing 13.6, and **WaveFunctionStringFromConstant()**, shown in Listing 13.7.

Listing 13.6   The WaveFormatStringFromConstant() General Function from WAVPLAY2.BAS

```
Function WaveFormatStringFromConstant (FormatNumber As Long)
    Dim Result As String
```

```
Select Case FormatNumber
  Case WAVE_FORMAT_1M08
      Result = "11.025 kHz, Mono,    8 bit"
  Case WAVE_FORMAT_1S08
      Result = "11.025 kHz, Stereo,  8 bit"
  Case WAVE_FORMAT_1M16
      Result = "11.025 kHz, Mono,   16 bit"
  Case WAVE_FORMAT_1S16
      Result = "11.025 kHz, Stereo, 16 bit"
  Case WAVE_FORMAT_2M08
      Result = "22.05  kHz, Mono,    8 bit"
  Case WAVE_FORMAT_2S08
      Result = "22.05  kHz, Stereo, 8 bit"
  Case WAVE_FORMAT_2M16
      Result = "22.05  kHz, Mono,   16 bit"
  Case WAVE_FORMAT_2S16
      Result = "22.05  kHz, Stereo, 16 bit"
  Case WAVE_FORMAT_4M08
      Result = "44.1   kHz, Mono,    8 bit"
  Case WAVE_FORMAT_4S08
      Result = "44.1   kHz, Stereo, 8 bit"
  Case WAVE_FORMAT_4M16
      Result = "44.1   kHz, Mono,   16 bit"
  Case WAVE_FORMAT_4S16
      Result = "44.1   kHz, Stereo, 16 bit"
  Case Else
      Result = "Invalid Wave Format"
  End Select
WaveFormatStringFromConstant = Result
End Function
```

Listing 13.7   The WaveFunctionStringFromConstant() General Function
from WAVPLAY2.BAS

```
Function WaveFunctionStringFromConstant (FunctionNumber As Long)
    Dim Result As String

    Select Case FunctionNumber
      Case WAVECAPS_PITCH
          Result = "Pitch Control"
      Case WAVECAPS_PLAYBACKRATE
          Result = "Playback Rate Control"
      Case WAVECAPS_VOLUME
          Result = "Volume Control"
      Case WAVECAPS_LRVOLUME
          Result = "Separate Left-Right Volume Control"
      Case WAVECAPS_SYNC
          Result = "Synchronization"
      Case Else
          Result = "Invalid Function"
      End Select
    WaveFunctionStringFromConstant = Result
    End Function
```

Modifying Wave Data with the ChangeLevel() Procedure

One of the simplest things you can do to waveform sample data is change its overall playback volume, known as its amplitude. Each 8 or 16-bit sample represents an amplitude level. To change the overall amplitude, we can multiply each sample by some constant adjustment factor. To increase the amplitude, we raise the peaks of the waves by increasing the positive values and lower their troughs by decreasing the negative values; to decrease the amplitude, we do just the opposite. The only complicating factor is the number of different, incompatible waveform formats. To handle all twelve standard waveform formats, we need to handle four cases. Here's why: The sampling rate doesn't make any difference when it comes to amplitude scaling, so all we need consider are the bit resolution and the number of channels, which gives us four cases. In fact, because the two channels in stereo sample data work just like two separate monaural channels, we could get away with just two cases, one for 8-bit samples and one for 16-bit. However, for more advanced effects, such as reverb and echo (coming up shortly), we will often need to account for the number of channels. Take a look at Listing 13.8 to see how I handled this situation.

Listing 13.8   The ChangeLevel() General Procedure from WAVPLAY2.BAS

```
Sub ChangeLevel (hTheWaveSampleData As Integer, LevelChange As Integer)
    Dim SelWaveSampleData As Integer
    Dim Position As Long
    Dim LevelFactor As Single
    Dim TempValue As Integer
    Dim MonoEightBitSample As MonoEightBitSamples
    Dim StereoEightBitSample As StereoEightBitSamples
    Dim MonoSixteenBitSample As MonoSixteenBitSamples
    Dim StereoSixteenBitSample As StereoSixteenBitSamples
    Dim BytesRead As Long
    Dim BytesWritten As Long
    Dim Dummy As Integer

    SelWaveSampleData = GlobalHandleToSel(hTheWaveSampleData)
    LevelFactor = 1 + LevelChange / 100
    Select Case WaveFormatConstantFromFormat(PCMWaveFmtRecord)
      Case WAVE_FORMAT_1M08, WAVE_FORMAT_2M08, WAVE_FORMAT_4M08
        'MsgBox "Mono 8-bit"
        For Position = 0 To (WaveHeader.dwBufferLength - 1)
            BytesRead = MemoryRead(SelWaveSampleData, Position,
                        MonoEightBitSample, 1)
            TempValue = (Asc(MonoEightBitSample.Char) - 128) * LevelFactor
            MonoEightBitSample.Char = Chr$(MaxInt(MinInt(TempValue, 127), -128) + 128)
```

```
         BytesWritten = MemoryWrite(SelWaveSampleData, Position,
                      MonoEightBitSample, 1)
      Next Position
   'MsgBox "Completed " + Str$(Position) + " Iterations out of " +
    Str$(WaveHeader.dwBufferLength)
 Case WAVE_FORMAT_1S08, WAVE_FORMAT_2S08, WAVE_FORMAT_4S08
   'MsgBox "Stereo 8-bit"
   For Position = 0 To (WaveHeader.dwBufferLength - 2) Step 2
      BytesRead = MemoryRead(SelWaveSampleData, Position,
                   StereoEightBitSample, 2)
      TempValue = (Asc(StereoEightBitSample.LeftChar) - 128) * LevelFactor
      StereoEightBitSample.LeftChar = Chr$(MaxInt(MinInt(TempValue, 127),
                          -128) + 128)
      TempValue = (Asc(StereoEightBitSample.RightChar) - 128) * LevelFactor
      StereoEightBitSample.RightChar = Chr$(MaxInt(MinInt(TempValue, 127),
                           -128) + 128)
      BytesWritten = MemoryWrite(SelWaveSampleData, Position,
                      StereoEightBitSample, 2)
      Next Position
   'MsgBox "Completed " + Str$(Position) + " Iterations out of " +
    Str$(WaveHeader.dwBufferLength)
 Case WAVE_FORMAT_1M16, WAVE_FORMAT_2M16, WAVE_FORMAT_4M16
   'MsgBox "Mono 16-bit"
   For Position = 0 To (WaveHeader.dwBufferLength - 2) Step 2
      BytesRead = MemoryRead(SelWaveSampleData, Position,
                   MonoSixteenBitSample, 2)
      MonoSixteenBitSample.Sample =
        MaxInt(MinInt(MonoSixteenBitSample.Sample * LevelFactor, 32767),
        -32768)
      BytesWritten = MemoryWrite(SelWaveSampleData, Position,
                      MonoSixteenBitSample, 2)
      Next Position
   'MsgBox "Completed " + Str$(Position\2) + " Iterations out of " +
    Str$(WaveHeader.dwBufferLength\2)
 Case WAVE_FORMAT_1S16, WAVE_FORMAT_2S16, WAVE_FORMAT_4S16
   'MsgBox "Stereo 16-bit"
   For Position = 0 To (WaveHeader.dwBufferLength - 4) Step 4
      BytesRead = MemoryRead(SelWaveSampleData, Position,
                   StereoSixteenBitSample, 4)
      StereoSixteenBitSample.LeftSample =
        MaxInt(MinInt(StereoSixteenBitSample.LeftSample * LevelFactor,
        32767), -32768)
      StereoSixteenBitSample.RightSample =
        MaxInt(MinInt(StereoSixteenBitSample.RightSample * LevelFactor,
        32767), -32768)
      BytesWritten = MemoryWrite(SelWaveSampleData, Position,
                      StereoSixteenBitSample, 4)
      Next Position
   'MsgBox "Completed " + Str$(Position \ 2) + " Iterations out of " +
    Str$(WaveHeader.dwBufferLength \ 2)
  End Select
End Sub
```

If we take one case in isolation, the code looks much simpler:

```
SelWaveSampleData = GlobalHandleToSel(hTheWaveSampleData)
LevelFactor = 1 + LevelChange / 100
Select Case WaveFormatConstantFromFormat(PCMWaveFmtRecord)
   Case WAVE_FORMAT_1M08, WAVE_FORMAT_2M08, WAVE_FORMAT_4M08
      'MsgBox "Mono 8-bit"
      For Position = 0 To (WaveHeader.dwBufferLength - 1)
         BytesRead = MemoryRead(SelWaveSampleData, Position,
                     MonoEightBitSample, 1)
         TempValue = (Asc(MonoEightBitSample.Char) - 128) * LevelFactor
         MonoEightBitSample.Char = Chr$(MaxInt(MinInt(TempValue, 127), -128) + 128)
         BytesWritten = MemoryWrite(SelWaveSampleData, Position,
                     MonoEightBitSample, 1)
      Next Position
   'MsgBox "Completed " + Str$(Position) + " Iterations out of " +
      Str$(WaveHeader.dwBufferLength)
```

For 8-bit, monaural sample data, the function reads through the global memory block byte by byte. For each sample, it shifts the value to a zero baseline by subtracting 128, multiplies the value by the level adjustment factor, shifts it back to a 128 baseline, and rewrites the sample to its position in the global memory block. The 16-bit samples are even easier to handle because their values are already signed integers, so all we have to do is multiply them by the **LevelFactor**.

As a case *selector*, we feed the wave format information to another general function called **WaveFormatConstantFromFormat()**, shown in Listing 13.9. This function uses the sampling rate, bit resolution, and number of channels stored in a record of type **PCMWAVEFORMAT** to derive one of the twelve standard wave format constants.

Listing 13.9   The WaveFormatConstantFromFormat() General Function from WAVPLAY2.BAS

```
Function WaveFormatConstantFromFormat (ThePCMWaveFormatRecord As PCMWAVEFORMAT)
   As Long
   Dim SampleRateFactor As Long
   Dim ResolutionFactor As Long
   Dim ChannelsFactor As Long

   SampleRateFactor = (Log(ThePCMWaveFormatRecord.wf.nSamplesPerSec \ 11025) /
                     Log(2)) * 4
   ResolutionFactor = (ThePCMWaveFormatRecord.wBitsPerSample \ 8 - 1) * 2
   ChannelsFactor = ThePCMWaveFormatRecord.wf.nChannels - 1
   WaveFormatConstantFromFormat = 2 ^ (SampleRateFactor + ResolutionFactor +
                     ChannelsFactor)
End Function
```

Implementing the AddEcho() Procedure

It's a little harder to add echo to waveform audio than it is to adjust the volume, but not much. The old-fashioned analog way to create an electronic echo is to take the output of the monitor head on a tape recorder and feed it back to the record head upstream. By adjusting the gain on this feedback loop, an engineer can control the decay rate of the echo—in other words, the change in loudness from one repetition to the next. To change the period of the echo—the delay between repetitions—you have to change the tape speed, because the heads are usually mounted in fixed positions along the tape path.

With a little digital wizardry, we can reproduce the effect of the analog tape loop method, and in the process gain some flexibility. Unlike the tape process, we'll be starting with a complete recording of the original sound, to which we will add echo. For each sample in the waveform recording, we'll pick up an earlier sample, adjust its amplitude, and add the two together. The distance between the two samples will depend on the sampling rate, the number of bytes per sample (a function of both bit resolution and the number of channels), and the time delay we choose. Take a look at the **AddEcho()** procedure in Listing 13.10.

Listing 13.10   The AddEcho() Procedure from WAVPLAY2.BAS

```
Function AddEcho (hTheWaveSampleData As Integer, Delay As Integer, EchoGain As Integer)
    Dim hNewWaveSampleData As Integer
    Dim EchoPeriod As Long
    Dim GainFactor As Single
    Dim lpTheWaveSampleData As Long
    Dim lpNewWaveSampleData As Long
    Dim SelWaveSampleData As Integer
    Dim LastSamplePosition As Long
    Dim Position As Long
    Dim BytesRead As Long
    Dim BytesWritten As Long
    Dim Dummy As Integer

    Dim MonoEightBitSample As MonoEightBitSamples
    Dim PrevMonoEightBitSample As MonoEightBitSamples
    Dim StereoEightBitSample As StereoEightBitSamples
    Dim PrevStereoEightBitSample As StereoEightBitSamples
    Dim MonoSixteenBitSample As MonoSixteenBitSamples
    Dim PrevMonoSixteenBitSample As MonoSixteenBitSamples
    Dim StereoSixteenBitSample As StereoSixteenBitSamples
    Dim PrevStereoSixteenBitSample As StereoSixteenBitSamples
    Const TrailingEchoes = 2

    GainFactor = EchoGain / 50
    EchoPeriod = Delay * PCMWaveFmtRecord.wf.nSamplesPerSec \ 1000
```

```
Select Case WaveFormatConstantFromFormat(PCMWaveFmtRecord)
  Case WAVE_FORMAT_1M08, WAVE_FORMAT_2M08, WAVE_FORMAT_4M08
    'MsgBox "Mono 8-bit"
    hTheWaveSampleData = ExtendGlobalMemBlock(hTheWaveSampleData,
                          WaveHeader.dwBufferLength,
                          WaveHeader.dwBufferLength + EchoPeriod *
                          TrailingEchoes)
    SelWaveSampleData = GlobalHandleToSel(hTheWaveSampleData)
    LastSamplePosition = WaveHeader.dwBufferLength + EchoPeriod *
                          TrailingEchoes - 1
    PrevMonoEightBitSample.Char = Chr$(128)
    ' Initialize new bytes to midpoint value.
    For Position = WaveHeader.dwBufferLength To LastSamplePosition
        BytesWritten = MemoryWrite(SelWaveSampleData, Position,
                        PrevMonoEightBitSample, 1)
    Next Position
    ' Mix in echo.
    For Position = EchoPeriod To LastSamplePosition
        BytesRead = MemoryRead(SelWaveSampleData, Position,
                      MonoEightBitSample, 1)
        ' Retrieve contents of byte at (Position-Period).
        BytesRead = MemoryRead(SelWaveSampleData, Position - EchoPeriod,
                      PrevMonoEightBitSample, 1)
        MonoEightBitSample.Char = Chr$(((Asc(MonoEightBitSample.Char) - 128)
                                  + (Asc(PrevMonoEightBitSample.Char) - 128)
                                  * GainFactor) \ 2 + 128)
        BytesWritten = MemoryWrite(SelWaveSampleData, Position,
                        MonoEightBitSample, 1)
    Next Position
    WaveHeader.dwBufferLength = WaveHeader.dwBufferLength + EchoPeriod *
                                TrailingEchoes
    MsgBox "Completed " + Str$(Position) + " iterations out of " +
      Str$(WaveHeader.dwBufferLength)
  Case WAVE_FORMAT_1S08, WAVE_FORMAT_2S08, WAVE_FORMAT_4S08
    'MsgBox "Stereo 8-bit"
    EchoPeriod = EchoPeriod * 2
    hTheWaveSampleData = ExtendGlobalMemBlock(hTheWaveSampleData,
                          WaveHeader.dwBufferLength,
                          WaveHeader.dwBufferLength + EchoPeriod *
                          TrailingEchoes)
    SelWaveSampleData = GlobalHandleToSel(hTheWaveSampleData)
    LastSamplePosition = WaveHeader.dwBufferLength + EchoPeriod *
                          TrailingEchoes - 2
    PrevStereoEightBitSample.LeftChar = Chr$(128)
    PrevStereoEightBitSample.RightChar = Chr$(128)
    ' Initialize new bytes to midpoint value.
    For Position = WaveHeader.dwBufferLength To LastSamplePosition Step 2
        BytesWritten = MemoryWrite(SelWaveSampleData, Position,
                        PrevStereoEightBitSample, 2)
    Next Position
    ' Mix in echo.
    For Position = EchoPeriod To LastSamplePosition
        BytesRead = MemoryRead(SelWaveSampleData, Position,
                      StereoEightBitSample, 2)
```

```
        ' Retrieve contents of byte at (Position-Period).
        BytesRead = MemoryRead(SelWaveSampleData, Position - EchoPeriod,
                  PrevStereoEightBitSample, 2)
        StereoEightBitSample.LeftChar =
          Chr$(((Asc(StereoEightBitSample.LeftChar) - 128) +
          (Asc(PrevStereoEightBitSample.LeftChar) - 128) * GainFactor) \ 2 + 128)
        StereoEightBitSample.RightChar =
          Chr$(((Asc(StereoEightBitSample.RightChar) - 128) +
          (Asc(PrevStereoEightBitSample.RightChar) - 128) * GainFactor) \ 2 + 128)
        BytesWritten = MemoryWrite(SelWaveSampleData, Position,
                     StereoEightBitSample, 2)
      Next Position
    WaveHeader.dwBufferLength = WaveHeader.dwBufferLength + EchoPeriod *
                        TrailingEchoes
  MsgBox "Completed " + Str$(Position) + " iterations out of " +
    Str$(WaveHeader.dwBufferLength)
Case WAVE_FORMAT_1M16, WAVE_FORMAT_2M16, WAVE_FORMAT_4M16
  'MsgBox "Mono 16-bit"
  EchoPeriod = EchoPeriod * 2
  hTheWaveSampleData = ExtendGlobalMemBlock(hTheWaveSampleData,
                    WaveHeader.dwBufferLength,
                    WaveHeader.dwBufferLength + EchoPeriod *
                    TrailingEchoes)
  SelWaveSampleData = GlobalHandleToSel(hTheWaveSampleData)
  LastSamplePosition = WaveHeader.dwBufferLength + EchoPeriod *
                    TrailingEchoes - 2
  For Position = EchoPeriod To LastSamplePosition Step 2
      BytesRead = MemoryRead(SelWaveSampleData, Position,
                MonoSixteenBitSample, 2)
      ' Retrieve contents of byte at (Position-Period).
      BytesRead = MemoryRead(SelWaveSampleData, Position - EchoPeriod,
                PrevMonoSixteenBitSample, 2)
      MonoSixteenBitSample.Sample = (MonoSixteenBitSample.Sample +
                          PrevMonoSixteenBitSample.Sample *
                          GainFactor) \ 2
      BytesWritten = MemoryWrite(SelWaveSampleData, Position,
                   MonoSixteenBitSample, 2)
    Next Position
  WaveHeader.dwBufferLength = WaveHeader.dwBufferLength + EchoPeriod *
                        TrailingEchoes
Case WAVE_FORMAT_1S16, WAVE_FORMAT_2S16, WAVE_FORMAT_4S16
  'MsgBox "Stereo 16-bit"
  EchoPeriod = EchoPeriod * 4
  hTheWaveSampleData = ExtendGlobalMemBlock(hTheWaveSampleData,
                    WaveHeader.dwBufferLength, WaveHeader.dwBufferLength
                    + EchoPeriod * TrailingEchoes)
  SelWaveSampleData = GlobalHandleToSel(hTheWaveSampleData)
  LastSamplePosition = WaveHeader.dwBufferLength + EchoPeriod *
                    TrailingEchoes - 4
  For Position = EchoPeriod To LastSamplePosition Step 4
      BytesRead = MemoryRead(SelWaveSampleData, Position,
                StereoSixteenBitSample, 4)
      ' Retrieve contents of byte at (Position-Period).
      BytesRead = MemoryRead(SelWaveSampleData, Position - EchoPeriod,
```

```
                        PrevStereoSixteenBitSample, 4)
                StereoSixteenBitSample.LeftSample =
                  (StereoSixteenBitSample.LeftSample +
                  PrevStereoSixteenBitSample.LeftSample * GainFactor) \ 2
                StereoSixteenBitSample.RightSample =
                  (StereoSixteenBitSample.RightSample +
                  PrevStereoSixteenBitSample.RightSample * GainFactor) \ 2
                BytesWritten = MemoryWrite(SelWaveSampleData, Position,
                             StereoSixteenBitSample, 4)
            Next Position
        WaveHeader.dwBufferLength = WaveHeader.dwBufferLength + EchoPeriod *
                             TrailingEchoes
      End Select
    End Function
```

This procedure takes three arguments: a handle to the waveform sample data, the echo **Delay** in milliseconds, and the **EchoGain** given as a whole percentage (here we use 50 for a fifty percent dropoff rate, rather than 0.5).

Just as in the **ChangeLevel()** procedure, the sampling rate is irrelevant, except to determine the **EchoPeriod**. So we can divide all twelve standard waveform data formats into just four cases, based on bit resolution and number of channels.

We need some room at the end of the sound for the trailing echoes, so the first thing we do in each of the four cases is to extend the sample data. I have arbitrarily set the value of **TrailingEchoes** to **2**. The number you use will depend on how much memory you're willing to commit to the waveform sample data, and how much you *attenuate* (reduce the amplitude) the feedback sample with each iteration. With only two extra iterations, you'll often hear a distinct cutoff before the sound entirely fades away. If you wish, increase the value of **TrailingEchoes** until you get the effect you want (you may wish to pass this value in as another argument of the procedure). To pad the waveform sample data in preparation for the echo, we call another general function, **ExtendGlobalMemoryBlock()**, which appears in Listing 13.11. (Once again, I'll leave it to you to add the appropriate error checking—you may ask Windows for another block of global memory whenever you wish, but it may not have any left to give.)

Listing 13.11 The ExtendGlobalMemoryBlock() General Function from WAVPLAY2.BAS.

```
Function ExtendGlobalMemBlock (hMemoryBlock As Integer, OldLength As Long,
  NewLength As Long) As Integer
    Dim hNewMemoryBlock As Integer
    Dim lpNewMemoryBlock As Long
    Dim lpMemoryBlock As Long
    Dim Dummy As Integer
```

```
hNewMemoryBlock = GlobalAlloc(GMEM_MOVEABLE Or GMEM_ZEROINIT, NewLength)
lpMemoryBlock = GlobalLock(hMemoryBlock)
lpNewMemoryBlock = GlobalLock(hNewMemoryBlock)
hmemcpy lpNewMemoryBlock, lpMemoryBlock, OldLength
Dummy = GlobalUnlock(hMemoryBlock)
hMemoryBlock = GlobalFree(hMemoryBlock)
Dummy = GlobalUnlock(hNewMemoryBlock)
ExtendGlobalMemBlock = hNewMemoryBlock
End Function
```

After it obtains the handle to the new global memory block, the function may then need to initialize the new bytes. The **GMEM_ZEROINIT** flag will set all the unused bytes in the block to 0, but for the 8-bit sample data the baseline is 128. The 16-bit formats require no further initialization.

There is no need to change the sample data prior to the first echo, so the **For** loops that mix in the echo effect begin not at the first byte in the sample, but at an offset equal to the echo period, as in this line from the stereo 16-bit format case:

```
For Position = EchoPeriod To LastSamplePosition Step 4
```

When you mix waveform sample data, you need to decide whether to attenuate the overall amplitude of the sample to avoid exceeding the limits of the 8- or 16-bit integer values, or to *clip* the sample at those limits. Clipping is the effect that occurs when you flatten out the top or bottom of a waveform. In **AddEcho()** I have averaged the two samples, which effectively scales them to prevent the mixed result from exceeding the amplitude limits. This will not always sound right. Imagine that you're processing a sound with a steady amplitude—some loud, continuous noise, like a train clattering along its tracks. If that sound already peaks near the limits of the amplitude range, then the averaging method will cause the original sound to suddenly drop its amplitude by half when the first echo begins.

For a more accurate sound, you should use the clipping method. Here's the code for 8-bit clipping:

```
TempValue% = ((Asc(MonoEightBitSample.Char) - 128) +
  (Asc(PrevMonoEightBitSample.Char) - 128) * GainFactor) \ 2 + 128
MonoEightBitSample.Char = Chr$(MinInt(MaxInt(TempValue%, 0), 255))
```

And this code is for 16-bit clipping:

```
TempValue% = (MonoSixteenBitSample.Sample + PrevMonoSixteenBitSample.Sample *
  GainFactor) \ 2
MonoSixteenBitSample.Sample = MinInt(MaxInt(TempValue%, -32768), 32767)
```

Clipping will cause popping and other noise, so if you choose this method, make sure the wave samples start out with low enough peak levels that clipping will rarely occur. You'll still get better results than you would with averaging.

On a more basic level, the biggest problem with this procedure, and also with **ChangeLevel()**, is speed. Some of the performance problems come from VB's interpreted math processing, which can be much slower than similar processing in Holy Trinity languages. But one major performance factor is the number of calls to the ToolHelp API functions, **MemoryRead()** and **MemoryWrite()**. To create an echo effect, we need to call the read function twice and the write function once for each sample. Every function call takes time, especially when you're dealing with operations on global memory blocks. To fine-tune the **ChangeLevel()** and **AddEcho()** procedures, you might try buffering larger chunks of the global memory blocks with arrays. In **ChangeLevel()**, you could use just one buffer; in **AddEcho()**, you would need two, one for the current samples and one for the echo samples. With array buffers, you could reduce the number of global memory operations by a factor of up to 65,536!

The Declarations for WAVPLAY.BAS

WAVPLAY2.BAS has grown considerably since the version we developed in Chapter 3. To support all these functions, you'll need some API functions, data structures, and variables. You'll find them all in the declarations section of the code module, shown in Listing 13.12.

Listing 13.12   The Declarations Section of WAVPLAY2.BAS

```
Option Explicit

Type WAVEOUTCAPS
    wMid As Integer
    wPid As Integer
    vDriverVersion As Integer
    szPName As String * 32
    dwFormats As Long
    wChannels As Integer
    dwSupport As Long
    End Type

Type WAVEFORMAT
    wFormatTag As Integer
    nChannels As Integer
    nSamplesPerSec As Long
    nAvgBytesPerSec As Long
```

```
        nBlockAlign As Integer
    End Type

Type PCMWAVEFORMAT
    wf As WAVEFORMAT
    wBitsPerSample As Integer
    End Type

Type WAVEHDR
    lpData As Long
    dwBufferLength As Long
    dwBytesRecorded As Long
    dwUser As Long
    dwFlags As Long
    dwLoops As Long
    lpNext As Long
    reserved As Long
    End Type

Type FOURCC
    Chars As String * 4
    End Type

Type MMIOINFO
    dwFlags As Long
    fccIOProc As FOURCC
    lpIOProc As Long
    wErrorRet As Integer
    wReserved As Integer
    ' Fields maintained by MMIO functions during buffered IO.
    cchBuffer As Long
    pchBuffer As Long
    pchNext As Long
    pchEndRead As Long
    pchEndWrite As Long
    lBufOffset As Long
    ' Fields maintained by I/O procedure.
    lDiskOffset As Long
    adwInfo As String * 12
    ' Other fields maintained by MMIO.
    dwReserved1 As Long
    dwReserved2 As Long
    hMMIO As Integer
    End Type

 ' RIFF chunk information data structure.
 Type MMCKINFO
    CkId As FOURCC
    CkSize As Long
    fccType As FOURCC
    dwDataOffset As Long
    dwFlags As Long
    End Type
```

```
Declare Function waveOutGetDevCaps Lib "MMSystem" (ByVal wDeviceID As Integer,
    lpCaps As WAVEOUTCAPS, ByVal wSize As Integer) As Integer
Declare Function waveOutOpen Lib "MMSystem" (lphWaveOut As Integer, ByVal
    wDeviceID As Integer, lpFormat As Any, ByVal dwCallBack As Long, ByVal
    dwCallBack As Long, ByVal dwFlags As Long) As Integer
Declare Function waveOutClose Lib "MMSystem" (ByVal hWaveOut As Integer) As Integer
Declare Function waveOutPrepareHeader Lib "MMSystem" (ByVal hWaveOut As Integer,
    lpWaveOutHdr As Any, ByVal wSize As Integer) As Integer
Declare Function waveOutUnprepareHeader Lib "MMSystem" (ByVal hWaveOut As
    Integer, lpWaveOutHdr As Any, ByVal wSize As Integer) As Integer
Declare Function waveOutWrite Lib "MMSystem" (ByVal hWaveOut As Integer,
    lpWaveOutHdr As Any, ByVal wSize As Integer) As Integer
Declare Function mmioOpen Lib "MMSystem" (ByVal szFilename As String, lpMMIOINFO
    As Any, ByVal dwOpenFlags As Long) As Integer
Declare Function mmioClose Lib "MMSystem" (ByVal hMMIO As Integer, ByVal wFlags
    As Integer) As Integer
Declare Function mmioDescend Lib "MMSystem" (ByVal hMMIO As Integer, lpCk As
    Any, lpCkParent As Any, ByVal wFlags As Integer) As Integer
Declare Function mmioAscend Lib "MMSystem" (ByVal hMMIO As Integer, lpCk As Any,
    ByVal wFlags As Integer) As Integer
Declare Function mmioRead Lib "MMSystem" (ByVal hMMIO As Integer, pCh As Any,
    ByVal cCh As Long) As Long
Declare Function mmioReadToGlobal Lib "MMSystem" Alias "mmioRead" (ByVal hMMIO
    As Integer, ByVal lpBuffer As Long, ByVal cCh As Long) As Long
Declare Function lstrcpy Lib "Kernel" (lpString1 As Any, lpString2 As Any) As Long


Global Const WAVE_MAPPER = -1          ' Device ID for Wave Mapper.
Global Const MMIO_READ = &H0&
Global Const MMIO_WRITE = &H1&
Global Const MMIO_READWRITE = &H2&

Global Const MMIO_FINDCHUNK = &H10     ' mmioDescend: find a chunk by ID
Global Const MMIO_FINDRIFF = &H20      ' mmioDescend: find a LIST chunk

Global Const WHDR_DONE = &H1           ' done bit

' flags for dwFlags parameter in waveOutOpen() and waveInOpen()
Global Const WAVE_FORMAT_QUERY = &H1

Global Const WAVECAPS_PITCH = &H1           ' Supports pitch control.
Global Const WAVECAPS_PLAYBACKRATE = &H2    ' Supports playback rate control.
Global Const WAVECAPS_VOLUME = &H4          ' Supports volume control.
Global Const WAVECAPS_LRVOLUME = &H8        ' Supports separate left-right
                                            '   volume control.
Global Const WAVECAPS_SYNC = &H10

Global Const WAVE_INVALIDFORMAT = &H0 ' Invalid Format
Global Const WAVE_FORMAT_1M08 = &H1   ' 11.025 kHz, Mono,   8 bit
Global Const WAVE_FORMAT_1S08 = &H2   ' 11.025 kHz, Stereo, 8 bit
Global Const WAVE_FORMAT_1M16 = &H4   ' 11.025 kHz, Mono,   16 bit
Global Const WAVE_FORMAT_1S16 = &H8   ' 11.025 kHz, Stereo, 16 bit
Global Const WAVE_FORMAT_2M08 = &H10  ' 22.05  kHz, Mono,   8 bit
Global Const WAVE_FORMAT_2S08 = &H20  ' 22.05  kHz, Stereo, 8 bit
Global Const WAVE_FORMAT_2M16 = &H40  ' 22.05  kHz, Mono,   16 bit
```

```
Global Const WAVE_FORMAT_2S16 = &H80  ' 22.05  kHz, Stereo, 16 bit
Global Const WAVE_FORMAT_4M08 = &H100 ' 44.1   kHz, Mono,   8 bit
Global Const WAVE_FORMAT_4S08 = &H200 ' 44.1   kHz, Stereo, 8 bit
Global Const WAVE_FORMAT_4M16 = &H400 ' 44.1   kHz, Mono,  16 bit
Global Const WAVE_FORMAT_4S16 = &H800 ' 44.1   kHz, Stereo, 16 bit

Type MonoEightBitSamples
    Char As String * 1
    End Type

Type StereoEightBitSamples
    LeftChar As String * 1
    RightChar As String * 1
    End Type

Type MonoSixteenBitSamples
    Sample As Integer
    End Type

Type StereoSixteenBitSamples
    LeftSample As Integer
    RightSample As Integer
    End Type

Dim hWaveOut As Integer
Dim WaveHeader As WAVEHDR
Global PCMWaveFmtRecord As PCMWAVEFORMAT
Global hWaveSampleData As Integer
```

Completing the Form-Level Code

We've already covered the longest procedure in the form module, **DeviceCapsOption_Click()**. The other event procedures delegate most of their responsibilities to the general functions and procedures in the code module. You'll find all the code from WAVPLAY2.FRM in Listing 13.13.

Listing 13.13   WAVPLAY2.FRM

```
Option Explicit

Sub DeviceCapsOption_Click ()
    Dim Result As Integer
    Dim CapsRecord As WAVEOUTCAPS
    Dim MajorVersion As Integer
    Dim MinorVersion As Integer
    Dim ProductName As String
    Dim Counter As Integer

    Result = waveOutGetDevCaps(0, CapsRecord, Len(CapsRecord))
    If Result = 0 Then
        Picture1.Cls
        Picture1.Print "Manufacturer's Driver ID: "; CapsRecord.wMid
```

```
    Picture1.Print "Product ID: "; CapsRecord.wPid
    MajorVersion = CapsRecord.vDriverVersion \ 256
    MinorVersion = CapsRecord.vDriverVersion Mod 256
    Picture1.Print "Driver Version: "; MajorVersion; ".";
      MinorVersion'Str$(CapsRecord.vDriverVersion)
    ProductName = Left$(CapsRecord.szPName, InStr(CapsRecord.szPName, Chr$(0)) - 1)
    Picture1.Print "Product Name: "; ProductName
    Picture1.Print "Wave Formats Supported:"
    For Counter = 0 To 11
        If CapsRecord.dwFormats And 2 ^ Counter Then
            Picture1.Print "     "; WaveFormatStringFromConstant(2 ^ Counter)
        End If
        Next Counter
    Picture1.Print "Number of Channels: "; Str$(CapsRecord.wChannels)
    Picture1.Print "Device Functions Supported:"
    For Counter = 0 To 4
        If CapsRecord.dwSupport And 2 ^ Counter Then
            Picture1.Print "     "; WaveFunctionStringFromConstant(2 ^ Counter)
        End If
        Next Counter
    End If
End Sub


Sub EchoOption_Click ()
    Dim Dummy As Integer

    Screen.MousePointer = 11
    PlayOption.Enabled = False
    Dummy = AddEcho(hWaveSampleData, 1000, 50)
    PlayOption.Enabled = True
    Screen.MousePointer = 0
    End Sub


Sub Form_Load ()
    PlayOption.Enabled = False
    VolumeOption.Enabled = False
    EchoOption.Enabled = False
    EffectsMenu.Enabled = False
    End Sub


Sub Form_Unload (Cancel As Integer)
    CloseWavePlay
    End Sub


Sub OpenOption_Click ()
    PlayOption.Enabled = False
    VolumeOption.Enabled = False
    EchoOption.Enabled = False
    EffectsMenu.Enabled = False
    FileOpenDialog.Action = 1
    If OpenWaveFile(FileOpenDialog.Filename) Then
        PlayOption.Enabled = True
```

```
            VolumeOption.Enabled = True
            EchoOption.Enabled = True
            EffectsMenu.Enabled = True
            Picture1.Cls
            Picture1.Print "Format: "; WaveFormatConstantFromFormat(PCMWaveFmtRecord)
            Picture1.Print "   Sample Rate: "; PCMWaveFmtRecord.wf.nSamplesPerSec; " Hz"
            Picture1.Print "    Resolution: "; PCMWaveFmtRecord.wBitsPerSample
            Picture1.Print "      Channels: "; PCMWaveFmtRecord.wf.nChannels
        End If
    End Sub

Sub PlayOption_Click ()
    Dim Dummy As Integer

    Dummy = WaveOut()
    End Sub

Sub QuitOption_Click ()
    Unload WavePlay
    End
    End Sub

Sub VolumeOption_Click ()
    Dim Dummy As Integer

    Screen.MousePointer = 11
    PlayOption.Enabled = False
    ChangeLevel hWaveSampleData, -50
    PlayOption.Enabled = True
    Screen.MousePointer = 0
    End Sub
```

Real-Time Audio Effects

In the previous project we explored ways to manipulate waveform data at the byte level. By using the low-level sound functions in the multimedia API, we were able to load a WAVE file into memory and trigger instant replay. On the other hand, while we were also able to modify the individual digital sample values to change the overall amplitude of the recording and to add echo effects, those operations were anything but instantaneous.

Imagine what we could do if we could manipulate wave data on the fly. We could combine WAVE files to produce effects for the ears that were as compelling and interactive as sprite animation is to the eyes. But clearly, based on our experience so far, it wouldn't be possible in VB to do something even so basic as mixing multiple WAVE files in real time. VB just doesn't have the horsepower...not by itself, that is.

Introducing WaveMix

As Microsoft continues to expand and refine the multimedia features of Windows, they have occasionally tossed us new components with which to tinker. One of the hottest libraries lately is a real-time waveaudio mixer, known appropriately as *WaveMix*. Although Microsoft officials are quick to remind us that this is not a *supported product*, the author of the library, Angel Diaz, has been answering all sorts of questions by way of CompuServe (GO WINMM). There are two consequences to using an unsupported product. First, because it is a work in progress, it may have bugs. And second, future releases may not provide complete backward compatibility. But WaveMix is so useful and so easy to use, it's worth tolerating these minor inconveniences. And someday, when it matures enough, WaveMix may become an offical component of the Windows Multimedia System. If it does, you can be among the privileged few who can claim they were listening to it before it went commercial.

WaveMix is contained entirely in a single file called WAVEMIX.DLL. Although it will work fine by itself, WAVEMIX.DLL can be configured by setting various constants in a file called WAVEMIX.INI, an unusual feature for a DLL.

Mixing Waves in Real Time

The WaveMix API consists of 12 functions. In this project we'll use most of them. Follow these steps to see just how useful this product can be:

1. Install WAVEMIX.DLL and test it out.
2. Create a form with seven Command Buttons.
3. Add the API declarations to the WAVEMIX.BAS code module (Listing 13.14).
4. Add the event procedures to WAVEMIX.FRM.

You'll find this project in the subdirectory \VBMAGIC in the files WAVEMIX.MAK, WAVEMIX.FRM, and WAVEMIX.BAS. You'll also need WAVEMIX.DLL and WAVEMIX.INI, which are located in the directory \WAVEMIX. The sample WAVE files 1.WAV through 7.WAV are supplied by Microsoft with the WAVEMIX.DLL. They too are located in the \WAVEMIX directory.

Installing and Testing WaveMix

Before you can run the demonstration program, you have to install the WaveMix DLL. This couldn't be much simpler. Copy the files WAVEMIX.DLL and

WAVEMIX.INI from the directory \WAVEMIX on the companion CD-ROM into your \WINDOWS\SYSTEM directory. That's it.

Next, load and run WAVEMIX.MAK. The program displays a simple form with seven Command Buttons, as shown in Figure 13.3.

To play any of the seven sounds individually, simply click on a button. To play more than one sound simultaneously, click several buttons. If you click on the same button repeatedly, the WAVE file attached to that button will be queued up to play once for each click.

To stop the program, use the Control menu, or the Quit option on the form's own File menu. If you stop the program with the VB End button or menu option, the waveaudio device driver will become locked. If this happens, the only way to reactivate the waveaudio device is to restart Windows.

Create the Form

For this project we'll need just one form. In the sample program on the companion CD-ROM, I haved named it WaveMixForm, but we won't reference the form name anywhere in the program so you may name it whatever you wish.

Place a Command Button on the form and set its **Name** property to PlayWaveButton. Then add six more Command Buttons with the same name. When you add the second button, VB will ask you if you wish to create a control array. Click on the Yes button. Then add the five remaining buttons. Set the button captions to "1" through "7."

We'll also need a File menu with one option, Quit. If you wish, you can dispense with the File menu and place the Quit option directly on the menu bar. Set the **Name** property of the Quit option to QuitOption.

The WaveMix API

In some ways, the WaveMix API resembles the GDI, although it's much simpler. You prepare to play waveaudio through the mixer by calling a function that returns a handle to a mixer *session*. You then use that handle to open *channels* and *waves*, which is a little like creating a GDI device context and

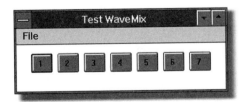

Figure 13.3 *WAVEMIX.FRM at runtime.*

selecting in drawing objects and bitmaps. When you're done playing sound, you have to close the channels and waves, and release the *session*.

A complete session with WaveMix actually requires at least eight steps, four to set things up, one to play the WAVE clip, and three to shut down:

1. Call either **WaveMixInit()** or **WaveMixConfigureInit()** to initialize the DLL and acquire a handle to a mix session.

2. Call **WaveMixOpenWave()** to open a WAVE file. If you're working in a Holy Trinity language, you can also open wave resources. Or if you wish, you may open waves you've loaded into memory with the multimedia IO functions.

3. Call **WaveMixOpenChannel()** to open one or more of the eight available mixer channels.

4. Call **WaveMixActivate()** to grab the waveaudio output device. This function enables your application to share the device with other applications.

5. Call **WaveMixPlay()** to feed a WAVE to a channel.

6. Call **WaveMixCloseChannel()** to close one or more open channels.

7. Call **WaveMixFreeWave()** to release a WAVE file or resource.

8. Call **WaveMixCloseSession()** to end the mixer session.

Along with these essential functions, the API includes three others. The first function, **WaveMixFlushChannel()**, will clear the queue of WAVEs waiting to play on the specified channel, and will stop the WAVE that is currently playing. You can flush a single channel, or all open channels with a single call.

WaveMixPump() works like a specialized version of the VB function **DoEvents**. WaveMix works by slicing off and adding together small chunks of sample data from each of the open channels. It passes these mixed chunks to the waveaudio device through the device driver's queue. WaveMix has to perform all that arithmetic at least as fast as the waveaudio device can play it. At sampling rates that begin at 11.025 KHz, that's quite a juggling act! If your program does a lot of processing, however, WaveMix will not get enough processor time to prepare these buffers, and the device driver's queue will empty, causing playback interruptions. To keep WaveMix from falling behind, scatter calls to **WaveMixPump()** throughout your program.

The last function, **WaveMixGetInfo()**, will retrieve some basic information about the WaveMix DLL, including its version number, its compilation date, and a list of supported wave formats.

The declarations for all twelve WaveMix functions, along with their required data structures and constants, appear in Listing 13.14.

Listing 13.14   WAVEMIX.BAS

```
Option Explicit

Type MIXCONFIG
    wSize As Integer
    dwFlags As Long
    wChannels As Integer
    wSamplingRate As Integer '(11=11025, 22=22050, 44=44100 Hz)
    End Type

Type MIXPLAYPARAMS
    wSize As Integer
    hMixSession As Integer
    iChannel As Integer
    lpMixWave As Long
    hWndNotify As Integer
    dwFlags As Long
    wLoops As Integer ' = &HFFFF means loop forever
    End Type

Type WAVEMIXINFO
    wSize As Integer
    Version As Integer
    Date As String * 12
    dwFormats As Long
    End Type

Type Boolean
    Byte As String * 1
    End Type

Declare Function WaveMixInit Lib "WaveMix.DLL" () As Integer
Declare Function WaveMixConfigureInit Lib "WaveMix.DLL" (lpConfig As MIXCONFIG)
    As Integer
Declare Function WaveMixActivate Lib "WaveMix.DLL" (ByVal hMixSession As Inte-
    ger, ByVal fActivate As Integer) As Integer
Declare Function WaveMixOpenWave Lib "WaveMix.DLL" (ByVal hMixSession As Inte-
    ger, ByVal szWaveFilename As String, ByVal hInst As Integer, ByVal dwFlags As
    Long) As Long
Declare Function WaveMixOpenChannel Lib "WaveMix.DLL" (ByVal hMixSession As
    Integer, ByVal iChannel As Integer, ByVal dwFlags As Long) As Integer
Declare Function WaveMixPlay Lib "WaveMix.DLL" (lpMixPlayParams As
    MIXPLAYPARAMS) As Integer
Declare Function WaveMixFlushChannel Lib "WaveMix.DLL" (ByVal hMixSession As
    Integer, ByVal iChannel As Integer, ByVal dwFlags As Long) As Integer
Declare Function WaveMixCloseChannel Lib "WaveMix.DLL" (ByVal hMixSession As
    Integer, ByVal iChannel As Integer, ByVal dwFlags As Long) As Integer
Declare Function WaveMixFreeWave Lib "WaveMix.DLL" (ByVal hMixSession As Inte-
    ger, ByVal lpMixWave As Long) As Integer
Declare Function WaveMixCloseSession Lib "WaveMix.DLL" (ByVal hMixSession As
    Integer) As Integer
Declare Sub WaveMixPump Lib "WaveMix.DLL" ()
```

```
Declare Function WaveMixGetInfo Lib "WaveMix.DLL" (lpWaveMixInfo As WAVEMIXINFO)
    As Integer

' Wave Format Constants for WAVEMIXINFO
Global Const WAVE_FORMAT_1M08 = &H1    ' 11.025 kHz, Mono,   8 bit
Global Const WAVE_FORMAT_1S08 = &H2    ' 11.025 kHz, Stereo, 8 bit
Global Const WAVE_FORMAT_1M16 = &H4    ' 11.025 kHz, Mono,   16 bit
Global Const WAVE_FORMAT_1S16 = &H8    ' 11.025 kHz, Stereo, 16 bit
Global Const WAVE_FORMAT_2M08 = &H10   ' 22.05  kHz, Mono,   8 bit
Global Const WAVE_FORMAT_2S08 = &H20   ' 22.05  kHz, Stereo, 8 bit
Global Const WAVE_FORMAT_2M16 = &H40   ' 22.05  kHz, Mono,   16 bit
Global Const WAVE_FORMAT_2S16 = &H80   ' 22.05  kHz, Stereo, 16 bit
Global Const WAVE_FORMAT_4M08 = &H100  ' 44.1   kHz, Mono,   8 bit
Global Const WAVE_FORMAT_4S08 = &H200  ' 44.1   kHz, Stereo, 8 bit
Global Const WAVE_FORMAT_4M16 = &H400  ' 44.1   kHz, Mono,   16 bit
Global Const WAVE_FORMAT_4S16 = &H800  ' 44.1   kHz, Stereo, 16 bit

' Flag values for MIXPLAYPARAMS.
Global Const WMIX_QUEUEWAVE = &H0
Global Const WMIX_CLEARQUEUE = &H1
Global Const WMIX_USELRUCHANNEL = &H2
Global Const WMIX_HIGHPRIORITY = &H4
Global Const WMIX_WAIT = &H8

' Flag values for MIXCONFIG.
Global Const WMIX_CONFIG_CHANNELS = &H1
Global Const WMIX_CONFIG_SAMPLINGRATE = &H2


' Flag values for WaveMixOpenWave().
Global Const WMIX_FILE = &H1
Global Const WMIX_RESOURCE = &H2
Global Const WMIX_MEMORY = &H4

' Flag values for WaveMixOpenChannel().
Global Const WMIX_OPENSINGLE = 0   ' Opens the single channel specified by iChannel.
Global Const WMIX_OPENALL = 1      ' Opens all the channels, iChannel is ignored.
Global Const WMIX_OPENCOUNT = 2    ' Opens iChannel Channels (e.g. if iChannel = 4
                                   ' will create channels 0-3).

' Flag values for WaveMixFlushChannel() and WaveMixCloseChannel().
Global Const WMIX_ALL = &H1        ' Stops sound on all the channels, iChannel
                                   ' is ignored.
Global Const WMIX_NOREMIX = &H2    ' Prevents the currently submited blocks from
                                   ' being remixed to exclude the new channel.
```

NOTE: *Microsoft's preliminary documentation for WaveMix is located in the file WAVEMIX.TXT, in the \ WAVEMIX subdirectory on the companion CD-ROM. In this directory you will also find a file named MIXDESCR.DOC, a brief document in Word for Windows format that discusses the mixer's theory of operation.*

Adding the Event Procedures to the Form Module

In this demonstration program, we'll handle the four steps that open and prepare a WaveMix session in the **Form_Load()** event procedure, as shown in Listing 13.15.

Listing 13.15   The Form_Load() Event Procedure from WAVEMIX.FRM

```
Sub Form_Load ()
    Dim Counter As Integer
    Dim RetValue As Integer

    WaveMixConfiguration.wSize = Len(WaveMixConfiguration)
    WaveMixConfiguration.dwFlags = WMIX_CONFIG_CHANNELS Or WMIX_CONFIG_SAMPLINGRATE
    WaveMixConfiguration.wChannels = 2
    WaveMixConfiguration.wSamplingRate = 11
    hThisMixSession = WaveMixConfigureInit(WaveMixConfiguration)
    WaveFiles(1) = "f:\wavemix\041094\1.wav"
    WaveFiles(2) = "f:\wavemix\041094\2.wav"
    WaveFiles(3) = "f:\wavemix\041094\3.wav"
    WaveFiles(4) = "f:\wavemix\041094\4.wav"
    WaveFiles(5) = "f:\wavemix\041094\5.wav"
    WaveFiles(6) = "f:\wavemix\041094\6.wav"
    WaveFiles(7) = "f:\wavemix\041094\7.wav"
    For Counter = 1 To 7
        lpMixWaves(Counter) = WaveMixOpenWave(hThisMixSession, WaveFiles(Counter),
                          0, WMIX_FILE)
    Next Counter
    RetValue = WaveMixOpenChannel(hThisMixSession, 0, WMIX_ALL)
    If RetValue Then
        MsgBox "Unable to open channels.", 16, "WaveMix Error"
        Unload WaveMixForm
        End
    End If
    RetValue = WaveMixActivate(hThisMixSession, True)
End Sub
```

In this procedure we're calling **WaveMixConfigureInit()**, which takes one argument, a structure of type **MIXCONFIG**. The alternative function, **WaveMixInit()**, takes no argument, but instead gets its initialization data from the WAVEMIX.INI file, which must be located in the same directory as WAVEMIX.DLL, usually \WINDOWS\SYSTEM.

In the call to **WaveMixOpenWave()** we use the constant **WMIX_FILE** to indicate that we want the DLL to open the WAVE data files for us, rather than look for WAVE resources, or for copies pre-loaded into memory. Since we can't load resources in VB, the third parameter of this function, **hInst**, will always be **0**.

Rather than open seven channels, one by one, we call **WaveMixOpenChannel()** with the **WMIX_ALL** flag, which opens all eight mixer channels. We have only seven WAVE files to play, so the eighth channel will remain idle; if you wish, you can add a WAVE file of your own. In this case, the function will ignore its second argument, **iChannel**, which normally specifies the channel to open.

Finally, we call **WaveMixActivate()** to turn on the mixer session.

Playing the Waves

We feed the WAVEs to the mixer channels in the **PlayWaveButton_Click()** event procedure, as shown in Listing 13.16.

Listing 13.16   The PlayWaveButton_Click() Event Procedure from WAVEMIX.FRM

```
Sub PlayWaveButton_Click (Index As Integer)
    Dim RetValue As Integer
    Dim MixPlayParameters As MIXPLAYPARAMS

    MixPlayParameters.wSize = Len(MixPlayParameters)
    MixPlayParameters.hMixSession = hThisMixSession
    MixPlayParameters.iChannel = Index
    MixPlayParameters.lpMixWave = lpMixWaves(Index + 1)
    MixPlayParameters.hWndNotify = 0
    MixPlayParameters.dwFlags = WMIX_HIGHPRIORITY
    MixPlayParameters.wLoops = 0
    RetValue = WaveMixPlay(MixPlayParameters)
    End Sub
```

Instead of a long list of parameters, **WaveMixPlay()** takes a single argument, a pointer to a structure of type **MIXPLAYPARAMS**, which contains the actual control parameters. In the **MixPlayParameters** record we associate a WAVE with a channel. There is no relationship between the order in which you open WAVEs and the order in which you open channels. WAVEs are assigned to channels only in the call to **WaveMixPlay()**. In fact, you may feed the same wave to multiple channels. You may also feed multiple WAVEs to the same channel; WaveMix will play them in the order submitted.

Besides the handle to the session, the channel number, and the pointer to the open WAVE sample data, the structure also holds three other parameters. The **hWndNotify** field can accept a handle to a window. When it has finished playing the submitted WAVE, WaveMix will send a notification message to the window specified by that handle. However, without the addition of a custom control, we cannot intercept that message from a VB program, so we set the handle to NULL (zero).

The fifth field, **dwFlags**, specifies how the newly submitted WAVE should affect the queue for the channel and the waveaudio device. There are five flag constants:

WMIX_QUEUEWAVE will simply add the new WAVE to the existing queue.

WMIX_CLEARQUEUE will clear the queue before submitting the new waveform data.

WMIX_HIGHPRIORITY—the flag used in the sample program—causes WaveMix to cancel and remix the data already submitted to the device driver, which can prevent a noticeable delay between the call to **WaveMixPlay()** and actual playback on the device.

WMIX_USELRUCHANNEL causes WaveMix to play the WAVE on the first available, or least recently used channel. The documentation says that you should use this flag in combination with either **WMIX_QUEUEWAVE** or **WMIX_CLEARQUEUE**, but not both.

WMIX_WAIT will queue the WAVE, but will not begin playback until the next time **WaveMixPlay()** is called without the wait flag. You can use this feature to queue up several WAVEs for simultaneous playback.

To prevent a playback delay when you resubmit a WAVE to the same channel you have two options. You can combine the flags **WMIX_CLEARQUEUE** and **WMIX_HIGHPRIORITY**:

```
MixPlayParameters.dwFlags = WMIX_HIGHPRIORITY Or WMIX_CLEARQUEUE
```

Or you can use the function **WaveMixFlushChannel()** to clear the channel before you submit the next WAVE:

```
RetValue = WaveMixFlushChannel(hThisMixSession, Index, WMIX_NOREMIX)
```

You may ask WaveMix to repeat a WAVE by setting the **wLoops** field. To force the WAVE to loop indefinitely, set this field to &HFFFF, which causes the WAVE to repeat until you flush, pre-empt, or close the channel.

Completing the Form Module

The remaining code in the form module includes a handful of declarations, and the housekeeping event procedures, as shown in Listing 13.17.

Listing 13.17   The Remaining Declarations and Event Procedures from WAVEMIX.FRM

```
Option Explicit

Dim WaveMixConfiguration As MIXCONFIG
Dim hThisMixSession As Integer
```

```
Dim WaveFiles(7) As String
Dim lpMixWaves(7) As Long

Sub Form_Activate ()
    Dim RetValue As Integer

    RetValue = WaveMixActivate(hThisMixSession, True)
    End Sub

Sub Form_Deactivate ()
    Dim RetValue As Integer

    RetValue = WaveMixActivate(hThisMixSession, False)
    End Sub

Sub Form_Unload (Cancel As Integer)
    Dim Counter As Integer
    Dim RetValue As Integer

    RetValue = WaveMixCloseChannel(hThisMixSession, 0, WMIX_ALL)
    For Counter = 1 To 7
        lpMixWaves(Counter) = WaveMixFreeWave(hThisMixSession, lpMixWaves(Counter))
        Next Counter
    RetValue = WaveMixCloseSession(hThisMixSession)
    End Sub

Sub QuitOption_Click ()
    Unload WaveMixForm
    End
    End Sub
```

Recording Waveaudio

Besides all the playback features we've covered in this chapter and in Chapters 3 and 4, the multimedia system also supports WAVE recording. For many of the **waveOut** functions, you will find corresponding **waveIn** functions. However, because of VB's inability to support callback functions, the easiest way to record WAVE data is to use the MCI.

Using MCI to Record Waveaudio

In this brief project we'll use the API function **mciSendString()** to record Waveaudio. Follow these steps to see how this works:

1. Create a simple form with three Command Buttons.
2. Add the form code, including the declarations for **mciSendString()** and a few variables (Listing 13.18).

You'll find this program in the subdirectory \VBMAGIC in the files
WAVERCRD.MAK and *WAVERCRD.FRM*.

Running the Program

When you run WAVERCRD.MAK, it will display a small form with three Command Buttons, as shown in Figure 13.4.

Make sure you have some kind of input audio source ready, such as a microphone or an audio CD playing in your CD-ROM drive. You may need to select an input source using the mixer application that came with your sound card. For specific instructions, consult the user guide for your sound card.

When your input source is ready, click on the Record Command Button to begin recording. Wait a few seconds, then click on the Command Button labeled Stop and Save. You may then click on the Play Command Button to replay your recording.

Creating the Form

Place three Command Buttons on a new form, and name them RecordButton, StopButton, and PlayButton. The complete property list, declarations section, and program code for this project appears in Listing 13.18.

Listing 13.18   WAVERCRD.FRM

```
VERSION 2.00
Begin Form WaveRecordForm
    Caption         =   "Wave Recording"
    ClientHeight    =   3156
```

Figure 13.4 *WAVERCRD.FRM at runtime.*

```
ClientLeft       =    876
ClientTop        =    1524
ClientWidth      =    3072
Height           =    3576
Left             =    828
LinkTopic        =    "Form1"
ScaleHeight      =    3156
ScaleWidth       =    3072
Top              =    1152
Width            =    3168
Begin CommandButton StopButton
   Caption       =    "&Stop and Save"
   Height        =    552
   Left          =    720
   TabIndex      =    2
   Top           =    1380
   Width         =    1572
End
Begin CommandButton PlayButton
   Caption       =    "&Play"
   Height        =    552
   Left          =    720
   TabIndex      =    1
   Top           =    2340
   Width         =    1692
End
Begin CommandButton RecordButton
   Caption       =    "&Record"
   Height        =    552
   Left          =    660
   TabIndex      =    0
   Top           =    360
   Width         =    1692
End
End
Option Explicit

Declare Function mciSendString Lib "MMSystem" (ByVal lpstrCommand As String,
   ByVal lpstrReturnString As String, ByVal wReturnLength As Integer, ByVal
   hCallback As Integer) As Long

Dim CommandString As String
Dim ReturnString As String * 255
Dim RetValue As Long

Sub PlayButton_Click ()
   Dim CommandString As String

   CommandString = "play " & App.Path & "\TestFile.Wav"
   RetValue = mciSendString(CommandString, ReturnString, 256, 0)
   End Sub
```

```
Sub RecordButton_Click ()
    RetValue = mciSendString("Open New type WaveAudio alias wave", ReturnString,
        256, 0)
    RetValue = mciSendString("set wave bitpersample 8", ReturnString, 256, 0)
    RetValue = mciSendString("set wave samplespersec 11025", ReturnString, 256, 0)
    RetValue = mciSendString("set wave channels 2", ReturnString, 256, 0)
    RetValue = mciSendString("record wave", ReturnString, 256, 0)
    End Sub

Sub StopButton_Click ()
    Dim CommandString As String

    RetValue = mciSendString("stop wave", ReturnString, 256, 0)
    CommandString = "save wave " & App.Path & "\TestFile.Wav"
    RetValue = mciSendString(CommandString, ReturnString, 256, 0)
    RetValue = mciSendString("close wave", ReturnString, 256, 0)
    End Sub
```

With a handful of MCI commands, and the functions we explored earlier in this chapter and in Chapters 3 and 4, you can create your own complete WAVE recording and editing system.

Learn to successfully add
music to your programs
with MIDI.

Using the
Musical Instrument
Digital Interface

t the 1982 convention of the National Association of Music Manufacturers,
a revolution started in the electronic music industry. Korg and Kawai, two
of the largest makers of electronic musical instruments, drove the Golden
Spike of the music industry when they linked together their instruments with
the new Musical Instrument Digital Interface (MIDI). The music industry has
never looked back. MIDI now occupies a prominent place and has appeared
in hundreds of thousands of recordings and live performances. Almost any
electronic device from the humblest portable keyboards to 48-channel studio
mixers, includes a set of MIDI ports.

These simple five pin connectors offer some of the most thrilling opportu-
nities for budding multimedia moguls. But, along with its phenomenal benefits, MIDI has also opened the door to corridors of confusion. Before you
can fully appreciate MIDI's potential, you need to grasp some MIDI funda-
mentals. Let's take a closer look at what MIDI does and how it works, and
then we'll explore how to access MIDI devices from our VB apps.

Everything You Need to Know about MIDI

Most MIDI devices—electronic keyboards, modular synthesizers, audio mixers, drum machines, and so on—are external. They talk to each other over a three-wire cable. You might not realize it but your sound card includes a MIDI compatible synthesizer. This MIDI device lives inside your computer and it talks directly to your computer's bus. Most sound cards let you hook up additional MIDI devices through a set of MIDI ports known as *In*, *Out*, and *Through*.

MIDI is actually a real-time interactive network. In theory, any device that includes at least one MIDI In and one MIDI Out port can talk to any other MIDI device. Many MIDI devices also offer a MIDI Through port to pass along data that comes in the MIDI In port. MIDI devices are not limited to three ports, however. In fact, many products provide several ports in various combinations of the three types.

The Musical Connection

When most people hear the term "MIDI," they think of musical applications. After all, the letter "M" in MIDI stands for Musical. But as we explore MIDI's musical features, keep in mind that it has grown far beyond its original specifications.

At the hardware level, MIDI provides a simple asynchronous serial interface that transmits data in ten bit chunks at a rate of 31.25 kilobaud (31,250 bits per second). The ten bits include a start bit, eight data bits, and a stop bit. Although we won't be dealing with many hardware issues in this chapter, you'll want to remember the transmission rate when you create your MIDI apps.

The data that travels through the MIDI cable controls electronic musical instruments—synthesizers. Before MIDI, in the late 1970s, as these instruments began to acquire the sophistication of digital electronics, their manufacturers developed various proprietary systems for interconnecting their products. Their main goal was to create integrated musical workshops so that musicians could compose and play music on several instruments simultaneously. This required at least one synthesizer, along with a device that could record what was played as a *sequence* of control events, or keypresses, just like a player piano roll. With such as system, you could later substitute a different note, change the duration of a note, or eliminate a note entirely without re-recording the entire passage. And because you were only recording keystrokes (rather than analog waveforms) you could even change the tempo of the music without changing its pitch, or transpose the pitch without changing the tempo. These recording devices became known as *sequencers*. And once that problem was solved, it didn't take long for most manufacturers to recognize the need for a standard protocol to link sequencers and synthesizers. That's how MIDI was born. Figure 14.1 shows a typical MIDI hardware setup.

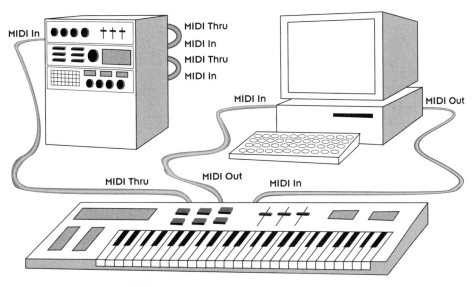

Figure 14.1 *A typical MIDI hardware setup.*

Once you can make a sequencer talk to a synthesizer, you can make synthesizers talk to each other. If you plug the MIDI Out port of one instrument into the MIDI In port of a second instrument, you can play the second synthesizer from the keyboard of the first. Most manufacturers now offer their major models in two versions, one with a keyboard and one without. Keyboardless versions are usually called *synthesizer modules* and they often come in "rack mount" cabinets. In the pre-MIDI era, keyboard players like Rick Wakeman and Keith Emerson, often appeared on stage in synthesizer pods, surrounded by walls of keyboards. Like space aliens in their cockpits, they flailed around from instrument to instrument, which made for a flashy performance, but created a setup nightmare. Today, performing keyboardists may play one or two keyboards on stage, controlling dozens of instruments stacked neatly out of the way in racks.

A Look at MIDI Messages

MIDI devices communicate by sending each other messages. Messages are divided into two general categories—*channel* and *system*—and into five types—*voice, mode, system common, system real-time,* and *system exclusive.*

The first category, *channel messages*, includes *voice messages* and *mode messages*. These messages are grouped into the channel message category because they are transmitted on individual channels rather than globally to all devices in the MIDI network. To understand how MIDI devices identify channels, let's take some time to review the structure of a MIDI message.

As shown in Figure 14.2, a MIDI message includes a *status byte* and up to two *data bytes*. It's easy to identify a status byte because all status bytes have their most significant bit set to 1. Conversely, the most significant bit of any data byte is set to 0. This convention holds for all standard MIDI messages and not just channel messages. Therefore, the data in each byte must be encoded in the seven remaining bits.

MIDI devices transmit all messages on the same cable, regardless of their channel assignments. In the early days of MIDI, musicians and recording engineers were accustomed to 48 track audio mixers, tangled patch panels, and fat umbilical cords stuffed with wire. These folks had a hard time understanding that they didn't need a separate cable for each MIDI channel. The four low-order bits of each status byte identify which channel it belongs to. Four bits produce 16 possible combinations, so MIDI supports 16 channels over a single cable string. (Keep in mind that although MIDI users and vendors number the channels from 1 through 16, internally they are numbered 0 through 15.) The three remaining bits identify the message. Three bits encode eight possible combinations, so channel messages could come in eight flavors, but they don't. A status byte with all four high-order bits set to 1 indicates a system common message—the second general category, which we'll get to after we tackle the channel messages. So there are only seven channel messages.

The Channel Voice Messages

Most of the channel messages are voice messages, as shown in Table 14.1. Voice messages:

- Instruct the receiving instrument to assign particular sounds to its *voices*
- Turn notes on and off
- Send *controller* signals that can alter how the currently active note(s) sounds

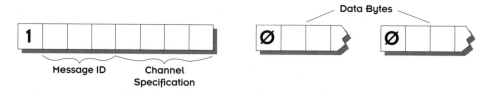

Figure 14.2　*How MIDI messages are structured.*

Table 14.1 *MIDI Channel Voice Messages*

Voice Message	Status Byte Hex Value	Number of Data Bytes
Note Off	&H8x	2
Note On	&H9x	2
Polyphonic Aftertouch	&HAx	2
Control Change	&HBx	2
Program Change	&HCx	1
Aftertouch	&HDx	1
Pitch Bend	&HEx	1 or 2

A voice is the portion of the synthesizer that produces sound. Most modern synthesizers have several voices, that is, they have several circuits that work independently and simultaneously to produce sounds of different *timbre* and *pitch*. Timbre is the sound that the instrument will imitate, such as a flute, cello, or a helicopter. Pitch is the musical note that the instrument plays. To play two notes together, the synthesizer uses two voices. Those voices may play two notes with the same timbre, or may play two notes of different timbres. A Control Change message *modulates* the current note by altering its pitch, volume, or timbre to produce various effects, such as vibrato or tremolo.

Voice messages are followed by either one or two data bytes. A Note On message, for example, is followed by two bytes, one to identify the note, and one to specify the *velocity*. The velocity specifies how the note should sound. For example, if the synthesizer's voice is set to sound like a piano, the velocity could determine how loudly the note should be played. (In the keyboard world, the faster you strike a piano key, the louder it plays.) To play note number 80 with maximum velocity on channel 13, the MIDI device would send these three hexadecimal byte values:

```
&H9C &H50 &H7F
```

To turn off the note, it would send either the Note Off message:

```
&H8C &H50 &H00
```

or the Note On message with a velocity of 0:

```
&H9C &H50 &H00
```

NOTE: *The Note Off channel voice message accepts a velocity because some synthesizers can use the* release velocity *to determine how a note should decay once it has been shut off. Almost any instrument will accept a Note On message with a velocity of 0 in lieu of a Note Off message.*

Often you will hear musicians and synthesizer technicians use the term *patches*. Each synthesizer make and model offers unique controls for designing and setting timbres. A patch is the control settings that define a particular timbre. The actual contents of a patch depend on the particular instrument, so rather than sending the whole patch to the instrument through MIDI (although this is also possible), the Program Change voice message sends a number from 0 to 127 to select a patch already stored in the instrument's own *voice bank* memory. For example, to set the instrument on channel 13 to its patch 104, you would send it the MIDI message:

&HCC &H68

Four of the channel voice messages—Control Change, Polyphonic Aftertouch, Aftertouch, and Pitch Bend—signal a *controller* change. For example, when a saxophone player blows harder, his instrument may sound harsher. By cleverly programming the synthetic saxophone, a keyboard musician can use a slider, foot pedal, or some other device to simulate the breath control of a sax player. Let's take a look at these voice message types.

Pitch Bend was so common on synthesizers when the MIDI specification was created that it was given its own MIDI message (&HEx). This message signals the synthesizer to raise or lower the pitch of currently active notes on the channel. Pitch Bend messages do not contain note values. The value of the Pitch Bend message bytes reflects the degree to which the pitch bend controller (usually a wheel or lever beside the keyboard) has been moved up or down. The degree to which the pitch changes is up to the instrument itself.

Like Pitch Bend, *Aftertouch* was considered valuable and common enough to be granted its own MIDI message types. The first type of Aftertouch, known as *Polyphonic Aftertouch* (&HAx), transmits a value on a particular channel, for a particular note, that indicates the degree of pressure on the key after it has been struck. Many electronic keyboards now support this feature, which enables keyboard players to get some of the control that other musicians get by changing the pressure on their mouthpieces or bows. The other Aftertouch control message (&HDx) is used when an instrument supports aftertouch, but not on individual notes. In other words, a change in pressure on one key will affect all the notes currently playing on the channel.

The creators of the MIDI specification realized that other types of controllers were found on some instruments, and that more would follow. So they created one general purpose channel voice message (&HBx) to handle them. The first data byte of the Control Change message selects the controller type, and the second byte specifies its current value. You'll find a complete listing of the pre-defined controller types in the *MIDI 1.0 Detailed Specification* (see the bibliography). Actually, the Control Change message supports only 121 controllers, numbered 0 through 120. The remaining 7 values are reserved for the Channel Mode Messages.

The Channel Mode Messages

Mode messages determine how an instrument will process MIDI voice messages. Now that you understand how to send MIDI channel voice messages, you'll have an easier time understanding how to send channel mode messages. Unfortunately, some of the modes themselves have caused more confusion than any other aspect of MIDI.

Channel Mode messages are a special case of the Control Change message. They always begin with a status byte containing the value &HBx, where x is the channel number. The difference between a Control Change message and a Channel Mode message, which share the same status byte value, is in the first data byte. Data byte values 121 through 127 have been reserved in the Control Change message for the channel mode messages. These are listed in Table 14.2.

Table 14.2 *The Channel Mode Messages*

First Data Byte Value	Description	Meaning of Second Data Byte
&H79	Reset All Controllers	None; set to 0
&H7A	Local Control	0 = Off; 127 = On
&H7B	All Notes Off	None; set to 0
&H7C	Omni Mode Off	None; set to 0
&H7D	Omni Mode On	None; set to 0
&H7E	Mono Mode On (Poly Mode Off)	0 means that the number of channels used is determined by the receiver; all other values set a specific number of channels, beginning with the current *basic channel*
&H7F	Poly Mode On (Mono Mode Off)	None; set to 0

Of these messages, the least understood—and therefore most creatively interpreted by instrument manufacturers—are Omni Mode On, Omni Mode Off, Mono Mode On, and Poly Mode On. Actually, modes are independent of the mode messages; the messages just change the mode on the fly. The intent of these modes is to determine how an instrument responds to incoming channel voice messages.

Omni Mode means that the instrument responds to messages on all 16 channels. So if Note On messages are transmitted on all channels, the instrument in Omni Mode will attempt to play them all, up to the maximum number of voices it has available. Some synthesizers can play only one note at a time. These are called *monophonic* instruments. Others, known as *polyphonic* instruments can play 8, 16, 32, or some other number of simultaneous notes. If a device with only 8 voices receives 15 simultaneous Note On messages, it will play only the first or last 8.

For most real-world applications, Omni Mode isn't discerning enough (it isn't discerning at all). Most polyphonic instruments can play not only a multitude of simultaneous notes, they can also play them with a variety of patches. So one synthesizer can sound like a whole band. In Poly Mode, each channel is assigned a patch. All notes on each channel play with the same timbre. For example, you could set channel 1 to play bass, channel 2 to play piano, and channel 3 to play drums. In Mono Mode, only one note can play at a time on each channel. Poly Mode has some powerful capabilities, but we don't have room to discuss them here. For detailed coverage of MIDI modes order a copy of the *MIDI 1.0 Detailed Specification*.

The System Messages

The second general category of MIDI messages are the *system messages*, which include *system common messages*, *system real-time messages*, and *system exclusive messages*. These messages carry information that is not channel specific, such as timing signals for synchronization, positioning information in pre-recorded MIDI sequences, and detailed setup information for the destination device.

There are four types of system common messages, as shown in Table 14.3.

The six system real-time messages, listed in Table 14.4, primarily affect sequencer playback and recording. These messages have no data bytes.

The third type of system message, the system exclusive message, is used to transfer data between devices. For example, you may wish to store patch setups for an instrument on a computer using a *patch librarian* program. You can then transfer those patches to the synthesizer by means of a system exclusive message. The name *system exclusive* means that these are messages exclusively for

Table 14.3   *The MIDI System Common Messages*

System Common Message	Status Byte Hex Value	Number of Data Bytes
MIDI Time Code	&HF1	1
Song Position Pointer	&HF2	2
Song Select	&HF3	1
Tune Request	&HF6	None

Table 14.4   *The MIDI System Real-Time Messages*

System Real Time Message	Status Byte Hex Value
Timing Clock	&HF8
Start Sequence	&HFA
Continue Sequence	&HFB
Stop Sequence	&HFC
Active Sensing	&HFE
System Reset	&HFF

a particular device, or type of device, rather than universal messages that all MIDI compatible products should recognize. A system exclusive message is just a stream of bytes, all with their high bits set to 0, bracketed by a pair of system exclusive start and end messages (&HF0 and &HF7).

The MIDI Offspring

Since the introduction of the MIDI protocol, four other MIDI standards have appeared:

- MIDI Show Control 1.0
- MIDI Machine Control 1.0
- Standard MIDI Files 1.0
- General MIDI System, Level 1

The MIDI Show Control and MIDI Machine Control standards specify a set of system exclusive messages that can control various types of non-musical equipment. The Show Control focuses specifically on stage lighting and sound control systems, although it is designed to control just about any kind of performance system, including mechanical stages. The Machine Control standard specifies system exclusive messages to operate audio and video recorders.

The biggest problem that surfaced after the widespread adoption of the MIDI protocol was in sequencer file formats. Shortly after the introduction of the first MIDI-equipped synthesizers, several sequencer programs appeared. Sequencer programs allow musicians and composers to record and playback MIDI information. With a sequencer, one person can compose and play an entire symphony, using nothing more than a computer and a few synthesizers. All these programs, no matter which platform they supported, adhered to the MIDI communication protocol. They had to or they wouldn't work. But the files in which they stored their data were another matter. Each software developer created its own proprietary format, which meant that you couldn't create a music sequence with one program and play it back with another. So in 1988, The International MIDI Association published the second component of the MIDI standard, *Standard MIDI Files 1.0.* Standard MIDI files are built from *chunks*, which contain some header information and a series of data bytes. Sound familiar? Although not identical, MIDI standard files and RIFF files have quite a bit in common. In fact, a Windows MIDI file is actually a standard MIDI file embedded in a RIFF chunk.

Standard MIDI files made it possible for musicians to share their files, regardless of hardware and software platforms. But this new standard highlighted another problem. The *tracks* in a MIDI sequencer file may specify a program number, which determines the instrument sound, or patch, with which that track should be played. But every instrument has its own assortment of patches. So while program number 30 on one synthesizer might be a brass section patch, the same program number on another instrument could be a tympani drum, or a sci-fi phaser gun. Playback of a standard MIDI file might produce all the right notes on all the wrong instruments. The General MIDI System standard attempts to solve this problem by offering a standard program list, consisting of the 128 most common patch types, from pianos to gunshots (literally—General MIDI program 1 is Acoustic Grand Piano, and program 128 is Gunshot). General MIDI also specifies a layout for percussion instruments, called the General MIDI Percussion Map. Percussion is a special case because non-melodic percussion sounds, such as drums, cymbals, and cowbells, need to occupy only one note position, so you can theoretically fit up to 128 separate percussion sounds in one patch. General MIDI includes 47 percussion sounds, and specifies that percussion should be transmitted on MIDI channel 10.

General MIDI is considered a *system* rather than a *specification* because not all instruments need to comply. That in fact would defeat the purpose of programmable synthesizers, which enable artists to continually invent new sounds. Some synthesizer modules are designed specifically for use as General MIDI devices, and come pre-programmed with compliant patches. Other synthesizers support a General MIDI mode, but also provide a separate programmable patch bank. And some instruments don't support General MIDI at all, unless you program and arrange the patches yourself.

MIDI and Windows

The Windows Multimedia System fully supports MIDI. Besides the standard MCI commands that enable us to play (but not record) MIDI files, there are 29 low-level MIDI functions in the API, with which we can send and receive MIDI messages over any of the 16 channels. To use these functions you'll need either a sound card equipped with MIDI ports, or a dedicated MIDI adapter.

MIDI Connections

Most sound cards today provide a combination joystick/MIDI port in the form of a 15-pin connector. To use this port for MIDI, you'll need an adapter cable, usually available from the card's manufacturer, to convert the 15-pin connector to either two or three 5-pin DIN connectors, as shown in Figure 14.3. If your adapter cable provides three MIDI ports, there will be one of each type (In, Out, and Through). If only two are present, they will likely be In and Out ports.

Three of the most common brands of PC sound cards, The Creative Labs Soundblaster series, the Media Vision Pro Audio Spectrum series, and the Advanced Gravis Ultrasound, all use the same type of MIDI cable. The professional level Multisound card from Turtle Beach Systems has no joystick port,

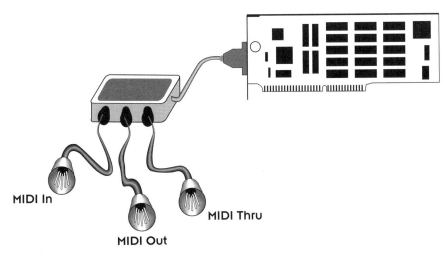

Figure 14.3 *A typical sound card with its MIDI adapter cable attached.*

but provides a 9-pin connector to which you may attach a special MIDI cable, available from the manufacturer.

It's important not to confuse the on-board synthesizer on your sound card with the card's MIDI capabilities. You don't need a sound card at all to use the MIDI multimedia functions. You can just install a MIDI port adapter, such as the Roland MPU-401, which would enable you to exchange MIDI data with any external MIDI device, including synthesizers, drum machines, sequencers, even other computers. The synthesizer on your sound card acts like just another MIDI device; you play notes on it by sending it MIDI messages. How your on-board synthesizer responds to MIDI depends partly on the settings in the Windows MIDI Mapper.

The Windows MIDI Mapper

For some reason, the Windows MIDI Mapper has inspired just about as much fear and loathing as any other Windows feature. That could be because Microsoft slipped it in with little fanfare, and even less explanation. However, the purpose and operation of the MIDI Mapper is really pretty simple.

The MIDI Mapper, an applet located in the Windows Control Panel, helps Windows achieve some level of device independence between MIDI devices. For example, not all sound cards have their internal patches organized according to General MIDI guidelines. The Patch Maps section of the MIDI Mapper provides a way to map General MIDI patch numbers to the actual patches in the sound card, as shown in Figure 14.4.

The Key Maps dialog box, shown in Figure 14.5, is used to re-map notes. Why would you need to do this, you ask? There are two reasons. The MIDI 1.0 Detailed Specification places middle C at note 60 (&H3C). Some older devices, especially those not specifically designed to support MIDI, may use a different note position mapping. You can use the Key Maps dialog box to re-map the device's own note positions to the standard configuration.

You can also use the Key Maps dialog box to map percussion instruments to the General MIDI layout. For example, in General MIDI, note 35 is an Acoustic Bass Drum. Some devices place that instrument at note 47, one octave higher, so the Key Map can be used to re-map it.

The MIDI Mapper also includes the MIDI Setups dialog box, shown in Figure 14.6, which enables you to re-map channels and select patch maps for each channel individually. The patch map is device-specific. In other words, if you play all music on one instrument, whether that's the on-board synthesizer on your sound card, or a single external instrument connected to your MIDI Out port, the patch map would be the same on all channels. If you connect multiple instruments into the MIDI chain, by linking the Through port of each

MIDI Patch Map: 'MT32'

1 based patches

Src Patch	Src Patch Name	Dest Patch	Volume %	Key Map Name
0	Acoustic Grand Piano	0	100	[None]
1	Bright Acoustic Piano	1	100	[None]
2	Electric Grand Piano	3	100	[None]
3	Honky-tonk Piano	7	100	[None]
4	Rhodes Piano	5	100	[None]
5	Chorused Piano	6	100	[None]
6	Harpsichord	17	100	[None]
7	Clavinet	21	100	[None]
8	Celesta	22	100	[None]
9	Glockenspiel	101	100	[None]
10	Music Box	101	100	[None]
11	Vibraphone	98	100	[None]
12	Marimba	104	100	[None]
13	Xylophone	103	100	[None]
14	Tubular Bells	102	100	[None]
15	Dulcimer	105	100	[None]

OK   Cancel   Help

Figure 14.4   *The MIDI Patch Map dialog box allows you to map General MIDI patch numbers to the actual patches in the sound card.*

MIDI Key Map: '+1 octave'

Src Key	Src Key Name	Dest Key
35	Acoustic Bass Drum	47
36	Bass Drum 1	48
37	Side Stick	49
38	Acoustic Snare	50
39	Hand Clap	51
40	Electric Snare	52
41	Low Floor Tom	53
42	Closed Hi Hat	54
43	High Floor Tom	55
44	Pedal Hi Hat	56
45	Low Tom	57
46	Open Hi Hat	58
47	Low-Mid Tom	59
48	High-Mid Tom	60
49	Crash Cymbal 1	61
50	High Tom	62

OK   Cancel   Help

Figure 14.5   *The MIDI Key Maps dialog box allows you to re-map notes and to map percussion instruments to the General MIDI system.*

instrument to the In port of the next, then you may need a separate patch map for each one. In this case, you would use the MIDI Mapper to assign the patch map to the channel or channels on which the corresponding instrument is waiting for MIDI messages. This may seem complicated, but it really simplifies things when it comes time to play music. By mapping all instruments to the General MIDI patch numbers, you can send MIDI messages that select the correct patches on each instrument without considering each instrument's unique patch layout. So device-*specific* MIDI Setups produce device-*independent* operation.

The construction of a complete MIDI setup is a three step process:

1. Create the necessary key maps.
2. Create the patch maps, using the appropriate key maps if needed.
3. Create the MIDI Setup, assigning Source Channels to Destination Channels, Ports, and Patch Maps.

The installation program for your sound card's drivers should have installed the Windows MIDI drivers and any required MIDI Mapper setups.

If you look at the setup shown in Figure 14.6, you'll notice that the activated channels are divided into two groups. Channels 1 through 10 are set to

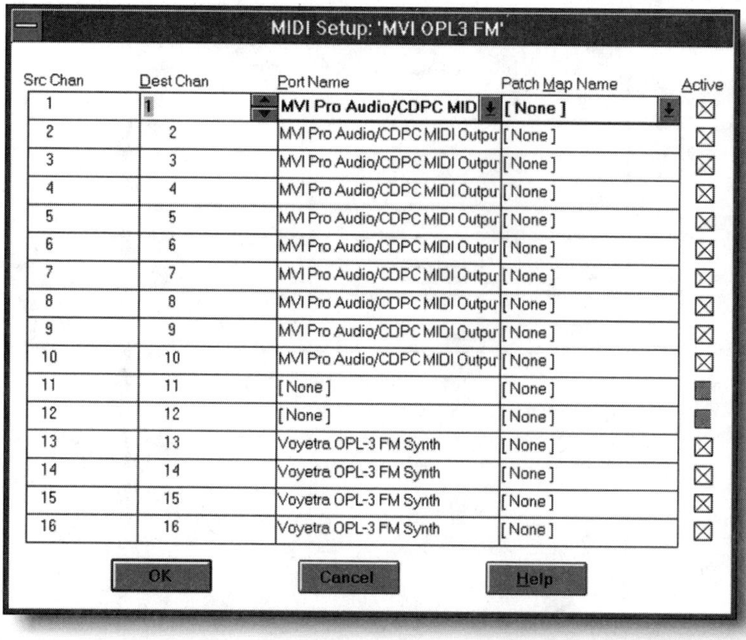

MIDI Setup: 'MVI OPL3 FM'

Src Chan	Dest Chan	Port Name	Patch Map Name	Active
1	1	MVI Pro Audio/CDPC MID	[None]	☒
2	2	MVI Pro Audio/CDPC MIDI Outpu	[None]	☒
3	3	MVI Pro Audio/CDPC MIDI Outpu	[None]	☒
4	4	MVI Pro Audio/CDPC MIDI Outpu	[None]	☒
5	5	MVI Pro Audio/CDPC MIDI Outpu	[None]	☒
6	6	MVI Pro Audio/CDPC MIDI Outpu	[None]	☒
7	7	MVI Pro Audio/CDPC MIDI Outpu	[None]	☒
8	8	MVI Pro Audio/CDPC MIDI Outpu	[None]	☒
9	9	MVI Pro Audio/CDPC MIDI Outpu	[None]	☒
10	10	MVI Pro Audio/CDPC MIDI Outpu	[None]	☒
11	11	[None]	[None]	■
12	12	[None]	[None]	■
13	13	Voyetra OPL-3 FM Synth	[None]	☒
14	14	Voyetra OPL-3 FM Synth	[None]	☒
15	15	Voyetra OPL-3 FM Synth	[None]	☒
16	16	Voyetra OPL-3 FM Synth	[None]	☒

OK　　Cancel　　Help

Figure 14.6 *The MIDI Mapper Setup dialog box allows you to assign a patch map to each MIDI channel.*

MVI Pro Audio/CDPC MIDI Output, while channels 13 through 16 are set to Voyetra OPL-3 FM Synth. The setting on the first ten channels causes them to send their output to an external MIDI device, completely bypassing the on-board synthesizer. The second group of channels do just the opposite; they send all messages to the internal device, the OPL-3 FM synthesizer chip. These groupings reflect Microsoft's own contribution to the standardization of MIDI files and devices, at least as far as Windows is concerned!

Windows recognizes two general types of synthesizers: *Base-Level* and *Extended-Level*. These two categories reflect the capabilities of the devices. A Base-Level device can play at least three distinct, simultaneous patches, each assigned to its own channel, with at least six simultaneous notes. The notes may be distributed in any way across the three channels. So at one point during playback, one channel can be used to play a single note, the second channel can play two notes, and the third channel can play three notes. Then later in the same sequence, the voices can shift, so the first channel can play four notes, while the third channel plays the remaining two notes. This is called *dynamic voice allocation*. In addition to the minimum of six simultaneous melodic notes, a Base-Level device must also support a minimum of three simultaneous percussion notes. The melodic parts are played from MIDI channels 13, 14, and 15, while percussion is played from channel 16.

Extended-Level MIDI devices can play at least nine distinct and simultaneous patches, on nine separate channels, with a minimum of sixteen simultaneous, dynamically allocated notes. The percussion channel should support an additional sixteen simultaneous notes. The melodic voices play on channels 1 through 9, with percussion on channel 10. Channels 11 and 12 are unassigned.

Most of the popular sound cards available today, especially those based on the OPL FM synthesizer chips, meet or exceed the Base-Level requirements. Only a few products meet the Extended-Level specification. And some of the cards that act as if they were Extended-Level devices fail to comply fully with the guidelines, usually by offering fewer than the 32 recommended voices.

To provide device-independent support for MIDI sequencer files, Microsoft recommends that any Windows compatible file should contain two versions of the sequence: one that will play on a Base-Level device and one that will play on an Extended-Level device. The file CANYON.MID that comes with Windows 3.1 is an example of such a file. The MIDI playback system will pump out data on all 14 assigned channels, but if the MIDI Setup is correct, as shown in the MIDI Mapper, only one set of tracks will play on any given device.

Sending MIDI Messages

You've already seen how to play a MIDI file with MCI commands in Chapters 3 and 10. It's as simple as sending the string "Play filename.MID" with either the **mciExecute()** or **mciSendString()** functions. But now that you know something about MIDI messages and where they go, let's use the low-level MIDI API functions to send some messages directly to the device. We'll begin with a simple experiment so you can see how the functions work. Then we'll explore the VB MIDI Piano, a nifty little program created by MIDI programming wizard Arthur Edstrom, of Artic Software, Inc.

Sending MIDI Messages

It takes only a handful of API functions to open and use a MIDI device. In this project we'll try them out. Here are the steps to follow:

1. Open a code module and declare the midiOut API functions (Listing 14.1).

2. Create the form and fill in the form code (Listing 14.2).

 You'll find this project in the subdirectory \VBMAGIC in the files MIDIOUT1.MAK, MIDIOUT1.FRM, and MIDI1.BAS.

Running the Program

When you run the program, it will display a small form with two Command Buttons, as shown in Figure 14.7.

Click on the button labeled Open MIDI Device. Its caption will change to Close MIDI Device. Click on the Send Note button once to turn on a note, and again to turn it off. If you hear nothing, make sure the MIDI channel is set properly for your sound card or external MIDI device. You may want to check the MIDI Setup dialog box in the MIDI Mapper applet to determine which channels are active. Also, don't forget to check all your volume settings, including those in your multimedia mixer program and on any physical devices, such as the amplifier controls and the output level of an external synthesizer.

Figure 14.7   *The MIDIOUT1.FRM form at runtime.*

When you're done testing, click on the Close MIDI Device button and end the program.

Declaring the midiOut API Functions

We'll place the four API function declarations in their own code module, called MIDI1.BAS, shown in Listing 14.1. This code module will contain no functions or procedures.

Listing 14.1 MIDI1.BAS

```
Option Explicit

Declare Function midiOutOpen Lib "MMSystem" (hMidiOut As Integer, ByVal DeviceId
    As Integer, ByVal dwCallback As Long, ByVal dwInstance As Long, ByVal dwFlags
    As Long) As Integer
Declare Function midiOutShortMsg Lib "MMSystem" (ByVal hMidiOut As Integer,
    ByVal MidiMessage As Long) As Integer
Declare Function midiOutClose Lib "MMSystem" (ByVal hMidiOut As Integer) As Integer

Global Const MIDI_MAPPER = -1
```

Let's take a look at how these functions work.

The **midiOutOpen()** function takes five arguments. In the first argument, **hMidiOut**, we pass an integer variable, which the function will fill with a handle to the device. The second argument, **DeviceId** specifies which MIDI device to open. Most systems have only one MIDI device, and its **DeviceId** is 0. To select the MIDI Mapper, pass the constant **MIDI_MAPPER**, which has a decimal value of -1.

The arguments **dwCallback** and **dwInstance** specify either the address of a callback function, or a handle for a window callback. As I explained in earlier chapters, VB does not support callbacks, so we'll set both these arguments to NULL (0). Later in this chapter, when we talk about MIDI input, I'll show you how to use a custom control to service window callbacks. The fifth argument, **dwFlags** also relates to callbacks. Its only defined flags are **CALLBACK_WINDOW** and **CALLBACK_FUNCTION**.

The function **midiOutShortMsg()** requires only two arguments. The first, as usual, takes the handle set by **midiOutOpen()**. In the second argument, we pass the MIDI message as a four byte long integer. The least significant byte contains the status byte, the actual MIDI command. The next higher-order byte contains the first data byte, if needed. And the third byte contains the second data byte, if needed. The highest-order byte is always set to &H00.

The third and last function declared for this project, **midiOutClose()** takes nothing but the handle to the device.

All three of these functions return integer values that indicate error conditions. If no error occurs, they return 0.

Creating the Form Module

If you're creating this program from the ground up, start with a small form. Place two Command Buttons on it. Set their **Name** properties to OpenButton and SendMessageButton. Set their initial **Caption** properties to Open MIDI Device and Send Note, respectively. Then place a Text Box on the form. **Name** it ChannelText, and give it an initial **Text** property value of 16. You may also want to place a Label beside the Text Box, as I did in the sample program on the companion CD. Next, we can fill in the code.

This bare-bones program requires only four event procedures and a handful of variables, as shown in Listing 14.2.

Listing 14.2　The Code and Declarations from MIDIOUT1.FRM

```
Option Explicit

Dim NoteToggle As Integer
Dim hMidiOut As Integer
Dim MidiDeviceOpen As Integer
Dim MidiChannel As Integer

Sub Form_Load ()
    MidiDeviceOpen = False
    End Sub

Sub Form_Unload (Cancel As Integer)
    Dim RetValue As Integer

    RetValue = midiOutClose(hMidiOut)
    End Sub

Sub OpenButton_Click ()
    Dim RetValue As Integer

    If MidiDeviceOpen Then
        RetValue = midiOutClose(hMidiOut)
        OpenButton.Caption = "Open MIDI Device"
      Else
        RetValue = midiOutOpen(hMidiOut, MIDI_MAPPER, 0, 0, 0)
        OpenButton.Caption = "Close MIDI Device"
      End If
    MidiDeviceOpen = Not MidiDeviceOpen
    End Sub

Sub SendMessageButton_Click ()
    Dim RetValue As Integer
    Dim MidiShortMessage As Long
```

```
MidiChannel = (Abs(Val(ChannelText.Text)) - 1) Mod 16
NoteToggle = Not NoteToggle
If NoteToggle Then
    ' Note On = &H9x, where x = channel
    ' Middle C = &H3C
    ' Velocity of 64 = &H40
    MidiShortMessage = &H403C90 + MidiChannel
    SendMessageButton.Caption = "Stop Note"
  Else
    ' Note On = &H9x, where x = channel
    ' Middle C = &H3C
    ' Velocity of 0 = Note Off = &H00
    MidiShortMessage = &H3C90 + MidiChannel
    SendMessageButton.Caption = "Send Note"
  End If
RetValue = midiOutShortMsg(hMidiOut, MidiShortMessage)
End Sub
```

Most of the action takes place in the **SendMessageButton_Click()** event procedure. After we make sure we're transmitting on a valid MIDI channel, we set **NoteToggle**, which determines whether we're about to turn a note on or off. If **NoteToggle** is True, we send a Note On message, &H9x. By adding the channel number of 0 to 15 to the long integer, we really affect only the four low-order bits of the lowest-order byte. The second byte is set to &H3C, which will select Middle C, and the third byte is set to the median velocity, &H40. To turn off the note, we can cheat by re-transmitting the Note On message with a velocity of 0.

The Visual Basic MIDI Piano

This program, contributed by Arthur Edstrom of Artic Software, Inc., was written as a tutorial for all the folks hanging around in the Visual Basic forum on CompuServe (GO MSBASIC) who expressed an interest in VB MIDI programming. Here are the steps to follow to create this program:

1. Create the form (Listing 14.3).
2. Add the form code (Listing 14.4).
3. Add a code module (Listing 14.5) with function declarations and three general procedures.

You'll find this project in the directory \VBPIANO in the files PIANO.MAK, ABOUTBX1.FRM, PIANO2.FRM, PIANO.BAS, MIDPIANO.WAV and PATCH.INI. You'll also need the THREED.VBX custom control, which the VB Setup program normally installs in the \WINDOWS\SYSTEM directory.

Playing the Visual Basic MIDI Piano

When you run the program, it will first play a welcome message from the program's author, and display its About Box, as shown in Figure 14.8

After this splash screen disappears, the program will display its main form, a piano keyboard with several scroll bars, as shown in Figure 14.9.

Use the scroll bars to select the MIDI channel and set the volume (or in MIDI terms, the velocity). You may also shift the octave of the keyboard up or down, change the current patch, and if your sound card supports stereo, set the left-to-right balance, known as the *pan*.

You can press and hold several notes in succession by holding down the mouse button and dragging the pointer across the piano keyboard. To acti-

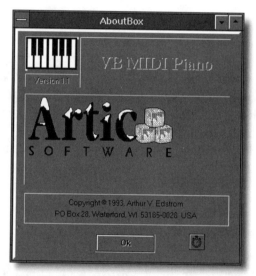

Figure 14.8   *The About Box from the VB MIDI Piano.*

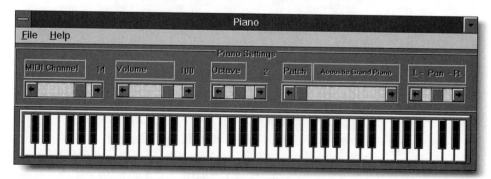

Figure 14.9   *The PIANO2.FRM form from the VB MIDI Piano, at runtime.*

vate selected notes, hold the button and drag off the keyboard, then back on again over the keys of your choice. To release all the currently active notes, release the mouse button while the pointer is over the piano keyboard, or release the mouse button and press it again over another key.

Creating the Main Form

Although you could burn a lot of time designing a bitmap keyboard with sprites to indicate keypresses, Arthur has found a much simpler, and very attractive alternative. The keys are actually a control array called **PanelWhite()**, consisting of 65 SSPanel controls (the Toolbox button for the SSPanels will appear when you load the THREED.VBX file into your project). To color the keys, the **BackColor** property is set either to pure black (&H000000) or pure white (&HFFFFFF). On all keys, the **BorderWidth** property is set to 2, the **BevelOuter** is set to 2 - Raised, and **RoundedCorners** is set to True. The **BevelWidth** property is set on the black keys to 1, and on the white keys to 2. To indicate a keypress, the program changes **BevelOuter** to 0 - None.

The remaining controls consist of Scroll Bars and Labels, set in SSPanel controls to get the 3D effect. For a complete list of the non-keyboard controls and their properties, see Listing 14.3.

Listing 14.3   The Non-Keyboard Controls from PIANO2.FRM

```
VERSION 2.00
Begin Form Piano
    BackColor       =   &H00C0C0C0&
    BorderStyle     =   1  'Fixed Single
    Caption         =   "Piano"
    ClientHeight    =   2388
    ClientLeft      =   684
    ClientTop       =   1680
    ClientWidth     =   9516
    ClipControls    =   0   'False
    Height          =   3132
    Icon            =   PIANO2.FRX:0000
    Left            =   636
    LinkTopic       =   "Form1"
    MaxButton       =   0   'False
    ScaleHeight     =   2388
    ScaleWidth      =   9516
    Top             =   984
    Width           =   9612
    Begin SSPanel Panel3D3
        Alignment       =       6  'Center - TOP
        AutoSize        =       3  'AutoSize Child To Panel
        BackColor       =       &H00C0C0C0&
        BevelWidth      =       3
```

```
        BorderWidth     =    0
        Font3D          =    3   'Inset w/light shading
        ForeColor       =    &H00808080&
        Height          =    975
        Left            =    90
        Outline         =    -1  'True
        TabIndex        =    20
        Top             =    1290
        Width           =    9315
    Begin SSFrame SSFrame4
        Alignment       =    2   'Center
        Caption         =    "Piano Settings"
        Font3D          =    3   'Inset w/light shading
        ForeColor       =    &H00000000&
        Height          =    1245
        Left            =    0
        ShadowColor     =    1   'Black
        ShadowStyle     =    1   'Raised
        TabIndex        =    0
        Top             =    0
        Width           =    9585
        Begin SSPanel SSPanel6
            Alignment       =    6   'Center - TOP
            AutoSize        =    3   'AutoSize Child To Panel
            BackColor       =    &H00C0C0C0&
            BevelInner      =    1   'Inset
            BorderWidth     =    2
            Caption         =    "SSPanel6"
            Font3D          =    3   'Inset w/light shading
            ForeColor       =    &H00808080&
            Height          =    375
            Left            =    2070
            TabIndex        =    18
            Top             =    720
            Width           =    1695
            Begin HScrollBar HScrollVolume
                Height          =    276
                LargeChange     =    10
                Left            =    48
                Max             =    127
                TabIndex        =    19
                Top             =    48
                Value           =    50
                Width           =    1596
            End
        End
    End
    Begin SSPanel SSPanel5
        Alignment       =    6   'Center - TOP
        AutoSize        =    3   'AutoSize Child To Panel
        BackColor       =    &H00C0C0C0&
        BevelInner      =    1   'Inset
        BorderWidth     =    1
        Caption         =    "SSPanel5"
```

```
      Font3D          =    3   'Inset w/light shading
      ForeColor       =    &H00808080&
      Height          =    375
      Left            =    5520
      TabIndex        =    16
      Top             =    720
      Width           =    2415
      Begin HScrollBar HScrollPatch
         Height          =    300
         LargeChange     =    10
         Left            =    36
         Max             =    127
         TabIndex        =    17
         Top             =    36
         Value           =    1
         Width           =    2340
      End
   End
   Begin SSPanel SSPanel2
      Alignment       =    6   'Center - TOP
      AutoSize        =    3   'AutoSize Child To Panel
      BackColor       =    &H00C0C0C0&
      BevelInner      =    1   'Inset
      BorderWidth     =    1
      Caption         =    "SSPanel2"
      Font3D          =    3   'Inset w/light shading
      ForeColor       =    &H00808080&
      Height          =    375
      Left            =    180
      TabIndex        =    14
      Top             =    720
      Width           =    1680
      Begin HScrollBar HScrollMIDIChannel
         Height          =    300
         LargeChange     =    2
         Left            =    36
         Max             =    15
         TabIndex        =    15
         Top             =    36
         Value           =    1
         Width           =    1608
      End
   End
   Begin SSPanel VolumeLabel
      Alignment       =    4   'Right Justify - MIDDLE
      AutoSize        =    3   'AutoSize Child To Panel
      BackColor       =    &H00C0C0C0&
      BevelOuter      =    0   'None
      BorderWidth     =    1
      Caption         =    "100"
      Font3D          =    3   'Inset w/light shading
      ForeColor       =    &H00000000&
      Height          =    228
```

```
        Left            =    3348
        TabIndex        =    13
        Top             =    396
        Width           =    372
     End
     Begin SSPanel MidiChannelOutLabel
        Alignment       =    4   'Right Justify - MIDDLE
        AutoSize        =    3   'AutoSize Child To Panel
        BackColor       =    &H00C0C0C0&
        BevelOuter      =    0   'None
        BorderWidth     =    1
        Caption         =    "1"
        Font3D          =    3   'Inset w/light shading
        ForeColor       =    &H00000000&
        Height          =    225
        Left            =    1575
        TabIndex        =    12
        Top             =    390
        Width           =    300
     End
     Begin SSPanel SSPanel10
        AutoSize        =    3   'AutoSize Child To Panel
        BackColor       =    &H00C0C0C0&
        BevelInner      =    2   'Raised
        BevelOuter      =    1   'Inset
        BorderWidth     =    0
        Caption         =    "L  -  Pan  - R"
        FloodShowPct    =    0   'False
        Font3D          =    3   'Inset w/light shading
        ForeColor       =    &H00000000&
        Height          =    375
        Left            =    8100
        TabIndex        =    11
        Top             =    300
        Width           =    1185
     End
     Begin SSPanel SSPanel9
        Alignment       =    1   'Left Justify - MIDDLE
        AutoSize        =    3   'AutoSize Child To Panel
        BackColor       =    &H00C0C0C0&
        BevelInner      =    2   'Raised
        BevelOuter      =    1   'Inset
        BorderWidth     =    0
        Caption         =    "Volume"
        FloodShowPct    =    0   'False
        Font3D          =    3   'Inset w/light shading
        ForeColor       =    &H00000000&
        Height          =    375
        Index           =    0
        Left            =    2070
        TabIndex        =    10
        Top             =    300
        Width           =    1230
```

```
End
Begin SSPanel PatchLabel
    AutoSize          =    3   'AutoSize Child To Panel
    BackColor         =    &H00C0C0C0&
    BevelInner        =    2   'Raised
    BevelOuter        =    1   'Inset
    BorderWidth       =    0
    Caption           =    "Electric Piano 2 "
    Font3D            =    3   'Inset w/light shading
    FontBold          =    -1  'True
    FontItalic        =    0   'False
    FontName          =    "Small Fonts"
    FontSize          =    6
    FontStrikethru    =    0   'False
    FontUnderline     =    0   'False
    ForeColor         =    &H00000000&
    Height            =    375
    Left              =    6150
    TabIndex          =    9
    Top               =    300
    Width             =    1785
End
Begin SSPanel SSPanel8
    Alignment         =    1   'Left Justify - MIDDLE
    AutoSize          =    3   'AutoSize Child To Panel
    BackColor         =    &H00C0C0C0&
    BevelInner        =    2   'Raised
    BevelOuter        =    1   'Inset
    BorderWidth       =    0
    Caption           =    "Patch"
    Font3D            =    3   'Inset w/light shading
    ForeColor         =    &H00000000&
    Height            =    375
    Left              =    5535
    TabIndex          =    8
    Top               =    300
    Width             =    615
End
Begin SSPanel SSPanel7
    Alignment         =    1   'Left Justify - MIDDLE
    AutoSize          =    3   'AutoSize Child To Panel
    BackColor         =    &H00C0C0C0&
    BevelInner        =    2   'Raised
    BevelOuter        =    1   'Inset
    BorderWidth       =    0
    Caption           =    "MIDI Channel "
    Font3D            =    3   'Inset w/light shading
    ForeColor         =    &H00000000&
    Height            =    375
    Left              =    180
    TabIndex          =    7
    Top               =    300
    Width             =    1275
```

```
End
Begin SSPanel Panel3D1
    Alignment          =   6   'Center - TOP
    AutoSize           =   3   'AutoSize Child To Panel
    BackColor          =   &H00C0C0C0&
    BevelInner         =   1   'Inset
    BorderWidth        =   2
    Caption            =   "SSPanel6"
    Font3D             =   3   'Inset w/light shading
    ForeColor          =   &H00808080&
    Height             =   375
    Left               =   8100
    TabIndex           =   5
    Top                =   720
    Width              =   1215
    Begin HScrollBar HScrollPan
        Height          =   276
        LargeChange     =   10
        Left            =   48
        Max             =   127
        TabIndex        =   6
        Top             =   48
        Width           =   1116
    End
End
Begin SSPanel Panel3D2
    Alignment          =   6   'Center - TOP
    AutoSize           =   3   'AutoSize Child To Panel
    BackColor          =   &H00C0C0C0&
    BevelInner         =   1   'Inset
    BorderWidth        =   2
    Caption            =   "SSPanel6"
    Font3D             =   3   'Inset w/light shading
    ForeColor          =   &H00808080&
    Height             =   375
    Left               =   4050
    TabIndex           =   3
    Top                =   720
    Width              =   1200
    Begin HScrollBar HScrollOctave
        Height          =   276
        LargeChange     =   10
        Left            =   48
        Max             =   4
        TabIndex        =   4
        Top             =   48
        Value           =   2
        Width           =   1104
    End
End
Begin SSPanel SSPanel9
    Alignment          =   1   'Left Justify - MIDDLE
    AutoSize           =   3   'AutoSize Child To Panel
```

```
    BackColor         =   &H00C0C0C0&
    BevelInner        =   2   'Raised
    BevelOuter        =   1   'Inset
    BorderWidth       =   0
    Caption           =   "Octave"
    FloodShowPct      =   0   'False
    Font3D            =   3   'Inset w/light shading
    ForeColor         =   &H00000000&
    Height            =   375
    Index             =   1
    Left              =   4050
    TabIndex          =   2
    Top               =   300
    Width             =   735
End
Begin SSPanel LabelOctave
    Alignment         =   4   'Right Justify - MIDDLE
    AutoSize          =   3   'AutoSize Child To Panel
    BackColor         =   &H00C0C0C0&
    BevelOuter        =   0   'None
    BorderWidth       =   1
    Caption           =   "1"
    Font3D            =   3   'Inset w/light shading
    ForeColor         =   &H00000000&
    Height            =   225
    Left              =   4950
    TabIndex          =   1
    Top               =   390
    Width             =   300
End
End
Begin Menu File
    Caption       =   "&File"
    Begin Menu Exit
        Caption       =   "E&xit"
    End
End
Begin Menu help
    Caption       =   "&Help"
    Begin Menu About
        Caption       =   "&About"
    End
End
End
```

Coding the VB MIDI Piano Form Module

The code for the piano program, shown in Listing 14.4, is simple. One difference between this program and the simple experiment we created in
MIDIOUT1.MAK is that this code uses decimal values for MIDI messages. In
your own programs use whichever numeric base you wish. The messages will
work either way.

Listing 14.4   The Code in PIANO2.FRM

```
Dim NoteCatchCount As Integer
Dim NoteOnCatcher(1024) As Integer


Sub About_Click ()
    AboutBox1.Show Modal
End Sub

Sub Exit_Click ()
    X% = MidiOutClose(hmidioutcopy)
    End
End Sub

Sub Form_Load ()
    Screen.MousePointer = 11
    Piano.Left = 0
    Piano.Top = 0

    ' Open Midi Driver
    MidiOutOpenPort

    HScrollMIDIChannel.Value = 13
    HScrollPatch.Value = 0
    HScrollVolume.Value = 100
    HScrollPan.Value = 64
    HScrollOctave.Value = 2
    Screen.MousePointer = 0
End Sub

Sub Form_Unload (Cancel As Integer)
    X% = MidiOutClose(hmidioutcopy)
End Sub

Sub HScrollMIDIChannel_Change ()
    ' Change Midi Channel to Vscroll1 value.
    MidiChannelOut = HScrollMIDIChannel.Value

    ' Display new channel.
    MidiChannelOutLabel.Caption = Str$(MidiChannelOut + 1)

    ' Sets the Patch & Volume for the current Midi Channel Out.
    HScrollPatch.Value = MidiPatch(MidiChannelOut)
    HScrollVolume.Value = MidiVolume(MidiChannelOut)
    HScrollPan.Value = MidiPan(MidiChannelOut)
    HScrollOctave.Value = Octave(MidiChannelOut) / 12
End Sub

Sub HScrollOctave_Change ()
    LabelOctave.Caption = Str$(HScrollOctave.Value)
    Octave(MidiChannelOut) = (HScrollOctave.Value * 12)
End Sub
```

```
Sub HScrollPan_Change ()
    MidiPan(MidiChannelOut) = HScrollPan.Value

    ' 05-16-92 Pan Midi Out routine
    MidiEventOut = 176 + MidiChannelOut
    MidiNoteOut = 10
    MidiVelOut = MidiPan(MidiChannelOut)
    SendMidiOut
End Sub

Sub HScrollPatch_Change ()
    ' Sets the Patch for the current Midi Channel Out.
    MidiPatch(MidiChannelOut) = HScrollPatch.Value
    ReadPatch

    ' 05-15-92 Patch Midi Out routine
    MidiEventOut = &HC0 + MidiChannelOut
    MidiNoteOut = MidiPatch(MidiChannelOut)
    MidiVelOut = 0
    SendMidiOut

End Sub

Sub HScrollVolume_Change ()
    MidiVelocity = HScrollVolume.Value
    MidiVolume(MidiChannelOut) = HScrollVolume.Value
    VolumeLabel.Caption = Str$(MidiVelocity)
End Sub

Sub PanelWhite_DragDrop (Index As Integer, Source As Control, X As Single, Y As Single)
    For nn = 0 To NoteCatchCount - 1
        MidiEventOut = 144 + MidiChannelOut
        MidiVelOut = 0
        MidiNoteOut = NoteOnCatcher(nn)
        SendMidiOut
        Piano.PanelWhite(NoteOnCatcher(nn) - Octave(MidiChannelOut)).BevelOuter = 2
    Next nn
    NoteCatchCount = 0
End Sub

Sub PanelWhite_DragOver (Index As Integer, Source As Control, X As Single, Y As
    Single, State As Integer)
    'If still on same note, discard.
    If NoteCatchCount > 0 Then
        If NoteOnCatcher(NoteCatchCount - 1) = Index + Octave(MidiChannelOut) Then
            Exit Sub
        End If
    End If

    Piano.PanelWhite(Index).BevelOuter = 0

    MidiEventOut = 144 + MidiChannelOut
    MidiVelOut = MidiVelocity
```

```
MidiNoteOut = Index + Octave(MidiChannelOut)
SendMidiOut

'Since drag/drop is being used, we must keep track of the note being played.
NoteOnCatcher(NoteCatchCount) = MidiNoteOut
If NoteCatchCount < 750 Then 'Don't let array get out of range
    NoteCatchCount = NoteCatchCount + 1
End If

End Sub
```

The playing action takes place in the **PanelWhite_DragOver()** event procedure, while the **PanelWhite_DragDrop()** event procedure handles the Note Off messages.

To enable the user to successively press and hold two or more piano keys, the program uses drag and drop operations to activate piano keys instead of **Click** or **MouseDown** events. A **DragOver** event occurs whenever you press the mouse button on a control that has DragMode enabled either because its **DragMode** property is set to Automatic, or because one of the control's other event procedures calls the **Drag** method. The **DragOver** event occurs even on the control that started the drag operation. This would cause the procedure to repeatedly activate the same note, also repeatedly adding it to the **NoteOnCatcher** array until the mouse cursor has moved off the key. So the first part of **PanelWhite_DragOver()** checks whether the current control index is the same as the previous one. If so, it exits the procedure:

```
If NoteCatchCount > 0 Then
    If NoteOnCatcher(NoteCatchCount - 1) = Index + Octave(MidiChannelOut) Then
        Exit Sub
    End If
End If
```

The next five lines in **PanelWhite_DragOver()** set up and send the MIDI Note On message:

```
Piano.PanelWhite(Index).BevelOuter = 0
MidiEventOut = 144 + MidiChannelOut
MidiVelOut = MidiVelocity
MidiNoteOut = Index + Octave(MidiChannelOut)
SendMidiOut
```

The variables **MidiVelocity** and **MidiChannelOut** are set by the HScrollVolume and the HScrollMidiChannel Scroll Bars. **SendMidiOut()** is a general procedure located in the PIANO.BAS code module, which we'll get to shortly.

To handle the simultaneous notes, the program keeps a list of active notes in an array of integers called **NoteOnCatcher**. The variable **NoteCatchCount** is used to keep track of the number of active notes held in the array. The last part of the **PanelWhite_DragOver()** event procedure updates this list:

```
NoteOnCatcher(NoteCatchCount) = MidiNoteOut
If NoteCatchCount < 750 Then 'Don't let array get out of range
    NoteCatchCount = NoteCatchCount + 1
End If
```

The **PanelWhite_DragDrop()** event procedure runs through the list, sending Note On messages with 0 velocity to shut off each note, and changing the **BevelOuter** property back to 2 - Raised.

The VB MIDI Piano Code Module

With the exception of the call to the API function **GetPrivateProfileString()**, the code in PIANO.BAS, shown in Listing 14.5, should be familiar to you if you studied the previous project.

Listing 14.5   The Complete Code and Declarations from PIANO.BAS

```
' MIDI Functions Windows 3.1
Declare Function MidiOutOpen Lib "mmsystem.dll" (hMidiOut As Long, ByVal DeviceId
    As Integer, ByVal C As Long, ByVal I As Long, ByVal F As Long) As Integer
Declare Function MidiOutShortMsg Lib "mmsystem.dll" (ByVal hMidiOut As Integer,
    ByVal MidiMessage As Long) As Integer
Declare Function MidiOutClose Lib "mmsystem.dll" (ByVal hMidiOut As Integer) As
    Integer

' Other API Functions
Declare Function GetPrivateProfileString Lib "kernel" (ByVal Sname$, ByVal
    Kname$, ByVal Def$, ByVal Ret$, ByVal Size%, ByVal Fname$) As Integer
Declare Function sndPlaySound Lib "mmsystem" (ByVal lpsSound As String, ByVal
    wFlag As Integer) As Integer

Global MidiEventOut, MidiNoteOut, MidiVelOut As Long
Global hMidiOut As Long
Global hMidiOutCopy As Integer
Global MidiOpenError As String

Global Const MODAL = 1
Global Const ShiftKey = 1

' The Patch number array used for current patch for each midi channel.
' The Volume array used for each channel's volume setting.
' TrackChannel is an array for the current midi channel that the Track on the
    midi is set to.
Global MidiPatch(16), MidiVolume(16), TrackChannel(16), MidiPan(16), Octave(16)
    As Integer
```

```
' The current midi channel out set on Piano form.
Global MidiChannelOut As Integer

' The Velocity (Volume) of notes for current midi channel.
Global MidiVelocity As Integer

'Boolean for if CapsLock has been pressed or not?
Global CapsLock As Integer

' NoteRepeat used to stop the same key from repeating. CapsLock detects if it is down.
Global NoteRepeat As Integer

Sub MidiOutOpenPort ()
    MidiOpenError = Str$(MidiOutOpen(hMidiOut, -1, 0, 0, 0))
    hMidiOutCopy = hMidiOut
End Sub

Sub ReadPatch ()
    Dim Sname As String, Ret As String, Ext As String
    Ret = String$(255, 0)
    Default1$ = Ret
    Sname = "General MIDI"
    Ext = Str$(MidiPatch(MidiChannelOut))
    FileName$ = App.Path & "\PATCH.INI"
    nSize = GetPrivateProfileString(Sname, Ext, Default1$, Ret, Len(Ret), FileName$)
    Piano.PatchLabel.Caption = Ret
End Sub

Sub SendMidiOut ()
    Dim MidiMessage As Long
    Dim lowint As Long
    Dim highint As Long

    lowint = (MidiNoteOut * 256) + MidiEventOut
    highint = (MidiVelOut * 256) * 256

    MidiMessage = lowint + highint
    X% = MidiOutShortMsg(hMidiOutCopy, MidiMessage)
End Sub
```

The function **GetPrivateProfileString()** is a standard Windows API function that reads data from .INI files. For a complete description of this function, consult any good Windows API reference. The purpose of this function in this program is to read the list of patch names from the file PATCH.INI.

Receiving MIDI Messages

One of the most difficult multimedia features to use from VB is MIDI input. Unlike WAVE audio, which can be recorded with MCI commands, MIDI provides no MCI input support—only low-level functions. And that creates a problem.

All the low-level recording functions in the Windows Multimedia System use callbacks to request buffers or to report activity. In the MIDI functions, the callback function is where incoming MIDI messages are passed to an application. Since VB provides no support for user-definable callback functions, we cannot capture MIDI input from our VB programs—that is, unless we use a custom control.

Windows Callbacks

Many Windows API functions support either of two kinds of callbacks: a *callback function*, or a *window message callback*. In general, callback functions are needed to handle precision timing and synchronous processes, while window message callbacks are used for tasks where response time is less critical.

To use a callback function, you pass the actual memory address of the function to the API function. The API function then calls your callback function when it has completed an operation. This arrangement enables the API function to perform complex processes, then interrupt all other activity on the system when it's ready to return the result.

To use a window message callback, you pass a handle to the window that needs to receive the callback notification. When messages are used for callbacks, the API function simply posts a message to a window. The message is then delivered when it reaches the front of the message queue.

Some functions, like **midiInOpen()**, support either type of callback. But there's a catch. MIDI data is time-critical. The human ear—or more accurately, the human brain—can detect minute variations in time, down to about two milliseconds. This means that if you're going to faithfully record MIDI input you need precision down to one millisecond.

The multimedia high-resolution timer can provide this kind of precision, but only when you use a callback function. For each MIDI message it receives from the Input port, the MIDI device driver calls the specified callback function, and passes it the MIDI message and an accurate time stamp. When you request a window message callback for the MIDI input device, however, the multimedia system doesn't even bother to time-stamp the callback message. It is assumed in the design of the MIDI API that window message callbacks can't be used for real-time musical event recording. But even with the limitations of window message callbacks, you can still do some impressive things.

The Visual Basic Messenger Custom Control

Since we can't pass callback functions or add our own event procedures to handle callback messages, the only way to receive MIDI messages in VB is to use a custom control. Fortunately, a programmer named James Tyminski has written one and published it as shareware. The *VB Messenger* is a custom control that intercepts all kinds of windows messages, and provides an event procedure where we can insert VB code, just as we do for any of VB's built-in event handlers.

> *The distribution copy of VB Messenger is located in the directory \VBMSSNGR. VB Messenger is a shareware product. For information on how to register your copy, see the file README.TXT in the \VBMSSNGER directory. If you wish, you can register your copy through the CompuServe Shareware Registration Forum (GO SWREG), registration number 961. Shareware registered through this forum will be billed to your CompuServe account.*

In our next project, we'll use the VB Messenger to capture incoming MIDI messages.

Receiving MIDI Messages

In this project we'll use the VB Messenger custom control to intercept a window callback message and trap incoming MIDI messages.

1. Create the form MIDIIN1.FRM.
2. Add the code for the **Form_Load()** and **StartStopButton_Click()** event procedures (Listings 14.6 and 14.7).
3. Add the **VBMsg1_WindowsMessage()** event procedure (Listing 14.8).
4. Fill in the declarations and housekeeping event procedures in the form module (Listing 14.9).
5. Add the code module MIDI2.BAS, and insert the global declarations and the declarations for the MIDI input functions (Listing 14.10).

> *You'll find this project in the subdirectory \VBMAGIC in the files MIDIIN1.MAK, MIDIIN1.FRM, and MIDI2.BAS. You'll also need the VB Messenger custom control. You'll find it in the \VBMSSNGR subdirectory. Copy the file VBMSG.VBX to your \WINDOWS\SYSTEM directory.*

Running the Program

To run this program you'll need an external MIDI controller, such as a professional or portable keyboard with a MIDI Out port. Use a standard MIDI cable to connect the MIDI Out port of the instrument to the MIDI In port on your computer's MIDI adapter. (You can find MIDI cables at most music stores.) This program does not discriminate channels, so you can set your external MIDI device to transmit data on any of the 16 MIDI channels.

Run the program and click on the Start button as shown in Figure 14.10. If the program locates any valid MIDI Input devices, it will display their names in the List Box. These names are determined by the manufacturer of the MIDI adapter or sound card and its driver. Choose the device whose name contains some reference to the MIDI In port. You can then click on the Start button to open the selected device. If the device is valid, "Device Open" appears in the Picture Box at right, indicating that the form window has received an **MM_MIM_OPEN** message from the device driver. When you press the keys of your MIDI controller keyboard, you should see the MIDI Note On and Note Off messages appear in the Picture Box at right. The messages are displayed as three decimal values. The first number in each line displays the value of the status byte. The second and third numbers display the values of the data bytes.

When you are finished, click on the Command Button, now labeled Stop, or use the form's Control menu to select the Close option. If you close the program by selecting the End option from the VB menu, you may lock up the device driver. In this situation, you will need to restart Windows to reactivate the MIDI device.

Creating the Form

Create a form named MidiInTest, set its **Caption** to Test MIDI In, and save it under the filename MIDIIN1.FRM. Place a List Box on the form, named MidiDevList. Then add a Command Button, named StartStopButton, and a Picture Box. Set the **ScaleMode** property of the Picture Box to 3 - Pixel.

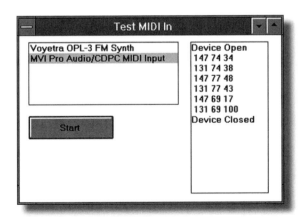

Figure 14.10 *The form MIDIIN1.FRM at runtime.*

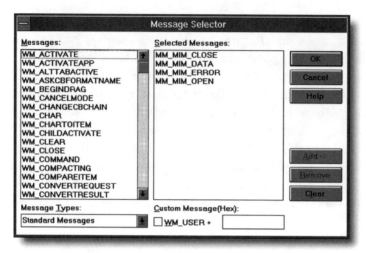

Figure 14.11   *You use the Message Selector dialog box to set up the VB Messenger control at design time.*

Finally, add a VB Messenger control to the form. Like a Timer control, the VB Messenger control is invisible at runtime, so you can place it anywhere on the form. We need to set up this control by telling it which windows messages to detect. First, select the **(Message Selector)** property, then click on the "..." button in the Properties window to open the Message Selector dialog box, shown in Figure 14.11.

In the Message Types list box in the lower-left corner of the dialog box, select Multimedia Messages. Then from the Messages list box in the upper-left corner, select **MM_MIM_OPEN**, **MM_MIM_CLOSE**, **MM_MIM_ERROR**, and **MM_MIM_DATA**. At runtime, when any of the message types you selected is intercepted, it will trigger the VB Messenger control's **WindowMessage()** event procedure.

Adding the Form Code

The first thing we need to do is query the MIDI device driver for the number of MIDI Input devices and their capabilities. We'll then list that information in the MidiDevList List Box, as shown in Listing 14.6.

Listing 14.6   The Form_Load() Event Procedure from MIDIIN1.FRM

```
Sub Form_Load ()
    Dim NumMidiInDevices As Integer
    Dim DevCounter As Integer
    Dim RetValue As Integer
    Dim DeviceCaps As MIDIINCAPS
```

```
VBMsg1.SubClasshWnd = MidiInTest.hWnd
StartButton.Enabled = False
NumMidiInDevices = midiInGetNumDevs()
For DevCounter = 0 To NumMidiInDevices - 1
    RetValue = midiInGetDevCaps(DevCounter, DeviceCaps, Len(DeviceCaps))
    MidiDevList.AddItem DeviceCaps.szPName
    MidiDevList.ItemData(MidiDevList.NewIndex) = DevCounter
    Next DevCounter
End Sub
```

The first line of the **FormLoad()** event procedure sets the **SubClasshWnd** property of the VB Messenger control to the window handle of the main form, **MidiInTest.hWnd**. To Holy Trinity programmers, subclassing a window or control basically means adding new capabilities to an existing type of object. By adding the ability to respond to MIDI input messages, we are effectively subclassing the form window. By setting this property, we instruct the VB Messenger control to intercept all messages to the specified window that match the types we selected at design time (in the control's Message Selector dialog box).

The API function **midiInGetNumDevs()**, which takes no arguments, returns the number of MIDI Input devices installed in the system. We use that number, captured in the integer variable **NumMidiInDevices** to step through the devices and interrogate them with **midiInGetDevCaps()**. This function takes three arguments: a zero-based device number, a **MIDIINCAPS** record passed by reference, and the size of the **MIDIINCAPS** record. For the complete declarations of these functions and the **MIDIINCAPS** structure, see Listing 14.10.

Before we can start MIDI input, we need to open the appropriate device, which we do in the **StartStopButton_Click()** event procedure, shown in Listing 14.7.

Listing 14.7 The StartStopButton_Click Event Procedure from MIDIIN1.FRM

```
Sub StartStopButton_Click ()
    Dim RetValue As Integer
    Dim NumMidiDevices As Integer

    If Not MidiInActive Then
        VBMsg1.SubClasshWnd = MidiInTest.hWnd
        RetValue = midiInOpen(hMidiIn, InputDeviceNumber, MidiInTest.hWnd, 0,
                CALLBACK_WINDOW)
        If RetValue = 0 Then
            RetValue = midiInReset(hMidiIn)
            RetValue = midiInStart(hMidiIn)
            MidiInActive = True
            StartButton.Caption = "Stop"
            MidiDevList.Enabled = False
```

```
        Else
           MsgBox "Unable to open Midi Device.", 48, "Midi Device Error"
        End If
    Else
      RetValue = midiInStop(hMidiIn)
      RetValue = midiInClose(hMidiIn)
      MidiInActive = False
      StartButton.Caption = "Start"
      MidiDevList.Enabled = True
    End If
  End Sub
```

The **midiInOpen()** function takes five arguments:

```
Declare Function midiInOpen Lib "MMSystem" (lphMidiIn As Integer, ByVal
    uDeviceID As Integer, ByVal dwCallback As Long, ByVal dwInstance As Long,
    ByVal dwFlags As Long) As Integer
```

The first, **lphMidiIn**, is a variable that the function will set to the handle of the open device. In the second argument, **uDeviceID**, we specify which device to open. The device numbers are zero-based, so the first device is number 0, the second is number 1, etc. In the third argument, **dwCallback**, we pass either the address of a callback function, or the handle to a window that can receive a message callback. **dwInstance**, the fourth argument, is used when **dwCallback** contains a function address; it is used to pass data to the callback function. Since we can't use a callback function, we always set **dwInstance** to 0. In **dwFlags** we pass a flag that indicates which type of callback to use. In **StartStopButton_Click()** we pass the flag constant **CALLBACK_WINDOW**, which has a value of &H10000.

If we successfully open the device, we call two more functions, **midiInReset()** and **midiInStart()** to reset the device and begin receiving MIDI messages. You can use **midiInStart()** and its sibling, **midiInStop()**, to temporarily suspend MIDI input without closing and re-opening the device. When we're ready to shut down the device, we call **midiInStop()** followed by **midiInClose()**. We use the form-level integer variable **MidiInActive** to keep track of whether the device is open or closed. In the **StartStopButton_Click()** event procedure, we open the device if **MidiInActive** is False; otherwise, we close it.

The WindowsMessage Event

The **VBMsg_WindowsMessage()** event procedure, shown in Listing 14.8, is triggered whenever the MIDI device sends the form any of the four windows message types we selected in the VB Messenger control's Message Selector dialog box.

Listing 14.8 The VBMsg1_WindowsMessage() Event Procedure from MIDIIN1.FRM

```
Sub VBMsg1_WindowMessage (hWindow As Integer, Msg As Integer, wParam As Integer,
    lParam As Long, RetVal As Long, CallDefProc As Integer)
    Dim MidiDataByte2 As Integer
    Dim MidiDataByte1 As Integer
    Dim MidiStatusByte As Integer
    Dim RetValue As Integer
    Dim AreaToScroll As RECT
    Dim LineHeight As Integer

    ' Scroll Picture Box 1 line.
    LineHeight = Picture1.TextHeight("A")
    If (Picture1.CurrentY > (Picture1.ScaleHeight - LineHeight)) Then
        AreaToScroll.Top = 0
        AreaToScroll.Left = 0
        AreaToScroll.Right = Picture1.ScaleWidth
        AreaToScroll.Bottom = Picture1.ScaleHeight
        RetValue = ScrollDC(Picture1.hDC, 0, -LineHeight, AreaToScroll,
                    AreaToScroll, 0, ByVal 0&)
        Picture1.Line (0, Picture1.ScaleHeight - LineHeight)-
          (Picture1.ScaleWidth, Picture1.ScaleHeight), Picture1.BackColor, BF
        Picture1.CurrentX = 0
        Picture1.CurrentY = Picture1.ScaleHeight - LineHeight
    End If
    Select Case Msg
      Case MM_MIM_OPEN
        Picture1.Print "Device Open"
      Case MM_MIM_CLOSE
        Picture1.Print "Device Closed"
      Case MM_MIM_ERROR
        Picture1.Print "DEVICE ERROR"
      Case Else
        MidiDataByte2 = lParam \ 65536
        MidiDataByte1 = (lParam Mod 65536) \ 256
        MidiStatusByte = lParam Mod 256
        ' Filter out Active Sensing messages, MIDI Status 254.
        If MidiStatusByte <> 254 Then
            Picture1.Print Str$(MidiStatusByte) & Str$(MidiDataByte1) &
              Str$(MidiDataByte2)
          End If
      End Select
    End Sub
```

This event procedure first uses the Windows API function **ScrollDC()** to scroll the Picture Box, which makes it possible to display a continuously scrolling list of MIDI messages.

In the **Case Else** clause of the **Select Case** statement, we unpack and display the MIDI message, which is passed along with the window message in its **lParam**, a long integer value. The lowest-order byte contains the status byte, the MIDI message code. The second-order byte contains the first data

byte, and the third-order byte contains the second data byte. I have filtered out MIDI message 254, which is a MIDI System Real Time Message called Active Sensing. Some MIDI devices continually send this message to announce their presence on the MIDI cable string. My Roland controller keyboard sends this message about three times per second, which would flood the Picture Box, making it difficult to see any other messages.

Completing the Form Module

Listing 14.9 contains the declarations and remaining event procedures from MIDIIN1.FRM.

Listing 14.9   The Declarations and Remaining Event Code from MIDIIN1.FRM

```
Option Explicit

Declare Function ScrollDC Lib "User" (ByVal hDC As Integer, ByVal dx As Integer,
    ByVal dy As Integer, lprcScroll As RECT, lprcClip As RECT, ByVal hRgnUpdate As
    Integer, lprcUpdate As Any) As Integer

Dim hMidiIn As Integer
Dim MidiInActive As Integer
Dim InputDeviceNumber As Integer

Sub Form_Unload (Cancel As Integer)
    Dim RetValue As Integer

    RetValue = midiInStop(hMidiIn)
    RetValue = midiInClose(hMidiIn)

    End Sub

Sub MidiDevList_Click ()
    InputDeviceNumber = MidiDevList.ItemData(MidiDevList.ListIndex)
    StartStopButton.Enabled = True
    End Sub
```

The Code Module

The MIDI2.BAS code module contains nothing but declarations, as shown in Listing 14.10.

Listing 14.10   MIDI2.BAS

```
Option Explicit

Type MIDIINCAPS
    wMid As Integer
```

```
    wPid As Integer
    vVersion As Integer
    szPname As String * 128
    End Type

Type RECT
    Left As Integer
    Top As Integer
    Right As Integer
    Bottom As Integer
    End Type

Declare Function midiInOpen Lib "MMSystem" (lphMidiIn As Integer, ByVal
    uDeviceID As Integer, ByVal dwCallback As Long, ByVal dwInstance As Long,
    ByVal dwFlags As Long) As Integer
Declare Function midiInClose Lib "MMSystem" (ByVal hMidiIn As Integer) As Integer
Declare Function midiInReset Lib "MMSystem" (ByVal hMidiIn As Integer) As Integer
Declare Function midiInStart Lib "MMSystem" (ByVal hMidiIn As Integer) As Integer
Declare Function midiInStop Lib "MMSystem" (ByVal hMidiIn As Integer) As Integer
Declare Function midiInGetNumDevs Lib "MMSystem" () As Integer
Declare Function midiInGetDevCaps Lib "MMSystem" (ByVal wDeviceId As Integer,
    lpCaps As MIDIINCAPS, ByVal wSize As Integer) As Integer

Global Const CALLBACK_WINDOW = &H10000
Global Const MM_MIM_OPEN = &H3C1
Global Const MM_MIM_CLOSE = &H3C2
```

Beyond MIDI Basics

The API functions we have used in this chapter represent the core of the MIDI programming interface. The multimedia system contains many other functions. Some handle MIDI System Exclusive messages (known in Windows as MIDI Long Messages). Among the others are functions that control playback volume on the internal mixer, that translate error codes into string messages, and that manage synthesizer patches. With the help of VB Messenger, or a custom control that supports callback functions, you can use the MIDI API to write your own MIDI utilities and sequencers.

You may also wish to review some of the other projects we've explored in earlier chapters to discover other applications for the VB Messenger custom control, especially the wave audio projects in Chapter 13. Both the standard Windows wave audio functions and the functions in the WaveMix library support callback notifications. With a little help from this handy control you can increase the utility of these functions.

Chapter 15

Ah, the sounds of music. Join me as we explore the MCI commands that make it possible for you to turn your CD-ROM drive into a big Discman.

Working with the Media Control Interface (MCI)

n Chapter 4 we created a simple test program that we could use to test various MCI command strings. But throughout this book, the only command we've used is **play**. The MCI offers many useful commands, including some that retrieve status information from devices, such as track number, track length, frame number, current position, and a variety of other useful items. In this chapter, we'll try out some of these commands by building an audio CD player with some cool features.

Windows Multimedia's "Simple" Devices

The MCI supports two types of devices, simple devices and compound devices. Up to this point, we've been using compound devices, which consist of a device driver and a data file. The waveaudio device is a compound device because without a WAVE file, it has nothing to do. Simple devices require no data file, usually because their data is loaded directly into the device on some kind of device-specific medium, such as an audio CD, a video cassette, a video laser disk, or a digital audio tape (DAT). Although the MCI has no control over which data is being played on a simple device, it usually has pretty extensive control over general operation, including rewind, fast forward, play, record, and stop.

Of the compound devices, the most common and easiest to use is a CD-ROM drive. Since CD audio enjoys a widely adopted standard, we can write programs based on MCI commands that will work on any CD loaded into any CD-ROM drive. Almost all CD-ROM drives come with analog audio outputs. If you have a CD-ROM drive, chances are pretty good you've already used it to play audio disks. If not, check your installation guide for the proper connections to your sound card or external amplifier.

Trying MCI Commands

Before we code anything, let's try a few MCI commands. We'll use the program MCIPlay, which we completed in Chapter 4, to send commands to our CD-ROM drives. Load your favorite disk, then run MCIPLAY3.MAK. Alternately, you can use the File, Make EXE File command on the VB menu to make MCIPLAY3.EXE. You can then run the program without first opening VB through either the File Manager or the Program Manager.

Begin by opening the device, as shown in Figure 15.1.

To execute this command, select the mciSendString button. If all goes well, the Error text box should say "The specified command was carried out." If not, then the device may not be available, either because the driver is not installed, or because another application, such as the Media Player, already has it open.

To start playing the disk, enter the command "Play CDAudio" in the Command String text box, and again select the mciSendString button. The disk should begin playing.

Next, let's query the device for the number of tracks on the CD. Enter the command "status CDAudio number of tracks" in the Command String text box, then select the mciSendString button. The answer to your query should appear in the Return String text box, as shown in Figure 15.2.

If you send the command, "status CDAudio current track," the device will return the number of the current track.

Try a few other commands. For a complete list of available MCI commands, see the Microsoft *Multimedia Programmer's Reference*, or the Waite Group's *Windows API New Testament*. When you're done, be sure to release the device by sending the message "close CDAudio."

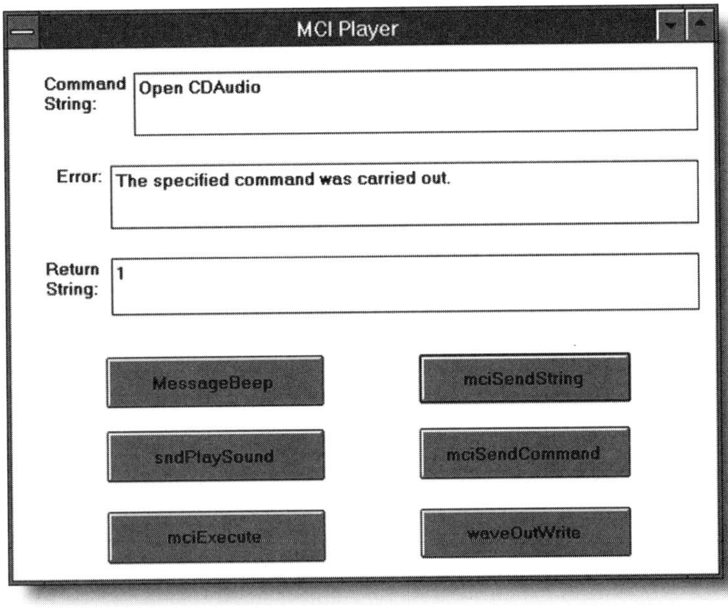

Figure 15.1 MCIPlay3 with the Open CDAudio command in the Command String text box.

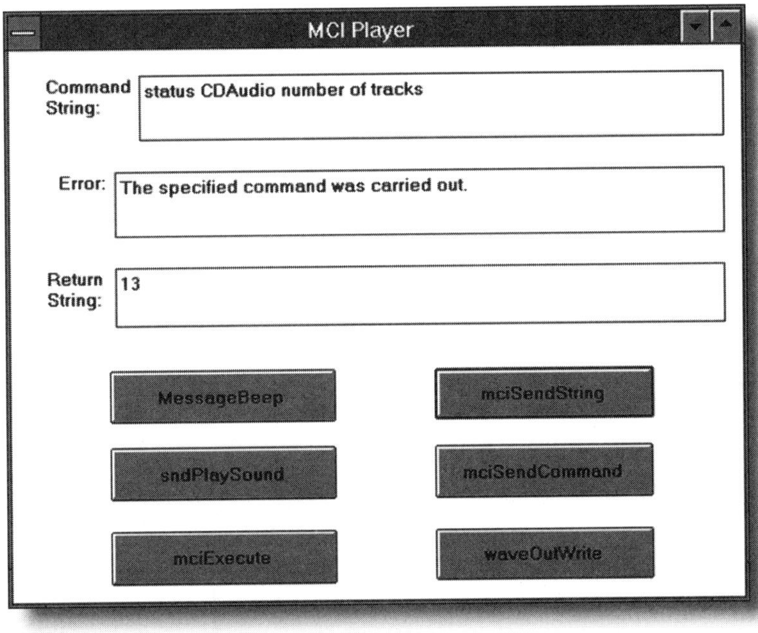

Figure 15.2 The result of an MCI status inquiry.

Using MCI to Play Redbook Audio

Because just about everyone who works in multimedia has a CD-ROM drive, let's begin this chapter with by building a couple of CD player projects that demonstrate the capabilities of the MCI.

One-Step CD Player

I like to listen to music, especially while I'm working on a multimedia project. But I prefer not to mess around with complex gizmos, like over-powered, feature-packed monster CD players. I just want to pop in a CD and let it play. In this project, we'll build a simple CD player that can detect whether a CD is loaded in the drive, and if so, play it. Here are the steps to follow:

1. Create a simple form.
2. Add the declaration for **mciSendString()** (Listing 15.1).
3. Write a general function called **SendMCICommand()** (Listing 15.2).
4. Add the event code (Listing 15.3).

> *You'll find this project in the subdirectory \VBMAGIC in the files ONESTEP.MAK, ONESTEP.FRM, and ONESTEP.FRX.*

Running the One-Step CD Player

When you run ONESTEP.MAK, it will appear as an icon on your desktop (I have chosen the EAR.ICO icon from the VB icon library). To play a CD, insert it into the drive. As soon as the program detects that a disk has been loaded, it will issue the **play** command.

To pause the CD, double-click on the ONESTEP icon to restore the program window and click on the Pause check box, as shown in Figure 15.3. Click the check box again to resume playback.

Figure 15.3   *ONESTEP.MAK as a restored window at runtime.*

To change CDs, simply remove the one that's playing and insert another. Within two or three seconds, the new disk will begin to play.

Use the Control menu, from either the minimized or restored state, to terminate the program. When you close the program, it will stop playback and close the CDAudio device.

Creating the Form

This program uses a simple form with only three controls: a timer, a label, and a check box. Figure 15.4 shows the form at design time. Set the **Name** property of the form to OneStepF1, and set its **Caption** property to "One Step CD Player." Set the **Interval** property of Timer1 to 1000 milliseconds, and make sure that **Enabled** is set to True. For Label1, set the **Caption** property to "Now Playing Track:" and set its **Alignment** property to 0 - Left Justify. Finally, set the **Name** property of the check box to PauseCheck, and set its **Caption** property to "&Pause."

Declare the API Function

This program requires only one API function, **mciSendString()**. Add its declaration to the declarations section of ONESTEP.FRM, as shown in Listing 15.1.

Listing 15.1   The Declarations Section of ONESTEP.FRM

```
Option Explicit

Declare Function mciSendString Lib "MMSystem" (ByVal lpstrCommand As String,
ByVal lpstrReturnString As String, ByVal wReturnLength As Integer, ByVal
hCallback As Integer) As Integer
```

Encapsulate the API Function

To simplify the calls to **mciSendString()**, I have written a general function called **SendMCICommand()** (shown in listing 15.2), which will take a command string as its one and only argument, and will return the contents of the return string filled in by the API function.

Figure 15.4   The form ONESTEP.FRM at design time.

Listing 15.2　The SendMCICommand General Function from ONESTEP.FRM

```
Function SendMCICommand (TheCommand As String) As String
    Dim Dummy As Integer
    Dim ReturnString As String

    ReturnString = String$(128, " ")
    Dummy = mciSendString(TheCommand, ReturnString, 127, 0)
    SendMCICommand = ReturnString

    End Function
```

Filling In the Event Code

Now we can fill in the four brief event procedures that make this program tick, as shown in Listing 15.3.

Listing 15.3　The Event Code from ONESTEP.FRM

```
Sub Form_Load ()
    Dim ReturnString As String

    ReturnString = SendMCICommand("Open CDAudio")
    End Sub

Sub Form_QueryUnload (Cancel As Integer, UnloadMode As Integer)
    Dim ReturnString As String

    ReturnString = SendMCICommand("stop CDAudio")
    ReturnString = SendMCICommand("close CDAudio")
    End Sub

Sub PauseCheck_Click ()
    Dim ReturnString As String

    If PauseCheck.Value = 1 Then
        Timer1.Enabled = False
        ReturnString = SendMCICommand("pause CDAudio")
    Else
        Timer1.Enabled = True
        ReturnString = SendMCICommand("play CDAudio")
    End If
    End Sub

Sub Timer1_Timer ()
    Dim ReturnString As String

    ReturnString = SendMCICommand("status CDAudio media present")
    If Left$(ReturnString, 4) = "true" Then
        ReturnString = SendMCICommand("status CDAudio mode")
        If Not (Left$(ReturnString, 7) = "playing") Then
            ReturnString = SendMCICommand("play CDAudio")
```

```
        Else
          ReturnString = SendMCICommand("status CDAudio current track")
          Label1.Caption = "Now Playing Track: " & Left$(ReturnString, 2)
        End If
    End If
End Sub
```

One time each second, the **Timer1_Timer()** event procedure checks whether a CD is loaded in the drive by sending the message "status CDAudio media present." If it is, the return string will contain the literal string value "true"; otherwise, it will contain "false." The API function **mciSendString()** returns a string with a null terminator between the return value and the blank padding, which prevents the VB **RTrim$()** function from returning a clean string. For this reason, I've used the **Left$()** function instead to grab just the number of characters needed for comparison.

If the drive contains a CD, the **Timer1_Timer()** event procedure sends a second status command to determine whether it is already playing. If not, it sends the **play** command. If the disk is already playing, it sends a third status command to retrieve the current track number, so we can display it on the form whenever it's restored.

For this simple program, we've used eight MCI commands. That's not too bad when you consider that the CDAudio device supports over three dozen command string combinations. In the next project, we'll try out a few more.

The Smart CD Player

In this project, we'll take even greater control over the CDAudio device. We'll even use MCI commands to uniquely identify each CD we load in the drive so we can store and display their titles. Here are the steps to follow:

1. Create the form (Listing 15.4).
2. Write the **Form_Load()** event procedure (Listing 15.5).
3. Write the **ActivityTimer_Timer()** event procedure (Listing 15.6).
4. Complete the form code (Listing 15.7).
5. Fill in the code module (Listing 15.8).

You'll find this project in the subdirectory \VBMAGIC in the files CDPLAYER.MAK, CDPLAYER.FRM, CDPLAYER.BAS, and MINMAX.BAS. You'll also need the SPIN.VBX custom control, which the VB Setup program normally installs in your \WINDOWS\SYSTEM directory.

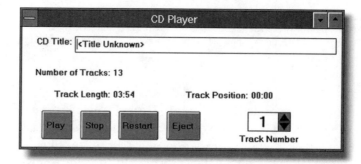

Figure 15.5   *CDPLAYER.FRM at runtime.*

Running the Smart CD Player

When you run the program CDPLAYER.MAK, it will display the form shown in Figure 15.5.

The first time you load a CD into the drive, the program will display <Title Unknown> in the CD Title text box. To assign the correct title, enter it in the text box. The next time you stop or eject the disk, the program will save its title record.

Use the spin control to select the starting track, or leave it at the beginning of the disk, and select the Play button to begin playback.

When you load a disk that has been assigned a title, the program will use track and timing information to identify it and display its title. You may edit the title whenever you wish by simply modifying the contents of the text box.

Creating the Form

This simple program has more controls than any other project in this book. For the complete list of controls and their properties, see Listing 15.4.

Listing 15.4   The Form and Control Properties from CDPLAYER.FRM

```
Begin Form CDPlayerF1
    Caption         =   "CD Player"
    ClientHeight    =   2328
    ClientLeft      =   1224
    ClientTop       =   1532
    ClientWidth     =   6420
    Height          =   2748
    Left            =   1176
    LinkTopic       =   "Form1"
    ScaleHeight     =   2328
    ScaleWidth      =   6420
    Top             =   1260
    Width           =   6515
```

```
Begin CommandButton RestartButton
    Caption         =    "Restart"
    Height          =    552
    Left            =    1980
    TabIndex        =    12
    Top             =    1520
    Width           =    792
End
Begin Timer ActivityTimer
    Interval        =    1000
    Left            =    5880
    Top             =    660
End
Begin CommandButton EjectButton
    Caption         =    "Eject"
    Height          =    552
    Left            =    2940
    TabIndex        =    9
    Top             =    1520
    Width           =    672
End
Begin SpinButton TrackSelectSpin
    Height          =    372
    Left            =    5150
    Top             =    1520
    Width           =    252
End
Begin TextBox CDTitleText
    Height          =    312
    Left            =    1080
    TabIndex        =    2
    Top             =    180
    Width           =    5232
End
Begin CommandButton StopButton
    Caption         =    "Stop"
    Height          =    552
    Left            =    1200
    TabIndex        =    1
    Top             =    1520
    Width           =    612
End
Begin CommandButton PlayButton
    Caption         =    "Play"
    Height          =    552
    Left            =    420
    TabIndex        =    0
    Top             =    1520
    Width           =    612
End
Begin Label Label5
    Alignment       =    2    'Center
    Caption         =    "Track Number"
```

```
         Height          =    192
         Left            =    4320
         TabIndex        =    13
         Top             =    2040
         Width           =    1332
      End
      Begin Label NumberOfTracksLabel
         Height          =    252
         Left            =    1860
         TabIndex        =    11
         Top             =    780
         Width           =    432
      End
      Begin Label Label4
         Alignment       =    1   'Right Justify
         Caption         =    "Number of Tracks:"
         Height          =    252
         Left            =    120
         TabIndex        =    10
         Top             =    780
         Width           =    1592
      End
      Begin Label TrackPositionLabel
         Height          =    252
         Left            =    4620
         TabIndex        =    8
         Top             =    1200
         Width           =    1212
      End
      Begin Label Label3
         Alignment       =    1   'Right Justify
         Caption         =    "Track Position:"
         Height          =    252
         Left            =    3300
         TabIndex        =    7
         Top             =    1200
         Width           =    1272
      End
      Begin Label TrackLengthLabel
         Height          =    252
         Left            =    1860
         TabIndex        =    6
         Top             =    1200
         Width           =    1152
      End
      Begin Label Label2
         Alignment       =    1   'Right Justify
         Caption         =    "Track Length:"
         Height          =    252
         Left            =    600
         TabIndex        =    5
         Top             =    1200
         Width           =    1212
      End
```

```
Begin Label TrackNumberLabel
    Alignment       =   2   'Center
    BorderStyle     =   1   'Fixed Single
    Caption         =   "4"
    FontBold        =   -1  'True
    FontItalic      =   0   'False
    FontName        =   "MS Sans Serif"
    FontSize        =   13.8
    FontStrikethru  =   0   'False
    FontUnderline   =   0   'False
    Height          =   372
    Left            =   4560
    TabIndex        =   4
    Top             =   1520
    Width           =   612
End
Begin Label Label1
    Alignment       =   1   'Right Justify
    Caption         =   "CD Title:"
    Height          =   312
    Left            =   180
    TabIndex        =   3
    Top             =   180
    Width           =   852
End
End
```

Beginning the Form Code

All the event procedures in CDPLAYER.FRM call the API function **mciSendString()** for one reason or another. Let's begin by looking at the **Form_Load()** event procedure, shown in Listing 15.5.

Listing 15.5   The Form_Load() Event Procedure from CDPLAYER.FRM

```
Sub Form_Load ()
    Dim CurrentMode As String

    OpenTitleFile
    mciResult = mciSendString("close CDAudio", ReturnString, 127, 0)
    mciResult = mciSendString("open CDAudio shareable", ReturnString, 127, 0)
    If mciResult <> 0 Then
        MsgBox "Unable to Open CD Audio Device", 15, "MCI Error"
        End
    Else
        mciResult = mciSendString("set CDAudio time format tmsf", ReturnString, 127, 0)
        mciResult = mciSendString("status CDAudio mode", ReturnString, 127, 0)
        CurrentMode = CleanString(ReturnString)
        DiskIdentified = False
        UserWantsToPlay = (CurrentMode = "playing")
        ActivityTimer.Enabled = True
    End If
End Sub
```

Oddly enough, this event procedure starts by closing the CDAudio device. This is a precautionary measure to cover the possibility that the device was left open in a previous session (particularly helpful when you're debugging a new program that terminates prematurely after opening the device). The variables **mciResult** and **ReturnString** occur frequently in this program, so I decided to declare them as globals in the code module, which we'll discuss later.

After making sure the device is properly closed, the procedure then attempts to re-open it. Most device drivers will return an error if no disk is loaded in the drive, or if another program has the device open, so it's common for the open operation to fail. That's why I chose to trap the error for this particular call to **mciSendString()**. If you wish, you can trap the individual error types and report the specific reason for the failure of the device to open.

If the device does open successfully, we send the command string "set CDAudio time format tmsf" to change the time format, so we can set the playback position in terms of tracks. From this point on, timing and positioning information will appear in this format: track number, minutes, seconds, and frames, in the form tt:mm:ss:ff. For CD audio, the frame count doesn't appear to mean anything. Time format strings are right-padded; that is, 5, 5:00, 5:00:00, and 5:00:00:00 all specify track 5 and 5:1:30 and 5:1:30:00 both specify 1 minute and thirty seconds into track 5.

The last MCI command string we send in the load event, "status CDAudio mode," checks the current status of the drive. It's possible to start the CDPLAYER program while a disk is already playing. Some CD-ROM drives have front panel controls that function even when the drive is under MCI control, which means you can load a disk and start it playing without first loading the CDPLAYER. It's also possible to accidentally or intentionally leave a disk playing by loading another program with CD playback capabilities, such as the Windows Media Player, starting a disk, then exiting the program. When CDPLAYER loads, if it finds that the CD drive is already playing a disk, it will allow it to continue without interruption.

Finally, we enable the ActivityTimer control, which is where most of the real action takes place in this program. Let's take a look.

The ActivityTimer_Timer() Event Procedure

As you have probably surmised, a device like the CDAudio player is the perfect candidate for an event-driven interface. Each time the device changes status, we can respond to a message, which is represented in VB by an event procedure. When the device locates a track, it could send a "track found" message; when the track starts playing, it could send a "playing" message;

and when the track is finished, it could send a "play complete" message. Unfortunately, that's not how the MCI works.

The MCI does support a window callback with a message called **MM_MCINOTIFY**, which we could trap with the VB Messenger custom control (discussed in Chapter 14). But since these messages are posted only when an operation is completed or aborted, it can become extremely confusing to sort them out. And notification messages don't help at all when it comes to monitoring the progress of an operation, such as the current position within a playing track.

Instead of messing around with messages, we'll use a *polling* technique. We'll set a timer control to trigger at 1 second intervals (1000 milliseconds). In the **Timer** event, we'll use the MCI command string "status CDAudio mode" to query the device for its current mode. We'll then use the resulting information to select the appropriate action. Listing 15.6 shows how the **ActivityTimer_Timer()** event procedure works.

Listing 15.6   The ActivityTimer_Timer() Event Procedure from CDPLAYER.FRM

```
Sub ActivityTimer_Timer ()
    Dim CurrentMode As String
    Dim TrackPosition
    Dim CurrentTrackNumber As String
    Dim CurrentPositionHours As Integer
    Dim StartPositionHours As Integer
    Dim CurrentPositionMinutes As Integer
    Dim StartPositionMinutes As Integer
    Dim CurrentPositionSeconds As Integer
    Dim StartPositionSeconds As Integer

    mciResult = mciSendString("status CDAudio mode", ReturnString, 127, 0)
    CurrentMode = CleanString(ReturnString)
    Select Case CurrentMode
        ' Insert whatever activity handling you wish in this
        ' Select Case statement.
        Case "not ready"
          UserWantsToPlay = False
          DiskIdentified = False
          'MsgBox "CD Drive Not Ready"
        Case "open"
          UserWantsToPlay = False
          DiskIdentified = False
          'MsgBox "Drive Open"
        Case "paused"
          UserWantsToPlay = False
        Case "playing", "stopped"
          If Not DiskIdentified Then
              CurrentTitleRecordNumber = GetDiskTitleRecord(DiskTitleRecord)
              If CurrentTitleRecordNumber <> 0 Then
```

```
            CDTitleText.Text = DiskTitleRecord.Title
          Else
            CDTitleText.Text = "<Title Unknown>"
          End If
        DiskIdentified = True
      End If
    mciResult = mciSendString("status CDAudio number of tracks",
            ReturnString, 127, 0)
    NumberOfTracksLabel.Caption = CleanString(ReturnString)
    mciResult = mciSendString("status CDAudio current track", ReturnString,
            127, 0)
    CurrentTrackNumber = CleanString(ReturnString)
    TrackNumberLabel.Caption = CurrentTrackNumber
    mciResult = mciSendString("status CDAudio length track " &
            CurrentTrackNumber, ReturnString, 127, 0)
    TrackLengthLabel.Caption = Left$(CleanString(ReturnString), 5)

    mciResult = mciSendString("status CDAudio position", ReturnString, 127, 0)
    CurrentPositionHours = Val(Mid$(ReturnString, 4, 2)) \ 60
    CurrentPositionMinutes = Val(Mid$(ReturnString, 4, 2)) Mod 60
    CurrentPositionSeconds = Val(Mid$(ReturnString, 7, 2))

    mciResult = mciSendString("status CDAudio position track " &
            CurrentTrackNumber, ReturnString, 127, 0)
    StartPositionHours = Val(Mid$(ReturnString, 4, 2)) \ 60
    StartPositionMinutes = Val(Mid$(ReturnString, 4, 2)) Mod 60
    StartPositionSeconds = Val(Mid$(ReturnString, 7, 2))

    TrackPosition = TimeSerial(CurrentPositionHours, CurrentPositionMinutes,
            CurrentPositionSeconds) - TimeSerial(StartPositionHours,
            StartPositionMinutes, StartPositionSeconds)
    TrackPositionLabel.Caption = Format$(TrackPosition, "nn:ss")
    ' Restart playback after a track change.
    If (CurrentMode = "stopped") And UserWantsToPlay Then
        mciResult = mciSendString("play CDAudio", ReturnString, 127, 0)
      End If
  Case "seeking"
  'Case "stopped"
  End Select
End Sub
```

In this program, we want to monitor the identity of the disk and the current playback position. In the *open* and *not ready* modes, we can't get any information from the disk, so all we can do is reset our status variables, **UserWantsToPlay** and **DiskIdentified**. In the *seeking* mode, all we can do is wait until the device locates the requested position, so we do nothing. Most of the action takes place when the device is either *stopped* or *playing*. In these two modes, we can get track and position information. We can then use the information to identify the disk or display its statistics on the form.

If we haven't identified the title of the disk yet, we can call the general function **GetDiskTitleRecord()** (Listing 15.8), which is located in the code module CDPLAYER.BAS. The integer variable **DiskIdentified** will keep the program from continually looking up the title whenever the **Timer** event fires. After we identify the title, we query the device for track and position information, which we use to display the current track number, the track length in minutes and seconds, and the current position within the track.

Unfortunately, the status command doesn't offer a "position within track" option, so we have to calculate our position within the current track by subtracting the starting position of the track from our current absolute position (our position relative to the beginning of the disk). For this task, we use the VB **TimeSerial()** function to calculate our offset into the track. The MCI tmsf format does not report hours, so we use integer division and the **Mod** operator to split the minutes field into hours and minutes. Notice that the MCI CDAudio driver cannot handle intervals longer than 99 minutes, 59 seconds. Other MCI device drivers, such as the MIDI Sequencer and Videodisc Player, support time formats that include a field for hours.

The frequency of these status messages can have a significant impact on system performance. When you request information from the device, the API function must wait for a response from the driver, which in turn must wait for a response from the CD-ROM drive. Status queries can cause noticeable system pauses. To improve general system performance while CDPLAYER is running, you may wish to reduce the number of status queries by eliminating real-time position tracking ("status CDAudio position") or by increasing the timer **Interval** to decrease MCI activity.

Finishing the Form Code

The remaining event code in CDPLAYER.FRM sends simple MCI messages to start and stop playback, to close the device, to eject the disk (not supported on all drives), and to select tracks, as shown in Listing 15.7.

Listing 15.7   The Declarations and Remaining Event Procedures from CDPLAYER.FRM

```
Option Explicit

Dim UserWantsToPlay As Integer
Dim DiskIdentified As Integer
Dim DiskTitleRecord As DiskTitleRecords
```

```
Sub EjectButton_Click ()
    mciResult = mciSendString("stop CDAudio", ReturnString, 127, 0)
    If DiskIdentified Then
        DiskTitleRecord.Title = CDTitleText.Text
        SaveDiskTitleRecord DiskTitleRecord, CurrentTitleRecordNumber
    End If
    mciResult = mciSendString("set CDAudio door open", ReturnString, 127, 0)
    UserWantsToPlay = False
    End Sub

Sub Form_Unload (Cancel As Integer)
    Dim mciResult As Integer

    mciResult = mciSendString("close CDAudio", ReturnString, 127, 0)
    End Sub

Sub PlayButton_Click ()
    mciResult = mciSendString("play CDAudio", ReturnString, 127, 0)
    If mciResult = 0 Then
        UserWantsToPlay = True
    End If
    End Sub

Sub RestartButton_Click ()
    mciResult = mciSendString("seek CDAudio to start", ReturnString, 127, 0)
    End Sub

Sub StopButton_Click ()
    mciResult = mciSendString("stop CDAudio", ReturnString, 127, 0)
    UserWantsToPlay = False
    If DiskIdentified Then
        DiskTitleRecord.Title = CDTitleText.Text
        SaveDiskTitleRecord DiskTitleRecord, CurrentTitleRecordNumber
    End If
    End Sub

Sub TrackSelectSpin_SpinDown ()
    Dim NewPosition As Integer

    NewPosition = MaxInt(Val(TrackNumberLabel.Caption) - 1, 1)
    mciResult = mciSendString("seek CDAudio to " & Str$(NewPosition),
            ReturnString, 127, 0)
    If UserWantsToPlay Then
        mciResult = mciSendString("play CDAudio", ReturnString, 127, 0)
    End If
    End Sub

Sub TrackSelectSpin_SpinUp ()
    Dim NewPosition As Integer

    NewPosition = MinInt(Val(TrackNumberLabel.Caption) + 1,
            Val(NumberOfTracksLabel.Caption))
    mciResult = mciSendString("seek CDAudio to " & Str$(NewPosition),
```

```
ReturnString, 127, 0)
    If UserWantsToPlay Then
        mciResult = mciSendString("play CDAudio", ReturnString, 127, 0)
    End If
End Sub
```

The only noteworthy code in these event procedures is in **TrackSelect-Spin_SpinDown()** and **TrackSelectSping_SpinUp()**. When you reposition the device with a **seek** command, the device driver will halt playback (at least it does on my system; this may depend on the device driver version). We can restart playback with a **play** command, but we don't want to do this arbitrarily, because the user may want to change tracks while the drive is stopped. To manage this problem, I created the variable **UserWantsToPlay** so I could distinguish between the current drive mode and the status selected by the operator. Clicking on the Play button sets **UserWantsToPlay** to True; clicking on the Stop button sets the variable to False. If the drive stops upon seeking, but **UserWantsToPlay** is still True, then we just issue another **play** command.

The Code Module

The code module, shown in Listing 15.8, contains the global declarations and the code that manages the disk title file, CDTITLES.DAT.

Listing 15.8   CDPLAYER.BAS

```
Option Explicit

Declare Function mciSendString Lib "MMSystem" (ByVal lpstrCommand As String,
ByVal lpstrReturnString As String, ByVal wReturnLength As Integer, ByVal
hCallback As Integer) As Long

Type DiskTitleRecords
    IDNumber As Long
    Title As String * 128
    End Type


Global mciResult As Integer
Global ReturnString As String * 128
Global CDTitleFile As Integer
Global CurrentTitleRecordNumber As Integer

Function CleanString (MessyString As String) As String
    CleanString = Left$(MessyString, InStr(MessyString, Chr$(0)) - 1)
    End Function

Function GetDiskTitleRecord (AnyDiskTitleRecord As DiskTitleRecords)
    Dim NumberOfTracks As Integer
```

```
    Dim DiskLength As Long
    Dim DiskID As Long
    Dim RecordPosition As Integer
    Dim Found As Integer

    mciResult = mciSendString("status CDAudio number of tracks", ReturnString, 127, 0)
    NumberOfTracks = Val(CleanString(ReturnString))
    mciResult = mciSendString("set CDAudio time format milliseconds",
            ReturnString, 127, 0)
    mciResult = mciSendString("status CDAudio length", ReturnString, 127, 0)
    DiskLength = Val(CleanString(ReturnString))
    DiskID = NumberOfTracks * DiskLength
    mciResult = mciSendString("set CDAudio time format tmsf", ReturnString, 127, 0)

    RecordPosition = 0
    Do
        RecordPosition = RecordPosition + 1
        Get CDTitleFile, RecordPosition, AnyDiskTitleRecord
        Found = (DiskID = AnyDiskTitleRecord.IDNumber)
        Loop Until Found Or EOF(CDTitleFile)
    If Found Then
        GetDiskTitleRecord = RecordPosition
      Else
        GetDiskTitleRecord = 0
        AnyDiskTitleRecord.IDNumber = DiskID
      End If
    End Function

Sub OpenTitleFile ()
    Dim AnyTitleRecord As DiskTitleRecords

    CDTitleFile = 1
    Open App.Path & "\CDTitles.Dat" For Random As CDTitleFile Len =
    Len(AnyTitleRecord)
    End Sub

Sub SaveDiskTitleRecord (AnyDiskTitleRecord As DiskTitleRecords, RecordPosition
As Integer)
    Dim FileSize As Integer

    If RecordPosition <> 0 Then
        Put CDTitleFile, RecordPosition, AnyDiskTitleRecord
      Else
        FileSize = LOF(CDTitleFile) \ Len(AnyDiskTitleRecord)
        RecordPosition = FileSize + 1
        Put CDTitleFile, RecordPosition, AnyDiskTitleRecord
      End If
    End Sub
```

In the general function **GetDiskTitleRecord()**, we temporarily change the time format to milliseconds. We multiply the total length of the disk in milliseconds by the number of tracks to create a unique *signature* for the disk.

Although it's possible, it's extremely unlikely that any two CDs will have the same signature. For each CD, we store a record with two fields:

```
Type DiskTitleRecords
    IDNumber As Long
    Title As String * 128
    End Type
```

We store the signature in the **IDNumber** field, and the CD title in the **Title** field. Each time the user loads a disk in the CD-ROM drive, the **ActivityTimer_Timer()** event procedure (shown in Listing 15.6) calls **GetDiskTitleRecord()**, which calculates the disk's signature and searches CDTITLES.DAT for a record with a matching **IDNumber**. If it finds an existing record, it returns the record position; if not, it returns 0. In the **StopButton_Click()** and **EjectButton_Click()** event procedures (Listing 15.7) we call the **SaveDiskTitleRecord()** general procedure, passing it the current **DiskTitleRecord** and the record position returned by **GetDiskTitleRecord()**. If the record position is non-zero, **SaveDiskTitleRecord()** replaces the existing record. If the record position is zero, **SaveDiskTitleRecord()** appends a new record to the end of the file. The record is replaced every time you stop or eject the disk, so you can modify the title any time you wish.

> **NOTE:** *Pressing the manual eject button on the drive itself will not trigger the **EjectButton_Click()** event, which means that it will not rewrite the title record. If your drive does not support automatic eject, you must use the program's Stop button to store the title record before you eject the disk. You may also wish to experiment with the* open *and* not ready *drive modes to trigger file updates.*

Suggested Enhancements

This kind of program is a hacker's wonderland. You can add features to this basic framework until it does anything you ever imagined you might want from your Discman—except make it portable enough to carry in the next triathalon. Here are a few suggestions:

- Add a second file to hold song titles.
- Replace the binary file system with an Access database.
- Add features to maintain the database, such as a delete option.
- Add random and programmable play ordering.

- Add a musician's practice loop that will repeat the same passage indefinitely.

- Dress up the screen with original artwork and animated buttons.

Don't Underestimate the MCI

Each MCI device supports its own set of commands. Many commands are the same or similar from one device to another, but be careful not to overlook hidden capabilities. Even the innocent-looking **play** command changes from one device to another. For example, in the Videodisc command set, the **play** command can control the speed of playback, and can even order the disc to play in reverse.

The number and type of MCI devices is growing steadily. If you're planning to purchase a laser disc player, a semi-professional VCR, a DAT tape deck, or any other piece of equipment that might be useful in multimedia production, be sure to investigate MCI support. Most of these devices will connect to your computer by way of a serial port, which means they won't require additional IRQs, DMA channels, or I/O addresses.

Don't assume, however, that all MCI devices are created equal. If a manufacturer claims that its product supports MCI, ask for some assurance in the form of a return policy. Not everyone understands just what it means to support MCI. Simple play, stop, and rewind functions won't do you any good when you try to perform step-frame AVI captures.

MCI devices can add a whole new dimension to your multimedia projects, especially those that do not need to run exclusively on a self-contained PC. For museum and kiosk systems, for example, you can really punch up your presentations with separate screens and speakers attached to MCI-controlled videodisc players, VCRs, audio tape players, or any number of other devices. And who knows where MCI and Windows multimedia are headed in the future?

Chapter 16

Video on my PC, really? Yes, really. Take a peek into this chapter as we explore Video for Windows' Visual Basic support that allows even you to create smooth-motion pictures on your PC.

The PC Video Revolution

F or better or for worse, video has been a major propellant of the multimedia revolution. The labels of successful multimedia titles often proclaim the number of minutes of video they contain. And regardless of how much or how little video appears in any particular multimedia product, it's still usually the first thing that most of us want to see. Isn't it amazing that people who spend an average of four hours every day looking at full-color, full-motion television get so excited when they see a tiny, 10-second video clip on their computer screens?

I don't know why PC video gets us so excited. Maybe because it hints at the virtual-reality future where pre-recorded video clips will be replaced by interactive 3D adventures through worlds both real and imaginary. It doesn't really matter. Any good salesperson will tell you that you must grab your users' attention or your message will be lost. When well done, video can get their attention and deliver the message with a single punch.

Video for Windows

Video for Windows (VfW), Microsoft's contribution to the world of digital video, is an extension for Windows that enables applications to digitize and play video clips captured from conventional analog video sources, such as camcorders, laserdisks, VCRs, and professional video decks. You're probably already thinking of the first blockbuster you'll be creating with this technology, but hold on. Unfortunately, digital video has a long way to go before it will allow you to collaborate with the likes of Steven Spielberg.

The current state of the art doesn't even match the poor quality pictures we're accustomed to seeing on television. American TV has a vertical resolution of 525 lines. Because TV is still an analog system, it's hard to precisely measure horizontal resolution. To some extent, horizontal resolution depends on the TV receiver, but the maximum is equivalent to roughly 700 pixels. If we could play full-screen digital video on our PC monitors, we would be looking at resolutions ranging from 640 by 480 pixels to over 1280 by 1024 pixels. Unfortunately, the current standard frame size for most video clips is only 160 by 120 pixels. It's possible to play full-screen digital video on our screens, but only with assistance from one of several proprietary hardware systems.

One of the key ideas behind VfW is that it requires no special hardware for playback. To achieve the data throughput necessary to spray bitmaps on the screen fast enough to simulate motion while simultaneously playing synchronized stereo digital audio using nothing but software, something had to be sacrificed—okay, many things had to be sacrificed. Although the current standard frame size for most video clips is 160 by 120 pixels, VfW also supports two other standard resolutions, 240 by 180 and 320 by 240 pixels. The problem with these larger dimensions is that most PCs can't decompress and display them fast enough to play them smoothly, especially from CD-ROM. Even at the largest size, unstretched digital video clips fill only one quarter of a 640 by 480 VGA display.

In the future, hardware video decompressors may become as common as sound cards are now. Unfortunately, that will require some kind of standard. Right now it's too early to settle on a video compression standard. Each of the competing systems offers unique advantages. If you've been through the agonizing torture of configuring your own multimedia PC, you know that the last thing we need is a separate card for each video format. Hardware video playback will not become common until either all the best features have been combined into a single standard, or a single card can be manufactured that will support multiple compression standards.

How it Works

VfW is based on a system called *audio-video interleave*. A basic VfW file, which carries the extension .AVI, contains a series of alternating bitmaps and wave data segments. Unlike bitmap files, the data in an .AVI file is usually compressed. In fact, it's the compression that makes it possible to move the data around fast enough to look like motion pictures. Uncompressed, 60 seconds of 15 frame per second video at 160 by 120 would fill 51,840,000 bytes! That's 864,000 bytes per second—with no sound. Most hard disk drives and controllers could not pump that much data into memory quickly enough to support smooth playback, and no consumer-level CD-ROM drive comes close to that data transfer rate. But compression often reduces the size of an .AVI file by a factor of 10 or more. This heavy compression, known as *lossy* compression, noticeably degrades the image quality, but without it, software-only video playback would not be possible on current desktop computers.

The task of the VfW system is to identify which compression-decompression algorithm, or *codec*, has been used to prepare a particular video clip, then to use that codec to reconstitute the data, separate it into video and audio elements, and feed it to the display system and sound card fast enough that it looks and sounds something like miniature television. This is a monumental task that will tax even the brawniest of PCs.

> **NOTE:** *For detailed coverage of PC video production and digital video capture, see* How to Digitize Video *by Nels Johnson with Fred Gault and Mark Florence of The San Francisco Canyon Company. John Wiley & Sons, Inc., 1994.*

.AVI files can get pretty complicated. VfW version 1.1a supports multiple streams, which means that a single file can contain multiple sound tracks, MIDI music data, even multiple video tracks. Some codecs support 24-bit color, while others use 8-bit color and palettes. Palettes are confusing enough when they apply to nice quiet, static bitmaps; in digital video files, palettes are utterly unnerving. Each time a scene changes, the palette can change, which means that the palette manager has to perform a quick change, right in the middle of a running video clip. To manage all this data and turn it into something that resembles video requires the services of several special libraries. Together, these libraries make up the VfW system and its API.

Video for Windows for Programmers

If you combined all the Windows API features we've used so far in this book—from bitblts and ROPs, to animation and wave audio—and injected them with steroids, you might end up with something about half as complex as the VfW API. Fortunately, you don't need to grasp all the inner workings of this powerful system to use video in your own multimedia projects. As a matter of fact, in the *Programmer's Guide* from the Video for Windows Development Kit, Microsoft discourages us from too quickly peeking under the hood. Instead, they provide high-level tools in the form of .VBXs and *window classes* (for Holy Trinity programmers) that enable us to capture, play, and edit video clips from within our own applications by sending messages or setting properties. After you've grasped the overall design of the video system, if you still feel the need for greater control, you can dive right into the low-level interface. The Developer's Kit includes plenty of sample code to get you started.

Video for Windows comprises six main modules:

- The AVICAP.DLL contains the functions that perform video capture. These functions provide a high-level interface to .AVI file I/O and to the video and audio device drivers. The CAPWNDX.VBX primarily calls on the functions in this library.

- The MSVIDEO.DLL handles onscreen video operation with a special set of *DrawDib* functions, which act like a turbo-charged form of **StretchDIBits()**. These functions also support the *Installable Compression Manager* (ICM), which allows them to display frames from compressed video. Both the CAPWNDX.VBX and MCIWNDX.VBX custom controls use functions in this library to display video on the screen.

- The MCIAVI.DRV driver contains the MCI command interpreter for VfW.

- The AVIFILE.DLL supports higher-level file access to .AVI files than provided by the standard multimedia I/O (mmio) functions (which we used to play wave audio in Chapters 4 and 13). AVIFILE functions manage .AVI files in terms of *video frames* and *data streams*. The purpose of streams is to provide synchronized playback of multiple data channels, such as video, audio soundtrack, MIDI background music, and multilingual narration. You can even write your own file handlers to support other non-standard streams.

- The Installable Compression Manager (ICM) manages the codecs, the drivers that *com*press and *de*compress video data stored in .AVI files. Several codecs already exist, including Microsoft Video 1, Intel's Indeo Video, and SuperMac's CinePak. The other modules in VfW access the codecs by way of the ICM.

- The Audio Compression Manager (ACM) provides services similar to the ICM, but works on wave audio data rather than on video. The ACM may be used independently of VfW to provide wave audio compression whenever it is needed. Once you have installed the ACM (this is done automatically when you install the VfW runtime library), decompression occurs automatically whenever the multimedia system encounters a compressed WAVE file. If the ACM is installed on your system, you'll find an applet called Sound Mapper in your Windows Control Panel. Sound Mapper is an interface that enables configuration of the audio codecs and control over the mappings between waveaudio devices and the compression drivers. One of the standard drivers, the Microsoft PCM Converter, is especially interesting because it enables playback of high-resolution, high sample rate WAVE files on sound cards with lesser capabilities.

The printed version of the *Programmer's Guide* from the VfW Development Kit is over 700 pages long! Obviously, we can't cover all the details of VfW in this chapter, so instead we'll focus on the VB support provided by the DK's two custom controls, CAPWNDX.VBX and MCIWNDX.VBX. Before we can get started, you'll need to install both the VfW runtime library, which will enable your system to play .AVI files, and the VfW Development Kit.

Installing the Video for Windows Runtime Library

To play .AVI files requires no special hardware. You don't even need a sound card—if you don't mind silent movies. But you do need to install the VfW runtime library, which includes an assortment of files and requires a few additions to your Windows INI files.

The companion CD-ROM for this book includes the \VFW11A subdirectory, which itself includes several further subdirectories:

```
\VFW11A
        \RUNTIME
                \DISKS
                        \FRN
                                \DISK1
                        \GER
                                \DISK1
                        \USA
                                \DISK1
                \SETUPSRC
        \VFWDK
```

To install the VfW runtime library, open the Program Manager and select File, Run. Then use the Browse dialog box to locate SETUP.EXE in the subdirectory \VFW11A\RUNTIME\DISKS\USA\DISK1. The runtime libraries will be installed in your \WINDOWS\SYSTEM directory. To activate the VfW drivers, you must restart Windows.

To test the VfW drivers, load the Media Player, then open its Device menu. If the VfW drivers have been correctly installed, you should find an option on this menu called Video for Windows. Select this option to display the Open dialog box. Locate a file with the extension .AVI. You'll find several on the companion CD-ROM. Once you have loaded an .AVI file, select the play button. The video clip will appear in its own window somewhere on your screen.

With the VfW drivers installed, you can play almost any .AVI file. You'll find hundreds of them on clip art disks, on BBSs, and on public networks such as CompuServe and the Internet. To make your own video clips, you'll need a video capture card and either a camcorder or a VCR (or both). Playback quality will vary from clip to clip, depending on the performance of your computer and video display system, and on the frame size, frame rate, and compression method used to prepare each clip. Even the content of the video sequence itself can significantly affect performance; most of the methods used to compress video use a technique called *delta compression*, which works best when there are few changes from one frame to the next. If your system has trouble playing a clip from CD-ROM, try copying the file to your hard drive. CD-ROM drives—even fast ones—are still considerably slower than hard disks.

> **NOTE:** *If you create products that include .AVI files, you'll also need to include the VfW runtime library. The contents of the subdirectories \VFW11A\RUNTIME\DISKS\USA\DISK1, ..\FRN\DISK1, and ..\GER\DISK1 are freely redistributable. The source code for the setup program is located in \VFW11A\RUNTIME\SETUPSRC. You may use this source code to incorporate the video runtime setup into your application's own setup program. For more information on runtime redistribution and the setup source, see the file DEV_KIT.TXT in the \VFWDK subdirectory.*

Installing the Video for Windows Development Kit

The Video for Windows Development Kit is almost as easy to install as the runtime library. Open the Program Manager and select File, Run from the menu. Then use the Browse option to locate the program SETUP.EXE in the \VFW11A\VFWDK subdirectory. Select this program and follow the instructions for installation

The setup program will create a directory structure with eight subdirectories off the main subdirectory (usually \VFWDK). The \VFWDK\SAMPLES subdirectory will contain 26 subdirectories of its own, one for each sample program. The \VFWDK\TOOLS subdirectory will contain one subdirectory called \DEBUG. The VfW DK will require a total of approximately 13 megabytes of disk space.

The setup program will also create a program group called VfW 1.1 DK, which will include an icon for the Read Me file, several of the sample programs (including two VB programs), and the Programmer's Guide, a lengthy help file that contains the complete documentation for the Development Kit.

NOTE: *For more information on the directory structure created by the VFWDK, see the DEV_KIT.TXT file in the \VFW11A subdirectory.*

Video Capture

The most complex process in PC video is the conversion of analog video into digital data. If you've used a video capture card, then you're probably already familiar with VidCap, the VfW capture utility. With VidCap you can specify the frame size, compression method, and frame rate, along with audio resolution and sampling rate, and a variety of other parameters. You may then select one of four capture techniques: streaming video capture, streaming video capture with MCI control, step-frame capture with MCI control, and single-frame capture. VidCap and its companion utility, VidEdit, are components of the commercial Video for Windows product, available through retail channels, but are also often bundled with video capture hardware—they are not included in the VfW Development Kit. However, with a lot of help from the CAPWNDX.VBX custom control, which does come with the VfW DK, we can create a VB program with most of VidCap's capabilities.

Capturing Video with the CAPWNDX.VBX Custom Control

You may find that the controls of the VfW capture program, VidCap, are not arranged well for your particular application. Or, you may want to embed video capture capabilities in your own applications, such as a video e-mail system. With the CAPWNDX.VBX custom control we can build our own video capture utilities. In this project, we'll write a simple video capture program. Here are the steps to follow:

1. Create the form VIDCAP1.FRM.
2. Add the event procedures to the form.

You'll find this project in the subdirectory \VBMAGIC in the files VIDCAP1.MAK and VIDCAP1.FRM. You'll also need the THREED.VBX custom control, usually installed in your \WINDOWS\SYSTEM subdirectory by VB Setup, and the CAPWNDX.VBX, which you should first copy from \VFWDK\BIN to \WINDOWS\SYSTEM.

Running the Video Capture Program

The first thing you need to run this program is a properly installed and tested video capture card. Any card that supports VfW will work. Luckily, this pretty much includes every card on the market. I use the Intel Smart Video Recorder (ISVR) because it supports real-time capture and compression, which saves both time and disk space. Creative Labs makes several video capture cards, including their VideoBlaster series and the VideoSpigot. And don't forget to check out the Pro MovieStudio from Media Vision, and VideoLogic's Captivator. Each card requires unique installation procedures, so follow the documentation carefully.

VIDCAP1 has only one VB form. Figure 16.1 shows the form at runtime.

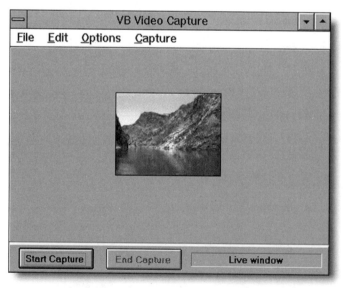

Figure 16.1   *VIDCAP1.FRM at runtime.*

To capture a video sequence:

1. Set up your video source (usually either a camcorder or a VCR), and make sure it is properly connected with the appropriate cables to your video capture card and sound card.
2. Run VIDCAP1.MAK.
3. Access the dialog boxes from the Options menu commands that allow you to choose a video format (such as 160 by 120 pixels) and a video source.
4. To begin capture, either select Capture, Video... from the menu bar, or click on the Start Capture button. If the capture is working, the cursor will change to an hourglass.
5. To end capture, either press Esc or click the right mouse button.

To replay the captured video sequence:

1. Open the Media Player.
2. Select Option, Video for Windows to display the Open dialog box.
3. Use the Open dialog box to locate and select the file CAPTURE.AVI (set in the sample program to be created in C:\).
4. Click on the Play button.

Creating the Form

The centerpiece of VIDCAP1 is the CAPWNDX.VBX custom control. When you place this control on a form, it appears as a black rectangle. This will become the video preview window. CAPWNDX has no buttons, labels, captions, or scroll bars of its own. To manipulate its features we have to set some properties. CAPWNDX has only two event procedures, **Status()** and **Error()**, and 54 properties, shown in Table 16.1.

Table 16.1   *The Properties List for CAPWNDX.VBX*

Property	Purpose
AudioBits	Specifies 8 or 16 bit audio.
AudioChannels	Specifies 1 for mono or 2 for stereo audio.
AudioRate	Specifies audio sampling rate of 11025, 22050, or 44100 Hz.
CaptureAudio	Set to True to capture audio along with video.
Capture	Set to True to begin capture; False to stop capture.
CaptureHitOK	If set to True, will display a prompt to press Enter before capture begins.

(continued)

Table 16.1   *The Properties List for CAPWNDX.VBX (continued)*

CaptureDOSMem	If True, this property uses memory under 1 Mb boundary to buffer capture data (the best choice for large direct-to-disk captures); if False, it uses extended memory to buffer capture (the best choice when the entire sequence will fit in memory).
CaptureUseLimit	Set to True to automatically stop capture after number of seconds specified in CaptureLimit property.
CaptureLimit	Limit captures to the specified number of seconds.
VideoRate	Specifies the frame rate; usually set to 15 or fewer frames, depending on capabilities of host machine and frame dimensions.
SingleFrameOpen	Set to True to prepare for single frame capture.
SingleFrame	Each time this property is set to True, it captures a single frame, appends it to the current capture file, and resets itself to False.
SingleFrameClose	Closes the single frame capture mode.
Yield	Set to True to allow other Windows applications to continue execution during video capture (I wouldn't try this).
CaptureAbort	If Yield is True, then the Esc key will no longer stop video capture; instead, you must set the property to True to end background capture.
CaptureStop	Set to True to stop step-frame capture. MCI commands will then be used to rerun the capture sequence on the source device to capture the audio tracks.
CaptureFile	Specifies the path and filename of the capture file.
CaptureFileSize	Used to preallocate a file large enough to hold the captured sequence; preallocation improves performance.
CaptureSave	Specifies a path and filename to which the capture file will be copied. This allows the maintenance of a permanently preallocated and defragmented capture file which is then copied to a destination file upon completion of capture. Copy occurs upon assignment of the filename to the property.
DriverNum	Specifies the capture driver to use; zero based.
Connect	Set to True to connect to the capture driver; the connection occurs automatically when capture begins, but to preview video before the capture, you must set Connect to True.
DriverName	Returns a string containing the name of the driver specified in the DriverNum property.
DriverVersion	Returns a string containing the version of the driver specified in the DriverNum property.
MCIDeviceEnable	Set to True to enable MCI capture control; currently requires a Sony VISCA compatible video source.

(continued)

Table 16.1   *The Properties List for CAPWNDX.VBX (continued)*

MCIDeviceName	A string used to specify the MCI device from which to capture.
MCIStartMS	Specifies the starting time for the capture on the source device (in milliseconds).
MCIStepCapture	Set to True to enable step frame capture.
MCIStopMS	Specifies the ending time for the capture on the source device (in milliseconds).
EditCopy	Set to True to copy the current frame to the Clipboard; automatically resets to False after the procedure.
CanOverlay	Read-only; indicates whether the device supports video overlay (display of live analog video to a window on the screen).
Overlay	If set to True, disables preview and displays live video in the capture window.
PalCreate	When set to True, automatically constructs a palette for the video being captured; applies only to 8-bit capture devices.
PalCreateManual	Set to True to add the palette of the current frame to an accumulator; set to False to build a palette from the accumulated color data.
PalNumColors	Specifies the number of colors in the palette created by either PalCreate or PalCreateManual: 2 to 256.
PalNumFrames	Specifies the number of frames examined by PalCreate to produce a palette for the entire sequence; if the sequence includes frequent scene changes, set this number high (defaults to 20 frames).
PalSave	Specifies the path and filename of a file in which to save the palette; copy occurs upon assignment of the filename.
PalOpen	Specifies the path and filename of a palette to use for 8-bit capture.
PreviewRate	Specifies the refresh rate of the preview window when Preview is set to True.
Preview	Set to True to activate Preview, which periodically samples the incoming video stream and displays the frames.
Error	Returns a string containing a description of the latest error.
ErrorNum	Returns the number of the latest error.
Status	Returns a string containing a description of the status of the capture process.
VideoCompressionDlg	Set to True to display a dialog box that enables the user to select the real-time compression method to use during capture. The actual dialog box depends on the current driver and data format.
VideoDisplayDlg	Set to True to display a dialog box that enables the user to choose display options. This dialog box is driver dependent and is not always available.

(continued)

Table 16.1   *The Properties List for CAPWNDX.VBX (continued)*

VideoFormatDlg	Set to True to display a dialog box that enables the user to choose the video format, such as dimensions and color depth (8-bit, 24-bit, etc.). This dialog box is driver dependent, and is not always available.
VideoSourceDlg	Set to True to display a dialog box that enables the user to choose a video source. This dialog box is driver dependent, and is not always available.
AutoSize	Set to True to cause the control window to resize itself to the video image; set to False to stretch the video image to fit the control window.
Left	Specifies the position of the left side of the control within the form or other container.
Height	Specifies the height of the control window.
Top	Specifies the position of the top of the control window within the form or other container.
Width	Specifies the width of the control window.
Name	Specifies the VB control name within the application.
Visible	Set to True to display the control; set to False to hide it.
BorderStyle	Set to True to display a single-pixel width border; set to False for no border.

Most of the other controls in this program are menu options, as shown in Listing 16.1.

Listing 16.1   The Controls and Properties from VIDCAP1.FRM

```
VERSION 2.00
Begin Form VidCap1F1
    BorderStyle     =   3   'Fixed Double
    Caption         =   "VB Video Capture"
    ClientHeight    =   3960
    ClientLeft      =   2460
    ClientTop       =   4500
    ClientWidth     =   5892
    Height          =   4704
    Left            =   2412
    LinkTopic       =   "Form1"
    ScaleHeight     =   3960
    ScaleWidth      =   5892
    Top             =   3804
    Width           =   5988
    Begin SSPanel Panel3D2
        Align       =   1   'Align Top
        Alignment   =   8   'Center - BOTTOM
        BackColor   =   &H00C0C0C0&
        Font3D      =   0   'None
```

```
   Height          =    3432
   Left            =    0
   TabIndex        =    3
   Top             =    0
   Width           =    5892
   Begin CommonDialog CaptureFileDialog
      DefaultExt    =    ".AVI"
      Filter        =    "Video (*.avi)|*.avi"
      Left          =    5340
      Top           =    2940
   End
   Begin CAPWND CapWnd1
      AudioBits     =    8
      AudioChannels =    1
      AudioRate     =    11025
      AutoSize      =    -1   'True
      CaptureAudio  =    -1   'True
      CaptureDOSMem =    0    'False
      CaptureFile   =    "C:\CAPTURE.AVI"
      CaptureHitOK  =    0    'False
      CaptureLimit  =    0
      CaptureUseLimit =  0    'False
      Connect       =    0    'False
      DriverNum     =    0
      Height        =    1872
      Left          =    60
      MCIDeviceEnable =  0    'False
      MCIDeviceName =    ""
      MCIStartMS    =    0
      MCIStepCapture =   0    'False
      MCIStopMS     =    0
      Overlay       =    0    'False
      PalNumColors  =    256
      PalNumFrames  =    20
      Preview       =    0    'False
      PreviewRate   =    1
      Top           =    120
      VideoRate     =    15
      Width         =    1992
      Yield         =    0    'False
   End
End
Begin SSPanel Panel3D1
   Align           =    2    'Align Bottom
   Alignment       =    8    'Center - BOTTOM
   BackColor       =    &H00C0C0C0&
   Font3D          =    0    'None
   Height          =    492
   Left            =    0
   TabIndex        =    0
   Top             =    3468
   Width           =    5892
```

```
Begin SSPanel StatusPanel
    Alignment       =   8   'Center - BOTTOM
    BackColor       =   &H00C0C0C0&
    BevelOuter      =   1   'Inset
    Caption         =   "Status Panel"
    Font3D          =   0   'None
    Height          =   252
    Left            =   3360
    TabIndex        =   4
    Top             =   120
    Width           =   2412
End
Begin CommandButton EndCaptureButton
    Caption         =   "End Capture"
    Enabled         =   0   'False
    Height          =   372
    Left            =   1800
    TabIndex        =   2
    Top             =   60
    Width           =   1392
End
Begin CommandButton StartButton
    Caption         =   "Start Capture"
    Height          =   372
    Left            =   180
    TabIndex        =   1
    Top             =   60
    Width           =   1392
End
End
Begin Menu FileMenu
    Caption         =   "&File"
    Begin Menu LoadPaletteOption
        Caption         =   "&Load Palette"
    End
    Begin Menu SetCapFileOption
        Caption         =   "&Set Capture File"
    End
    Begin Menu Break1
        Caption         =   "-"
    End
    Begin Menu SaveAsOption
        Caption         =   "Save &Captured Video As..."
    End
    Begin Menu SavePaletteOption
        Caption         =   "Save &Palette"
    End
    Begin Menu SaveFrameOption
        Caption         =   "Save Single &Frame"
        Enabled         =   0   'False
    End
    Begin Menu Break2
        Caption         =   "-"
    End
```

```
      Begin Menu ExitOption
         Caption        =    "E&xit"
      End
   End
   Begin Menu EditMenu
      Caption       =    "&Edit"
      Begin Menu CopyOption
         Caption        =    "&Copy Frame"
         Shortcut       =    ^C
      End
      Begin Menu PastePalOption
         Caption        =    "Paste &Palette"
         Enabled        =    0    'False
      End
      Begin Menu Break3
         Caption        =    "-"
      End
      Begin Menu PreferencesOption
         Caption        =    "Pre&ferences"
         Enabled        =    0    'False
      End
   End
   Begin Menu OptionsMenu
      Caption       =    "&Options"
      Begin Menu AudioCaptureOption
         Caption        =    "Capture &Audio"
      End
      Begin Menu Break4
         Caption        =    "-"
      End
      Begin Menu VideoFormatOption
         Caption        =    "&Video Format"
      End
      Begin Menu VideoSourceOption
         Caption        =    "Video &Source"
      End
      Begin Menu VideoDisplayOption
         Caption        =    "Video &Display"
      End
      Begin Menu Break5
         Caption        =    "-"
      End
      Begin Menu PreviewOption
         Caption        =    "&Preview Video"
      End
      Begin Menu OverlayOption
         Caption        =    "&Overlay Video"
      End
   End
   Begin Menu CaptureMenu
      Caption       =    "&Capture"
      Begin Menu SingleFrameOption
         Caption        =    "&Single Frame"
      End
```

```
    Begin Menu FramesOption
        Caption          =    "&Frames..."
        Enabled          =    0    'False
    End
    Begin Menu CaptureVideoOption
        Caption          =    "&Video..."
    End
    Begin Menu PaletteOption
        Caption          =    "&Palette..."
        Enabled          =    0    'False
    End
    End
End
```

Adding the Event Code

The overwhelming bulk of the code in the event procedures sets the properties of the CapWnd1 control, as shown in Listing 16.2. This program has no code module. In fact, it has no general procedures or functions, or even any variables! CapWnd1 is virtually a program in itself.

Listing 16.2   The Event Procedures from VIDCAP1.FRM

```
Option Explicit

Sub AudioCaptureOption_Click ()
    If Not AudioCaptureOption.Checked Then
        CapWnd1.AudioBits = 8
        CapWnd1.AudioChannels = 1
        CapWnd1.AudioRate = 22050
        CapWnd1.CaptureAudio = True
        AudioCaptureOption.Checked = True
    Else
        CapWnd1.CaptureAudio = False
        AudioCaptureOption.Checked = False
    End If
    End Sub

Sub CaptureVideoOption_Click ()
    CapWnd1.DriverNum = 0
    CapWnd1.Connect = True
    CapWnd1.CaptureLimit = 20 '20 seconds
    CapWnd1.CaptureUseLimit = True
    CapWnd1.VideoRate = 15
    CapWnd1.Capture = True
    End Sub

Sub CapWnd1_Error ()
    If CapWnd1.ErrorNum > 0 Then
        MsgBox CapWnd1.Error, , "Video Capture Error"
    End If
    End Sub
```

```
Sub CapWnd1_Status ()
    StatusPanel.Caption = CapWnd1.Status
    End Sub

Sub CopyOption_Click ()
    CapWnd1.EditCopy = True
    End Sub

Sub EndCaptureButton_Click ()
    CapWnd1.CaptureStop = True
    End Sub

Sub ExitOption_Click ()
    Unload VidCap1F1
    End
    End Sub

Sub Form_Load ()
    CapWnd1.Top = Panel3D2.Height \ 2 - CapWnd1.Height \ 2
    CapWnd1.Left = Panel3D2.Width \ 2 - CapWnd1.Width \ 2
    CapWnd1.DriverNum = 0
    CapWnd1.Connect = True
    OverlayOption.Enabled = CapWnd1.CanOverlay
    End Sub

Sub LoadPaletteOption_Click ()
    CaptureFileDialog.DefaultExt = ".PAL"
    CaptureFileDialog.Filter = "Palette (*.pal)|*.pal"
    CaptureFileDialog.Action = 1
    CapWnd1.PalOpen = CaptureFileDialog.Filename
    End Sub

Sub OverlayOption_Click ()
    If CapWnd1.CanOverlay Then
        If OverlayOption.Checked Then
            CapWnd1.Overlay = False
            OverlayOption.Checked = False
          Else
            CapWnd1.Overlay = True
            OverlayOption.Checked = True
          End If
      End If
    End Sub

Sub PreviewOption_Click ()
    If Not PreviewOption.Checked Then
        CapWnd1.PreviewRate = CapWnd1.VideoRate
        CapWnd1.Preview = True
        PreviewOption.Checked = True
      Else
        CapWnd1.Preview = False
        PreviewOption.Checked = False
      End If
    End Sub
```

```
Sub SaveAsOption_Click ()
    CaptureFileDialog.DefaultExt = ".avi"
    CaptureFileDialog.Filter = "Video (*.avi)|*.avi"
    CaptureFileDialog.Action = 1
    CapWnd1.CaptureSave = CaptureFileDialog.Filename
    End Sub

Sub SavePaletteOption_Click ()
    CaptureFileDialog.DefaultExt = ".pal"
    CaptureFileDialog.Filter = "Palette (*.pal)|*.pal"
    CaptureFileDialog.Action = 1
    CapWnd1.PalSave = CaptureFileDialog.Filename
    End Sub

Sub SetCapFileOption_Click ()
    CaptureFileDialog.DefaultExt = ".AVI"
    CaptureFileDialog.Filter = "Video (*.avi)|*.avi"
    CaptureFileDialog.Action = 1
    CapWnd1.CaptureFile = CaptureFileDialog.Filename
    End Sub

Sub SingleFrameOption_Click ()
    CapWnd1.SingleFrameOpen = True
    CapWnd1.SingleFrame = True
    CapWnd1.SingleFrameClose = True
    End Sub

Sub StartButton_Click ()
    CapWnd1.DriverNum = 0
    CapWnd1.Connect = True
    CapWnd1.CaptureLimit = 20 '20 seconds
    CapWnd1.CaptureUseLimit = True
    CapWnd1.VideoRate = 15
    CapWnd1.Capture = True
    End Sub

Sub VideoDisplayOption_Click ()
    CapWnd1.VideoDisplayDlg = True
    End Sub

Sub VideoFormatOption_Click ()
    CapWnd1.VideoFormatDlg = True
    CapWnd1.Top = Panel3D2.Height \ 2 - CapWnd1.Height \ 2
    CapWnd1.Left = Panel3D2.Width \ 2 - CapWnd1.Width \ 2
    End Sub

Sub VideoSourceOption_Click ()
    CapWnd1.VideoSourceDlg = True
    End Sub
```

If you can't get what you need from CAPWNDX.VBX, you can resort to the
API functions. But realize that this will not be a trivial enterprise. The custom

control handles a myriad of details for us, including .AVI file access, interaction with the ICM, and screen updates using the high-speed DrawDIB functions. To get all this stuff working, you'll need callback functions and fast memory management. As much as I hate to admit it, the VfW API may lie outside the domain of practical VB programming. To write a more sophisticated capture program or any kind of video editor you may find it easier to implement the lower-level functions in one of the Holy Trinity languages. You can always pack the complex code into custom controls or DLLs, and use VB to create the user interface, just as we did in VIDCAP1.MAK.

The Playback's the Thing

We've already used the easiest method to replay a video clip, the MCI Play command. When you play a .AVI file with MCI, the driver will open up its own window somewhere on the screen. With a little more work, we can instruct the driver to display the video in a specific window.

Playing Video in a Window with the MCI

In this project we'll use the **mciSendString()** function to open, position, and play a video clip in a VB form. Here are the steps to follow:

1. Create a form.
2. Write the general procedure **PlayVideo()** (Listing 16.3).
3. Add the general procedure **GetWordFrom()** (Listing 16.4) to the form.
4. Fill in the **Form_Click()** event procedure (Listing 16.5) and the declarations section (Listing 16.6) for the form.

You'll find this project in the subdirectory \VBMAGIC in the files AVIPLAY1.MAK, AVIPLAY1.FRM, and MINMAX.BAS.

Running the Program

When you run this simple program, it will display a small, blank form. To play the video clip (the filename is hard-coded), click anywhere in the client area of the form. The clip will play in the center of the form, as shown in Figure 16.2.

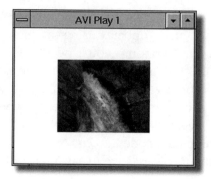

Figure 16.2 *AVIPLAY1.FRM at runtime.*

Creating the Form

This form has no controls. Set the **Name** property of the form to AVIPlay1F1, and set its **ScaleMode** property to 3 - Pixel.

Adding PlayVideo() General Procedure

The general procedure **PlayVideo()**, shown in Listing 16.3, consists primarily of a series of calls to **mciSendString()**.

Listing 16.3 The PlayVideo() General Procedure from AVIPLAY1.FRM

```
Sub PlayVideo (FileName As String, ByVal hWindow As Integer, ByVal DestWidth As
    Integer, ByVal DestHeight As Integer)
    Dim MCIError As Integer
    Dim CommandString As String
    Dim ReturnString As String * 128
    Dim DummyString As String
    Dim ClipWidth As Integer
    Dim ClipHeight As Integer
    Dim XPos As Integer
    Dim YPos As Integer

    'Open AVI device.
    CommandString = "Open " & FileName & " alias VidClip"
    MCIError = mciSendString(CommandString, ByVal ReturnString,
            Len(ReturnString) - 1, 0)

    'Set output window.
    CommandString = "Window VidClip handle " & Str$(hWindow)
    MCIError = mciSendString(CommandString, ByVal ReturnString,
            Len(ReturnString) - 1, 0)

    'Get dimensions of clip in window.
    CommandString = "Where VidClip destination"
    MCIError = mciSendString(CommandString, ByVal ReturnString,
            Len(ReturnString) - 1, 0)
```

```
DummyString = GetWordFrom(ReturnString)
DummyString = GetWordFrom(ReturnString)
ClipWidth = Val(GetWordFrom(ReturnString))
ClipHeight = Val(GetWordFrom(ReturnString))
XPos = MaxInt(0, DestWidth - ClipWidth) \ 2
YPos = MaxInt(0, DestHeight - ClipHeight) \ 2

'Re-position clip in center of window.
CommandString = "Put VidClip destination at " & Str$(XPos) & " " &
                Str$(YPos)
CommandString = CommandString & " " & Str$(ClipWidth) & " " & Str$(ClipHeight)
MCIError = mciSendString(CommandString, ByVal ReturnString,
          Len(ReturnString) - 1, 0)

'Play clip.
MousePointer = 11
CommandString = "Play VidClip wait"
MCIError = mciSendString(CommandString, ByVal ReturnString,
          Len(ReturnString) - 1, 0)
MousePointer = 0

'Close the device.
CommandString = "Close VidClip"
MCIError = mciSendString(CommandString, ByVal ReturnString,
          Len(ReturnString) - 1, 0)

End Sub
```

Instead of simply sending the **Play** command, causing the driver to open its own window, play the clip, and close the device, we'll send the **Open** command, allowing us to send further instructions before we commence playback. The path and filename can become unwieldy to repeat in every command, so we'll use a shorthand name, **VidClip**, known to MCI as an *alias*. In each subsequent command, we'll use this alias to refer to this instance of the .AVI file and device.

After we open the device, we send the **Window** command with its handle parameter to specify the output window, which, in this case, is the handle of AVIPlay1F1. To pass the handle, we need to convert it to a string. The conversion is no problem because handles are just integer values.

Before we can center the video clip in the window, we need to know its dimensions. The command **Where <devicename> destination** will return a string containing four integer values separated by spaces. These values represent the left, top, width, and height of the clip, positioned relative to the window's client area and scale mode. The Windows API does not recognize VB twips, so make sure the form's **ScaleMode** property is set to 3 - Pixel. To parse out the string and extract the width and height values, we'll borrow the general function **GetWordFrom()**, which we created for the hypertext system. We don't need the left and top positions, so we toss them out by assigning them to **DummyString**. Once we have the **ClipWidth** and **ClipHeight**, we can calculate the proper position for the clip within the window. We then send the **Put <devicename> destination at** command with **XPos**, **YPos**, **ClipWidth**, and **ClipHeight** as its arguments (all converted to strings, of course) to center the image.

Finally, we send the **Play <devicename> wait** command to play the clip, followed by the **Close <devicename>** command to close the device and release the driver.

Adding GetWordFrom() General Function

Be sure to add **GetWordFrom()** to the form module, as shown in Listing 16.4.

Listing 16.4   The GetWordFrom() General Function from AVIPLAY1.FRM

```
Function GetWordFrom (AnyString As String) As String
    Dim TempString As String

    If InStr(AnyString, " ") = 0 Then
        TempString = AnyString
        AnyString = ""
      Else
        TempString = Left$(AnyString, InStr(AnyString, " "))
        AnyString = Mid$(AnyString, InStr(AnyString, " ") + 1)
      End If
    If (InStr(".,?!", Right$(TempString, 1)) > 0) And (Len(TempString) > 1) Then
        AnyString = Right$(TempString, 1) & AnyString
        TempString = Left$(TempString, Len(TempString) - 1)
      End If
    GetWordFrom = TempString
    End Function
```

Adding the Form_Click() Event Procedure

The only event procedure in this program, **Form_Click()**, exists solely to call **PlayVideo()**.

Listing 16.5   The Form_Click Event Procedure from AVIPLAY1.FRM

```
Sub Form_Click ()
    PlayVideo "c:\vbmagic\video\watrfall.avi", AVIPlay1F1.hWnd,
      AVIPlay1F1.ScaleWidth, AVIPlay1F1.ScaleHeight
    End Sub
```

Finally, don't forget to add the declaration for **mciSendString()**.

Listing 16.6   The Declarations Section from AVIPLAY1.FRM

```
Option Explicit

Declare Function mciSendString Lib "MMSystem" (ByVal lpstrCommand As String,
    ByVal lpstrReturnString As String, ByVal wReturnLength As Integer, ByVal
    hCallback As Integer) As Long
```

The MCIWNDX.VBX Custom Control

For the quickest and cleanest way to play .AVI files from within a VB program, use the MCIWNDX.VBX custom control, supplied with the VfW DK. Figure 16.3 shows how this control appears on a form.

Like the MCI.VBX included in the Professional Edition of VB, this control will operate any MCI device, but there are some important differences:

- MCI.VBX cannot send complete MCI command strings, so it cannot use all the features offered by all the MCI device drivers. Also, the only return values available to MCI.VBX are those for which control properties have been defined. MCI.VBX cannot support new devices, or newly added features in existing MCI device drivers. MCIWNDX.VBX, on the other hand, can send any valid MCI command string to any MCI device, and can retrieve return strings.

- MCI.VBX offers a set of nine control buttons: Back, Eject, Next, Pause, Play, Prev, Record, Step, and Stop. MCIWNDX.VBX offers only a Play/ Stop button and a slider for positioning.

- MCI.VBX does not support window-oriented devices, such as video and animation. MCIWNDX.VBX provides its own display window.

MCIWNDX.VBX has six event procedures, listed in Table 16.2, and 35 properties, listed in Table 16.3.

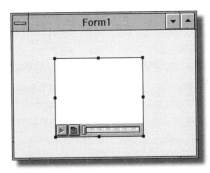

Figure 16.3   *The MCIWNDX.VBX custom control as it appears in a VB form.*

Table 16.2   *The Event Procedures Supported by MCIWNDX.VBX*

Event Procedure	Purpose
Error()	Occurs whenever an MCI command causes an error.
MediaChange()	Occurs whenever a device is opened or closed; for example, when you change the file to be played, or change the disk in the CD-ROM drive.
ModeChange()	Occurs whenever the mode—open, not ready, playing, stopped, paused, seeking, or recording—of a device changes.
Notify()	Occurs when the notify flag is used with an MCI command to indicate the success or failure of an operation.
PositionChange()	Occurs repeatedly as the file or media position changes during seek, play, or record operations. *Caution: use the **WantPosEvent** property to enable or disable this event, and use the **TimerFreq** property to keep the event from firing too frequently.*
SizeChange()	Occurs whenever the display window changes size, such as when the user resizes the video playback window, or when the **AutosizeWindow** property is set to True and activated.

Table 16.3   *The Properties List for MCIWNDX.VBX*

Property	Purpose
Command	Set this string property to the MCI command string you wish to execute. Just like any other MCI string command, except that you must omit the alias or device name. The field will clear once the command is executed. The error code will be stored in the **Error** property; the return string will be stored in the **CommandReturn** property.
CommandReturn	Will contain any information returned by the latest MCI command executed.
DeviceID	Returns the ID of the currently open device. Not often used.
Device	A string containing the name of the current device.
FileName	For simple devices, set this string property to a device name, such as "CDAudio." For compound devices, set it to a path and filename. If you set this property to a question mark, the control will display a file open dialog box.
Speed	With this integer property you can control the playback speed of many MCI devices. Normal speed, or 100%, is represented by a value of 1000. Specify lower values for slower operation, higher values for faster speeds.
TimeFormat	Returns the current time format of the open device.
Volume	As in the Speed property, a value of 1000 represents normal audio volume.
End	Returns the end position of the current device element in the current time format.

(continued)

Table 16.3 *The Properties List for MCIWNDX.VBX (continued)*

Length	Returns the length of the current device element in the current time format.
Position	Returns the current position of the device in the current time format.
PositionString	Returns the current position in string format, such as TT:MM:SS:FF.
Start	Returns the starting position of the current device element in the current time format.
Error	Returns the error code of the latest MCI command executed.
ErrorDlg	Set to True if you want the control to display an Error dialog box whenever a command fails.
ErrorString	Returns the current error message as a string.
Mode	Returns the current mode of the device (see the ModeChange() event in Table 16.2).
TimerFreq	Determines the number of milliseconds between PositionChange() events; defaults to 500 milliseconds.
WantPosEvent	Set to True to enable PositionChange() events.
AutosizeMovie	Set to True if you want the image stretched (or squished) to fit the current display window.
AutosizeWindow	Set to True if you want the display window to resize itself to match the dimensions of the current device element (animation or video file).
BorderStyle	Set to True for a single pixel border or False for no border.
Zoom	Used to resize a visual device element (animation or video file). Specify integer percentages such as 100 (default), 200 for double size, 33 for one-third size, etc.
NewDevice	Opens a recordable device, such as waveaudio, for recording with no existing device element. Similar to the MCI string command open new waveaudio.
Left	Specifies or returns the current left position of the control in its container.
Top	Specifies or returns the current top position of the control in its container.
Height	Specifies or returns the current height of the control.
Width	Specifies or returns the current width of the control.
Menu	Set to True to enable the pop-up control menu.
Playbar	Set to True to display the user controlled play controls (Play/Stop button, Menu button, and position scroll bar). If False, all operation must occur under program control.
Record	Set to True to enable display of recording controls when appropriate. The AVIVideo device does not support recording under MCI control.
Repeat	Set to True to enable automatic repeat. Not supported by all MCI devices.
Name	The VB control instance name.
Enabled	Set to True to enable control at runtime.
Visible	Set to True to display the control at runtime, or False to hide the control.

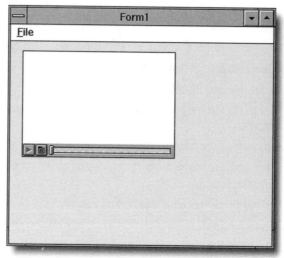

Figure 16.4 *AVIPLAY2.FRM at design time.*

Playing Video with MCIWNDX.VBX

The MCIWNDX.VBX custom control makes it a breeze to play video when and where you want it. In this very simple program we'll center the control on a form and display the Playbar so playback can be controlled at runtime.

 You'll find this project in the subdirectory \VBMAGIC in the files AVIPLAY2.MAK, AVIPLAY2.FRM, and MINMAX.BAS. You'll also need to copy MCIWNDX.VBX from the subdirectory \VFWDK\BIN to your \WINDOWS\SYSTEM subdirectory.

Creating the AVIPlay2 Form

This project requires nothing more than a form with a simple File menu and a single MCIWNDX.VBX control, as shown in Figure 16.4.

The form code includes just four brief event procedures and one general procedure, as shown in Listing 16.7.

Listing 16.7   AVIPLAY2.FRM

```
VERSION 2.00
Begin Form AVIPlay2F1
    Caption         =    "Form1"
    ClientHeight    =    3924
    ClientLeft      =    876
```

```
            ClientTop        =    1848
            ClientWidth      =    5256
            Height           =    4668
            Left             =    828
            LinkTopic        =    "Form1"
            ScaleHeight      =    3924
            ScaleWidth       =    5256
            Top              =    1152
            Width            =    5352
            Begin MCIWND MCIWnd1
               AutosizeMovie    =    -1    'True
               AutosizeWindow   =    -1    'True
               ErrorDlg         =    0     'False
               Filename         =    ""
               Height           =    276
               Left             =    240
               Menu             =    -1    'True
               Playbar          =    -1    'True
               Record           =    0     'False
               Repeat           =    0     'False
               Speed            =    1000
               TimeFormat       =    ""
               TimerFreq        =    500
               Top              =    180
               Volume           =    1000
               WantPosEvent     =    -1    'True
               Width            =    3072
               Zoom             =    100
            End
            Begin Menu FileMenu
               Caption          =    "&File"
               Begin Menu OpenOption
                  Caption          =    "&Open File"
               End
               Begin Menu QuitOption
                  Caption          =    "&Quit"
               End
            End
         End
Option Explicit

Sub MCIWnd1_MediaChange (Media As String)
    ResizeMCIWindow
    AVIPlay2F1.Caption = UCase$(Media)
    End Sub

Sub MCIWnd1_SizeChange ()
    ResizeMCIWindow
    End Sub

Sub OpenOption_Click ()
    MCIWnd1.Filename = "?"
    End Sub
```

```
Sub QuitOption_Click ()
    End
    End Sub

Sub ResizeMCIWindow ()
    MCIWnd1.Left = MaxInt(0, (AVIPlay2F1.ScaleWidth - MCIWnd1.Width) \ 2)
    MCIWnd1.Top = MaxInt(0, (AVIPlay2F1.ScaleHeight - MCIWnd1.Height) \ 2)
    End Sub
```

Adding Video to the Magic Hypermedia Engine

In the last version of the Magic Hypermedia Engine, HYPRMED2.MAK (see Chapter 10), we still used the simple MCI **Play** command to run .AVI files. Each time we activated a video with either a hypertext hotlink or an image hotspot, VfW would open and play the video clip in a floating window. This works, but it doesn't give us the control we need for tight multimedia presentations. For instance, we might want to overlay a video clip on a still image to emphasize the connection between them. The other problem is that the VfW floating window sometimes disappears behind other windows, including our own hypermedia form. Now that we know how to properly control video, however, we can play clips not only when we want, but also where we want. So let's get to it!

Windowed Video in the Hypermedia Engine

For our final project, let's use the MCIWNDX.VBX custom control to position video clips within the Hypermedia form. Here are the steps:

1. Copy HYPRMED2.MAK, HYPRMED2.FRM, and HYPRMED2.BAS to HYPRMED3.MAK, HYPRMED3.FRM, and HYPRMED3.BAS respectively.

2. Add the control MCIWnd1 to the form.

3. Modify the **DoHypermediaJump()** general procedure in HYPRMED3.BAS (Listing 16.8).

4. Modify the **TextPictureBox_MouseDown()** and **ImagesPictureBox_MouseDown()** event procedures in HYPRMED3.FRM (Listing 16.9).

5. Test the new version with a mini multimedia title about the Grand Canyon.

You'll find this project in the subdirectories \VBMAGIC and \GRANDCAN in the files HYPRMED3.MAK, HYPRMED3.FRM, HYPRMED3.BAS, HOTSPOT5.BAS, HYPRTXT6.BAS,

DATACONS.BAS, GLOBCONS.BAS, and MINMAX.BAS. This project also requires the custom control MCIWNDX.VBX, which you should copy from the subdirectory \VFWDK\BIN to your \WINDOWS\SYSTEM subdirectory.

Modifying the Form

Before we change any of the code, let's figure out how and where we're going to position the MCIWnd1 control on the Hypermedia form. In anticipation of the demonstration mini-multimedia presentation I'm going to show you shortly, I have decided to re-arrange the main text and image display areas of the form. The mini-project contains some panoramic photographs. To get the maximum impact from these images, let's split the screen lengthwise, instead of vertically as we did in the two previous versions of the Hypermedia engine.

The video display window is usually small, 160 by 120 pixels. For the mini-project I thought it might be nice to overlay the video window over the images Picture Box, as shown in Figure 16.5.

If you haven't already, add the MCIWNDX.VBX file to your project with the File, Add File menu option. Then draw the control in the **PictureFrame** Frame control, not in the **ImagesPictureBox**. Anchor the upper-left corner where

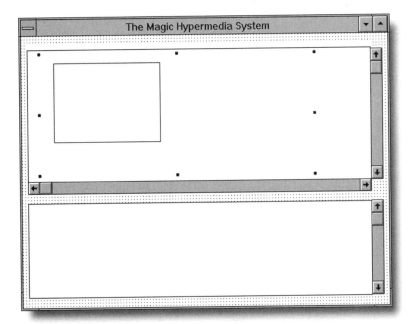

Figure 16.5 HYPRMED3.FRM at design time.

you want it to appear throughout the presentation. The **AutosizeWindow** property will cause the **Height** and **Width** of the control to change automatically as each clip is loaded. If you wish, you can modify the program code to change the **Left** and **Top** positions as well.

We'll need to set a few of the properties of the MCIWnd1 control. For this project, we'll disable all user control over playback by setting the **Menu** and **Playbar** properties to False. Next, we'll want the video clip to determine the window size, rather than stretching to the existing dimensions, so we'll set the **AutosizeMovie** property to False, and the **AutosizeWindow** property to True. To keep the control from appearing prematurely, we'll set its **Visible** property to False.

Modifying DoHypermediaJump()

In the previous version of **DoHypermediaJump()**, we examined the filename extension in the **TargetString** to determine whether it referenced an image file (.BMP or .DIB), or a multimedia file (.WAV, .MID, or .AVI) playable with MCI. We'll use the same technique in the new version, but we'll replace the **If** statement with **Select Case**, as shown in Listing 16.8.

Listing 16.8　The DoHypermediaJump() General Procedure from HYPRMED3.BAS

```
Sub DoHypermediaJump (TargetString As String, TheTextPicture As PictureBox,
    TheImagePicture As PictureBox, TheScrollBar As VScrollBar, TheMCIControl As MCIWND)
    Dim Dummy As Integer
    Dim FileExt As String

    If Left$(Right$(TargetString, 4), 1) = "." Then
        FileExt = UCase$(Right$(TargetString, 3))
        TargetString = Left$(App.Path, 2) & TargetString
        Select Case FileExt
          Case "MID", "WAV"
            Dummy = mciExecute("Play " + TargetString)
          Case "BMP", "DIB"
            TheImagePicture.Picture = LoadPicture(TargetString)
            TheImagePicture.Left = 0
            TheImagePicture.Top = 0
            ActivateHotspots UCase$(TargetString)
          Case "AVI", "MOV"
            TheMCIControl.Filename = TargetString
            TheMCIControl.Visible = True
            TheMCIControl.Command = "Play wait"
            TheMCIControl.Command = "Close"
            TheMCIControl.Visible = False
          Case Else
            MsgBox "Unable to locate media file " & TargetString, 48, "Hyperlink
```

```
            Error"
        End Select
    Else
        LoadSubject TargetString, TheTextPicture, TheScrollBar
    End If
End Sub
```

To maintain the re-useability of this code module, we added a fifth argument to the procedure, through which we can pass the MCIWnd1 control. Everything else in this procedure remains the same, except for the addition of the **Case** clause that handles .AVI (Video for Windows) and .MOV (Quicktime for Windows) files. To play a video file, we set the MCIWnd1 control's **Filename** property to the **TargetString**. We then show the control by changing its **Visible** property to True. Next, we send the **Play** command with the **wait** flag, which freezes the program until the video finishes playing. And finally, we hide the control again.

The MouseDown() Event Procedures

The **TextPictureBox_MouseDown()** and **ImagesPictureBox_Mouse-Down()** event procedures in HYPRMED3.FRM each calls **DoHypermedia-Jump()**. We've added a new argument to that procedure, so we need to modify the calls in the two **MouseDown()** events, as shown in Listing 16.9.

Listing 16.9 The TextPictureBox_MouseDown() and ImagesPictureBox_MouseDown() Event Procedures from HYPRMED3.FRM

```
Sub TextPictureBox_MouseDown (Button As Integer, Shift As Integer, X As Single,
    Y As Single)
    Dim TargetString As String

    TargetString = TargetFromPointInText(X, Y)
    If Len(TargetString) > 0 Then
        DoHypermediaJump TargetString, TextPictureBox, ImagesPictureBox,
          TextVScroll, MCIWnd1
    End If
End Sub

Sub ImagesPictureBox_MouseDown (Button As Integer, Shift As Integer, X As
    Single, Y As Single)
    Dim TargetString As String

    TargetString = TargetFromPointInImage(X, Y)
    If Len(TargetString) > 0 Then
        DoHypermediaJump TargetString, TextPictureBox, ImagesPictureBox,
          TextVScroll, MCIWnd1
    End If
End Sub
```

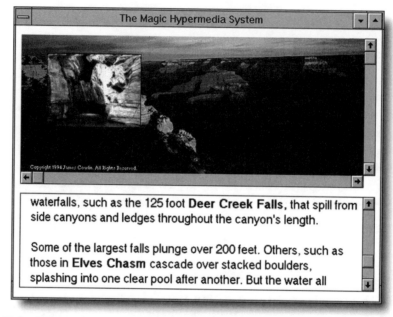

Figure 16.6   *The Grand Canyon demonstration mini-title.*

The Grand Canyon Mini-Multimedia Presentation

To demonstrate the final version of the Magic Hypermedia Engine, I've taken some material from a title my company is developing for commercial release early next year. Take a look at Figure 16.6 for an idea of what you'll see. The subdirectory \GRANDCAN on the CD-ROM contains a complete copy of HYPRMED3, along with an IMAGES.MDB hotspot database file, and the source text file, HYPRMED3.TXT, shown in Listing 16.10. The pictures, WAVE audio file, and video clips for this project are located on the companion CD-ROM in the subdirectories \GRANDCAN\IMAGES, \GRANDCAN\SOUND, and \GRANDCAN\VIDEO.

Listing 16.10   The Source Text from the Grand Canyon Mini-Multimedia Project, HYPRMED3.TXT

```
###The Grand Canyon
The ##Colorado River|The Colorado River~ in
##Grand Canyon|\grandcan\images\yakidawn.bmp~
slices through nearly two billion years of
geological history. And yet, the gaping canyon
itself, a gorge of such immense proportions
that it defies measure by the naked eye, has
itself existed for no more than eight million
```

years or so—a brief instant in geological time.
###The Colorado River
A vertical mile below the crowded
##south rim|\grandcan\images\grndview.bmp~
visitor's areas and lodges, the stream that
appeared to quietly thread its way along the
##canyon's|The Grand Canyon~ floor
becomes a temperamental tyrant.

For long stretches the broad river,
often more than 100 yards across, rolls serenely
and steadily between walls of polished rock
and occasional sandy beaches. Then suddenly it
##roars|\grandcan\sound\rapids.wav~ to life
in a thundering ##rapid|Rapids~.
###Rapids
Most rapids in the ##Grand Canyon|The Grand Canyon~
occur where debris from side canyons has poured
out and constricted the stream. ##Deubendorff
Rapid|\grandcan\video\dubendrf.avi~ is an
example of such a rapid. Here the river squeezes
past a broad debris fan, consisting primarily
of boulders, gravel, and sand that have been
driven out of Galloway Canyon by flash floods.
These deep water rapids give
##river runners|River Running~ their thrills
with less danger than more technical rivers
whose smaller, shallower rapids are often strewn
with boulders and hazardous hydraulics.
###Hidden Sights
Among the most popular of riverside attractions
within the ##Grand Canyon|The Grand Canyon~
are the many side streams, springs, and
waterfalls, such as the 125 foot ##Deer Creek
Falls|\grandcan\video\deercrk.avi~, that
spill from side canyons and ledges throughout
the canyon's length.

Some of the largest falls plunge over 200
feet. Others, such as those in
##Elves Chasm|\grandcan\video\elves.avi~ cascade
over stacked boulders, splashing into one
clear pool after another. But the water all
eventually finds its way into the
##great river|The Colorado River~.
###River Running
Since Major John Wesley Powell first explored
the ##Colorado River|The Colorado River~ all
the way through the ##Grand Canyon|The Grand
Canyon~ in 1869, no more than 500,000 people
have repeated the journey. Compare that
to the nearly 5,000,000 visitors that crowd
the South rim's ##scenic views|\grandcan
\images\winter.bmp~ and lodges every year.

```
Today, skilled boatmen and their passengers
travel the river in a variety of craft,
from kayak to ##inflatable rafts|\grandcan
\images\rapid1.bmp~ to 32 foot ##pontoon
boats|\grandcan\video\dubendrf.avi~, capable
of carrying 18 people and enough supplies
to last over a week.

River travelers experience the canyon in a
completely different way from rim visitors,
many of whom come and go, completely unaware
of the spectacular ##sights|Hidden Sights~
hidden deep within the many side canyons.
```

With the code we've developed in this book and the shareware authoring tools you'll find on the companion CD_ROM, you have a rich toolkit. But don't stop here. These projects are meant to illustrate the basic principles of multimedia programming in Windows. Don't be afraid to change them. Create the effects *you* need to drive *your* presentation. Interactive multimedia at its best is not just informative, it's exciting. Visual Basic and the Windows API can deliver the power you need to turn your favorite subject into a multimedia extravaganza.

Appendix A

Visual Basic Multimedia Adventure Set Installation Guide

You'll find all the source code from *Visual Basic Multimedia Adventure Set* on the companion CD-ROM, most of it in the subdirectory \VBMAGIC. The Visual Basic MIDI Piano is located in its own subdirectory, \VBPIANO.

The CD-ROM also contains the complete Microsoft Video for Windows (VfW) system, including the runtime library, production utilities, and Development Kit. These items are located in various subdirectories under the main \VFW11A subdirectory.

For a variety of fun and useful shareware programs, take a look at the subdirectories under \SHARWARE. The Buyer's Guide at the end of the book contains a brief description of each program. We've tried to select just a few of the best products available so you won't have to wade through hundreds of programs to find those that you can really use. There are many other excellent shareware multimedia products available through BBSs, commercial online services, and CD-ROM compilations. By excluding a program, we do not mean in any way to imply that it is useless or inferior. We simply did not have time to test and review them all.

Look in the subdirectories for a variety of art, music, waveaudio, and video clips. You can use this material to test the programs in the book. For information on copyright restrictions and how to obtain more clips from these vendors, be sure to check out the README.TXT files located in each vendor's subdirectory.

The images located in the subdirectories \VBMAGIC, \VBMAGIC\IMAGES, \GRANDCAN, \GRANDCAN\IMAGES, and \GRANDCAN\VIDEO are provided as a courtesy of the artists, and are for your own use only. Please do not redistribute any of these photographs, illustrations, or video clips.

Installing the VB Programs

We chose not to provide a Setup program for the *Adventure Set* programs. Setup programs tend to behave like black boxes, creating directories, copying files, and modifying your .INI files behind your back. To get the most from this code, you need to understand not only how it works, but how to make it work on your system. Fortunately, it's simple. Just copy the \VBMAGIC subdirectory and its \VBMAGIC\IMAGES subdirectory to your hard drive. Important: Keep in mind that all of the source files and programs are saved on the CD-ROM with "read-only" attributes. To use these files, you'll need to change the attributes to "read-write" after you copy the files to you hard disk. We've included two .BAT files, PROGINST.BAT and INSTDEMO.BAT, to help you copy all these files to you hard disk. For most of the programs, that's all there is to it. A few programs, however, require custom controls (.VBX files) or dynamic link libraries (.DLL files), which are located in their own subdirectories on the CD-ROM. Make sure to read through the following items carefully:

- The program WAVEMIX.MAK, explained in Chapter 13, requires the WAVEMIX.DLL, located on the CD-ROM in the subdirectory \SHARWARE\WAVEMIX. Copy that file to your \WINDOWS\SYSTEM subdirectory. WaveMix is provided as a courtesy by Microsoft Corporation. It is not a supported product. There is no registration fee.

- The MIDIIN1.MAK program, explained in Chapter 14, requires the VB Messenger custom control. This control is located on the CD-ROM in the \SHARWARE\VBMSG subdirectory in the file VBMSG.VBX. Copy that file to your \WINDOWS\SYSTEM subdirectory. The distribution version of VB Messenger is provided as a courtesy by its author, James Tyminski. VB Messenger is not free software. For information on how to obtain a registered copy of this handy custom control, see the README.TXT file in the \SHARWARE\VBMSG subdirectory.

- The programs VIDCAP1.MAK, AVIPLAY2.MAK, and HYPRMED3.MAK, explained in Chapter 16, require the CAPWNDX.VBX and MCIWNDX.VBX custom controls, which are installed on your hard drive by the VfW Development Kit Setup program. To install the VfW Development Kit, follow the instructions in Chapter 16, in the section *Installing the Video for Windows Development Kit*. After you've run the Setup program, you'll find the .VBX files on your hard drive in the subdirectory \VFWDK\BIN. Copy them both to your \WINDOWS\SYSTEM subdirectory.

Note: In the source code directories you'll also find executable versions of all the Adventure Set programs. Most of the programs will run directly from the CD-ROM, but several update data files, which they expect to find in the directory from which they are invoked. You should copy all the programs to your hard drive to test them properly.

Installing Video for Windows

To play .AVI video clips on your system, you must install the VfW runtime library, version 1.1a. Follow the instructions in Chapter 16, in the section *Installing the Video for Windows Runtime Library*. The VfW runtime setup will copy numerous files to your \WINDOWS\SYSTEM subdirectory, will modify your WIN.INI and SYSTEM.INI files, and will install an updated version of the Windows Media Player.

Appendix B

Visual Basic Multimedia Adventure Set Related Products

This guide provides information on useful products that can greatly help you develop Visual Basic multimedia applications. The commercial products are listed first, and the shareware products are listed at the end. The shareware products mentioned are provided on the companion CD-ROM.

Adobe Premiere V1.1 ($295)

Adobe Systems, Inc.
1585 Charleston Rd.
P.O. Box 7900
Mountain View, CA 94039-7900
800-833-6687

Adobe Premiere for Windows offers PC users an intuitive, cost-effective way to create digital movies for a variety of uses. It makes it easy to combine video footage, audio recordings, animation, still images, and graphics to create digital movies. The program supports the use of all common media types, including still images in DIB, TIFF, Adobe Photoshop, and PCX formats, sound in AIFF and WAV formats, video content in AVI and QuickTime formats, and animation in Autodesk Animator (FLC/FII) and PICT formats. Adobe Premiere 1.1 for Windows now includes software for capturing live video and audio to a computer, instead of requiring a separate software utility program.

Visual/db ($149)

AJS Publishing, Inc.
P.O. Box 83220
Los Angeles, CA 90083
800-992-3383

Visual/db is a complete relational Database Management System for Microsoft's Visual Basic for Windows. Employ Visual/db's powerful routines to create, read, and write dBASE III-type database, index, and memo files, and give your Visual Basic applications extensive DBMS capabilities. Visual/db is implemented entirely in Visual Basic source code so you have total control over its implementation. With Visual/db's online context-sensitive help, an easy and natural access method, and industry-standard files, you will find that writing full-featured database programs with an attractive Windows interface could not be easier or faster.

Morphology 101 ($39.95)

Andover Advanced Technologies
239 Littleton Rd., Suite 2A
Westford, MA 01886
800-274-9674

Morphology 101 is the first multimedia product that includes a comprehensive interactive tutorial on professional morphing techniques. The interactive tutorial uses animations to illustrate basic techniques such as point placement and morphing between images of different size and shape. It includes a guide to file formats, compression algorithms, and special effects. Its advanced sections also show how to use transition images to bring still images to life, how to do a liquid metal morph, and how to avoid spider webs and ghosting. The clips can be used royalty-free in any computer presentation or application you create, even when those presentations or applications are for resale.

Sound Choice ($69)

Cambium
P.O. Box 296-H
Scarsdale, NY 10583-8796
800-231-1779
FAX 914-472-6729

Sound Choice is a CD-ROM based, MPC clip music library and Windows software package. The royalty-free, impeccably recorded compositions include classical, rock, jazz, contemporary, new age, and more. Each volume contains more than 25 main selections and more than 75 pre-edited "bumpers," totaling over 100 individual clips and 900 music files in CD Audio, six WAV, and two MIDI formats. Three of the WAV formats are state-of-the art ADPCM compressed, offering superb quality with reduced disk usage.

The powerful software features a scalable, interactive database, and enables you to audition and edit music files. Cross-platform developers can output WAV and device-independent MIDI files for Windows, and AIFF and extended MIDI for Macintosh.

JPEG Image Compressor VBX ($199)

Crisp Technology Inc.
20198 Pacifica Drive
Cupertino, CA 95014
408-257-0588

JPEG VBX is a custom control for immediate JPEG compression and decompression. It allows you to add image files to your Visual Basic applications, access image data faster, and access more hard disk space. By applying JPEG compression and decompression technology for BMP, TARGA, TIFF, GIF, PCX, and DIB files, JPEG VBX allows you to develop Visual Basic multimedia applications with more efficiency and flexibility. The product's powerful features include support of Visual C++; color reduction and dithering; the ability to display true color, 256 color, VGA, and Monochrome images; redrawing, scrolling, smoothing, resizing, and printing functions; and the ability to read, write, and display BMP, TARGA, TIFF, GIF, PCX, DIB, and JPEG image files.

ImageMan/VB ($295)

Data Techniques, Inc.
340 Bowditch Street, Suite 6
Burnsville, NC 28714
800-955-8015

ImageMan/VB is the first custom control to offer sophisticated image processing and scanner support for Visual Basic users. ImageMan provides complete image processing support for all the popular raster and vector image formats. The product's scanner control supports the industry standard TWAIN scanner interface, giving your application instant support for dozens for popular scanners. It even provides complete multi-page scanning support, including the ability to save multi-page TIFF and DCX files. ImageMan has advanced features such as rotation, brightness and contrast enhancement, color manipulation, color reduction, and more—all accessible via custom properties, eliminating the need to declare and call functions.

ProVoice for Windows ($595)

First Byte
19840 Pioneer Avenue
Torrance, CA 90503
800-556-6141

ProVoice for Windows allows developers to add synthesized speech to their Windows applications. ProVoice for Windows supports most Windows 3.1 programming languages through a DLL interface. Your program simply passes text strings to a speech driver, which translates the text into audible speech. All of the necessary tools and examples are provided to manipulate the ProVoice speech technology with ease.

1000 of the World's Greatest Sound Effects ($39.95)

Interactive Publishing Corporation
c/o Corporate Mailing Inc.
26 Parsipanny Rd.
Whippany, NY 07981
800-472-8777

1000 of the World's Greatest Sound Effects is a dual-platform CD-ROM sound effects studio that also provides sophisticated sound shaping, editing, and digital recording tools. The product, which contains effects like a roaring tiger, exploding dynamite, and a cruise ship whistle, offers its samples royalty-free. They are recorded in both 8-bit and high-fidelity 16-bit digital audio formats.

The product's Sound Finder utility categorizes each effect for quick access, testing, and copying. As a bonus, the title also includes Multimedia Sound Studio, which allows the user to play, record, and edit sounds all in the digital domain. It also offers compatibility with MIDI-equipped musical instruments and sequencers, as well as audio CDs. A sophisticated WAVE editor provides even greater control over customizing and shaping sounds, while the Attach utility allows sound effects to be activated by system events, for that perfect default alarm.

Action! 3.0 ($199)

MacroMedia
600 Townsend Street
San Francisco, CA 94103
800-288-4797

Action! is a multimedia presentation program for Windows that gives users the power to integrate graphics, motion, digital video, animations, sound, and interactivity into compelling business presentations. It has a scene sorter, outliner, drawing tools, and spell checker. Users can then add sound, motion, digital video, and special effects to make their messages stand out. For $299, users can receive the Action! CD-ROM bundle, which includes ClipMedia and Turtle Beach Wave Tools.

ImageKnife/VBX, Pro Pack V1.3 ($299)

Media Architects, Inc.
1075 NW Murray Rd. #230
Portland, OR 97229-5501
503-297-5010

ImageKnife is a data-aware custom control for Visual Basic and Visual C++ that provides simple, but comprehensive image handling including: display (with pan and zoom), format conversion (TIFF, BMP, DIB, PCX, GIF, TARGA, JPEG), and image processing (rotate, sharpen, matrix filter, and so on). ImageKnife supports True Color (24-bit), Super VGA (8-bit), VGA (4-bit), and monochrome images. Its color processing includes color reduction, palette remapping, optimization, and more. The product provides easy multiple image operations (compositing, masking, and so on), quality printing to Windows graphics-capable devices, and access to image data via a DIB handle or scanline get/put functions. A fully documented browser sample application is included. ImageKnife supports TWAIN-compliant image acquisition devices.

Media-Pedia Video Clips

Media-Pedia Inc.
22 Fisher Avenue
Wellesley, MA 02181
617-235-5617
FAX orders: 800-633-7332

Media-Pedia Video Clips videotape is a collection of over 150 royalty-free video clips with synchronized natural sound effects. It contains more than 50 minutes of professionally shot and selected clips from all decades of the twentieth century including aerial, time-lapse, slow motion, and point-of-view cinematography. The product is $195 in VHS, $295 in S-VHS and Hi8, $395 in 3/4SP, and $495 in BETACAM SP. Available for an introductory price of $49 is Media-Pedia Video Clips on CD-ROM for Windows in .AVI format compressed with Intel Indeo video technology.

Windows Sound System 2.0 Software ($49.95)

Microsoft Corporation
One Microsoft Way
Redmond, WA 98052
800-426-9400

Windows Sound System 2.0 is a high-quality audio software solution that optimizes the audio capabilities of the Windows 3.1 operating system. It provides sophisticated sound tools that enhance multimedia presentations and allow you to interact with Windows applications using audio. Key features include Voice Pilot, which enables the computer to listen to and recognize your voice as you command it through Windows applications; ProofReader, which allows the computer to read back spreadsheet numbers and other financial data; and the Quick Recorder Expanded View, which provides sophisticated audio editing tools ideally suited for multimedia presentations. With Quick Recorder, you can also embed voice notes in documents, spreadsheets, and email messages. For more information, contact your local reseller.

Picture++ ($425)

Rainbow Imaging
460 East 79th Street, Suite 19A
New York, NY 10021
212-794-2717

Picture++ is a high-performance, professional imaging library that lets you build world-class imaging applications with a complete set of fast, versatile imaging capabilities for Windows. Comprehensive, field-proven file format support for reading/writing/converting BMP, DIB, TIFF, PCX, TGA, GIF, DCX, and JPEG image files, with a full range of compression methods including Packbits, RLE, LZW, CCITT G3 and G4, and JPEG. A single set of functions uniformly handles all image types from B/W to full color, providing image editing, image type conversion, clipboard support, color control (hue, saturation, brightness, contrast), TWAIN scanner support, and printing. Advanced image display capabilities provide selectable options for color reduction, dithering, palette creation (including default, optimized, native, and user-defined palettes), and optimized palette sharing for simultaneously displaying of multiple images with different palettes. Picture++ provides state-of-the-art, field-proven performance in leading commercial applications and retail multimedia products. ImageKnife can be distributed royalty-free. Call vendor for full information and a free file viewer demo.

LiveWindows Video Library ($395)

Software Interphase
82 Cucumber Hill Road
Foster, RI 02825-1212
800-542-2742

LiveWindows is a collection of routines written completely in assembly language to provide device-independent control of the LW/TV card and other similar cards such as the Video Blaster, WIN/TV, and Super VideoWindows. LiveWindows provides real-time display and scaling of live video within a window or multiple windows on the VGA screen. The video can be frame-grabbed in 1/30 of a second. It can be stored in YUV, TARGA 24, TIFF-G, TIFF-R, or Windows BMP 24-bit formats. The digitized image can be processed by using a variety of image processing functions including brightness, contrast, inversion, b/w and color filtering, posterization, sharpening, smoothing, vertical and horizontal edge detection, and a user-definable convolution matrix.

VGA text and graphics can overlay video for titling and "sub-caption" needs. LiveWindows includes a library of functions, many example programs, a manual/tutorial, and a demo program.

ImagePals 2 ($199; $129 through 10/31/94)

Ulead Systems, Inc.
970 W. 190th Street, Ste. 520
Torrance, CA 90502
800-858-5323

ImagePals 2 is the indispensable management tool for users of image, graphic, animation, video, and sound files. Catalog your files into visual thumbnail albums for quick and easy access. Convert files among all popular file formats for compatibility with your favorite programs. ImagePals provides seamless integration by dragging and dropping your files into your publishing, presentation, and multimedia applications. ImagePals 2 also includes a complete library of image editing tools to help you create vivid, dramatic images every time. You can even create exciting multimedia slide show presentations of your files complete with audio background and visual transition effects.

MediaStudio ($349; $149 through 10/31/94)

Ulead Systems, Inc.
970 W. 190th Street, Ste. 520
Torrance, CA 90502
800-858-5323

MediaStudio allows you to unleash your creativity and produce captivating multimedia business presentations, training materials, and proposals. It unites video, audio, and image editing in one easy-to-use program. Browse through the Album—a visual catalog of all your image, graphic, animation, audio, and video files—to easily locate the clip you need. Transform your images with Image Editor or Morph Editor by adding a splash of color, morphing your images, or applying one of the many special effects including fish eye, whirlpool, and more. Or bump up the volume on your audio track with a comprehensive range of audio filters. Then bring it all together in Video Editor. Create video-in-video overlays and special effects, add flying text, then mix in your audio tracks to complete your multimedia production.

Useful Visual Basic Shareware Tools

Here is a list and short description of the useful Visual Basic shareware tools that are provided on the companion CD-ROM. You'll find more detailed information about each product by reading the description file that is included with each product (see the subdirectories in the directory \SHARWARE on the CD-ROM).

3DFXPLUS   A custom DLL for creating special 3D effects in your VB programs.

CANIMATE   A unique custom control for performing animation.

CDR_13   A program used for doing digitization directly from CDs.

COOL   A full-featured WAVE editor for Windows written by David Johnston.

CSRPLUS   A DLL that provides a collection of icons and backdrop patterns for VB (or any Windows programming environment) complete with easy-to-use functions for utilizing the new, appealing graphics in your own applications. You get nearly 100 new cursors and 18 eye-appealing backdrop patterns.

MUSICF   A useful music truetype font.

SPECTRUM   A small utility program that provides a real-time display of the power spectrum of the signal present on the Wave Input device of a Windows multimedia PC—typically the signal coming in through the microphone socket on the sound card.

VBMSG A custom control that allows you to tap into the power of Windows by intercepting Windows messages while still providing Visual Basic's ease of use. With VB Messenger, you can subclass a Visual Basic form or control (or any Windows control or window) to intercept messages that are intended for the form or control.

WAVEMIX A DLL utility that allows multiple WAVE files to be played simultaneously. It is designed to be as simple to use as possible but still have the power to do what is required by games. The DLL supports eight channels of simultaneous wave play, the ability to queue up waves along the same channel, and wave completion notification.

WINJAMMR A full-featured MIDI sequencer for Windows. It uses standard MIDI files, giving you access to a huge number of songs. WinJammer also contains a companion program called WinJammer Player, which is used to play MIDI song files in the background.

Bibliography

Aitken, Peter. *The Visual Basic for Windows Insider.* Coriolis Group Books. New York: John Wiley & Sons, Inc., 1993.

> *Aitken, an extremely popular writer of books and articles for both users and programmers, reaches into his VB toolkit and digs out numerous tips and techniques that will benefit any VB programmer. Look here for some handy code, all lucidly explained. Although not focused exclusively on the Windows API, this book does cover several API functions, including the global memory functions found in ToolHelp.DLL.*

Appleman, Daniel. *Visual Basic Programmer's Guide to the Windows API.* Emeryville: Ziff-Davis Press, 1993.

> *Almost all Windows API references are written for C programmers. But not all API functions are useful to VB programmers, and to call many of those that are, you need to know a little VB witchcraft. This indispensable reference covers the Windows API from a VB programmer's perspective. For example, all functions are listed with their proper VB declarations. Appleman also explains some of the peculiar ways in which VB interacts with Windows so you can make better use of the API. Includes a complete table of the 256 ternary raster operations.*

Conger, James L. *The Waite Group's Windows API Bible: The Definitive Programmer's Reference.* Mill Valley: Waite Group Press, 1992.

> *If you plan to spend any time in the Windows basements, you'll need a reference to the thousand or so functions buried there. All the API reference books have their strengths and weaknesses. I have used Conger's book extensively, so I'm attached to it. In particular I like the way he's organized the functions into related groups, such as Chapter 11, "Painting the Screen" and Chapter 15, "Bitmaps." Most API references come alphabetized. This one is alphabetized within categories. And for added convenience, it includes a fully alphabetized jump table right inside the front and back covers, along with a tear-out quick reference card that lists all the Windows messages and the Windows functions with their parameter lists.*

Conger, James L. *The Waite Group's Windows API New Testament*. Mill Valley: Waite Group Press, 1992.

> *This companion to* The Waite Group's Windows API Bible *covers all of the extensions added in Windows 3.1, including OLE, ToolHelp, and best of all, the Multimedia Extensions.*

Heiny, Loren. *Advanced Graphics Programming Using C/C++*. New York: John Wiley & Sons, Inc., 1993.

> *Although aimed at C programmers, Heiny's coverage of graphics programming techniques will benefit anyone with an interest in 3D ray tracing, image processing, and* polymorphic tweening *(morphing, as popularized by the movie* Terminator II *and Michael Jackson's* Black or White *music video).*

Holzner, Steven and The Peter Norton Computing Group. *Advanced Visual Basic*. New York: Brady, 1992.

> *This book includes a good chapter on the use of API calls from within Visual Basic programs.*

The International MIDI Association. *MIDI 1.0 Detailed Specification: Document Version 4.1.1, February, 1990.*

> *Available only from the publisher:*
> *The International MIDI Association*
> *5316 West 57th Street*
> *Los Angeles, CA 90056*
> *818-598-0088*
>
> *Also available:*
> *Standard MIDI Files 1.0*
> *General MIDI System, Level 1*
> *MIDI Show Control (MSC) 1.0*

Johnson, Nels with Fred Gault and Mark Florence. *How to Digitize Video*. New York: John Wiley & Sons, Inc., 1994.

> *Written by the principals of The San Francisco Canyon Company, creators of QuickTime for Windows, this book contains comprehensive coverage of PC and Macintosh digital video, from the proper way to handle tape cartridges to scaling, frame rates, and compression strategies.*

Microsoft Corporation. *Microsoft Windows 3.1 Programmer's Reference: Volumes 1 through 4.* Redmond: Microsoft Press, 1992.

> *Third-party references are great for sample code and interpretation, but sometimes you need to go directly to the source. If you program in Windows, regardless of what other API references you may keep your fingers in, you should own a copy of the original document. Then, when some function fails to work as you expected, you can try to reconcile your own code with the documentation in at least two sources. Remember, the documentation for every function, message, and macro you find in a third-party API reference began with the information in these books, Microsoft's original SDK manuals.*

Microsoft Corporation. *Microsoft Windows Multimedia Authoring and Tools Guide.* Redmond: Microsoft Press, 1991.

> *Although it provides few specifics, this volume of Microsoft's Multimedia trilogy offers an overview of multimedia production techniques.*

Microsoft Corporation. *Microsoft Windows Multimedia Programmer's Reference.* Redmond: Microsoft Press, 1991.

> *If you do any extensive multimedia programming, you'll need this guide. None of the other Windows reference guides I've seen so far includes the Multimedia APIs and messages.*

Microsoft Corporation. *Microsoft Windows Multimedia Programmer's Workbook.* Redmond: Microsoft Press, 1991.

> *The* Programmer's Reference *does not provide examples, but the* Workbook *does. Microsoft could have included a more detailed discussion of the various interfaces, but even so, you may get further faster than you would with the* Programmer's Reference *alone.*

Petzold, Charles. *Programming Windows 3.1: Third Edition.* Redmond: Microsoft Press, 1992.

> *This is Microsoft's official guide to programming for Windows. It's also a remarkably accessible and well written book. If you want to know how to write Windows programs from the ground up, read Petzold.*

Thomas, Zane with Robert Arnson and Mitchell Waite. *Visual Basic How-To: Second Edition.* Corte Madera: Waite Group Press, 1993.

Every programmer needs an occasional hint. This 800-page volume is loaded with them. Every time I browse through the 100 or so mini-projects in this book, I pick up new ideas for my own programs. Many of the projects use API functions, sometimes extensively.

Index

The Visual Basic Multimedia Adventures Contest

Don't miss your chance to win over $2,500 dollars in hot multimedia development tools. Enter The Coriolis Group's VB Multimedia Adventures contest and show us the best multimedia applications that you've created with the tools, software, and multimedia files included in this book. All you need is your PC, Visual Basic, and your imagination.

Here are the prizes you can win:

1. The first place winner will receive over $2,500 worth of multimedia development goodies including Microsoft's Widows Sound System, ProVoice for Windows, ImageKnife, Picture ++, and Media Studio.
2. The second place winner will receive $1,000 worth of multimedia tools and add-on products for VB.
3. The third place winner will receive books, software, and multimedia tools worth $500.
4. The first 20 place winners will receive a free subscription *to PC TECH-NIQUES* Magazine, their choice of a Coriolis Group Book, and a "way cool" Coriolis Group T-shirt.

What to Submit

Send your multimedia creation with source code to The Coriolis Group. Please make sure you include the entry form on the next page along with your software. Mark each disk with your name, phone number, and name of your multimedia entry. If you need to archive your entry, submit it as a self-extracting archive. You may also submit your entry on CD-ROM or Syquest cartridge. You can submit as many entries as you like, but you must submit one entry at a time.

Contest Guidelines

1. All entries must be sent by February 1, 1995.
2. The entry must be created using Microsoft's Visual Basic and any of the tools and products included in this book.

3. Each entry will be judged on the basis of content, creativity and design, user interface, usefulness, and educational and/or entertainment value, by a panel of judges from The Coriolis Group and the multimedia industry.

4. All winners will be notified by May 1, 1995. For the names of all winners, send a self-addressed, stamped envelope to The Coriolis Group, Visual Basic Multimedia Adventures Contest, 7721 E. Gray Road, Suite 204, Scottsdale, AZ 85260.

5. The Coriolis Group will not return any entries unless a self-addressed envelope with sufficient postage is provided with the entry for return. The Coriolis Group is not responsible for lost or damaged entries.

6. The Coriolis Group reserves the right to demonstrate the winning entries in a future edition of the *Visual Basic Multimedia Adventure Set* book and *PC TECHNIQUES* Magazine, and other national publications.

7. No purchase is necessary. This contest is subject to all federal, state, local, and provincial laws and regulations and is void where prohibited. This contest is not open to employees of The Coriolis Group, IDG, any Coriolis Group distributor, or the families of any of the above.

So what are you waiting for? Here's the perfect opportunity to show the world what you can do, have some fun, and win some valuable prizes.

Name _____ Daytime Phone _____

Address _____

City_____ State _____ Zip_____

File Name _____

Brief Discription of Entry _____

_____

_____

Send entries to: **VB Multimedia Contest**
The Coriolis Group
7721 E. Gray Rd., Suite 204
Scottsdale, AZ 85260

I signify that the enclosed is my own original work and that I abide by all rules described here.

Signature _____

Adventure Set License Agreement

Please read this Coriolis Adventure Set software license agreement carefully before you buy this product and use the software contained on the enclosed CD-ROM.

1. By opening the accompanying software package, you indicate that you have read and agree with the terms of this licensing agreement. If you disagree and do not want to be bound by the terms of this licensing agreement, return this product in whole for refund to the source from which you purchased it.

2. The entire contents of this CD-ROM and the compilation of the software contained therein are copyrighted and protected by both U.S. copyright law and international copyright treaty provisions. Each of the programs, including the copyrights in each program, is owned by the respective author, and the copyright in the entire work is owned by The Coriolis Group, Inc. You may copy any or all of this software to your computer system.

3. The CD-ROM contains source code presented in the book, utilities, tools, multimedia demonstration software, and multimedia files including sound, video, music, and pictures. You may use the source code, utilities, tools, and multimedia files presented in the book and included on the CD-ROM to develop your own applications for both private and commercial use unless other restrictions are noted on the CD-ROM by the author of the file.

4. You may not decompile, reverse engineer, disassemble, create a derivative work, or otherwise use the programs except as stated in this agreement.

5. The Coriolis Group, Inc. and the author specifically disclaim all other warranties, express or implied, including but not limited to implied warranties of merchantability and fitness for a particular purpose with respect to defects in the disk, the program, source code, and sample files contained therein, and/or the techniques described in the book, and in no event shall The Coriolis Group and/or the author be liable for any loss of profit or any other commercial damage, including but not limited to special, incidental, consequential, or other damages.

6. The Coriolis Group, Inc. will replace any defective CD-ROM without charge if the defective CD-ROM is returned to The Coriolis Group, Inc. within 90 days from the date of purchase.

7. The source code and sample program files presented in this book are available on a 3 1/2" 1.44MB disk. You can obtain this disk by sending your request to: The Coriolis Group, Attn: VB Multimedia Adventures Disk, 7721 E. Gray Rd., Suite 204, Scottsdale, AZ 85260, or call 602-483-0192. A $5 shipping and handling fee is required.

READ THE MAGAZINE
OF TECHNICAL EXPERTISE!

Published by The Coriolis Group

For years, Jeff Duntemann has been known for his crystal-clear, slightly-bemused explanations of programming technology. He's one of the few in computer publishing who has never forgotten that English is the one language we all have in common. Now he's teamed up with author Keith Weiskamp and created a magazine that brings you a selection of readable, practical technical articles six times a year, written by himself and a crew of the very best technical writers working today. Michael Abrash, Tom Swan, Jim Mischel, Keith Weiskamp, David Gerrold, Brett Glass, Michael Covington, Peter Aitken, Marty Franz, Jim Kyle, and many others will perform their magic before your eyes, and then explain how *you* can do it too, in language that you can understand.

If you program under DOS or Windows in C, C++, Pascal, Visual Basic, or assembly language, you'll find code you can use in every issue. You'll also find essential debugging and optimization techniques, programming tricks and tips, detailed product reviews, and practical advice on how to get your programming product finished, polished and ready to roll.

Don't miss another issue—subscribe today!

☐ 1 Year $21.95   ☐ 2 Years $37.95

☐ $29.95 Canada; $39.95 Foreign   ☐ $53.95 Canada; $73.95 Foreign

Total for subscription: _____
Arizona orders please add 6% sales tax: _____
Total due, in US funds:_____

Send to:
PC TECHNIQUES
7721 E. Gray Road, #204
Scottsdale AZ 85260

Name _____
Company _____
Address _____
City/State/Zip _____
Phone _____

Phone
(602) 483-0192
Fax
(602) 483-0193

VISA/MC # _____   Expires: _____

Signature for charge orders: _____

Learn the Secrets of Game Programming!

Enter the $2,500
Arcade Game
Contest!
Details
inside

Action Arcade
Adventure Set

3.5" Disk
packed with
valuable C source code
and a graphics library
Over $500 Value

Adventure Set
Features:

• Amazing
game engine
and visual
game editor

• Complete
arcade game
with dazzling
graphics and
fast animation

• Hot game
coding secrets

The best way
to create
action arcade
games in C

Diana Gruber

CORIOLIS
GROUP
BOOKS

**Win over $2,500
in free software!**

Enter the Action
Arcade Adventures
Contest. Details on
inside book cover!

Only $39.95
$49.95 Canada
Call 800-410-0192
Outside U.S.: 602-483-0192

Create your own fast-action scrolling arcade game
with Diana Gruber's *Action Arcade Adventure Set*.
This amazing book/software set includes a complete scrolling arcade game engine, game editor,
and Fastgraph/Light Shareware Graphics Library!

CORIOLIS GROUP BOOKS

FAX us your order at (602) 483-0193

CAUTION
POWERFUL MUSIC LIBRARY
ENCLOSED ON YOUR COMPANION CD-ROM

Cambium™ SOUND CHOICE Lite

Your companion CD-ROM contains Cambium SOUND CHOICE Lite, a powerful MPC music library with full-featured Windows™ software. The **Visual Basic Multimedia Adventure Set** helps you create multimedia projects in Visual Basic. SOUND CHOICE empowers your project with the best and most comprehensive music available, royalty-free. No cheap synthesis. No elevators. No embarrassments. Just great music that's intelligent, emotive, and crafted for multimedia. From Classical to Rock, the captivating textures, melodies, and rhythms of SOUND CHOICE will make the projects you create in Visual Basic and other authoring environments sparkle.

The Software

Using music in your projects has never been easier or more effective. It's intuitive. It's comprehensive. It's even fun.

- Search for music files by tempo, style, or customized key words
- Audition and edit across multiple SOUND CHOICE volumes
- Choose from pre-edited transitional and finale selections
- Customize music files by looping or fading
- Print and export log reports of your session

It's Royalty-Free

Integrate SOUND CHOICE into your project and you pay no fees, sign no forms, suffer no penalties for early withdrawal. Music to the ears of your accounting and legal departments. See license for details.

The Upgrade

The larger your music library, the greater depth and scope your multimedia projects can have. While this Lite version offers you our full functioning software, it contains only about 20% of the music available on each of the complete SOUND CHOICE volumes, and does not include the CD Audio versions. Upgrade to one or more full volumes of SOUND CHOICE by calling (800) 231-1779. Enjoy the musical power and flexibility of 25-30 main selections, over 100 individual clips, and over 800 music files per volume. Make an impact with music. Use the best. Upgrade now and receive any full volume of SOUND CHOICE for just $69.

Installation

1. Insert the CD-ROM into your CD-ROM drive

2. From the Program Manager select File, Run D:\SDCHOICE\SETUP (where D is the drive letter of your CD-ROM drive)

3. Please follow the setup instructions on the screen

4. For the thrill of your life, after setup is complete, select the Quick Tour in your Sound Choice Program Group

Cambium Upgrades: (800) 231-1779